Cognition

8e

exploring the science of the mind

Daniel Reisberg

REED COLLEGE

W. W. NORTON & COMPANY
Independent Publishers Since 1923

W. W. Norton & Company has been independent since its founding in 1923, when William Warder Norton and Mary D. Herter Norton first published lectures delivered at the People's Institute, the adult education division of New York City's Cooper Union. The firm soon expanded its program beyond the Institute, publishing books by celebrated academics from America and abroad. By midcentury, the two major pillars of Norton's publishing program—trade books and college texts—were firmly established. In the 1950s, the Norton family transferred control of the company to its employees, and today—with a staff of five hundred and hundreds of trade, college, and professional titles published each year—W. W. Norton & Company stands as the largest and oldest publishing house owned wholly by its employees.

Editor: Sheri L. Snavely
Senior Associate Editor: Gerra Goff
Project Editor: Taylere Peterson
Manuscript Editor: Alice Vigliani
Production Manager: Jane Searle
Managing Editor, College: Marian Johnson
Managing Editor, College Digital Media: Kim Yi
Media Editor: Kaitlin Coats
Associate Media Editor: Christina Fuery
Media Project Editors: Danielle Belfiore and Diane Cipollone
Media Editorial Assistant: Emilia Pesantes
Ebook Production Manager: Sophia Purut
Marketing Manager: Ken Barton
Design Director: Rubina Yeh
Art Director: Jillian Burr
Designer: Lisa Buckley
Photo Editor: Thomas Persano
Permissions Associate: Patricia Wong
Permissions Manager: Megan Schindel
Composition/Illustrations: Graphic World, Inc.
Manufacturing: Transcontinental Beauceville

Permission to use copyrighted material is included in the credits section of this book, which begins on page C1.

Library of Congress Cataloging-in-Publication Data

Names: Reisberg, Daniel, author.
Title: Cognition : exploring the science of the mind / Daniel Reisberg.
Description: Eighth Edition. | New York, NY: W. W. Norton & Company, 2021.
  | Revised edition of the author's Cognition, [2018] | Includes
  bibliographical references and index.
Identifiers: LCCN 2021022097 | **ISBN 9780393877601** (paperback)
  | ISBN 9780393877403 (epub)
Subjects: LCSH: Cognitive psychology.
Classification: LCC BF201 .R45 2021 | DDC 153—dc23
LC record available at https://lccn.loc.gov/2021022097

W. W. Norton & Company, Inc., 500 Fifth Avenue, New York, NY 10110
wwnorton.com

W. W. Norton & Company Ltd., 15 Carlisle Street, London W1D 3BS

1 2 3 4 5 6 7 8 9 0

With the hope
of reminding
people of the
power and
relevance of science.

Brief Contents

Contents

Preface

I began writing the first edition of this book in 1994—almost three decades ago. Working on the book, I soon found, was a glorious intellectual adventure. I had to examine my field, asking myself which claims, and which findings, were solid enough, and important enough, so that they deserved some space on the pages. I had to find ways to make the linkages clear among the various strands of research. I had to work through the challenge of finding a presentation that was orderly and persuasive. And as an extra pleasure, I wanted to find ways that (I hoped) would make the material as interesting for readers as it is for me.

Now, in 2021, we're about to release the Eighth Edition, and I have to say: Working on the book, for all the same reasons, is still a pleasure. In addition, I've now gained the further reward of watching my field evolve and advance, with new findings and new conceptualizations. But I've also been gratified to see how many of the field's claims have remained solidly in place—a strong indication of the power of our science. And, of course, I've also been gratified by the fact that my colleagues have enough respect for the book so that they've sustained it across these many editions.

But maybe I should begin with the real start of this journey: I was a college sophomore when I took my first course in cognitive psychology, and, remarkably, I decided almost immediately that I wanted to spend the rest of my professional life working in this domain. What was it that caught me from the very beginning? Part of the answer lies in the fact that I could see that cognitive psychologists were pursuing fabulous questions, questions that have intrigued humanity for thousands of years: Why do we think the things we think? Why do we believe the things we believe? What is "knowledge," and how secure (how complete, how accurate) is our knowledge of the world around us?

But alongside of these lofty questions, I also saw that cognitive psychologists were simultaneously pursuing more immediate, personal issues: How can I help myself to remember more of the material that I'm studying in my classes? Is there some better way to solve the problems I encounter? Why is it that my roommate can study with music on, but I can't?

And there was more—because cognitive psychologists were also asking questions with powerful implications for society. For example, when eyewitnesses report what they saw at a crime, should we trust them? If a newspaper raises questions about a candidate's integrity, how will voters react?

Of course, as a college student and even more so now, I wanted more than interesting questions—I also wanted answers to these questions, and this was another reason I found cognitive psychology so exciting. Indeed, now looking back over the last years, it's plain that the field has made extraordinary progress, providing us with a rich understanding of the nature of memory, the processes of thought, and the content of knowledge. There are of course many things still to be discovered—that's part of the fun. Even so, cognitive psychology has a lot to say about all of the questions just posed and many more as well. We can speak to the specific questions and to the general, to the theoretical issues and to the practical. Our research has uncovered principles useful for improving the process of education, and we have made discoveries of considerable importance for the legal system. What I've learned as a cognitive psychologist has changed how I think about my own memory; it's changed how I make decisions; it's changed how I draw conclusions when I'm thinking about events in my life.

On top of all this, I've always been excited about the connections that cognitive psychology makes possible. In the academic world, intellectual disciplines are often isolated from one another, sometimes working on closely related problems without even realizing it. In the last decades, though, cognitive psychology has forged rich connections with its neighboring disciplines, and in this book we'll touch on topics in philosophy, neuroscience, law, economics, linguistics, politics, computer science, and medicine. These connections bring obvious benefits, since insights and information can be traded back and forth between the domains. But these connections also highlight the importance of the material we'll be examining, since the connections make it clear that the issues before us are of interest to a wide range of scholars. This provides a strong signal that we're working on questions of considerable power and scope.

In this edition, as in all its predecessors, I've tried to convey all this excitement. I've done my best to describe the questions being asked within my field, the substantial answers we can provide for these questions, and, finally, some indications of how cognitive psychology is (and has to be) interwoven with other intellectual endeavors.

I've also had other goals in writing this text. In my own teaching, I've always tried to maintain a balance among many different elements. The nuts and bolts of how our science proceeds are, of course, important. But just as important are the results provided by the science, the practical implications of our research findings, and the theoretical framework that holds all of these pieces together. I've tried to find the same balance in this text. Perhaps most important, though, I try, both in my teaching and throughout this book, to "tell a good story," one that conveys how the various pieces of our field fit together into a coherent package. Of course, I want the evidence for our claims to be in view, so that readers can see how our field tests its hypotheses and why our claims must be taken seriously. But I've also put a strong emphasis on the flow of ideas—how new theories lead to new experiments, and how those experiments can lead to new theories.

The notion of "telling a good story" also emerges in another way: I've always been impressed by the ways in which the different parts of cognitive psychology are interlocked. Our claims about attention, for example, have immediate implications for how we can theorize about memory; our theories of object recognition are linked to our proposals for how knowledge is stored in the mind. Linkages like these are intellectually satisfying, because they ensure that the pieces of the puzzle really do fit together. But, in addition, these linkages make the material within cognitive psychology easier to learn—and easier to remember. Indeed, if I were to emphasize one crucial fact about memory, it would be that memory is best when the memorizer perceives the organization and interconnections within the material being learned. (We'll discuss this point further in Chapter 6.) With an eye on this point, I've therefore made sure to highlight the interconnections among various topics, so that readers can appreciate the beauty of our field and can also be helped in their learning by the orderly nature of our theorizing.

Over the various editions of this book, I've also added another dimension: It's a pleasure when student questions pull a discussion in an unexpected direction. Sometimes students ask how the materials you're discussing might be related to something they've observed for themselves, outside of the course. I've tackled some of their questions in a Cognition Outside the Lab feature, one for every chapter. And sometimes students ask questions about the possible linkage between the material and one of their own interests—and so a student interested in health or medicine might ask how cognitive psychology matters for her domain, and a student interested in technology might ask a question pointing in that direction. With an eye on questions like these, I've added a series of essays, at least four per chapter, exploring how cognitive psychology matters for issues in education, in law, in health or medicine, and in technology. I hope these essays are fun for readers, and I also hope these essays convey the importance and applicability of our field. One essay is featured at the end of each chapter, and the full set is collected in the online Applying Cognitive Psychology reader at digital.wwnorton.com/cognition8.

Have I met all of these goals? You, the readers, will need to be the judges of this. I would love to hear from you about what I've done well in the book and what I could have done better; what I've covered (but should have omitted) and what I've left out. I'll do my best to respond to every comment. You can reach me via email (reisberg@reed.edu); I've been delighted to get comments from readers about previous editions, and I hope for more emails with this edition.

An Outline of the Eighth Edition

The book's 15 chapters are designed to cover the major topics within cognitive psychology. The chapters in Part 1 lay the foundation. Chapter 1 provides the conceptual and historical background for the subsequent chapters.

In addition, this chapter seeks to convey the extraordinary scope of the field and why, therefore, research on cognition is so important. The chapter also highlights the relationship between theory and evidence in cognitive psychology, and it discusses the logic on which this field is built.

Chapter 2 then offers a brief introduction to the study of the brain. Most of cognitive psychology is concerned with the functions that our brains make possible, and not the brain itself. Nonetheless, our understanding of cognition has certainly been enhanced by the study of the brain, and throughout this book we'll use biological evidence as one means of evaluating our theories. Chapter 2 is designed to make this evidence fully accessible to the reader—by providing a quick survey of the research tools used in studying the brain, an overview of the brain's anatomy, and also an example of how we can use brain evidence as a source of insight into cognitive phenomena.

Part 2 of the book considers the broad issue of how we gain information from the world. Chapter 3 covers visual perception. At the outset, this chapter links to the previous (neuroscience) chapter with descriptions of the eyeball and the basic mechanisms of early visual processing. In this context, the chapter introduces the crucial concept of parallel processing and the prospect of mutual influence among separate neural mechanisms. From this base, the chapter builds toward a discussion of the perceiver's activity in shaping and organizing the visual world, and the text explores this point by discussing the rich topics of perceptual constancy and perceptual illusions.

Chapter 4 discusses how we recognize the objects that surround us. This seems a straightforward matter—what could be easier than recognizing a cell phone, or a coffee cup, or the letter G? As we'll see, however, recognition is surprisingly complex, and discussion of this complexity allows me to amplify key themes introduced in earlier chapters: how active people are in organizing and interpreting the information they receive from the world; the degree to which people supplement that information by relying on prior experience; and the ways in which this knowledge can be built into a network.

Chapter 5 then considers what it means to "pay attention." The first half of the chapter is concerned largely with selective attention—cases in which you seek to focus on a target while ignoring distractors. The second half of the chapter is concerned with divided attention ("multitasking")—that is, cases in which you seek to focus on more than one target, or more than one task, at the same time. Here, too, we'll see that seemingly simple processes turn out to be more complicated than one might suppose.

Part 3 turns to the broad topic of memory. Chapters 6, 7, and 8 start with a discussion of how information is "entered" into long-term storage, but then they turn to the complex interdependence between how information is first learned and how that same information is subsequently retrieved. A recurrent theme in this section is that learning that's effective for one sort of task, one sort of use, may be quite ineffective for other uses. This theme is examined in several contexts, and it leads to an exploration of research on unconscious memories—so-called memory without awareness. These chapters also offer a broad assessment of human memory: How accurate are our memories? How complete? How long-lasting? These issues are pursued both with regard to theoretical treatments of memory and also with regard to the practical consequences of memory research, including the application of this research to the assessment, in the courtroom, of eyewitness testimony.

The book's Part 4 is about knowledge. Earlier chapters show over and over that humans are, in many ways, guided in their thinking and experiences by what they already know—that is, the broad pattern of knowledge they bring to each new experience. This invites the questions posed by Chapters 9, 10, and 11: What is knowledge? How is it represented in the mind? Chapter 9 tackles the question of how "concepts," the building blocks of our knowledge, are represented in the mind. Chapters 10 and 11 focus on two special types of knowledge. Chapter 10 examines our knowledge about language; Chapter 11 considers visual knowledge and examines what is known about mental imagery.

The chapters in Part 5 are concerned with the topic of thinking. Chapter 12 examines how each of us draws conclusions from evidence—including cases in which we are trying to be careful and deliberate in our judgments, and also cases of informal judgments of the sort we often make in our everyday lives. The chapter then turns to the question of how we reason from our beliefs—how we check on whether our beliefs are correct, and how we draw conclusions based on things we already believe. The chapter also considers the practical issue of how errors in thinking can be diminished through education.

Chapter 13 is also about thinking, but with a different perspective: This chapter considers some of the ways people differ from one another in their ability to solve problems and in their creativity. We'll consider both "Big-C Creativity" (the creativity evident in groundbreaking scientific discoveries or remarkable artistic achievements) and also "little-c creativity" (the creativity evident when you find a new way to organize your day or a clever way to cheer up a friend). Then, in Chapter 14, we turn to another way in which people differ—in their intelligence. We all know individuals who are incredibly smart and other individuals who are less so. What is it exactly that separates these people? Can the difference be measured in a meaningful way? This chapter also addresses the often heated, often misunderstood debate about how different groups—especially American Whites and African Americans—might (or might not) differ in their intellectual capacities.

The final chapter in the book does double service. First, it pulls together many of the strands of contemporary research relevant to the topic of consciousness—what consciousness is, and what consciousness is for. In addition, most readers will reach this chapter at the end of a full semester's work, a point at which they are well served by a review of the topics already covered and ill served by the introduction of much new material. Therefore, this chapter draws many of its themes and evidence from previous chapters, and in that way it serves as a review of points that appear earlier in the book. Chapter 15 also highlights the fact that we're using these materials to approach some of the greatest questions ever asked about the mind, and in that way this chapter should help to convey some of the power of the material we've been discussing throughout the book.

New in the Eighth Edition

What's new in this edition? Overall, I've taken steps to streamline the presentation, and so this edition is actually briefer than the previous one. Even so, every chapter contains new material, in most cases because readers specifically requested the new content. Chapter 2, for example, now includes a discussion of how researchers sometimes study the brain by *manipulating* it (chemically, electrically, or genetically) and, with that, an exploration of the ethics of manipulating another creature's brain. Chapter 4 includes expanded coverage of the neural bases for object recognition. Chapter 5 has an enlarged discussion of feature binding. Chapter 8 broadens its treatment of flashbulb memories and also its discussion of memories for events that were *traumatic* when they occurred. Chapter 9 has been recast to help readers see why the study of conceptual knowledge is so important; it also includes expanded coverage of the neural underpinnings of conceptual knowledge. Chapter 10 has been updated with examples more familiar to readers (and so there's discussion of how changes in the way people think about *gender* is encouraging changes in the way people use *pronouns*). This chapter also now includes fuller coverage of how language gets used in actual conversations. Chapter 11 has broader coverage of how people differ both in their visualization abilities and (as a separate matter) in their spatial skills. Chapter 12 offers consideration of why many people rigidly endorse false claims (and dismiss any challenges to their claims as "fake news"). The material in Chapters 13 and 14 had been presented in a single chapter in the previous edition; the separation of these two chapters now makes the material much more approachable and allows coverage of the role of *sleep* in problem solving, the nature of brainstorming, and more.

Other Special Features

In addition, I have (of course) held on to features that were newly added in the previous edition—including the **Cognition Outside the Lab** features in each chapter. For example, in Chapter 4, in discussing how word recognition proceeds, I tackle the question of how the choice of font can influence readers (sometimes in good ways and sometimes not). In Chapter 7, I've written about cryptoplagiarism, a pattern in which you can steal another person's ideas without realizing it!

I've also kept the **Test Yourself** questions, because I take seriously the research indicating that these brief reviews, as straightforward as they are, help students to retain the material. I've also retained (and expanded) an art program that showcases the many points of contact between cognitive psychology and cognitive neuroscience.

This edition also retains the "**What if . . .**" section that launches each chapter. The "What if . . ." material serves several aims. First, the mental capacities described in each chapter (the ability to recognize objects, the ability to pay attention, and so on) are crucial for our day-to-day functioning;

to help readers understand this point, most of the "What if . . ." sections explore what someone's life is like if they lack the relevant capacity. Second, the "What if . . ." sections are rooted in concrete, human stories; they talk about specific individuals who lack these capacities. I hope these stories will be thought-provoking for readers, motivating them to engage the material in a richer way. And third, most of the "What if . . ." sections involve people who have lost the relevant capacity through some sort of brain damage. These sections therefore provide another avenue through which to highlight the linkage between cognitive psychology and cognitive neuroscience.

This edition also includes (and has now updated) a section, introduced in the previous edition, on **Research Methods**. In previous editions, this material was covered in the appendix, but it is now separated from the main text in a section easily accessible to all readers—but set to the side to accommodate readers (or instructors) who prefer to focus on the book's substantive content. This coverage of methods is included in the online Norton Teaching Tools for instructors to access and distribute to students, and is divided into separate essays for each chapter, so that it can be used on a chapter-by-chapter basis. This organization will help readers see, for each chapter, how the research described in the chapter unfolds, and it will simultaneously provide a context for each methods essay so that readers can see why the methods are so important.

This coverage of methods is no substitute for a research methods course, but nonetheless it's sequenced in a manner that builds toward a broad understanding of how the scientific method plays out in our field. An early essay, for example, works through the question of what a "testable hypothesis" is and why this is so important; another essay explains the power of random assignment; another discusses how we deal with confounds. One of the essays comments on the "replication crisis" that is currently being widely discussed in psychology. In all cases, though, my hope is that this coverage will guide readers toward a sophisticated understanding of why our research is as it is—and why, therefore, our research is so persuasive.

The previous edition had also introduced two types of "themed essays" accompanying each chapter. One series of essays focuses on **Cognitive Psychology and Education** and explores how cognitive psychology is connected to students' own learning. We are, after all, talking about memory, and students obviously are engaged in an endeavor of putting lots of new information—information they're learning in their courses—into their memories. We're talking about attention, and students often struggle with the chore of keeping themselves "on task" and "on target." In light of these points, these Education essays build a bridge between the content in the chapter and the concerns that impact students' lives. This will, I hope, make the material more useful for students and also make it clear just how important an enterprise cognitive psychology is.

A separate series of essays focuses on **Cognitive Psychology and the Law**. Here, I've drawn on my own experience in working with law enforcement and the legal system. In this work, I'm called on to help juries understand how eyewitnesses might be certain in their recollection, but mistaken. I also work with police officers to help them elicit as much information from a witness as possible, without leading the witness in any way. Based on this experience, these essays discuss how the material in each chapter might be useful for the legal system. These essays will, I hope, be immediately interesting for readers and will also make it obvious why it's crucial that the science be done carefully and well—so that we bring only high-quality information into the legal system.

The reader reaction to these essays has been positive, and that encouraged me to add two new series of essays for the Eighth Edition, with the goal of making contact with an even wider range of student interests. One of the new series, **Cognitive Psychology and Health**, discusses ways in which cognitive psychology matters for questions about health and medicine. The essay for Chapter 7, for example, explores whether patients undergoing surgery (and therefore who have been anesthetized) might nonetheless have memories for their surgical procedures. Chapter 9's essay relies on what we know about *categories* to explore whether there might be better procedures for diagnosing mental illness. Chapter 11's essay examines claims that visualization techniques can be useful for pain management.

The other new series, **Cognitive Psychology and Technology**, examines the interaction between our field and questions of technology. Chapter 2's essay, for example, discusses high-tech means of detecting whether someone is telling lies or not. Chapter 4's essay treats the state of the art (and the concerns about) face-recognition software. Chapter 5's essay explores the cognitive psychology of why some content goes "viral" on the Internet. Chapter 10's essay discusses the "vocabulary" used in texting, and Chapter 13's considers the prospects for computer creativity.

As with the essays in the previous edition, I hope that these new ones are fun and engaging for readers. And, throughout, I hope that these essays make it clear just how important, and how influential, the field of cognitive psychology is. Some of the essays are included in the printed text (one at the end of each chapter). The full set, though, is available in the online Applying Cognitive Psychology reader at https://digital.wwnorton.com/cognition8.

Finally, and as in the previous edition, I've also included **Demonstrations** in both the online Applying Cognitive Psychology reader and the Interactive Instructor's Guide. Many of these demos are miniature versions of experimental procedures, allowing students to see for themselves what these experiments involve and also allowing them to see just how powerful many of the effects are. Readers who want to run the demos for themselves as they read along certainly can; instructors who want to run the demos within their classrooms (as I sometimes have) are certainly encouraged to do so. Instructors who want to use the demos in discussion sections, aside from the main course, can do that as well. In truth, I suspect that some demos will work better in one of these venues and that other demos will work better in others; but in all cases I hope the Demonstrations help bring the material to life—putting students directly in contact with both our experimental methods and our experimental results.

As in previous editions, this version of *Cognition* also comes with various teaching and learning tools.

For Students & Instructors

InQuizitive

Built by one of my cognitive psychology colleagues, InQuizitive adaptive assessment, entirely new for this edition, incorporates research-based psychological principles—like retrieval practice and learning by doing—in order to maximize student retention and comprehension. A variety of interactive question types, guiding answer-specific feedback, and personalized question sets based on each student's areas for improvement are designed to help students grasp key course concepts. Motivating, gamelike elements engage students and direct them back into the text when they need to review.

ZAPS 3.0

The ZAPS 3.0 Interactive Labs are easy-to-use lab activities that invite students to actively engage in the scientific process. Students participate in interactive experimental trials, analyze the resulting data, read about the concepts illustrated by the research, and complete assessment questions along the way. ZAPS Version 3.0 is more interactive than ever before, with streamlined content, added formative assessment, enhanced visuals, and a new suite of accompanying instructor support tools.

Applying Cognitive Psychology Reader

The new online Applying Cognitive Psychology reader contains brief application essays, described earlier and all written by me, that show how cognitive psychology is linked to four key domains: law, education, and—entirely new to the Eighth Edition—technology and health. Also included in the reader are Demonstrations: easy-to-execute activities that I've created for use either in the classroom or as assignments to students to experience on their own.

Norton Testmaker

Norton Testmaker brings *Cognition*'s assessment materials online and makes it easy to build customized, data-driven assessments. Instructors can search and filter test bank questions by chapter, question type, difficulty level, learning objective, and more. You can customize test bank questions to fit your course, or simply "grab and go" with Testmaker's ready-to-use chapter review quizzes. Easily export your tests and quizzes to Microsoft Word or Common Cartridge files for your learning management system.

Norton Teaching Tools

The Norton Teaching Tools site is a searchable, sortable database of author-created resources for engaging students in active and applied learning, in the classroom or online. The Norton Teaching tools for the Eighth Edition include expanded and refreshed Suggested Video Clips, Applying Cognitive Psychology essays with accompanying discussion prompts, author-created Demonstrations, support for teaching with ZAPS 3.0, Lecture PowerPoints, Chapter Outlines, and more.

The video clips were initially selected by me, but the set of clips has now been expanded for this edition. My students love these clips—including (among many others) multiple demonstrations of change blindness; a video of a patient with neglect syndrome trying to draw a picture; and an excerpt from a documentary about Stephen Wiltshire, the "living camera." These videos make the course material vivid and concrete, and they are a fabulous addition to any lecture presentation.

Resources for Your LMS

Easily add high-quality Norton digital resources to your online, hybrid, or lecture courses. All activities can be accessed within your existing learning management system, and graded activities are configured to report to the LMS course grade book.

Acknowledgments

Finally, let me turn to the happiest of chores—thanking all of those who have contributed to this book. I begin with those who helped with the previous editions: Bob Crowder (Yale University) and Bob Logie (University of Aberdeen) both read the entire text of the first edition, and the book was unmistakably improved by their insights. Other colleagues read, and helped me enormously with, specific chapters: Enriqueta Canseco-Gonzalez (Reed College), Rich Carlson (Pennsylvania State University), Henry Gleitman (University of Pennsylvania), Lila Gleitman (University of Pennsylvania), Peter Graf (University of British Columbia), John Henderson (Michigan State University), Jim Hoffman (University of Delaware), Frank Keil (Cornell University), Mike McCloskey (Johns Hopkins University), Hal Pashler (University of California, San Diego), Steve Pinker (Massachusetts Institute of Technology), and Paul Rozin (University of Pennsylvania).

The second edition was markedly strengthened by the input and commentary provided by Martin Conway (University of Bristol), Kathleen Eberhard (Notre Dame University), Howard Egeth (Johns Hopkins University), Bill Gehring (University of Michigan), Steve Palmer (University of California, Berkeley), Henry Roediger (Washington University), and Eldar Shafir (Princeton University).

In the third edition, I was again fortunate to have the advice, criticism, and insights provided by a number of colleagues who, together, made the book better than it otherwise could have been, and I'd like to thank Rich Carlson (Penn State), Richard Catrambone (Georgia Tech), Randall Engle (Georgia Tech), Bill Gehring and Ellen Hamilton (University of Michigan), Nancy Kim (Rochester Institute of Technology), Steve Luck (University of Iowa), Michael Miller (University of California, Santa Barbara), Evan Palmer, Melinda Kunar, and Jeremy Wolfe (Harvard University), Chris Shunn (University of Pittsburgh), and Daniel Simons (University of Illinois).

A number of colleagues also provided their insights and counsel for the fourth edition. I'm therefore delighted to thank Ed Awh (University of Oregon), Glen Bodner (University of Calgary), William Gehring (University of Michigan),

Katherine Gibbs (University of California, Davis), Eliot Hazeltine (University of Iowa), William Hockley (Wilfrid Laurier University), James Hoffman (University of Delaware), Helene Intraub (University of Delaware), Vikram Jaswal (University of Virginia), Karsten Loepelmann (University of Alberta), Penny Pexman (University of Calgary), and Christy Porter (College of William and Mary).

Then, even more people to thank for their help with the fifth edition: Karin M. Butler (University of New Mexico), Mark A. Casteel (Penn State University, York), Alan Castel (University of California, Los Angeles), Robert Crutcher (University of Dayton), Kara D. Federmeier (University of Illinois, Urbana-Champaign), Jonathan Flombaum (Johns Hopkins University), Katherine Gibbs (University of California, Davis), Arturo E. Hernandez (University of Houston), James Hoeffner (University of Michigan), Timothy Jay (Massachusetts College of Liberal Arts), Timothy Justus (Pitzer College), Janet Nicol (University of Arizona), Robyn T. Oliver (Roosevelt University), Raymond Phinney (Wheaton College, and his comments were especially thoughtful!), Brad Postle (University of Wisconsin, Madison), Erik D. Reichle (University of Pittsburgh), Eric Ruthruff (University of New Mexico), Dave Sobel (Brown University), Martin van den Berg (California State University, Chico), and Daniel R. VanHorn (North Central College).

For the sixth edition: Michael Dodd (University of Nebraska, Lincoln), James Enns (University of British Columbia), E. Christina Ford (Penn State University), Danielle Gagne (Alfred University), Marc Howard (Boston University), B. Brian Kuhlman (Boise State University), Guy Lacroix (Carleton University), Ken Manktelow (University of Wolverhampton), Aidan Moran (University College Dublin, Ireland), Joshua New (Barnard College), Janet Nicol (University of Arizona), Mohammed K. Shakeel (Kent State University), David Somers (Boston University), and Stefan Van der Stigchel (Utrecht University).

For the seventh edition, I'm delighted to thank: Alan Castel (University of California, Los Angeles), Jim Hoelzle (Marquette University), Nate Kornell (Williams College), and Stefanie Sharman (Deakin University).

And now, happily, for the current edition: Dr. H. Bliss (Mississippi University for Women), Elena Festa (Brown University), Bryan Fox (University of Missouri, Kansas City), Özge Gürcanlı (Rice University), Stephanie Huette (University of Memphis), Daniel Koo (Gallaudet University), Cara Laney (The College of Idaho), Lindsey Lilienthal (Penn State Altoona), Anne McLaughlin (North Carolina State University), Catherine D. Middlebrooks (University of California, Los Angeles), Matthew O'Brien (Palomar Community College), Celeste Pilegard (University of California, San Diego), Erin M. Sparck (University of California, Los Angeles), Mark Stefani (Norwich University) and Meagan M. Wood (Valdosta State University).

I also want to thank the people at Norton. I've had a succession of terrific editors, and I'm grateful to Gerra Goff, Ken Barton, Sheri Snavely, Aaron Javsicas, and Jon Durbin for their support and fabulous guidance over the years. There's no question that the book is stronger, clearer, and better because of their input and advice. I also want to thank Taylere Peterson for doing a fabulous job of keeping this project on track. I'm delighted with the design that Rubina Yeh, Jillian Burr, and Lisa Buckley created. Thomas Persano has been truly great in dealing with my sometimes-zany requests for photographs, and I'm often amazed by his ability to find exactly the right photo for my often-specialized needs. Many thanks to Kaitlin Coats, Christina Fuery, Emilia Pesantes, Danielle Belfiore, Diane Cipollone and the crew that has developed and produced the teaching and learning tools for this book, including InQuizitive and ZAPS 3.0. I'd also like to thank Jane Searle and Sophia Purut for managing the production of the print text and ebook. Thanks in advance to Casey Johnson, Dorothy Laymon and the Norton sales team; I am, of course, deeply grateful for all you do.

And I once again get to celebrate the pleasure of working with Alice Vigliani as manuscript editor. I've worked with dozens of manuscript editors and it's clear: Alice is the best. She's skilled; she is thoughtful; she's blessed with wonderful perspicacity; and she's also fun to work with. Our working relationship is evolving into a friendship, for which I am deeply grateful. And someday, I really want to visit her marvelous garden.

Finally, it brings me joy to reiterate with love the words I said in the previous edition: In countless ways, Friderike makes all of this possible and worthwhile. She forgives me the endless hours at the computer, tolerates the tension when I'm feeling overwhelmed by deadlines, and is always ready to read my pages and offer thoughtful, careful, instructive insights. My gratitude to, and love for, her are boundless.

Daniel Reisberg
Portland, Oregon

part 1

The Foundations of Cognitive Psychology

What is cognitive psychology? In Chapter 1, we'll define this discipline and offer a sketch of what this field can teach us. We'll also provide a brief history to explain why cognitive psychology has taken the form that it has.

Chapter 2 has a different focus. At many points in this book, we'll draw insights from the field of cognitive neuroscience—the effort toward understanding our mental functioning through study of the brain and nervous system. To make sure this biological evidence is useful, though, we need some background, and that's the main purpose of Chapter 2. There, we offer a rough mapping of what's where in the brain, and we'll describe the functioning of many of the brain's parts. As we'll see, though, each of the brain's parts is highly specialized in what it does. As a result, mental achievements such as reading, remembering, or deciding depend on the coordinated functioning of many brain regions, each contributing its own small bit to the overall achievement.

chapter **1**

The Science of
the Mind

Almost everything you do, or feel, or say depends on your *cognition*—what you know, what you remember, and what you think. As a result, the book you're now reading—a textbook on cognition—describes the foundation for virtually every aspect of who you are.

As an illustration of this theme, in a few pages we'll consider the way in which your ability to cope with grief depends on your memory. We'll also discuss the role that memory plays in shaping your self-image—and, therefore, your self-esteem. As another example, we'll discuss a case in which your understanding of a simple story depends on the background knowledge that you supply. Examples like these make it clear that cognition matters in an extraordinary range of circumstances, and it's on this basis that our focus in this book is on the intellectual foundation of almost every aspect of human experience.

The Scope of Cognitive Psychology

When the field of cognitive psychology was first launched, it was understood to be the scientific study of knowledge, and this broad definition led immediately to a series of questions: How is knowledge acquired? How is knowledge retained so that it's available when needed? How is knowledge used—whether as a basis for making decisions or as a means of solving problems?

These are great questions, and it's easy to see that answering them might be quite useful. For example, imagine that you're studying for next Wednesday's exam, but for some reason the material just won't "stick" in your memory. You find yourself wishing, therefore, for a better strategy to use in studying and memorizing. What would that strategy be? Is it possible to have a "better memory"?

As a different case, let's say that while you're studying, your friend is moving around in the room, and you find this quite distracting. Why can't you just shut out your friend's motion? Why don't you have better control over your attention and your ability to concentrate?

Here's one more example: You're looking at your favorite social media site, and you're horrified to learn how many people have decided to vote for candidate X. How do people decide whom to vote for? For that matter, how do people decide what college to attend, or which car to buy, or even what to have for dinner? And how can we help people make better decisions—so that, for example, they choose healthier foods, or vote for the candidate who (in your view) is preferable?

preview of chapter themes

- The chapter begins with a description of the scope of cognitive psychology. The domain of this field includes activities that are obviously "intellectual" (such as remembering, paying attention, or making judgments) but also a much broader range of activities that depend on these intellectual achievements.

- What form should a "science of the mind" take? We discuss the difficulties in trying to study the mind by means of direct observation. But we also explore why we must study the mental world if we're to understand behavior; the reason is that our behavior depends in crucial ways on how we *perceive* and *understand* the world around us.

- Combining these themes, we come to the view that we must study the mental world *indirectly*. But as we will see, the method for doing this is the method used by most sciences.

Before we're through, we'll consider evidence pertinent to all of these questions. Let's note, though, that in these examples, things aren't going as you might have wished: You remember less than you want to; you can't ignore a distraction; the voters make a choice you don't like. What about the other side of the picture? What about the remarkable intellectual feats that humans achieve—brilliant deductions or creative solutions to complex problems? In this text, we'll also discuss these cases and explore how people manage to accomplish the great things they do.

CELEBRATING HUMAN ACHIEVEMENTS

Many of this text's examples involve *failures* or *limitations* in our cognition. But we also need to explain the incredible intellectual achievements of our species—the complex problems we've solved and the extraordinary devices we've invented.

The Broad Role of Memory

The questions we've mentioned so far might make it sound like cognitive psychology is concerned just with your functioning as an intellectual—your ability to remember, or to pay attention, or to think through options when making a choice. As we've said, though, the relevance of cognitive psychology is much broader—thanks to the fact that a huge range of your actions, thoughts, and feelings *depend on your cognition*. As one way to convey this point, let's ask: When we investigate how memory functions, what's at stake? Or, to turn this around, what aspects of your life depend on memory?

You obviously rely on memory when you're taking an exam—memory for what you learned during the term. Likewise, you rely on memory when you're at the supermarket and trying to remember the cheesecake recipe so that you can buy the right ingredients. You also rely on memory when you're reminiscing about childhood. But what else draws on memory?

Consider this simple story (adapted from Charniak, 1972):

> Betsy wanted to bring Jacob a present. She shook her piggy bank. It made no sound. She went to look for her mother.

This four-sentence tale is easy to understand, but *only because you provided important bits of background*. For example, you weren't at all puzzled about why Betsy was interested in her piggy bank; you weren't puzzled, specifically, about why the story's first sentence led naturally to the second. This is because you already knew (a) that the things one gives as presents are often things bought for the occasion (rather than things already owned), (b) that buying things requires money, and (c) that money is sometimes stored in piggy banks. Without these facts, you would have wondered why a desire to give a gift would lead someone to her piggy bank. (Surely you didn't think Betsy intended to give the piggy bank itself as the present!) Likewise, you immediately understood why Betsy *shook* her piggy bank. You didn't suppose that she was shaking it in frustration or trying to find out if it would make a good percussion instrument. Instead, you understood that she was trying to determine its contents. But you knew this fact only because you already knew (d) that Betsy was a child (because few adults keep their money in piggy banks), (e) that children don't keep track of how much money is in their banks, and (f) that piggy banks are made out of opaque material (and so a child can't simply look into the bank to see what's inside). Without these facts, Betsy's shaking of the bank would make no sense. Similarly, you understood what it meant that the bank made no sound. That's because you know (g) that it's usually coins (not bills) that are kept in piggy banks, and (h) that coins make noise when they're shaken. If you didn't know these facts, you might have interpreted the bank's silence, when it was shaken, as good news, indicating perhaps that the bank was jammed full of $20 bills—an inference that would have led you to a very different expectation for how the story would unfold from there.

A SIMPLE STORY

What is involved in your understanding of this simple story? Betsy wanted to bring Jacob a present. She shook her piggy bank. It made no sound. She went to look for her mother.

TRYING TO FOCUS

Often, you want to focus on just one thing, and you want to shut out the other sights and sounds that are making it hard for you to concentrate. What steps should you take to promote this focus and to avoid distraction?

Of course, there's nothing special about the "Betsy and Jacob" story, and we'd uncover a similar reliance on background knowledge if we explored how you understand some other narrative, or follow a conversation, or comprehend a movie. Our suggestion, in other words, is that many (perhaps all) of your encounters with the world depend on your supplementing your experience with knowledge that you bring to the situation. And perhaps this has to be true. After all, if you didn't supply the relevant bits of background, then anyone telling the "Betsy and Jacob" story would need to spell out all the connections and all the assumptions. The story would have to include all the facts that, *with* memory, are supplied by you. As a result, the story would have to be much longer, and the telling of it much slower. The same would be true for every story you hear, every conversation you participate in. Memory is thus crucial for each of these activities.

Amnesia and Memory Loss

Here is a different sort of example: In Chapter 7, we will consider cases of clinical *amnesia*—cases in which someone, because of brain damage, has lost the ability to remember certain materials. These cases are fascinating at many levels and provide key insights into what memory is *for*. Without memory, what is disrupted?

H.M. was in his mid-20s when he had brain surgery intended to control his severe epilepsy. The surgery was, in a narrow sense, a success, and H.M.'s epilepsy was brought under control. But this gain came at an enormous cost, because H.M. essentially lost the ability to form new memories. He survived for more than 50 years after the operation, and across those years he had little trouble remembering events *prior* to the surgery. But H.M. seemed completely unable to recall any event that occurred *after* his operation. If asked what he'd had for breakfast, or about books he'd read recently, he had no clue. If asked questions about last week, or even an hour ago, he recalled nothing.

This memory loss had massive consequences for H.M.'s life. For example, he had an uncle he was very fond of, and he occasionally asked his hospital visitors how his uncle was doing. Unfortunately, the uncle died sometime after H.M.'s surgery, and H.M. was told this sad news. The information came as a horrible shock, but because of his amnesia, H.M. soon forgot about it.

Sometime later, because he'd *forgotten* about his uncle's death, H.M. again asked how his uncle was doing and was again told of the death. But with no memory of having heard this news before, he was once more hearing it "for the first time," with the shock and grief every bit as strong as it was initially. Indeed, each time he heard this news, he was hearing it "for the first time." With no memory, he had no opportunity to live with the news, to adjust to it. As a result, his grief could not subside. Without memory, H.M. had no way to come to terms with his uncle's death.

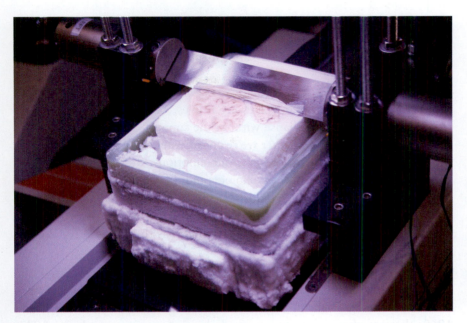

H.M.'S BRAIN

When H.M. died in 2008, the world learned his full name—Henry Molaison. Throughout his life, H.M. had cooperated with researchers in many studies of his memory loss. Even after his death, H.M. is contributing to science: His brain (shown here) was frozen and has now been sliced into sections for detailed anatomical study. Unfortunately, though, there has been debate over who "owns" H.M.'s brain and how we might interpret some observations about his brain (see, for example, Dittrich, 2016).

A different glimpse of memory function comes from H.M.'s comments about what it felt like to be in his situation. Let's start here with the notion that for those of us without amnesia, numerous memories support our conception of who we are: We know whether we deserve praise for our good deeds or blame for our transgressions because we remember those good deeds and transgressions. We know whether we've kept our promises or achieved our goals because, again, we have the relevant memories. None of this is true for people who suffer from amnesia, and H.M. sometimes commented that in important ways, he didn't know who he was. He didn't know if he should be proud of his accomplishments or ashamed of his crimes; he didn't know if he'd been clever or stupid, honorable or dishonest, industrious or lazy. In a sense, then, without a memory, there is no self. (For discussion, see Stanley et al. 2020.)

What, then, is the scope of cognitive psychology? As we mentioned earlier, this field is sometimes defined as the scientific study of the acquisition, retention, and use of knowledge. We've now seen, though, that "knowledge" (and so the study of how we gain and use knowledge) is relevant to a huge range of concerns. Our self-concept, it seems, depends on our knowledge (and, in particular, on our memory for various episodes in our past). Our

TEST YOURSELF

1. Why is memory crucial for behaviors and mental operations that don't in any direct or explicit way ask you to "remember"?
2. What aspects of H.M.'s life were disrupted as a result of his amnesia?

emotional adjustments to the world rely on our memories. Even our ability to understand a simple story—or, presumably, our ability to understand any experience—depends on our supplementing that experience with some knowledge.

The suggestion, then, is that cognitive psychology can help us understand capacities relevant to every moment of our lives. Activities that don't appear to be intellectual would collapse without the support of our cognitive functioning. The same is true whether we're considering our physical movements through the world, our social lives, our emotions, or any other domain. This is the scope of cognitive psychology and, in a real sense, the scope of this book.

The Cognitive Revolution

The enterprise that we call "cognitive psychology" is roughly 60 years old, and the emergence of this field was in some ways dramatic. Indeed, the science of psychology went through a succession of changes in the 1950s and 1960s that are often referred to as psychology's "cognitive revolution." This "revolution" involved a new style of research, aimed initially at questions we've already met: questions about memory, decision making, and so on. But this new type of research, and its new approach to theorizing, soon influenced other domains, with the result that the cognitive revolution dramatically changed the intellectual map of our field.

To understand what this revolution was all about, let's look at two earlier traditions in psychology, because, in some ways, it was the *limitations* of these traditions that gave rise to cognitive psychology. (For readers interested in a broader history of cognitive psychology, though, see Benjamin, 2008; Broadbent, 1958; Malone, 2009; Mandler, 2011.)

The Limits of Introspection

In the late 19th century, Wilhelm Wundt (1832–1920) and his student Edward Bradford Titchener (1867–1927) launched a new research enterprise, and it was their work that led to the modern field of experimental psychology. In Wundt and Titchener's view, though, psychology needed to focus on the study of conscious mental events—feelings, thoughts, perceptions, and recollections. These early researchers obviously knew, however, that there is no way for you to experience my thoughts, or I yours. The only person who can experience or observe your thoughts is you. Wundt and his colleagues concluded, therefore, that the only way to study thoughts is through **introspection,** or "looking within"—a method in which people observe and record the content of their own mental lives and the sequence of their own experiences.

Wundt and Titchener insisted, though, that this introspection could not be casual. Instead, introspectors had to be meticulously trained: They were given a vocabulary to describe what they observed; they were taught to be as

complete as possible; and above all, they were trained simply to report their experiences, with a minimum of interpretation.

This style of research was enormously influential for several years, but psychologists gradually became disenchanted with it, and it's easy to see why. As one concern, these investigators soon had to acknowledge that some thoughts are *un*conscious, which meant that introspection was limited as a research tool. After all, by its very nature introspection is the study of conscious experiences, so of course it can tell us nothing about unconscious events.

Indeed, we now know that unconscious thought plays a huge part in our mental lives. For example, which is bigger: a flea or an elephant? Surely, the moment you read this question, the answer "popped" into your thoughts without any effort. But, in fact, there's good reason to think that this simple judgment requires a series of steps. These steps take place outside of aware-ness; and so, if we rely on introspection as our means of studying mental events, we have no way of examining these processes.

But there's another, deeper problem with introspection. In order for any science to proceed, there must be some way to test its claims; otherwise, we have no means of separating correct assertions from false ones, accurate descriptions of the world from fictions. Along with this requirement, sci-ence needs some way of resolving disagreements. If you claim that Earth has one moon and I insist that it has two, we need some way of determin-ing who is right. Otherwise, our "science" will become a matter of opinion, not fact.

With introspection, this testability of claims is often unattainable. To see why, imagine that I insist my headaches are worse than yours. How could we ever test my claim? It might be true that I describe my headaches in extreme terms: I talk about them being "agonizing" and "excruciating." But that might only show that I like to use extravagant descriptions; those words might reveal my tendency to exaggerate (or to complain), not the actual severity of my headaches. Similarly, it might be true that I need bed rest whenever one of my headaches strikes. Does that mean my headaches are truly intolerable? It might mean instead that I'm self-indulgent and rest even when I feel mild pain. Perhaps our headaches are identical, but you're stoic about yours and I'm not.

How, therefore, should we test my claim about my headaches? What we need is some way of directly comparing my headaches to yours, and that would require transplanting one of my headaches into your experience, or vice versa. Then one of us could make the appropriate comparison. But (setting fantasy to the side) there's no way to do this, leaving us, in the end, unable to determine whether my headache reports are distorted or accurate. We're left, in other words, with the brute fact that our only information about my headaches is what comes through the filter of my description, and we have no way to know how (or whether) that filter is coloring the evidence.

For science, this is unacceptable. Ultimately, we do want to understand conscious experience, and, in later chapters, we'll talk (for example) about the conscious experience of mental imagery; in Chapter 15, we'll talk about consciousness itself. In these settings, though, we'll rely on introspection as a source of observations *that need to be explained*. In other words, we won't rely on introspective data as a means of evaluating our hypotheses—because, usually, we can't. If we want to test hypotheses, we need data we can rely on, and, among other requirements, this means data that aren't dependent on a particular point of view or a particular descriptive style. Scientists generally achieve this objectivity by making sure the raw data are out in plain view, so that you can inspect my evidence, and I can inspect yours. In that way, we can be certain that neither of us is distorting or misreporting the facts. And that is precisely what we cannot do with introspection.

The Years of Behaviorism

Historically, the concerns just described led many psychologists to abandon introspection as a research tool. Instead, they argued, psychology needed objective data, and that meant data out in the open for all to observe.

What sorts of data does this allow? First, an organism's *behaviors* are observable in the right way: You can watch my actions, and so can anyone else who is appropriately positioned. Therefore, observations of behavior provide objective data and thus grist for the scientific mill. Likewise, *stimuli* in the world are in the same "objective" category: These are measurable, recordable, physical events.

In contrast, someone's *beliefs, preferences, hopes,* and *expectations* cannot be directly observed, cannot be objectively recorded. These "mentalistic" notions can be observed only via introspection; and introspection, we've suggested, has little value as a scientific tool. Therefore, a scientific psychology needs to avoid these invisible internal entities.

This perspective led to the **behaviorist movement**, a movement that dominated psychology in America for the first half of the 20th century. The movement was in many ways successful and uncovered a range of principles concerned with how behavior changes in response to various stimuli (including the stimuli we call "rewards" and "punishments"). By the late 1950s, however, psychologists were convinced that a lot of our behavior could not be explained in these terms. The reason, basically, is that the ways people act, and the ways they feel, are guided by how they *understand* or *interpret* the situation, and not by the objective situation itself. Therefore, if we follow the behaviorists' instruction and focus only on the objective situation, we will often misunderstand why people are doing what they're doing and make the wrong predictions about how they'll behave in the future. To put this point another way, the behaviorist perspective demands that we not talk about mental entities such as beliefs, memories, and so on, because these things cannot be studied directly and so cannot be studied scientifically. Yet it seems that these subjective entities play a pivotal role in guiding behavior, and so we *must* consider them if we want to understand behavior.

Evidence supporting these assertions is threaded throughout the chapters of this book. Over and over, we'll find it necessary to mention people's

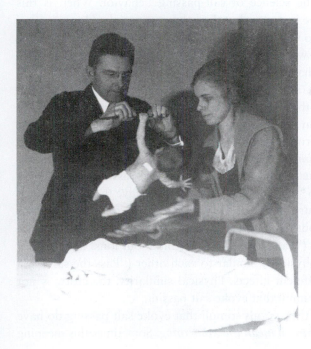

JOHN B. WATSON

John B. Watson (1878–1958) was a prominent advocate for the behaviorist movement. Given his focus on learning and learning histories, it's not surprising that Watson was intrigued by babies' behavior and learning. Here, he tests the grasp reflex displayed by human infants. Rosalie Rayner (1898–1935), Watson's assistant and wife, played an important role in his research, although many accounts offer little mention of her contribution.

perceptions and strategies and understanding, as we explain how they perform various tasks and accomplish various goals. Indeed, we've already seen an example of this pattern. Imagine that we present the "Betsy and Jacob" story to people and then ask various questions: Why did Betsy shake her piggy bank? Why did she go to look for her mother? People's responses will surely reflect their understanding of the story, which in turn depends on far more than the physical stimulus—that is, the 29 syllables of the story itself. If we want to predict someone's responses to these questions, therefore, we'll need to refer to the stimulus (the story itself) *and also* to the person's knowledge and understanding of this stimulus.

Here's a different example that makes the same general point. Imagine you're sitting in the dining hall. A friend produces this physical stimulus: "Pass the salt, please," and you immediately produce a bit of salt-passing behavior. In this exchange, there is a physical stimulus (the words your friend uttered) and an easily defined response (your passing of the salt), and so this simple event seems fine from the behaviorists' perspective—the elements are out in the open and can be objectively recorded. But note that the event would have unfolded in the same way if your friend had offered a different stimulus. "Could I have the salt?" would have done the trick. Ditto for "Salt, please!" or "Hmm, this sure needs salt!" If your friend is both loquacious and obnoxious, the utterance might have been: "Excuse me, but after briefly contemplating the gustatory qualities of these comestibles, I have discerned that their sensory qualities would be enhanced by the addition of a number of sodium and chloride ions, delivered in roughly equal proportions and in crystalline form; could you aid me in this endeavor?" You might giggle (or snarl) at your friend, but you would still pass the salt.

Now let's work on the science of salt-passing behavior. When is this behavior produced? We've just seen that the behavior is evoked by a number of different stimuli, and so we surely want to ask: What do these stimuli have in common? If we can answer that question, we're on our way to understanding why these stimuli all have the same effect.

The problem, though, is that if we focus on the observable, objective aspects of these stimuli, they actually have little in common. After all, the sounds being produced in that long statement about sodium and chloride ions are rather different from the sounds in the utterance "Salt, please!" And in many circumstances, *similar* sounds would not lead to salt-passing behavior. Imagine that your friend says, "Salt the pass" or "Sass the palt." These are acoustically similar to "Pass the salt" but wouldn't have the same impact.

It seems, then, that our science of salt passing won't get very far if we insist on talking only about the physical stimulus. Stimuli that are physically different from each other ("Salt, please" and the bit about ions) have similar effects. Stimuli that are physically similar to each other ("Pass the salt" and "Sass the palt") have different effects. Physical similarity, therefore, is not what unites the various stimuli that evoke salt passing.

It's clear, though, that the various stimuli that evoke salt passing do have something in common: *They all mean the same thing*. Sometimes this meaning

PASSING THE SALT

If a friend requests the salt, your response will depend on how you understand your friend's words. This is a simple point, echoed in example after example, but it is the reason why a rigid behaviorist perspective cannot explain your behavior.

derives from the words themselves ("Please pass the salt"). In other cases, the meaning depends on certain pragmatic rules. (For example, you understand that the question "Could you pass the salt?" isn't a question about arm strength, although, interpreted literally, it might be understood that way.) In all cases, though, it seems plain that to predict your behavior in the dining hall, we need to ask what these stimuli *mean to you*. This seems an extraordinarily simple point, but it is a point, echoed by countless other examples, that indicates the impossibility of a complete behaviorist psychology.[1]

The Intellectual Foundations of the Cognitive Revolution

One might think, then, that we're caught in a trap. On one side, it seems that the way people act is shaped by how they *perceive* the situation, how they *understand* the stimuli, and so on. If we want to explain behavior, then, we have no choice. We need to talk about the mental world. But, on the other side, the only direct means of studying the mental world is introspection, and introspection is scientifically unworkable. Therefore: We need to study the mental world, but we can't.

The solution to this impasse, however, was suggested years ago by the philosopher Immanuel Kant (1724–1804). To use Kant's **transcendental method**, you begin with the observable facts and work backward from these observations. In essence, you ask: How could these observations have come about? What must be the underlying *causes* that led to these *effects*?

This method, sometimes called "inference to best explanation," is at the heart of most modern science. Physicists, for example, routinely use this method to study objects or events that cannot be observed directly. To take just one case, no physicist has ever observed an electron, but this hasn't stopped physicists from learning a great deal about electrons. How do the physicists proceed? Even though electrons themselves aren't observable, their presence often leads to observable results—in essence, *visible effects* from an *invisible cause*. For example, electrons leave observable tracks in cloud chambers and can produce momentary fluctuations in a magnetic field. Physicists use these observations in the same way a police detective uses clues—asking what the "crime" must have been like if it left this and that clue. (A size 11 footprint? That probably tells us what size feet the criminal has, even though no one saw his feet. A smell of tobacco smoke? That suggests the criminal was a smoker. And so on.) In the same way, physicists observe the clues that electrons leave behind, and from this information they form hypotheses about what electrons must be like in order to have produced those effects.

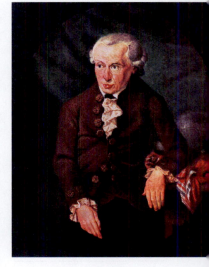

IMMANUEL KANT

Philosopher Immanuel Kant (1724–1804) made major contributions to many fields, and his transcendental method enabled him to ask what qualities of the mind make experience possible.

---

1. The behaviorists themselves quickly realized this point. As a result, modern behaviorism has abandoned the radical rejection of mentalistic terms. The behaviorism being criticized here is a historically defined behaviorism, and it's this perspective that, in large measure, gave birth to modern cognitive psychology.

Of course, physicists (and other scientists) have a huge advantage over a police detective. If the detective has insufficient evidence, she can't arrange for the crime to happen again in order to produce more evidence. (She can't say to the robber, "Please visit the bank again, but this time leave a lot of fingerprints.") Scientists, in contrast, can arrange for a repeat of the "crime" they're seeking to explain—they can arrange for new experiments, with new measures. Better still, they can set the stage in advance, to maximize the likelihood that the "culprit" (in our example, the electron) will leave useful clues behind. They can, for example, add new recording devices to the situation, or place various obstacles in the electron's path. In this way, scientists can gather more data, including data crucial for testing the predictions of a particular theory. This prospect—of reproducing experiments and varying the experiments to test hypotheses—is what gives science its power. It's what enables scientists to assert that their hypotheses have been rigorously tested, and it's what gives scientists assurance that their theories are correct.

Psychologists work in the same fashion—and the notion that we *could* work in this fashion was one of the great contributions of the cognitive revolution. The idea is this: We know that we need to study mental processes; that's what we learned from the limitations of classical behaviorism. But we also know that mental processes cannot be observed directly; we learned that from the downfall of introspection. Our path forward, therefore, is to study mental processes *indirectly*, relying on the fact that these processes, themselves invisible, have visible consequences: measurable delays in producing a response, performances that can be assessed for accuracy, errors that can be scrutinized and categorized. By examining these (and other) effects produced by mental processes, we can develop—and *test*—hypotheses about what the mental processes must have been. In this way, we use Kant's method, just as physicists (or biologists, or chemists, or astronomers) do, to develop a science that does not rest on direct observation.

The Path from Behaviorism to the Cognitive Revolution

Cognitive psychologists have applied the Kantian logic to explain how people remember, make decisions, pay attention, or solve problems. In each case, we begin with a particular performance—say, a problem that someone solved—and hypothesize a series of unseen mental events that made the performance possible. We then do further tests, asking (say) whether other examples of problem solving unfold as we'd expect, based on our hypothesis. We continue this process until we're sure that our hypothesis (and only our hypothesis) fits with the full pattern of evidence.

This pattern of theorizing has become the norm in psychology (and not just in cognitive psychology)—a powerful indication that the cognitive revolution did indeed change the entire field. But what triggered the revolution?

What happened in the 1950s and 1960s that propelled psychology forward in this way? It turns out that multiple forces were in play.

One contribution came from within the behaviorist movement itself. We've discussed concerns about classical behaviorism, and some of those concerns were voiced early on by Edward Tolman (1886–1959)—a researcher who can be counted both as a behaviorist and as one of the forerunners of cognitive psychology. Prior to Tolman, most behaviorists argued that learning could be understood simply as a *change in behavior*. Tolman argued, however, that learning involved something more abstract: the acquisition of new knowledge.

In one of Tolman's studies, rats were placed in a maze day after day. For the initial 10 days, no food was available anywhere in the maze, and the rats wandered around with no pattern to their movements. Across these days, therefore, there was no change in behavior—and so, according to the conventional view, no learning. But, in fact, there was learning, because *the rats were learning the layout of the maze*. That became clear on the 11th day of testing, when food was introduced into the maze in a particular location. The next day, the rats, placed back in the maze, ran immediately to that location. Indeed, their behavior was essentially identical to the behavior of rats who had had many days of training with food in the maze (Tolman, 1948; Gleitman, 1963).

What happened here? Across the initial 10 days, the rats were acquiring what Tolman called a "cognitive map" of the maze. In the early days of the procedure, however, the rats had no motivation to use this knowledge. On Days 11 and 12, though, the rats gained a reason to use what they knew, and at that point they revealed their knowledge. The key point, though, is that—even for rats—we need to talk about (invisible) mental processes (e.g., the formation of cognitive maps) if we want to explain behavior.

A different spur to the cognitive revolution also arose out of behaviorism— but this time from a strong *critique* of behaviorism. B. F. Skinner (1904–1990) was an influential American behaviorist, and in 1957 he applied his style of analysis to humans' ability to learn and use language, arguing that language use could be understood in terms of behaviors and rewards (Skinner, 1957). Two years later, the linguist Noam Chomsky (1928–) published a ferocious rebuttal to Skinner's proposal, and convinced many psychologists that an entirely different approach was needed for explaining language learning and language use, and perhaps for other achievements as well.

Chomsky's argument was complex, but (among other points) he noted that Skinner's view could not explain the *creativity* of language—that is, our ability to produce and understand sentences we've never encountered before. Chomsky argued that this creativity was rooted in abstract principles (including rules of syntax) that demanded a type of theorizing incompatible with Skinner's approach. (For more on Chomsky's contribution and the principles governing language, see Chapter 10.)

ULRIC NEISSER

Many intellectual developments led to the cognitive revolution. A huge boost, though, came from the work of Ulric Neisser (1928–2012). The title of his book, *Cognitive Psychology* (1967) gave the new field its name, and the book brought together a succession of topics that both summarized the content of the new field and also set the research agenda for many years. Neisser's influence was so large that many scholars refer to him as the "father of cognitive psychology."

European Roots of the Cognitive Revolution

Research psychology in the United States was, we've said, dominated by the behaviorist movement for many years. Other perspectives, however, flourished in Europe, and fed into and strengthened the cognitive revolution. In Chapter 3, we will describe some of the theorizing that grew out of the Gestalt psychology movement—a movement based in Berlin in the early decades of the 20th century. (Many of the Gestaltists fled to the United States in the years leading up to World War II and became influential figures in their new home.) Gestalt psychologists argued that behaviors, ideas, and perceptions are organized in a way that cannot be understood through a part-by-part, element-by-element, analysis of the world. Instead, they claimed, the elements take on meaning only as part of the whole— and therefore psychology needed to understand the nature of the "whole." This position had many implications, including an emphasis on the role of perceivers in organizing their experiences. As we will see, this notion— that perceivers shape their own experience—is a central theme for modern cognitive psychology.

Another crucial figure was British psychologist Frederic Bartlett (1886–1969). Although he was working in a very different tradition from the Gestalt psychologists, Bartlett also emphasized the ways in which each of us shapes and organizes our experience. Bartlett claimed that people spontaneously fit their experiences into a mental framework, or "schema," and rely on this schema both to interpret the experience as it happens and to aid memory later on. We'll say more about Bartlett's work (found primarily in his book *Remembering*, published in 1932) in Chapter 8.

Computers and the Cognitive Revolution

Tolman, Chomsky, the Gestaltists, and Bartlett disagreed on many points. Even so, a common theme ran through their theorizing: These scholars agreed that we can't explain humans' (or even rats') behavior unless we explain what is going on within the mind—whether our emphasis is on cognitive maps, schemas (or schemata), or some other form of knowledge. But, in explaining this knowledge and how the knowledge is put to use, where should we begin? What sorts of processes or mechanisms might we propose?

In the 1950s, computer scientists were making enormous progress in developing new hardware and software. Computers are, of course, capable of information storage and retrieval ("memory") and can do tasks that seemingly involve decision making and problem solving. Perhaps it was inevitable, then, that computer scientists would seek to create genuinely intelligent computers, and in the 1950s the field of "artificial intelligence" made rapid progress (e.g., Newell & Simon, 1959).

Psychologists were intrigued by these developments and began to explore the possibility that the human mind followed procedures similar to

FREDERIC BARTLETT

Frederic Bartlett (1886–1969) was the first professor of experimental psychology at the University of Cambridge. He is best known for his studies of memory and the notion that people spontaneously fit their experiences into a "schema," and they rely on the schema both to guide their understanding and (later) to guide their memory.

those used in computers. As a result, psychological data were soon being explained in terms of "buffers" and "gates" and "central processors," terms borrowed from computer technology (e.g., Miller, 1956; Miller et al., 1960). This approach was certainly evident in the work of Donald Broadbent (1926–1993). This British psychologist was one of the earliest researchers to use the language of computer science in explaining human cognition—for example, in his theorizing about how people focus their attention when working in complex environments.

Other psychologists soon followed this lead, and so, to explain how people loaded information into memory or how they made decisions, researchers hypothesized a series of information-processing events that made the performance possible. As we will see, hypotheses cast in these terms led psychologists to predict a range of new observations, and in this way both organized the available information and led to many new discoveries.

Research in Cognitive Psychology: The Diversity of Methods

Cognitive psychologists continue to frame many hypotheses in these computer-based terms, but we've also developed other options for theorizing. For example, before we're done in this book, we'll also discuss hypotheses framed in terms of the strategies a person is relying on, or the inferences she is making. No matter what the form of the hypothesis, though, we then run tests, following the logic we've already described: In other words, we derive predictions from the hypothesis, along the lines of "If this is the mechanism behind the original findings, then things should work differently in *this* circumstance or *that* one." Then, we gather data to test those predictions. And of course, if the data don't line up with the predictions, then a new hypothesis is needed.

But what methods do we use, and what sorts of data do we collect? The answer, in brief, is that we use *diverse* methods and collect many types of data. In other words, what unites cognitive psychology is the logic behind our research, and not an allegiance to any particular procedure in the laboratory.

Thus, in some settings, we ask how well people perform a particular task. In tests of memory, for example, we might ask *how complete* someone's memory is (does the person remember all of the objects in view in a picture?) and also *how accurate* the memory is (does the person perhaps remember seeing a banana when, actually, no banana was in view?). We can also ask how performance changes if we change the "input" (how well does the person remember a story, rather than a picture?), and we can change the person's circumstances (how is memory changed if the person is happy, or afraid, when hearing the story?). We can also manipulate the person's plans or strategies (what happens if we teach the person some sort of memorization technique?), and we can compare different people (children vs. adults; novices at a task vs. experts; people with normal vision vs. people who have been blind since birth).

TEST YOURSELF

3. Why is introspection limited as a source of scientific evidence?
4. Why do modern psychologists agree that we *have* to refer to mental states (what you believe, what you perceive, what you understand) in order to explain behavior?
5. Describe at least one historical development that laid the groundwork for the cognitive revolution.

A different approach relies on measurements of *speed*. The idea here is that mental operations are fast but do take a measurable amount of time, and by examining the **response time (RT)**—that is, how long someone needs to make a particular response—we can gain important insights into what's going on in the mind. For example, imagine that we ask you: "Yes or no: Do cats have whiskers?" And then: "Yes or no: Do cats have heads?" Both questions are absurdly easy, so there's no point in asking whether you're accurate in your responses—it's a sure bet that you will be. We can, however, measure your response times to questions like these, with intriguing results. For example, if you're forming a mental picture of a cat when you're asked these questions, you'll be faster for the "heads" question than the "whiskers" question. If you think about cats without forming a mental picture, the pattern reverses—you'll be faster for the "whiskers" question. In Chapter 11, we'll use results like these to test hypotheses about how ideas—and mental pictures in particular—are represented and analyzed in your mind.

We can also gain insights from observations focused on the brain and nervous system. Over the last few decades, cognitive psychology has formed a productive partnership with the field of **cognitive neuroscience**, the effort toward understanding humans' mental functioning through close study of the brain and nervous system. But here, too, numerous forms of evidence are available. We'll say more about these points in the next chapter, but for now let's note that we can learn a lot by studying people with damaged brains and also people with healthy brains. Information about damaged brains comes from the field of **clinical neuropsychology**, the study of brain function that uses, as its main data source, cases in which damage or illness has disrupted the working of some brain structure. We've already mentioned H.M., a man whose memory was massively disrupted as an unexpected consequence of surgery. As a different example, in Chapter 12 we'll consider cases in which someone's ability to make ordinary decisions (Coke or Pepsi? Wear the blue sweater or the green one?) is disrupted if brain centers involved in *emotion* are disrupted; observations like these provide crucial information about the role of emotion in decision making.

Information about healthy brains comes from **neuroimaging techniques**, which enable us, with some methods, to scrutinize the precise structure of the brain and, with other methods, to track the moment-by-moment pattern of activation within someone's brain. We'll see in Chapter 7, for example, that different patterns of brain activation during learning lead to different types of memory, and we'll use this fact as we ask what the types of memory are.

There's no reason for you, as a reader, to memorize this catalogue of different types of evidence. That's because we'll encounter each of these forms of data again and again in this text. Our point for now is simply to highlight the fact that there are multiple tools with which we can test, and eventually confirm, various claims. Indeed, relying on these tools, cognitive psychology has learned a tremendous amount about the mind. Our research has brought us powerful new theories and enormously useful results. Let's dive in and start exploring what the science of the mind has taught us.

TEST YOURSELF

6. Describe at least three types of evidence that cognitive psychologists routinely rely on.

Research in cognitive psychology sometimes addresses deep theoretical issues, such as what it means to be "rational" or what the function of consciousness might be. But our research also has broad practical implications, with studies providing important lessons for how we should conduct our daily lives.

To explore these practical implications, I've written "themed essays" for each of the upcoming chapters in this book. Starting with Chapter 2, there is, for each chapter, first, an essay describing how the material in that chapter can be applied to an issue that's important for *education*. Second, for each chapter, there's (at least) one essay discussing how the chapter's content might shape the way we think about the *legal system*. Third, every chapter also has an essay that explores the relationship between cognitive psychology and questions about *health* and medicine. Finally, for each chapter, there's also an essay that examines a linkage between cognitive psychology and the world of *technology*. To give readers a taste of—and easy access to—these essays, one of them is included at the end of each chapter in this volume. The full set of essays, though, can be found on the web at https://digital.wwnorton.com/cognition8.

It's certainly possible to read this book without any attention to these various essays. Even so, I hope that readers will be curious to explore some of them—perhaps in one of the four categories (education, law, health, or technology) that's of special interest, or perhaps by sampling across the categories.

So what are these themed essays all about? Some of the lessons from cognitive psychology are obvious. For example, research on memory can help students who are trying to learn new materials in the classroom; studies of how people draw conclusions can help people draw smarter, more defensible conclusions. Following these leads, one group of essays explores how the material in the chapter can be applied to questions about *education*. For example, the essay for Chapter 4 will teach you how to speed-read (but will also explain the limitations of speed-reading, with the aim of helping you decide when to speed-read, and when not). The essay for Chapter 8 will describe some steps you can take to avoid forgetting the materials you learned last week, or even last year.

The *law* essays have a different focus, and to see the point, think about what happens in a criminal investigation. Eyewitnesses provide evidence, based on what they paid attention to during a crime and what they remember. Police officers question the witnesses, trying to get the most out of what each witness recalls—but without leading the witness in any way. Then, the police try to deduce, from the evidence, who the perpetrator was. Later, during the trial, jurors listen to evidence and make a judgment about the defendant's innocence or guilt.

Cast in these terms, it should be obvious that an understanding of *attention, memory, reasoning,* and *judgment* (to name just a few processes) is directly relevant to what happens in police investigations and the courts. The essay for Chapter 7, for example, explores a research-based procedure for helping witnesses recall more of what they've observed. The essay for Chapter 8 discusses how *jurors* remember the evidence they've heard during a trial.

Research in cognition also matters—and may be crucial—when we explore questions about medicine and *health*. The essay for Chapter 5, for example, discusses the risk that radiologists might overlook a tumor visible in an X-ray. The essay for Chapter 6 discusses the role of "prospective memory" in helping someone to follow a doctor's instructions. The essay for Chapter 9 uses what we know about mental categories to evaluate the diagnosis of mental disorders.

Finally, a lot of your daily routine is shaped by *technology*, and it turns out that cognitive psychology has implications here, too. So the essay for Chapter 4, for example, discusses the status of face-recognition software; the essay for Chapter 5 explores why it is that some content on the web "goes viral." The essay for Chapter 9 discusses how the tech world is stretching some of our concepts, when, for example, the word "smart" is used by a company selling "smart toilets."

I hope that all of these essays—with themes, as I've said, of *education, law, health,* and *technology*—are interesting, useful for readers, and maybe even fun. But I also hope that the range of these essays helps convey a message that was central to this entry chapter: Virtually every aspect of our lives depends on, and is shaped by, our cognition. When we're exploring cognitive psychology, therefore, we're exploring a central aspect of who we are and how we function, and I hope these essays, examining a wide range of implications of our science, help to drive that point home!

COGNITIVE PSYCHOLOGY AND THE LEGAL SYSTEM

Eyewitnesses in the courtroom rely on what they *remember* about key events, and what they remember depends crucially on what they *perceived* and *paid attention to*. Therefore, our understanding of memory, perception, and attention can help the legal system in its evaluation of witness evidence.

chapter review

SUMMARY

• Cognitive psychology is concerned with how people remember, pay attention, and think. The importance of all these issues arises partly from the fact that most of what we do, say, and feel is guided by things we already know. One example is our comprehension of a simple story, which turns out to be heavily influenced by the knowledge we supply.

• Cognitive psychology emerged as a separate discipline in the late 1950s, and its powerful impact on the wider field of psychology has led many academics to speak of this emergence as the cognitive revolution. One predecessor of cognitive psychology was the 19th-century movement that emphasized introspection as the main research tool for psychology. But psychologists soon became disenchanted with this movement for several reasons: Introspection cannot inform us about unconscious mental events; and even with conscious events, claims rooted in introspection are often untestable because there is no way for an independent observer to check the accuracy or completeness of an introspective report.

• The behaviorist movement rejected introspection as a method, insisting instead that psychology speak only of mechanisms and processes that are objective and out in the open for all to observe. However, evidence suggests that our thinking, behavior, and feelings are often shaped by our perception or understanding of the events we experience. This is problematic for the behaviorists: Perception and understanding are exactly the sorts of mental processes that the behaviorists regard as subjective and not open to scientific study.

• In order to study mental events, psychologists have turned to a method in which one focuses on observable events but then asks what (invisible) events must have taken place in order to make these (visible) effects possible.

• Many factors contributed to the emergence of cognitive psychology in the 1950s and 1960s. Tolman's research demonstrated that even in rats, learning involved the acquisition of new knowledge and not just a change in behavior. Chomsky argued powerfully that a behaviorist analysis was inadequate as an explanation for language learning and language use. Gestalt psychologists emphasized the role of perceivers in organizing their experiences. Bartlett's research showed that people spontaneously fit their experiences into a mental framework, or schema.

• Early theorizing in cognitive psychology often borrowed ideas from computer science, including early work on artificial intelligence.

• Cognitive psychologists rely on a diverse set of methods and collect many types of data. Included are measures of the quality of someone's performance, measures of response speed, and, in some cases, methods that allow us to probe the underlying biology.

KEY TERMS

introspection (p. 8)
behaviorist movement (p. 11)
transcendental method (p. 13)
response time (RT) (p. 18)

cognitive neuroscience (p. 18)
clinical neuropsychology (p. 18)
neuroimaging techniques (p. 18)

TEST YOURSELF AGAIN

1. Why is memory crucial for behaviors and mental operations that don't in any direct or explicit way ask you to "remember"?

2. What aspects of H.M.'s life were disrupted as a result of his amnesia?

3. Why is introspection limited as a source of scientific evidence?

4. Why do modern psychologists agree that we *have to* refer to mental states (what you believe, what you perceive, what you understand) in order to explain behavior?

5. Describe at least one historical development that laid the groundwork for the cognitive revolution.

6. Describe at least three types of evidence that cognitive psychologists routinely rely on.

THINK ABOUT IT

1. The chapter argues that in a wide range of settings, our behaviors and our emotions depend on what we know, believe, and remember. Can you come up with examples of your own that illustrate this reliance on cognition in a circumstance that doesn't seem, on the surface, to be one that involves "intellectual activity"?

2. Some critics of Darwin's theory of evolution via natural selection argue this way: "Darwin's claims can never be tested, because of course no one was around to observe directly the processes of evolution that Darwin proposed." Why is this assertion misguided, resting on a false notion of how science proceeds?

DEMONSTRATIONS

For demonstrations of key concepts in cognitive psychology, take a look at the Online Demonstrations.

- Demonstration 1.1: The Broad Impact of Background Knowledge

- Demonstration 1.2: Understanding Depends on Background Knowledge

ZAPS COGNITION LABS

Go to ZAPS online cognition labs to conduct hands-on experiments on key concepts.

INQUIZITIVE

It's time to complete your study experience! Go to InQuizitive to practice actively with this chapter's concepts and get personalized feedback along the way.

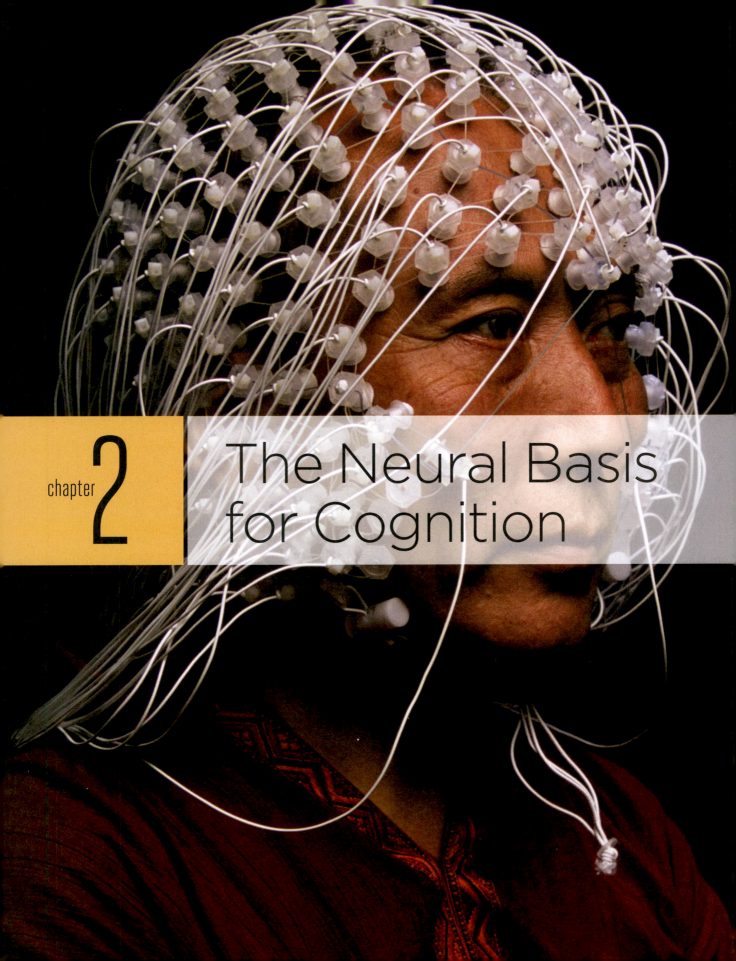

chapter **2**

The Neural Basis
for Cognition

what if... Throughout this text, we'll be examining ordinary achievements. Someone asks, "Where'd you grow up?" and you immediately answer. You're meeting a friend at the airport, and you recognize her the moment she steps into view. An instructor says, "Listen carefully," and you have no trouble focusing your attention.

Ordinary or not, achievements like these are crucial for you, and your life would be massively disrupted if you couldn't draw information from memory, recognize your friends, or choose where you point your attention. As a way of dramatizing this point, we'll begin each chapter by asking: What would happen to someone if one of these fundamental capacities *didn't work* as it normally does? What if . . . ?

The disorder known as Capgras syndrome (Capgras & Reboul-Lachaux, 1923) is relatively rare, but can result from various injuries to the brain (Ellis & De Pauw, 1994) and is sometimes found in people with Alzheimer's syndrome (Harwood et al., 1999). Someone with this syndrome is fully able to recognize the people in her world—her husband, parents, friends—but is utterly convinced that some of these people are not who they appear to be. The real husband or the real son, the afflicted person insists, has been kidnapped (or worse). The person now in view, therefore, must be a fraud of some sort, impersonating the (allegedly) absent person.

Imagine what it's like to have this disorder. You turn to your father and angrily shout, "You look like my father, sound like him, and act like him. But I can tell that you're not my father! *Who are you? And what have you done with my real father?!*"

Often, a person with Capgras syndrome insists there are slight differences between the "impostors" and the people they have supposedly replaced—subtle changes in personality or appearance. Of course, no one else detects these changes (because there have been no changes!), and this can lead the person with the syndrome to paranoid suspicions about why a loved one has vanished and why no one else will acknowledge the replacement. In the extreme, these suspicions can lead a Capgras sufferer to desperate steps. In some cases, patients with this syndrome have murdered the supposed impostor in an attempt to end the charade. In one case, a Capgras patient was convinced his father had been replaced by a robot and so decapitated him in order to look for the batteries and microfilm in his head (Blount, 1986).

- We begin by exploring the example of Capgras syndrome to illustrate how seemingly simple achievements actually depend on many parts of the brain. We also highlight the ways that the study of the brain can illuminate questions about the mind.

- We then survey the brain's anatomy, emphasizing the function carried out by each region. Identification of these functions is supported by neuroimaging data, which can assess the activity levels in different areas, and by studies of the effects of brain damage.

- We then take a closer look at the various parts of the cerebral cortex—the most important part of the brain for cognitive functioning. These parts include the motor areas, the sensory areas, and the so-called association cortex.

- Finally, we turn to the individual cells that make up the brain—the neurons and glia—and discuss the basic principles of how these cells function.

What is going on here? The answer lies in the fact that face recognition involves two separate systems in the brain. One system leads to a cognitive appraisal ("I know what my father looks like, and I can see that you closely resemble him"), and the other to a more global, emotional appraisal ("You look familiar to me and also trigger a warm response in me"). When these two appraisals agree, the result is a confident recognition ("You obviously are my father"). In Capgras syndrome, though, the emotional processing is disrupted, leading to an intellectual identification without a familiarity response (Ellis & Lewis, 2001; Ellis & Young, 1990; Ramachandran & Blakeslee, 1998): "You resemble my father but trigger no sense of familiarity, so you must be someone else." The result? Confusion and bizarre speculation about why a loved one has been kidnapped and replaced—and a level of paranoia that can, as we have seen, lead to homicide.

Explaining Capgras Syndrome

Is this account the right way to think about Capgras syndrome? One line of evidence comes from neuroimaging techniques that provide researchers with high-quality, three-dimensional "pictures" of living brains. We'll have more to say about neuroimaging later; but first, what do these techniques tell us about Capgras syndrome?

The Neural Basis for Capgras Syndrome

One type of neuroimaging provides a portrait of the physical makeup of the brain: What's where? How are structures shaped or connected to one another? Are there structures present (such as tumors) that shouldn't be there, or structures that are missing (because of disease or birth defects)? This information about structure was gained in older studies from positron emission tomography (PET scans). Newer studies rely on magnetic resonance imaging (MRI scans; see **Figure 2.1**). These scans suggest a link between Capgras syndrome and abnormalities in several brain areas (Edelstyn & Oyebode, 1999; also see O'Connor et al., 1996). One site of damage is in the temporal lobe (see **Figure 2.2**), particularly on the right side of the head. This damage disrupts circuits involving the **amygdala**, an almond-shaped structure that—in the intact brain—serves as an "emotional evaluator," helping an organism detect stimuli associated with threat or danger (see **Figure 2.3**). The amygdala is also important for detecting positive stimuli—indicators of safety or available rewards. With *damaged* amygdalae, therefore, people with Capgras syndrome won't experience the warm sense of feeling safe and secure when looking at a loved one's familiar face. This lack of an emotional response is probably why these faces don't feel familiar to them, and it is fully in line with the two-systems hypothesis we've already sketched.

FIGURE 2.1 NEUROIMAGING

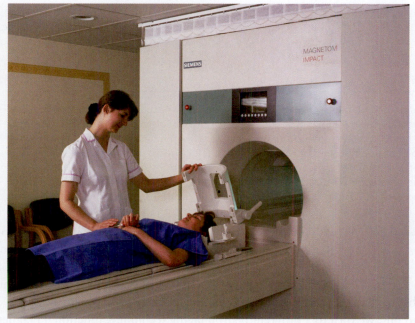

Scanners like this one are used for both MRI and fMRI scans. MRI scans tell us about the structure of the brain; fMRI scans tell us which portions of the brain are especially active during the scan. An fMRI scan usually results in color images, with each hue indicating a particular activity level.

FIGURE 2.2 THE LOBES OF THE HUMAN BRAIN

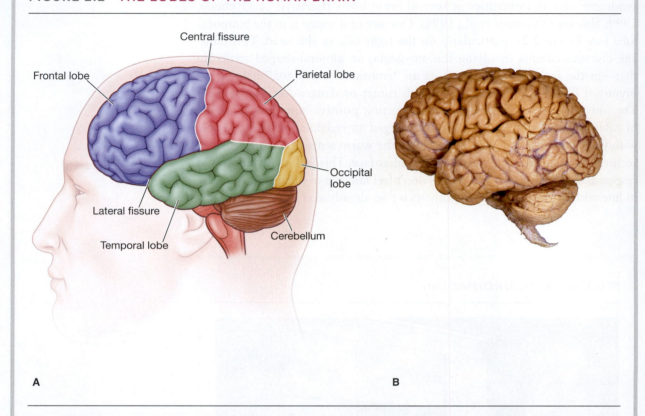

A

B

Panel A identifies the various lobes and some of the brain's prominent features. Actual brains, however, are uniformly colored, as shown in the photograph in Panel B. The four lobes of the forebrain surround (and hide from view) the midbrain and most of the hindbrain. (The cerebellum is the only part of the hindbrain that is visible in the figure, and, in fact, the temporal lobe has been pushed upward a bit in the left panel to make the cerebellum more visible.) This side view shows the left cerebral hemisphere; the structures on the right side of the brain are similar. However, the two halves of the brain have somewhat different functions, and so the results of brain injury depend on which half is damaged. The symptoms of Capgras syndrome, for example, result from damage to specific sites on the right side of the frontal and temporal lobes.

Patients with Capgras syndrome also have abnormalities in the frontal lobe, in the right **prefrontal cortex**. What is this area's normal function? To find out, we turn to a different neuroimaging technique, functional magnetic resonance imaging (fMRI), which enables us to track moment-by-moment activity levels in a living brain. (We'll say more about fMRI in a later section.) This technique allows us to answer such questions as: When a person is reading, which brain regions are particularly active? How about when a person is listening to music? With data like these, we can ask which tasks make heavy use of a brain area, and from that base we can draw conclusions about that brain area's function.

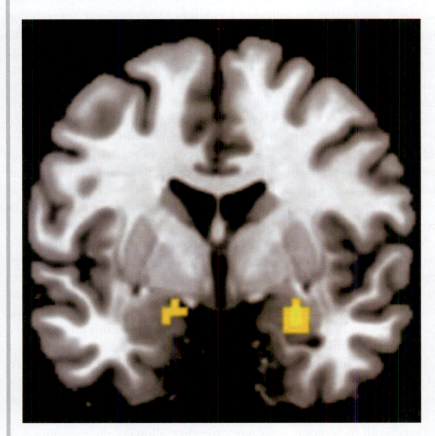

FIGURE 2.3 THE AMYGDALA AS AN "EMOTIONAL EVALUATOR"

The areas shown in yellow marks the location of the amygdala. In this image, the yellow is a reflection of increased activity created by a fear memory—the memory of receiving an electric shock.

Studies show that the prefrontal cortex is especially active when a person is doing tasks that require planning or careful analysis. How is this relevant to Capgras syndrome? With damage to the frontal lobe, Capgras patients may be less able to keep track of what is real and what is not, what is sensible and what is not. As a result, weird beliefs can emerge unchecked, including delusions (about robots and the like) that you or I would find totally bizarre. (For more on Capgras syndrome, see Ellis & Lewis, 2001; Ramachandran & Blakeslee, 1998.)

What Do We Learn from Capgras Syndrome?

Our understanding of Capgras syndrome draws on evidence from cognitive psychology and cognitive neuroscience. We use both perspectives to test (and, ultimately, to confirm) the hypothesis we've offered. In addition, just as both perspectives can illuminate Capgras syndrome, both *can be illuminated by* the syndrome. That is, we can use Capgras syndrome (and other biological evidence) to illuminate broader issues about the nature of the mind and brain.

For example, Capgras syndrome suggests that the amygdala plays a crucial role in supporting the feeling of familiarity. Other evidence suggests that the amygdala helps people remember the emotional events of their lives (e.g., Buchanan & Adolphs, 2004) and also plays a role in decision making (e.g., Bechara et al., 2003). Facts like these tell us a lot about the functions that make cognition possible and, specifically, tell us that our theorizing needs to include a broadly useful "emotional evaluator," involved in many cognitive processes. Moreover, Capgras syndrome tells us that this emotional evaluator works in a fashion separate from the evaluation of factual information, and this observation gives us a way to think about occasions in which your evaluation of the facts points toward one conclusion, while an emotional evaluation points toward a different conclusion. These are valuable clues as we try to understand the processes that support ordinary remembering or decision making.

What does Capgras syndrome teach us about the brain itself? One lesson involves the fact that many parts of the brain are needed for even the simplest achievement. In order to recognize your father, for example, one part of your brain needs to store the memory of what he looks like. Another part of the brain is responsible for analyzing the visual input you receive when looking at a face. Yet another brain area has the job of comparing this now-analyzed input to the information provided from memory, asking whether there's a match. Another site provides the emotional evaluation of the input. A different site presumably assembles the data from all these other sites—and registers the fact that the face being inspected does match the factual recollection of your father's face, and also produces a warm sense of familiarity.

Usually, all these brain areas work together, allowing the recognition of your father's face to go smoothly forward. If they don't work together—that is, if coordination among these areas is disrupted—yet another area works to make sure you offer reasonable hypotheses about this disconnect, and not zany ones. (In other words, if your father looks less familiar to you on some occasion, you're likely to explain this by saying, "I guess he must have gotten new glasses" rather than "I bet he's been replaced by a robot.")

Plainly, then, this simple task—seeing your father and recognizing who he is—requires multiple brain areas. The same is true of most tasks, and in this way Capgras syndrome illustrates this crucial aspect of brain function.

The Study of the Brain

In order to discuss Capgras syndrome, we needed to refer to different brain areas and had to rely on several different research techniques. In this way, the syndrome also illustrates another point—that this is a domain in which we need some technical foundations before we can develop our theories. Let's start building those foundations.

The human brain weighs (on average) a bit more than 3 pounds (roughly 1.4 kg) and is roughly the size of a small melon. This compact structure, however, has been estimated to contain 86 billion nerve cells (Azevedo et al.,

2009). Each of these cells is connected to 10,000 or so others—for a total of 860 trillion connections. The brain also contains a huge number of *glial cells*, and we'll have more to say about all of these individual cells later on in the chapter. For now, though, how should we begin our study of this densely packed, incredibly complex organ?

Let's start with a simple fact we've already met: that different parts of the brain perform different jobs. Scientists have known this fact about the brain for many years, thanks to clinical evidence showing that the symptoms produced by brain damage depend heavily on the location of the damage. In 1848, for example, a horrible construction accident caused Phineas Gage to suffer damage in the frontmost part of his brain (see **Figure 2.4**), and this damage led to severe personality and emotional problems. In 1861, physician Paul Broca noted that damage in a different location, on the left side of the brain, led to a disruption of language skills. In 1911, Édouard Claparède (1911/1951) reported his observations with patients who suffered from profound memory loss produced by damage in still another part of the brain.

FIGURE 2.4   PHINEAS GAGE

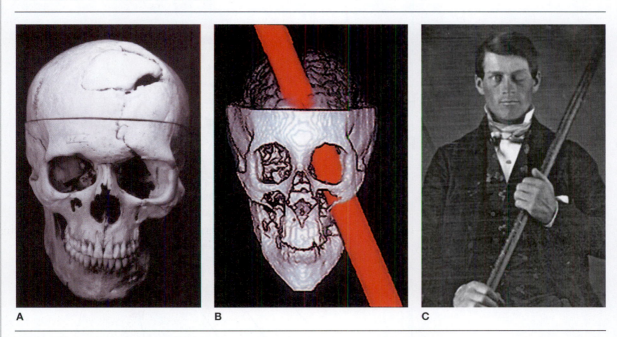

A   B   C

Phineas Gage was working as a construction foreman when some blasting powder misfired and launched a piece of iron into his cheek and through the front part of his brain. Remarkably, Gage survived and continued to live a fairly normal life, but his pattern of intellectual and emotional impairments provides valuable cues about the function of the brain's frontal lobes. Panel A is a photo of Gage's skull; the drawing in Panel B depicts the iron bar's path as it blasted through his head. Panel C is an actual photograph of Gage, and he's holding a bizarre souvenir of his experience—the actual bar that went through his brain!

Clearly, therefore, we need to understand brain functioning with reference to brain anatomy. Where was the damage that Gage suffered? Where was the damage in Broca's patients or Claparède's? In this section, we fill in some basics of brain anatomy.

Hindbrain, Midbrain, Forebrain

The human brain is divided into three main structures: the hindbrain, the midbrain, and the forebrain. The **hindbrain** is located at the very top of the spinal cord and includes structures crucial for controlling key life functions. It's here, for example, that the rhythm of heartbeats is regulated. The hindbrain also plays an essential role in maintaining the body's overall posture and balance; it also helps control the brain's level of alertness.

The largest area of the hindbrain is the **cerebellum**. For many years, investigators believed this structure's main role was in the coordination of bodily movements. Research indicates, however, that the cerebellum plays various other roles and that damage to this organ can cause problems in spatial reasoning, in discriminating sounds, and in integrating the input received from various sensory systems (Bower & Parsons, 2003).

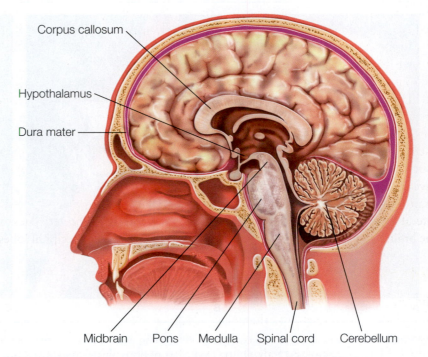

Corpus callosum

Hypothalamus

Dura mater

Midbrain   Pons   Medulla   Spinal cord   Cerebellum

GROSS ANATOMY OF A BRAIN SHOWING BRAIN STEM

The pons and medulla are part of the hindbrain. The medulla controls vital functions such as breathing and heart rate. The pons (Latin for "bridge") is the main connection between the cerebellum and the rest of the brain.

The **midbrain** has several functions. It plays an important part in coordinating the precise movements of the eyes as they explore the visual world. Also in the midbrain are circuits that relay auditory information from the ears to areas in the forebrain where this information is processed and interpreted. Still other structures in the midbrain help to regulate the experience of pain.

For our purposes, though, the most interesting brain region (and, in humans, the largest region) is the **forebrain**. Drawings of the brain (like the one shown in Figure 2.2) show little other than the forebrain, because this structure surrounds (and so hides from view) the midbrain and most of the hindbrain. Of course, only the outer surface of the forebrain—the **cortex**—is visible in such pictures. In general, the word "cortex" (from the Latin word for "tree bark") refers to an organ's outer surface, and many organs each have their own cortex; what's visible in the drawing is the cerebral cortex.

The cortex is just a thin covering on the outer surface of the forebrain; on average, it's a mere 3 mm thick. Nonetheless, there's a lot of cortical tissue; by some estimates, the cortex makes up 80% of the human brain. This considerable volume is made possible by the fact that the cerebral cortex, thin as it is, is a rather large sheet of tissue; if stretched out flat, it would cover more than 300 in², or roughly 2,000 cm². (For comparison, an extra-large pizza is about 1,600 cm²—that is, 20% smaller than the area of the cortex.) But the cortex isn't stretched flat; it's crumpled up and jammed into the limited space inside the skull. It's this crumpling that produces the brain's most obvious visual feature—the wrinkles, or **convolutions**, that cover the brain's outer surface.

Some of the "valleys" between the wrinkles are actually deep grooves that divide the brain into different sections. The deepest groove is the **longitudinal fissure**, running from the front of the brain to the back, and separating the left **cerebral hemisphere** from the right. Other fissures divide the cortex in each hemisphere into four lobes (again, look back at Figure 2.2). The **frontal lobes** form the front of the brain, right behind the forehead. The **central fissure** divides the frontal lobes on each side of the brain from the **parietal lobes**, the brain's topmost part. The bottom edge of the frontal lobes is marked by the **lateral fissure**, and below it are the **temporal lobes**. Finally, at the very back of the brain, connected to the parietal and temporal lobes, are the **occipital lobes**.

Subcortical Structures

Hidden from view, underneath the cortex, are many **subcortical structures**. One of these structures, the **thalamus**, acts as a relay station for nearly all the sensory information going to the cortex. Directly underneath the thalamus is the **hypothalamus**, a structure that plays a crucial role in controlling behaviors that serve specific biological needs—behaviors that include eating, drinking, and sexual activity.

Surrounding the thalamus and hypothalamus is another set of structures that form the **limbic system**. Included here is the amygdala, and close by is the

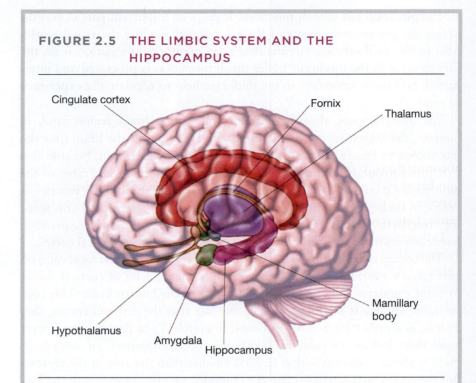

FIGURE 2.5   THE LIMBIC SYSTEM AND THE HIPPOCAMPUS

Cingulate cortex

Fornix

Thalamus

Hypothalamus

Amygdala

Hippocampus

Mamillary body

Color is used in this drawing to help you visualize the arrangement of these brain structures. Imagine that the cortex is semitransparent, allowing you to look into the brain to see the (subcortical) structures highlighted here. The limbic system includes a number of subcortical structures that play a crucial role in learning and memory and in emotional processing.

hippocampus, both located underneath the cortex in the temporal lobe (see **Figure 2.5**). These structures are essential for learning and memory, and the patient H.M., discussed in Chapter 1, developed his profound amnesia after surgeons removed large portions of these structures—strong confirmation of their role in the formation of new memories.

We mentioned earlier that the amygdala plays a key role in emotional processing, and this role is reflected in many findings. For example, presentation of scary faces causes high levels of activity in the amygdala (Williams et al., 2006). Likewise, people ordinarily show more complete, longer-lasting memories for emotional events, compared to similar but emotionally flat events. This memory advantage for emotional events is especially pronounced in people who showed greater activation in the amygdala while they were witnessing the event in the first place. Conversely, the memory advantage for emotional events is diminished (and may not be observed at all) in people who (through sickness or injury) have suffered damage to the amygdalae.

Lateralization

Virtually all parts of the brain come in pairs, and so there is a hippocampus on the left side of the brain and another on the right, a left-side amygdala and a right-side one. The same is true for the cerebral cortex itself: There is a temporal cortex (i.e., a cortex of the temporal lobe) in the left hemisphere and another in the right, a left occipital cortex and a right one, and so on. In all cases, cortical and subcortical, the left and right structures in each pair have roughly the same shape and the same pattern of connections to other brain areas. Even so, there are differences in function between the left- and right-side structures, with each left-hemisphere structure playing a somewhat different role from the corresponding right-hemisphere structure.

Let's remember, though, that the two halves of the brain work together—the functioning of one side is closely integrated with that of the other side. This integration is made possible by the **commissures**, thick bundles of fibers that carry information back and forth between the two hemispheres. The largest commissure is the **corpus callosum**, but several other structures also make sure that the two brain halves work as partners in almost all mental tasks.

In certain cases, though, there are medical reasons to sever the corpus callosum and some of the other commissures. (For many years, this surgery was a last resort for extreme cases of epilepsy.) The person is then said to be a "split-brain patient"—with communication between the brain halves severely limited. Research with these patients has taught us a great deal about the specialized function of the brain's two hemispheres. It has confirmed, for example, that many aspects of language processing are lodged in the left hemisphere, while the right hemisphere seems crucial for a number of tasks involving spatial judgment.

However, it's important not to overstate the contrast between the two brain halves, and it's misleading to claim (as some people do) that we need to silence our "left-brain thinking" in order to be more creative, or that intuitions grow out of "right-brain thinking." These claims do begin with a kernel of truth, because some elements of creativity depend on specialized processing in the right hemisphere (see, e.g., Kounios & Beeman, 2015). Even so, whether we're examining creativity or any other capacity, the two halves of the brain have to work together, with each hemisphere making its own contribution to the overall performance. Therefore, "shutting down" or "silencing" one hemisphere, even if that were biologically possible, wouldn't allow you new achievements, because the many complex, sophisticated skills we each display (including creativity, intuition, and more) depend on the whole brain. In other words, our hemispheres are not cerebral competitors, each trying to impose its style of thinking on the other. Instead, the hemispheres pool their specialized capacities to produce a seamlessly integrated, single mental self. (For a glimpse, though, of the pattern of specialization between the hemispheres, see **Figure 2.6**.)

TEST YOURSELF

2. What is the cerebral cortex?
3. What are the four major lobes of the forebrain?
4. Identify some of the functions of the hippocampus, the amygdala, and the corpus callosum.

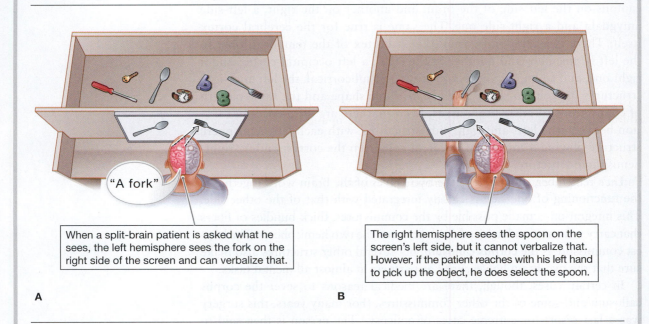

FIGURE 2.6 STUDYING SPLIT-BRAIN PATIENTS

"A fork"

When a split-brain patient is asked what he sees, the left hemisphere sees the fork on the right side of the screen and can verbalize that.

The right hemisphere sees the spoon on the screen's left side, but it cannot verbalize that. However, if the patient reaches with his left hand to pick up the object, he does select the spoon.

A

B

In this experiment, the patient is shown two pictures, one of a spoon and one of a fork (Panel A). If asked what he sees, his response is controlled by the left hemisphere, which has seen only the fork (because it's in the right visual field). However, if asked to pick up the object shown in the picture, the patient—reaching with his left hand—picks up the spoon (Panel B). That happens because the left hand is controlled by the right hemisphere, and this hemisphere receives visual information from the left-hand side of the visual world.

Sources of Evidence about the Brain

How can we learn about these various structures—and many others that we haven't named? Cognitive neuroscience relies on many types of evidence to study the brain and nervous system.

Data from Neuropsychology

We've already encountered one form of evidence—the study of individuals who have suffered brain damage through accident, disease, or birth defect. The study of these cases falls within the domain of *neuropsychology*: the study of the brain's structures and how they relate to brain function. Within neuropsychology, the specialty of *clinical neuropsychology* seeks (among other goals) to understand the functioning of intact, undamaged brains by means of careful scrutiny of cases involving brain damage.

Data drawn from clinical neuropsychology will be important throughout this text. For now, though, we emphasize that the symptoms resulting from brain damage depend on the site of the damage. A **lesion** (a specific area of damage) in the hippocampus produces memory problems but not language disorders; a lesion in the occipital cortex produces problems in vision but spares the other sensory modalities. Likewise, the consequences of brain lesions depend on which hemisphere is damaged. Damage to the left side of the frontal lobe, for example, is likely to produce a disruption of language use; damage to the right side of the frontal lobe generally doesn't have this effect. In obvious ways, then, these patterns confirm the claim that different brain areas perform different functions. In addition, these patterns provide a rich source of data that help us develop and test hypotheses about those functions.

Data from Neuroimaging

Further insights come from **neuroimaging techniques.** There are several types of neuroimaging, but they all produce precise, three-dimensional pictures of a living brain. Some neuroimaging procedures provide *structural* imaging, generating a detailed portrait of the shapes, sizes, and positions of the brain's components. Other procedures provide *functional* imaging, which tells us about activity levels throughout the brain.

For many years, **computerized axial tomography (CT scans)** was the primary tool for structural imaging, and **positron emission tomography (PET scans)** was used to study the brain's activity. CT scans provide three-dimensional X-ray pictures of the brain. PET scans, in contrast, start by introducing a tracer substance such as glucose into the patient's body; the molecules of this tracer have been tagged with a low dose of radioactivity, and the scan keeps track of this radioactivity, allowing us to tell which tissues are using more of the glucose (the body's main fuel) and which ones are using less.

For each type of scan, the primary data (X-rays or radioactive emissions) are collected by detectors placed around the person's head. A computer then compares the signals received by each of the detectors and uses this information to construct a three-dimensional map of the brain—a map of structures from a CT scan, and a map showing activity levels from a PET scan.

More recent studies use two newer techniques, mentioned earlier in the chapter. **Magnetic resonance imaging (MRI scans)** relies on the magnetic properties of the atoms that make up the brain tissue, and provides fabulously detailed structural images. A closely related technique, **functional magnetic resonance imaging (fMRI scans)**, provides functional imaging. The fMRI scans measure the oxygen content in blood flowing through each region of the brain; this provides an index of the level of neural activity in that region—and so, overall, can offer us an incredibly precise picture of the brain's moment-by-moment activities.

Data from Electrical Recording

Neuroscientists have another technique in their tool kit: electrical recording of the brain's activity. To explain this point, though, we need to say a bit about how the brain functions. As we said early on, the brain contains

PET SCANS

PET scans measure how much glucose (the brain's fuel) is being used at specific locations within the brain; this provides a measurement of each location's activity level at a certain moment in time. In the figure, the brain is viewed from above, with the front of the head at the top and the back of the head at the bottom. The various colors indicate relative activity levels (an actual brain is uniformly colored), using the palette shown on the right side of the figure. Dark blue indicates a low level of activity; red indicates a high level. And as the figure shows, visual processing involves increased activity in the occipital lobe.

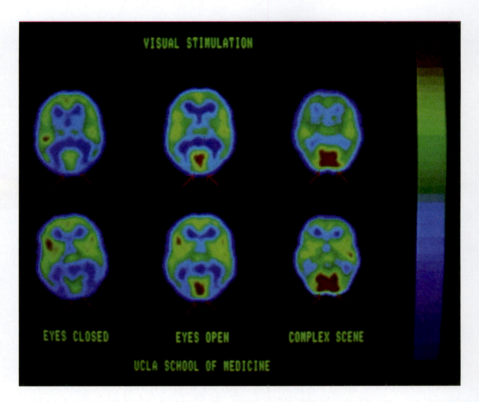

billions of nerve cells—"neurons"—and it is the neurons that do the brain's main work. (We'll say more about these cells later in the chapter.) Neurons vary in their functioning, but for the most part they communicate with one another via chemical signals called "neurotransmitters." Once a neuron is "activated," it releases the transmitter, and this chemical can then activate (or, in some cases, *de*-activate) other, adjacent neurons. The adjacent neurons "receive" this chemical signal and, in turn, send their own signal onward to other neurons.

Let's be clear, though, that the process we just described is communication *between* neurons: One neuron releases the transmitter substance, and this activates (or de-activates) another neuron. But there's also communication *within* each neuron. The reason, basically, is that neurons have an "input" end and an "output" end. The "input" end is the portion of the neuron that's most sensitive to neurotransmitters; this is where the signal from other neurons is received. The "output" end is the portion that releases neurotransmitters, sending the signal on to other neurons. These two ends can sometimes be far apart. (For example, some neurons in the body run from the base of the spine down to the toes; for these cells, the input and output ends might be a full meter apart.) The question, then, is how neurons get a signal from one end of the cell to the other.

The answer involves an electrical pulse, made possible by a flow of charged atoms (ions) in and out of the neuron (again, we'll say more about

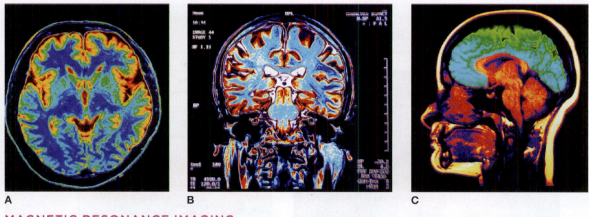

MAGNETIC RESONANCE IMAGING

Magnetic resonance imaging produces magnificently detailed pictures of the brain. Panel A shows an "axial view"—a "slice" of the brain viewed from the top of the head (the front of the head is at the top of the image). Clearly visible is the longitudinal fissure, which divides the left cerebral hemisphere from the right. Panel B, a "coronal view," shows a slice of the brain viewed from the front. Again, the separation of the two hemispheres is clearly visible, as are some of the commissures linking the two brain halves. Panel C, a "sagittal view," shows a slice of the brain viewed from the side. Here, many of the structures in the limbic system (see Figure 2.5) are easily seen.

this process later in the chapter). The amount of electrical current involved in this ion flow is tiny; but many millions of neurons are active at the same time, and the current generated by all of them together is strong enough to be detected by electrodes placed on the surface of the scalp. This is the basis for *electroencephalography*—a recording of voltage changes occurring at the scalp that reflect activity in the brain underneath. This procedure generates an **electroencephalogram (EEG)**—a recording of the brain's electrical activity.

Often, EEGs are used to study broad rhythms in the brain's activity. For example, an *alpha rhythm* (with the activity level rising and falling 7 to 10 times per second) can usually be detected in the brain of someone who is awake but calm and relaxed; a *delta rhythm* (with the activity rising and falling roughly 1 to 4 times per second) is observed when someone is deeply asleep. A much faster *gamma rhythm* (between 30 and 80 cycles per second) has received a lot of research attention, with a suggestion that this rhythm plays a key role in creating conscious awareness (e.g., Crick & Koch, 1990; Dehaene, 2014; Fiebelkorn & Kastner, 2020).

Sometimes, though, we want to know about electrical activity in the brain over a shorter period—for example, when the brain is responding to a specific input or a particular stimulus. In this case, we measure changes in the EEG in the brief periods just before, during, and after the event. These changes are referred to as **event-related potentials** (see **Figure 2.7**).

FIGURE 2.7 RECORDING THE BRAIN'S ELECTRICAL ACTIVITY

A

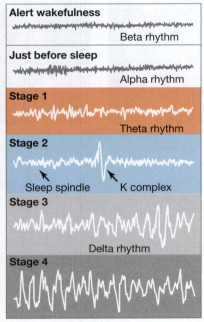

B

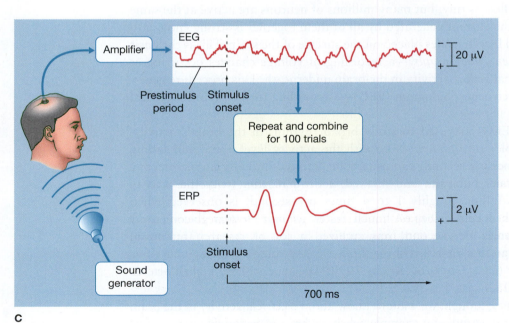

C

To record the brain's electrical signals, researchers generally use a cap that has electrodes attached to it. The procedure is easy and entirely safe—it can even be used to measure brain signals in a baby (Panel A). In some procedures, researchers measure recurrent rhythms in the brain's activity, including rhythms that distinguish the stages of sleep (Panel B). In other procedures, they measure brain activity produced in response to a single event—such as the presentation of a well-defined stimulus (Panel C).

Manipulations of Brain Function

Most of the methods we've considered so far involve *observation* of the brain's functioning. Researchers also use techniques to *manipulate* the brain's function. For example, some studies scrutinize what happens if various chemicals are introduced into the body—for example, chemicals known to interfere with (or, in some cases, promote) the activity of specific neurotransmitters. Other studies explore brain function by stimulating specific sites with (mild) electrical inputs. In still other studies, researchers rely on an option made possible by modern genetic research. These studies are almost always done with mice and rats and involve direct manipulation of the genes, in order to ask how adding or subtracting genetic material alters brain function. For example, in a classic study, researchers developed a mouse strain that lacked a certain type of cell in the hippocampus. These mice exhibited poor learning in a variety of tasks, powerfully confirming the role of these cells in supporting learning (Wilson & Tonegawa, 1997).

Of course, these studies of brain manipulation remind us of the importance of *ethical considerations* in designing research. Is it ethically appropriate to manipulate the brain of another creature? Scientists take this question quite seriously, and any study (not just a study of brain manipulation) goes forward only after careful review (usually by a committee in the researcher's home institution) that asks whether risks have been minimized, and whether any remaining risks are fully justified by the likely benefits of the research.

The Power of Combining Techniques

Each of the research tools we've described has strengths and weaknesses. MRI data, for example, tell us about the shape and size of brain structures, but tell nothing about the activity levels within these structures. In contrast, fMRI studies do tell us about brain activity, and they can locate the activity rather precisely (within a millimeter or two). But this technique is less precise about *when* the activity took place, typically summarizing the brain's activity over a period of several seconds, with no clear indication of when, within this time window, the activity took place. EEG data give more precise information about timing but are much weaker in indicating *where* the activity took place.

Researchers deal with these limitations by means of a strategy commonly used in science: We seek data from multiple sources, so that the strengths of one technique can make up for the shortcomings of another. As a result, some studies combine EEG recordings with fMRI scans, with the EEGs telling us when certain events took place in the brain, and the scans telling us where the activity took place. Likewise, some studies combine fMRI scans with CT data, so that findings about brain activation can be linked to a detailed portrait of the person's brain anatomy.

Researchers also face another complication: the fact that these techniques usually provide only *correlational data*. To understand the concern, let's look at an example. A brain area called the **fusiform face area (FFA)** is especially active whenever a face is being perceived (see **Figure 2.8**)—and so there is a correlation between a mental activity (perceiving a face) and a pattern of brain activity. Does this mean the FFA is needed for face perception? A different possibility is that the FFA activation may just be a by-product of face perception and doesn't play a crucial role. As an analogy, think about the fact that a car's speedometer becomes "more activated" (i.e., shows a higher value) whenever the car goes faster. That doesn't mean that the speedometer

FIGURE 2.8 BRAIN ACTIVITY AND AWARENESS

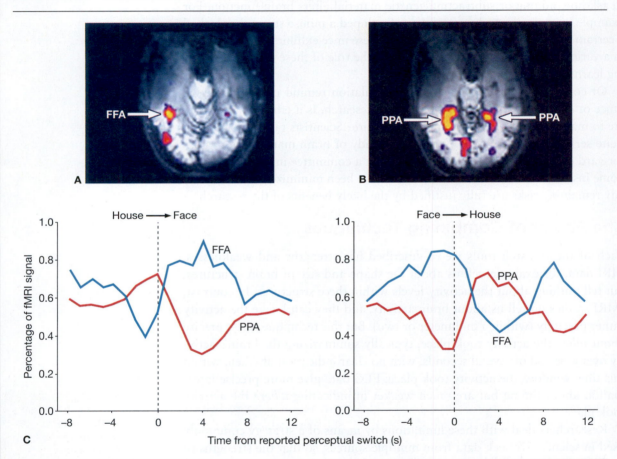

Panel A shows an fMRI scan of a subject looking at faces. Activation levels are high in the fusiform face area (FFA), an area that is apparently more responsive to faces than to other visual stimuli. Panel B shows a scan of the same subject looking at pictures of places; now, activity levels are high in the parahippocampal place area (PPA). Panel C compares the activity in these two areas when the subject has a picture of a face in front of one eye and a picture of a house in front of the other eye. When the viewer's perception shifts from the house to the face, activation increases in the FFA. When the viewer's perception shifts from the face to the house, PPA activation increases. In this way, the activation level reflects what the subject is aware of, and not just the pattern of incoming stimulation.

(AFTER TONG ET AL., 1998)

causes the speed or *is necessary* for the speed. The car would go just as fast and would, for many purposes, perform just as well if the speedometer were removed. The speedometer's state, in other words, is correlated with the car's speed but in no sense causes (or promotes, or is needed for) the car's speed.

In the same way, neuroimaging data can tell us that a brain area's activity is correlated with a particular function, but we need other data to determine whether the brain site plays a role in *causing* (or supporting, or allowing) that function. In many cases, those other data come from the study of brain lesions. If damage to a brain site disrupts a particular function, it's an indication that the site does play some role in supporting that function. (And, in fact, the FFA does play an important role in face recognition.)

Also helpful here is a technique called **transcranial magnetic stimulation (TMS)**. This technique creates a series of strong magnetic pulses at a specific location on the scalp, and these pulses activate the neurons directly underneath this scalp area (Helmuth, 2001). TMS can thus be used as a means of asking what happens if we stimulate certain neurons. In addition, because this stimulation *disrupts* the ordinary function of these neurons, it produces a (temporary) lesion—allowing us to identify, in essence, what functions are compromised when a particular bit of brain tissue is briefly "turned off." In these ways, the results of a TMS procedure can provide crucial information about the functional role of that brain area.

Localization of Function

Drawing on all these techniques, neuroscientists have learned a great deal about the function of specific brain structures. This type of research effort is referred to as the **localization of function**, an effort (to put it crudely) aimed at figuring out what's happening where within the brain.

Localization data are useful in many ways. For example, think back to the discussion of Capgras syndrome earlier in this chapter. Brain scans told us that people with this syndrome have damaged amygdalae, but how is this damage related to the symptoms of the syndrome? More broadly, what problems does a damaged amygdala create? To tackle these questions, we rely on localization of function—in particular, on data showing that the amygdala is involved in many tasks involving emotional appraisal. This combination of points helped us to build our claims about this syndrome and, in general, claims about the role of emotion within the ordinary experience of "familiarity."

As a different illustration, consider the experience of calling up a "mental picture" before the "mind's eye." We'll have more to say about this experience in Chapter 11, but we can already ask: How much does this experience have in common with ordinary seeing—that is, the process that unfolds when we place a real picture before someone's eyes? As it turns out, localization data reveal enormous overlap between the brain structures needed for these two activities (visualizing and actual vision), telling us immediately that these activities have a great deal in common (see **Figure 2.9**). So, again, we build on localization—this time, to identify how exactly two mental activities are related to each other.

TEST YOURSELF

5. What is the difference between *structural imaging* of the brain and *functional imaging*? What techniques are used for each?
6. What do we gain from *combining* different methods in studying the brain?
7. What is meant by the phrase "localization of function"?

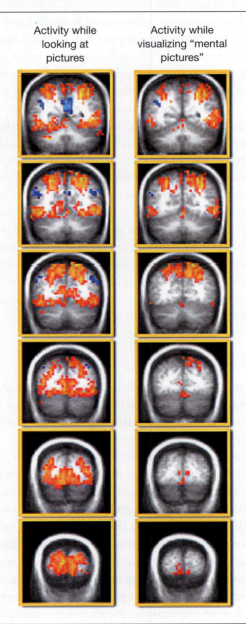

FIGURE 2.9   A PORTRAIT OF THE BRAIN AT WORK

Activity while looking at pictures

Activity while visualizing "mental pictures"

These fMRI images show different "slices" through the living brain, revealing levels of activity in different brain sites. Regions that are more active are shown in yellow, orange, and red; lower activity levels are indicated in blue. The first column shows brain activity while a person is making judgments about simple pictures. The second column shows brain activity while the person is making the same sort of judgments about "mental pictures," visualized before the "mind's eye."

The Cerebral Cortex

As we've noted, the largest portion of the human brain is the cerebral cortex—the thin layer of tissue covering the cerebrum, or forebrain. This is the brain area in which an enormous amount of information processing takes place, and it includes many distinct regions, each with its own function. These regions are traditionally divided, though, into three categories. *Motor areas* contain brain tissue crucial for organizing and controlling bodily movements. *Sensory areas* contain tissue essential for organizing and analyzing the information received from the senses. Finally, the *association areas* support many functions, including the essential (but not well-defined) human activity we call "thinking."

Motor Areas

Certain regions of the cerebral cortex serve as "departure points" for signals leaving the cortex and controlling muscle movement. Other areas are the "arrival points" for information coming from the eyes, ears, and other sense organs. In both cases, these areas are called "primary projection areas," with the departure points known as the **primary motor projection areas** and the arrival points contained in regions known as the **primary sensory projection areas**.

Evidence for the motor projection area comes from studies in which investigators apply mild electrical current to this area in anesthetized animals. This stimulation often produces specific movements, so that current applied to one site causes a movement of the left front leg, while current applied to a different site causes the ears to prick up. These movements show a pattern of **contralateral control,** with stimulation to the left hemisphere leading to movements on the right side of the body, and vice versa.

Why are these areas called "projection areas"? The term is borrowed from mathematics and from the discipline of map making, because these areas seem to form "maps" of the external world, with particular positions on the cortex corresponding to particular parts of the body or particular locations in space. In the human brain, the map that constitutes the motor projection area is located on a strip of tissue toward the rear of the frontal lobe, and the pattern of mapping is illustrated in **Figure 2.10**. In this illustration, a drawing of a person has been overlaid on a depiction of the brain, with each part of the person alongside of the brain area that controls its movement. The figure shows that areas of the body that we can move with great precision (e.g., fingers and lips) have a lot of cortical area devoted to them; areas of the body over which we have less control (e.g., the shoulder and the back) receive less cortical coverage.

Sensory Areas

Information arriving from the skin senses (your sense of touch or your sense of temperature) is projected to a region in the parietal lobe, just behind the motor projection area. This is labeled the "somatosensory" area in Figure 2.10.

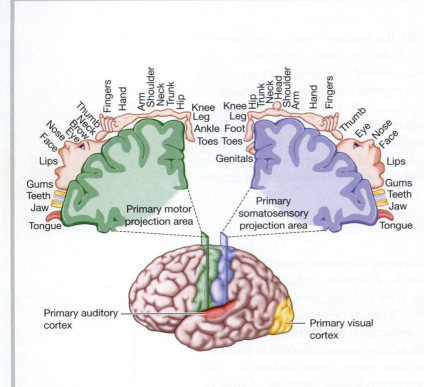

FIGURE 2.10 THE PRIMARY PROJECTION AREAS

The primary motor projection area is located at the rearmost edge of the frontal lobe, and each region within this projection area controls the motion of a specific body part, as illustrated on the top left. The primary somatosensory projection area, receiving information from the skin, is at the forward edge of the parietal lobe; each region within this area receives input from a specific body part. The primary projection areas for vision and hearing are located in the occipital and temporal lobes, respectively. These two areas are also organized systematically. For example, in the visual projection area, adjacent areas of the brain receive visual inputs that come from adjacent areas in visual space.

If a patient's brain is stimulated in this region (with electrical current or touch), the patient will typically report a tingling sensation in a specific part of the body. Figure 2.10 also shows the region (in the temporal lobes) that functions as the primary projection area for hearing (the "auditory" area). If the brain is directly stimulated here, the patient will hear clicks, buzzes, and hums. An area in the occipital lobes is the primary projection area for vision; stimulation here causes the patient to see flashes of light or visual patterns.

The sensory projection areas differ from each other in important ways, but they also have features in common—and they're features that parallel the attributes of the motor projection area. First, each of these areas provides a "map" of the sensory environment. In the somatosensory area, each part of the body's surface is represented by its own region on the cortex; areas of the body that are near to one another are represented by similarly nearby areas in the brain. In the visual area, each region of visual space has its own cortical representation, and adjacent areas of visual space are usually represented by adjacent brain sites. In the auditory projection area, different frequencies of sound have their own cortical sites, and adjacent brain sites are responsive to adjacent frequencies.

Second, in each of these sensory maps, the assignment of cortical space is governed by function, not by anatomical proportions. In the parietal lobes, parts of the body that aren't very discriminating with regard to touch—even if they're physically large—get relatively little cortical area. Other, more sensitive areas of the body (the lips, tongue, and fingers) get much more space. In the occipital lobes, more cortical surface is devoted to the fovea, the part of the eyeball that is most sensitive to detail. (For more on the fovea, see Chapter 3.) And in the auditory areas, some frequencies of sound get more cerebral coverage than others. It's surely no coincidence that these "advantaged" frequencies are those essential for the perception of speech.

Finally, we also find evidence here of contralateral connections. The somatosensory area in the left hemisphere, for example, receives its main input from the right side of the body; the corresponding area in the right hemisphere receives its input from the left side of the body. Likewise for the visual projection areas, although here the projection is not contralateral with regard to body parts. Instead, it's contralateral with regard to physical space. Specifically, the visual projection area in the right hemisphere receives information from both the left eye and the right, but the information it receives corresponds to the left half of visual space (i.e., all of the things visible to your left when you're looking straight ahead). The reverse is true for the visual area in the left hemisphere. It receives information from both eyes, but from only the right half of visual space. The pattern of contralateral organization is also evident—although not as clear-cut—for the auditory cortex, with roughly 60% of the nerve fibers from each ear sending their information to the opposite side of the brain.

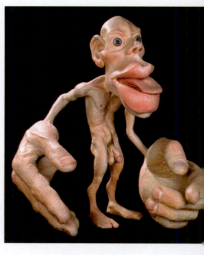

THE SENSORY HOMUNCULUS

An artist's rendition of what a man would look like if his appearance were proportional to the area allotted by the somatosensory cortex to his various body parts.

Association Areas

The areas described so far, both motor and sensory, make up only a small part of the human cerebral cortex—roughly 25%. The remaining cortical areas are referred to as the **association cortex**, although this terminology is falling out of use, partly because this large volume of brain tissue can be subdivided further on both functional and anatomical grounds. These subdivisions are perhaps best revealed by the diversity of symptoms that result if the cortex is damaged in one or another specific location. For example, some lesions in the frontal lobe produce **apraxias**, disturbances in the initiation or organization of voluntary action. Other lesions (generally in the occipital cortex, or in the rearmost part of the parietal lobe) lead to **agnosias**, disruptions in the ability to identify familiar objects. Agnosias usually affect one modality only—so a patient with visual agnosia, for example, can recognize a fork by touching it but not by looking at it. A patient with auditory agnosia, by contrast, might be unable to identify familiar voices but might still recognize the face of the person speaking.

Still other lesions (usually in the parietal lobe) produce **unilateral neglect syndrome**, in which the individual seems to ignore half of the visual world. A patient afflicted with this syndrome will shave only half of his face and eat food from only half of his plate. If asked to read the word "parties," he will read "ties," and so on.

Damage in other areas causes still other symptoms. We mentioned earlier that lesions in areas near the deep groove that separates the frontal and temporal lobes can result in disruption to language capacities, a problem referred to as **aphasia**.

Finally, damage to the frontmost part of the frontal lobe, the prefrontal area, causes problems in planning and implementing strategies. In some cases, patients with damage here show problems in inhibiting their own behaviors, relying on habit even in situations in which habit is inappropriate. Frontal lobe damage can also (as we mentioned in our discussion of Capgras syndrome) lead to a variety of confusions, such as whether a remembered episode actually happened or was simply imagined.

We'll say more about these diagnostic categories—aphasia, agnosia, neglect, and more—in upcoming chapters, where we'll consider these disorders in the context of other things that are known about object recognition, attention, and so on. Our point for the moment, though, is simple: These clinical patterns make it clear that the so-called association cortex contains many subregions, each specialized for a particular function, but with all of the subregions working together in virtually all aspects of our daily lives.

Brain Cells

Our brief tour so far has described some of the large-scale structures in the brain. For many purposes, though, we need to zoom in for a closer look, in order to see how the brain's functions are actually carried out.

Neurons and Glia

We've already mentioned that the human brain contains many billions of **neurons** and a comparable number of **glia**. The glia perform many functions. They help to guide the development of the nervous system in the fetus and young infant; they support repairs if the nervous system is damaged; they also control the flow of nutrients to the neurons. Specialized glial cells also provide a layer of electrical insulation surrounding parts of some neurons; this insulation dramatically increases the speed with which neurons can send their signals. (We'll return to this point in a moment.) Finally, some research suggests the glia may also constitute their own signaling system within the brain, separate from the information flow provided by the neurons (e.g., Bullock et al., 2005; Gallo & Chitajullu, 2001).

There is no question, though, that the main flow of information through the brain—from the sense organs inward, from one part of the brain to the others, and then from the brain outward—is made possible by the neurons. Neurons come in many shapes and sizes (see **Figure 2.11**), but in general, neurons have three major parts. The **cell body** is the portion of the cell that contains the neuron's nucleus and all the elements needed for the normal metabolic activities of the cell. The **dendrites** are usually the "input" side of the neuron, receiving signals from many other neurons. In most neurons, the dendrites are heavily branched, like a thick and tangled bush. The **axon** is the "output" side of the neuron; it sends neural impulses to other neurons (see

TEST YOURSELF

8. What is a projection area in the brain? What's the role of the motor projection area? The sensory projection area?

9. What does it mean to say that the brain relies on contralateral connections?

FIGURE 2.11   NEURONS

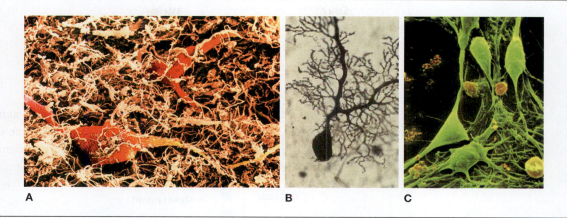

Panel A shows neurons from the spinal cord (stained in red); Panel B shows neurons from the cerebellum; Panel C shows neurons from the cerebral cortex.

Figure 2.12). Axons can vary enormously in length—the giraffe, for example, has neurons with axons that run the full length of its neck.

The Synapse

We've mentioned that communication from one neuron to the next is generally made possible by a chemical signal: When a neuron has been sufficiently stimulated, it releases a minute quantity of a **neurotransmitter**. The molecules of this substance drift across the tiny gap between neurons and latch on to the dendrites of the adjacent cell. If the dendrites receive enough of this substance, the next neuron will "fire," and so the signal will be sent along to other neurons.

Notice, then, that neurons usually don't touch each other directly. Instead, at the end of the axon there is a gap separating each neuron from the next. This entire site—the end of the axon, plus the gap, plus the receiving membrane of the next neuron—is called a **synapse**. The bit of the neuron that releases the transmitter into this space between neurons is the **presynaptic membrane**, and the bit of the neuron on the other side of the gap, affected by the transmitters, is the **postsynaptic membrane**.

When the neurotransmitters arrive at the postsynaptic membrane, they cause changes in this membrane that allow certain ions to flow into and out of the postsynaptic cell (see **Figure 2.13**). If these ionic flows are relatively small, then the postsynaptic cell quickly recovers and the ions are transported back to where they were initially. But if the ionic flows are large enough, they trigger a response in the postsynaptic cell. In formal terms, if the incoming

FIGURE 2.12   REGIONS OF THE NEURON

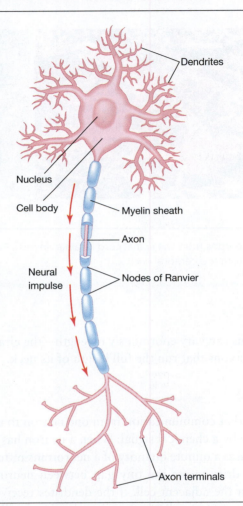

Most neurons have three identifiable regions. The *dendrites* are the part of the neuron that usually detects incoming signals. The *cell body* contains the metabolic machinery that sustains the cell. The *axon* is the part of the neuron that transmits a signal to another location. When the cell fires, neurotransmitters are released from the terminal endings at the tip of the axon. The myelin sheath is created by glial cells that wrap around the axons of many neurons. The gaps in between the myelin cells are called the nodes of Ranvier.

signal reaches the postsynaptic cell's **threshold**, then the cell fires. That is, it produces an **action potential**—a signal that moves down its axon, which in turn causes the release of neurotransmitters at the next synapse, potentially causing the next cell to fire.

In some neurons, the action potential moves down the axon at a relatively slow speed. For other neurons, specialized glial cells are wrapped around the

FIGURE 2.13 SCHEMATIC VIEW OF SYNAPTIC TRANSMISSION

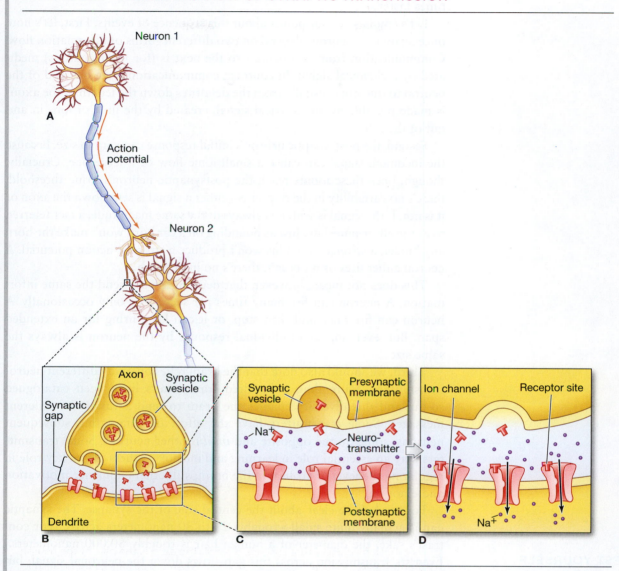

Neuron 1

Action
potential

Neuron 2

B

Axon

Synaptic
vesicle

Synaptic
gap

Dendrite

C

Synaptic
vesicle

Presynaptic
membrane

Na$^+$

Neuro-
transmitter

Postsynaptic
membrane

D

Ion channel

Receptor site

Na$^+$

(Panel A) Neuron 1 transmits a message across the synaptic gap to Neuron 2. The neurotransmitters are initially stored in structures called "synaptic vesicles" (Panel B). When a signal travels down the axon, the vesicles are stimulated and some of them burst (Panel C), ejecting neurotransmitter molecules into the synaptic gap and toward the postsynaptic membrane. (Panel D) Neurotransmitter molecules settle on receptor sites, ion channels open, and sodium (NA$^+$) floods in.

axon, creating a layer of insulation called the **myelin sheath** (see Figure 2.12). Because of the myelin, ions can flow in or out of the axon only at the gaps between the myelin cells. As a result, the signal traveling down the axon has to "jump" from gap to gap, and this greatly increases the speed at which the signal is transmitted. For neurons without myelin, the signal travels at speeds below 10 m/s; for "myelinated" neurons, the speed can be ten times faster.

Let's emphasize four points about this sequence of events. First, let's note once again that neurons depend on two different forms of information flow. Communication from one neuron to the next is (for most neurons) mediated by a chemical signal. In contrast, communication from one end of the neuron to the other (usually from the dendrites down the length of the axon) is made possible by an electrical signal, created by the flow of ions in and out of the cell.

Second, the postsynaptic neuron's initial response can vary in size, because the incoming signal can cause a small ionic flow or a large one. Crucially, though, once these inputs reach the postsynaptic neuron's firing threshold, there's no variability in the response—either a signal is sent down the axon or it is not. If the signal is sent, it is always of the same magnitude, a fact referred to as the **all-or-none law**. Just as pounding on a car horn won't make the horn any louder, a stronger stimulus won't produce a stronger action potential. A neuron either fires or it doesn't; there's no in-between.

This does not mean, however, that neurons always send the same information. A neuron can fire many times per second or only occasionally. A neuron can fire once and then stop, or it can keep firing for an extended span. But, even so, each individual response by the neuron is always the same size.

Third, we should also note that the brain relies on many different neurotransmitters. More than a hundred transmitters have been catalogued so far, and this diversity enables the brain to send a variety of different messages. Some transmitters have the effect of stimulating subsequent neurons; some do the opposite and *inhibit* other neurons. Some transmitters play an essential role in learning and memory; others play a key role in regulating the level of arousal in the brain; still others influence motivation and emotion.

Fourth, let's be clear about the central role of the synapse. The synaptic gap is actually quite small—roughly 20 to 30 nanometers across. (For contrast's sake, the diameter of a human hair is roughly 80,000 nanometers.) Even so, transmission across this gap slows down the neuronal signal, but this is a tiny price to pay for the advantages created by this mode of signaling: Each neuron receives information from (i.e., has synapses with) many other neurons, and this allows the "receiving" neuron to integrate information from many sources. This pattern of many neurons feeding into one also makes it possible for a neuron to "compare" signals and to adjust its response to one input according to the signal arriving from a different input. In addition, communication at the synapse is *adjustable*. This means that the strength of a synaptic connection can be altered by experience, and this adjustment is crucial for the process of *learning*—the storage of new knowledge and new skills within the nervous system.

TEST YOURSELF

10. What are glia? What are dendrites? What is an axon? What is a synapse?
11. What does it mean to say that neurons rely on two different forms of information flow, one chemical and one electrical?

Of the many drugs that influence the brain, alcohol is among the most readily available and frequently consumed. Alcohol influences the entire brain, and we can detect alcohol's effects even at low levels of intoxication—for example, with measures of motor skills or response time.

Alcohol's effects are more visible, though, in some functions than in others, and so someone who's quite intoxicated can still perform many activities at a fairly normal level. In contrast, just one or two drinks can be enough to undermine activities that depend on the brain's prefrontal cortex. This is the brain region that's essential for the mind's *executive function*—the system that allows you to control your thoughts and behaviors. (We'll say more about executive function in upcoming chapters.) As a result, alcohol undercuts your ability to resist temptation or to overcome habit. Impairments in executive function also erode your ability to make thoughtful decisions and draw sensible conclusions.

In addition, alcohol can produce impairments in memory, including "alcoholic blackouts." So-called fragmentary blackouts, in which the person remembers some bits of an experience but not others, are actually quite common. In one study, college students were asked: "Have you ever awoken after a night of drinking not able to remember things that you did or places where you went?" More than half of the students indicated that, yes, this had happened to them at some point; 40% reported they'd had a blackout within the previous year (White et al., 2002).

How drunk do you have to be in order to experience a blackout? Many authorities point to a blood alcohol level of 0.25 (roughly nine or ten drinks for someone of average weight), but other factors also matter. For example, blackouts are more common if you become drunk rapidly—as when you drink on an empty stomach, or when you gulp alcohol rather than sipping it.

Let's combine these points about blackouts, though, with our earlier observation about alcohol's uneven effects. It's possible for someone to be quite drunk, and therefore suffer an alcoholic blackout, even if the person seems alert and coherent during the drunken episode. To see some of the serious problems this can cause, consider a pattern that often emerges in cases involving allegations of sexual assault. Victims of assault sometimes report that they have little or no memory of the sexual encounter; they therefore assert that they were barely conscious during the event and surely incapable of giving consent.

This assertion is entirely reasonable: If someone was drunk enough to end up with a blackout, then that person was likely impaired to a degree that would interfere with decision making—and so the person could not have given any consent that was legitimate or meaningful. Therefore, there was indeed no consent. But, even so, the person might have been functioning in a way that seemed mostly normal (able to converse, to move around) and may even have expressed consent in words or actions.

In this situation, then, an accused person might have had reason to believe there was consent for the sexual activity, even though the complainant is correct in saying that they couldn't have given (and therefore didn't give) meaningful consent. There's ongoing debate about how to deal with these situations, but surely one path forward is to avoid this sort of circumstance—by drinking only in safe settings or by keeping a strict limit on your drinking.

Coding

This discussion of individual neurons leads to a further question: How do these microscopic nerve cells manage to represent a specific idea or a specific content? Let's say that right now you're thinking about your favorite song. How is this information represented by neurons? The issue here is referred to as **coding**, and there are many options for what the neurons' "code" might be (Gallistel, 2017). As one option, we might imagine that a specific group of neurons somehow represents "favorite song," so that whenever you're thinking about the song, it's precisely these neurons that are activated. Or, as a different option, the song might be represented by a broad *pattern* of neuronal activity. If so, "favorite song" might be represented in the brain by something like "Neuron X firing strongly while Neuron Y is firing weakly and Neuron Z is not firing at all" (and so on for thousands of other neurons). In this scheme, the same neurons might be involved in the representation of other sounds, but with different patterns. So—to continue our example—Neuron X might also be involved in the representation of the sound of a car engine, but for this sound it might be part of a pattern that includes Neurons Q, R, and S also firing strongly, and Neuron Y not firing at all.

As it turns out, the brain uses both forms of coding. For example, in Chapter 4 we'll see that some neurons do seem to be associated with a particular content. In fact, researchers documented a cell in one of the people they tested that fired whenever a picture of Jennifer Aniston was in view, and didn't fire in response to pictures of other faces. Another cell (in a different person's brain) fired whenever a picture of the Sydney Opera House was shown, but didn't fire when other buildings were in view (Quiroga et al., 2005)! These seem to be cases in which an idea (in particular, a certain visual image) is represented by specific neurons in the brain.

In other cases, ideas and memories are represented in the brain through widespread patterns of activity. This sort of "pattern coding" is, for example, certainly involved in the neural mechanisms through which you plan, and then carry out, particular motions—like reaching out to turn a book page or lifting your foot to step over an obstacle (Georgopoulos, 1990, 1995). We'll return to pattern coding in Chapter 9, when we discuss the notion of a *distributed representation*.

Moving On

We have now described the brain's basic anatomy and have also taken a brief look at the brain's microscopic parts—the individual neurons. But how do all of these elements, large and small, function in ways that enable us to think, remember, learn, speak, or feel? As a step toward tackling this issue, the next chapter takes a closer look at the portions of the nervous

TEST YOURSELF

12. How is information coded, or represented, in the brain?

system that allow us to *see*. We'll use the visual system as our example for two reasons. First, vision is the modality through which humans acquire a huge amount of information, whether by reading or simply by viewing the world around us. If we understand vision, therefore, we understand the processes that bring us much of our knowledge. Second, investigators have made enormous progress in mapping out the neural "wiring" of the visual system, offering a detailed and sophisticated portrait of how this system operates. As a result, an examination of vision provides an excellent illustration of how the study of the brain can proceed and what it can teach us.

COGNITIVE PSYCHOLOGY AND THE LAW

the adolescent brain

We've known for years that adolescents engage in a variety of risky behaviors. Some become criminals. Some become drug users. Indeed, evidence suggests that a wide range of concerning behaviors (including theft, carrying a weapon, reckless driving, and unprotected sex) are more likely during adolescence than at any other time of life.

These patterns are influenced by many factors, including the fact that the brain continues to mature during the first decades of life, with some brain regions reaching adult levels of functioning early, and other regions reaching their full functioning only later. Specifically, the speed and efficiency of functioning in the brain's prefrontal cortex reaches fully adult levels only when someone is in their 20s. This brain region is associated with a range of mental processes relevant to decision making—including careful judgment of evidence, thoughtful planning, and the weighing of consequences. The prefrontal cortex is also crucial in situations in which a person needs to inhibit impulses and suppress inappropriate thoughts and actions. It is easy to see, therefore, how a not-yet-fully-mature prefrontal cortex could leave someone open to risky choices.

In addition, neuroimaging data suggest that adolescent brains often show particularly strong activation in the brain's limbic system (including areas in and around the amygdala) that are involved in the response to incentives and emotion-laden inputs. This brain activity may help us understand the increased emotional reactivity displayed by many adolescents, and it may create a situation in which these young adults are especially responsive to the excitement and immediate rewards often associated with risky behaviors.

Now let's put these points together: If limbic regions reach their full functioning relatively early, and prefrontal regions reach their functioning only later, there will be a period of time in which there is an imbalance—with a strong responsiveness to incentives and emotions, and a somewhat weaker

ADOLESCENT RISK-TAKING

Adolescents and young adults are strong and agile, and so they're often terrific athletes. But they're also risk takers. Notice that this fellow (photographed in Latvia) is well off the ground with no knee pads, no elbow pads, and—most important—no helmet.

ability to evaluate consequences, inhibit impulses, and make good choices (Casey et al., 2008). It may be this combination that leads to the behaviors often seen in young adults.

All of this matters for the legal system in countless ways. Consider, as one example, what happens in a police interrogation room. Police often do all they can to persuade suspects to confess to a crime, and, for this purpose, they use a range of techniques that many people consider to be coercive. These techniques are troubling and especially so for younger people. One study examined a large set of wrongful convictions (Gross et al., 2005). Among adults, 13% of the suspects had been persuaded to give (false) confessions. The percentage jumps to more than 40% if we focus on cases with juvenile suspects, and to 75% among the youngest juveniles (12 to 15 years old) in the data set.

This pattern can be understood, in part, with reference to brain development: These younger suspects tend to be impulsive in their decision making and inclined to discount risk. They are also likely to be keenly sensitive to immediate gratification, and so may feel a powerful pull toward saying what the police want them to say; if they do, they'll get the immediate "reward" of escaping the intense pressure of the interrogation room. At the same time, these younger suspects are likely to be less sensitive to the long-term repercussions of their offering a (false) confession. This combination—impulsive decision making, keen sensitivity to immediate reward, diminished sensitivity to long-term consequences—is dangerous in many settings, and it's certainly dangerous if you're suspected of, and being questioned about, a crime.

Here is a different, and certainly more extreme, example: Relatively few countries use the death penalty, and for many years the United States was the only country on the planet that executed young people for some crimes. It was only in 2005 that the United States Supreme Court ruled that people could not be sentenced to death for crimes committed when they were under the age of 18.

But, if not the death penalty, how are young people punished? In the United States, roughly 12,000 people are serving a life sentence for crimes committed when they were under the age of 18 (The Sentencing Project, 2019). Many of them are serving life sentences that explicitly rule out any possibility of parole; in other words, these young people, having been convicted for a crime they committed as teenagers, will stay in prison until they die. However, in 2012 the Supreme Court issued a ruling (in *Miller v. Alabama*) that limited the use of this in-jail-forever sentence. The ruling still allowed this sort of sentence, but it rejected the notion that state laws could make this sort of sentence a requirement for some types of crimes. Instead, the Court argued, judges in each case must consider the defendant's youth and the nature of the crime before putting the adolescent behind bars with no hope ever for release.

Debate continues about all of these issues and sits alongside the broader debate over the ways in which the U.S. legal system prosecutes and punishes crimes. In the meantime, there is no question that the behavior of adolescents is different from the behavior of older adults, and no question that part of this contrast lies in biological facts that no one (the adolescent, a parent, a police officer) can change.

For more on this topic:

Casey, B. J., Jones, R. M., & Hare, T. A. (2008). The adolescent brain. *Annals of the New York Academy of Sciences, 1124*(1), 111–126.

Gross, S. R., Jacoby, K., Matheson, D. J., Montgomery, N., & Patil, S. (2005). Exonerations in the United States 1989 through 2003. *Journal of Criminal Law and Criminology, 95*(2), 523–560.

The Sentencing Project (2019). *Youth sentenced to life imprisonment.* https://www.sentencingproject.org/publications/youth-sentenced -life-imprisonment/

chapter review

SUMMARY

- The brain is divided into several different structures, but of particular importance for cognitive psychology is the forebrain. In the forebrain, each cerebral hemisphere is divided into the frontal lobe, parietal lobe, temporal lobe, and occipital lobe. In understanding these brain areas, one important source of evidence comes from studies of brain damage, enabling us to examine what sorts of symptoms result from lesions in specific brain locations. This has allowed a localization of function, an effort that is also supported by neuroimaging research, which shows that the pattern of activation in the brain depends on the particular task being performed.

- Different parts of the brain perform different jobs; but for virtually any mental process, different brain areas must work together in a closely integrated way. When this integration is lost (as it is, for example, in Capgras syndrome), bizarre symptoms can result.

- The primary motor projection areas are the departure points in the brain for nerve cells that initiate muscle movement. The primary sensory projection areas are the main points of arrival in the brain for information from the eyes, ears, and other sense organs. These projection areas generally show a pattern of contralateral control, with tissue in the left hemisphere sending or receiving its main signals from the right side of the body, and vice versa. Each projection area provides a map of the environment or the relevant body part, but the assignment of space in this map is governed by function, not by anatomical proportions.

- Most of the forebrain's cortex has traditionally been referred to as the association cortex, but this area is subdivided into specialized regions. This subdivision is reflected in the varying consequences of brain damage, with lesions in the occipital lobes leading to visual agnosia, damage in the temporal lobes leading to aphasia, and so on. Damage to the prefrontal area causes many different problems, but these are generally in the forming and implementing of strategies.

- The brain's functioning depends on neurons and glia. The glia perform many functions, but the main flow of information is carried by the neurons. Communication from one end of the neuron to the other is electrical and is governed by the flow of ions in and out of the cell. Communication from one neuron to the next is generally chemical, with a neuron releasing neurotransmitters that affect neurons on the other side of the synapse.

KEY TERMS

amygdala (p. 27)
prefrontal cortex (p. 28)
hindbrain (p. 32)
cerebellum (p. 32)
midbrain (p. 33)
forebrain (p. 33)
cortex (p. 33)
convolutions (p. 33)

longitudinal fissure (p. 33)
cerebral hemisphere (p. 33)
frontal lobes (p. 33)
central fissure (p. 33)
parietal lobes (p. 33)
lateral fissure (p. 33)
temporal lobes (p. 33)
occipital lobes (p. 33)

TEST YOURSELF AGAIN

1. What are the symptoms of Capgras syndrome, and why do they suggest a two-part explanation for how people recognize faces?

2. What is the cerebral cortex?

3. What are the four major lobes of the forebrain?

4. Identify some of the functions of the hippocampus, the amygdala, and the corpus callosum.

5. What is the difference between *structural imaging* of the brain and *functional imaging*? What techniques are used for each?

6. What do we gain from *combining* different methods in studying the brain?

7. What is meant by the phrase "localization of function"?

8. What is a projection area in the brain? What's the role of the motor projection area? The sensory projection area?

9. What does it mean to say that the brain relies on contralateral connections?

10. What are glia? What are dendrites? What is an axon? What is a synapse?

11. What does it mean to say that neurons rely on two different forms of information flow, one chemical and one electrical?

12. How is information coded, or represented, in the brain?

THINK ABOUT IT

1. People often claim that humans only use 10% of their brains. Does anything in this chapter help us in evaluating this claim?

2. People claim that you need to "liberate your right brain" in order to be creative. What's true about this claim? What's false about this claim?

DEMONSTRATIONS & APPLYING COGNITIVE PSYCHOLOGY ESSAYS

For demonstrations of key concepts in cognitive psychology, take a look at the Online Demonstrations. To explore more of the practical applications of cognitive psychology in themed essays, visit the online reader.

Online Demonstrations

- Demonstration 2.1: Brain Anatomy
- Demonstration 2.2: Temporary Fatigue-Created Brain Dysfunction
- Demonstration 2.3: "Acuity" in the Somatosensory System
- Demonstration 2.4: The Speed of Neural Transmission

Online Applying Cognitive Psychology Essays

- Cognitive Psychology and Education: Food Supplements and Cognition
- Cognitive Psychology and Technology: Lie Detection
- Cognitive Psychology and Health: Stroke

ZAPS COGNITION LABS

Go to ZAPS online cognition labs to conduct hands-on experiments on key concepts.

INQUIZITIVE

It's time to complete your study experience! Go to InQuizitive to practice actively with this chapter's concepts and get personalized feedback along the way.

Learning about the World around Us

In setting after setting, you rely on your knowledge and beliefs. But where does knowledge come from? The answer, usually, is *experience*, but this invites another question: What is it that makes experience possible? Tackling this issue will force us to examine mental processes that turn out to be surprisingly complex.

In Chapter 3, we'll ask how you manage to perceive the world around you. We'll start with events in the eyeball and then move to how you organize and interpret the visual information you receive. We'll also consider the ways in which you can *mis*interpret this information, so that you're vulnerable to illusions. Chapter 4 then takes a further step and asks how you manage to recognize and categorize the objects that you see. We'll start with a simple case—how you recognize printed letters—but then turn to the recognition of more complex (three-dimensional) objects.

In both chapters, we'll discuss the active role that you play in shaping your experience. We'll see, for example, that your perceptual apparatus doesn't just "pick up" the visual information that's available to you. You don't, in other words, just open your eyes and let the information "flow in." Instead, we'll discuss the ways in which you supplement and interpret the information you receive. In Chapter 3, we'll see that this activity begins very early in the sequence of biological events that support visual perception. In Chapter 4, these ideas will lead us to a mechanism made up of very simple components but shaped by a broad pattern of knowledge.

Chapter 5 then turns to the study of attention. Paying attention turns out to be a complex achievement involving many elements. We'll discuss how these elements can limit what people achieve—and so part of what's at stake in Chapter 5 is the question of what people ultimately can or cannot accomplish, and whether there may be ways to escape these apparent limits on human performance.

chapter 3

Visual Perception

what if... You look around the world and instantly, effortlessly, recognize the objects that surround you—words on this page, objects in the room where you're sitting, things you can view out the window. Perception, in other words, seems fast, easy, and automatic. But even so, there is complexity here, and your ability to perceive the world depends on many separate and complicated processes.

Consider the disorder *akinetopsia* (Cooper & O'Sullivan, 2016; Otsuka-Hirota et al., 2014; Zeki, 1991). This condition is rare, and part of what we know comes from a single patient—L.M.—who developed this disorder at age 43 because of a blood clot in her brain. L.M. was completely unable to perceive motion—even though other aspects of her vision (e.g., her ability to recognize objects, to see color, or to discern detail in a visual pattern) seemed normal.

Because of her akinetopsia, L.M. can detect that an object *now* is in a position different from its position a moment ago, but she reports seeing "nothing in between." As a way of capturing this experience, think about what you see when you're looking at really slow movement. If, for example, you stare at the hour hand on a clock as it creeps around the clock face, you cannot discern its motion. But you can easily see the hand is now pointing, say, at the 4, and if you come back a while later, you can see that it's closer to the 5. In this way, you can *infer* motion from the change in position, but you can't *perceive* the motion. This is your experience with very slow movement; L.M., suffering from akinetopsia, has the same experience with *all* movement.

What's it like to have this disorder? L.M. complained, as one concern, that it was hard to cross the street because she couldn't tell which cars were moving and which ones were parked. (She eventually learned to judge the movement of traffic by listening to cars' *sounds* as they approached, even though she couldn't see their movement.)

Other problems caused by akinetopsia are more surprising. For example, L.M. complained about difficulties in following conversations, because she was essentially blind to the speaker's lip movement or changing facial expressions. She also felt insecure in social settings. If more than two people were moving around in a room, she felt anxious because "people were suddenly here or there, but [she had] not seen them moving" (Zihl et al., 1983, p. 315). Or, as a different example:

- We explore vision—humans' dominant sensory modality. We discuss the mechanisms through which the visual system detects patterns in the incoming light, but we also showcase the *activity* of the visual system in interpreting and shaping the incoming information.

- We also highlight the ways in which perception of one aspect of the input is shaped by perception of other aspects—so that the detection of simple features depends on how the overall form is organized, and the perception of size depends on the perceived distance of the target object.

- We emphasize that the interpretation of the visual input is usually accurate—but the same mechanisms can lead to illusions, and the study of those illusions can often illuminate the processes through which perception functions.

She had trouble in everyday activities like pouring a cup of coffee. She couldn't see the fluid level's gradual rise as she poured, so she didn't know when to stop pouring. For her, "the fluid appeared to be frozen, like a glacier" (Zihl et al., 1983, p. 315; also Schenk et al., 2005; Zihl et al., 1991).

We will have more to say about cases like this later in the chapter. For now, though, let's note the specificity of this disorder—a disruption of movement perception, with other aspects of perception still intact. Let's also highlight the important point that each of us is, in countless ways, dependent on our perceptual contact with the world. That point demands that we ask: What makes this perception possible?

The Visual System

You receive information about the world through multiple sensory modalities: You hear the sound of the approaching train, you smell the freshly baked bread, you feel the tap on your shoulder. There's no question, though, that for humans vision is the dominant sense. This is reflected in how much brain area is devoted to vision compared to any of the other senses. It's also reflected in many aspects of our behavior. For example, if visual information conflicts with information received from other senses, you usually place your trust in vision. This is the basis for ventriloquism, in which you see the dummy's mouth moving while the sounds themselves are coming from the dummy's master. Vision wins out in this contest, and so you experience the illusion that the voice is coming from the dummy.

The Photoreceptors

How does vision operate? The process begins, of course, with light. Light is produced by many objects in our surroundings—the sun, lamps, candles—and then reflects off other objects. In most cases, it's this reflected light—reflected from this book page or from a friend's face— that launches the processes of visual perception. Some of this light hits the front surface of the eyeball, passes through the **cornea** and the **lens**, and then hits the **retina**, the light-sensitive tissue that lines the back of the eyeball (see **Figure 3.1**). The cornea and lens focus the incoming light, just as a camera lens might, so that a sharp image is cast onto the retina. The focusing is made possible by a band of muscle that surrounds the lens. When the muscle tightens, the lens bulges somewhat, creating the proper shape for focusing the images cast by nearby objects. When the muscle relaxes, the lens returns to a flatter shape, allowing the proper focus for objects farther away.

On the retina, there are two types of **photoreceptors**—specialized neural cells that respond directly to the incoming light. One type, the **rods**, are sensitive to very low levels of light and so play an essential role whenever you're moving around in semidarkness. But the rods are also color-blind: They can distinguish different intensities of light (and in that way contribute to your

---

FIGURE 3.1   THE HUMAN EYE

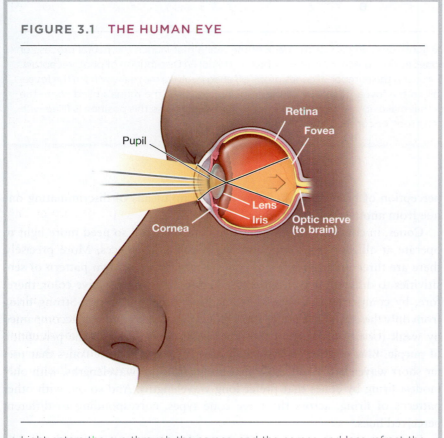

Light enters the eye through the cornea, and the cornea and lens refract the light rays to produce a sharply focused image on the retina. The iris can open or close to control the amount of light that reaches the retina. The retina is made up of three main layers: the rods and cones, which are the photoreceptors; the bipolar cells; and the ganglion cells, whose axons make up the optic nerve.

FIGURE 3.2 RODS AND CONES

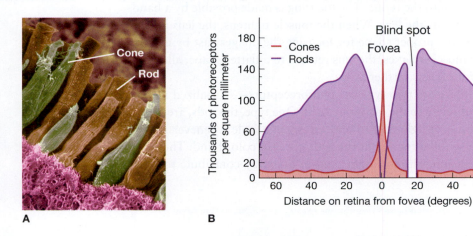

A   **B**

(Panel A) Rods and cones are the light-sensitive cells at the back of the retina that launch the neural process of vision. In this (colorized) photo, cones appear green; rods appear brown. (Panel B) Distribution of photoreceptors. Cones are most frequent at the fovea, and the number of cones drops off sharply as we move away from the fovea. In contrast, there are no rods at all on the fovea. There are neither rods nor cones at the retina's blind spot—the position at which the neural fibers that make up the optic nerve exit the eyeball. Because this position is filled with these fibers, there's no space for any rods or cones.

perception of brightness), but they provide no means of discriminating one hue from another (see **Figure 3.2**).

Cones, in contrast, are less sensitive than rods and so need more light to operate at all. But cones are sensitive to color differences. More precisely, there are three different types of cones, each having its own pattern of sensitivities to different wavelengths (see **Figure 3.3**). You perceive color, therefore, by comparing the outputs from these three cone types. Strong firing from only the cones that prefer short wavelengths, for example, accompanied by weak (or no) firing from the other cone types, leads to the perception of purple. Blue is signaled by equally strong firing from the cones that prefer short wavelengths and those that prefer medium wavelengths, with only modest firing by cones that prefer long wavelengths. And so on, with other patterns of firing, across the three cone types, corresponding to different perceived hues.

Cones have another function: They enable you to perceive fine detail. The ability to see detail is referred to as **acuity**, and acuity is much higher for the cones than it is for the rods. This explains why you point your eyes toward a target whenever you want to learn more about it. What you're actually doing is positioning your eyes so that the image of the target falls onto the **fovea**, the very center of the retina. Here, cones far outnumber rods (and, in fact,

FIGURE 3.3 WAVELENGTHS OF LIGHT

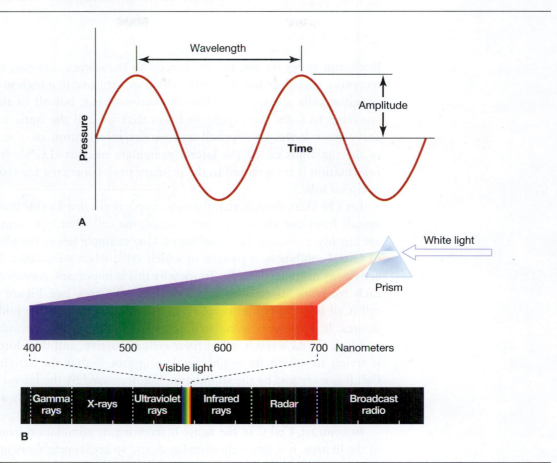

The physics of light are complex, but for many purposes light can be thought of as a wave (Panel A), and the shape of the wave can be described in terms of its amplitude and its wavelength (i.e., the distance from "crest" to "crest"). The wavelengths our visual system can sense are only a tiny part of the broader electromagnetic spectrum (Panel B; the numbers shown are the wavelengths measured in nanometers). Light with a wavelength longer than 750 nanometers is invisible to us, although we feel these longer infrared waves as heat. Ultraviolet light, which has a wavelength shorter than 360 nanometers, is invisible to us. That leaves the narrow band of wavelengths between 750 and 360 nanometers—the so-called visible spectrum. Within this spectrum, we usually see wavelengths close to 400 nanometers as violet, those close to 700 nanometers as red, and those in between as the rest of the colors in the rainbow.

the center of the fovea has no rods at all). As a result, this is the region of the retina with the greatest acuity.

In portions of the retina more distant from the fovea (i.e., portions of the retina in the so-called visual periphery), the rods predominate. This distribution explains why you're better able to see very dim lights out of the corner of your eyes. Indeed, sailors and astronomers have known for hundreds of years that when looking at a barely visible star, it's best not to look directly at the star's location. By looking slightly away from the star, they ensure that the star's image falls outside of the fovea and onto a region of the retina dense with the more light-sensitive rods.

Lateral Inhibition

Rods and cones do not report directly to the cortex. Instead, the photo-receptors stimulate **bipolar cells**, which in turn excite **ganglion cells**. The ganglion cells are spread across the entire retina, but all of their axons converge to form the bundle of fibers that we call the **optic nerve**. This nerve tract leaves the eyeball and carries information to a way station in the thalamus called the **lateral geniculate nucleus (LGN)**; from there, information is transmitted to the primary projection area for vision, in the occipital lobe.

Let's be clear, though, that the optic nerve is not just a cable that conducts signals from one site to another. Instead, the cells that link retina to brain are already analyzing the visual input. One example lies in the phenomenon of **lateral inhibition**, a pattern in which cells, when stimulated, inhibit the activity of neighboring cells. To see why this is important, consider two cells, each receiving stimulation from a brightly lit area (see **Figure 3.4**). One cell (Cell B in the figure) is receiving its stimulation from the middle of the lit area. It is intensely stimulated, but so are its neighbors (including Cell A and Cell C). As a result, all of these cells are active, and therefore each one is trying to inhibit its neighbors. The upshot is that the activity level of Cell B is *increased* by the stimulation but *decreased* by the lateral inhibition it's receiving from its neighbors. This combination leads to only a moderate level of activity in Cell B.

In contrast, Cell C in the figure is receiving its stimulation from the edge of the lit area. It is intensely stimulated, and so are its neighbors *on one side*. Therefore, this cell will receive inhibition from one side but not from the other (in the figure: inhibition from Cell B but *not* from Cell D), so it will be less inhibited than Cell B (which is receiving inhibition from both sides). Thus, Cells B and C initially receive the same input, but C is less inhibited than B and so ends up firing more strongly than B.

Notice that this dynamic actually highlights a surface's edges, because the response of cells detecting the edge of the surface (such as Cell C) will be stronger than that of cells detecting the middle of the surface (such as Cell B). In fact, by *increasing* the response by Cell C and *decreasing* the response by Cell D, lateral inhibition exaggerates the contrast at the edge—a process called **edge enhancement**. This process is of enormous importance, because it's highlighting information that defines an object's shape—information essential for figuring out what the object is. And let's emphasize that this edge enhancement occurs at a very early stage of the visual processing. In other words, the information sent to the brain isn't a mere copy of the incoming stimulation; instead, the steps of interpretation and analysis begin immediately, in the eyeball. (For a

TEST YOURSELF

1. What are the differences between rods and cones? What traits do these cells *share*?
2. What is lateral inhibition? How does it contribute to edge perception?

FIGURE 3.4 LATERAL INHIBITION

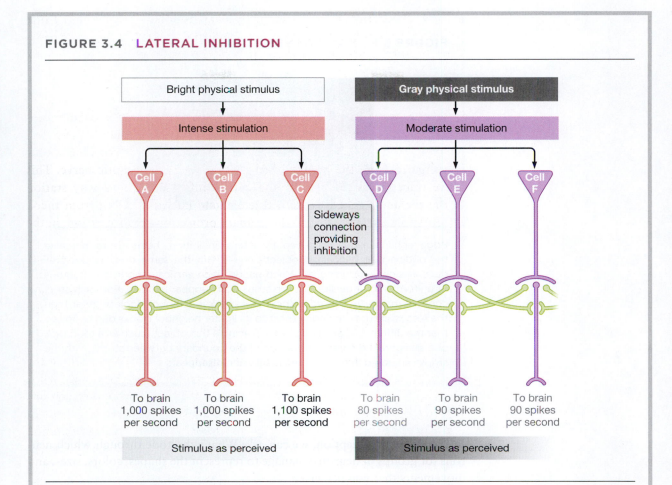

Cell B receives strong inhibition from all its neighbors, because its neighbors are intensely stimulated. Cell C, in contrast, receives inhibition only from one side (because its neighbor on the other side, Cell D, is only moderately stimulated). As a result, Cells B and C start with the same input, but Cell C, receiving less inhibition, sends a stronger signal to the brain, emphasizing the edge in the stimulus. The same logic applies to Cells D and E, and it explains why Cell D sends a weaker signal to the brain. Note, by the way, that the spikes per second numbers, shown in the figure, are hypothetical and intended only to illustrate lateral inhibition's effects.

demonstration of an illusion caused by this process—the so-called **Mach bands**—see **Figure 3.5**.)

Visual Coding

In Chapter 2, we introduced the idea of coding in the nervous system. This term refers to the relationship between activity in the nervous system and the stimulus (or idea or operation) that is somehow represented by that activity.

FIGURE 3.5   MACH BANDS

Edge enhancement, produced by lateral inhibition, helps us to perceive the outline that defines an object's shape. But the same process can produce illusions—including the Mach bands. Each vertical strip in this figure is of uniform light intensity, but the strips don't appear uniform. For each strip, contrast makes the left edge (next to its darker neighbor) look brighter than the rest, while the right edge (next to its lighter neighbor) looks darker. To see that the differences are illusions, try placing a thin object (such as a toothpick or a straightened paper clip) on top of the boundary between strips. With the strips separated in this manner, the illusion disappears.

In the study of perception, we can ask: What's the code through which neurons (or groups of neurons) manage to represent the shapes, colors, sizes, and movements that you perceive?

Single Neurons and Single-Cell Recording

Part of what we know about the visual system—actually, part of what we know about the entire brain—comes from a technique called **single-cell recording**. As the name implies, this is a procedure through which investigators can record, moment by moment, the pattern of electrical changes within a single neuron.

We mentioned in Chapter 2 that when a neuron fires, each response is the same size; this is the *all-or-none law*. But neurons can vary in *how often* they fire, and when investigators record the activity of a single neuron, what they're usually interested in is the cell's firing rate, measured in "spikes per second." The investigator can then vary the circumstances (either in the external world or elsewhere in the nervous system) in order to learn what makes the cell fire more and what makes it fire less. In this way, we can figure out what job the neuron does within the broad context of the entire nervous system.

The technique of single-cell recording has been used with enormous success in the study of vision. In a typical procedure, the animal being studied is first immobilized.[1] Electrodes are then placed just outside a neuron in the animal's optic nerve or brain. Next, a computer screen is placed in front of the animal's eyes, and various patterns are flashed on the screen: circles, lines at various angles, or squares of various sizes at various positions. Researchers can then ask: Which patterns cause that neuron to fire? To what visual inputs does that cell respond?

By analogy, we know that a smoke detector is a smoke detector because it "fires" (i.e., makes noise) when smoke is on the scene. We know that a motion detector is a motion detector because it "fires" when something moves nearby. But what kind of detector is a given neuron? Is it responsive to any light in any position within the field of view? In that case, we might call it a "light detector." Or is it perhaps responsive only to certain shapes at certain positions (and therefore is a "shape detector")? With this logic, we can map out precisely what the cell responds to—what kind of detector it is. More formally, this procedure allows us to define the cell's **receptive field**—that is, the size and shape of the area (the "field") in the visual world to which that cell responds.

Multiple Types of Receptive Fields

In 1981, the neurophysiologists David Hubel and Torsten Wiesel were awarded the Nobel Prize for their exploration of the mammalian visual system (e.g., Hubel & Wiesel, 1959, 1968). They documented the existence of specialized neurons within the brain, each of which has a different type of receptive field—that is, a different kind of visual trigger. For example, some neurons seem to function as "dot detectors." These cells fire at their maximum rate when light is presented in a small, roughly circular area in a specific position within the field of view. Presentations of light just outside of this area cause the cell to fire at less than its usual "resting" rate, so the input must be precisely positioned to make this cell fire. **Figure 3.6** depicts such a receptive field.

These cells are often called **center-surround cells,** to mark the fact that light presented to the central region of the receptive field has one influence, while light presented to the surrounding ring has the opposite influence. If both the center and the surround are strongly stimulated, the cell will fire neither more nor less than usual. For this cell, a strong uniform stimulus is equivalent to no stimulus at all.

Other cells fire at their maximum only when a stimulus containing an edge of just the right orientation appears within their receptive fields. These cells, therefore, can be thought of as "edge detectors." Some of these cells fire at their maximum rate when a horizontal edge is presented; others, when a vertical edge is in view; still others fire at their maximum to orientations in

TORSTEN WIESEL AND DAVID HUBEL

Much of what we know about the visual system is based on the pioneering work done by David Hubel (left) and Torsten Wiesel (right). This pair of researchers won the 1981 Nobel Prize for their discoveries. (They shared the Nobel with Roger Sperry for his independent research on the cerebral hemispheres.)

---

1. Actually, the animal is first anesthetized, and care is taken throughout the procedure to protect the animal's health and well-being. These points are demanded by proper research ethics, but they are also important for the science—because ultimately we want to understand how neurons function in a normal, healthy organism.

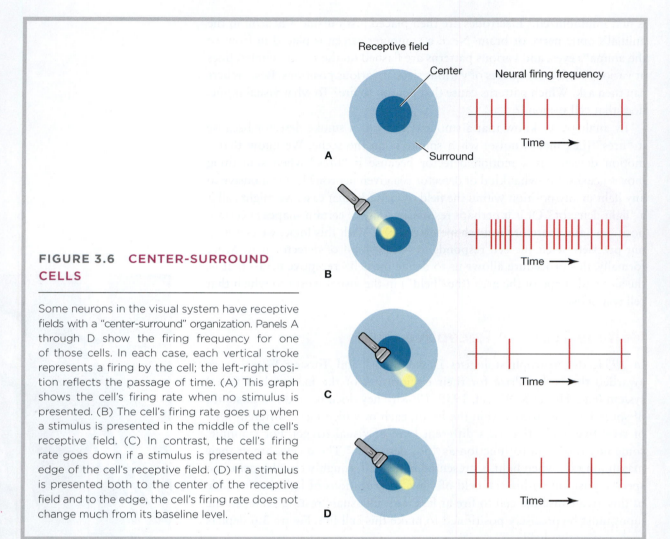

Receptive field

Center

Surround

Neural firing frequency

Time →

Time →

Time →

Time →

A

B

C

D

FIGURE 3.6 CENTER-SURROUND CELLS

Some neurons in the visual system have receptive fields with a "center-surround" organization. Panels A through D show the firing frequency for one of those cells. In each case, each vertical stroke represents a firing by the cell; the left-right position reflects the passage of time. (A) This graph shows the cell's firing rate when no stimulus is presented. (B) The cell's firing rate goes up when a stimulus is presented in the middle of the cell's receptive field. (C) In contrast, the cell's firing rate goes down if a stimulus is presented at the edge of the cell's receptive field. (D) If a stimulus is presented both to the center of the receptive field and to the edge, the cell's firing rate does not change much from its baseline level.

between horizontal and vertical. Note, though, that in each case these orientations merely define the cells' "preference," because these cells are not oblivious to edges of other orientations. If a cell's preference is for, say, horizontal edges, then the cell will still respond to other orientations—but the farther the edge is from the cell's preferred orientation, the weaker the firing will be, and edges sharply different from the cell's preferred orientation (e.g., a vertical edge for a cell that prefers horizontal) will elicit virtually no response (see **Figure 3.7**).

Other cells, elsewhere in the visual cortex, have receptive fields that are more specific. Some cells fire maximally only if an angle of a particular size appears in their receptive fields; others fire maximally in response to corners and notches. Still other cells appear to be "movement detectors" and fire strongly if a stimulus moves, say, from right to left across the cell's receptive field. Other cells favor left-to-right movement, and so on through the various possible directions of movement.

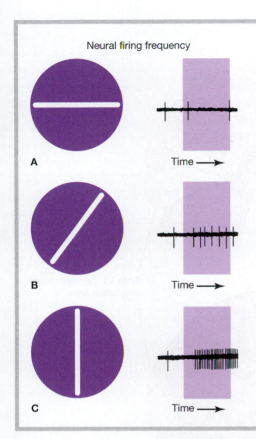

Neural firing frequency

A

Time →

B

Time →

C

Time →

FIGURE 3.7 ORIENTATION-SPECIFIC VISUAL FIELDS

Some cells in the visual system fire only when the input contains a line segment at a certain orientation. For example, one cell might fire very little in response to a horizontal line, fire only occasionally in response to a diagonal, and fire at its maximum rate only when a vertical line is present. In this figure, the circles show the stimulus that was presented. The right side shows records of neural firing. As in Figure 3.6, each vertical stroke represents a firing by the cell; the left-right position reflects the passage of time. (AFTER HUBEL, 1963)

Parallel Processing in the Visual System

This proliferation of cell types highlights an important principle—namely, that the visual system relies on a "divide and conquer" strategy, with different types of cells, located in different areas of the cortex, each specializing in a particular kind of analysis. This pattern is plainly evident in **Area V1**, the site on the occipital lobe where axons from the LGN first reach the cortex (see **Figure 3.8**). In this brain area, some cells fire to (say) horizontals in *this* position in the visual world, others to horizontals in *that* position, others to verticals in specific positions, and so on. The full ensemble of cells in this area provides a detector for every possible stimulus, making certain that no matter what the input is or where it's located, some cell will respond to it.

The pattern of specialization is also evident when we consider other brain areas. **Figure 3.9**, for example, reflects one summary of the brain areas known to be involved in vision. The details of the figure aren't crucial, but it is noteworthy that some of these areas (V1, V2, V3, V4, PO, and MT) are in the occipital cortex; other areas are in the parietal cortex; others are in the temporal cortex. (We'll have more to say in a moment about these areas outside of the occipital cortex.) Most important, each area seems to have its own

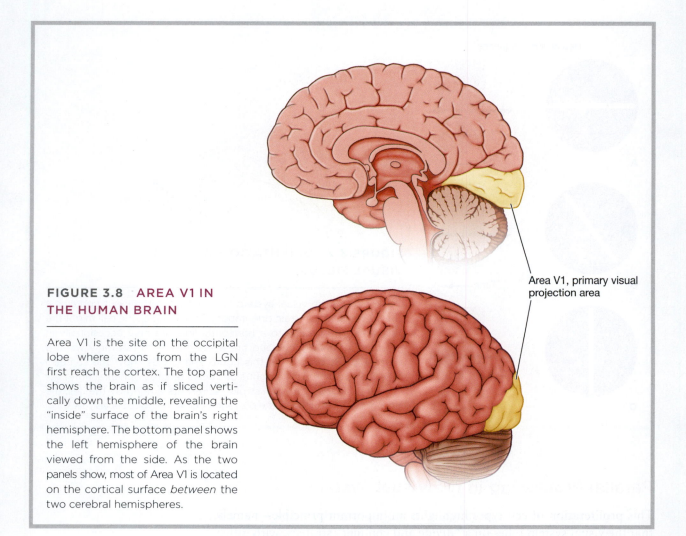

FIGURE 3.8 · AREA V1 IN THE HUMAN BRAIN

Area V1 is the site on the occipital lobe where axons from the LGN first reach the cortex. The top panel shows the brain as if sliced vertically down the middle, revealing the "inside" surface of the brain's right hemisphere. The bottom panel shows the left hemisphere of the brain viewed from the side. As the two panels show, most of Area V1 is located on the cortical surface *between* the two cerebral hemispheres.

Area V1, primary visual projection area

function. Neurons in Area MT, for example, are acutely sensitive to direction and speed of movement. (This area, named for its position in the brain, is the brain region that has suffered damage in cases involving akinetopsia.) Cells in Area V4 fire most strongly when the input is of a certain color and a certain shape.

Let's also emphasize that all of these specialized areas are active at the same time, so that (for example) cells in Area MT are detecting movement in the visual input at the same time that cells in Area V4 are detecting shapes. In other words, the visual system relies on **parallel processing**, with many different steps (in this case, different kinds of analysis) going on simultaneously. (Parallel processing is usually contrasted with **serial processing**, in which steps are carried out one at a time—i.e., in a series.)

One advantage of this simultaneous processing is speed: Brain areas trying to discern the shape of the incoming stimulus don't need to wait until the

FIGURE 3.9 THE VISUAL PROCESSING PATHWAYS

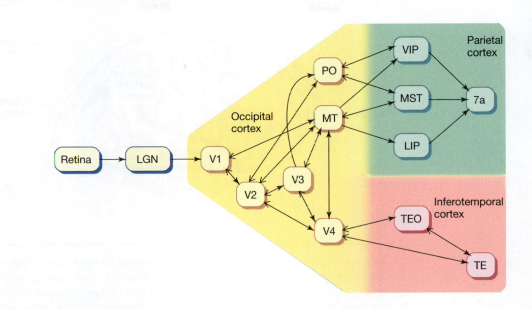

Each box in this figure refers to a specific location within the visual system. Notice that vision depends on many brain sites, each performing a specialized type of analysis. Note also that the flow of information is complex, so there's no strict sequence of "this step" of analysis followed by "that step." Instead, everything happens at once, with a great deal of back-and-forth communication among the various elements.

motion analysis or the color analysis is complete. Instead, all of the analyses go forward immediately when the input appears before the eyes, with no waiting time.

Another advantage of parallel processing is the possibility of mutual influence among multiple systems. To see why this matters, consider the fact that sometimes your interpretation of an object's motion depends on your understanding of the object's three-dimensional shape. This suggests that it might be best if the perception of shape happened first. That way, you could use the results of this processing step as a guide to later analyses. In other cases, though, the relationship between shape and motion is reversed. In these cases, your interpretation of an object's three-dimensional shape depends on what you can see of its motion. To allow for this possibility, it might be best if the perception of motion happened first, so that it could guide the subsequent analysis of shape.

How does the brain deal with these contradictory demands? Parallel processing provides the answer. Since both sorts of analysis go on simultaneously, each type of analysis can be informed by the other. Put differently, neither the shape-analyzing system nor the motion-analyzing system gets priority.

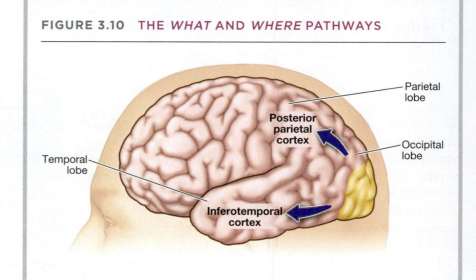

FIGURE 3.10 THE *WHAT* AND *WHERE* PATHWAYS

Parietal lobe

Posterior parietal cortex

Occipital lobe

Temporal lobe

Inferotemporal cortex

Information from the primary visual cortex at the back of the head is transmitted to the inferotemporal cortex (the so-called *what* system) and to the posterior parietal cortex (the *where* system). The term "inferotemporal" refers to the lower part of the temporal lobe. The term "posterior parietal cortex" refers to the rearmost portion of this cortex.

Instead, the two systems work concurrently and "negotiate" a solution that satisfies both systems (Van Essen & DeYoe, 1995).

Parallel processing is easy to document throughout the visual system. As we've seen, the retina contains two types of specialized receptors (rods and cones) each doing its own job (e.g., the rods detecting stimuli in the periphery of your vision, and the cones detecting hues and detail at the center of your vision). Both types of receptors function at the same time—another case of parallel processing.

Parallel processing is also evident when we move beyond the occipital cortex. As **Figure 3.10** shows, some of the activation from the occipital lobe is passed along to the cortex of the temporal lobe. This pathway, called the ***what*** **system**, plays a major role in the identification of visual objects, telling you whether the object is a cat, an apple, or whatever. At the same time, activation from the occipital lobe is also passed along a second pathway, leading to the parietal cortex, in what is called the ***where*** **system**. This system guides your action based on your perception of where objects are located—above or below you, to your right or to your left. (See Goodale & Milner, 2004; Humphreys & Riddoch, 2014; Ungerleider & Haxby, 1994. For complications, though, see Borst et al., 2011; de Haan & Cowey, 2011.)

The contrasting roles of these two systems can be revealed in many ways, including studies of brain damage. Patients with lesions in the *what* system show visual agnosia—an inability to recognize visually presented objects, including such common things as a cup or a pencil. However, these patients show little disorder in recognizing visual orientation or in reaching. The reverse pattern occurs with patients who have suffered lesions in the *where* system: They have difficulty in reaching, but no problem in object identification (Damasio et al., 1989; Farah, 1990; Goodale, 1995).

Other data also echo the broad theme of parallel processing within the visual system. For example, we noted earlier that different brain areas are critical for the perception of color, motion, and form. If this is right, then someone who has suffered damage in just one of these areas might show problems in the perception of color but not the perception of motion or form, or problems in the perception of motion but not the perception of form or color. These predictions are correct. As we mentioned at the chapter's start, some patients suffer damage to the motion system and so develop akinetopsia (Zihl et al., 1983). For such patients, the world is described as a succession of static photographs. They're unable to report the speed or direction of a moving object; as one patient put it, "When I'm looking at the car first, it seems far away. But then when I want to cross the road, suddenly the car is very near" (Zihl et al., 1983, p. 315).

Other patients suffer a specific loss of color vision through damage to the central nervous system, even though their perception of form and motion remains normal (Damasio, 1985; Gazzaniga et al., 2019). To them, the entire world is clothed only in "dirty shades of gray."[2]

Cases like these provide dramatic confirmation of the separateness of our visual system's various elements and the ways in which the visual system is vulnerable to very specific forms of damage. (For further evidence with neurologically intact participants, see Bundesen et al., 2003.)

Putting the Pieces Back Together

Let's emphasize once again, therefore, that even the simplest of our intellectual achievements depends on an array of highly specialized brain areas working together in parallel. This was evident in Chapter 2 in our consideration of Capgras syndrome, and the same pattern has emerged in our description of the visual system. Here, too, the many parts of the visual system must work together: the rods and the cones; the *what* system and the *where* system; areas specialized for the perception of color and areas specialized for the perception of detail.

We've identified several advantages that come from this division of labor and the parallel processing it allows. But the division of labor also creates a problem: If multiple brain areas contribute to an overall task, how is their functioning coordinated? When you see an athlete make an astonishing jump, the jump itself is registered by motion-sensitive neurons, but your recognition of the athlete depends on shape-sensitive neurons. How are the pieces put back together? When you reach for a coffee cup but stop midway

---

2. This is different from ordinary color blindness, which is usually present from birth and results from abnormalities that are outside the brain itself—for example, abnormalities in the photoreceptors.

because you see that the cup is empty, the reach itself is guided by the *where* system; the fact that the cup is empty is registered by the *what* system. How are these two streams of processing coordinated?

Investigators refer to this broad issue as the **binding problem**—the task of reuniting the various elements of a scene, elements that are initially addressed by different systems in different parts of the brain. And obviously this problem is solved. What you perceive is not an unordered catalogue of sensory elements. Instead, you perceive a coherent, integrated perceptual world. Apparently, this is a case in which the various pieces of Humpty Dumpty are reassembled to form an organized whole.

Visual Maps and Firing Synchrony

Look around you. Your visual system registers whiteness and blueness and brownness; it also registers a small cylindrical shape (your coffee cup), a medium-sized rectangle (this book page), and a much larger rectangle (your desk). How do you put these pieces together so that you see that it's the coffee cup, and not the book page, that's blue; the desktop, and not the cup, that's brown?

There is debate about how the visual system solves this problem, but we can identify three elements that contribute to the solution. One element is *spatial position*. The part of the brain registering the cup's shape is separate from the parts registering its color or its motion; nonetheless, these various brain areas all have something in common. They each keep track of where the target is—where the cylindrical shape was located, and where the blueness was; where the motion was detected, and where things were still. As a result, the reassembling of these pieces can be done with reference to position. In essence, you can overlay the map of *which forms are where* on top of the map of *which colors are where* to get the right colors with the right forms, and likewise for the map showing *which motion patterns are where*.

Information about spatial position is, of course, useful for its own sake: You have a compelling reason to care whether the tiger is close to you or far away, or whether the bus is on your side of the street or the other. But in addition, location information apparently provides a frame of reference used to solve the binding problem. Given this double function, we shouldn't be surprised that spatial position is a major organizing theme in all the various brain areas concerned with vision, with each area seeming to provide its own map of the visual world.

Spatial position, however, is not the whole story. Evidence also suggests that the brain uses special *rhythms* to identify which sensory elements belong with which. Imagine two groups of neurons in the visual cortex. One group of neurons fires maximally whenever a vertical line is in view; another group fires maximally whenever a stimulus is in view moving from a high position to a low one. Let's also imagine that right now a vertical line is presented and it is moving downward; as a result, both groups of neurons are firing strongly. How does the brain encode the fact that these attributes are bound together, different aspects of a single object? There is evidence that the visual system marks this fact by means of **neural synchrony**: If the neurons detecting a vertical line are firing in synchrony with those signaling movement, then these attributes are registered as belonging to the same object. If they aren't in synchrony, then the features aren't bound together (Buzsáki & Draguhn, 2004; Csibra et al., 2000; Elliott & Müller, 2000; Fries et al., 2001).

What causes this synchrony? How do the neurons become synchronized in the first place? Here, another factor is crucial: *attention*. We'll have more to say about attention in Chapter 5, but for now let's note that attention plays a key role in binding together the separate features of a stimulus. (For a classic statement of this argument, see Treisman & Gelade, 1980; Treisman et al., 1977. For more recent discussion, see Fiebelkorn & Kastner, 2020; Harris et al., 2020; and also Chapter 5.)

Evidence for attention's role comes from many sources, including the fact that when we overload perceivers' attention, they often make **conjunction errors**. This means that they correctly detect the features present in a visual display, but then make mistakes about how the features are bound together. Thus, for example, someone shown a blue *H* and a red *T* might report seeing a blue *T* and a red *H*—an error in binding.

Likewise, recording of brain activity indicates that synchronized neural firing occurs in an animal's brain when the animal is attending to a specific stimulus, but does not occur in neurons activated by an unattended stimulus (e.g., Buschman & Miller, 2007; Saalmann et al., 2007; Womelsdorf et al., 2007). Results like these bolster the claim that attention plays a central part in solving the binding problem.

Before moving on, let's also emphasize the many ways in which information is represented in the brain. In Chapter 2, we noted that the brain uses different chemical signals (i.e., different neurotransmitters) to transmit different types of information. We now see that there is information reflected in *which* cells are firing, *how often* they are firing, whether the cells are firing in *synchrony* with other cells, and (it turns out) also the *rhythm* in which they are firing. Plainly, this is a system of considerable complexity!

Form Perception

So far in this chapter, we've been discussing the detection of simple attributes in the stimulus—color, motion, and the catalogue of features. But this detection is just the start of the process, because the visual system still has to assemble these features into recognizable wholes. We've mentioned the binding problem as part of this "assembly"—but binding isn't the whole story. This point is reflected in the fact that our perception of the world is organized in ways that the stimulus input is not—a point documented early in the 20th century by a group called the "Gestalt psychologists."[3] The Gestaltists argued that the organization is contributed by the perceiver;

---

3. *Gestalt* is the German word for "shape" or "form." The Gestalt psychology movement was committed to the view that theories about perception and thought need to emphasize the organization of patterns, not just focus on a pattern's elements.

TEST YOURSELF

3. How do researchers use single-cell recording to reveal a cell's receptive field?
4. What are the advantages of parallel processing in the visual system? What are the disadvantages?
5. How is firing synchrony relevant to the solution of the binding problem?

this is why, they claimed, the perceptual whole is often different from the sum of its parts. Years later, Jerome Bruner (1973) voiced related claims and coined the phrase "beyond the information given" to describe some of the ways our perception of a stimulus differs from (and goes beyond) the stimulus itself.

Consider the form shown on the top of **Figure 3.11**: the **Necker cube**. This drawing is an example of a **reversible (or ambiguous) figure**—so called because people perceive it first one way and then another. Specifically, this form can be perceived as a drawing of a cube viewed from above (in which case it's similar to the cube marked A in the figure); it can also be perceived as a cube viewed from below (so that it's similar to the cube marked B). Let's be clear, though, that this isn't an "illusion," because neither of these interpretations is "wrong," and the drawing itself (and, therefore, the information reaching your eyes) is fully compatible with either interpretation. Put differently, the Necker cube is entirely neutral with regard to the shape's configuration in depth; the lines on the page don't specify which is the "proper" interpretation. Your perception of the cube, however, is not neutral. Instead, you perceive the cube as having one configuration or the other—similar either to Cube A or to Cube B. Your perception goes beyond the information given in the drawing, by specifying an arrangement in depth.

FIGURE 3.11 THE NECKER CUBE

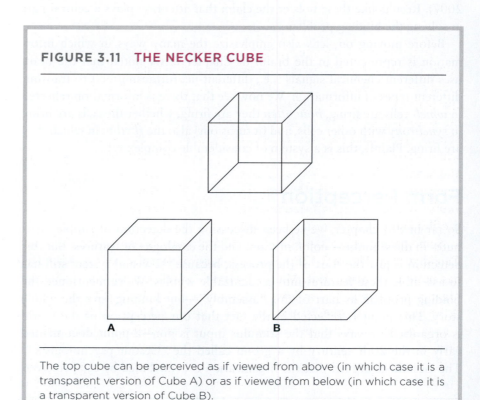

A   B

The top cube can be perceived as if viewed from above (in which case it is a transparent version of Cube A) or as if viewed from below (in which case it is a transparent version of Cube B).

FIGURE 3.12 AMBIGUOUS FIGURES

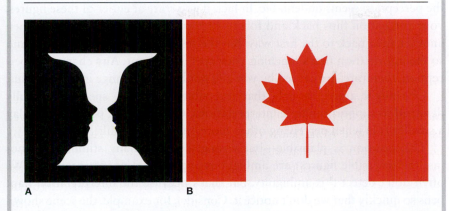

Some stimuli easily lend themselves to reinterpretation. The figure in Panel A, for example, is perceived by many to be a white vase or candlestick on a black background; others see it as two black faces shown in profile. Some people argue that a similar ambiguity exists in the Canadian flag, with two pointy-nosed profiles pointing toward the leaf's stem (Panel B).

The same point can be made for many other stimuli. **Figure 3.12A** (after Rubin, 1915, 1921) can be perceived either as a vase centered in the picture or as two profiles facing each other. The drawing by itself is compatible with either of these perceptions, and so, once again, the drawing is neutral with regard to perceptual organization. In particular, it is neutral with regard to **figure/ground organization**, the determination of what is the figure (the depicted object, displayed against a background) and what is the ground. Your perception of this drawing, however, isn't neutral about this point. Instead, your perception somehow specifies that you're looking at the vase and not the profiles, or that you're looking at the profiles and not the vase.

Some people assert that figure/ground ambiguity is also detectable in the Canadian flag (**Figure 3.12B.**) Since 1965, the centerpiece of Canada's flag has been a red maple leaf. Many observers, however, note that a different organization is possible, at least for part of the flag. In their view, the flag depicts two profiles, shown in white against a red backdrop. Each profile has a large pointy nose, an open mouth, and a prominent brow ridge, and the profiles are looking downward, toward the flag's center.

In all these examples, then, your perception contains information—about how the form is arranged in depth, or about which part of the form is figure and which is ground—that is not contained within the stimulus itself. Apparently, this is information contributed by you, the perceiver.

The Gestalt Principles

With figures like the Necker cube or the vase/profiles, your role in shaping the perception seems undeniable. In fact, if you stare at either of these figures, your perception flips back and forth—first you see the figure one way, then another, then back to the first way. But the stimulus itself isn't changing, and so the information that's reaching your eyes is constant. Any changes in perception, therefore, are caused by *you* and not by some change in the stimulus.

One might argue, though, that reversible figures are special—carefully designed to support multiple interpretations. On this basis, perhaps you play a smaller role when perceiving other, more "natural" stimuli.

This position is plausible—but wrong, because many stimuli (and not just the reversible figures) are ambiguous and in need of interpretation. We often don't detect this ambiguity, but that's because the interpretation happens so quickly that we don't notice it. Consider, for example, the scene shown in **Figure 3.13**. It's almost certain that you perceive segments B and E as being united, forming a complete apple, but notice that this information isn't

---

FIGURE 3.13   THE ROLE OF INTERPRETATION IN PERCEIVING AN ORDINARY SCENE

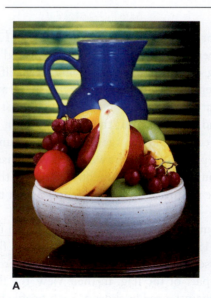
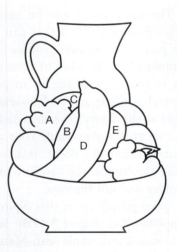

A   B

Consider the still life (Panel A) and an overlay designating five different segments of the scene (Panel B). For this picture to be perceived correctly, the perceptual system must first decide what goes with what—for example, that Segment B and Segment E are different bits of the same object (even though they're separated by Segment D) and that Segment B and Segment A are different objects (even though they're adjacent and the same color).

provided by the stimulus; instead, it's your interpretation. (If we simply go with the information in the figure, it's possible that segments B and E are parts of entirely different fruits, with the "gap" between the two fruits hidden by the banana.) It's also likely that you perceive the banana as entirely banana-shaped and therefore continuing downward out of your view, into the bowl, where it eventually ends with the sort of point that's normal for a banana. In the same way, surely you perceive the horizontal stripes in the background as continuous and merely hidden from view by the pitcher. (You'd be surprised if we removed the pitcher and revealed a pitcher-shaped gap in the stripes.) But, of course, the stimulus doesn't in any way "guarantee" the banana's shape or the continuity of the stripes; these points are, again, just your interpretation.

Even with this ordinary scene, therefore, your perception goes "beyond the information given"—and so the unity of the two apple slices and the continuity of the stripes is "in the eye of the beholder," not in the stimulus itself. Of course, you don't feel like you're "interpreting" this picture or extrapolating beyond what's on the page. But your role becomes clear the moment we start cataloguing the differences between your perception and the information that's truly present in the photograph.

Your interpretation of a stimulus isn't, however, careless or capricious. Instead, you're guided by a few straightforward principles that the Gestalt psychologists catalogued many years ago—and so they're referred to as the **Gestalt principles**. For example, your perception is guided by *proximity* and *similarity*: If, within the visual scene, you see elements that are close to each other, or elements that resemble each other, you assume these elements are parts of the same object (**Figure 3.14**). You also tend to assume that contours

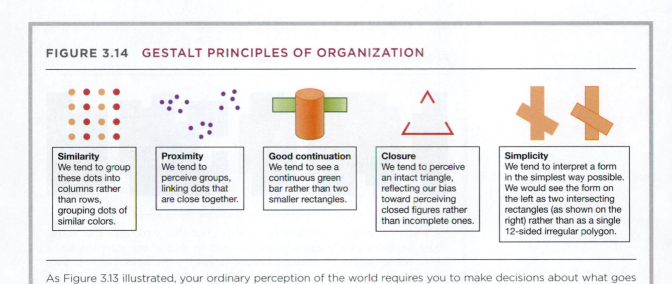

FIGURE 3.14   GESTALT PRINCIPLES OF ORGANIZATION

Similarity
We tend to group these dots into columns rather than rows, grouping dots of similar colors.

Proximity
We tend to perceive groups, linking dots that are close together.

Good continuation
We tend to see a continuous green bar rather than two smaller rectangles.

Closure
We tend to perceive an intact triangle, reflecting our bias toward perceiving closed figures rather than incomplete ones.

Simplicity
We tend to interpret a form in the simplest way possible. We would see the form on the left as two intersecting rectangles (as shown on the right) rather than as a single 12-sided irregular polygon.

As Figure 3.13 illustrated, your ordinary perception of the world requires you to make decisions about what goes with what—which elements are part of the same object, and which elements belong to different objects. Your decisions are guided by a few simple principles, catalogued many years ago by the Gestalt psychologists.

are smooth, not jagged, and you avoid interpretations that involve coincidences. (For perspective on these principles and Gestalt psychology in general, see Wagemans, Elder, et al., 2012; Wagemans, Feldman, et al., 2012.)

These perceptual principles are straightforward, but they're essential if your perceptual apparatus is going to make sense of the often ambiguous, often incomplete information provided by your senses. In addition, it's worth mentioning that everyone's perceptions are guided by the same principles, and that's why you generally perceive the world in the same way that other people do. Each of us imposes our interpretation on the perceptual input, but we all tend to impose the same interpretation because we're all governed by the same rules.

Organization and Features

We've now considered two broad topics—the detection of simple attributes in the stimulus, and the ways in which you organize those attributes. In thinking about these topics, you might want to think about them as separate steps. First, you collect information about the stimulus, so that you know (for example) what corners or angles or curves are in view—the **visual features** contained within the input. Then, once you've gathered the "raw data," you interpret this information. That's when you "go beyond the information given"—deciding how the form is laid out in depth (as in Figure 3.11), deciding what is figure and what is ground (Figure 3.12), and so on.

The idea, then, is that perception might be divided (roughly) into an "information gathering" step followed by an "interpretation" step. This view, however, is *wrong*, and, in fact, it's easy to show that in many settings, your interpretation of the input happens *before* you start cataloguing the input's basic features, not after. Consider **Figure 3.15**. Initially, these shapes seem to

---

FIGURE 3.15   A HIDDEN FIGURE

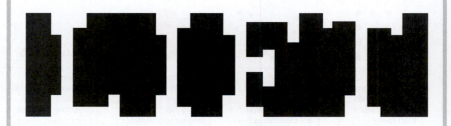

Initially, these dark shapes have no meaning, but after a moment the hidden figure becomes clearly visible. Notice, therefore, that at the start the figure seems not to contain the features needed to identify the various letters. Once the figure is reorganized, with the white parts (not the dark parts) making up the figure, the features are easily detected. Apparently, the analysis of features depends on how the figure is first organized by the viewer.

have no meaning, but after a moment most people discover the word hidden in the figure. That is, people find a way to reorganize the figure so that the familiar letters come into view. But let's be clear about what this means. At the start, the form seems not to contain the features needed to identify the *L*, the *I*, and so on. Once the form is reorganized, though, it does contain these features, and the letters are immediately recognized. In other words, with one organization, the features are absent; with another, they're plainly present. It would seem, then, that the features themselves depend on how the form is organized by the viewer—and so the features are as much "in the eye of the beholder" as they are in the figure itself.

As a different example, you have no difficulty reading the word printed in **Figure 3.16**, although most of the features needed for this recognition are absent. You easily "provide" the missing features, though, thanks to the fact that you interpret the black marks in the figure as shadows cast by solid letters. Given this interpretation and the extrapolation it involves, you can easily "fill in" the missing features and read the word.

How should we think about all of this? On one hand, your perception of a form surely has to start with the stimulus itself and must be governed by what's in that stimulus. After all, no matter how you try to interpret Figure 3.16, it won't look to you like a photograph of Queen Elizabeth— the basic features of the queen are just not present, and your perception respects this obvious fact. This suggests that the features must be in place *before* an interpretation is offered, because the features govern the interpretation. But, on the other hand, Figures 3.15 and 3.16 suggest that the opposite is the case: that the features you find in an input depend on how the figure is interpreted. Therefore, it's the interpretation, not the features, that must be first.

The solution to this puzzle builds on ideas that we've already met: Many aspects of the brain's functioning depend on parallel processing, with different brain areas all doing their work at the same time. In addition, the various brain areas all influence one another, so that what's going on in one

---

FIGURE 3.16 MISSING FEATURES

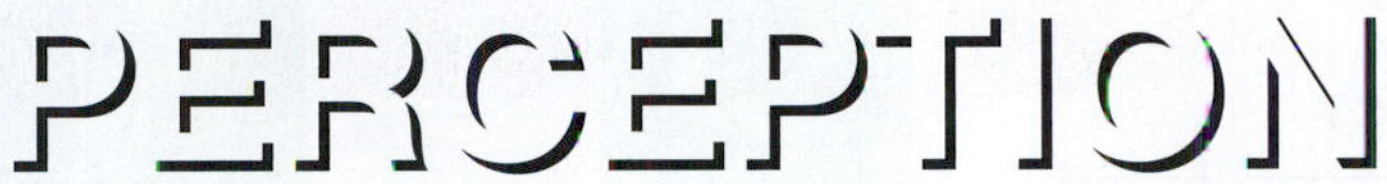

PERCEPTION

People have no trouble reading this word, even though most of the features needed for recognition are absent from the stimulus. People easily "supply" the missing features, illustrating once again that the analysis of features depends on how the overall figure has been interpreted and organized.

TEST YOURSELF

6. What evidence tells us that perception goes beyond (i.e., includes more information than) the stimulus input?

7. What are the Gestalt principles, and how do they influence visual perception?

8. What evidence is there that the perception of an overall form depends on the detection of features? What evidence is there that the detection of features depends on the overall form?

brain region is shaped by what's going on elsewhere. In this way, the brain areas that analyze a pattern's basic features do their work at the same time as the brain areas that analyze the pattern's large-scale configuration, and these brain areas interact so that the perception of the features is guided by the configuration, and analysis of the configuration is guided by the features. In other words, neither type of processing "goes first." Neither has priority. Instead, they work together, with the result that the perception that is achieved makes sense at both the large-scale and fine-grained levels.

Constancy

We've now seen many indications of the perceiver's role in "going beyond the information given" in the stimulus itself. This theme is also evident in another aspect of perception: the achievement of **perceptual constancy**. This term refers to the fact that we perceive the constant properties of objects in the world (their sizes, shapes, and so on) even though the sensory information we receive about these attributes changes whenever our viewing circumstances change.

Consider the perception of size. If you happen to be far away from the object you're viewing, then the image cast onto your retinas by that object will be relatively small. If you approach the object, then the image size will increase. This change in image size is a simple consequence of physics, but you're not fooled by this variation. Instead, you manage to achieve **size constancy**—you correctly perceive the sizes of objects despite the changes in retinal-image size created by changes in viewing distance.

Similarly, if you view a door straight on, the retinal image will be rectangular; but if you view the same door from an angle, the retinal image will have a different shape (see **Figure 3.17**). Still, you achieve **shape constancy**—that is, you correctly perceive the shapes of objects despite changes in the

FIGURE 3.17 SHAPE CONSTANCY

If you change your viewing angle, the shape of the retinal image cast by a target changes. In this figure, the door viewed straight on casts a rectangular image on your retina; the door viewed from an angle casts a trapezoidal image. Nonetheless, you generally achieve shape constancy.

retinal image created by shifts in your viewing angle. You also achieve **brightness constancy**—you correctly perceive the brightness of objects whether they're illuminated by dim light or strong sun.

Unconscious Inference

How do you achieve each of these forms of constancy? One hypothesis focuses on relationships within the retinal image. In judging size, for example, you generally see objects against some background, and this can provide a basis for comparison with the target object. To see how this works, imagine that you're looking at a dog sitting on the kitchen floor. Let's say the dog is half as tall as the nearby chair and hides eight of the kitchen's floor tiles from view. If you take several steps back from the dog, none of these relationships change, even though the sizes of all the retinal images are reduced. Size constancy, therefore, might be achieved by focusing not on the images themselves but on these unchanging relationships (see **Figure 3.18**).

Relationships do contribute to size constancy, and that's why you're better able to judge size when comparison objects are in view or when the target you're judging sits on a surface that has a visual texture (like the floor tiles in the example). But these relationships don't tell the whole story. Size constancy is achieved even when the visual scene offers no basis for comparison (if, for example, the object to be judged is the only object in view), provided that other cues signal the *distance* of the target object (Harvey & Leibowitz, 1967; Holway & Boring, 1947).

How does your visual system use this distance information? More than a century ago, the physicist Hermann von Helmholtz offered a hypothesis. Helmholtz started with the fact that there's a simple inverse relationship

A   B

FIGURE 3.18 AN INVARIANT RELATIONSHIP THAT PROVIDES INFORMATION ABOUT SIZE

One proposal is that you achieve size constancy by focusing on *relationships* in the visual scene. For example, the dog sitting nearby on the kitchen floor (Panel A) is half as tall as the chair and hides eight of the kitchen's floor tiles from view. If you take several steps back from the dog (Panel B), none of these relationships change, even though the sizes of all the retinal images are reduced. By focusing on the relationships, then, you can see that the dog's size hasn't changed.

between distance and retinal image size: If an object doubles its distance from the viewer, the size of its image is reduced by half. If an object triples its distance, the size of its image is reduced to a third of its initial size. This relationship is guaranteed to hold true because of the principles of optics, and the relationship makes it possible for perceivers to achieve size constancy by means of a simple calculation. Of course, Helmholtz knew that we don't run through a conscious calculation every time we perceive an object's size, but he believed we're calculating nonetheless—and so he referred to the process as an **unconscious inference** (Helmholtz, 1909).

What is the calculation that enables you to perceive size correctly? It's multiplication: the size of the image on the retina, multiplied by the distance between you and the object. (We'll have more to say about how you know this distance in a later section.) As an example, imagine an object that, at a distance of 10 ft, casts an image on the retina that's 4 mm across. Because of straightforward principles of optics, the same object, at a distance of 20 ft, casts an image of 2 mm. In both cases, the product—10×4 or 20×2—is the same. If, therefore, your size estimate depends on that product, your size estimate won't be thrown off by viewing distance—and that's exactly what we want (see **Figure 3.19**).

FIGURE 3.19   **THE RELATIONSHIP BETWEEN IMAGE SIZE AND DISTANCE**

Closer objects cast larger retinal images

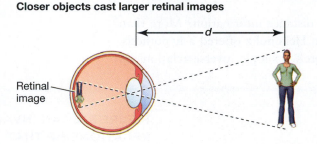

Retinal image

Farther objects cast smaller retinal images

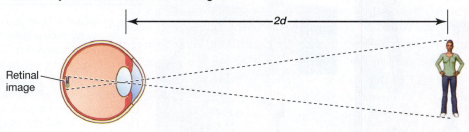

Retinal image

If you view an object from a greater distance (marked "d" in the figure), the object casts a smaller image on your retina. Nonetheless, you generally achieve size constancy—perceiving the object's actual size. Helmholtz proposed that you achieve constancy through an unconscious inference—essentially multiplying the image size by the distance.

What's the evidence that size constancy does rely on this sort of inference? In many experiments, researchers have shown participants an object and, without changing the object's retinal image, have changed the apparent distance of the object. (There are many ways to do this—lenses that change how the eye has to focus to bring the object into sharp view, or mirrors that change how the two eyes have to angle inward so that the object's image is centered on both foveas.) If people are—as Helmholtz proposed—using distance information to judge size, then these manipulations should affect size perception. Any manipulation that makes an object seem farther away (without changing retinal image size) should make that object seem bigger (because, in essence, the perceiver would be "multiplying" by a larger number). Any manipulation that makes the object seem closer should make it look smaller. And, in fact, these predictions are correct—a powerful confirmation that people do use distance to judge size.

A similar proposal explains how people achieve shape constancy. Here, you take the slant of the surface into account and make appropriate adjustments—again, an unconscious inference—in your interpretation of the retinal image's shape. Likewise for brightness constancy: Perceivers are sensitive to how a surface is oriented relative to the available light sources, and they take this information into account in estimating how much light is reaching the surface. Then, they use this assessment of lighting to judge the surface's brightness (e.g., whether it's black or gray or white). In all these cases, therefore, it appears that the perceptual system does draw some sort of unconscious inference, taking viewing circumstances into account in a way that enables you to perceive the constant properties of the visual world.

Illusions

The process of taking information into account—whether it's distance (in order to judge size), viewing angle (to judge shape), or illumination (to judge brightness)—is crucial for achieving constancy. More than that, it's another indication that you don't just "receive" visual information; instead, you *interpret* it.

Interpretation is, overall, an essential part of your perception and generally helps you perceive the world correctly. The role of interpretation becomes especially clear, however, in circumstances in which you *misinterpret* the information available to you and end up misperceiving the world. Consider the two tabletops shown in **Figure 3.20**. The table on the left looks quite a bit longer and thinner than the one on the right; a tablecloth that fits one table surely won't fit the other. Objectively, though, the parallelogram depicting the left tabletop is exactly the same shape as the one depicting the right tabletop. If you were to cut out the shape on the page depicting the left tabletop, rotate it, and slide it onto the right tabletop, they'd be an exact match. (Not convinced? Just lay another piece of paper on top of the page, trace the left tabletop, and then move your tracing onto the right tabletop.)

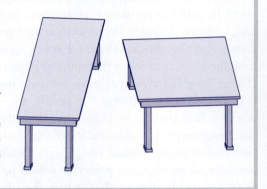

FIGURE 3.20 TWO TABLETOPS

These two tabletops seem to have very different shapes and sizes. However, this contrast is an illusion—and the shapes drawn here (the two parallelograms depicting the tabletops) are identical in shape and size. The illusion is caused by the same mechanisms that, in most circumstances, allow you to achieve constancy.

Why do people misperceive these shapes? The answer involves the normal mechanisms of shape constancy. Cues to depth in this figure cause you to perceive the figure as a drawing of three-dimensional objects, each viewed from a particular angle. This leads you—quite automatically—to adjust for the (apparent) viewing angles in order to perceive the two tabletops, and it's this adjustment that causes the illusion. Notice, then, that this illusion about shape is caused by a misperception of depth: You misperceive the depth relationships in the drawing and then take this faulty information into account in interpreting the shapes. (For a related illusion, see **Figure 3.21**.)

FIGURE 3.21 THE MONSTER ILLUSION

The two monsters appear rather different in size. But, again, this is an illusion, because the two drawings are exactly the same size. The illusion is created by the distance cues in the picture, which make the monster on the right appear to be farther away. This (mis)perception of distance leads to a (mis)perception of size.

FIGURE 3.22 A BRIGHTNESS ILLUSION

The central square (third row, third column) appears much brighter than the square marked by the arrow. Once again, though, this is an illusion. If you don't believe it, use your fingers or pieces of paper to cover everything in the figure except for these two squares.

A different example is shown in **Figure 3.22**. It seems obvious to most viewers that the center square in this checkerboard (third row, third column) is a brighter shade than the square indicated by the arrow. But, in truth, the shade of gray shown on the page is identical for these two squares. What has happened here? The answer again involves the normal processes of perception. First, the mechanisms of lateral inhibition (described earlier) play a role here in producing a *contrast effect*: The central square in this figure is surrounded by dark squares, and the contrast makes the central square look brighter. The square marked at the edge of the checkerboard, however, is surrounded by white squares; here, contrast makes the marked square look darker.

But, in addition, the visual system also detects that the central square is in the shadow cast by the cylinder. Your vision compensates for this fact—again, an example of unconscious inference that takes the shadow into account in judging brightness—and therefore powerfully magnifies the illusion.

The Perception of Depth

We've now argued that perceivers take distance, slant, and illumination into account in judging size, shape, and brightness. But to do this, they need to know what the distance is ("How far away is the target object?"), what the viewing angle is ("Am I looking at the shape straight on or at an angle?"), and what the illumination is. Otherwise, they'd have no way to take these factors into account and, therefore, no way to achieve constancy.

Let's pursue this issue by asking how people judge *distance*. We've said that distance perception is crucial for size constancy, but, of course, information about distance is also valuable for its own sake. If you want to walk down a hallway without bumping into obstacles, you need to know which obstacles are close to you and which ones are far off. If you wish to caress a

9. What does it mean to say that size constancy may depend on an unconscious inference? An inference about what?
10. How do the ordinary mechanisms of constancy lead to visual illusions?

loved one, you need to know where he or she is; otherwise, you're likely to swat empty space when you reach out with your caress or (worse) poke your loved one in the eye. Plainly, then, you need to know where objects in your world are located.

Binocular Cues

The perception of distance depends on various **distance cues**—features of the stimulus that indicate an object's position. One cue comes from the fact that your eyes look out on the world from slightly different positions; as a result, each eye has a slightly different view. This difference between the two eyes' views is called **binocular disparity**, and it provides important information about distance relationships in the world.

Binocular disparity can lead to the perception of depth even when no other distance cues are present. For example, the bottom panels of **Figure 3.23** show the views that each eye would receive while looking at a pair of nearby objects. If we present each of these views to the appropriate eye (e.g., by drawing the views on two cards and placing one card in front of each eye), we can obtain a striking impression of depth.

Monocular Cues

Binocular disparity is a powerful determinant of perceived depth. But we can also perceive depth with one eye closed; plainly, then, there are depth cues that depend only on what each eye sees by itself. These are the **monocular distance cues**.

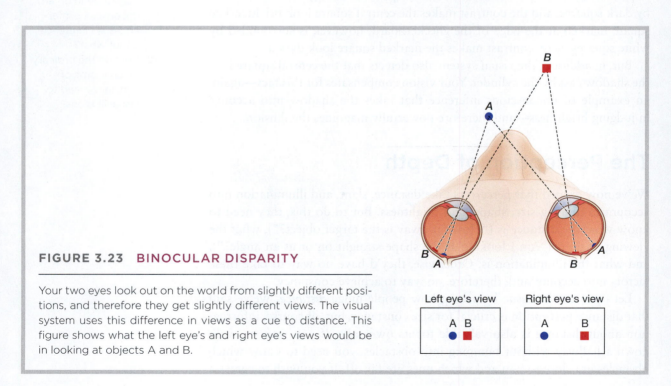

FIGURE 3.23   BINOCULAR DISPARITY

Your two eyes look out on the world from slightly different positions, and therefore they get slightly different views. The visual system uses this difference in views as a cue to distance. This figure shows what the left eye's and right eye's views would be in looking at objects A and B.

One monocular cue depends on the adjustment that the eye must make in order to see the world clearly. We mentioned earlier that in each eye, muscles adjust the shape of the lens to produce a sharply focused image on the retina. The amount of adjustment depends on how far away the viewed object is—there's a lot of adjustment for nearby objects, less for those a few steps away, and virtually no adjustment at all for objects more than a few meters away. It turns out that perceivers are sensitive to the amount of adjustment and use it as a cue indicating how far away the object is.

Other monocular cues have been exploited by artists for centuries to create an impression of depth on a flat surface—that is, within a picture—and that's why these cues are called **pictorial cues**. In each case, these cues rely on straightforward principles of physics. For example, imagine a situation in which a man is trying to admire a car, but a mailbox is in the way (see **Figure 3.24A**). In this case, the mailbox will inevitably block the view simply because light can't travel through an opaque object. This fact about the physical world provides a cue you can use in judging distance. The cue is known as **interposition**—the blocking of your view of one object by some other object. In **Figure 3.24B**, interposition tells the man that the mailbox is closer than the car.

In the same way, distant objects produce a smaller retinal image than do nearby objects of the same size; this is a fact about optics. But this physical fact again provides perceptual information you can use. In particular, it's the basis for the cue of **linear perspective**, the name for the pattern in

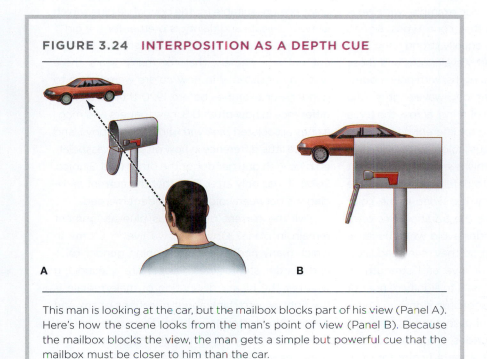

FIGURE 3.24   INTERPOSITION AS A DEPTH CUE

A

B

This man is looking at the car, but the mailbox blocks part of his view (Panel A). Here's how the scene looks from the man's point of view (Panel B). Because the mailbox blocks the view, the man gets a simple but powerful cue that the mailbox must be closer to him than the car.

The Meaning of Color

Vision provides you with an enormous amount of information that is immediately useful—telling you (among other things) about the identity and position of objects in your surroundings, and how (or whether) the objects are moving. But vision does far more than this, because vision also adds pleasure, aesthetic value, and a dimension of meaning to our lives.

Even relatively simple aspects of vision can create a mood, convey information, or set a context that guides our behavior. Consider just one aspect of vision: *color.* The actual perception of color is largely determined by our biology: Human retinas have three types of cones, and the types differ in how they respond to different wavelengths of light. The perception of color is then governed by the pattern of firing in these three cone types. As the chapter describes, strong firing from the cones that prefer short wavelengths, for example, with weak (or no) firing from the other cone types, signals purple. Blue is signaled by equally strong firing from the cones that prefer short wavelengths and those that prefer medium wavelengths, with only modest firing by cones that prefer long wavelengths. And so on, with other patterns of firing, across the three cone types, corresponding to different hues.

The *meaning* of various colors, in contrast, is not set by our biology; this is evident in the fact that the meanings seem to differ from one culture to another. In many countries, *white* is the color indicating purity and so is the traditional color of bridal gowns; in India, brides avoid white because it's a symbol of mourning, so they're instead likely to wear *red,* a symbol of love and strength. In Western countries, red is used to signify danger or warning (think of the color of stop signs). In China, though, red is used to symbolize good luck or happiness, and so Chinese brides, like Indian brides, often wear red. *Orange* is a sacred color for Buddhists and the color of monks' robes; this hue has no such meaning in most Western countries. (For a different view, though, suggesting more sharing of color associations from one country to the next, see Jonauskaite et al., 2020 and Tham et al., 2020.)

Even within a single culture, the meaning of colors can change from one historical period to the next. For example, many modern U.S. hospitals immediately put a pink cap onto newborn baby girls, and a blue cap on newborn boys. There is dispute, however, about the historical origins of this pattern. One author has argued that the gender assignment of pink and blue used to be the *reverse* of what it is now (Paoletti, 2012). In support of this claim, consider advice offered by a 1918 magazine published for companies that manufactured baby clothes: "There has been a great diversity of opinion on this subject, but the generally accepted rule is pink for the boy and blue for the girl. The reason is that pink being a more decided and stronger color, is more suitable for the boy; while blue, which is more delicate and dainty, is prettier for the girl."

Other evidence, though, suggests yet a different pattern—namely, that for many years there was no consistency in how colors were linked to gender. For example, before 1920 there was little difference in how often U.S. newspapers and magazines associated *pink* with girls or with boys, and likewise little difference in how often they associated *blue* with one gender or the other (Del Giudice, 2017). It was only after 1920 that the current associations between color and gender emerged.

Will the current pink versus blue assignment remain in place? Obviously, we live in a time in which many people are questioning gender roles and gender stereotypes. People are questioning whether the binary distinction of male/female is the right way to think about questions of sex and gender. No matter how these discussions unfold, though, the historical and cultural differences in color meaning remind us that in understanding visual perception, we need to consider both the relevant biology and the powerful influence of our cultural surroundings.

FIGURE 3.25 EFFECT OF CHANGES IN TEXTURE GRADIENT

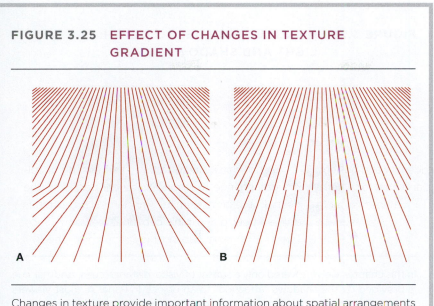

A

B

Changes in texture provide important information about spatial arrangements in the world. Examples here show (Panel A) an upward tilt and (Panel B) a sudden drop.

which parallel lines seem to converge as they get farther and farther from the viewer.

A related cue is provided by texture gradients. Consider what meets your eye when you look at cobblestones on a street or patterns of sand on a beach. The retinal projection of the sand or cobblestones shows a pattern of change in which the elements of the texture grow smaller and smaller as they become more distant. This pattern of change by itself can reveal the spatial layout of the relevant surfaces. If, in addition, there are discontinuities in these textures, they can tell you even more about how the surfaces are laid out (see **Figure 3.25**; Gibson, 1950, 1966).

The Perception of Depth through Motion

Whenever you move your head, the images projected by objects in your view move across your retinas. For reasons of geometry, the projected images of nearby objects move more than those of distant ones, and this pattern of motion in the retinal images gives you another distance cue, called **motion parallax**.

A different cue relies on the fact that the pattern of stimulation across the entire visual field changes as you move forward. This change in the visual input—termed **optic flow**—provides another type of information about depth and plays a large role in the coordination of bodily movements (Gibson, 1950, 1979).

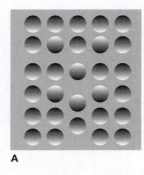
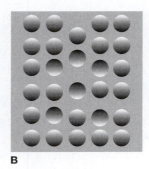

A   B

In this chapter, we've covered only a subset of visual distance cues. Another cue is provided by the shadows "attached" to an object. In Panel A, most viewers will say that the figure contains six "bulges" in a smiley-face configuration. In Panel B, the same figure has been turned upside down. Now, the bulges appear to be "dents." The reason is the location of the shadows. When the shadow is at the bottom, the object looks convex—a point that makes sense because in our day-to-day lives light almost always comes from above us, not below.

The Role of Redundancy

One might think that the various distance cues all end up providing the same information—each one tells you which objects are close by and which ones are distant. On that basis, it might be efficient for the visual system to focus on just one or two cues and ignore the others. The fact is, however, that you use all these cues, as well as several others we haven't described (e.g., see **Figure 3.26**).

Why is our visual system influenced by so many cues, especially since these cues do, in fact, often provide redundant information? It's because different distance cues become important in different circumstances. For example, binocular disparity is a powerful cue, but it's informative only when objects are relatively close by. (For targets farther than 30 ft away, the two eyes receive virtually the same image.) Likewise, motion parallax tells you a great deal about the spatial layout of your world, but only if you're moving. Texture gradients are informative only if there's a suitably uniform texture in view. So while these various cues are often redundant, each type of cue can provide information when the others cannot. By being sensitive to them all, you're able to judge distance in nearly any situation you encounter. This turns out to be a consistent theme of perception—with multiple cues to distance, multiple cues to illumination, multiple paths through which to detect motion, and so on. The result is a system that sometimes seems inelegant and inefficient, but it's one that guarantees flexibility and versatility.

TEST YOURSELF

11. What are the monocular cues to distance?
12. Why is it helpful that people rely on several different cues in judging distance?

virtual reality

We obviously move around in a three-dimensional world. For centuries, though, people have been trying to create an *illusion* of 3-D with displays that are actually flat. Painters during the Renaissance, for example, developed great skill in the use of "pictorial cues" (including visual perspective) to create a sense of depth on a flat canvas. This skill led, for some artists, to the technique of trompe l'oeil (French for "deceive the eye"), which could leave people truly puzzled about whether an object was painted or actually present. Panel C in the figure on the following page shows a modern version—created by a talented sidewalk artist.

A different technique relies on binocular ("two-eyed") vision. Consider the Holmes stereoscope (invented by a man whose son was a Supreme Court justice for 30 years!). This wooden device (Panel A in the figure below) allows the presentation of a pair of pictures, one to each eye. The two pictures show the same scene but viewed from slightly different vantage points, and these "stereoviews" produce a compelling sense of depth.

The same principle—and your capacity for "stereovision"—is used with the "virtual reality" (VR) accessory that works with many smartphones. The accessory, often made of cardboard, places a lens in front of each eye so that you'll be comfortable pointing your eyes straight ahead (as if you were looking at something far away), even though you're actually looking at an image just an inch or so away. With this setup, your phone displays two views of the

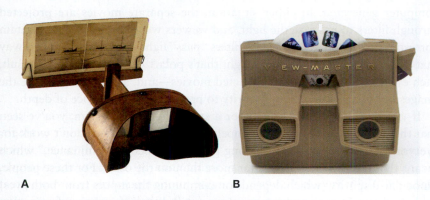

A   **B**

CLASSICAL USES OF BINOCULAR DISPARITY

Binocular disparity was the principle behind the stereoscope (Panel A), a device popular in the 19th century that presented a slightly different photograph to each eye, creating a vivid sense of depth. The View-Master (Panel B), a popular children's toy, works the same way. The photos on the wheel are actually in pairs—and so, at any rotation, the left eye views one photo in the pair (the one at 9 o'clock on the wheel) and the right eye views a slightly different photo (the one at 3 o'clock), one that shows the same scene from a slightly different angle. Again, the result is a powerful sense of depth.

C

D

MODERN SIMULATIONS OF 3-D

Panel C shows a chalk drawing on a flat (and entirely undamaged) sidewalk. By manipulating pictorial cues, though, the artist creates a compelling illusion of depth—with a car collapsed into a pit that in truth isn't there at all. Panel D shows one of the devices used to turn a smartphone into a "virtual reality" viewer.

same scene (one view to each eye), viewed from slightly different angles. Your eyes "fuse" these inputs into a single image, but that doesn't mean you ignore the differences between the inputs. Instead, your brain manages to figure out how the scene must have been arranged in order to produce these two different views, and it's the end product of this computation that you experience as a three-dimensional scene.

3-D movies work the same way. There are actually *two separate movies* projected onto the theater's screen. In some cases, the movies were shot from slightly different positions; in other cases, the two perspectives were computer generated. In either situation, the separate movies are projected through filters to polarize the light, and viewers wear eyeglasses that contain corresponding filters. The eyeglass filters "pass" light that's polarized in a way that matches the filter, and block light that's polarized differently. As a result, each eye sees only one of the projected movies—and, again, viewers fuse the images but use the binocular disparity to produce the experience of depth.

If you've enjoyed a 3-D movie or a smartphone VR system, you've seen that the sense of depth is quite compelling. But these systems don't work for everyone. Some people have a strong pattern of "ocular dominance," which means that they rely on one eye far more than on the other. For these people, binocular disparity (which depends on combining the inputs from both eyes) loses its force. However, these people can still draw information from other (monocular or motion-based) cues, and so they can enjoy the same movies as anyone else.

chapter review

SUMMARY

- One aspect of brain functioning that has been mapped in considerable detail is the visual system. This system takes its main input from the rods and cones on the retina. Then, information is sent via the optic nerve to the brain. An important point is that cells in the optic nerve do much more than transmit information; they also begin the analysis of the visual input. This is reflected in the phenomenon of lateral inhibition, which leads to edge enhancement.

- Part of what we know about the brain comes from single-cell recording, which can record the electrical activity of an individual neuron. In the visual system, this recording has allowed researchers to map the receptive fields of many cells. The mapping has provided evidence for a high degree of specialization among the various parts of the visual system, with some parts specialized for the perception of motion, others for the perception of color, and so on. The various areas function in parallel, and this parallel processing allows great speed. It also allows mutual influence among multiple systems.

- Parallel processing begins in the optic nerve and continues throughout the visual system. For example, the *what* system (in the temporal lobe) appears to be specialized for the identification of visual objects; the *where* system (in the parietal lobe) seems to identify where an object is located.

- The reliance on parallel processing creates a problem of reuniting the various elements of a scene so that these elements are perceived in an integrated way. This is the binding problem. One key in solving this problem lies in the fact that different brain systems are organized in terms of maps, so that spatial position can be used as a framework for reuniting the separately analyzed aspects of the visual scene.

- Visual perception requires more than the "pick-up" of features. Those features must be organized into wholes—a process apparently governed by the so-called Gestalt principles. The visual system also must interpret the input, a point that is especially evident with reversible figures. Crucially, though, these interpretive steps aren't separate from, and occurring after, the pickup of elementary features, because the features themselves are shaped by the perceiver's organization of the input.

- The active nature of perception is also evident in perceptual constancy. We achieve constancy through a process of unconscious inference, taking one aspect of the input (e.g., the distance to the target) into account in interpreting another aspect (e.g., the target's size). This process is usually quite accurate, but it can produce illusions.

- The perception of distance relies on many cues—some dependent on binocular vision, and some on monocular vision. The diversity of cues lets us perceive distance in a wide range of circumstances.

KEY TERMS

cornea (p. 65)

lens (p. 65)

retina (p. 65)

photoreceptors (p. 65)

rods (p. 65)

cones (p. 66)

acuity (p. 66)

fovea (p. 66)

bipolar cells (p. 68)
ganglion cells (p. 68)
optic nerve (p. 68)
lateral geniculate nucleus (LGN) (p. 68)
lateral inhibition (p. 68)
edge enhancement (p. 68)
Mach band (p. 69)
single-cell recording (p. 70)
receptive field (p. 71)
center-surround cells (p. 71)
Area V1 (p. 73)
parallel processing (p. 74)
serial processing (p. 74)
what system (p. 76)
where system (p. 76)
binding problem (p. 78)
neural synchrony (p. 78)
conjunction errors (p. 79)

Necker cube (p. 80)
reversible (or ambiguous) figure (p. 80)
figure/ground organization (p. 81)
Gestalt principles (p. 83)
visual features (p. 84)
perceptual constancy (p. 86)
size constancy (p. 86)
shape constancy (p. 86)
brightness constancy (p. 87)
unconscious inference (p. 88)
distance cues (p. 92)
binocular disparity (p. 92)
monocular distance cues (p. 92)
pictorial cues (p. 93)
interposition (p. 93)
linear perspective (p. 93)
motion parallax (p. 95)
optic flow (p. 95)

TEST YOURSELF AGAIN

1. What are the differences between rods and cones? What traits do these cells *share*?

2. What is lateral inhibition? How does it contribute to edge perception?

3. How do researchers use single-cell recording to reveal a cell's receptive field?

4. What are the advantages of parallel processing in the visual system? What are the disadvantages?

5. How is firing synchrony relevant to the solution of the binding problem?

6. What evidence tells us that perception goes beyond (i.e., includes more information than) the stimulus input?

7. What are the Gestalt principles, and how do they influence visual perception?

8. What evidence is there that the perception of an overall form depends on the detection of features? What evidence is there that the detection of features depends on the overall form?

9. What does it mean to say that size constancy may depend on an unconscious inference? An inference about what?

10. How do the ordinary mechanisms of constancy lead to visual illusions?

11. What are the monocular cues to distance?

12. Why is it helpful that people rely on several different cues in judging distance?

THINK ABOUT IT

1. The chapter emphasizes the *active nature* of perception—and the idea that we don't just "pick up" information from the environment; instead, we *interpret* and *supplement* that information. What examples of this pattern can you think of—either from the chapter or from your own experience?

2. Chapter 2 argued that the functioning of the brain depends on the coordination of many specialized operations. How does that claim, about the brain in general, fit with the discussion of visual perception in this chapter?

DEMONSTRATIONS & APPLYING COGNITIVE PSYCHOLOGY ESSAYS

For demonstrations of key concepts in cognitive psychology, take a look at the Online Demonstrations. To explore more of the practical applications of cognitive psychology in themed essays, visit the online reader.

Online Demonstrations

- Demonstration 3.1: Foveation
- Demonstration 3.2: Eye Movements
- Demonstration 3.3: The Blind Spot and the Active Nature of Vision
- Demonstration 3.4: Satanic Messages? The Power of Suggestion
- Demonstration 3.5: A Brightness Illusion
- Demonstration 3.6: A Size Illusion and a Motion Illusion

Online Applying Cognitive Psychology Essays

- Cognitive Psychology and Education: An "Educated" Eye
- Cognitive Psychology and Health: Treatments for Blindness
- Cognitive Psychology and the Law: Viewing Opportunity

ZAPS COGNITION LABS

Go to ZAPS online cognition labs to conduct hands-on experiments on key concepts.

👁 INQUIZITIVE

It's time to complete your study experience! Go to InQuizitive to practice actively with this chapter's concepts and get personalized feedback along the way.

chapter **4**

Recognizing
Objects

what if... In Chapter 3, we discussed some of the steps involved in visual perception—steps allowing you to see that the object in front of you is, let's say, brown, large, and moving. But you don't leave things there; you also *recognize* objects and can identify what they are (perhaps: a UPS truck). This sort of recognition is usually easy for you, so you have no difficulty in recognizing the vast array of objects in your world—trucks, squirrels, shoes, frying pans, and more. But, easy or not, recognition relies on processes that are surprisingly sophisticated, and your life would be massively disrupted if you couldn't manage this (seemingly simple) achievement.

We mentioned in Chapter 2 that certain types of brain damage produce a disorder called "agnosia." In some cases, patients suffer from apperceptive agnosia—they seem able to see an object's shape and color and position, but they can't put these elements together to per-ceive the entire object. For example, one patient—D.F.—suffered from brain damage in the sites shown in **Figure 4.1**. D.F. was asked to copy drawings that were in plain view (**Figure 4.2A**). The resulting attempts are shown in **Figure 4.2B**. Let's be clear, though, that the problem here is not some lack of drawing ability. **Figure 4.2C** shows what happened when D.F. was asked to draw various forms *from memory*. Plainly, D.F. can draw; the problem instead is in her ability to see and assemble the various elements that she sees.

Other patients suffer from associative agnosia. They can see but cannot link what they see to their basic visual knowledge. One remark-able example comes from a case described by neurologist Oliver Sacks:

> "What is this?" I asked, holding up a glove.
> "May I examine it?" he asked, and, taking it from me, he proceeded to examine it. "A continuous surface," he announced at last, "infolded in itself. It appears to have"—he hesitated—"five outpouchings, if this is the word."
> "Yes," I said cautiously. ". . . Now tell me what it is."
> "A container of some sort?"
> "Yes," I said, "and what would it contain?"
> "It would contain its contents!" said Dr. P., with a laugh. "There are many possibilities. It could be a change purse, for example, for coins of five sizes. It could . . ." (Sacks, 1985, p. 14)

preview of chapter themes

- Recognition of visual inputs begins with features, but it's not just the features that matter. How easily people recognize a pattern also depends on how frequently or recently they have viewed the pattern and on whether the pattern is well formed (such as letter sequences with "normal" spelling patterns).

- We explain these findings in terms of a feature net—a network of detectors, each of which is "primed" according to how often or how recently it has fired. The network relies on distributed knowledge to make inferences, and this process gives up some accuracy in order to gain efficiency.

- The feature net can be extended to other domains, including the recognition of three-dimensional objects. However, the recognition of faces requires a different sort of model, sensitive to configurations rather than to parts.

- Finally, we consider top-down influences on recognition. The existence of these influences tells us that object recognition is not a self-contained process. Instead, knowledge external to object recognition is imported into and clearly shapes the process.

FIGURE 4.1   D.F.'S LESIONS

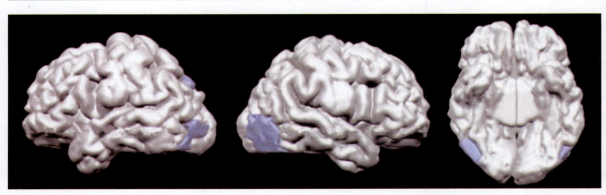

A Lesions in subject D.F.

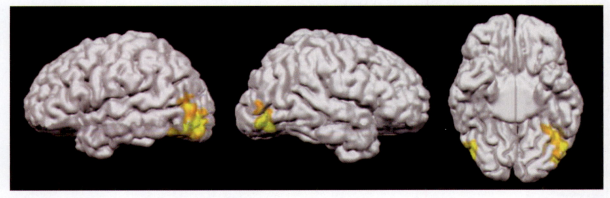

B Location of LOC in neurologically intact subjects

Panel A shows the location of the brain damage in D.F. Panel B shows the areas in the lateral occipital complex (LOC) that are especially activated when neurologically healthy people are recognizing objects.

FIGURE 4.2   DRAWINGS FROM PATIENT D.F.

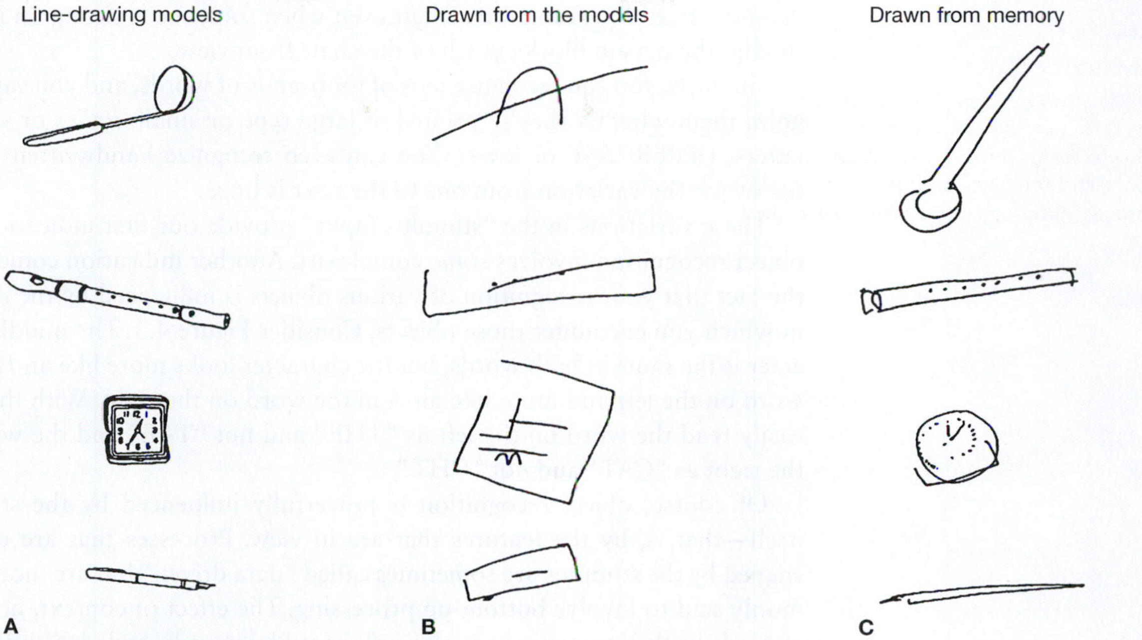

Line-drawing models	Drawn from the models	Drawn from memory
A	B	C

Patients who suffer from apperceptive agnosia can see, but they can't organize the elements they see in order to perceive an entire object. This deficit was evident when patient D.F. was asked to copy the drawings shown in Panel A. Her attempts are shown in Panel B. The problem is not in her drawing ability, because D.F.'s performance was much better (as shown in Panel C) when she was asked to draw the same forms from memory, rather than from a model.

Dr. P. does what he can to figure out what he is seeing. Nonetheless, his agnosia profoundly disrupts his life. Sacks describes one incident in which Dr. P. failed to put on his shoe, because he didn't recognize it as a shoe. Then, at the end of their time together, Sacks reports that Dr. P. "reached out his hand and took hold of his wife's head, tried to lift it off, to put it on. He had apparently mistaken his wife for a hat!" (Sacks, 1985, p. 11).

Plainly, then, object recognition may not be a glamorous skill, but it is one we all rely on for even our most ordinary interactions with the world. What are the processes that make object recognition possible?

Recognition: Some Early Considerations

You're able to recognize a huge number of different objects (cats, cups, coats), various actions (crawling, climbing, clapping), and different sorts of situations (crises, comedies). You also recognize variations of each of these things—cats standing up and cats sitting down, cats running and cats asleep.

You recognize objects even when your information is incomplete. For example, you can still recognize a cat if only its head and one paw are visible behind a tree. You recognize a chair even when someone is sitting on it, even though the person blocks much of the chair from view.

Similarly, you can recognize tens of thousands of words, and you can recognize them whether they're printed in large type or small, *italics* or straight letters, UPPERCASE or lower. You can even recognize handwritten words, for which the variation from one to the next is huge.

These variations in the "stimulus input" provide our first indication that object recognition involves some complexity. Another indication comes from the fact that your recognition of various objects is influenced by the *context* in which you encounter those objects. Consider **Figure 4.3**. The middle character is the same in both words, but the character looks more like an *H* in the word on the left and more like an *A* in the word on the right. With this, you easily read the word on the left as "THE" and not "TAE" and the word on the right as "CAT" and not "CHT."

Of course, object recognition is powerfully influenced by the stimulus itself—that is, by the features that are in view. Processes that are directly shaped by the stimulus are sometimes called "data driven" but are more commonly said to involve **bottom-up processing**. The effect of context, however, reminds us that recognition is also influenced by your knowledge and expectations. As a result, your reading of Figure 4.3 is guided by your knowledge that "THE" and "CAT" are common words while "TAE" and "CHT" are not. This sort of influence—relying on your knowledge—is sometimes called "concept driven," and processes shaped by knowledge are said to involve **top-down processing**.

What mechanism underlies both the top-down and the bottom-up influences? In the next section, we'll consider a classic proposal for what the mechanism might be. We'll then build on this base as we discuss more recent elaborations of this proposal.

FIGURE 4.3 CONTEXT INFLUENCES PERCEPTION

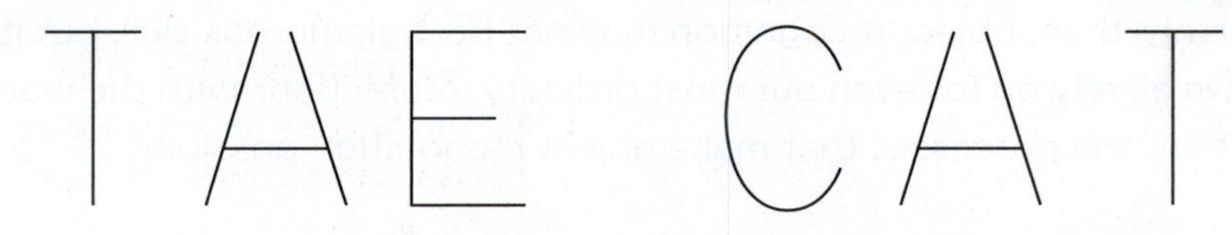

TAE CAT

You are likely to easily read this sequence as "THE CAT," recognizing the middle symbol as an *H* in one case and as an *A* in the other.   (AFTER SELFRIDGE, 1955)

The Importance of Features

Common sense suggests you recognize an elephant because you see the trunk, the thick legs, and the large body. Likewise, you know a lollipop is a lollipop because you see the circle shape on top of the straight stick. It seems, then, that you often recognize objects by recognizing their *parts*. But how do you recognize the parts themselves? How, for example, do you recognize the trunk on the elephant or the circle in the lollipop? The answer may be simple: Perhaps you recognize the parts by looking at *their* parts—such as the arcs that make up the circle in the lollipop, or the (roughly) parallel lines that identify the elephant's trunk.

To put this more generally, recognition might begin with the identification of visual features in the input pattern—the vertical lines, curves, diagonals, and so on. With these features appropriately catalogued, you can start assembling the larger units. If you detect a horizontal together with a vertical, you know you're looking at a right angle; if you've detected four right angles, you know you're looking at a square.

This broad proposal lines up well with the evidence we discussed in Chapter 3. There, we saw that specialized cells in the visual system do seem to act as feature detectors, firing (producing an action potential) whenever the relevant input (i.e., the appropriate feature) is in view. Also, we've already noted that people can recognize many variations on the objects they encounter—cats in different positions, *A*'s in different fonts or different handwritings. An emphasis on features, though, might help with this point. The various *A*'s, for example, differ from one another in overall shape, but they do have certain things in common: two inwardly sloping lines and a horizontal crossbar. Focusing on features, therefore, might allow us to concentrate on elements shared by the various *A*'s and so might allow us to recognize *A*'s despite their apparent diversity.

The importance of features is also evident in **visual search tasks**—tasks in which study participants are asked to examine a display and judge whether a particular target is present or not. This search is remarkably efficient when someone is searching for a target defined by a simple feature—for example, finding a vertical segment in a field of horizontals or a green shape in a field of red shapes. But people are generally slower in searching for a target defined as a *combination* of features (see **Figure 4.4**). This is just what we would expect if feature analysis is an early step in your analysis of the visual world—and separate from the step in which you combine the features you've detected.

Word Recognition

Several lines of evidence, therefore, indicate that object recognition does begin with the detection of simple features. Then, once this detection has occurred, separate mechanisms put the features together, assembling them

THE VARIABILITY OF STIMULI WE RECOGNIZE

We recognize cats from the side or the front, whether we see them close up or far away.

TEST YOURSELF

1. What is the difference between bottom-up and top-down processing?
2. What is the evidence that features play a special role in object recognition?

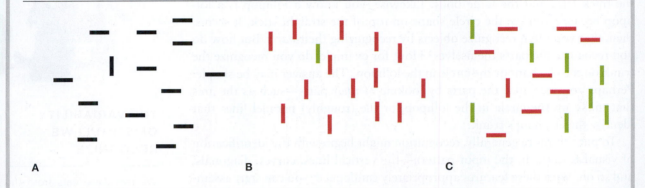

FIGURE 4.4 VISUAL SEARCH

A   B   C

In Panel A, you can immediately spot the vertical, distinguished from the other shapes by just one feature. Likewise, in Panel B, you can immediately spot the lone green bar in the field of reds. But in Panel C, it takes longer to find the one red vertical, because now you need to search for a combination of features—not just for red or vertical, but for the one form that has both of these attributes.

into complete objects. But how exactly does this assembly proceed? Let's fill in some more facts that we can then use as a guide to our theory building.

Factors Influencing Recognition

In many studies, participants have been shown stimuli for just a brief duration—perhaps 20 or 30 ms (milliseconds; for comparison, this is less than one-quarter of the duration of an average eyeblink). Older research did this by means of a **tachistoscope**, a device designed to present stimuli for precisely controlled amounts of time. More modern research uses computers, but the brief displays are still called "tachistoscopic presentations."

Each stimulus is followed by a post-stimulus **mask**—often, a random pattern of lines and curves, or a random jumble of letters such as "XJDKEL." The mask interrupts any continued processing that participants might try to do for the stimulus just presented. In this way, researchers can be certain that a stimulus presented for (say) 20 ms is visible for exactly 20 ms and no longer.

Can people recognize these briefly visible stimuli? The answer depends on many factors, including how *familiar* the stimulus is. If the stimulus is a word, we can measure familiarity by counting how often that word appears in print; more recent studies count how often each word appears in social media, or blogs, or (for some groups) television subtitles (Brysbaert et al., 2018). No matter how they're obtained, though, these counts are an excellent predictor of tachistoscopic recognition. In one early experiment, Jacoby and Dallas (1981) showed participants words that were either frequent (appearing at least 50 times in every million printed words) or infrequent (occurring

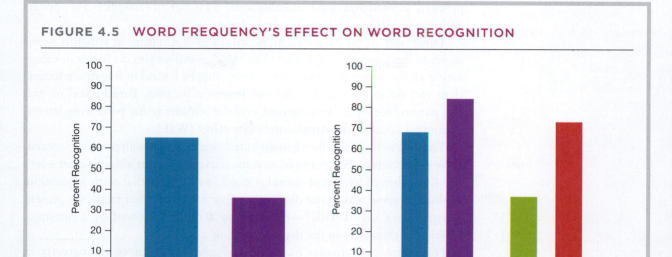

FIGURE 4.5   WORD FREQUENCY'S EFFECT ON WORD RECOGNITION

In one study, recognition was much more likely for words appearing often in print, in comparison to words appearing only rarely—an effect of frequency (Panel A). Similarly, words that had been viewed recently were more often recognized, an effect of recency that in this case creates a benefit called "repetition priming" (Panel B).

(AFTER JACOBY & DALLAS, 1981)

only 1 to 5 times per million words of print). Participants viewed these words for 35 ms, followed by a mask. Under these circumstances, they recognized almost twice as many of the frequent words (see **Figure 4.5A**).

Another factor influencing recognition is recency of view. If participants view a word and then, soon after, view it again, they'll recognize the word more readily the second time around. The first exposure "primes" the participant for the second exposure; specifically, this is a type of **priming** referred to as **repetition priming**.

As an example, participants in one study read a list of words aloud. The participants were then shown a series of words in a tachistoscope. Some of these words were from the earlier list and so had been primed; others were unprimed. For words that were high in frequency, 68% of the unprimed words were recognized, compared to 84% of the primed words. For words low in frequency, 37% of the unprimed words were recognized, compared to 73% of the primed words (see **Figure 4.5B**; Jacoby & Dallas, 1981).

The Word-Superiority Effect

Figure 4.3 suggests that the recognition of a letter depends on its context—and so an ambiguous letter is read as an *A* in one setting but as an *H* in another setting. But context also has another effect: Even when a letter is properly printed and quite unambiguous, it's *easier to recognize* if it appears within a word than if it appears in isolation.

This result seems paradoxical, because this is a setting in which it seems easier to do "more work" rather than "less"—and so you do better in recognizing all the letters that make up a word (maybe a total of five or six letters) than you do in recognizing just one letter on its own. Paradoxical or not, this pattern is easy to demonstrate, and the advantage for perceiving letters-in-context is called the **word-superiority effect** (**WSE**).

The WSE is generally demonstrated with a "two-alternative, forced-choice" procedure. For example, in some trials we present a single letter—let's say *K*—followed by a post-stimulus mask, and follow that with a question: "Which of these was in the display: an *E* or a *K*?" In other trials, we present a word—let's say "DARK"—followed by a mask, followed by a question: "Which of these was in the display: an *E* or a *K*?"

Note that participants have a 50-50 chance of guessing correctly in either of these situations, and so any contribution from guessing is the same for letters as it is for words. Also, for the word stimulus, both of the letters we've asked about are plausible endings for the stimulus; either ending would create a common word ("DARE" or "DARK"). Therefore, participants who saw only part of the display (perhaps "DAR") couldn't use their knowledge of the language to figure out the display's final letter. In order to choose between *E* and *K*, therefore, participants really need to have seen the relevant letter—and that is exactly what we want.

In this procedure, accuracy rates are reliably higher in the word condition. Apparently, recognizing an entire word is easier than recognizing isolated letters (see **Figure 4.6**; Johnston & McClelland, 1973; Reicher, 1969; Rumelhart & Siple, 1974; Wheeler, 1970).

FIGURE 4.6   THE WORD-SUPERIORITY EFFECT

The word-superiority effect is usually demonstrated with a two-alternative, forced-choice procedure (which means that a participant can get a score of 50% just by guessing randomly). Performance is much better if the target letter is shown in context—within an entire word—than if it is shown on its own.

(AFTER JOHNSTON & McCLELLAND, 1973)

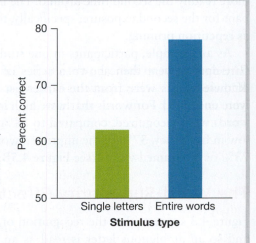

Degree of Well-Formedness

The term "word-superiority effect" may, however, be misleading, because we observe a related effect with *nonwords* like "FIKE" or "LAFE." These letter strings aren't in any dictionary and they're not familiar, but they *look like* English strings and (related) are easy to pronounce. And, crucially, strings like these produce a context effect that promotes recognition.

There are many ways to demonstrate this point, but the most direct method simply involves presenting letter strings and asking participants to report what they saw. If we show a string like "HZYQ" for, say, a 30-ms exposure, participants may report that they only saw a flash and no letters at all; at best, they may report a letter or two. But with the same 30-ms exposure, participants will generally recognize (and be able to report) strings like "FIKE" or "LAFE," although they do even better if the stimuli presented are actual, familiar words.

How should we think about these findings? One approach emphasizes the statistically defined regularities in English spelling. Specifically, we can work through lists of words, counting how often (for example) the letter combination "FI" occurs, or the combination "LA," or "HZ." We can do the same for three-letter sequences ("FIK," "LAF," and so on). These counts will give us a tally that reveals which letter combinations are more probable in English spelling and which are less probable. We can then use this tally to evaluate new strings—asking, for any string, whether its letter sequences are high-probability ones (occurring often) or low-probability (occurring rarely).

These statistical measures allow us to evaluate how "well-formed" a letter string is—that is, how well the letter sequence conforms to the usual spelling patterns of English—and **well-formedness** is a good predictor of word recognition: The more English-like the string is, the easier it will be to recognize. This well-documented pattern has been known for more than a century (see, e.g., Cattell, 1885) and has been replicated in many studies (e.g., Gibson et al., 1964; Miller et al., 1954).

Making Errors

The data seem to indicate, therefore, that you're somehow guided by your knowledge of spelling patterns when you look at, and recognize, the words you encounter—and so you have an easier time with letter strings that conform to these patterns, compared to strings that do not.

The influence of spelling patterns is also evident in the mistakes you make. With brief exposures, word recognition is good but not perfect, and the errors that occur are systematic: There's a strong tendency to misread less-common letter sequences as if they were more-common patterns. So, for example, "TPUM" is likely to be misread as "TRUM" or even "DRUM." But the reverse errors are rare: "DRUM" is unlikely to be misread as "TRUM" or "TPUM."

TEST YOURSELF

3. What is repetition priming, and how is it demonstrated?
4. What procedure demonstrates the word-superiority effect?
5. What's the evidence that word perception is somehow governed by the rules of ordinary spelling?

These errors can sometimes be quite large—so that someone shown "TPUM" for a few milliseconds might instead perceive "TRUMPET." But, large or small, the errors show the pattern described: Misspelled words, partial words, or nonwords are read in a way that brings them into line with normal spelling. In effect, people perceive the input as being more regular than it actually is. Once again, therefore, recognition seems to be guided by (or, in this case, misguided by) some knowledge of spelling patterns.

Feature Nets and Word Recognition

What lies behind this pattern of evidence? What are the processes inside of us that lead to the findings we've described? Our understanding of these points grows out of a theory published many years ago (Selfridge, 1959). Let's start with that theory, and then use it as our base as we look at more modern work.

The Design of a Feature Net

Imagine that we want to design a system that will recognize the word "CLOCK" whenever it is in view. How might our "CLOCK" detector work? One option is to "wire" this detector to a *C*-detector, an *L*-detector, an *O*-detector, and so on. Then, whenever these letter detectors are activated, this would activate the word detector. But what activates the letter detectors? Maybe the *L*-detector is "wired" to a horizontal-line detector and also a vertical-line detector, as shown in **Figure 4.7**. When these feature detectors are activated, this activates the letter detector.

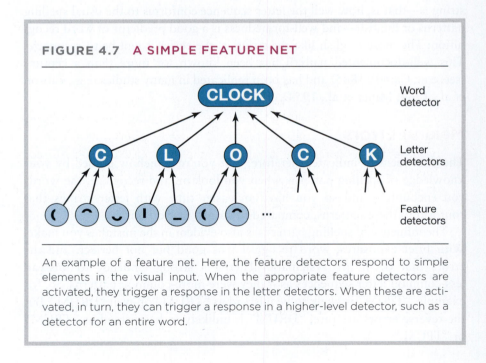

FIGURE 4.7   A SIMPLE FEATURE NET

An example of a feature net. Here, the feature detectors respond to simple elements in the visual input. When the appropriate feature detectors are activated, they trigger a response in the letter detectors. When these are activated, in turn, they can trigger a response in a higher-level detector, such as a detector for an entire word.

You encounter printed material in a wide range of fonts. In fact, most computers offer hundreds of font choices, from Chathura and CHOMSKY, to BPreplay and *Aguafina Script*. You also come across hand-written material, and of course people differ enormously in their handwriting. Despite this variety, you're able to read almost everything you see—somehow rising above the variations from one bit to the next.

These variations do matter, however, and someone's poor handwriting or their use of an obscure font can make your reading less fluent. What effects this will have, though, depend on the circumstances.

In one study, college students read a passage printed either in a clear font (Times New Roman) or in a difficult font (Italicized Juice ITC). Students in both groups were then asked to rate the *intelligence* of the author who'd written the passage (Oppenheimer, 2006). Remarkably, the students who read the less-clear font rated the author as less intelligent. They had noticed that the Juice ITC passage was difficult to read, but they seemed not to realize that the problem was the font. Instead, they decided that the lack of fluency was the author's fault: The passage was hard to read because the author hadn't been clear enough. Therefore, they decided, the author was an unskilled writer and probably not intelligent!

Another experiment, though, showed an *advantage* for a (slightly) obscure font (Diemond-Yauman et al., 2011). College students were asked to read made-up facts about space aliens—for example, that the Norgletti are 2 ft tall and eat flower petals. Half of the students read these facts in a clear font (**Arial printed in pure black**), and half read the facts in a less clear font (e.g., Bodoni MT, printed in 60% grayscale). When tested later, participants who'd seen the clear print remembered 73% of the facts; participants who'd seen the less clear print recalled 86% of the facts. What was going on here? We'll see in Chapter 6 that memory is promoted by active engagement with the to-be-remembered materials, and it seems that the somewhat obscure font promoted that sort of engagement—and so created what (in Chapter 6) we'll refer to as "desirable difficulty" in the learning process. (For other evidence, focused on the font's *size,* see Halamish, 2018.)

What about other aspects of formatting? Evidence suggests that readers are sensitive to a word's overall *shape* and gain useful information from word shape. This is one of the reasons WHY IT IS MORE DIFFICULT TO READ CAPITALIZED TEXT. Capitalized words all have the same rectangular shape; gone are the portions of the letter that hang belong the line—the so-called descenders, like the bottom tail on a *g* or a *j*. Also gone are the portions of the letters that stick up (ascenders), like the top of an *h* or an *l*, or the dot over an *i*. Your reading slows down when these features aren't available, so you're slower when YOU READ BLOCK CAPITALS compared to the normal pattern of print.

Are there practical lessons here? In some cases, you might prefer the look of block capitals; but if so, be aware that this format slows reading a bit. In choosing a font, you should probably avoid the obscure styles (unless you want less-fluent reading!), but notice that a moderately challenging font can actually help readers to process and remember what you've written.

The idea is that there could be a network of detectors, organized in layers. The "bottom" layer is concerned with features, and that is why networks of this sort are often called **feature nets**. As we move "upward" in the network, each subsequent layer is concerned with larger-scale objects; using the term we introduced earlier, the flow of information would be *bottom-up*—from the lower levels toward the upper levels.

What does it mean to "activate" a detector? At any point in time, each detector in the network has a particular **activation level**, a level that reflects the status of the detector at that moment—roughly, how energized the detector is. When a detector receives some input, its activation level increases. A strong input will increase the activation level by a lot, and so will a series of weaker inputs. In either case, the activation level will eventually reach the detector's **response threshold**, and at that point the detector will *fire*—that is, send its signal to the other detectors to which it is connected.

These points parallel our description of neurons in Chapter 2, and that's no accident. If the feature net is to be a serious candidate for how humans recognize patterns, then it has to use the same sorts of building blocks that the brain does. However, let's be careful not to overstate this point: No one is suggesting that detectors are neurons or even large groups of neurons. Instead, detectors probably involve complex assemblies of neural tissue. Nonetheless, it's plainly attractive that the hypothesized detectors in the feature net function in a way that's biologically sensible.

Within the net, some detectors will be easier to activate than others—that is, some will require a strong input to make them fire, while others will fire even with a weak input. This difference is created in part by how activated each detector is to begin with. If the detector is moderately activated at the start, then only a little input is needed to raise the activation level to threshold, and so it will be easy to make this detector fire. If a detector is not at all activated at the start, then a strong input is needed to bring the detector to threshold, and so it will be more difficult to make this detector fire.

What determines a detector's starting activation level? As one factor, detectors that have fired recently will have a higher activation level (think of it as a "warm-up" effect). In addition, detectors that have fired frequently in the past will have a higher activation level (think of it as an "exercise" effect). Overall, then, activation level is dependent on principles of *recency* and *frequency*.

We now can put these mechanisms to work. Why are frequent words in the language easier to recognize than rare words? Frequent words, by definition, appear often in the things you read. Therefore, the detectors needed for recognizing these words have been frequently used, so they have relatively high levels of activation. Thus, even a weak signal (e.g., a brief or dim presentation of the word) will bring these detectors to their response threshold and will be enough to make them fire. As a result, the word will be recognized even with a degraded input.

Repetition priming is explained in similar terms. Presenting a word once will cause the relevant detectors to fire. Once they've fired, activation levels will be temporarily lifted (because of recency of use). Therefore, only a weak signal will be needed to make the detectors fire again. As a result, the word will be more easily recognized the second time around.

The Feature Net and Well-Formedness

The net we've described so far cannot, however, explain all of the data. Consider the effects of well-formedness: for instance, the fact that people are able to read letter strings like "PIRT" or "HICE" even when those strings are presented very briefly (or dimly or in low contrast), but not strings like "ITPR" or "HCEI." How can we explain this finding? One option is to add another layer to the net, a layer filled with detectors for *letter combinations*. In **Figure 4.8**, we've added a layer of **bigram detectors**—detectors of letter pairs. These detectors, like all the rest, will be triggered by lower-level detectors and send their output to higher-level detectors. And just like any other detector, each bigram detector will start out with a certain activation level, influenced by the frequency with which the detector has fired in the past and by the recency with which it has fired.

This turns out to be all the theory we need. You have never seen the sequence "HICE" before, but you have seen the letter pair *HI* (in "HIT," "HIGH," or "HILL") and the pair *CE* ("FACE," "MICE," "JUICE"). The detectors for these letter pairs, therefore, have high activation levels at the

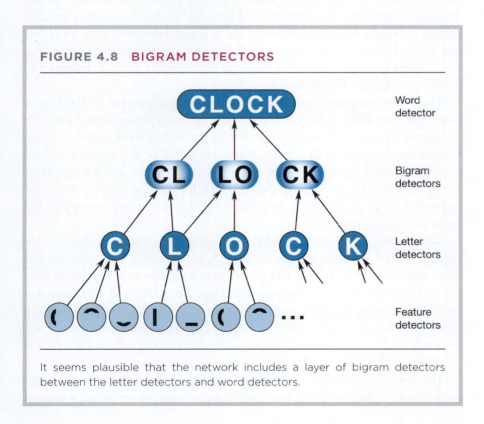

FIGURE 4.8   BIGRAM DETECTORS

It seems plausible that the network includes a layer of bigram detectors between the letter detectors and word detectors.

start, so they don't need much additional input to reach their threshold. As a result, these detectors will fire with only weak input. That will make the corresponding letter combinations easy to recognize, facilitating the recognition of strings like "HICE." None of this is true for "IJPV" or "RSFK." Because none of these letter combinations are familiar, these strings will receive no benefits from priming. As a result, a strong input will be needed to bring the relevant detectors to threshold, and so these strings will be recognized only with difficulty. (For more on bigram detectors and how they work, see Grainger et al., 2008; Grainger & Whitney, 2004. For some complications, see Rayner & Pollatsek, 2011.)

Ambiguous Inputs

The network we're describing has many advantages—including a capacity to deal sensibly with ambiguous or unclear inputs. Look again at Figure 4.3. The second character is exactly the same as the fifth, but the left-hand string is perceived as "THE" (and the character is identified as an *H*) and the right-hand string is perceived as "CAT" (and the character as an *A*).

What's going on here? Let's focus on the three characters on the left. Here the initial *T* and the final *E* are clearly in view, and so presumably the detectors for these letters will fire strongly in response. The middle character in this string, however, will likely trigger some of the features normally associated with an *A* but not all. As a result, with only some of the relevant feature detectors activated, the *A*-detector will fire only weakly. Likewise, that same middle character will trigger some of the features associated with an *H*, but not all, and so the *H*-detector, too, will fire only weakly. It seems, then, that at the letter level, the network's response is something like "*T*, followed by maybe-*A* or maybe-*H*, followed by *E*."

The confusion continues in the information sent upward to the bigram level. The detector for the *TH* bigram will receive a strong signal from the *T*-detector (because a *T* was clearly visible) but only a weak signal from the *H*-detector (because an *H* wasn't clearly visible). The *TA*-detector will get roughly the same input—a strong signal for its first letter, and a weak signal for its second. As a result, both the *TH*- and *TA*-detectors will be activated, but only weakly. At this level, then, the network's response is something like "maybe *TA* or maybe *TH*."

What's crucial, though, is what happens next. Your detector for the sequence *THE* is enormously well primed, because this is a sequence you often encounter. If there is a *TAE*-detector, it would be barely primed, since this is a string that's rarely encountered. Thus, the *THE*- and *TAE*-detectors might be receiving the same muddy message from the bigram level, but this input is sufficient only for the (well-primed) *THE*-detector, so only it will respond. In this way, the net will respond as if the ambiguous pattern was "THE," not "TAE."

The logic here boils down to this: In many settings, the network starts with a weak signal—perhaps because the input is sloppy, or perhaps because you only glanced at the input. No matter what produced the weak signal, though, a weak signal will likely be enough to trigger a well-primed detector, but not enough to trigger a less-primed detector. The priming, in turn, will depend on the principles of frequency and recency—and so will be shaped by what inputs the network has encountered in the past. As a result, the network has a bias built into it—a bias toward responding to current (and perhaps unclear) inputs in a fashion that mirrors how it has responded on previous occasions.

The same ideas will handle the word-superiority effect. To take a simple case, imagine that we present the letter *A* in the context "AT." If the presentation is brief enough, participants may see very little of the *A*, perhaps just the horizontal crossbar. This wouldn't be enough to distinguish among *A*, *F*, or *H*, and so all these letter detectors would fire weakly. If this were all the information the participants had, they'd be stuck. But let's imagine that the participants did perceive the second letter in the display, the *T*. It seems likely that the *AT* bigram is much better primed than the *FT* or *HT* bigrams. (That's because you often encounter words like "CAT" or "BOAT"; words like "SOFT" or "HEFT" are used less frequently.) Therefore, the weak firing of the *A*-detector would be enough to fire the *AT* bigram detector, while the weak firing for the *F* and *H* might not trigger their bigram detectors. In this way, a "choice" would be made at the bigram level that the input was "AT" and not something else. And, once this bigram has been detected, answering the question "Was there an *A* or an *F* in the display?" is easy. In this way, the letter will be better detected in context than in isolation. This isn't because context enables you to see more; instead, context allows you to make better use of what you see.

Recognition Errors

There is, however, a downside to all this. Imagine that we present the string "CQRN" to participants. If the presentation is brief enough, the participants might see only a subset of the string's features. Let's imagine that they register only the bottom curve of the string's second letter. This detection of this curve will weakly activate the *Q*-detector but also the *S*-detector, the *U*-detector, and the *O*-detector. The resulting pattern of network activation is shown in **Figure 4.9**.

This confusion at the letter level, though, will get sorted out at the bigram level. The *CO-*, *CU-*, *CQ-*, and *CS*-detectors will all get the same input—a strong signal for one of their letters (because we're hypothesizing that the *C* was clearly seen) and a weak signal for their other letter (because we've suggested that the second letter in the string wasn't clearly seen). This signal may not be enough to trigger a *CU-*, *CQ-*, or *CS*-detector, because these detectors are not well primed, and therefore will be activated only by a strong input. But the signal will be enough to trigger the *CO*-detector. This bigram is often encountered, so the detector is well primed and can therefore be activated with only a moderate input.

If the input actually had been "CORN," but with the second letter not easily visible, then the sequence of events we just described would be a good

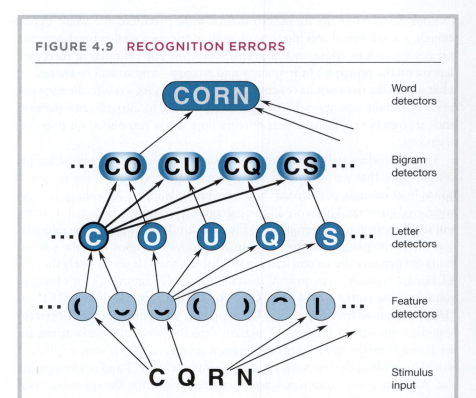

FIGURE 4.9   RECOGNITION ERRORS

If "CQRN" is presented briefly, not all of its features will be detected. Perhaps only the bottom curve of the Q is detected, and this will weakly activate various other letters having a bottom curve, including O, U, and S. This will lead to a weak signal being sent to the bigram detectors (The signal is weak because each bigram is receiving a strong signal from the C-detector, but only a weak signal for the bigram's second letter.) However, this weak signal is enough to trigger the well-primed CO-detector, and so the input will be (mistakenly) recognized as "CORN."

thing: The pattern of priming would lead to the CO-detector firing, but not detectors for CU or CQ or CS, and so the network would, in essence, recover from confusion that was caused, at the letter level, by the poor-quality input. But if the input was "CQRN" (as suggested in the figure), the same dynamic will cause the network to misread the stimulus—misperceiving the stimulus as "CORN" when the stimulus was actually something else.

This logic helps us understand why recognition errors tend to make the input look more regular than it really is. As we've already suggested, the pattern of priming biases the network toward a principle we might summarize as "when in doubt, assume that the input falls into the frequent pattern." But, of course, there is no process of reasoning or inference here; instead, the network's response is an automatic and mechanical consequence of what's primed (and therefore easy to trigger) and what's not.

Let's be clear, though, that the bias built into the network *facilitates* perception whenever the input is, in fact, a frequent word, and these (by definition) are the words you encounter most of the time. The bias will pull the network toward errors if the input happens to have an unusual spelling pattern, but (by definition) these inputs are less common in your experience. On this basis, then, the network's bias inevitably helps perception more often than it hurts.

Distributed Knowledge

In the last few sections, we've considered how the network operates. Let's pause, though, to reflect on what it is that makes this operation possible. Doing so will allow us to highlight two themes that characterize this network and also—it turns out—many aspects of the brain's functioning.

In a variety of ways, the network seems to be guided by knowledge of spelling patterns. We've noted that letter strings are easier to recognize if they follow normal spelling. We've also discussed the fact that letters are better recognized in context—but only if the context has a sensible spelling pattern. Still more evidence comes from the errors people make, which consistently "shift" the perception toward patterns of normal spelling.

To explain these results, we've suggested that the network "knows" (for example) that *CO* is a common bigram in English, while *CS* is not, and also "knows" that *THE* is a common sequence but *TAE* is not. The network seems to rely on this "knowledge" in "choosing" its "interpretation" of unclear or ambiguous inputs.

We've wrapped quotation marks around several of these words, though, to emphasize that the sense in which the net "knows" facts about spelling, or the sense in which it "chooses interpretations," is a little peculiar. In reality, knowledge about spelling patterns isn't explicitly stored anywhere in the network. Nowhere within the net is there a sentence like "*CO* is a common bigram in English; *CS* is not." Instead, this memory (if we even want to call it that) is manifest only in the fact that the *CO*-detector happens to be more primed than the *CS*-detector. And, of course, the *CO*-detector doesn't "know" anything about its priming advantage, nor does the *CS*-detector know anything about its disadvantage. Instead, each one simply does its job, and in the course of doing their jobs, sometimes a "competition" will take place between these detectors. When these competitions occur, they'll be "decided" by activation levels: The better-primed detector will be more likely to respond and therefore more likely to influence subsequent events. That's the entire mechanism through which these "knowledge effects" arise—as a direct consequence of priming and activation levels.

To put this idea into technical terms, the network's "knowledge" is not **locally represented** anywhere; it isn't stored in a particular location or built into a specific process. That's why we cannot look just at the level of priming in the *CO*-detector and conclude that this detector represents a frequently seen bigram. Nor can we look at the *CS*-detector and conclude that it represents a rarely seen bigram. Instead, we need to look at the relationship between these priming levels, and we also need to look at how this relationship will lead to one detector being more influential than the other. In this way, knowledge about bigram frequencies is contained within the network via a **distributed representation**; it's knowledge, in other words, that's represented by a pattern of activations distributed across the network and detectable only if we consider how the entire network functions.

What seems remarkable about the feature net, then, lies in how much can be accomplished with a distributed representation, and so with simple, mechanical elements correctly connected to one another. The net appears to make inferences and to know the rules of spelling. But the actual mechanics of the net involve neither inferences nor knowledge (at least, not in any conventional sense). You and I can see how the inferences unfold by taking a bird's-eye view and considering how all the detectors work together as a system. But nothing in the net's functioning depends on the bird's-eye view. Instead, the activity of each detector is locally determined—influenced by just those detectors feeding into it. When all these detectors work together, the result is a process that acts as if it knows the rules. But the rules themselves play no role in guiding the network's moment-by-moment activities.

Efficiency versus Accuracy

Here's our second broad theme about the network's functioning: The network sometimes makes mistakes, misreading some inputs and misinterpreting some patterns. We've described, for example, a case in which the network will "misread" a string like "CQRN" and (mistakenly) respond as though the input was (the correctly spelled) "CORN." In some ways, this is a good thing, because *humans* make recognition errors, and we're proposing that the network functions as people do. But let's also emphasize that these errors are produced by the same mechanisms that are responsible for some of the network's advantages—its ability to deal with ambiguous inputs, for example, or cases in which you've only had an incomplete view of the pattern before your eyes. If (for example) someone's handwriting presents you with a sloppy version of the words "THE CAT" (like the version in Figure 4.3), it's a good thing that the pattern of priming in your detectors helps you to read it. If those same patterns of priming occasionally mislead you (and they do), that's just the price you pay for a mechanism that can handle unclear or partial inputs.

But this framing of the issue raises a question: Do you need to pay this price? After all, you could, if you wished, read by scrutinizing the input character by character. That way, if a letter were missing or misprinted, you'd be sure to detect it. But, with this strategy, reading would be incredibly inefficient—partly because the speed with which you move your eyes is relatively slow (no more than four or five eye movements per second). In contrast, it's possible to make inferences about a page with remarkable speed, and this leads readers to adopt the obvious strategy: They read some of the letters and make

TEST YOURSELF

6. How does a feature net explain the word-frequency effect?

7. How does a feature net explain the types of *errors* people make in recognizing words?

8. What are the benefits, and what are the costs, associated with the feature net's functioning?

inferences about the rest—with a small cost in accuracy, but a huge gain in efficiency. Put differently, readers accept the possibility of error, because the alternative is a process that would be unacceptably slow.

Descendants of the Feature Net

We mentioned early on that we were discussing the "classic" version of the feature net. This discussion has enabled us to bring a number of themes into view—including the trade-off between efficiency and accuracy and the idea of distributed knowledge built into a network's functioning.

Over the years, though, researchers have offered improvements on this basic conceptualization, and in the next sections we'll consider two of these improvements. We'll look first at a proposal that highlights the role of *inhibitory* connections among detectors. Then we'll turn to a proposal that applies the network idea to the recognition of complex three-dimensional objects.

The McClelland and Rumelhart Model

In the network we've considered so far, activation of one detector serves to activate other detectors. Other models add a mechanism through which detectors can *inhibit* one another, so that the activation of one detector can *decrease* the activation in other detectors.

One influential model of this sort was proposed years ago by McClelland and Rumelhart (1981); a portion of their model is illustrated in **Figure 4.10**. This network, like the one we've been discussing, is better able to identify well-formed strings than irregular strings; this net is also more efficient in identifying characters in context as opposed to characters in isolation. However, several attributes of this net make it possible to accomplish all this without bigram detectors.

In Figure 4.10, **excitatory connections**—connections that allow one detector to activate its neighbors—are shown as red arrows; for example, detection of a *T* serves to "excite" the "TRIP" detector. Other connections are *inhibitory*, and so (for example) detection of a *G* deactivates, or inhibits, the "TRIP" detector. These **inhibitory connections** are shown in the figure with dots. In addition, this model allows for more complicated signaling than we've used so far. In our discussion, we have assumed that lower-level detectors trigger upper-level detectors, but not the reverse. The flow of information, it seemed, was a one-way street. In the McClelland and Rumelhart model, though, higher-level detectors (word detectors) can influence lower-level detectors, and detectors at any level can also influence other detectors at the same level (e.g., letter detectors can inhibit other letter detectors; word detectors can inhibit other word detectors).

To see how this would work, let's say that the word "TRIP" is briefly shown, allowing a viewer to see enough features to identify only the *R*, *I*, and *P*. Detectors for these letters will therefore fire, in turn activating the detector

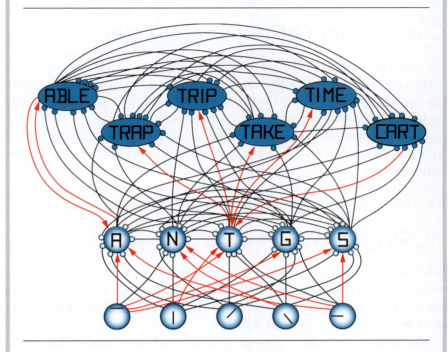

FIGURE 4.10 AN ALTERNATE CONCEPTION OF THE FEATURE NETWORK

The McClelland and Rumelhart (1981) pattern-recognition model includes both excitatory connections (indicated by red arrows) and inhibitory connections (indicated by connections with dots). Connections within a specific level are also possible—so that, for example, activation of the "TRIP" detector will inhibit the detectors for "TRAP," "TAKE," and "TIME."

for "TRIP." Activation of this word detector will inhibit the firing of other word detectors (e.g., detectors for "TRAP" and "TAKE"), so that these other words are less likely to arise as distractions or competitors with the target word.

At the same time, activation of the "TRIP" detector will also excite the detectors for its component letters—that is, detectors for T, R, I, and P. The R-, I-, and P-detectors, we've assumed, were already firing, so this extra activation "from above" has little impact. But the T-detector wasn't firing before. The relevant features were on the scene but in a degraded form (thanks to the brief presentation), and this weak input wasn't enough to trigger an unprimed detector. But once the excitation from the "TRIP" detector primes the T-detector, it's more likely to fire, even with a weak input.

In effect, then, activation of the word detector for "TRIP" implies that this is a context in which a T is quite likely. The network therefore responds to this suggestion by "preparing itself" for a T. Once the network is suitably prepared (by the appropriate priming), detection of this letter is facilitated. In this way, the detection of a letter sequence (the word "TRIP") makes the network more sensitive to elements that are likely to occur within that sequence. That is exactly what we need in order for the network to be responsive to the regularities of spelling patterns.

Let's also note that the two-way communication that's in play here fits well with how the nervous system operates: Neurons in the eyeballs send activation to the brain but also *receive* activation from the brain; neurons in the lateral geniculate nucleus (LGN) send activation to the visual cortex but also *receive* activation from the cortex. Facts like these make it clear that visual processing is not a one-way process, with information flowing simply from the eyes toward the brain. Instead, signaling occurs in both an ascending (toward the brain) and a descending (away from the brain) direction, just as the McClelland and Rumelhart model claims.

Recognition of Three-Dimensional Objects

The McClelland and Rumelhart model—like the feature net we started with—was designed as an account of how people recognize *printed language*. But, of course, we recognize many objects other than print, including the three-dimensional objects that fill our world—chairs and lamps and cars and trees. Can these objects also be recognized by a feature network? The answer turns out to be yes.

One proposal involves a network theory known as the **recognition by components (RBC) model** (Hummel & Biederman, 1992; Hummel, 2013). This model includes several important innovations, one of which is the inclusion of an intermediate level of detectors, sensitive to **geons** (short for "geometric ions"). The idea is that geons might serve as the basic building blocks of all the objects we recognize—geons are, in essence, the alphabet from which all objects are constructed.

Geons are simple shapes, such as cylinders, cones, and blocks (see **Figure 4.11A**), and according to Biederman (1987, 1990), we only need 30 or so different geons to describe every object in the world, just as 26 letters are all we need to spell all the words of English. These geons can be combined in various ways—in a top-of relation, or a side-connected relation, and so on—to create all the objects we perceive (see **Figure 4.11B**).

The RBC model, like the other networks we've been discussing, uses a hierarchy of detectors. The lowest-level detectors are feature detectors, which respond to edges, curves, angles, and so on. These detectors in turn activate the geon detectors. Higher levels of detectors are then sensitive to combinations of geons. More precisely, geons are assembled into complex arrangements called "geon assemblies," which explicitly represent the relations between geons (e.g., top-of or side-connected). These assemblies, finally, activate the *object model*, a representation of the complete, recognized object.

The presence of the geon and geon-assembly levels within this hierarchy offers several advantages. For one, geons can be identified from virtually any

FIGURE 4.11 GEONS

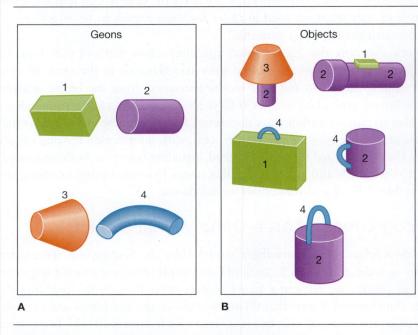

| Geons | Objects |

Panel A shows four different geons; Panel B shows how these geons can be assembled into objects. The numbers in Panel B identify the specific geons—for example, a bucket contains Geon 4 top-connected to Geon 2.

angle of view. Thus, no matter what your position is relative to a cat, you'll be able to identify its geons and identify the cat. Moreover, it seems that most objects can be recognized from just a few geons. As a consequence, geon-based models like RBC can recognize an object even if many of the object's geons are hidden from view.

Object Recognition and the Brain

Modern research continues to refine these network models, and has also examined how the processes we've described are implemented in the brain. Some of the evidence comes from recording from cells in the inferotemporal (IT) cortex, near the terminus of the *what* pathway (see Figure 3.10). Cells in this area seem to have specific "targets" and fire most strongly when the target is in view. Researchers located one cell, for example, that was most highly activated when a human hand was in view; the cell even fired (although less strongly) in response to a mitten shape (which lacked distinct fingers; see **Figure 4.12**). Other cells in this brain region fire selectively when *faces* are in view. (We'll return to the topic of face recognition in a moment.)

FIGURE 4.12 SINGLE-CELL RECORDINGS FROM A "HAND DETECTOR" CELL

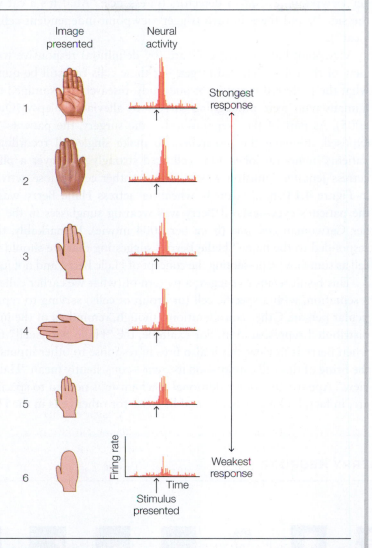

Neurons in the inferotemporal cortex fire in response to complex inputs. The neural activity shown here was from a cell responsive to hand shapes. The cell even fired (although weakly) to a mitten shape that lacked distinct fingers.

It seems plausible that cells in the IT cortex are the biological foundation for what we've been calling "word detectors" or "object detectors." As one complication, though, some of the brain's cells fire strongly only to a particular view of an object—that is, the object viewed from a particular angle. If the same object is viewed from a different angle, the cell's response is reduced.

Other cells, in contrast, fire strongly to virtually any view of the target object, and so these cells are said to be "viewpoint independent." Presumably, in our hierarchy of detectors, cells responding directly to the input's shape trigger viewpoint-*dependent* detectors (in essence: "Aha! It's a cat viewed from the side"), and these in turn trigger viewpoint-independent cells ("Aha! It's a cat").

Viewpoint-independent cells are (by definition) responsive to almost any view of the cell's preferred target, but these cells can still be quite specific in what the preferred target is. In one study, researchers examined the brains of humans who were undergoing surgery to alleviate epilepsy (Quiroga et al., 2005). As part of the preparation for the surgery, the patients' brains were exposed, allowing the researchers to make single-cell recordings from the patients' temporal lobes. One cell fired strongly whenever a photograph of actress Jennifer Anniston was in view; another cell (whose activity is shown in **Figure 4.13**) fired strongly whenever actress Halle Berry was in front of the patient's eyes—even if Berry was wearing sunglasses in the photo, or in her Catwoman costume (from her 2004 movie). Remarkably, this cell even responded to the name "Halle Berry," suggesting that we should think of this cell as somehow representing the concept of Halle Berry, and not just her image.

This result seems to suggest a pattern of (what we earlier called) local representation, with a specific cell (or group of cells) serving to represent a particular person. Other considerations, though, remind us of the importance of distributed representation. For example, the "Halle Berry cell" fires strongly when Berry is in view, but it also fires in response to other inputs. As a result, the firing of this cell cannot—on its own—consistently mean "Halle Berry is in view." Apparently, some additional mechanism is needed to specify when you are, in fact, looking at Berry (and likewise for other cells in the IT cortex). To

TEST YOURSELF

9. How does the McClelland and Rumelhart model differ from the older, "classical" version of the feature net?

10. What aspects of the recognition by components (RBC) proposal allow this model to handle the recognition of three-dimensional objects?

FIGURE 4.13   A HALLE BERRY NEURON?

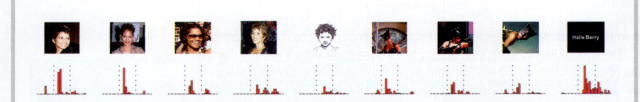

Researchers recorded the activity in a single neuron in the hippocampus of a patient undergoing epilepsy surgery. Each of these pictures shows an input that was placed in front of the patient's eyes, together with the cell's response to that input. The dotted lines indicate when the input was presented and when it was removed from view. The neuron fired strongly in response to pictures of Berry, even when she appeared in her Catwoman costume, and even when her name was presented.

put the matter differently, we simply do not know yet exactly what the pattern of activity is in the brain that represents each of the inputs you can recognize.

Face Recognition

As we said at the start, you're able to recognize many different patterns—printed words, items of clothing, animals in the zoo, and much, much more. Network models like the ones we've been discussing seem useful in all of these domains. In each case, we start with a layer of feature detectors, and then the output from these detectors is passed from level to level within a recognition hierarchy, with each successive level handling more complex combinations. There's one type of recognition, however, that seems to demand a different approach: the recognition of *faces*.

Faces Are Special

Damage to the visual system, we've said, can produce a disorder known as agnosia—an inability to recognize certain stimuli—and one type of agnosia specifically involves the perception of faces. People who suffer from **prosopagnosia** generally have normal vision. Indeed, they can look at a photograph and correctly say whether the photo shows a man's face or a woman's, and whether it belongs to someone young or someone old. But they can't recognize individual faces—not even of their own parents or children, whether from photographs or "live." They can't recognize the faces of famous performers or politicians. In fact, they can't recognize *themselves* (and so they sometimes think they're looking through a window at a stranger when they're actually looking at themselves in a mirror).

Often, this condition is the result of brain damage, but in some people it appears to be present from birth, without any detectable brain damage (e.g., Duchaine & Nakayama, 2006). Whatever its origin, prosopagnosia seems to imply the existence of special neural structures involved almost exclusively in the recognition of faces. Presumably, prosopagnosia results from some problem or limitation in the functioning of this brain tissue. (See Behrman & Avidan, 2005; Busigny et al., 2010; De Renzi et al., 1991. For a related condition, involving an inability to recognize *voices*, see Shilowich & Biederman, 2016.)

The special nature of face recognition is also suggested by a pattern that is the *opposite* of prosopagnosia. Some people seem to be "super-recognizers" and are magnificently accurate in face recognition, even though they have no special advantage in other perceptual or memory tasks (e.g., Bobak et al., 2015; Davis et al., 2020; Russell et al., 2009; Tree et al., 2017). Compared to most people, super-recognizers do far better in tests of face memory, including memory of faces they viewed only briefly or long ago. They show superior performance when tested with degraded images of faces (e.g., images that are viewed from a distance or from an odd angle). They're also more successful in tasks that require "face matching"—that is, judging whether two different views of a face actually show the same person.

There are certainly advantages to being a super-recognizer, but also some disadvantages. On the plus side, being able to remember faces is obviously a benefit for a politician or a salesperson; super-recognizers also seem to be more accurate as eyewitnesses (e.g., in selecting a culprit from a police line-up). In fact, London's police force now has a special unit of super-recognizers involved in many aspects of crime investigation (Keefe, 2016; also see Bate, Bennetts, et al., 2019; Bate, Frowd, et al., 2019). On the downside, though, being a super-recognizer can produce some social awkwardness. Imagine approaching someone and cheerfully announcing, "I know you! You used to work at the grocery store on Main Street." The other person (who, let's say, actually left that job eight years ago) might find this puzzling, perhaps creepy, and maybe even alarming.

What about the rest of us—people who are neither prosopagnosic nor super-recognizers? It turns out that people differ widely in their ability to remember and recognize faces (Bindemann et al., 2012; Lander et al., 2018; DeGutis et al., 2013; Noyes et al., 2018; Tardif et al., 2019; Wilmer, 2017). In fact, the performance differences, from one person to the next, are easy to measure, and there are online face-memory tests that can help you find out how your abilities compare to those of other people. (If you're curious, point your browser at the Cambridge Face Memory Test.)

No matter what the level of performance, though, face recognition seems to involve processes different from those used for other forms of recognition. For example, the recognition of ordinary objects (pictures of houses, for example, or teacups) is disrupted somewhat if you view an upside-down picture of the object. But this effect is small compared to the disruption produced by viewing faces upside down; in other words, faces show a powerful **inversion effect**. In one study, four categories of stimuli were considered: right-side-up faces, upside-down faces, right-side-up pictures of common objects other than faces, and upside-down pictures of common objects. As **Figure 4.14** shows, performance suffered for all of the upside-down

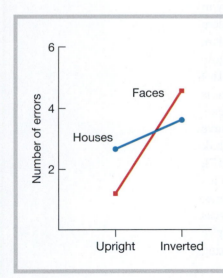

FIGURE 4.14 FACES AND THE INVERSION EFFECT

People's memory for faces is quite good, when compared with memory for other pictures (in this case, pictures of houses). However, performance is very much disrupted when the pictures of faces are inverted. Performance with houses is also worse with inverted pictures, but the effect of inversion is much smaller. (AFTER YIN, 1969)

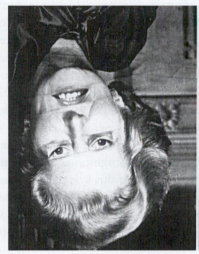

FIGURE 4.15 PERCEPTION OF UPSIDE-DOWN FACES

The left-hand picture looks some-what odd, but the two pictures still look relatively similar to each other. Now, try turning the book upside down (so that the faces are upright). In this position, the left-hand face (now on the right) looks ghoulish, and the two pictures look very different from each other. Our perception of upside-down faces is apparently quite different from our perception of upright faces.

(AFTER THOMPSON, 1980)

(i.e., inverted) stimuli. However, this effect was much larger for faces than for other kinds of stimuli, such as houses (Bruyer, 2001; Yin, 1969; also see McKone et al., 2007; Rosenthal et al., 2018).

The role of orientation in face recognition can also be illustrated informally. **Figure 4.15** shows two upside-down photographs of former British prime minister Margaret Thatcher (from Thompson, 1980). You can probably tell that something is odd about these pictures, but now try turning the book upside down so that the faces are right side up. As you can see, the difference between the faces is striking, and yet this fiendish contrast is largely lost when the faces are upside down. (Also see Rhodes et al., 1993; Valentine, 1988.)

It seems, then, that face recognition is strongly dependent on orientation in ways that other forms of object recognition are not. Here, though, we need to acknowledge a debate. According to some authors, the recognition of faces really is in a category by itself, distinct from all other forms of recognition (e.g., Kanwisher et al., 1997). Other authors, however, offer a different perspective: They agree that face recognition is special but argue that certain other types of recognition, in addition to faces, are special in the same way. As one line of evidence, they argue that prosopagnosia isn't just a disorder of face recognition. In one case, for example, a prosopagnosic bird-watcher lost not only the ability to recognize faces but also the ability to distinguish the different types of warblers (Bornstein, 1963; Bornstein et al., 1969). Another patient with prosopagnosia lost the ability to tell cars apart; she could locate her car in a parking lot only by reading all the license plates until she found her own (Damasio et al., 1982).

Likewise, in Chapter 2, we mentioned neuroimaging data showing that a particular brain site—the fusiform face area (FFA)—is specifically responsive to faces. (See, e.g., Kanwisher & Yovel, 2006; for a description of other brain areas involved in face recognition, see Gainotti & Marra, 2011.) One study, however, suggests that tasks requiring subtle distinctions among birds, or among cars, can also produce high levels of activation in this brain area (Gauthier et al., 2000; also Bukach et al., 2006). This finding suggests that the neural tissue "specialized" for faces isn't used *only* for faces. (For more on this debate, see, on one side, Grill-Spector et al., 2004; McKone et al., 2007; Weiner & Grill-Spector, 2013. On the other side, see Gauthier, 2020; Richler & Gauthier, 2014; Stein et al., 2016; Wallis, 2013; Zhao et al., 2016.)

What should we make of all this? There's no question that humans have a specialized recognition system that's crucial for face recognition. This system certainly involves the FFA in the brain, and damage to this system can cause prosopagnosia. What's controversial is how exactly we should describe this system. According to some authors, the system is truly a *face* recognition system and will be used for other stimuli only if those stimuli happen to be "face-like" (see Kanwisher & Yovel, 2006). According to other authors, this specialized system needs to be defined more broadly: It is used whenever you are trying to recognize specific individuals within a highly familiar category (e.g., Gauthier et al., 2000). The recognition of faces certainly has these traits (e.g., you distinguish Sol from George from Jacob within the familiar category of "faces"), but other forms of recognition may have the same traits (e.g., if a bird-watcher is distinguishing different types within the familiar category of "warblers").

So far, the data don't provide a clear resolution of this debate; both sides of the argument have evidence supporting their view. But let's focus on the key point of agreement: Face recognition is achieved by a process that's different from the process described earlier in this chapter. We need to ask, therefore, how face recognition proceeds.

Holistic Recognition

The networks we've considered so far all begin with an analysis of a pattern's *parts* (e.g., features, geons); the networks then assemble those parts into larger wholes. Face recognition, in contrast, seems not to depend on an inventory of a face's parts; instead, this process seems to depend on **holistic perception** of the face. In other words, face recognition depends on the face's overall configuration—the spacing of the eyes relative to the length of the nose, the height of the forehead relative to the width of the face, and so on. (For more on face recognition, see Duchaine & Nakayama, 2006; Hayward et al., 2016; Meltzer & Bartlett, 2019.)

Some of the evidence for this holistic processing comes from the *composite effect* in face recognition. In an early demonstration of this effect, Young, Hellawell, and Hay (1987) combined the top half of one face with the bottom half of another, and study participants were asked to identify just the top half (see **Figure 4.16A**). This task is difficult if the two halves are properly aligned. In this setting, participants seemed unable to focus only on

FIGURE 4.16 THE COMPOSITE EFFECT IN FACE RECOGNITION

Study participants were asked to identify the top half of composite faces like those in Panels A and B. This task was much harder if the halves were properly aligned (as seen in Panel A) and easier if the halves weren't aligned (as in Panel B). With the aligned faces, participants have a difficult time focusing on just the face's top (and so have a hard time recognizing Hugh Jackman—shown in Panel C). Instead, they view the face as a whole, and this context changes their perception of Jackman's features, making it harder to recognize him. (The bottom of the composite face belongs to Justin Timberlake, shown in Panel D.)

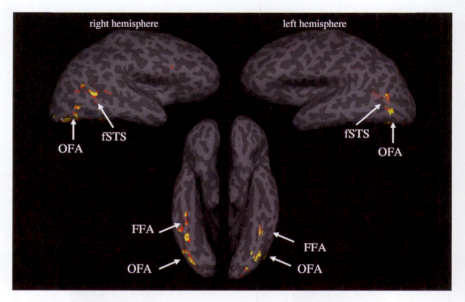

BRAIN AREAS CRUCIAL FOR FACE PERCEPTION

Several brain sites seem to be especially activated when people are looking at faces. These sites include the fusiform face area (FFA), the occipital face area (OFA), and the superior temporal sulcus (fSTS).

the top half; instead, they saw the top of the face as part of the whole. Thus, in the figure, it's difficult to see that the top half of the face is Hugh Jackman (shown in normal view in **Figure 4.16C**). This task is relatively easy, though, if the halves are misaligned (as in **Figure 4.16B**). Now, the stimulus itself breaks up the configuration, making it possible to view the top half on its own. (For related results, see Amishav & Kimchi, 2010; but also see Murphy et al., 2017.)

Of course, a face's features still matter in this holistic process. The key, however, is that the features can't be considered one by one, apart from the context of the face. Instead, the features matter because of the relationships they create. It's the relationships, not the features on their own, that guide face recognition. (See Fitousi, 2013; Rakover, 2013; Rhodes, 2012; Wang et al., 2012; but also see Richler & Gauthier, 2014.)

More work is needed to specify how the brain detects and interprets the relationships that define each face. Also, our theorizing will need to take some complications into account—including the fact that the recognition processes used for *highly familiar* faces may be different from the processes used for faces you've seen only a few times (Burton et al., 2015; Young & Burton, 2017). Evidence for this point comes from many sources, including a different pattern of brain activation when you're viewing a familiar face, compared to the activation when you're viewing a face for the first or second time (Wiese et al., 2019; see **Figure 4.17**).

FIGURE 4.17   BRAIN ACTIVITY WHEN VIEWING FAMILIAR AND UNFAMILIAR FACES

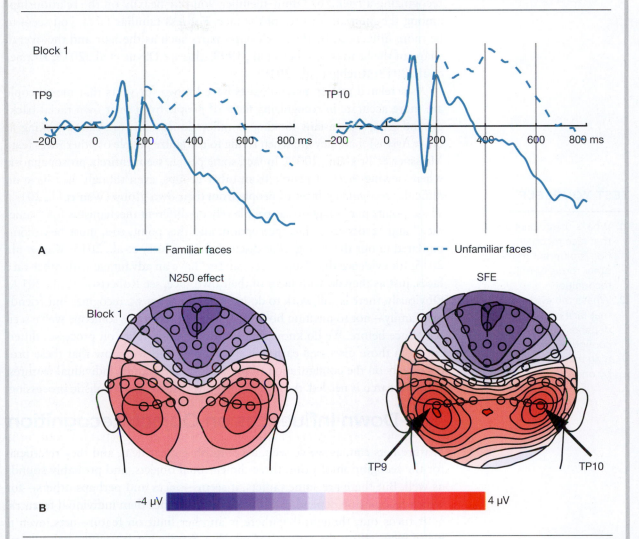

In a series of experiments, electrical activity in the brain was recorded while the study participants were viewing either familiar faces (faces of relatives or close friends) or unfamiliar faces. The left-hand side of Panel A shows the moment-by-moment activity recorded in the left hemisphere; the right-hand side of Panel A shows activity recorded in the right hemisphere. The two "heads" shown in Panel B reveal how the *difference* between familiar and unfamiliar faces was distributed across the scalp. The colors indicate the subtractive difference between conditions (activity produced by unfamiliar faces minus activity produced by familiar faces); the N250 effect is an electrical pattern measured between 200 and 400 m after the face is presented; the SFE ("sustained familiarity effect") is measured about 400 ms later.

People also seem to rely on different cues when recognizing familiar faces, in contrast to the face of someone they've just met. Specifically, when you're recognizing a friend or family member, you rely heavily on the relationships among the *internal* features of the face. For less familiar faces, you seem to be more influenced by the face's *outer parts* such as the hair and the overall shape of the head (Campbell et al., 1999; also see Devue et al., 2018; Kramer et al., 2018; Ritchie et al., 2018).

As a related matter, psychologists have known for years that most people are more accurate in recognizing faces of people from their own racial background (e.g., Caucasians looking at other Caucasians, or Asians looking at other Asians) than they are when trying to recognize people of other races (e.g., Meissner & Brigham, 2001). In fact, some people seem entirely prosopagnosic when viewing faces of people from other groups, even though they have no difficulty recognizing faces of people from their own group (Wan et al., 2017). These points may suggest that people rely on different mechanisms for "same-race" and "cross-race" face perception, and this point, too, must be accommodated in our theorizing. (For discussion, see Horry et al., 2015; Wan et al., 2015; for evidence that "super-recognizers" have an advantage with other-race faces, just as they do with faces of their own race, see Robertson et al., 2019.) Obviously, there is still work to do in explaining how we recognize our friends and family—not to mention how we manage to recognize someone we've seen only once before. We do know that face recognition relies on processes different from those discussed earlier in the chapter, and we know that these processes rely on the configuration of the face, rather than its individual features. More research is needed, though, to fill in the details of this holistic processing.

Top-Down Influences on Object Recognition

Feature nets can, as we've seen, accomplish a great deal, and they're crucial for the recognition of print, three-dimensional objects, and probably sounds as well. But there are some targets, it seems—faces and perhaps others—for which recognition depends on configurations rather than individual features.

It turns out, though, that there is another limit on feature nets, even if we're focusing on the targets for which a feature net *is* useful—print, common objects, and so on. Even in this domain, feature nets must be supplemented with additional mechanisms. This requirement doesn't undermine the importance of the feature net idea; feature nets are definitely needed as part of our theoretical account. The key word, however, is "part," because we need to place feature nets within a larger theoretical frame.

The Benefits of Larger Contexts

Earlier in the chapter, we saw that letter recognition is improved by context. For example, the letter *V* is easier to recognize in the context "VASE," or even the nonsense context "VIMP," than it is if presented alone. These are examples of top-down effects—effects driven by your knowledge and expectations. And these particular top-down effects, based on spelling patterns, are easily accommodated by the network: As we have discussed, priming (from recency and frequency of use) guarantees that detectors that have often been used in the past will be easier to activate in the future. In this way, the network "learns" which patterns are common and which are not, and it is more receptive to inputs that follow the usual patterns.

Other top-down effects, however, require a different type of explanation. Consider the fact that words are easier to recognize if you see them as part of a sentence than if you see them in isolation. There have been many formal demonstrations of this effect (for an overview, see DeLange et al., 2018), but for our purposes an informal example will work. Imagine that we tell research participants, "I'm about to show you a word very briefly on a computer screen; the word is the name of something that you can eat." If we forced the participants to guess the word at this point, they would be unlikely to name the target word. (There are, after all, many things you can eat, so the chances are slim of guessing just the right one.) But if we briefly show the word "CELERY," we're likely to observe a large priming effect; that is, participants are more likely to recognize "CELERY" with this cue than they would have been without the cue.

Think about what this priming involves. First, the participants need to understand each of the words in the instruction. If they didn't understand the word "eat" (e.g., if they mistakenly thought we had said, "something that you can beat"), we wouldn't get the priming. Second, the participants must understand the relations among the words in the instruction. For example, if they mistakenly thought we had said, "something that can eat you," we would expect a very different sort of priming. Third, the participants have to know some facts about the world—namely, the kinds of things that can be eaten; without this knowledge, we would expect no priming.

Obviously, then, this instance of priming relies on a broad range of knowledge, and there is nothing special about this example. We could observe similar priming effects if we tell someone that the word about to be shown is the name of a historical figure or that the word is related to the *Star Wars* movies. In each case, the instruction would facilitate perception, with the implication that in order to explain these various priming effects, we'll need to hook up our object-recognition system to a much broader library of information.

Here's a different example, this time involving what you *hear*. Participants in one study listened to a low-quality recording of a conversation. Some participants were told they were listening to an interview with a job candidate; others were told they were listening to an interview with a suspect in a criminal case (Lange et al., 2011). This difference in context had a powerful effect on what the participants heard. For example, the audio contained the sentence "I got scared when I saw what it'd done to him." Participants who thought they were listening to a criminal often mis-heard this statement and were sure they had heard ". . . when I saw what I'd done to him."

Where does all of this bring us? Examples like we're considering here tell us that we cannot view object recognition as a self-contained process. Instead, knowledge that is external to object recognition (e.g., knowledge about what is edible, or about the sorts of things a criminal might say) is imported into and influences the process. In other words, these examples (unlike the ones we considered earlier in the chapter) don't depend just on the specific stimuli you've encountered recently or frequently. Instead, what's crucial for this sort of priming is what you know coming into the experiment—knowledge derived from a wide range of life experiences.

We have, therefore, reached an important juncture. We've tried in this chapter to examine object recognition apart from other cognitive processes, considering how a separate object-recognition "module" might function, with the module then handing its product (the object it had recognized) on to subsequent processes. We have described how a significant piece of this process might unfold, but in the end we have run up against a problem—namely, top-down priming that draws on knowledge from outside of object recognition itself. (For neuroscience evidence that word and object recognition interacts with other sorts of information, see Carreiras et al., 2014; also **Figure 4.18.**) This sort of priming depends on what is in memory and on how that knowledge is accessed and used, and so we can't tackle this sort of priming until we've said more about memory, knowledge, and thought. We therefore must leave object recognition for now in order to fill in other pieces of the puzzle. We'll have more to say about object recognition in later chapters, once we have some additional theoretical machinery in place.

TEST YOURSELF

13. What's the evidence that word recognition (or object recognition in general) is influenced by processes separate from what has been seen recently or frequently?

FIGURE 4.18   THE FLOW OF TOP-DOWN PROCESSING

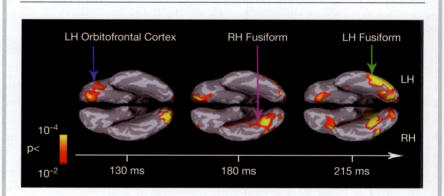

When viewers had only a very brief glimpse of a target object, brain activity indicating top-down processing was evident in the front part of the brain (the orbitofrontal cortex) 130 ms after the target came into view. Roughly 50 ms later (and so 180 ms after the target came into view), brain activity increased further back in the brain (in the right hemisphere's fusiform area), indicating successful recognition. This activity then spread into other visual areas in the subsequent moments (as is evident in the measurements taken 215 ms after the target came into view). This overall pattern, however, was not evident when object recognition was easy (because of a longer presentation of the target). Sensibly, top-down processing plays a larger role when bottom-up processing is somehow limited or inadequate.

speed-reading

Students often wish they could read more quickly, and, in fact, it's easy to teach people how to speed-read. It's important to understand, however, how speed-reading works, because this will help you see when speed-reading is a good idea—and when it's a terrible strategy.

As the chapter describes, in normal reading there's no need to look at every word on the page. Printed material (like language in general) follows predictable patterns, and so, having read a few words, you're often able to guess what the next words will be. And without realizing you're doing it, you're already exploiting this predictability. In reading this (or any) page, your eyes skip over many of the words, and you rely on rapid inference to fill in what you've skipped.

The same process is central for speed-reading. Courses that teach you how to speed-read actually encourage you to skip more, as you move down the page, and to rely more on inference. As a result, speed-reading isn't really "reading faster"; it is instead "reading less and inferring more."

How does this process work? First, before you speed-read some text, you need to lay the groundwork for the inference process—so that you'll make the inferences efficiently and accurately. Therefore, before you speed-read a text, you should skim through it quickly. Look at the figures and the figure captions. If there's a summary at the end or a preview at the beginning, read them. These steps will give you a broad sense of what the material is about, preparing you to make rapid—and sensible—inferences about the material.

Second, you need to make sure you do rely on inference, rather than word-by-word scrutiny of the page. To do this, read for a while holding an index card just under the line you're reading, or using your finger to slide along the line of print to indicate what you're reading at that moment. These procedures establish a physical marker that helps you keep track of where your eyes are pointing as you move from word to word.

This use of a pointer will become easy and automatic after a little practice, and once it does, you're ready for the key step. Rather than using the marker to *follow* your eye position, use the marker to lead your eyes. Specifically, try moving the index card or your finger a bit more quickly than you have so far, and try to move your eyes to "keep up" with this marker.

Of course, if you suddenly realize that you don't have a clue what's on the page, then you've been going too fast. Just move quickly enough so that you have to hustle along to keep up with your pointer. Don't move so quickly that you lose track of what you're reading.

This procedure will feel awkward at first, but it will become easier with practice, and you'll gradually learn to move the pointer faster and faster. As a result, you'll increase your reading speed by 30%, 40%, or more. But let's be clear about what's going on here: You're simply shifting the balance between how much input you're taking in and how much you're filling in the gaps with sophisticated guesswork. Often, this is a fine strategy. Many of the things you read are

WHEN SHOULD YOU SPEED-READ?

Students are often assigned an enormous amount of reading, so strategies for speed-reading can be extremely helpful. But it's important to understand why speed-reading works as it does; knowing this will help you decide when speed-reading is appropriate and when it's unwise.

highly predictable, so your inferences about the skipped words are likely to be correct. In settings like these, you might as well use the faster process of making inferences, rather than the slower process of looking at individual words.

But speed-reading is a bad bet if the material is hard to understand. In that case, you won't be able to figure out the skipped words via inference, so speed-reading will hurt you. Speed-reading is also a poor choice if you're trying to appreciate an author's style. If, for example, you speed-read Shakespeare's *Romeo and Juliet*, you probably will be able to make inferences about the plot, but you won't be able to make inferences about the specific words you're skipping over; you won't be able to make inferences about the language Shakespeare actually used. And, of course, if you miss the language of Shakespeare and miss the poetry, you've missed the point.

Speed-reading will enable you to zoom through many assignments. But don't speed-read material that's technical, filled with details that you'll need, or beautiful for its language. In those cases, you need to pay attention to the words on the page and not rely on your own inferences.

For more on this topic:

Rayner, K., Schotter, E. R., Masson, M. E. J., Potter, M. C., & Treiman, R. (2016). So much to read, so little time: How do we read, and can speed reading help? *Psychological Science in the Public Interest, 17*(1), 4–34.

chapter review

SUMMARY

- We easily recognize a wide range of objects in a wide range of circumstances. Our recognition is significantly influenced by context, which can determine how or whether we recognize an object. To study these achievements, investigators have often focused on the recognition of printed language, using this case to study how object recognition in general might proceed.

- Many investigators have proposed that recognition begins with the identification of features in the input pattern. Key evidence for this claim comes from visual search tasks, which show that searches for a target defined by a single feature are easy and extremely fast.

- To study word recognition, investigators often use tachistoscopic presentations. In these studies, words that appear frequently in the language are easier to identify than words that don't appear frequently, and so are words that have been recently viewed—an effect known as repetition priming. The data also show a pattern known as the word-superiority effect; this refers to the fact that letters are more readily perceived if they appear in the context of a word than if they appear in isolation. In addition, well-formed nonwords are more readily perceived than letter strings that do not conform to the rules of normal spelling. Another reliable pattern is that recognition errors, when they occur, are quite systematic, with the input typically perceived as being more regular than it actually is. These findings, taken together, indicate that recognition is influenced by the regularities that exist in our environment (e.g., the regularities of spelling patterns).

- We can understand these results in terms of a network of detectors. Each detector collects input and fires when the input reaches a threshold level. A network of these detectors can accomplish a great deal; for example, it can interpret ambiguous inputs, recover from its own errors, and make inferences about barely viewed stimuli.

- The feature net seems to "know" the rules of spelling and "expects" the input to conform to these rules. However, this knowledge is distributed across the entire network and emerges only through the network's parallel processing. This setup leads to enormous efficiency in our interactions with the world because it enables us to recognize patterns and objects with relatively little input and under diverse circumstances. But these gains come at the cost of occasional error. This trade-off may be necessary, though, if we are to cope with the informational complexity of our world.

- A feature net can be implemented in different ways—with or without inhibitory connections, for example. With some adjustments (e.g., the addition of geon detectors), the net can also recognize three-dimensional objects. However, some stimuli—for example, faces—probably are not recognized through a feature net but, instead, require a different sort of recognition system, one that is sensitive to relationships and configurations within the stimulus input.

- The feature net also needs to be supplemented to accommodate top-down influences on object recognition. These influences can be detected in the benefits of larger contexts in facilitating recognition and in forms of priming that depend on far more than just the specific stimuli you've encountered recently or frequently. These other forms of priming call for an interactive model that merges bottom-up and top-down processes.

KEY TERMS

bottom-up processing (p. 106)
top-down processing (p. 106)
visual search tasks (p. 107)
tachistoscope (p. 108)
mask (p. 108)
priming (p. 109)
repetition priming (p. 109)
word-superiority effect (WSE) (p. 110)
well-formedness (p. 111)
feature nets (p. 114)
activation level (p. 114)

response threshold (p. 114)
bigram detectors (p. 115)
local representation (p. 119)
distributed representation (p. 120)
excitatory connections (p. 121)
inhibitory connections (p. 121)
recognition by components (RBC) model (p. 123)
geons (p. 123)
prosopagnosia (p. 127)
inversion effect (p. 128)
holistic perception (p. 130)

TEST YOURSELF AGAIN

1. What is the difference between bottom-up and top-down processing?

2. What is the evidence that features play a special role in object recognition?

3. What is repetition priming, and how is it demonstrated?

4. What procedure demonstrates the word-superiority effect?

5. What's the evidence that word perception is somehow governed by the rules of ordinary spelling?

6. How does a feature net explain the word-frequency effect?

7. How does a feature net explain the types of *errors* people make in recognizing words?

8. What are the benefits, and what are the costs, associated with the feature net's functioning?

9. How does the McClelland and Rumelhart model differ from the older, "classical" version of the feature net?

10. What aspects of the recognition by components (RBC) proposal allow this model to handle the recognition of three-dimensional objects?

11. What's the evidence that face recognition is different from other forms of object recognition?

12. What's the evidence that face recognition depends on the face's configuration, rather than the features one by one?

13. What's the evidence that word recognition (or object recognition in general) is influenced by processes separate from what has been seen recently or frequently?

THINK ABOUT IT

1. Imagine that you were designing a mechanism that would recognize *items of clothing* (shirts, pants, jackets, belts). Would some sort of feature net be possible? If so, what would the net involve?

2. Imagine that you were designing a mechanism that would recognize different *smells* (roses, cinnamon, freshly mown grass, car exhaust). Do you think some sort of feature net would be possible? If so, what would the net involve?

DEMONSTRATIONS & APPLYING COGNITIVE PSYCHOLOGY ESSAYS

For demonstrations of key concepts in cognitive psychology, take a look at the Online Demonstrations. To explore more of the practical applications of cognitive psychology in themed essays, visit the online reader.

Online Demonstrations

- Demonstration 4.1: Features and Feature Combination
- Demonstration 4.2: The Broad Influence of the Rules of Spelling
- Demonstration 4.3: Inferences in Reading
- Demonstration 4.4: Face-Recognition Ability

Online Applying Cognitive Psychology Essays

- Cognitive Psychology and Technology: Face-Recognition Software
- Cognitive Psychology and Health: Hindsight
- Cognitive Psychology and the Law: Cross-Race Identification

ZAPS COGNITION LABS

Go to ZAPS online cognition labs to conduct hands-on experiments on key concepts.

INQUIZITIVE

It's time to complete your study experience! Go to InQuizitive to practice actively with this chapter's concepts and get personalized feedback along the way.

chapter **5** Paying Attention

what if... Right now, you're paying attention to this page, reading these words. But you could, if you chose, pay attention to the other people in the room, or your plans for the weekend, or even the feel of the floor under your feet.

What would your life be like if you couldn't control your attention in this way? Every one of us, of course, has had the maddening experience of being distracted when we're trying to concentrate. For example, there you are on the bus, trying to read your book. You have no interest in the conversation going on in the seats behind you, but you seem unable to shut it out, and so you make no progress in your book.

The frustration in this experience is fueled by the fact that usually you *can* control your attention, so it's irritating when you can't focus in the way you want to. The life challenge is much worse, though, for people who suffer from something called "unilateral neglect syndrome." This pattern is generally the result of damage to the parietal cortex, and patients with this syndrome ignore all inputs coming from one side of the body. Patients with neglect syndrome will, for example, eat food from only one side of the plate, wash only half of their face, and fail to locate sought-for objects if they're on the neglected side. Someone with this disorder cannot safely drive a car and, as a pedestrian, is likely to trip over unnoticed obstacles.

This syndrome typically results from damage to the *right* parietal lobe, and so the neglect is for the *left* side of space. (Remember the brain's contralateral organization; see Chapter 2.) Neglect patients will therefore read only the right half of words shown to them—they'll read "threat" as "eat," "parties" as "ties." If asked to draw a clock, they'll probably remember that the numbers from 1 to 12 need to be included, but they'll jam all the numbers onto the clock's right side.

Observations like these remind us how crucial the ability to pay attention is—so that you can focus on the things you want to focus on and not be pulled off track by distraction. But what is "attention"? As we'll see in this chapter, the ability to pay attention involves many independent elements.

preview of chapter themes

- Multiple mechanisms are involved in the seemingly simple act of paying attention, because people must take various steps to facilitate the processing of desired inputs. Without these steps, their ability to pick up information from the world is dramatically reduced.

- Many of the steps necessary for perception have a "cost": They require the commitment of mental resources. These resources are limited in availability, which is part of the reason you usually can't pay attention to two inputs at once—doing so would require more resources than you have.

- Divided attention (the attempt to do two things at once) can also be understood in terms of resources. You can perform two activities at the same time only if the activities don't require more resources than you have available.

- Some of the mental resources you use are specialized, which means they're required only for tasks of a certain sort. Other resources are more general, needed for a wide range of tasks. However, the resource demand of a task can be diminished through practice.

- We emphasize that attention is best understood not as a process or mechanism but as an *achievement*. Like most achievements, paying attention involves many elements, all of which help you to be aware of the stimuli you're interested in and not be pulled off track by irrelevant distractors.

Selective Attention

William James (1842–1910) is one of the historical giants of the field of psychology, and he is often quoted in the modern literature. One of his most famous quotes provides a starting point for this chapter. Roughly 130 years ago, James wrote:

> Everyone knows what attention is. It is the taking possession by the mind, in clear and vivid form, of one out of what seem several simultaneously possible objects or trains of thought. . . . It implies withdrawal from some things in order to deal effectively with others, and is a condition which has a real opposite in the confused, dazed, scatterbrained state which in French is called distraction. . . . (James, 1890, pp. 403–404)

In this quote, James is describing what modern psychologists call **selective attention**—that is, the skill through which a person focuses on one input or one task while ignoring other stimuli that are on the scene. But what does this skill involve? What steps do you need to take to achieve the focus that James described?

Dichotic Listening

Early studies of attention used a setup called **dichotic listening**: Participants wore headphones and heard one input in the left ear and a different input in the right ear. The participants were instructed to pay attention to one of these inputs—the **attended channel**—and to ignore the message in the other ear—the **unattended channel**.

To make sure participants were paying attention, investigators gave them a task called **shadowing**: Participants were required to repeat back what they were hearing, word for word, so that, as they listened, they were simply echoing what they heard on the attended channel. Participants quickly mastered this task, but, focused on shadowing, they heard remarkably little from the unattended channel. If asked, after a minute or so of shadowing, to report what the unattended message was about, they had no idea (e.g., Cherry, 1953). They couldn't even tell if the unattended channel contained a coherent message or random words. In fact, in one study, participants shadowed speech in the attended channel, while in the unattended channel they heard a text in Czech, read with English pronunciation. The individual sounds, therefore (the vowels, the consonants), resembled English, but the message itself was (for an English speaker) gibberish. After a minute of shadowing, only 4 of 30 participants detected the peculiar character of the unattended message (Treisman, 1964).

We can observe a similar pattern with *visual* inputs. Participants in one study viewed a video that many readers will already know, because the video has gone viral on the Internet. In this video, a team of players in white shirts is passing a basketball back and forth; people watching the video are urged to count how many times the ball is passed from one player to another. Interwoven with these players (and visible in the video) is another team, wearing black shirts, also passing a ball back and forth; viewers are instructed to ignore these players.

Viewers have no difficulty with this task, but, while doing it, they usually don't see another event that appears on the screen right in front of their eyes. Specifically, they fail to notice when someone wearing a gorilla costume walks through the middle of the game, pausing briefly to thump his chest before exiting. (See **Figure 5.1**; Neisser & Becklen, 1975; Simons & Chabris, 1999; also see Jenkins et al., 2005.)

People are not, however, altogether oblivious to the unattended channel. Research participants easily and accurately report whether the unattended

FIGURE 5.1   THE INVISIBLE GORILLA

In this procedure, participants are instructed to keep track of the ballplayers in the white shirts. Intent on their task, participants are oblivious to what the back-shirted players are doing, and—remarkably—they fail to see the person in the gorilla suit strolling through the scene.   (FIGURE PROVIDED BY DANIEL J. SIMONS.)

channel contained human speech, musical instruments, or silence. If the unattended channel did contain speech, participants can report whether the speaker was male or female, had a high or low voice, or was speaking loudly or softly. (For reviews of this early work, see Broadbent, 1958; Kahneman, 1973.) Apparently, then, *physical attributes* of the unattended channel are heard, even though participants are generally clueless about the unattended channel's *semantic content*.

In one study, though, participants were asked to shadow one passage while ignoring a second passage. Embedded within the unattended channel was a series of names, and roughly one third of the participants did hear their own name when it was spoken—even though (just like in other studies) they heard almost nothing else from the unattended input (Moray, 1959; for a modern confirmation, see Röer & Cowan, 2020).

And it's not just names that can "catch" your attention. Mention of a recently seen movie, or a favorite restaurant, will often be noticed in the unattended channel. More broadly, words with some personal importance are often noticed, even though the rest of the unattended channel is perceived only as an undifferentiated blur (Conway et al., 2001; Wood & Cowan, 1995).

Inhibiting Distractors

How should we think about all these results? How can we explain both the general insensitivity to the unattended channel and also the cases in which the unattended channel "leaks through"?

One option focuses on what you do with the *unattended* input. The proposal is that you somehow block processing of the inputs you're not interested in, much as a sentry blocks the path of unwanted guests but stands back and does nothing when legitimate guests are in view, allowing them to pass through the gate unimpeded. This sort of proposal was central for early theories of attention, which suggested that people erect a **filter** that shields them from potential distractors. Desired information (the attended channel) is not filtered out and so goes on to receive further processing (Broadbent, 1958).

What does it mean to "filter" something out? The key lies in the nervous system's ability to *inhibit* certain responses, and evidence suggests that you do rely on this ability to avoid certain forms of distraction. This inhibition, however, is rather specific, operating on a distractor-by-distractor basis. In other words, you might have the ability to inhibit your response to *this* distractor and the same for *that* distractor, but these abilities are of little value if some new, unexpected distractor comes along. In that case, you need to develop a new skill aimed at blocking the new intruder. (For more on the suppression of unwanted inputs, see Britton & Anderson, 2019; Chang & Egeth, 2019; Cunningham & Egeth, 2016; Frings & Wühr, 2014; Geng et al., 2019; Singh et al., 2018. For a glimpse of brain mechanisms that support this inhibition, see Payne & Sekuler, 2014; Wimmer et al., 2015.)

THE COCKTAIL PARTY EFFECT

We have all experienced some version of the so-called cocktail party effect. There you are at a party, deep in conversation. Other conversations are going on, but somehow you're able to "tune them out." All you hear is the single conversation you're attending to, plus a buzz of background noise. But now imagine that someone a few steps away from you mentions the name of a close friend of yours. Your attention is immediately caught, and you find yourself listening to that other conversation and (momentarily) oblivious to the conversation you had been engaged in. This experience, easily observed outside the laboratory, matches the pattern of experimental data.

The ability to ignore certain distractors—to shut them out—therefore needs to be part of our theory. Other evidence, though, indicates that this isn't the whole story. That's because you not only inhibit the processing of distractors, you also *promote* the processing of *desired* stimuli.

Inattentional Blindness

We saw in Chapters 3 and 4 that perception involves a lot of activity, as you organize and interpret the incoming stimulus information. It seems plausible that this activity requires some initiative and some resources from you—and evidence suggests that it does.

In one experiment, participants were told that they would see large "+" shapes on a computer screen, presented for 200 ms (a fifth of a second), followed by a pattern mask. If the horizontal bar of the "+" was longer than the vertical, participants were supposed to press one button; if the vertical bar was longer, they had to press a different button. As a complication, though, participants weren't allowed to look directly at the "+." Instead, they were told to point their eyes at a mark in the center of the computer screen—a **fixation target**—and the "+" shapes were shown just off to one side (see **Figure 5.2**).

For the first three trials of the procedure, events proceeded just as participants expected. On Trial 4, though, things were slightly different: While the

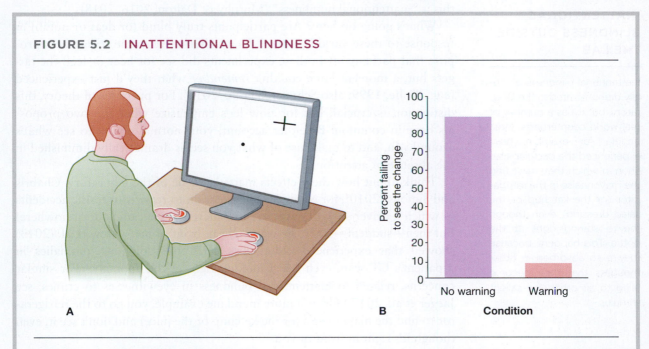

FIGURE 5.2   INATTENTIONAL BLINDNESS

Participants were instructed to point their eyes at the dot and to make judgments about the "+" shown just off to the side. However, the dot itself briefly changed to another shape. If participants weren't warned about this (and so weren't paying attention to the dot), they failed to detect this change—even though they had been pointing their eyes right at the dot the whole time.   (AFTER MACK & ROCK, 1998)

INATTENTIONAL BLINDNESS OUTSIDE THE LAB

Inattentional blindness is usually demonstrated in the laboratory, but it has a number of real-world counterparts. Most people, for example, have experienced the peculiar situation in which they can't find the mayonnaise in the refrigerator (or the ketchup or the salad dressing) even though they're staring right at the bottle. This happens because they're so absorbed in other thoughts that they become blind to an otherwise salient stimulus.

target "+" was on the screen, the fixation target disappeared and was replaced by one of three shapes—a triangle, a rectangle, or a cross. Then, the entire configuration (the "+" target and this new shape) was replaced by the mask.

Immediately after the trial, participants were asked: Was there anything different on this trial? Was anything present, or anything changed, that wasn't there on previous trials? Remarkably, 89% of the participants reported that there was no change; they had failed to see anything other than the (attended) "+." To probe the participants further, the researchers told them (correctly) that during the previous trial the fixation target had momentarily disappeared and had been replaced by a shape. The participants were then asked what that shape had been, and were given the choices of a triangle, a rectangle, or a cross (one of which, of course, was the right answer). The responses to this question were essentially random. Even when probed in this way, participants seemed not to have seen the shape directly in front of their eyes (Mack & Rock, 1998; also see Mack, 2003).

This pattern has been named **inattentional blindness** (Mack & Rock, 1998; also Mack, 2003; also see Redlich et al., 2021)—a pattern in which people fail to see a prominent stimulus, even though they're staring straight at it. In a similar effect, called "inattentional deafness," participants regularly fail to *hear* prominent stimuli if they aren't expecting them (Dalton & Fraenkel, 2012). In other studies, participants fail to feel stimuli if the inputs are unexpected; this is "inattentional numbness" (Murphy & Dalton, 2016, 2018).

What's going on here? Are participants truly blind (or deaf or numb) in response to these various inputs? As an alternative, some researchers propose that participants in these experiments did see (or hear or feel) the targets but, a moment later, couldn't *remember* what they'd just experienced (e.g., Wolfe, 1999; also Schnuerch et al., 2016). For purposes of theory, this distinction is crucial, but for now let's emphasize what the two proposals have in common: By either account, your normal ability to see what's around you, and to make use of what you see, is dramatically diminished in the absence of attention.

Think about how these effects matter outside of the laboratory. Chabris and Simons (2010), for example, call attention to reports of traffic accidents in which a driver says, "I never saw the bicyclist! He came out of nowhere! But then—suddenly—there he was, right in front of me." Drew et al. (2013) showed that experienced radiologists often miss obvious anomalies in a patient's CT scan, even when looking right at the anomaly. (For similar concerns, related to inattentional blindness in eyewitnesses to crimes, see Jaeger et al., 2017.) Or, as a more mundane example, you go to the refrigerator to find the mayonnaise (or the ketchup or the juice) and don't see it, even though it's right in front of you.

In these cases, we lament the neglectful driver and the careless radiologist, and your inability to find the mayo may cause you to worry that you're losing your mind (as well as your condiments). The reality, though, is that these cases of failing-to-see are entirely normal. Perception requires more than "merely" having a stimulus in front of your eyes. Perception requires some work.

Change Blindness

The active nature of perception is also evident in studies of **change blindness**—observers' inability to detect changes in scenes they're looking directly at. In some experiments, participants are shown pairs of pictures separated by a brief blank interval (e.g., Rensink et al., 1997; Rensink, 2018). The pictures in each pair are identical except for one aspect—a large jet engine easily visible in one picture but missing from the other; a man wearing a hat in one picture but not in the other; and so on (see **Figure 5.3**). Participants know

FIGURE 5.3   CHANGE BLINDNESS

In some change-blindness demonstrations, participants see one picture, then a second, then the first again, then the second, and must spot the difference between the two pictures. Here, we've displayed the pictures side by side, rather than putting them in alternation. Can you find the difference? For most people, it takes a surprising amount of time and effort to locate the differences—even though some of the differences are large. Apparently, having a stimulus directly in front of your eyes is no guarantee that you will perceive the stimulus.

FIGURE 5.4
CHANGE
BLINDNESS

In this video, every time there was a shift in camera angle, there was a change in the scene—so that the woman in the red sweater abruptly gained a scarf, the plates that had been red were suddenly white, and so on. When viewers watched the video, though, they noticed none of these changes.

that their task is to detect any changes in the pictures, but even so, the task is difficult. If the change involves something central to the scene, participants may need to look back and forth between the pictures a dozen times before they detect the change. If the change involves some peripheral aspect of the scene, as many as 25 alternations may be required.

A related pattern can be documented when participants watch videos. In one study, observers watched a movie of two women having a conversation. The camera first focused on one woman, then the other, just as it would in an ordinary TV show or movie. The crucial element of this experiment, though, was that certain aspects of the scene changed every time the camera angle changed. For example, from one camera angle, participants could plainly see the red plates on the table between the women. When the camera shifted to a different position, the plates' color had changed to white. In another shift, one of the women gained a prominent scarf that she didn't have on a fraction of a second earlier (see **Figure 5.4**). Most observers, however, noticed none of these changes (Levin & Simons, 1997; Shore & Klein, 2000; Simons & Rensink, 2005).

Incredibly, the same pattern can be documented with live (i.e., not filmed) events. In a remarkable study, an investigator (let's call him "Leon") approached pedestrians on a college campus and asked for directions to a certain building. During the conversation, two men carrying a door approached and deliberately walked *between* Leon and the research participant. As a result, Leon was momentarily hidden (by the door) from the participant's view, and in that moment Leon traded places with one of the men carrying the door. A second later, therefore, Leon was able to walk away, unseen, while the new fellow (who had been carrying the door) stayed behind and continued the conversation with the participant.

Roughly half of the participants failed to notice this switch. They continued the conversation as though nothing had happened—even though Leon and his replacement were different heights, had different hairstyles, and were wearing different clothes. When asked whether anything odd had happened in this event, many participants commented only that it was rude that the guys carrying the door had walked right through their conversation. (See Chabris & Simons, 2010; Simons & Ambinder, 2005; also see Most et al., 2001; Rensink, 2002; Seegmiller et al., 2011.)

Early versus Late Selection

It's clear, then, that people are often oblivious to stimuli directly in front of their eyes—whether the stimuli are simple displays on a computer screen, photographs, videos, or real-life events. Similarly, people are sometimes oblivious to prominent sounds in the environment. As we've said, though, there are two ways to think about these results. First, the studies may reveal genuine limits on *perception*, so that participants literally don't see (or hear) these stimuli; or, second, the studies may reveal limits on *memory*, so that participants do see (or hear) the stimuli but immediately forget what they've just experienced.

Which proposal is correct? One approach to this question hinges on *when* the perceiver selects the desired input and (correspondingly) when the perceiver stops processing the unattended input. According to the **early selection hypothesis**, the attended input is privileged from the start, so that the unattended input receives little analysis and therefore is never perceived. According to the **late selection hypothesis**, all inputs receive relatively complete analysis, and selection occurs after the analysis is finished. Perhaps the selection occurs just before the stimuli reach consciousness, so that we become aware only of the attended input. Or perhaps the selection occurs later still—so that all inputs make it (briefly) into consciousness, but then the selection occurs so that only the attended input is remembered.

Debate about this issue began over 50 years ago (Broadbent, 1958; Deutsch & Deutsch, 1963; Treisman, 1964), but more recent findings make it clear that each hypothesis captures part of the truth. On the one side, there are cases in which people seem unaware of distractors but are influenced by them anyway— so that the (apparently unnoticed) distractors guide the interpretation of the attended stimuli (e.g., Moore & Egeth, 1997; see **Figure 5.5**). This seems to be a case of *late selection*: The distractors are perceived (so that they do have an influence) but are selected out before they make it to consciousness.

FIGURE 5.5   UNCONSCIOUS PERCEPTION

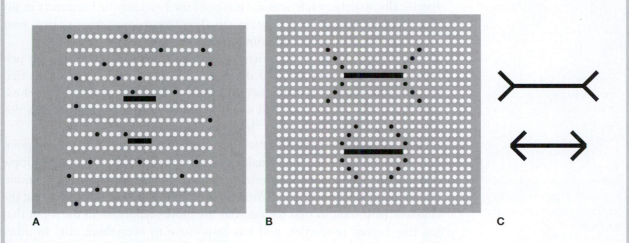

One study, apparently showing late selection, found that participants perceived (and were influenced) by background stimuli even though the participants did not *consciously* perceive these stimuli. The participants were shown a series of images, each containing a pair of horizontal lines; their task was to decide which line was longer. For the first three trials, the background dots in the display were arranged randomly (Panel A). For the fourth trial, the dots were arranged as shown in Panel B, roughly reproducing the configuration of a classic illusion (called the "Müller-Lyer illusion"); Panel C shows the standard form of this illusion. Participants in this study didn't perceive the "fins" consciously, but they were influenced by them—judging the top horizontal line in Panel B to be longer, fully in accord with the usual misperception of this illusion (Moore & Egeth, 1997).

TEST YOURSELF

1. What information do people reliably pick up from the *attended* channel? What do they pick up from the *unattended* channel?

2. How is inattentional blindness demonstrated? What situations outside of the laboratory seem to reflect inattentional blindness?

3. What evidence seems to confirm early selection? What evidence seems to confirm late selection?

But we can also find evidence for *early selection*, with distractor stimuli falling out of the stream of processing at a very early stage. Relevant evidence comes, for example, from studies that record the brain's electrical activity in the milliseconds after a stimulus has arrived. These studies confirm that the brain activity for attended inputs is distinguishable from that for unattended inputs just 80 ms or so after the stimulus presentation—a time interval in which early sensory processing is still under way (e.g., Hillyard et al., 1998; see **Figure 5.6**).

Other evidence suggests that attention can influence activity levels in the lateral geniculate nucleus (LGN; Kastner et al., 2006; McAlonan et al., 2008; Moore & Zirnsak, 2017). In this case, attention is changing the flow of signals within the nervous system even before the signals reach the brain. (For more on how attention influences the earliest stages of processing in the visual system, see Carrasco et al., 2004; McAdams & Reid, 2005; Yantis, 2008.)

Selection via Priming

Whether selection is early or late, it's clear that people often fail to see stimuli that are directly in front of them, in plain view. But what is the obstacle here? Why *don't* people perceive these stimuli?

In Chapter 4, we proposed that recognition requires a network of detectors, and we argued that these detectors fire most readily if they're suitably primed. In some cases, the priming is produced by your visual experience—specifically, whether each detector has been used recently or frequently in the past. But we suggested that priming can also come from another source: your expectations about what the stimulus will be.

The proposal here, then, is that you can literally prepare yourself for perceiving by priming the relevant detectors. The idea, in other words, is that you somehow reach into the network and deliberately activate just those detectors that, you believe, will soon be needed. Then, once primed in this way, those detectors will be on "high alert" and ready to fire.

A related idea comes from **biased competition theory**. The starting point here is that neurons in the visual cortex often receive inputs from multiple stimuli—perhaps the stimulus you hope to attend and also a distractor stimulus that happens to be nearby. Attention solves this problem by adjusting the neurons' priorities, so that the neurons are more responsive to the input that has the desired properties, and less responsive to everything else. In other words, attention creates a temporary "bias" in what the neuron is sensitive to—so that (for example) the neuron is more sensitive to inputs that are of a certain color, or inputs that arise from a particular location in space. This bias—again, created by attention—favors one input over another, with the result that the desired input is given further processing and the distractor input is not (Desimone & Duncan, 1995; for discussion, see Hollingworth & Luck, 2009; Hopf et al., 2006).

In either case, the proposal is that you can prime your own visual system—sometimes by activating detectors (so they're more easily triggered,

FIGURE 5.6 EVIDENCE FOR EARLY SELECTION

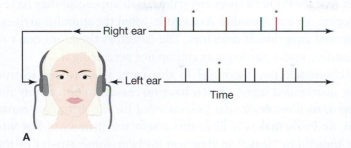

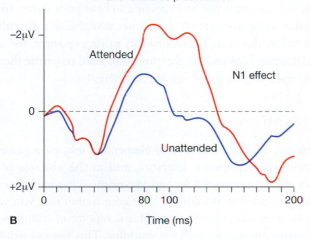

Participants were instructed to pay attention to the targets arriving in one ear, but to ignore targets in the other ear (Panel A; dots indicate which of the input signals were actually targets). During this task, researchers monitored the electrical activity in the participants' brains, with special focus on a brain wave termed the "N1" (so-called because the wave reflects a negative voltage roughly 100 ms after the target). As Panel B shows, the N1 effect was different for the attended and unattended inputs within 80 ms of the target's arrival—indicating that the attended and unattended inputs were processed differently from a very early stage. (FROM HILLYARD ET AL. "ELECTRIC SIGNS OF SELECTIVE ATTENTION IN THE HUMAN BRAIN," *SCIENCE* 182 © 1973 AAAS. REPRINTED WITH PERMISSION.)

and hence more sensitive), and sometimes by biasing detectors (so that they're more likely to respond to the desired input). Let's now add a further claim—that these activities have a "cost" attached to them. Specifically, you need to spend some effort or allocate some resources in order to do the priming, and these resources are in limited supply. As a result, there's a limit on just how much adjusting you can do.

We'll need to flesh out this proposal in several ways, but even so, we can already use it to explain some of the research findings. Why don't participants notice the shapes in the inattentional blindness studies? The answer lies in the fact that they don't expect any stimulus to appear, so they have no reason to prepare for any stimulus. As a result, when the stimulus arrives, it falls on unprepared (unprimed) detectors. The detectors therefore don't respond to the stimulus, so the participants end up not perceiving it.

What about selective listening? In this case, you've been instructed to *ignore* the unattended input, so you have no reason to devote any resources to this input. As a result, the detectors needed for the distractor message are unprimed, and this makes it difficult to hear the distractor. But why does attention sometimes "leak," so that you do hear some aspects of the unattended input? Think about what happens if your name is spoken on the unattended channel. The detectors for this stimulus are already primed, but this isn't because at that moment you're expecting to hear your name. Instead, the detectors for your name are primed simply because this is a stimulus you've often encountered in the past. Thanks to this prior exposure, the activation level of these detectors is already high; you don't need to prime them further. So they will fire even if your attention is elsewhere.

Spatial Attention

The idea before us, in short, has several elements. First, perception is facilitated by the priming of relevant detectors, and in the absence of priming, perception may not happen at all! Second, the priming is sometimes stimulus-driven—that is, produced by the stimuli (like your name) that you've encountered (recently or frequently) in the past. This is *repetition priming*—priming produced by a prior encounter with the stimulus. This type of priming takes no effort on your part and requires no resources. But third, another sort of priming is also possible. This priming is expectation-driven and under your control. In this form of priming, you deliberately prime detectors for inputs you think are upcoming, so that you're ready for those inputs when they arrive. You don't do this priming for inputs you have no interest in, and you *can't* do this priming for inputs you can't anticipate.

Important evidence for these claims comes from studies of **spatial attention**—your ability to focus attention on a specific location in space. These studies generally involve a simple task: Participants watch a computer screen and have to press a button as soon as a letter appears. The letter can appear either on the left side of the screen or on the right, but participants are required to keep their eyes pointed at a fixation mark at the center of the screen.

Let's look at an early study using this basic procedure (Posner et al., 1980). In some of the trials within this experiment, a neutral warning signal was presented just before the letter's arrival. Participants therefore knew a trial was about to start but had no information about where the stimulus would appear (on the left side of the screen or the right). For other trials, an arrow was used as the warning signal. Sometimes the arrow pointed left, sometimes right; and the arrow was generally an accurate predictor of the location of the stimulus-to-come. On 20% of the trials, however, the arrow misled participants about location (and so the arrow might point right, but then the letter appeared on the left).

When the arrow provided correct information (as it did most of the time), participants were reliably faster in detecting the target. The difference (in comparison to the neutral condition) isn't large, but let's keep the task in mind: All participants had to do was detect the letter's arrival; they didn't have to identify the letter or make any judgment about it. Even with this simple task, it pays to be prepared (see **Figure 5.7**).

What about the trials in which the arrow was pointing in the "wrong" direction? Response times in this condition were about 12% slower than those in the neutral condition. Apparently, if you're devoting more attention to (say) the left position, because that's where the arrow was pointing, you end up devoting *less* attention to the right. If the stimulus then shows up on the right, you're less prepared for it—and so slower in responding.

Many studies confirm this pattern: If participants have some advance information about the stimulus-to-come, they are more efficient in perceiving the stimulus and responding to it. If, however, participants are misled about the stimulus-to-come, they're less efficient (slower) in responding.

In some studies, like the one we just described, the advance information involves the spatial position of the stimulus-to-come. In other studies, the advance information involves the identity of the stimulus, and here too it pays be be prepared: If, for example, participants are expecting to see a letter "G," they respond more quickly if the stimulus is a "G," compared to a condition in which participants have no idea what the stimulus will be. But once again there's a cost to being misled, and so participants respond more slowly if they're expecting, let's say, a "G" and then actually see a "K" (e.g., Posner & Snyder, 1975).

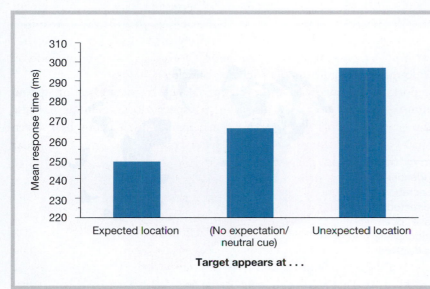

FIGURE 5.7 SPATIAL ATTENTION

In the Posner et al. (1980) study, participants simply had to press a button as soon as they saw the target. If the target appeared in the expected location, participants detected it a bit more quickly. If, however, participants were misled about the target's position (so that the target appeared in an unexpected location), their responses were slower than when the participants had no expectations at all.

Other studies show similar patterns (e.g., Hillyard & Münte, 1984; Liu et al., 2007). Thus, participants respond more quickly if the input has the color they are expecting, compared to a condition in which participants have no idea what the color will be. But they respond more slowly if they're misled—that is, if the color of the stimulus isn't what they were prepared for. Likewise for advance information about how the stimulus will be moving (and so participants are faster, for example, if they expect the stimulus to be moving left-to-right, and that's what they get).

Explaining the Costs and Benefits

The priming at issue in these studies is different from the *repetition priming* that we first met in Chapter 4. (For a view of some of the biological differences between these distinct forms of priming, see **Figure 5.8**; Corbetta & Shulman, 2002; Hahn et al., 2006; but also Moore & Zirnsak, 2017; Vossel et al., 2014.) The priming we're talking about now depends on your expectations for what's to come, and not just on the stimuli you've encountered in the past. In addition, the priming we're discussing now has a "cost" attached to it. We see this in the trials in which participants are misled, so that their expectation doesn't match the input they actually receive. As we've discussed, participants are worse off in these trials—when they're misled—than when they receive no prime at all; priming the "wrong" detectors, it seems, takes something away from other detectors.

What produces this cost? As an analogy, let's say that you have $50 to spend on groceries. You can spend more on ice cream if you wish, but if you do, you'll have less to spend on other foods. Any increase in the ice cream allotment must be covered by a decrease somewhere else. This trade-off arises, though, only because of the limited budget. If you had unlimited funds, you could spend more on ice cream and still have enough money for everything else.

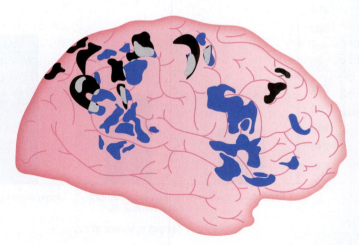

FIGURE 5.8 BIOLOGICAL MECHANISMS FOR THE TWO TYPES OF PRIMING

Brain sites shown in black have been identified in various studies as involved in expectation-based (sometimes called "goal directed") attention; sites shown in blue have been implicated in "stimulus-driven" attention. Sites shown in gray have been identified as involved in both types of attention.

Expectation-based priming shows the same pattern. If you expect a stimulus on the left (or, perhaps, a stimulus of a particular color or moving a certain way), this takes something away from the other detectors. Getting prepared for one target seems to make you less prepared for other targets. But we just said that this sort of pattern implies a limited "budget." If an unlimited supply of activation were available, you could prime some detectors and leave the others just as they were. However, that's not what happens, and in this fashion, expectation-based priming, by virtue of revealing costs when misled, reveals the presence of a **limited-capacity system**.

We can now put the pieces together. Ultimately, we need to explain the facts of selective attention, including the fact that while listening to one message you hear little content from other messages. To explain this, we've proposed that perceiving involves some work, and this work requires some **mental resources**—some process or capacity needed for performance, but in limited supply. That's why you can't listen to two messages at the same time; doing so would require more resources than you have. And now, finally, we're seeing evidence for those limited resources: The "costs" associated with mistaken expectations reveal the workings of a limited-capacity system, just as our hypothesis demands.

Attention as a Spotlight

We've said that expectation-based priming can involve a variety of stimulus dimensions: If you know what the stimulus will likely be (for example, a letter "B" rather than a "K"), you can prime yourself for that specific input. If you know what color the stimulus will likely be, or how it will be moving, you can prime yourself for these dimensions. Researchers are especially interested, though, in spatial attention, in part because this form of priming seems to influence very early processing stages in the visual system.

Researchers sometimes compare spatial attention to a spotlight beam that can "shine" anywhere in the visual field. The "beam" marks the region of space for which you are prepared, so inputs within the beam are processed more efficiently. The beam can be widely or narrowly focused (see **Figure 5.9**) and can be moved about at will as you explore (i.e., attend to) various aspects of the visual field.

Note, though, that the spotlight idea refers to movements of *attention*, not movements of the eyes. Of course, eye movements do play an important role in your selection of information from the world: If you want to learn more about something, you generally look at it. (For more on how you move your eyes to explore a scene, see Henderson, 2013; Moore & Zirnsak, 2017.) Even so, movements of the eyes can be separated from movements of attention, and it's attention, not the eyes, that's moving around in studies of spatial attention. We know this because of the timing of the effects. Eye movements are surprisingly slow, requiring 180 to 200 ms. But the benefits of primes can be detected within the first 150 ms after the priming stimulus is presented.

TEST YOURSELF

4. What are the differences between the way that stimulus-based priming functions and the way that expectation-based priming functions?
5. Why is there a "cost" associated with being misled by expectation-based priming?

Selection via Priming • **157**

FIGURE 5.9   ADJUSTING THE "BEAM" OF ATTENTION

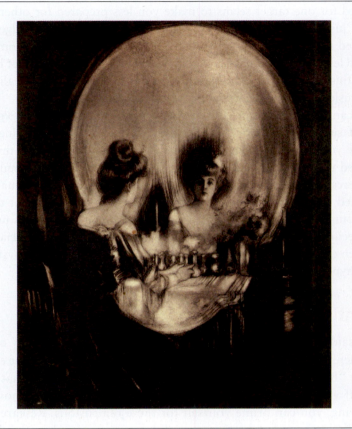

Charles Allan Gilbert's painting *All Is Vanity* can be perceived either as a woman at her dressing table or as a human skull. As you shift from one of these perceptions to the other, you need to adjust the spotlight beam of attention—to a narrow beam to see details (e.g., to see the woman) or to a wider beam to see the whole scene (e.g., to see the skull).

Therefore, the benefits of attention occur *prior to* any eye movement, so they cannot be a consequence of eye movements.

But what does it mean to "move attention"? The answer involves a network of sites in the frontal cortex and parietal cortex. According to one proposal (Posner & Rothbart, 2007; also Fiebelkorn & Kastner, 2020; see **Figure 5.10**), one cluster of sites (the *orienting* system) is needed to disengage attention from one target, shift attention to a new target, and then engage attention on the new target. A second set of sites (the *alerting* system) is responsible for maintaining an alert state in the brain. A third set of sites (the *executive* system) controls voluntary actions.

FIGURE 5.10 MANY BRAIN SITES ARE CRUCIAL FOR ATTENTION

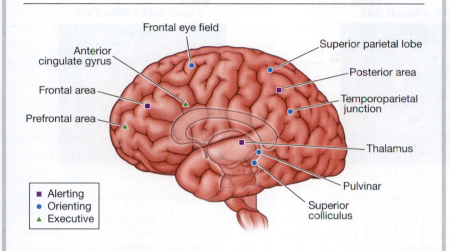

Many brain sites are important for controlling attention. Some sites play a pivotal role in *alerting* the brain, so that it is ready for an upcoming event. Other sites play a key role in *orienting* attention, so that you're focused on this position or that, on one target or another. Still other sites are crucial for controlling the brain's *executive* function—a function we'll discuss later in the chapter. (AFTER POSNER & ROTHBART, 2007)

These various sites form the "control system" for attention. Entirely different brain areas do the actual analysis of the incoming information (see **Figure 5.11**). The "control system" can, however, amplify (or, in some cases, inhibit) this analysis, with the result that processing of inputs you're interested in is enhanced, and processing of distractors is undermined. (See Corbetta & Shulman, 2002; Hampshire et al., 2007; Hon et al., 2006; Hung et al., 2005; for further discussion of the "spotlight" idea, see Cave, 2013; Rensink, 2012.)

All of these points echo a theme we first met in Chapter 2. There, we argued that most cognitive capacities depend on the activity of multiple brain regions, with each region providing a specialized process necessary for the overall achievement. As a result, a problem in any of these regions can disrupt the overall capacity, and if there are problems in several regions, the disruption can be substantial.

To see how these points play out, consider *attention deficit disorder* (a disorder often associated with *hyperactivity*; hence, the abbreviation *ADHD*). People with ADHD are often overwhelmed by the flood of information that's available to them, and they're unable to focus on their chosen target.

FIGURE 5.11   SELECTIVE ATTENTION ACTIVATES THE VISUAL CORTEX

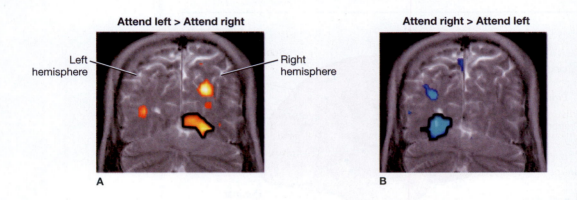

The brain sites that *control* attention are separate from the brain sites that do the actual analysis of the input. Thus, the intention to attend to, say, stimuli on the left is implemented through the many brain sites shown in Figure 5.10 However, these sites collectively activate a different set of sites—in the visual cortex—to promote the actual processing of the incoming stimuli. Shown here are activity levels in one participant (measured through fMRI scans) overlaid on a structural image of the brain (obtained through MRI scans). Keep in mind that because of the brain's contralateral organization, the intention to pay attention to the left side of space requires activation in the right hemisphere (Panel A); the intention to pay attention to the right requires activation in the left (Panel B).

Table 5.1 summarizes one proposal about this disorder. Symptoms of ADHD are listed in the left column; the right column identifies brain areas (i.e., neural networks) that may be the main source of each symptom. This proposal is not the only way to think about ADHD, but it illustrates the complex, many-part relationship between overall function (in this case, the ability to pay attention) and brain anatomy. (For more on ADHD, see Barkley et al., 2008; Brown, 2005; Seli et al., 2015; Zillmer et al., 2008.)

Where Do We "Shine" the "Beam"?

So far, we've been discussing *how* people pay attention, but we can also ask *what people pay attention to*. Where do people "shine" the "spotlight beam"? The answer has several parts. As a start, you pay attention to elements of the input that are visually prominent (Parkhurst et al., 2002) and also to elements that you think are interesting or important. Decisions about what's important, though, depend on the context. For example, **Figure 5.12** shows classic data recording a viewer's eye movements while inspecting a picture (Yarbus, 1967). The target picture is shown in the top left. Each of the other panels shows a three-minute recording of the viewer's eye movements; plainly, the pattern of movements depended on what the viewer was trying to learn about the picture.

TABLE 5.1 A PROPOSAL FOR THE LINKAGE BETWEEN ADHD SYMPTOMS AND NEURAL NETWORKS

Symptom Domains	Neural Networks
Problems in the alerting *system*	
Has difficulty sustaining attention	Right frontal cortex
Fails to finish	Right posterior parietal
Avoids sustained efforts	Locus ceruleus
Problems in the orienting *system*	
Is distracted by stimuli	Bilateral parietal
Does not appear to listen	Superior colliculus
Fails to pay close attention	Thalamus
Problems in the executive *system*	
Blurts out answers	Anterior cingulate
Interrupts or intrudes	Left lateral frontal
Cannot wait	Basal ganglia

This table summarizes an influential proposal about ADHD, linking the symptoms of the disorder to the three broad processes (*alerting, orienting,* and *executive*) described in the text, and then linking these processes to relevant brain areas (Swanson et al., 2000; for a different proposal, though, see Barkley et al., 2008).

In addition, your beliefs about the scene play an important role. You're unlikely to focus, for example, on elements of a scene that you think are entirely predictable, because you know you'll gain little information from inspecting these things (Brewer & Treyens, 1981; Friedman, 1979; Võ & Henderson, 2009). But you're also unlikely to focus on aspects of the scene that are totally unexpected. If, for example, you're walking through a forest, you won't be on the lookout for a stapler sitting on the ground, and so you may fail to notice the stapler (unless it's a bright color, or directly in your path). This point provides part of the basis for inattentional blindness and also leads to a pattern called the "ultra-rare item effect" (Mitroff & Biggs, 2014). The term refers to a pattern in which rare items are often overlooked; as the authors of one paper put it, "If you don't find it often, you often don't find it" (Evans et al., 2013).

These patterns are important for our theorizing, but they also have some troubling consequences. Consider the security inspectors at airports: They spend hours scrutinizing X-ray images of people's luggage, but they're looking for items (weapons, potential explosives) that, in truth, they encounter only rarely (if ever; **Figure 5.13**). It shouldn't be a surprise, therefore, when reports emerge of the inspectors overlooking a handgun or failing to spot a knife. These reports aren't evidence that the inspectors are poorly trained or careless; instead, the reports are simply a real-world confirmation of the ultra-rare item effect.

FIGURE 5.12   EYE MOVEMENT PATTERNS DEPEND ON THE PERSON'S GOALS

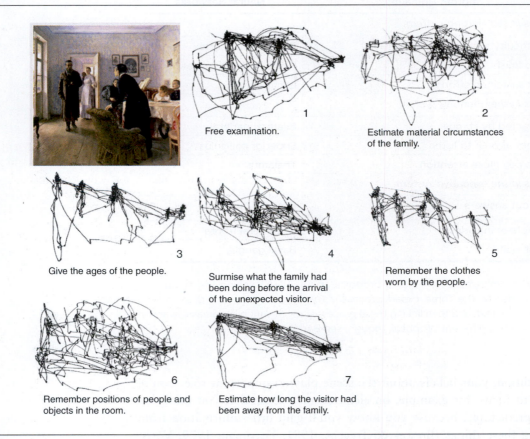

1. Free examination.

2. Estimate material circumstances of the family.

3. Give the ages of the people.

4. Surmise what the family had been doing before the arrival of the unexpected visitor.

5. Remember the clothes worn by the people.

6. Remember positions of people and objects in the room.

7. Estimate how long the visitor had been away from the family.

Participants were shown the picture in the top left. Each of the other panels shows a three-minute recording of one viewer's eye movements while inspecting the picture. The labels for each panel summarize the viewer's goal while looking at the picture. Plainly, the pattern of the movements depended on what the viewer was trying to learn.

Let's also note that people *differ* in what they pay attention to (e.g., Castelhano & Henderson, 2008), although some differences aren't surprising. For example, in looking at a scene, women are more likely than men to focus on how the people within the scene are dressed; men are more likely to focus on what the people look like (including their body shapes; Powers et al., 1979).

Perhaps more surprising are studies indicating differences from one *culture* to the next in how people pay attention. The underlying idea here is that people in the West (e.g., the United States, Canada, most of Europe) live in "individualistic" cultures that emphasize the achievements and qualities of the single person; therefore, in thinking about the world, Westerners are likely to focus on individual people, individual objects, and their attributes.

FIGURE 5.13 "IF YOU DON'T FIND IT OFTEN . . ."

Data both in the laboratory and in real-world settings tell us that people often overlook targets if the targets happen to be quite rare. As Evans et al. (2013) put it, "If you don't find it often, you often don't find it." This pattern has troubling implications for the security inspections routinely conducted at airports: The inspectors will see troubling items only rarely and, as a result, are likely to overlook those troubling items.

In contrast, people in East Asia (for example) have traditionally lived in "collectivist" cultures that emphasize the ways in which all people are linked to, and shaped by, the people around them. East Asians are therefore encouraged to think more holistically, with a focus on the context and how people and objects are related to one another. (See Nisbett, 2003; Nisbett et al., 2001; also Tardif et al., 2017. For a broad review, see Heine, 2015.) This linkage between culture and cognition isn't rigid, and so people in any culture can stray from these patterns. Even so, researchers have documented many manifestations of these differences from one culture to the next—including differences in how people pay attention. In one study, researchers tracked participants' eye movements while the participants were watching animated scenes on a computer screen (Masuda et al., 2008). In the initial second of viewing, there was little difference between the eye movements of American participants and Japanese participants: Both groups spent 90% of the time looking at the target person, located centrally in the display. But in the second and third seconds of viewing, the groups differed. The Americans continued to spend 90% of their time looking directly at the central figure (and so spent only 10% of their time looking at the faces of people visible in the scene's background); Japanese participants, in contrast, spent between 20% and 30% of their time looking at the faces in the background. (For related data, see Amer et al., 2016; Boduroglu et al., 2010; Masuda & Nisbett, 2006; for a challenge to this pattern, though, see Hakim et al., 2017.)

Finally, let's acknowledge that sometimes you choose what to pay attention to—a pattern called **endogenous control of attention**. But sometimes an element of the scene "seizes" your attention whether you like it or not;

FIGURE 5.14   EXOGENOUS CONTROL OF ATTENTION

SURGEON GENERAL'S WARNING: QUITTING SMOKING NOW GREATLY REDUCES SERIOUS HEALTH RISKS.

Marlboro

Public health officials would like the health warning for cigarettes to seize your attention, so that you can't overlook it. The tobacco industry, however, seems to have a different preference, and so "buries" the warning in the narrow bar near the bottom of this ad.

this pattern is called **exogenous control of attention**. Exogenous control is of interest to theorists, and it's also important for pragmatic reasons. For example, researchers have explored why some content "goes viral" on the Internet; part of the explanation may lie in the fact that some inputs—especially those with moral or emotional overtones—seize our attention in a largely uncontrollable fashion (Brady et al., 2020). Or, as different example, bear in mind that the people who design ambulance sirens or warning signals in an airplane cockpit want to make sure these stimuli cannot be ignored—so they, too, design inputs that grab your attention. In the same way, advertisers do all they can to ensure that their product name or logo will seize your attention even if you're intensely focused on something else (also see **Figure 5.14**).

Attending to Objects or Attending to Positions

A related question is concerned with the "target" of the attention "spotlight." To understand the issue, think about how an actual spotlight works. If a spotlight shines on a donut, then part of the beam will fall on the donut's hole and will illuminate part of the plate underneath the donut. Similarly, if the beam isn't aimed quite accurately, it may also illuminate the plate just to the left of the donut. The region illuminated by the beam, in other words, is defined purely in spatial terms: a circle of light at a particular position. That circle may or may not line up with the boundaries of the object you're shining the beam on.

Is this how attention works—so that you pay attention to whatever falls in a certain region of space? If this is the case, you might at times end up paying attention to part of this object, part of that. An alternative is that you pay attention to *objects* rather than to *positions in space*. To continue the example, the target of your attention might be the donut itself rather than its location. In that case, the plate just to the left and the bit of plate visible through the donut's hole might be close to your focus, but they aren't part of the attended object and so aren't attended.

Which is the correct view of attention? Do you pay attention to regions in space, no matter what objects (or parts of objects) fall in that region? Or do you pay attention to objects? It turns out that each view captures part of the truth.

One line of evidence comes from the study of people we mentioned at the chapter's start—people who suffer from *unilateral neglect syndrome* (see **Figure 5.15**, also see Chapter 2). Taken at face value, the symptoms shown by these patients support a space-based account of attention: The afflicted patients seem insensitive to all objects within a region that's defined spatially—namely, everything to the left of their current focus. If an object falls half within the region and half outside of it, then the spatial boundary is what matters, not the object's boundaries. This is clear, for example, in how these patients read words (likely to read "bother" as "her" or "carrot"

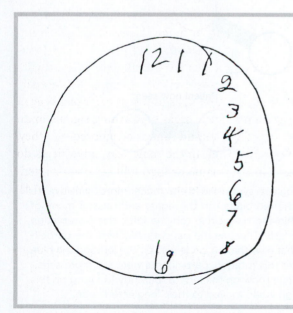

FIGURE 5.15 UNILATERAL NEGLECT SYNDROME

A patient with damage to the right parietal cortex was asked to draw a typical clock face. In his drawing, the patient seemed unaware of the left side, but he still recalled that all 12 numbers had to be displayed. The drawing shows how he resolved this dilemma.

as "rot")—responding only to the word's right half, apparently oblivious to the word's overall boundaries.

Other evidence, however, demands further theory. In one study, patients with neglect syndrome had to respond to targets that appeared within a barbell-shaped frame (see **Figure 5.16**). Not surprisingly, they were much more sensitive to the targets appearing within the red circle (on the right) and missed many of the targets appearing in the blue circle (on the left); this result confirms the patients' diagnosis. What's crucial, though, is what happened next. While the patients watched, the barbell frame was slowly spun around, so that the red circle, previously on the right, was now on the left and the blue circle, previously on the left, was now on the right.

If the patients consistently neglect a region of space, they should now be more sensitive to the (right-side) blue circle. But here's a different possibility: Perhaps these patients have a powerful bias to attend to the right side, and so initially they attend to the red circle. Once they have "locked in" to this circle,

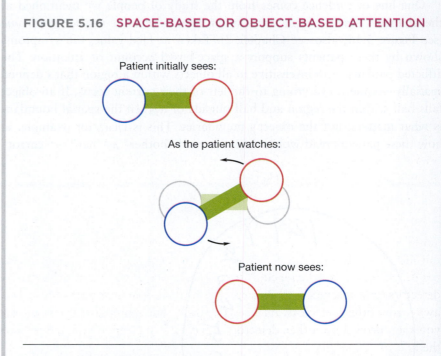

FIGURE 5.16   SPACE-BASED OR OBJECT-BASED ATTENTION

Patient initially sees:

As the patient watches:

Patient now sees:

Patients with unilateral neglect syndrome were much more sensitive to targets appearing within the red circle (on the right) and missed many of the targets appearing within the blue circle (on the left); this observation confirms their clinical diagnosis. Then, as the patients watched, the barbell-shaped frame rotated, so that now the red circle was on the left and the blue circle was on the right. After this rotation, participants were still more sensitive to targets in the red circle (now on the left), apparently focusing on this attended object even though it had moved to their "neglected" side.

however, it's the object, not the position in space, that defines their focus of attention. According to this view, if the barbell rotates, they will continue attending to the red circle (this is, after all, the focus of their attention), even though it now appears on their "neglected" side. This prediction turns out to be correct: When the barbell rotates, the patients' focus of attention seems to rotate with it (Behrmann & Tipper, 1999).

To describe these patients, therefore, we need a two-part account. First, the symptoms of neglect syndrome plainly reveal a spatially defined bias: These patients neglect half of space. But, second, once attention is directed toward a target, it's the target itself that defines the focus of attention; if the target moves, the focus moves with it. In this way, the focus of attention is object-based, not space-based. (For more on these issues, see Chen & Cave, 2006, 2019; Logie & Della Salla, 2005; Richard et al., 2008.)

And it's not just people with brain damage who show this complex pattern. People with intact brains also show a mix of space-based and object-based attention. We've already seen evidence for the spatial base: Studies of spatial attention show that participants can focus on a particular region of space *in preparation for* a stimulus (e.g., Posner et al., 1980). In this situation, the stimulus has not yet appeared; there is no object to focus on. Therefore, the attention must be spatially defined.

In other cases, though, attention is heavily influenced by object boundaries. For example, in some studies, participants have been shown displays with *visually superimposed* stimuli (e.g., Becklen & Cervone, 1983; Neisser & Becklen, 1975). Participants can usually pay attention to one of these stimuli and ignore the other. This selection cannot be space-based (because both stimuli are in the same place) and so must be object-based. (For more on the interplay between space-based and object-based attention, see Chen & Cave, 2019; Chen & Zelinsky, 2019; Cohen, 2012; Corbetta & Shulman, 2011.)

Feature Binding

We're almost finished with our discussion of selective attention, but there's one more topic to consider. So far, we've argued that expectation-based priming draws on a limited capacity system. Therefore, if you want to prime the detectors for a specific target or a specific location, you need to take resources away from other detectors. As a result, you'll be less prepared if it turns out you then need those other detectors—that is, if the input that arrives isn't the one you expected.

You might think, therefore, that you'd be better off if you had *un*limited capacity; then you could prime all of your detectors and so be ready for anything. However, this suggestion is wrong, because there's an important regard in which your limited capacity helps you. In Chapters 2 and 3, we emphasized that different analyses of the input all go on in the brain in parallel. In other words, you figure out the color of the object in front of you at the same time that you figure out its shape and its position. A separate step is then needed to put these elements together, so that you perceive a single, unified object. In other words, you need to solve the *binding problem*, so that you don't just perceive orange + round + close by + moving, but instead see the basketball sailing toward you.

Attention plays a key role in solving this problem. In other chapters, we discussed some of the evidence for this claim, including evidence from *visual search tasks*. We discussed these tasks in Chapter 4, when we mentioned that it's easy to search through a set of stimuli looking for a red object, for example, in a crowd of greens, or finding a round shape in a group of triangles. This was part of the evidence that *features* really do have priority in your perception.

Things are different, though, if you're searching for a target defined by a *combination* of features. Imagine, for example, that you're looking at a computer screen, and some of the lines in view are red and some are green. Some of the lines are horizontal and some are vertical. But there's just one line that's red *and* horizontal, and it's your job to find it. In this case, the time you'll need depends on how many items (in total) are in view; to put the matter simply, the larger the crowd to be searched through, the longer it takes.

To understand these results, imagine two participants, both hunting for the combination red + horizontal. One participant, shown in **Figure 5.17A**, is trying to take in the whole display. He'll quickly be able to catalogue all the features that are in view (because he's looking at all the inputs simultaneously), but he'll fail in his search for the red + horizontal combination: His catalogue of features tells him that both redness and horizontality are present, but the catalogue doesn't help him in figuring out if these features are linked or not. The observer in **Figure 5.17B**, in contrast, has focused his mental spotlight, so he's looking at just one stimulus at a time. This process is slower, because he'll have to examine the stimuli one by one, but this focusing gives the participant the information he needs: If, at any moment, he's only analyzing one item, he can be sure that the features he's detecting are all coming from that item. This tells him directly which features are linked to each other, and for this task (and for many other purposes as well), that's the key.

These ideas are essential for **feature integration theory** (Treisman & Gelade, 1980; for recent discussion, see Harris et al., 2020; Hochstein, 2020; Kristjánsson & Egeth, 2020; Wolfe, 2020). According to this conception, your early evaluation of the input does involve parallel processing of the entire display. This *preattentive stage* is efficient, but it puts you in a position akin to that of the observer in Figure 5.17A. The subsequent *focused attention stage*, in contrast, relies on mechanisms like those we've been discussing in the chapter. Specifically, expectation-based priming allows you to prepare the detectors for just one location, and this creates a processing advantage for stimuli in that location.

It seems, then, that the "limits" of attention are actually helpful for you. If you've primed the detectors for just one input, then you'll receive information from just that input. There will therefore be no risk of

FIGURE 5.17 THE COSTS AND BENEFITS OF SELECTION

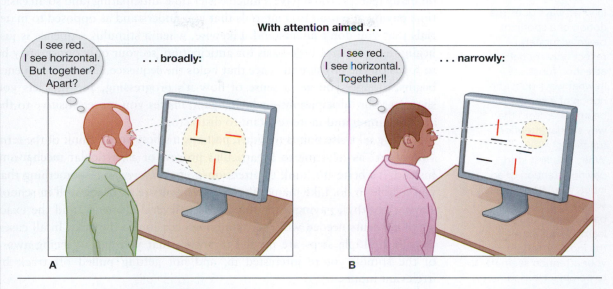

Focusing your attention involves a trade-off: If you focus your attention broadly, you can take in many inputs at once, and this is faster (because you don't have to search through the items one by one). But since you're taking in multiple inputs simultaneously, you may not know which feature belongs with which (Panel A). In contrast, if you focus your attention narrowly, you'll be slower in your search (because now you do have to search item-by-item), but with information coming from just one input, you'll know how the features are combined (Panel B).

confusion about where your information is coming from, and so (to continue our example) you'll know that the redness you're detecting and the orientation you're detecting are both aspects of the same object. In this way, the selectivity that's built into priming helps to "glue together" the various features of the input, moving you toward a solution to the binding problem.

Perceiving and the Limits on Cognitive Capacity: An Interim Summary

Let's pause to review. In some circumstances, you protect yourself from distraction by *inhibiting* the processing of specific unwanted inputs. More broadly, though, various mechanisms *facilitate* the processing of *desired* inputs. The key here is *priming*; and in most cases the priming depends on your ability to anticipate what the upcoming stimulus will be, so that you can make sure the processing pathway is ready for the stimulus when it arrives.

This priming makes you more responsive to the input when it does arrive, and this gives the input an advantage relative to other inputs. That advantage is what you want—so that you end up perceiving the desired input but don't perceive other inputs that happen to be present.

TEST YOURSELF

6. In what ways does the notion of a spotlight beam accurately reflect how spatial attention functions?

7. In what ways does the notion of a spotlight beam differ from the way spatial attention functions?

8. When you first start paying attention to an input, your attention seems to be space-based. Once you've learned a bit about the input, though, your attention seems to be object-based. How does this pattern fit with the idea that you pay attention by *anticipating* the input?

Notice, then, that your ability to pay attention often depends on your ability to anticipate the upcoming stimulus. This anticipation, in turn, depends on many factors. You'll have a much easier time anticipating (and so an easier time paying attention to) materials that you understand as opposed to materials that you don't understand. Likewise, when a stimulus sequence is just beginning, you have little basis for anticipation, so your only option may be to focus on the position in space that holds the sequence. Once the sequence begins, though, you get a sense of how it's progressing, and this lets you sharpen your anticipations—which, again, makes you more sensitive to the attended input and more resistant to distractors.

Putting all these points together, perhaps it's best not to think of the term "attention" as referring to a particular process or a particular mechanism. Instead, it's better to think of attention as an *achievement*—something that you're able to do. Like many other achievements (e.g., doing well in school, staying healthy), paying attention involves several elements, and the exact set of elements needed will vary from one occasion to the next. In all cases, though, multiple steps are needed to ensure that you end up being aware of the stimuli you're interested in, and not getting pulled off track by irrelevant inputs.

Divided Attention

So far in this chapter, we've emphasized situations in which you're trying to focus on a single input. If other tasks and other stimuli were on the scene, they were mere distractors. Sometimes, though, your goal is different: You want to "multitask"—that is, deal with multiple tasks, or multiple inputs, all at the same time. What can we say about this sort of situation—a situation involving **divided attention**?

Sometimes divided attention is easy. Almost anyone can walk and sing simultaneously; many people like to knit while they're holding a conversation or listening to a lecture. It's much harder, though, to do calculus homework while listening to a lecture; and trying to get your assigned reading done while watching TV is surely a bad bet. What lies behind this pattern? Why are some combinations difficult while others are easy?

Our first step toward answering these questions is already in view. We've proposed that perceiving requires resources that are in limited supply; the same is true for other tasks—remembering, reasoning, problem solving. They, too, require resources, and without these resources the processes cannot go forward. What are the resources? The answer includes a mix of things: certain mechanisms that do specific jobs, certain types of memory that hold on to information while you're working on it, energy supplies to keep the mental machinery going, and more. No matter what the resources are, though, a task will be possible only if you have the needed resources—just as a dressmaker can produce a dress only if he has the raw materials, the tools, the time needed, the energy to run the sewing machine, and so on.

All of this leads to an obvious proposal: You can perform concurrent tasks only if you have the resources needed for both. If the two tasks, when combined, require more resources than you've got, then divided attention will fail.

The Specificity of Resources

Imagine that you're hoping to read a novel while listening to an academic lecture. These tasks both involve the use of language, and so it seems likely that these tasks will have overlapping resource requirements. As a result, if you try to do the tasks at the same time, they're likely to *compete* for resources—and therefore this sort of multitasking will be difficult.

Now, think about the combination of *knitting* while listening to a lecture. These tasks are unlikely to interfere with each other. Even if all your language-related resources are in use for the lecture, this won't matter for knitting, because it's not a language-based task.

More broadly, the prediction here is that divided attention will be easier if the simultaneous tasks are very different from each other, because different tasks are likely to have distinct resource requirements. Resources consumed by Task 1 won't be needed for Task 2, so it doesn't matter for Task 2 that these resources are tied up in another endeavor.

Is this the pattern found in the research data? In an early study by Allport et al. (1972), participants heard a list of words presented through headphones into one ear, and their task was to shadow (i.e., repeat back) these words. At the same time, they were also presented with a second list. No immediate response was required to the second list, but later on, memory was tested for these items. In one condition, the second list (the memory items) consisted of words presented into the other ear, so the participants were hearing (and shadowing) a list of words in one ear while simultaneously hearing the memory list in the other. In another condition, the memory items were presented visually. That is, while the participants were shadowing one list of words, they were also seeing a different list of words on a screen before them. Finally, in a third condition, the memory items consisted of pictures, also presented on a screen.

These three conditions had the same requirements—shadowing one list while memorizing another. But the first condition (hear words + hear words) involved very similar tasks; the second condition (hear words + see words) involved less similar tasks; the third condition (hear words + see pictures), even less similar tasks. On the logic we've discussed, we should expect the most interference in the first condition and the least interference in the third. And that is what the data showed (see **Figure 5.18**).

The Generality of Resources

Similarity among tasks, however, is not the whole story. If it were, then we'd observe less and less interference as we consider tasks further and further apart. Eventually, we'd find tasks so different from each other that we'd

CAESAR THE MULTITASKER

Some writers complain about the hectic pace of life today and view it as a sad fact about the pressured reality of the modern world. But were things different in earlier times? More than 2,000 years ago, Julius Caesar was praised for his ability to multitask. (The term is new, but the capacity is not.) According to the Roman historian Suetonius, Caesar could write, dictate letters, and read at the same time. Even on the most important subjects, he could dictate four letters at once—and if he had nothing else to do, as many as seven letters at once. From a modern perspective, though, we can ask: Is any of this plausible? Perhaps it is—some people do seem especially skilled at multitasking (Just & Buchweitz, 2017; Redick et al., 2016), and maybe Caesar was one of those special people!

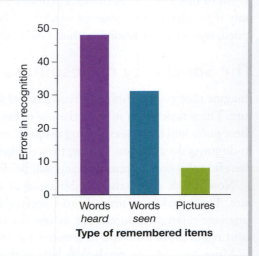

FIGURE 5.18   DIVIDED ATTENTION AMONG DISTINCT TASKS

Participants perform poorly if they are trying to shadow one list of words while *hearing* other words. They do somewhat better if shadowing while *seeing* other words. They do better still if shadowing while seeing *pictures*. In general, the greater the difference between two tasks, the easier it will be to combine the tasks.   (AFTER ALLPORT ET AL., 1972)

observe *no* interference at all between them. But that's not the pattern of the evidence.

Consider the common practice of talking on a cell phone while driving. When you're on the phone, the main stimulus information comes into your ear, and your primary response is by talking. In driving, the main stimulation comes into your eyes, and your primary response involves control of your hands on the steering wheel and your feet on the pedals. For the phone conversation, you're relying on language skills. For driving, you need spatial skills. Overall, it looks like there's little overlap in the specific demands of these two tasks, and so little chance that the tasks will compete for resources.

Data show, however, that driving and cell-phone use do interfere with each other. Even with a hands-free phone, drivers engaged in cell-phone conversations are more likely to be involved in accidents, more likely to overlook traffic signals, and slower to hit the brakes when they need to. (See Kunar et al., 2008; Levy & Pashler, 2008; Sanbonmatsu et al., 2016; Stothart et al., 2015; Strayer & Drews, 2007. For some encouraging data, though, on why phone-related accidents don't occur even more often, see Garrison & Williams, 2013; Medeiros-Ward et al., 2015.)

As a practical matter, therefore, talking on the phone while driving is a bad idea—even if the conversation is not particularly complex or fast paced (Kunar et al., 2018). In fact, by some estimates, the danger caused by driving while on the phone is comparable to the risk of driving while drunk. But, on the theoretical side, notice that the interference observed between driving and talking is interference between two hugely distinctive activities—a point that provides important information about the nature of the resource competition involved, and therefore the nature of mental resources.

Before moving on, we should mention that the results are somewhat different if the driver is talking to a passenger *in the car* rather than using the

FIGURE 5.19   CELL-PHONE USE AND DRIVING

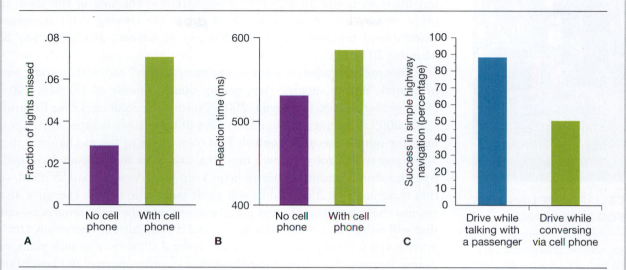

Many studies show that driving performance is impaired when the driver is on the phone (whether handheld or hands-free). While on the phone, drivers are more likely to miss a red light (Panel A) and are slower in responding to a red light (Panel B). Disruption is not observed, however, if the driver is conversing with a passenger rather than on the phone (Panel C). That's because passengers are likely to adjust their conversation to accommodate changes in driving—such as not speaking while the driver is navigating an obstruction.

(AFTER STRAYER & JOHNSTON, 2001)

phone. Conversations with passengers seem to cause little interference with driving (Drews et al., 2008; see **Figure 5.19**), and the reason is simple. If the traffic becomes complicated or the driver has to perform some tricky maneuver, the passenger can see this—either by looking out of the car's window or by noticing the driver's tension and focus. In these cases, passengers helpfully slow down their side of the conversation, which takes the load off of the driver, enabling the driver to focus on the road (Gaspar et al., 2014; Hyman et al., 2010).

Executive Control

The evidence is clear, then, that tasks as different as driving and talking compete with each other for some mental resource. But what is this resource, apparently needed for both verbal tasks and spatial ones, tasks with visual inputs and tasks with auditory inputs?

Actually, *multiple* resources are involved. Some resources serve (roughly) as an energy supply, drawn on by all tasks (e.g., Lavie, 2001, 2005; Lavie et al., 2009; Murphy et al., 2016). According to this perspective, tasks vary in the "load" they put on you, and the greater the load, the greater the interference with other tasks. In one study, drivers were asked to

CELL-PHONE DANGERS FOR PEDESTRIANS

It's not just driving that's disrupted by cell-phone use. Compared to pedestrians who aren't using a phone, pedestrians engaging in phone conversations tend to walk more slowly and more erratically, and they are less likely to check traffic before they cross a street. They're also less likely to notice things along their path. In one study, researchers observed pedestrians walking across a public square (Hyman et al., 2010). If a pedestrian was walking with a friend (and so engaged in a "live" conversation), there was a 71% chance the pedestrian would notice the unicycling clown just off the pedestrian's path. But if the pedestrian was on the phone (i.e., engaging in a telephonic conversation), the person had only a 25% chance of detecting the clown.

estimate whether their vehicle would fit between two parked cars (Murphy & Greene, 2016). When the judgment was difficult, participants were less likely to notice an unexpected pedestrian at the side of the road. In other words, higher perceptual load (from the driving task) increased inattentional blindness. (Also see Murphy & Greene, 2017; Murphy & Murphy, 2018.)

Other mental resources seem to be "mental tools" rather than some sort of mental "energy supply." (See, among others, Bourke & Duncan, 2005; Dehaene, Sergent, & Changeux, 2003; Norman & Shallice, 1986; Ruthruff et al., 2009; Vergauwe et al., 2010.) One of these tools is especially important: the mind's **executive control**. This term refers to the mechanisms that allow you to control your own thoughts, and these mechanisms have multiple functions. Executive control helps keep your current goals in mind, so that these goals (and not habit) will guide your actions. The executive also ensures that your mental steps are organized into the right sequence—one that will move you toward your goals. And if your current operations aren't moving you toward your goal, executive control allows you to shift plans, or change strategy. (For discussion of how the executive operates and how brain tissue enables executive function, see, among others, Engle, 2018; Karr et al., 2018; Miyake & Friedman, 2012; Shipstead et al., 2015; Vandierendonck et al., 2010.)

Executive control can only handle one task at a time, and this obviously puts limits on your ability to multitask—that is, to divide your attention. But executive control is also important when you're trying to do just a single task. Evidence comes from studies of people who have suffered damage to the prefrontal cortex (PFC), a brain area right behind the eyes. People with this damage (including Phineas Gage, whom we met in Chapter 2) can lead relatively normal lives, because in their day-to-day behavior they can often rely on habit or simply respond to prominent cues in their environment. With appropriate tests, though, we can reveal the disruption that results from frontal lobe damage. In one commonly used task, patients with frontal lesions are asked to sort a deck of cards into two piles. At the start, the patients have to sort the cards according to color; later, they need to switch strategies and sort according to the shapes shown on the cards. The patients have enormous difficulty in making this shift and continue to sort by color, even though the experimenter tells them again and again that they're placing the cards on the wrong piles (Goldman-Rakic, 1998). This is referred to as a **perseveration error,** a tendency to produce the same response over and over even when it's plain that the task requires a change in the response.

These patients also show a pattern of **goal neglect**—failing to organize their behavior in a way that moves them toward their goals. When one patient was asked to copy **Figure 5.20A**, the patient produced the drawing shown in **Figure 5.20B**. The copy preserves features of the original, but it seems that the patient drew the copy with no particular plan in mind. The large rectangle that defines the shape was never drawn, and the diagonal lines

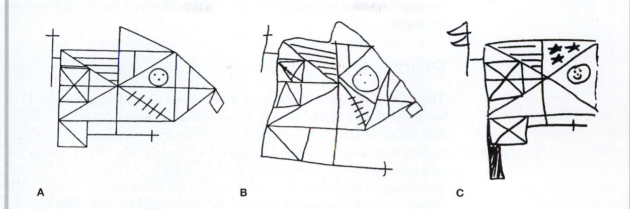

FIGURE 5.20 GOAL NEGLECT

A   B   C

Patients who had suffered damage to the prefrontal cortex were asked to copy the drawing in Panel A. One patient's attempt is shown in Panel B; the drawing is reasonably accurate but seems to have been drawn with no overall plan—for example, the large rectangle in the original, and the main diagonals, were created piecemeal rather than being used to organize the drawing. Another patient's attempt is shown in Panel C; this patient started to re-create the drawing but then got swept up in her own artistic impulses.

that organize the figure were drawn in a piecemeal fashion. Many details are correctly reproduced but weren't drawn in any sort of order; instead, these details were added whenever they happened to catch the patient's attention (Kimberg et al., 1998). Another patient, asked to copy the same figure, produced the drawing shown in **Figure 5.20C**. This patient started to draw the figure in a normal way, but then she got swept up in her own artistic impulses, adding stars and a smiley face (Kimberg et al., 1998). (For more on executive control, see Chapter 14.)

Divided Attention: An Interim Summary

Our consideration of *selective* attention drove us toward a several-part account, with one mechanism serving to block out unwanted distractors and other mechanisms promoting the processing of interesting stimuli. Now, in our discussion of *divided* attention, we again need several elements in our theory. Interference between tasks is increased if the tasks are similar to each other, presumably because similar tasks overlap in their processing requirements and make competing demands on mental resources that are specialized for that sort of task.

But interference can also be observed with tasks that are entirely different from each other—such as driving and talking on a cell phone. Therefore, our account needs to include resources that are quite general in their use and needed for a wide range of tasks. There are several of these general resources:

TEST YOURSELF

9. Why is it easier to divide attention between very different activities (e.g., knitting while listening to a lecture) than it is to divide attention between more similar activities?

10. What is executive control, and why does it create limits on your ability to divide your attention between two simultaneous tasks?

an energy supply needed for mental tasks, executive control, and others as well. No matter what the resource, though, the key principle will be the same: Tasks will interfere with each other if their combined demand for a resource is greater than the amount available—that is, if the demand exceeds the supply.

Practice

There's no question that talking on a cell phone while driving is risky. Even so, for a skilled driver, this bit of multitasking seems doable as long as the driving is straightforward and the conversation is simple. (For a cautionary note about this point, though, see Kunar et al., 2018.) Things fall apart, though, if the conversation becomes complex or the driving becomes challenging. Engaged in deep conversation, the driver misses a turn; while maneuvering through an intersection, the driver suddenly stops talking.

The situation is entirely different, though, for a *novice* driver. For someone who's just learning to drive, driving is difficult all by itself, even on a straight road with no traffic. If we ask the novice to do anything else at the same time—whether it's talking on a cell phone or even listening to the radio—we put the driver (and other cars) at substantial risk. Why is this? Why are things so different after practice?

Practice Diminishes Resource Demand

We've said that mental tasks require resources, with the particular resources required being dependent on the nature of the task. Let's now add another claim: As a task becomes more practiced, it requires *fewer* resources, or perhaps it requires *less frequent* use of these resources.

What causes this decrease? Consider executive control. There's little need for this control if you rely on habit or routine in performing a task. Early in practice, though, when a task is new, you haven't formed any relevant habits yet, so you have no habits to fall back on. As a result, executive control is needed all the time. Once you've done the task over and over, though, you do acquire a repertoire of suitable habits, and so the demand for executive control decreases. (For a glimpse of the neural basis of this shift, see Servant et al., 2018.)

How will this matter? We've already said that tasks interfere with each other if their combined resource demand is greater than the amount of resources available. Interference is less likely, therefore, if the "cognitive cost" of a task is low. In that case, you'll have an easier time accommodating the task within your "resource budget." And we've now added the idea that the resource demand (the "cost") will be lower after practice than before. Therefore, it's no surprise that practice makes divided attention easier—enabling the skilled driver to continue chatting with her passenger as they cruise down the highway, even though this combination is hopelessly difficult for the novice driver.

At the start of this chapter, we refer to common experiences like this one: You're trying to read a book—perhaps an assignment for one of your courses. You're in a public place, though, and two people nearby are chatting with each other. You have no interest in what they're talking about, and you really need to get through your reading assignment. But, no matter how hard you try, you find yourself unable to ignore their conversation, so your reading doesn't get done. What's going on here? Why can't you control what you're paying attention to?

Think about the mechanisms that allow you to pay attention. When you're reading or listening to something, you do what you can to anticipate the upcoming input, and that anticipation lets you prime the relevant detectors so that they'll be ready when the input arrives. As a result, the input falls onto "prepared" detectors and so you're more sensitive to the input—more likely to notice it, more likely to process it.

In contrast, you won't try to anticipate inputs you don't care about. With no anticipation, therefore, the input falls on unprepared detectors. You've done nothing to make yourself ready for these inputs, and so you remain relatively insensitive to them, just as you wish.

Now think about the situation with which we began. Perhaps you're trying to read something challenging. You'll therefore have some difficulty anticipating how the passage will unfold—what words or phrases will be coming up. Therefore, you'll have little basis for priming the soon-to-be-needed detectors, and so you won't be especially sensitive to the input when it arrives.

What about the conversation you're overhearing and hoping to ignore? Maybe it's unfolding according to a familiar script—for example, the people behind you on the bus, or on the other side of the room, are discussing romance or a popular movie. In this setting, with almost no thought you'll easily anticipate where this distractor conversation is going, and the anticipation will prime the relevant nodes in your mind, making you more sensitive to the input—the opposite of what you want.

Part of our explanation, then, lies in ease of anticipation. That's why you'll probably avoid distraction if the material you're trying to read is something you can anticipate (and so prime yourself for) and if the irrelevant conversation involves content you can't easily anticipate. In the extreme, imagine that the irrelevant conversation is in some foreign language that you don't speak; here, because there's no basis for anticipation, the distraction will be minimal.

But we also need another element in our explanation. Most people aren't distracted if they try to read while music is playing in the room or if there are traffic noises in the background. Why don't these (potential) distractors cause problems? Here, the key is resource competition. Reading a book and hearing a conversation both involve language, so these activities draw on the same mental resources and compete for those resources. But reading a book and hearing music (especially instrumental music) draw on different mental resources, so those activities don't compete for resources.

Automaticity

With practice in a task, then, the need for executive control is diminished, and we've mentioned one benefit of this: Your control mechanisms are available for other chores, allowing you to divide your attention in ways that would have been impossible before practice. This gain, however, comes at a price. With sufficient practice, task performance can go forward with *no* executive control, and so the performance is essentially *not controlled*. This can create a setting in which the performance goes forward "on auto-pilot"—and therefore goes forward, once triggered, whether you like it or not.

Psychologists use the term **automaticity** to describe tasks that are well practiced and involve little (or no) control. (For a classic statement, see Shiffrin & Schneider, 1977; also Moors, 2016; Moors & De Houwer, 2006.) The often-mentioned example is an effect known as **Stroop interference**. In the classic demonstration of this effect, study participants are shown a series of words and asked to name aloud the color of the ink used for each word. The trick, though, is that the words themselves are color names. So people might see the word "BLUE" printed in green ink and would have to say "green" out loud, and so on (see **Figure 5.21**; Stroop, 1935).

This task turns out to be extremely difficult. There's a strong tendency to read the printed words themselves rather than to name the ink color, and people make many mistakes in this task. Presumably, this reflects the fact that word recognition, especially for college-age adults, is enormously well practiced and therefore can proceed automatically. (For more on these issues, including debate about what exactly automaticity involves, see Besner et al., 2016; Engle & Kane, 2004; Labuschagne & Besner, 2015; Moors, 2016.)

Where Are the Limits?

Let's once again summarize where we are. Two simple ideas are key: First, tasks require resources, and second, you can't "spend" more resources than you have. These claims are central for almost everything we've said about selective and divided attention.

As we've seen, though, there are different types of resources, and the exact resource demand of a task depends on several factors. The nature of the task matters, of course, so that the resources required by a verbal task (e.g., reading) are different from those required by a spatial task (e.g., remembering a shape). The novelty of the task and the amount of flexibility the task requires also matter. Connected to this, *practice* matters, with well-practiced tasks requiring fewer resources.

What, then, sets the limits on divided attention? When can you do two tasks at the same time, and when not? The answer varies, case by case. If two tasks make competing demands on task-specific resources, the result will be interference. If two tasks make competing demands on task-general resources (the energy supply or executive control), then here, too, the result will be interference.

FIGURE 5.21   STROOP INTERFERENCE

Column A	Column B
ZYP	RED
QLEKF	BLACK
SUWRG	YELLOW
XCIDB	BLUE
WOPR	RED
ZYP	GREEN
QLEKF	YELLOW
XCIDB	BLACK
SUWRG	BLUE
WOPR	BLACK

As rapidly as you can, name out loud the colors of the *ink* in Column A. (You'll say, "black, green," and so on.) Next, do the same for Column B—again, naming out loud the colors of the ink. You'll probably find it much easier to do this for Column A, because in Column B you experience interference from the automatic habit of reading the words.

For these and other reasons, it again seems like we need a multipart theory of attention, with performance limited by different factors in different settings. This perspective draws us back to a claim we've made several times in this chapter: Attention cannot be thought of as a skill or a mechanism. Instead, attention is an achievement—an achievement of performing multiple activities simultaneously or an achievement of successfully avoiding distraction when you want to focus on a single task. And this achievement rests on an intricate base, so that many elements contribute to your ability to attend.

Finally, we have discussed various limits on human performance—that is, limits on how much you can do at any one time. How rigid are these limits? We've discussed the improvements in divided attention that are made possible by practice, but are there boundaries on what practice can accomplish? Can you gain new resources or find new ways to accomplish a task in order to avoid the bottleneck created by a limited resource? Some evidence indicates that the answer may be yes; if so, many of the

TEST YOURSELF

11. Why does practice decrease the resource demand of a task?

12. Why does practice create a situation in which you can lose control over your own mental steps?

claims made in this chapter must be understood as claims about what is usual, not about what is *possible*. (See Hirst et al., 1980; Spelke et al., 1976. For a neuroscience perspective, see Just & Buchweitz, 2017.) With this, some traditions in the world—Buddhist meditation traditions, for example—claim it's possible to *train* attention so that one has better control over one's mental life. How do these claims fit into the framework we've developed in this chapter? These are issues in need of exploration, and in truth, what's at stake here is a question about the boundaries on human potential, making these issues of deep interest for future researchers to pursue.

COGNITIVE PSYCHOLOGY AND TECHNOLOGY

"virality"

On the Internet and elsewhere, some topics and some bits of information seem to grab your attention. Then, once you've seen this new information, you may feel compelled to share it—by posting it on Facebook or retweeting it. And if other people react in the same way that you did, soon this information will have gone viral—and spread all over the world.

But what sorts of things, on the Internet and elsewhere, grab your attention, and so what sorts of things are likely to go viral? The answer surely has many parts, but two broad themes are important: First, information that might matter to you *emotionally* is likely to seize your attention. Second (and related), information with *moral* content often grabs your attention, because issues of morality (things that you consider good, and things that you consider bad or even evil) are likely central to your view of the world. In addition, your views of morality provide a key point of connection to groups that share your values, and your membership in these groups is likely important to you. This provides another reason why you're likely to focus on information with moral content.

How do these factors matter for the way people react to, and share, information on the Internet? A recent series of studies examined this issue (Brady et al., 2020). One step of this research relied on a procedure in which a series of words was presented in rapid succession, and participants had to report, at the end of the series, the two words that were in a different color from the rest. We know from prior studies that if the two target words are spaced far enough apart in the series, participants reliably spot both of them. But if the second target arrives in the series soon after the first, participants often miss it. Researchers describe this pattern as an "attentional blink," on the idea that right after the first target, participants seem to "blink" briefly and miss the second target if it arrives during this blink.

As a variant on this procedure, though, researchers in the Brady et al. study sometimes used words with a moral tone (*church, holy, pure*) for the second target, and sometimes used words with emotional tone (*weep, sad, afraid*). And sometimes the second target was a word that had both moral and emotional content (*hate, shame, ruin*). The question of interest was whether these words would be seen despite the attentional blink—that is, whether the words would grab the attention of participants who (because of the blink) were at that moment less attentive.

The results showed that the use of moral words as the second target did decrease the blink effect, and words that were emotional did so even more. Apparently, then, even in circumstances in which you're less attentive, these words grab your attention. But does this pattern in the laboratory tell us anything about social media? Think about a setting in which you're scanning through a list of posts on your favorite social media site. As your eyes run down the list, some posts grab your attention; might this pattern be linked to the results just described?

To explore this issue, the authors carried their research a step further: They examined the lab data word-by-word, asking which words were especially effective in "getting past" the attentional blink; in other words, how effective was each word at capturing attention? They then scrutinized a large collection of Twitter conversations, searching for tweets that used the words already tested in the lab. This enabled the researchers to estimate the "attention capture" strength of each tweet, using the lab measurements already available for that tweet's individual words. And now the bottom line: The greater the attention capture of the tweet (again: assessed through measurements of the words in the lab), the more likely the tweet was to be retweeted.

Here, as always, we urge caution about drawing conclusions from a single study, especially one that is relatively new (so that follow-up work remains to be done). Note also that the Twitter study describes a correlation, with some uncertainty about cause-effect relationships. Even so, this study offers an intriguing suggestion that we can use laboratory measures of attention to predict what sorts of content will be retweeted, and perhaps go viral, in the attention economy.

For more on this topic:

Brady, W. J., Gantman, A. P., & Van Bavel, J. J. (2020). Attentional capture helps explain why moral and emotional content go viral. *Journal of Experimental Psychology: General, 149*(4), 746–756.

Kozyreva, A., Lewandowsky, S., & Hertwig, R. (2020). Citizens versus the internet: Confronting digital challenges with cognitive tools. *Psychological Science in the Public Interest, 21*(3), 103–156.

chapter review

SUMMARY

• People are often oblivious to unattended inputs; they usually cannot tell if an unattended auditory input was coherent prose or random words, and they often do not detect unattended visual inputs, even though such inputs are right in front of their eyes. However, some aspects of the unattended inputs are detected. For example, people can report on the pitch of the unattended sound and whether it contained human speech or some other sort of noise. Sometimes they can also detect stimuli that are especially meaningful; some people, for example, hear their own name if it is spoken on the unattended channel.

• These results suggest that perception may require the commitment of mental resources, with some of these resources helping to prime the detectors needed for perception. This proposal is supported by studies of inattentional blindness—that is, studies showing that perception is markedly impaired if the perceiver commits no resources to the incoming stimulus information. The proposal is also supported by results showing that participants perceive more efficiently when they can anticipate the upcoming stimulus (and so can prime the relevant detectors). In many cases, the anticipation is spatial—if, for example, participants know that a stimulus is about to arrive at a particular location. This priming, however, seems to draw on a limited-capacity system, with the result that priming one stimulus or one position takes away resources that might be spent on priming some other stimulus.

• The ability to pay attention to certain regions of space has caused many researchers to compare attention to a spotlight beam, with the idea that stimuli falling "within the beam" are processed more efficiently than stimuli that fall "outside the beam." However, this spotlight analogy is potentially misleading. In many circumstances, people do seem to devote attention to identifiable regions of space, no matter what falls within those regions. In other circumstances, attention seems to be object-based, not space-based, and so people pay attention to specific objects, not specific positions.

• Perceiving seems to require the commitment of resources, and so do most other mental activities. This observation suggests an explanation for the limits on divided attention: It is possible to perform two tasks simultaneously only if the two tasks do not in combination demand more resources than are available. Some of the relevant mental resources, including executive control, are task-general, being required in a wide variety of mental activities. Other mental resources are task-specific, being required only for tasks of a certain type.

• Divided attention is influenced by practice, with the result that it is often easier to divide attention between familiar tasks than between unfamiliar tasks. In the extreme, practice may produce automaticity, in which a task seems to require virtually no mental resources but is also difficult to control. One proposal is that automaticity results from the fact that decisions are no longer needed for a well-practiced routine; instead, one can simply run off the entire routine, doing on this occasion just what one did on prior occasions.

KEY TERMS

selective attention (p. 144)
dichotic listening (p. 144)
attended channel (p. 144)
unattended channel (p. 144)
shadowing (p. 144)
filter (p. 146)
fixation target (p. 147)
inattentional blindness (p. 148)
change blindness (p. 149)
early selection hypothesis (p. 151)
late selection hypothesis (p. 151)
biased competition theory (p. 152)

spatial attention (p. 154)
limited-capacity system (p. 157)
mental resources (p. 157)
endogenous control of attention (p. 163)
exogenous control of attention (p. 164)
feature integration theory (p. 168)
divided attention (p. 170)
executive control (p. 174)
perseveration error (p. 174)
goal neglect (p. 174)
automaticity (p. 178)
Stroop interference (p. 178)

TEST YOURSELF AGAIN

1. What information do people reliably pick up from the *attended* channel? What do they pick up from the *unattended* channel?

2. How is inattentional blindness demonstrated? What situations outside of the laboratory seem to reflect inattentional blindness?

3. What evidence seems to confirm early selection? What evidence seems to confirm late selection?

4. What are the differences between the way that stimulus-based priming functions and the way that expectation-based priming functions?

5. Why is there a "cost" associated with being misled by expectation-based priming?

6. In what ways does the notion of a spotlight beam accurately reflect how spatial attention functions?

7. In what ways does the notion of a spotlight beam differ from the way spatial attention functions?

8. When you first start paying attention to an input, your attention seems to be space-based. Once you've learned a bit about the input, though, your attention seems to be object-based. How does this pattern fit with the idea that you pay attention by *anticipating* the input?

9. Why is it easier to divide attention between very different activities (e.g., knitting while listening to a lecture) than it is to divide attention between more similar activities?

10. What is executive control, and why does it create limits on your ability to divide your attention between two simultaneous tasks?

11. Why does practice decrease the resource demand of a task?

12. Why does practice create a situation in which you can lose control over your own mental steps?

THINK ABOUT IT

1. It's easy to keep your attention focused on materials that you *understand*. But if you try to focus on difficult material, your mind is likely to wander. Does the chapter help you in understanding why that is? Explain your response.

2. People claim that some forms of meditation training (including Buddhist meditation) can help those who do it become better at paying attention—staying focused and not suffering from distraction. Does the chapter help you in understanding why that might be? Explain your response.

DEMONSTRATIONS & APPLYING COGNITIVE PSYCHOLOGY ESSAYS

For demonstrations of key concepts in cognitive psychology, take a look at the Online Demonstrations. To explore more of the practical applications of cognitive psychology in themed essays, visit the online reader.

Online Demonstrations

- Demonstration 5.1: Shadowing
- Demonstration 5.2: Color-Changing Card Trick
- Demonstration 5.3: The Control of Eye Movements
- Demonstration 5.4: Automaticity and the Stroop Effect
- Demonstration 5.5: Meditation Exercise

Online Applying Cognitive Psychology Essays

- Cognitive Psychology and Education: ADHD
- Cognitive Psychology and Health: Inattentional Blindness in Medicine
- Cognitive Psychology and the Law: Guiding the Formulation of New Laws
- Cognitive Psychology and the Law: What Do Witnesses Pay Attention To?

ZAPS COGNITION LABS

Go to ZAPS online cognition labs to conduct hands-on experiments on key concepts.

INQUIZITIVE

It's time to complete your study experience! Go to InQuizitive to practice actively with this chapter's concepts and get personalized feedback along the way.

part 3

Memory

As you move through life, you encounter new facts, gain new skills, and have new experiences, so that later on you know things and can do things that you couldn't know or do before. How do these changes happen? How do you get new information into your memory, and then how do you retrieve this information when you need it? And how much trust can you put in this process? Why, for example, do people sometimes *not* remember things (including important things)? And why are memories sometimes *wrong*—so that in some cases you remember an event one way, but a friend remembers things differently?

We'll tackle all these issues in this section, and they will lead us to theoretical claims and practical applications. We'll offer suggestions, for example, about how students should study their class materials to maximize retention, and also what students can do later so that they'll hold on to what they learned at some earlier point.

In our discussion, several themes will emerge again and again. One theme concerns the active nature of learning: We'll see that passive exposure to information, with no intellectual engagement, leads to poor memory. From this base, we'll consider why some forms of engagement lead to especially good memory but other forms do not.

A second theme concerns the role of memory connections. In Chapter 6, we'll see that learning involves the creation of connections, and the more connections formed, the better the learning. In Chapter 7, we'll argue that these connections serve as "retrieval paths"—paths that, you hope, will lead you from your memory search's starting point to the information you're trying to recall. As we'll see, this idea has implications for when you will remember a previous event and when you won't.

Chapter 8 then explores a different aspect of the connections idea: Memory connections can actually be a source of memory errors, and we'll discuss what you can do to minimize error and to improve the completeness and accuracy of your recollection.

chapter **6**

The Acquisition of Memories and the Working-Memory System

what if... Clive Wearing is an accomplished scholar of Renaissance music. But at age 47 a virus damaged his brain, leaving him with profound amnesia. He is still articulate and intelligent, and still able to play music and conduct. But ever since the viral infection, he's been unable to form new memories. He can't recall any of the experiences he's had in the years since he suffered the brain damage. He can't even remember events that happened just moments ago, with a bizarre result: Every few minutes, Wearing realizes he can't recall anything from a few seconds back, and he concludes that he must have just woken up. He grabs his diary and writes "8:31 a.m.: Now I am really, completely awake." A short while later, though, he again realizes he can't recall the last seconds, and decides that *now* he has just woken up. He picks up his diary to record this event and immediately sees his previous entry. Puzzled, he crosses it out and replaces it with "9:06 a.m.: Now I am perfectly, overwhelmingly awake." But then the process repeats, and so this entry, too, gets scribbled out and a new entry reads "9:34 a.m.: Now I am superlatively, actually awake."

Alongside of this massive disruption, though, Wearing's love for his wife, Deborah, has not in any way been diminished by his amnesia. But here, too, the memory loss has powerful effects. Each time Deborah enters his room—even if she's been away just a few minutes—he races to embrace her as though it's been countless months since they last met. If asked directly, he has no recollection of her previous visits—including a visit that happened just minutes earlier.

We met a different case of amnesia in Chapter 1—patient H.M. He, too, was unable to recall his immediate past—and the many problems this produced included an odd sort of disorientation: If you were smiling at him, was it because you'd just said something funny? Or because he'd said something embarrassing? Or had you been smiling all along? As H.M. put it, "Right now, I'm wondering. Have I done or said anything amiss? You see, at this moment, everything looks clear to me, but what happened just before? That's what worries me" (Milner, 1970, p. 37; also see Corkin, 2013).

Cases like these remind us how profoundly our memories shape our everyday lives. But these cases also raise many questions: Why is it that Wearing still remembers who his wife is? Why did H.M. still remember his young years, even though he couldn't remember what he said five

A

B

CLIVE WEARING

Clive Wearing (shown here with his wife) developed profound amnesia as a result of viral encephalitis and now seems to have only a moment-to-moment consciousness. With no memory at all of what he was doing just seconds ago, he is often convinced he just woke up, and he repeatedly writes in his diary, "Now perfectly awake (1st time)." On the diary page shown here, he has recorded his thought, at 5:42 a.m., as his "1st act" because he has no memory of any prior activity. Soon after, though, he seems to realize again that he has no memory of any earlier events, and so he scribbles out the entry and now records that his bath is his "1st act." The sequence repeats over and over, with Wearing never recalling what he did before his current activity, and so he records act after act as his "first."

- We begin the chapter with a discussion of the broad architecture of memory. We then turn to a closer examination of one component of this architecture: working memory.

- We emphasize the active nature of working memory—activity that is especially evident when we discuss working memory's "central executive," a mental resource that serves to order, organize, and control our mental lives.

- The active nature of memory is also evident in the process of *rehearsal*. Rehearsal is effective only if the person engages the materials in some way; this is reflected, for example, in the contrast between deep processing (which leads to excellent memory) and mere maintenance rehearsal (which produces virtually no memory benefit).

- Activity during learning appears to establish *memory connections*, which can serve as retrieval routes when it comes time to remember the target material. For complex material, the best way to establish these connections is to seek to understand the material; the better the understanding, the better the memory will be.

minutes earlier? We'll tackle questions like these in this chapter and the next two.

Acquisition, Storage, and Retrieval

How does new information—whether it's a friend's phone number or a fact you hope to memorize for the bio exam—become established in memory? Are there ways to learn that are particularly effective? Then, once information is in storage, how do you locate it and "reactivate" it later? And why does searching through memory sometimes fail—so that, for example, you forget the name of that great restaurant downtown (but then remember the name when you're midway through a mediocre dinner someplace else)?

In tackling these questions, there's a logical way to organize our inquiry. Before there can be a memory, you need to gain, or "acquire," some new information. Therefore, **acquisition**—the process of gaining information and placing it into memory—should be our first topic. Then, once you've acquired this information, you need to hold it in memory until the information is needed. We refer to this as the **storage** phase. Finally, you *remember*. In other words, you somehow locate the information in the vast warehouse that is memory and you bring it into active use; this is called **retrieval**.

This organization seems logical; it fits, for example, with the way most "electronic memories" (e.g., computers) work. Information ("input") is provided to a computer (the acquisition phase). The information then resides in some dormant form, generally on the hard drive or perhaps in the cloud (the storage phase). Finally, the information can be brought back from this dormant form, often via a search process that hunts through the disk (the retrieval phase). And there's nothing special about the computer comparison here; "low-tech" information storage works the same way. Think about a file drawer—information is acquired (i.e., filed), rests in this or that folder, and then is retrieved.

Guided by this framework, we'll begin our inquiry by focusing on the acquisition of new memories, leaving discussion of storage and retrieval for later. We'll start with a simple model, emphasizing data collected largely in the 1970s. We'll then use this as the framework for examining more recent research, adding refinements to the model as we proceed.

The Route into Memory

For many years, theorizing in cognitive psychology focused on the flow of information through various "information-processing stages." One proposal was offered by Waugh and Norman (1965). Refinements were added by Atkinson and Shiffrin (1968), and their version of the proposal came to be known as the **modal model. Figure 6.1** shows a simplified depiction of this model.

Updating the Modal Model

According to the modal model, when information first arrives, it is stored briefly in **sensory memory**. This form of memory holds on to the input in "raw" sensory form—an *iconic memory* for visual inputs and an *echoic memory* for auditory inputs. A process of selection and interpretation then moves the information into **short-term memory**—the place where you hold information while you're working on it. Some of the information is then transferred into *long-term memory*, a much larger and more permanent storage place.

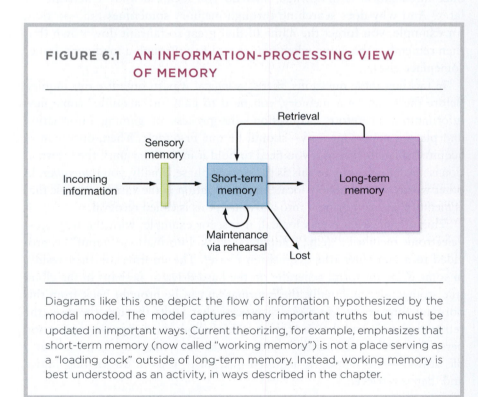

FIGURE 6.1   AN INFORMATION-PROCESSING VIEW OF MEMORY

Diagrams like this one depict the flow of information hypothesized by the modal model. The model captures many important truths but must be updated in important ways. Current theorizing, for example, emphasizes that short-term memory (now called "working memory") is not a place serving as a "loading dock" outside of long-term memory. Instead, working memory is best understood as an activity, in ways described in the chapter.

This proposal captures some important truths, but it needs to be updated in several ways. First, the idea of "sensory memory" plays a smaller role in current theorizing, so modern discussions of perception (like our discussion in Chapters 2 and 3) often make no mention of this memory. (For discussion of *visual* sensory memory, though, see Cappiello & Zhang, 2016; Pratte, 2018.) Second, most modern proposals use the term **working memory**, rather than "short-term memory," to emphasize the function of this memory. Ideas or thoughts in this memory are currently activated, currently being thought about, and so they're the ideas you're currently *working on*. **Long-term memory (LTM)**, in contrast, is the vast repository that contains all of your knowledge and beliefs—most of which you aren't thinking about (i.e., aren't working on) at this moment.

The modal model also needs updating in another way. Pictures like the one in Figure 6.1 suggest that working memory is a *storage place*, sometimes described as the "loading dock" just outside of the long-term memory "warehouse." The idea is that information has to "pass through" working memory on the way into longer-term storage. Likewise, the picture implies that memory retrieval involves the "movement" of information out of storage and back into working memory.

In contrast, contemporary theorists don't think of working memory as a "place" at all. Instead, working memory is simply the name we give to a *status*. When we say that ideas are "in working memory," we simply mean that these ideas are currently activated and being worked on by a specific set of operations.

We'll have more to say about this modern perspective before we're through. (For more on the evolution of the modal model, see Baddeley et al., 2019; Malmberg et al., 2019; but also Oberauer et al., 2018.) It's important to emphasize, though, that contemporary thinking preserves some key ideas from the modal model, including its claims about how working memory and long-term memory differ from each other. Let's identify those differences.

First, working memory is limited in size; long-term memory is enormous. In fact, long-term memory has to be enormous, because it contains all of your knowledge—including specific knowledge (e.g., how many siblings you have) and more general themes (e.g., that water is wet, that Dublin is in Ireland, that unicorns don't exist). Long-term memory also contains all of your *episodic* knowledge—that is, your knowledge about events, including events early in your life as well as more recent experiences.

Second, getting information into working memory is easy. If you think about a particular idea or some other type of content, then you're "working on" that idea or content, and so this information—by definition—is now in your working memory. In contrast, we'll see later in the chapter that getting information into long-term memory often involves some work.

Third, getting information out of working memory is also easy. Since (by definition) this memory holds the ideas you're thinking about right now, the information is already available to you. Finding information in long-term memory, in contrast, can sometimes be difficult and slow—and in some settings can fail completely.

W R T O
Y D S A
L M R E

ICONIC MEMORY

In a classic experiment (Sperling, 1960), participants viewed a grid like this one for just 50 ms. If asked to report all of the letters, participants could report just three or four of them. In a second condition, participants saw the grid and then immediately afterward heard a cue signaling which row they had to report. No matter which row they were asked about, participants could recall most of the row's letters. It seems, therefore, that participants could remember the entire display (in iconic memory) for a brief time and could "read off" the contents of any row when appropriately cued. The limitation in the report-all condition, then, came from the fact that iconic memory faded away before the participants could report on all of it.

Fourth, the contents of working memory are quite fragile. Working memory, we emphasize, contains the ideas you're thinking about right now. If your thoughts shift to a new topic, then new ideas will enter working memory, pushing out what was there a moment ago. Long-term memory, in contrast, isn't linked to your current thoughts, so it's much less fragile—information there remains in storage whether you're thinking about it right now or not.

Working Memory and Long-Term Memory: One Memory or Two?

Let's make these claims concrete by looking at some classic research findings. In many studies, researchers have asked participants to listen to a series of words, such as "bicycle, artichoke, radio, chair, palace." In a typical experiment, the list might contain 30 words and be presented at a rate of one word per second. Then, immediately after the last word is read, participants are asked to repeat back as many words as they can. They are free to report the words in any order they choose, and that's why this task is called a **free recall procedure**.

People usually remember 12 to 15 words in this test, in a consistent pattern. They're likely to remember the first few words on the list, something known as the **primacy effect**, and they're also likely to remember the last few words on the list, a **recency effect**. The resulting pattern is a U-shaped curve describing the relation between position within the series—or **serial position**—and the likelihood of recall (see **Figure 6.2**; Baddeley & Hitch, 1977; Glanzer & Cunitz, 1966; Murdock, 1962).

Explaining the Recency Effect

What produces this pattern? We've already said that working memory contains the material someone is *working on* at just that moment. In other words, this memory contains whatever the person is currently thinking about; and

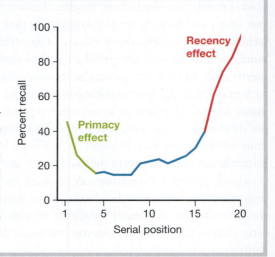

FIGURE 6.2 PRIMACY AND RECENCY EFFECTS IN FREE RECALL

Research participants in this study heard a list of 20 common words presented at a rate of one word per second. Immediately after hearing the list, the participants were asked to write down as many of the words on the list as they could recall. Participants had better recall for words at the beginning of the list (the primacy effect) and for words at the end of the list (the recency effect), compared to words in the middle of the list.

during the list presentation, the participants are obviously thinking about the words they're hearing. Therefore, it's these words that are in working memory. This memory, however, is limited in size, capable of holding only five or six words. Consequently, as participants try to keep up with the list presentation, they'll be placing the words *just heard* into working memory, and this action will bump the previous words out of working memory. As a result, as participants proceed through the list, their working memories will, at each moment, contain only the half dozen words that arrived most recently. Any words that arrived earlier than these will have been pushed out by later arrivals.

Of course, the last few words on the list don't get bumped out of working memory, because no further input arrives to displace them. Therefore, when the list presentation ends, those last few words stay in place. Moreover, our hypothesis is that materials in working memory are readily available—easily and quickly retrieved. When the time comes for recall, then, working memory's contents (the list's last few words) are accurately and completely recalled.

In short, the list's last few words are still in working memory when the list ends (because nothing has arrived to push out these items), and working memory's contents are easy to retrieve. This is the source of the recency effect.

Explaining the Primacy Effect

The primacy effect has a different source. We've suggested that it takes some work to get information into long-term memory (LTM), and it seems likely that this work requires some time and attention. So let's examine how participants allocate their attention to the list items.

As participants hear the list, they do their best to be good memorizers, and so when they hear the first word, they repeat it over and over to themselves ("bicycle, bicycle, bicycle")—a process known as **memory rehearsal**. When the second word arrives, they rehearse it, too ("bicycle, artichoke, bicycle, artichoke"). Likewise for the third ("bicycle, artichoke, radio, bicycle, artichoke, radio"), and so on through the list. Note, though, that the first few items on the list are privileged. For a brief moment, "bicycle" is the only word participants have to worry about, so it has 100% of their attention; no other word receives this privilege. When "artichoke" arrives a moment later, participants divide their attention between the first two words, so "artichoke" gets only 50% of their attention—less than "bicycle" got, but still a large share of the participants' efforts. When "radio" arrives, it has to compete with "bicycle" and "artichoke" for the participants' time, and so it receives only 33% of their attention.

Words arriving later in the list receive even less attention. Once six or seven words have been presented, the participants need to divide their attention among all these words, which means that each one receives only a small fraction of the participants' focus. As a result, words later in the list are rehearsed fewer times than words early in the list—a fact that can be confirmed simply by asking participants to rehearse out loud (Rundus, 1971).

This view of things leads immediately to our explanation of the primacy effect—that is, the observed memory advantage for the early list items. These early words didn't have to share attention with other words (because the other words hadn't arrived yet), so more time and more rehearsal were devoted to them than to any others. This means that the early words have a greater chance of being transferred into LTM—and so a greater chance of being recalled after a delay. That's what shows up in the data as the primacy effect.

Testing Claims about Primacy and Recency

In the procedure we've been discussing, participants recite what they remember immediately after the list's end. What happens if, instead, we delay recall by asking participants to perform some other task before they report the list items—for example, asking them to count backward by threes, starting from 201? Participants do this for just 30 seconds, and then they try to recall the list.

We've hypothesized that at the end of the list presentation, working memory still contains the list's last few items. But the task of counting backward itself requires working memory (e.g., to keep track of where you are in the counting sequence). Therefore, this chore will *displace* working memory's current contents; that is, it will bump the last few list items out of working memory. As a result, these items won't benefit from the swift and easy retrieval that working memory allows, and, of course, that retrieval was the presumed source of the recency effect. On this basis, the simple chore of counting backward, even if only for a few seconds, will eliminate the recency effect. In contrast, the counting backward should have no impact on recall of the items earlier in the list: These items are (by hypothesis) being recalled from long-term memory, not working memory, and there's no reason to think the counting task will interfere with LTM. (That's because LTM, unlike working memory, isn't dependent on current activity.)

Figure 6.3 shows that these predictions are correct. An activity interpolated, or inserted, between the list and recall essentially eliminates the recency effect, but it has no influence elsewhere in the list (Baddeley & Hitch, 1977; Glanzer & Cunitz, 1966; Postman & Phillips, 1965). In contrast, merely delaying the recall for a few seconds after the list's end, with no interpolated activity, has no impact. In this case, participants can continue rehearsing the last few items during the delay and so can maintain them in working memory. With no new materials coming in, nothing pushes the recency items out of working memory, and so, even with a delay, a normal recency effect is observed.

We'd expect a different outcome, though, if we manipulate long-term memory rather than working memory. In this case, the manipulation should affect all performance *except* for recency (which, again, is dependent on working memory, not LTM). For example, what happens if we slow down the presentation of the list? Now, participants will have more time to spend on all of the list items, increasing the likelihood of transfer into more permanent storage. This should improve recall for all items coming from LTM. Working

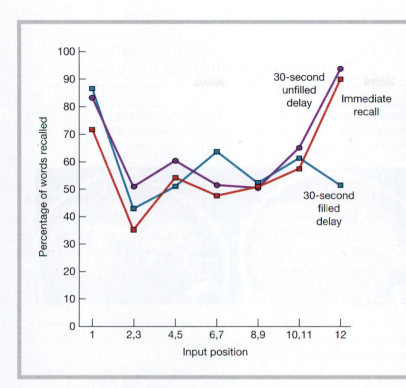

FIGURE 6.3   THE IMPACT OF INTERPOLATED ACTIVITY ON THE RECENCY EFFECT

With immediate recall (the red line in the figure), or if recall is delayed by 30 seconds with no activity during the delay (the purple line), a recency effect is detected. In contrast, if participants spend 30 seconds on some other activity between hearing the list and the subsequent memory test (the blue line), the recency effect is eliminated. This interpolated activity has no impact on the pre-recency portion of the curve (i.e., the portion of the curve other than the last few positions).

memory, in contrast, is limited by its size, not by ease of entry or ease of access. Therefore, the slower list presentation should have no influence on working-memory performance. Research results confirm these claims: Slowing the list presentation improves retention of all the pre-recency items but does not improve the recency effect (see **Figure 6.4**).

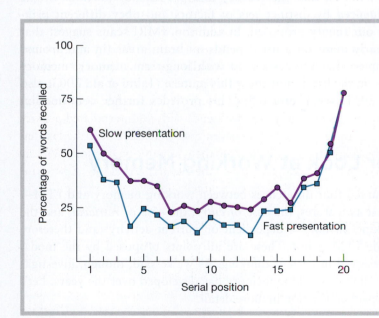

FIGURE 6.4   RATE OF LIST PRESENTATION AND THE SERIAL-POSITION EFFECT

Presenting the to-be-remembered materials at a slower rate improves pre-recency performance but has no effect on recency. The slow presentation rate in this case was 9 seconds per item; the faster rate was 3 seconds per item.

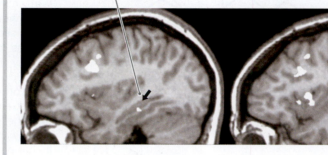

FIGURE 6.5 BRAIN REGIONS SUPPORTING WORKING MEMORY AND LONG-TERM MEMORY

Retrieval from long-term memory specifically activates the hippocampus.

Retrieval from working memory specifically activates the perirhinal cortex.

We can confirm the distinction between working and long-term memory with fMRI scans. These scans suggest that memory for early items on a list depends on brain areas (in and around the hippocampus) that are associated with long-term memory; memory for later items on the list do not show this pattern. (AFTER TALMI ET AL., 2005)

TEST YOURSELF

2. List the four ways in which (either in the modal model or in more recent views) working memory is different from long-term storage.

3. How is the primacy effect usually explained? How is the recency effect usually explained?

It seems, therefore, that the recency and pre-recency portions of the curve are influenced by distinct sets of factors and obey different principles, just as our theory proposed. In addition, fMRI scans suggest that memory for early items on a list depends on brain areas (in and around the hippocampus) that are associated with long-term memory; memory for later items on the list do not show this pattern (Talmi et al., 2005; also Eichenbaum, 2017; see **Figure 6.5**). This provides further confirmation for our model.

A Closer Look at Working Memory

Earlier, we counted four differences between working memory and LTM—the *size* of these two stores, the *ease of entry*, the *ease of retrieval*, and the fact that working memory is dependent on current activity (and therefore is *fragile*) while LTM is not. These are all points proposed by the modal model and preserved in current thinking. As we've said, though, investigators' understanding of working memory has developed over the years. Let's examine the newer conception in more detail.

The Function of Working Memory

Virtually all mental activities require the coordination of multiple pieces of information. Sometimes the relevant bits come into view one by one, so that you need to hold on to the early arrivers until the rest of the information is available, and only then weave all the bits together. Alternatively, sometimes the relevant bits are all in view at the same time—but you still need to hold on to them together, so that you can think about the relations and combinations. In either case, you'll end up with multiple ideas in your thoughts, all activated simultaneously, and thus several bits of information in the status we describe as "in working memory."

Framing things in this way makes it clear how important working memory is: You use it whenever you have multiple ideas in your mind, multiple elements that you're trying to combine or compare. Let's now add that people differ in the "holding capacity" of their working memories. Some people are able to hold on to (and work with) more elements, and some with fewer. How does this matter? To find out, we first need a way of *measuring* working memory's capacity, to determine if your memory capacity is above average, below, or somewhere in between. The procedure for obtaining this measurement, however, has changed over the years; looking at this change will help clarify what working memory *is* and what working memory *is for*.

Digit Span

For many years, the holding capacity of working memory was measured with a **digit-span task**. In this task, research participants hear a series of digits (e.g., "8, 3, 4") and must immediately repeat them back. If they do this successfully, they're given a slightly longer list (e.g., "9, 2, 4, 0"). If they can repeat this one without error, they're given a still longer list ("3, 1, 2, 8, 5"), and so on. The procedure continues until the participant starts to make errors—something that usually happens when the list contains more than seven or eight items. The number of digits a person can echo back without errors is referred to as that person's digit span.

Procedures such as this imply that working memory's capacity is typically around seven items—at least five and probably not more than nine. These estimates have traditionally been summarized by the statement that this memory holds **"7 plus-or-minus 2"** items (Chi, 1976; Dempster, 1981; Miller, 1956; Watkins, 1977).

If working memory can hold roughly seven items, though, what exactly is an "item"? Can people remember seven sentences as easily as seven words? Seven letters as easily as seven equations? In a classic paper, George Miller proposed that working memory holds 7 plus-or-minus 2 **chunks** (Miller, 1956). The term "chunk" doesn't sound scientific or technical, and that's useful because this informal terminology reminds us that a chunk doesn't hold a fixed quantity of information. Instead, Miller proposed, working memory holds 7 plus-or-minus 2 packages, and what those packages contain is largely up to the individual person.

The flexibility in how people "chunk" input can easily be seen in the span test. Imagine that we test someone's "letter span" rather than their "digit span," using the procedure already described. So the person might hear "R, L" and have to repeat this sequence back, and then "F, C, H," and so on. Eventually, let's imagine that the person hears a much longer list, perhaps one starting "H, A, P, T, R, O, S, L, U . . ." If the person thinks of these as individual letters, she'll only remember seven of them, more or less. But she might reorganize the list into "chunks" and, in particular, think of the letters as forming syllables ("HAP, TRO, SLU . . ."). In this case, she'll still remember 7 plus-or-minus 2 items, but the items are *syllables*, and by remembering the syllables she'll be able to report back at least a dozen letters and probably more.

How far can this process be extended? Chase and Ericsson (1982; Ericsson, 2003) studied a remarkable individual who happens to be a fan of track events. When he hears numbers, he thinks of them as finishing times for races. The sequence "3, 4, 9, 2," for example, becomes "3 minutes and 49.2 seconds, near world-record mile time." In this way, four digits become one chunk of information. This person can then retain 7 finishing times (7 chunks) in memory, and this can involve 20 or 30 digits! Better still, these chunks can be grouped into larger chunks, and these into even larger chunks. For example, finishing times for individual racers can be chunked together into heats within a track meet, so that, now, 4 or 5 finishing times (more than a dozen digits) become one chunk. With strategies like this and a lot of practice, this person has increased his apparent memory span from the "normal" 7 digits to 79 digits.

However, let's be clear that what has changed through practice is the person's chunking strategy, not the capacity of working memory itself. This is evident in the fact that when tested with sequences of letters, rather than numbers (so that he can't use his chunking strategy), this individual's memory span is a normal size—just 6 consonants. Thus, the 7-chunk limit is still in place for this man, even though (with numbers) he's able to make extraordinary use of these 7 slots.

Operation Span

Chunking provides one complication in our measurement of working memory's capacity. Another—and deeper—complication grows out of the very nature of working memory. Early theorizing about working memory, as we said, was guided by the modal model, and this model implies that working memory is something like a box in which information is stored or a location in which information can be displayed. The traditional digit-span test fits well with this idea. If working memory is like a box, then it's sensible to ask how much "space" there is in the box: How many slots, or spaces, are there in it? This is precisely what the digit span measures, on the idea that each digit (or each chunk) is placed in its own slot.

WORLD'S FASTEST MILE

When Chase and Ericsson conducted their classic studies, 3 minutes, 49.2 seconds was a bit slower than the record for the fastest mile. Now, some decades later, that record has been broken. In 1999, Hicham El Guerrouj of Morocco beat this time by more than 6 seconds. By the time you read this book, someone may have been even faster.

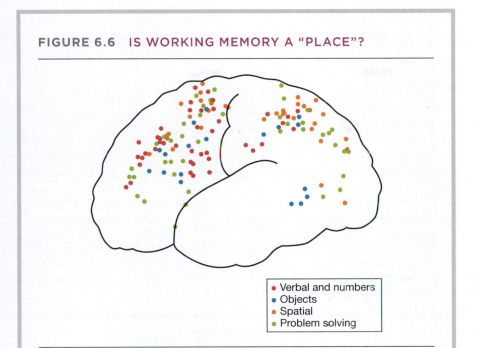

FIGURE 6.6   IS WORKING MEMORY A "PLACE"?

- ● Verbal and numbers
- ● Objects
- ● Spatial
- ● Problem solving

Modern theorists argue that working memory is not a place at all, but is instead the name we give for a certain set of mental activities. Consistent with this modern view, there's no specific location within the brain that serves as working memory. Instead, working memory is associated with a wide range of brain sites, as shown here.   (AFTER CABEZA & NYBERG, 2000)

We've suggested, though, that the modern conception of working memory is more dynamic—so that working memory is best thought of as a *status* (something like "currently activated") rather than as a *place*. (See, e.g., Christophel et al., 2017; also **Figure 6.6**.) On this basis, perhaps we need to rethink how we measure this memory's capacity—seeking a measure that reflects working memory's active operation.

Modern researchers therefore measure working memory's capacity in terms of **operation span**, a measure of this memory when it is "working." There are several ways to measure operation span, with the types differing in what "operation" they use (e.g., Bleckley et al., 2015; Chow & Conway, 2015). One type is *reading span*. To measure this span, a research participant might be asked to read aloud a series of sentences, like these:

Due to his gross inadequacies, his position as director was terminated abruptly.

It is possible, of course, that life did not arise on Earth at all.

Immediately after reading the sentences, the participant is asked to recall each sentence's final word—in this case, "abruptly" and "all." If she can do

FIGURE 6.7 DYNAMIC MEASURES OF WORKING MEMORY

$(7 \times 7) + 1 = 50$; dog
$(10/2) + 6 = 10$; gas
$(4 \times 2) + 1 = 9$; nose
$(3/1) + 1 = 5$; beat
$(5/5) + 1 = 2$; tree

Operation span can be measured in several different ways. In one procedure, participants must announce whether each of these "equations" is true or false, and then recall the words appended to each equation. If participants can do this with two equations, we ask them to do three; if they can do that, we ask them to try four. By finding out how far they can go, we measure their working-memory capacity.

this with these two sentences, she's asked to do the same task with a group of three sentences, and then with four, and so on, until the limit on her performance is located. This limit defines the person's **working-memory capacity**, or **WMC**. (For another way to measure operation span, see **Figure 6.7.**)

Let's think about what this task involves: storing materials (the ending words) for later use in the recall test, while simultaneously working with other materials (the full sentences). This juggling of processes, as the participant moves from one part of the task to the next, is exactly what working memory must do in day-to-day life. Therefore, performance in this test is likely to reflect the efficiency with which working memory will operate in more natural settings.

Is operation span a valid measure—that is, does it measure what it's supposed to? Our hypothesis is that someone with a higher operation span has a larger working memory. If this is right, then someone with a higher span should have an advantage in tasks that make heavy use of this memory. Which tasks are these? They're tasks that require you to keep multiple ideas active at the same time, so that you can coordinate and integrate various bits of information. So here's our prediction: People with a larger span (i.e., a greater WMC) should do better in tasks that require the coordination of different pieces of information.

Consistent with this claim, people with a greater WMC do have an advantage in tests of reasoning, assessments of reading comprehension, standardized academic tests (including the verbal SAT), and more. (See, e.g., Butler et al., 2011; Redick et al., 2016. For some complications, see Chow & Conway, 2015; Harrison et al., 2015; Kanerva & Kalakoski, 2016; Mella et al., 2015.)

These correlations between WMC and performance provide some indications about when it's helpful to have a larger working memory, which in turn helps us understand when and how working memory is used. In addition, it's important that these correlations are observed with the more active measure of working memory (operation span) but not with the more traditional (and more static) span measure. This point confirms the advantage of the more dynamic measures and strengthens the idea that we're now thinking about working memory in the right way: not as a passive storage box, but instead as a highly active information processor.

The Rehearsal Loop

Working memory's active nature is also evident in another way: in the actual structure of this memory. The key here is that working memory is actually a *system* with several components (Baddeley, 1986, 2012; Baddeley & Hitch, 1974; also see Logie & Cowan, 2015). At the center of the **working-memory system** is a set of processes we discussed in Chapter 5: the executive control processes that govern the selection and sequence of thoughts. In discussions of working memory, these processes have been playfully called the "central executive," as if there were a tiny agent embedded in your mind, running your mental operations. Of course, there is no agent, and the central executive is just a name we give to the set of mechanisms that do run the show.

The central executive is needed for the "work" in working memory; if you have to plan a response or make a decision, these steps require the executive. But in many settings, you need less than this from working memory. Specifically, there are settings in which you need to keep ideas in mind, not because you're analyzing them right now but because you're likely to need them soon. In this case, you don't need the executive. Instead, you can rely on the executive's "helpers," leaving the executive free to work on more difficult matters.

Let's focus on one of working memory's most important helpers, the **articulatory rehearsal loop**. To see how the loop functions, try reading the next few sentences while holding on to these numbers: "1, 4, 6, 3." Got them? Now read on. You're probably repeating the numbers over and over to yourself, rehearsing them with your inner voice. But this takes very little effort, so you can continue reading while doing this rehearsal. Nonetheless, the moment you need to recall the numbers (what were they?), they're available to you.

In this setting, the four numbers were maintained by working memory's rehearsal loop, and with the numbers thus out of the way, the central executive could focus on the processes needed for reading. That is the advantage of this system: With mere storage handled by the helpers, the executive is available for other, more demanding tasks.

How does the rehearsal loop work? To hold on to those numbers, you used **subvocalization**—silent speech—to launch the loop, and this production by the "inner voice" produced a representation of the numbers in the **phonological buffer**, a passive storage system used for holding a representation (essentially an "internal echo") of sound. In other words, you created an image in the "inner ear." This image started to fade away after a second or two, but you then subvocalized the numbers once again to create a new image, sustaining the material in this buffer. (For a glimpse of the biological basis for the "inner voice" and "inner ear," see **Figure 6.8**.)

Many lines of evidence confirm this proposal. For example, when people are holding information in working memory, they often make "sound-alike" errors: Having heard "F," they'll report back "S." When trying to remember the name "Tina," they'll slip and recall "Deena." The problem isn't that people mis-hear the inputs at the start; we know this because similar sound-alike confusions emerge if the inputs are presented *visually*. So, having seen "F," people are likely to report back "S"; they aren't likely in this situation to report back the similar-looking "E."

What produces this pattern? The cause lies in the fact that for this task people are relying on the rehearsal loop, which involves a mechanism (the

FIGURE 6.8   BRAIN ACTIVITY AND WORKING-MEMORY REHEARSAL

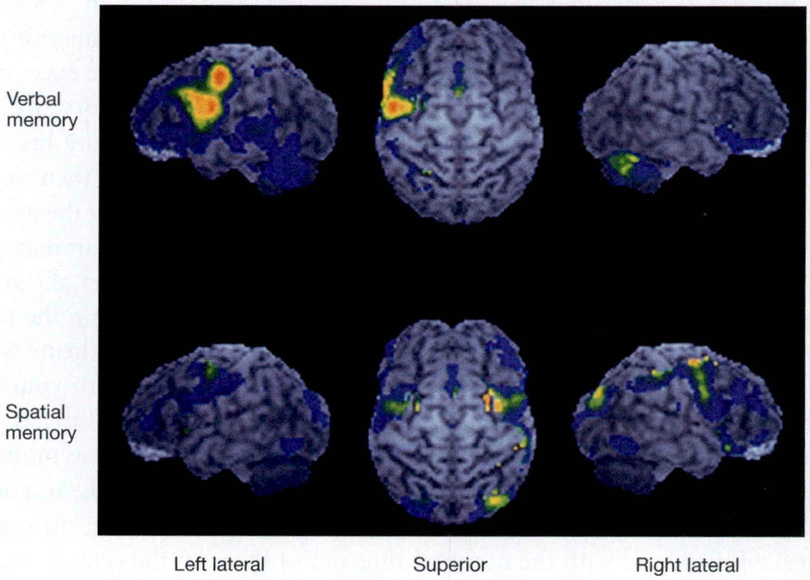

Verbal memory

Spatial memory

Left lateral   Superior   Right lateral

Color is used here as an indication of increased brain activity (measured in this case by positron emission tomography). When research participants are doing a verbal memory task (and using the articulatory loop), activation increases in areas ordinarily used for language production and perception. A very different pattern is observed when participants are doing a task requiring memory for spatial position. Notice, then, that the "inner voice" and "inner ear" aren't casual metaphors; instead, they involve mechanisms that are ordinarily used for overt speech and actual hearing.

(AFTER JONIDES, ET AL., 2005; ALSO SEE JONIDES ET AL., 2008)

"inner ear") that stores the memory items as (internal representations of) sounds. It's no surprise, therefore, that errors, when they occur, are shaped by this mode of storage.

As a test of this claim, we can ask people to take a span test while simultaneously saying "Tah-Tah-Tah" over and over, out loud. This **concurrent articulation task** obviously requires the mechanisms for speech production, and so these mechanisms are not available for other use, including subvocalization. (If you're directing your lips and tongue to produce the "Tah-Tah-Tah" sequence, you can't at the same time direct them to produce the sequence needed for the subvocalized materials.) By this logic, concurrent articulation blocks use of the rehearsal loop.

This manipulation has many effects. Let's start with measures of working memory's capacity (using the older *digit-span* procedure, as opposed to the more modern measure of *operation span*). In a digit-span test, people store some of the to-be-remembered items in the loop and other items via the central executive. (This is a poor use of the executive, underutilizing its talents, but that's okay here because the task doesn't require anything beyond mere storage.)

With concurrent articulation, though, the loop isn't available for use, so we're now measuring the capacity of working memory without the rehearsal loop. We should predict, therefore, that concurrent articulation, even though it's extremely easy, should cut memory span drastically. This prediction turns out to be correct. Span is ordinarily about seven items; with concurrent articulation, it drops by roughly a third—to around five items (Chincotta & Underwood, 1997; see **Figure 6.9**).

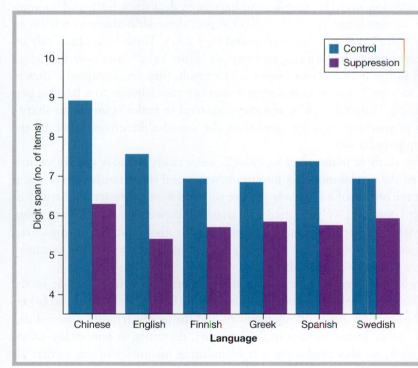

FIGURE 6.9   THE EFFECT OF CONCURRENT ARTICULATION ON SPAN

In the Control condition, participants were given a normal digit-span test. In the Suppression condition, participants were required to do concurrent articulation while taking the test. Concurrent articulation is easy, but it blocks use of the articulatory loop and consistently decreases memory span, from roughly seven items to five or so. And, plainly, this use of the articulatory loop is not an occasional strategy; instead, it can be found in a wide range of cultures and languages. (AFTER CHINCOTTA & UNDERWOOD, 1997)

With visually presented items, concurrent articulation should also eliminate the sound-alike errors. Repeatedly saying "Tah-Tah-Tah" blocks use of the articulatory loop, and it's in this loop, we've proposed, that the sound-alike errors arise. This prediction, too, is correct: With concurrent articulation and visual presentation of the items, sound-alike errors are largely eliminated.

The Working-Memory System

The working-memory system also includes other helpers in addition to the rehearsal loop, and these helpers substantially increase working memory's capacity—and are therefore quite useful whenever you're trying to keep multiple ideas in working memory all at the same time.

For example, the system also relies on a *visuospatial buffer*, used for storing visual materials such as mental images, in much the same way that the rehearsal loop stores speech-based materials. (We'll have more to say about mental images in Chapter 11.) Baddeley (the researcher who launched the idea of a working-memory system) has also proposed another component of the system: the *episodic buffer*. This component helps the executive organize information into a chronological sequence—so that, for example, you can keep track of a story you've just heard or a film clip you've just seen (e.g., Baddeley, 2000, 2012; Baddeley et al., 2009; Hitch et al., 2020). The role of this component is evident in patients with profound amnesia who seem unable to put new information into long-term storage, but who still can recall the flow of narrative in a story they just heard. This recall, it seems, relies on the episodic buffer—an aspect of working memory unaffected by the amnesia.

In addition, consider people who have been deaf since birth and communicate via sign language. We wouldn't expect these individuals to rely on an "inner voice" and an "inner ear"—and they don't. These individuals rely on a different helper for working memory: an "inner hand" (and covert sign language) rather than an "inner voice". As a result, they are disrupted if they're asked to wiggle their fingers during a memory task (similar to a hearing person saying "Tah-Tah-Tah"), and they also tend to make "same hand-shape" errors in working memory (similar to the sound-alike errors made by the hearing population).

With all these points in view, though, we're ready to move on. We've now updated the modal model in important ways, and in particular we've abandoned the notion of a relatively passive *short-term memory* serving largely as storage container. We've shifted to a dynamic conception of *working memory*, with the proposal that this term is merely the name for an organized set of activities—especially the complex activities of the central executive together with its various helpers.

But let's also emphasize that in this modern conception, just as in the modal model, working memory is quite fragile. Each shift in attention brings new information into working memory, and the newly arriving material displaces earlier items. Storage in this memory, therefore, is temporary. Obviously, then, we also need some sort of enduring memory storage, so that we

TEST YOURSELF

4. What does it mean to say that working memory holds 7 plus-or-minus 2 "chunks"? What is a chunk?

5. What evidence suggests that operation span is a better measure of working memory than the more standard digit-span measure?

6. How does the rehearsal loop manage to hold on to information with only occasional involvement by the central executive?

can remember things that happened an hour, or a day, or even years ago. Let's turn, therefore, to the functioning of long-term memory.

Entering Long-Term Storage: The Need for Engagement

We've already seen an important clue regarding how information gets established in long-term storage: In discussing the primacy effect, we suggested that the more an item is rehearsed, the more likely you are to remember that item later. To pursue this point, though, we need to ask what exactly rehearsal is and how it works to promote memory.

Two Types of Rehearsal

The term "rehearsal" doesn't mean much beyond "thinking about." In other words, when research participants rehearse an item on a memory list, they're simply thinking about that item—perhaps once, perhaps over and over; perhaps mechanically, perhaps with close attention to what the item means. There's considerable variety, therefore, within the activities that count as rehearsal, and psychologists find it useful to sort this variety into two broad types.

As one option, people can engage in **maintenance rehearsal**, in which they simply focus on the to-be-remembered items themselves, with little thought about what the items mean. This is a rote, mechanical process, recycling items in working memory by repeating them over and over. In contrast, **relational or elaborative rehearsal** involves thinking about what the to-be-remembered items mean and how they're related to one another and also to other things you already know.

Relational rehearsal is vastly superior to maintenance rehearsal for establishing information in memory. In fact, in many settings maintenance rehearsal provides no long-term benefit at all. As an informal demonstration of this point, consider the following experience. You're watching your favorite reality show on TV. The announcer says, "To vote for Contestant #4, text 4 to 21523!" You reach into your pocket for your phone but realize you left it in the other room. So you recite the number to yourself while scurrying for your phone, but then, just before you dial, you see that you've got a text message. You pause, read the message, and then you're ready to dial, but . . . you don't have a clue what the number was.

What went wrong? You certainly heard the number, and you rehearsed it a couple of times while moving to grab your phone. But despite these rehearsals, the brief interruption from reading the text message seems to have erased the number from your memory. This might seem like ultra-rapid forgetting, but it's not. Instead, you never established the number in memory in the first place, because in this setting you relied only on maintenance rehearsal. That kept the number in your thoughts while you were moving across the

WE DON'T REMEMBER THINGS WE DON'T PAY ATTENTION TO

To promote public safety, many buildings have fire extinguishers and automatic defibrillators positioned in obvious and easily accessible locations. But in a moment of need, will people in the building remember where this safety equipment is located? Will they even remember that the safety equipment is conveniently available? Research suggests they may not. Occupants of the building have passed by the safety equipment again and again— but have had no reason to notice the equipment. As a result, they're unlikely to remember where the equipment is located.

(AFTER CASTEL ET AL., 2012)

room, but it did nothing to establish the number in long-term storage. And when you try to dial the number after reading the text message, it's long-term storage that you need.

The idea, then, is that if you think about something only in a mindless and mechanical way, the item will be established only weakly (if at all) in your long-term memory. Similarly, consider the ordinary penny. Adults in the United States have probably seen pennies many thousands of times. Adults in other countries have seen their own coins just as often. If sheer exposure is what counts for memory, people should remember perfectly what these coins look like.

But, of course, most people have little reason to pay attention to the penny. Pennies are a different color from other coins, so they can be identified at a glance without further scrutiny. And if it's scrutiny that matters for memory—or, more broadly, *if we remember what we pay attention to and think about*—then memory for the coin should be quite poor.

The evidence on this point is clear: People's memory for the penny is remarkably bad. For example, most people know that Lincoln's head is on the "heads" side, but which way is he facing? Is it his right cheek that's visible or his left? What other markings are on the coin? Most people do very badly with these questions; their answers to the "Which way is he facing?" question are close to random (Nickerson & Adams, 1979). And performance is similar for people in other countries remembering their own coins. (Also see Bekerian & Baddeley, 1980; Rinck, 1999.)

As a related example, consider the logo that identifies Apple products—the iPhone, the iPad, or one of the Apple computers. You've probably seen this logo hundreds and perhaps thousands of time, but you've had no reason to pay attention to its appearance. The prediction, then, is that your memory for the logo will be quite poor—and this prediction is correct. In one study, only 1 of 85 participants was able to draw the logo correctly—with the bite on the proper side, the stem tilted the right way, and the dimple properly placed in the logo's bottom (Blake et al., 2015; see **Figure 6.10**).

FIGURE 6.10   MEMORY FOR AN OFTEN-VIEWED LOGO

Most people have seen the apple logo countless times, but they've no reason to pay attention to its features. As a result, they have poor memories for the features. Test yourself. Can you find the correct version among the options displayed here?

(THE ANSWER IS AT THE END OF THE CHAPTER.)

And—surprisingly—people who use an Apple computer (and therefore see the logo every time they turn on the machine) perform at a level not much better than people who use a PC.

Incidental Learning, Intentional Learning, and Depth of Processing

It seems clear, then, that passive exposure and maintenance rehearsal do little to promote memory. But, if so, what activities or strategies are more helpful?

Consider a student taking a course in college. The student knows that her memory for the course materials will be tested later (e.g., in the final exam). And presumably she'll take various steps to help herself remember: She may read through her notes again and again; she may discuss the material with friends; she may try outlining the material. Will these various techniques work—so that she'll have a complete and accurate memory when the exam takes place? And notice that the student is taking these steps in the context of wanting to memorize; she wants to do well on the exam! How does this motivation influence performance? In other words, how does the intention to memorize influence how or how well the material is learned?

In an early experiment, participants in one condition heard a list of 24 words; their task was to remember as many of the words as they could. This is **intentional learning**—learning that is deliberate, with an expectation that memory will be tested later. Other groups of participants heard the same 24 words but had no idea that their memories would be tested. This enables us to examine the impact of **incidental learning**—that is, learning in the absence of any intention to learn. One of the incidental-learning groups was asked simply, for each word, whether the word contained the letter *e*. A different incidental-learning group was asked to look at each word and to report how many letters it contained. Another group was asked to consider each word and to rate how pleasant it seemed.

Later, all the participants were tested—and asked to recall as many of the words as they could. (The test was as expected for the intentional-learning group, but a surprise for the other groups.) The results are shown in **Figure 6.11A** (Hyde & Jenkins, 1969). Performance was relatively poor for the "Find the *e*" and "Count the letters" groups but appreciably better for the "How pleasant?" group. What's striking, though, is that the "How pleasant?" group, with no intention to memorize, performed just as well as the intentional-learning ("Learn these!") group. The suggestion, then, is that the intention to learn doesn't add very much; memory can be just as good without this intention, provided that you approach the materials in the right way.

This broad pattern has been reproduced in many experiments (e.g., Bobrow & Bower, 1969; Jacoby, 1978; Slamecka & Graf, 1978; also see Craik, 2020). For example, consider a study by Craik and Tulving (1975). Their participants were led to do incidental learning (i.e., they didn't know their memories would be tested). For some of the words shown, the participants did **shallow processing**—that is, they engaged the material in a

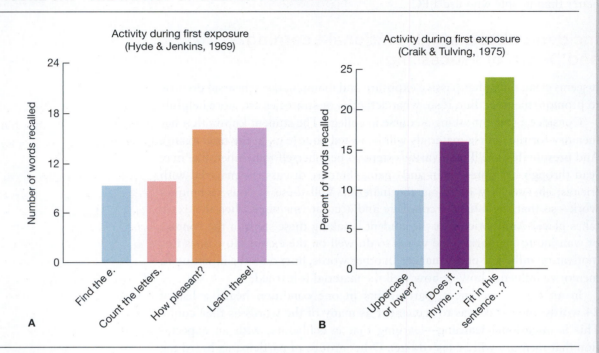

FIGURE 6.11   THE IMPACT OF DEEPER PROCESSING

Activity during first exposure
(Hyde & Jenkins, 1969)

Number of words recalled

Find the e.
Count the letters.
How pleasant?
Learn these!

A

Activity during first exposure
(Craik & Tulving, 1975)

Percent of words recalled

Uppercase or lower?
Does it rhyme...?
Fit in this sentence...?

B

The two sets of results shown here derive from studies described in the text, but they are part of an avalanche of data confirming the broad pattern: Shallow processing leads to poor memory. Deeper processing (paying attention to meaning) leads to much better memory. And what matters seems to be the level of engagement; the specific intention to learn (because participants know their memory will be tested later on) contributes little.

TEST YOURSELF

7. What is the difference between maintenance rehearsal and relational (or elaborative) rehearsal?

8. What does it mean to say, "It doesn't matter if you *intend* to memorize; all that matters for memory is how exactly you engage the material you encounter"?

9. What is deep processing, and what impact does it have on memory?

superficial way. Specifically, they had to say whether the word was printed in CAPITAL letters or not. (Other examples of shallow processing would be decisions about whether the words are printed in red or in green, high or low on the screen, etc.) For other words, the participants had to do a moderate level of processing: They had to judge whether each word shown *rhymed* with a cue word. Finally, for other words, participants had to do **deep processing**. This is processing that requires some thought about what the words *mean*; specifically, Craik and Tulving asked whether each word shown would fit into a particular sentence.

The results are shown in **Figure 6.11B**, and they indicate a huge effect of **level of processing**, with deeper processing (i.e., more attention to meaning) leading to better memory. In addition, Craik and Tulving confirmed the finding that the intention to learn adds little. That is, memory performance is roughly the same in conditions in which participants do shallow processing *with* an intention to memorize, and conditions in which they do shallow processing *without* this intention. Likewise, the outcome is the same whether people do deep processing *with* the intention to memorize or *without*. In

COGNITION outside the lab

Gender Differences?

Most of this book focuses on principles that apply to all people—young or old, sociable or shy, smart or slow. But, of course, people differ in many ways, leading us to ask: Are there differences in how people remember? As one aspect of this issue, researchers have sometimes asked whether men and women differ in their memories. (A separate question—largely unexplored—is how non-binary individuals might be distinctive in their memories; this is a question awaiting future research.)

Studies tell us that there's no overall difference between the genders in memory accuracy, or quantity of information retained, or susceptibility to outside influences that might pull memory off track. If we take a closer look, though, we do find some differences (e.g., Asperholm et al., 2019; Herlitz & Rehnman, 2014)—with studies indicating an advantage for women in remembering verbal materials, and other studies suggesting an advantage for men in remembering spatial arrangement.

In addition, bear in mind that people tend to remember what they paid attention to, and don't remember things they didn't attend to. From this base, it's not surprising that after viewing an event, women are more likely than men to recall the clothing people were wearing or their jewelry. Men, in contrast, are more likely than women to recall the people's body shapes. (Also see Chapter 5, p. 162.) There is also some indication that women may have better face memory—but only when remembering the faces of other women. These various differences are, of course, easy to understand. They're reflections of the "attention priorities" that Western culture encourages for men and women, priorities that derive from the conventional roles assumed (for better or worse) for each gender.

Let's note in addition that larger differences between men's and women's memory have been documented in Europe, North and South America, and Australia, in comparison to studies conducted in Asia (Asperholm et al., 2019). This pattern strongly suggests that we're looking at an influence of culture (which varies from country to country) rather than biology (which is essentially the same around the globe).

Other results suggest that women may also have better memory for emotional events than men do; but this, too, might be a difference in attention rather than a true difference in memory. Women are, in Western cultures, encouraged to pay attention to social dynamics, and in many settings are encouraged to be more emotionally responsive, more emotionally sensitive, than men. These points color the ways in which women pay attention to and think about an event—and ultimately how they remember the event.

In short, most of these differences (none of them profound) are likely to be a reflection of cultural bias. With this, it seems that men and women are much more similar in their cognition than they are different. But, in addition, these patterns remind us that what you remember now is dependent on what you paid attention to earlier. Therefore, if people differ in what they focus on, they'll remember different things later on.

study after study, what matters is how people approach the material they're seeing or hearing. It's that approach—that manner of engagement—that determines whether memory will be excellent or poor later on. The intention to learn seems, by itself, not to matter.

The Role of Meaning and Memory Connections

The message so far seems clear: If you want to remember the sentences you're reading in this text, or the materials you're learning in training sessions at your job, you should pay attention to what these materials mean. In other words, you should try to do deep processing. And if you do deep processing, it won't matter if you're trying hard to memorize the materials (intentional learning) or merely paying attention to the meaning because you find the material interesting, with no plan for memorizing (incidental learning).

But what lies behind these effects? Why does attention to meaning lead to good recall? Let's start with a broad proposal; we'll then fill in the evidence for this proposal.

Connections Promote Retrieval

Perhaps surprisingly, the benefits of deep processing may not lie in the learning process itself. Instead, deep processing may influence subsequent events. More precisely, attention to meaning may help you by facilitating *retrieval* of the memory later on. To understand this point, consider what happens whenever a library acquires a new book. On its way into the collection, the new book must be catalogued and shelved appropriately. These steps happen when the book arrives, but the cataloguing doesn't literally influence the arrival of the book into the building. The moment the book is delivered, it's physically in the library, catalogued or not, and the book doesn't become "more firmly" or "more strongly" in the library because of the cataloguing.

Even so, the cataloguing is crucial. If the book were merely tossed on a random shelf somewhere, with no entry in the catalogue, users might never be able to find it. Without a catalogue entry, users of the library might not even realize that the book was in the building. Notice, then, that cataloguing happens at the time of arrival, but the benefit of cataloguing isn't for the arrival itself. (If the librarians all went on strike, so that no books were being catalogued, books would continue to arrive, magazines would still be delivered, and so on. Again: The *arrival* doesn't depend on cataloguing.) Instead, the benefit of cataloguing is for events that happen after the book's arrival—cataloguing makes it possible (and maybe makes it *easy*) to find the book later on.

The same is true for the vast library that is your memory (after Miller & Springer, 1973). The task of learning is not merely a matter of placing information into long-term storage. Learning also needs to establish some

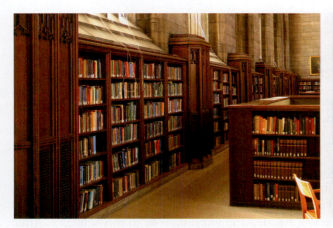

WHY DO MEMORY CONNECTIONS HELP?

When books arrive in a library, the librarians must catalogue them. This doesn't facilitate the "entry" of books into the library, because the books are in the building whether they're catalogued or not. But cataloguing makes the books much easier to find later on. Memory connections may serve the same function: The connections don't "bring" material into memory, but they do make the material "findable" in long-term storage later.

appropriate indexing; it must pave a path to the new information, so that this information can be retrieved at some future point. Thus, one of the main chores of memory acquisition is to lay the groundwork for memory retrieval.

But what is it that facilitates memory retrieval? There are, in fact, several ways to search through memory, but a great deal depends on memory *connections*. Connections allow one memory to trigger another, and then that memory to trigger another, so that you're "led," connection by connection, to the sought-after information. In some cases, the connections link one of the items you're trying to remember to some of the other items; if so, finding the first will lead you to the others. In other settings, the connections might link some aspect of the context-of-learning to the target information, so that when you think again about the context ("I recognize this room—this is where I was last week"), you'll be led to other ideas ("Oh, yeah, I read the funny story in this room"). In all cases, though, this triggering will happen only if the relevant connections are in place—and establishing those connections is a large part of what happens during learning.

This line of reasoning has many implications, and we can use those implications as a basis for testing whether this proposal is correct. But right at the start, it should be clear why, according to this account, deep processing (i.e., attention to meaning) promotes memory. The key is that attention to meaning involves thinking about relationships: "What words are related in meaning to the word I'm now considering? What words have *contrasting* meaning? What is the relationship between the start of this story and the way the story turned out?" Points like these are likely to be prominent when you're thinking about what some word (or sentence or event) means, and these points will help you to find (or, perhaps, to *create*) connections among your various ideas. It's these connections, we're proposing, that really matter for memory.

Elaborate Encoding Promotes Retrieval

If our proposal so far is correct, then attention to meaning is not the only way to improve memory. Other strategies should also be helpful, provided that they establish memory connections. As an example, consider another classic study by Craik and Tulving (1975). Participants were shown a word and then shown a sentence with one word left out. Their task was to decide whether the word fit into the sentence. For example, they might see the word "chicken" and then the sentence "She cooked the _____." The appropriate response would be yes, because the word does fit in this sentence. After a series of these trials, there was a surprise memory test, with participants being asked to remember all the words they had seen.

But there was an additional element in this experiment. Some of the sentences shown to participants were simple, while others were more elaborate. For example, a more complex sentence might be: "The great bird swooped down and carried off the struggling _____." Sentences like this one produced a large memory benefit—words were much more likely to be remembered if they appeared with these rich, elaborate sentences than if they had appeared in the simpler sentences (see **Figure 6.12**).

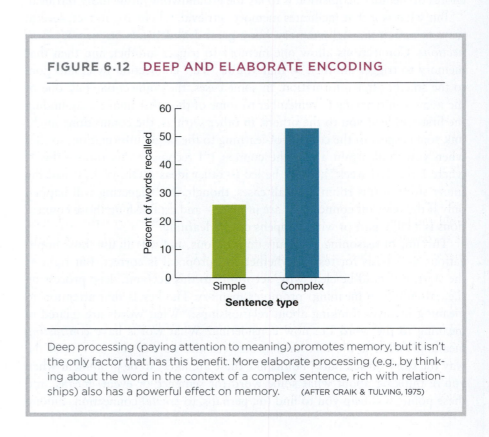

FIGURE 6.12 DEEP AND ELABORATE ENCODING

Deep processing (paying attention to meaning) promotes memory, but it isn't the only factor that has this benefit. More elaborate processing (e.g., by thinking about the word in the context of a complex sentence, rich with relationships) also has a powerful effect on memory. (AFTER CRAIK & TULVING, 1975)

Apparently, *elaborate* processing leads to better recall. Why? The answer hinges on memory connections. Maybe the "great bird swooped" sentence calls to mind a barnyard scene with a hawk carrying away a chicken. Or maybe it calls to mind thoughts about predator-prey relationships. One way or another, the richness of the sentence offers the potential for many connections as it calls other thoughts to mind, each of which can be connected to the target sentence. These connections, in turn, provide potential **retrieval paths**—paths that can, in effect, guide your thoughts toward the content to be remembered. All of this seems less likely for the simpler sentences, which will evoke fewer connections and so establish a narrower set of retrieval paths. Consequently, words associated with these sentences are less likely to be recalled later on.

Organizing and Memorizing

For thousands of years, people have longed for "better" memories and have developed various strategies that (they hoped) would help them remember. Here, too, we find a central role for many connections.

Mnemonics

The ancient Greeks devoted considerable effort to the development of **mnemonic strategies**—techniques specifically designed to improve memory—and, in fact, many of the mnemonics still in use date back to those times. It therefore seems appropriate that these techniques are named in honor of Mnemosyne, the goddess of memory in Greek mythology.

How do mnemonics work? The key is that these strategies provide a way to organize the to-be-remembered material. One type of mnemonic, often used for memorizing sequences of words, links the *first letters* of the words into some meaningful structure. Thus, children rely on ROY G. BIV to memorize the sequence of colors in the rainbow (*red, orange, yellow* . . .), and they learn the lines in music's treble clef via "Every Good Boy Deserves Fudge" or ". . . Does Fine" (the lines indicate the musical notes *E, G, B, D,* and *F*). Biology students use a sentence like "King Philip Crossed the Ocean to Find Gold and Silver" (or: ". . . to Find Good Spaghetti") to memorize the sequence of taxonomic categories: *kingdom, phylum, class, order, family, genus,* and *species.* (For another example, see **Figure 6.13.**)

Other mnemonic strategies involve the use of mental imagery, relying on "mental pictures" to link the to-be-remembered items to one another. (We'll have more to say about "mental pictures" in Chapter 11.) For example, imagine a student trying to memorize a list of word pairs. For the pair *eagle-train,* the student might imagine the eagle winging back to its nest with a locomotive in its beak. Classic research evidence indicates that images like this can be enormously helpful. It's important, though, that the images show the objects in some sort of relationship or interaction. It doesn't help just to form a picture of an eagle and a train sitting side-by-side (Wollen et al., 1972).

TEST YOURSELF

10. What does it mean to say, "The creation of memory connections often occurs at the time of learning, but the main benefit of those connections comes later, at the time of memory retrieval"?

11. In what ways is deep and elaborate processing superior to deep processing on its own?

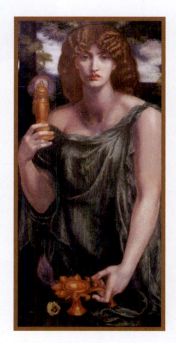

MNEMOSYNE

Strategies that are used to improve memory are known as mnemonic strategies, or mnemonics. The term derives from the name of the goddess of memory in Greek mythology—Mnemosyne (usually pronounced "neh-MAH-sin-ay").

FIGURE 6.13   MNEMONIC STRATEGIES

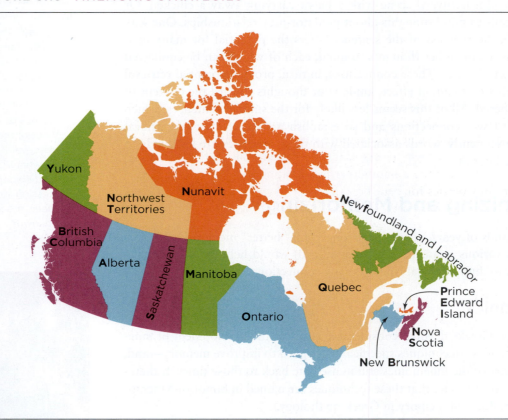

With a bit of creativity, you can make up mnemonics for memorizing all sorts of things. For example, can you name all ten of the Canadian provinces? Perhaps there is a great mnemonic available, but in the meantime, this one will do. It's a complicated mnemonic but unified by the theme of the early-morning meal: "**B**reakfast **C**ooks **A**lways **S**ell **M**ore **O**melets. **Q**uiche **N**ever **B**ought, **N**ever **S**old. **P**erhaps **E**ggs **I**n **N**ew **F**orms?" (You're on your own for remembering the three northern territories.)

A different type of mnemonic provides an external "skeleton" for the to-be-remembered materials, and mental imagery can be useful here, too. Imagine that you want to remember a list of largely unrelated items—perhaps the entries on your shopping list, or a list of questions you want to ask your adviser. For this purpose, you might rely on one of the so-called **peg-word systems**. These systems begin with a well-organized structure, such as this one:

One is a bun.

Two is a shoe.

Three is a tree.

Four is a door.

Five is a hive.

Six are sticks.

Seven is heaven.

Eight is a gate.

Nine is a line.

Ten is a hen.

This rhyme provides ten "peg words" ("bun," "shoe," etc.), and in memorizing something you "hang" the materials to be remembered on these "pegs." Let's imagine that you want to remember your shopping list. If you need to buy milk, you should form an association between milk and the first peg, "bun"—perhaps picturing a hamburger bun floating in pool of milk. If you also need to buy berries for your breakfast cereal, you should form an association between berries and the next peg, "shoe." (You could picture what your shoes would look like if they were filled with strawberries.) Then, when you get to the store, all you have to do is think through that silly rhyme again. When you think of "one is a bun," it's likely that the image of the hamburger bun (and therefore the milk) will come to mind. With "two is a shoe," you'll be reminded of the berries. And so on.

Hundreds of variations on these techniques—the first-letter mnemonics, visualization strategies, peg-word systems—are available, and crucially, these systems all work. They help you remember individual items, and they also help you remember those items in a specific sequence. **Figure 6.14** shows some of the data from one early study; many other studies confirm this pattern (e.g., Bower, 1970, 1972; Higbee, 1977; Roediger, 1980; Ross & Lawrence, 1968).

In fact, given the power of mnemonics, students are well advised to use these strategies in their studying. Bear in mind, though, that there's a downside to the use of mnemonics in educational settings. When using a mnemonic, you typically focus on just one aspect of the material you're trying to memorize—for example, just the first letter of the word to be remembered—and so you may cut short your effort toward understanding this material, and likewise your effort toward finding multiple connections between the material and other things you know.

To put this point differently, mnemonic use involves a trade-off. If you focus on just one or two memory connections, you'll spend little time thinking about other possible connections, including those that might help you understand the material. This trade-off will be fine if you don't care very much about the meaning of the material. (Do you care why, in taxonomy, "orders" are contained within "classes," rather than the other way around?) But the trade-off is troubling if you're trying to memorize material that is meaningful. In this case, you'd be better served by a memory strategy that seeks out *multiple* connections between the material you're trying to learn and things you already know. This effort toward multiple links will help you in two ways. First, it will foster your understanding of the material to

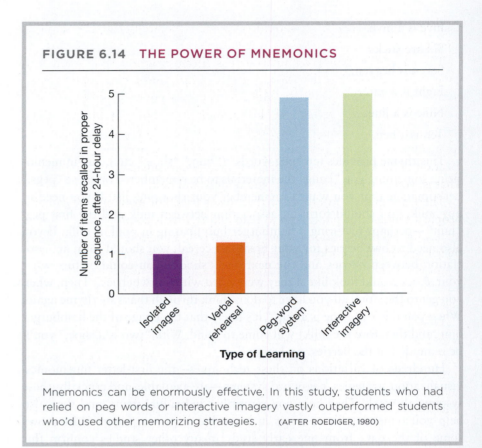

FIGURE 6.14   THE POWER OF MNEMONICS

Mnemonics can be enormously effective. In this study, students who had relied on peg words or interactive imagery vastly outperformed students who'd used other memorizing strategies.   (AFTER ROEDIGER, 1980)

be remembered, and so will lead to better learning. Second, it will help you retrieve this information later. We've already said that memory connections serve as retrieval paths, and the more paths there are, the easier it will be to find the target material later.

For these reasons, mnemonic use may not be the best approach in many situations. Still, the fact remains that mnemonics are immensely useful in some settings (What were those rainbow colors?), and this fits well with our overall theme: Mnemonics provide an organization for the material you're trying to learn. Organization connects the bits you're learning to one another, or perhaps to an external frame. And it's these connections that promote memory.

Understanding and Memorizing

We've now said a lot about how people memorize simple stimulus materials—items on a shopping list or colors that have to be learned in the right sequence. In day-to-day life, however, you typically want to remember more meaningful, more complicated, material. You want to remember the episodes you experience, the details of rich scenes you've observed, or the many-step arguments you've read in a book. Do the same memory principles apply to these cases?

The answer is clearly yes (although we'll have more to say about this issue in Chapter 8). In other words, your memory for events, or pictures, or complex bodies of knowledge is enormously dependent on your being able to organize the material to be remembered. With these more complicated materials, though, we've already suggested that your best bet for organization isn't some arbitrary skeleton like those used in mnemonics. Instead, the best organization of these complex materials is generally dependent on understanding. That is, you remember best what you understand best.

There are many ways to show that this is true. For example, we can give people a sentence or paragraph to read and test their comprehension immediately, by asking questions about the material. Sometime later, we can test their memory. The results are clear: The better the participants' understanding of a sentence or a paragraph, if questioned right after viewing the material, the greater the likelihood that they will remember the material after a delay (for classic data on this topic, see Bransford, 1979).

Likewise, consider the material you're learning right now in the courses you're taking. Will you remember this material 5 years from now, or 10, or 20? The answer depends on how well you understand the material, and one measure of understanding is the grade you earn in a course. With full and rich understanding, you're likely to earn an A; with poor understanding, your grade is likely to be lower. This leads to a prediction: If understanding is (as we've proposed) important for memory, then the higher someone's grade in a course, the more likely that person is to remember the course contents, even years later. This is exactly what the data show, with A students remembering the material quite well, and C students remembering much less (Conway et al., 1992).

The relationship between understanding and memory can also be demonstrated in another way: by *manipulating* whether people understand the material or not. For example, in an early experiment by Bransford and Johnson (1972, p. 722), participants read this passage:

The procedure is actually quite simple. First you arrange items into different groups. Of course one pile may be sufficient depending on how much there is to do. If you have to go somewhere else due to lack of facilities that is the next step; otherwise you are pretty well set. It is important not to overdo things. That is, it is better to do too few things at once than too many. In the short run, this may not seem important but complications can easily arise. A mistake can be expensive as well. At first, the whole procedure will seem complicated. Soon, however, it will become just another facet of life. It is difficult to foresee any end to the necessity for this task in the immediate future, but then, one never can tell. After the procedure is completed one arranges the materials into different groups again. Then they can be put into their appropriate places. Eventually they will be used once more and the whole cycle will then have to be repeated. However, that is part of life.

149162536496481

Examine this series of digits for a moment, and then turn away from the page and try to recall all 15 in their proper sequence. The chances are good that you will fail in this task—perhaps remembering the first few and the last few digits, but not the entire list. Things will go differently, though, if you discover the pattern within the list. Now, you'll easily be able to remember the full sequence. What is the pattern? Try thinking of the series this way: 1, 4, 9, 16, 25, 36. . . . Here, as always, organizing and understanding aid memory.

You're probably puzzled by the passage, and so are most research participants. The story is easy to understand, though, if we give it a title: "Doing the Laundry." In the experiment, some participants were given the title before reading the passage; others were not. Participants in the first group easily understood the passage and were able to remember it after a delay. Participants in the second group, reading the same words, weren't confronting a meaningful passage and did poorly on the memory test. (For related data, see Bransford & Franks, 1971; Sulin & Dooling, 1974. For another example, see **Figure 6.15**.)

Similar effects can be documented with nonverbal materials. The picture shown in **Figure 6.16** initially looks like a bunch of meaningless blotches; with some study, though, you may discover a familiar object. Wiseman and Neisser (1974) tested people's memory for this picture. Consistent with what we've seen so far, their memory was good if they understood the picture—and bad otherwise.

The Study of Memory Acquisition

This chapter has largely been about memory acquisition. How do we acquire new memories? How is new information, new knowledge, established in long-term memory? In more pragmatic terms, what is the best, most effective way to learn? We now have answers to these questions, but our discussion has highlighted two important themes: the substantial contribution from the memorizer, and also the interconnections among acquisition, retrieval, and storage.

The Contribution of the Memorizer

Over and over, we've seen that memory depends on *connections* among ideas, connections fostered by the steps you take in organizing and understanding the materials you encounter. Hand in hand with this, it appears that

FIGURE 6.16 COMPREHENSION ALSO AIDS MEMORY FOR PICTURES

People who perceive this picture as a pattern of meaningless blotches are unlikely to remember the picture. People who perceive the "hidden" form do remember the picture. (AFTER WISEMAN & NEISSER, 1974)

memories are not established by sheer contact with the items you're hoping to remember. If you're merely exposed to the items without giving them any thought, then subsequent recall of those items will be poor.

These points draw attention to the huge role played by the memorizer. If, for example, we wish to predict whether this or that event will be recalled, it isn't enough to know that someone was exposed to the event. Instead, we need to ask what the person was *doing* during the event. Did she only do maintenance rehearsal, or did she engage the material in some other way? If the latter, how did she think about the material? Did she pay attention to the appearance of the words or to their meaning? If she thought about meaning, was she able to understand the material? These considerations are crucial for predicting the success of memory.

The contribution of the memorizer is also evident in another way. We've argued that learning depends on making connections, but connections to what? If you want to connect the to-be-remembered material to other knowledge, to other memories, then you need to have that other knowledge—you need to have other (potentially relevant) memories that you can "hook" the new material onto.

This point helps us understand why sports fans have an easy time learning new facts about sports, and why car mechanics can easily learn new facts about cars, and why memory experts easily memorize new information about memory. In each situation, the person enters the learning situation with a considerable advantage—a rich framework that the new materials can be woven into. But, conversely, if someone enters a learning situation with little relevant background, then there's no framework, nothing to connect to, and learning will be more difficult. Plainly, then, if we want to predict someone's success in memorizing, we need to consider what other knowledge the individual brings into the situation.

The Links among Acquisition, Retrieval, and Storage

These points lead us to another important theme. Throughout this chapter, we've seen indications that claims about memory acquisition cannot be separated from claims about storage and retrieval. For example, why is memory acquisition improved by organization? We've suggested that organization provides retrieval paths, making the memories "findable" later on, and this is a claim about retrieval. Therefore, our claims about acquisition are intertwined with claims about retrieval.

Likewise, we've just noted that your ability to learn new material depends, in part, on your having a framework of prior knowledge to which the new materials can be tied. In this way, claims about memory acquisition need to be coordinated with claims about the nature of what is already in storage.

These interactions among acquisition, knowledge, and retrieval are crucial for our theorizing. But the interactions also have important implications for learning, for forgetting, and for memory accuracy. The next two chapters explore some of those implications.

TEST YOURSELF

14. Explain why memorizing involves a contribution from the memorizer, both in terms of what the memorizer *does* while memorizing, and also in terms of what the memorizer *knows* prior to the memorizing.

COGNITIVE PSYCHOLOGY AND EDUCATION

how should i study?

Throughout life, you encounter information that you hope to remember later—whether you're a student taking courses or an employee training for a new job. In these and many other settings, what helpful lessons can you draw from memory research?

For a start, bear in mind that the *intention to memorize*, on its own, has no effect. Therefore, you don't need any special "memorizing steps." Instead, you should focus on making sure you understand the material, because if you do, you're likely to remember it.

As a specific strategy, it's useful to spend a moment after a class, or after you've done a reading assignment, to quiz yourself about what you've just learned. "What are the new ideas here?" "Do these new ideas fit with other things I know?" "Do I know what evidence or arguments support the claims here?" Answering questions like these will help you find meaningful connections within the material you're learning, and between this material and other information already in your memory. In the same spirit, it's often useful to rephrase material you encounter, putting it into your own words. Doing this will force you to think about what the words mean—again, a good thing for memory.

Surveys suggest, however, that most students rely on study strategies that are more passive than this—in fact, far *too* passive. Many students try to learn materials by simply rereading the textbook or reading over their notes several times. The problem with these strategies should be obvious: As the chapter explains, memories are produced by active engagement with materials, not by passive exposure.

As a related point, it's often useful to study with a friend—so that they can explain topics to you, and you can do the same in return. Why does this help? In explaining things, you're forced into a more active role. Working with a friend is also likely to enhance your understanding, because each of you can help the other to understand bits you're having trouble with. You'll also benefit from hearing your friend's perspective on the materials. This additional perspective offers the possibility of creating new connections among ideas, making the information easier to recall later on.

Memory will also be better if you spread out your studying across multiple occasions—using *spaced learning* (e.g., spreading out your learning across several days) rather than *massed learning* (essentially, "cramming" all at once). It also helps to vary your focus while studying—working on your history assignment for a while, then shifting to math, then over to the novel your English professor assigned, and then back to history. There are several reasons for this, including the fact that spaced learning and a changing focus will make it likely that you'll bring a somewhat different perspective to the material each time you turn to it. This new perspective will let you see connections you didn't see before; and—again—these new connections provide retrieval paths that can promote recall.

Spaced learning also has another advantage. With this form of learning, some time will pass between the episodes of learning. (Imagine, for example, that you study your sociology text for a while on Tuesday night and then return to it on Thursday, so that two days go by between these study sessions.) This situation allows some amount of forgetting to take place, and that's actually helpful because now each episode of learning will require a bit more effort, a bit more thought. This stands in contrast to massed learning, in which your second and third passes through the material may only be separated by a few minutes. In this setting, the second and third passes may feel easy enough so that you zoom through them, with little engagement in the material.

Note an ironic point here: Spaced learning may be more difficult (because of the forgetting between sessions), but this difficulty leads to better learning overall. Researchers refer to this as "desirable difficulty"—difficulty that may seem like an obstacle when you're slogging through the material you hope to learn, but is nonetheless beneficial because it leaves you with more complete, more long-lasting memory.

MEANINGFUL CONNECTIONS

What sort of connections will help you to remember? The answer is that almost any connection can be helpful. Here's a silly—but useful—example. Students learning about the nervous system have to learn that *efferent* fibers carry information *away from* the brain and central nervous system, while *afferent* fibers carry information *inward*. How to keep these terms straight? It may be helpful to notice that efferent fibers carry information *exiting* the nervous system, while afferent fibers provide information *arriving* in the nervous system. And, as a bonus, the same connections will help you remember that you can have an *effect* on the world (an influence outward, from you), but that the world can also *affect* you (an influence coming inward, toward you).

What about mnemonic strategies, such as a peg-word system? These are enormously helpful—but often at a cost. When you're first learning something new, focusing on a mnemonic can divert your time and attention away from efforts at understanding the material, and so you'll end up understanding the material less well. You'll also be left with only the one or two retrieval paths that the mnemonic provides, not the multiple paths created by comprehension. In some circumstances these drawbacks aren't serious—and so, for example, mnemonics are often useful for memorizing dates, place names, or particular bits of terminology. But for richer, more meaningful material, mnemonics may hurt you more than they help.

Mnemonics can be more helpful, though, *after* you've understood the new material. Imagine that you've thoughtfully constructed a many-step argument or a complex derivation of a mathematical formula. Now, imagine that you hope to re-create the argument or the derivation later on—perhaps on an exam. In this situation, you've already achieved a level of mastery, and you don't want to lose what you've gained. Here, a mnemonic (like the peg-word system) might be quite helpful, enabling you to remember the full argument or derivation in its proper sequence.

Finally, let's emphasize that there's more to say about these issues. Our discussion here (like Chapter 6 itself) focuses on the "input" side of memory—getting information into storage, so that it's available for use later on. There are also steps you can take later that will help you to locate information in the vast warehouse of your memory, and still other steps that you can take to avoid forgetting materials you've already learned. Discussion of those steps, however, depends on materials we'll cover in Chapters 7 and 8.

For more on this topic . . .

Brown, P. C., Roediger, H. L. III, & McDaniel, M. A. (2014). *Make it stick: The science of successful learning.* Cambridge, MA: Belknap Press of Harvard University Press.

Carpenter, S. K., Witherby, A. E., & Tauber, S. K. (2020). On students' (mis)judgments of learning and teaching effectiveness. *Journal of Applied Research in Memory and Cognition, 9*, 137–151.

McCabe, J. A., Redick, T. S., & Engle, R. W. (2016). Brain-training pessimism, but applied memory optimism. *Psychological Science in the Public Interest, 17*(3), 187–191.

Putnam, A. L., Sungkhasettee, V. W., & Roediger, H. L. III (2016). Optimizing learning in college: Tips from cognitive psychology. *Perspectives on Psychological Science, 11*(5), 652–660.

chapter review

SUMMARY

- It is convenient to think of memorizing as having separate stages. First, one acquires new information (acquisition). Next, the information remains in storage until it is needed. Finally, the information is retrieved. However, this separation among the stages may be misleading. For example, in order to memorize new information, you form connections between this information and things you already know. In this way, the acquisition stage is intertwined with the retrieval of information already in storage.

- Information that is currently being considered is held in working memory; information that isn't currently active but is nonetheless in storage is in long-term memory. The distinction between these two forms of memory has traditionally been described in terms of the modal model and has been examined in many studies of the serial-position curve. The primacy portion of this curve reflects items that have had extra opportunity to reach long-term memory; the recency portion of this curve reflects the accurate retrieval of items currently in working memory.

- Psychologists' conception of working memory has evolved in important ways in the last few decades. Crucially, psychologists no longer think of working memory as a "storage container" or even as a "place." Instead, working memory is a status—and so we say items are "in working memory" when they're being actively thought about. This activity is governed by working memory's central executive. For mere storage, the executive often relies on low-level assistants, including the articulatory rehearsal loop and the visuospatial buffer, which work as mental scratch pads. The activity inherent in this overall system is reflected in the flexible way material can be chunked in working memory. The activity is also reflected in current measures of working memory, via operation span.

- Maintenance rehearsal serves to keep information in working memory and requires little effort, but it has little impact on subsequent recall. To maximize your chances of recall, elaborative rehearsal is needed, in which you seek connections within the material to be remembered or connections between the material to be remembered and things you already know.

- In many cases, elaborative processing takes the form of attention to meaning. This attention to meaning is called "deep processing," in contrast to attention to sounds or visual form, which is considered "shallow processing." Many studies have shown that deep processing leads to good memory performance later on, even if the deep processing occurred with no intention of memorizing the target material. In fact, the intention to learn has no direct effect on performance; what matters instead is how someone engages or thinks about the material to be remembered.

- Deep processing has beneficial effects by creating effective retrieval paths that can be used later on. Retrieval paths depend on connections linking one memory to another; each connection provides a path potentially leading to a target memory. Mnemonic strategies rely on the same mechanism and focus on the creation of specific memory connections, often tying the to-be-remembered material to a frame (e.g., a strongly structured poem).

- Perhaps the best way to form memory connections is to understand the material to be remembered. In understanding, you form many connections within the material to be remembered, as well as between this material and other knowledge. With all these retrieval paths, it becomes easy to locate this material in memory. Consistent with these suggestions, studies have shown a close correspondence between the ability to understand some material and the ability to recall that material later on. This pattern has been demonstrated with stories, visual patterns, numbers in series, and many other stimuli.

KEY TERMS

acquisition (p. 189)
storage (p. 189)
retrieval (p. 189)
modal model (p. 190)
sensory memory (p. 190)
short-term memory (p. 190)
working memory (p. 191)
long-term memory (LTM) (p. 191)
free recall procedure (p. 192)
primacy effect (p. 192)
recency effect (p. 192)
serial position (p. 192)
memory rehearsal (p. 193)
digit-span task (p. 197)
"7 plus-or-minus 2" (p. 197)
chunks (p. 197)
operation span (p. 199)

working-memory capacity (WMC) (p. 200)
working-memory system (p. 201)
articulatory rehearsal loop (p. 201)
subvocalization (p. 201)
phonological buffer (p. 201)
concurrent articulation task (p. 203)
maintenance rehearsal (p. 205)
relational (or elaborative) rehearsal (p. 205)
intentional learning (p. 207)
incidental learning (p. 207)
shallow processing (p. 207)
deep processing (p. 208)
level of processing (p. 208)
retrieval paths (p. 213)
mnemonic strategies (p. 213)
peg-word systems (p. 214)

TEST YOURSELF AGAIN

1. Define the terms "acquisition," "storage," and "retrieval."

2. List the four ways in which (either in the modal model or in more recent views) working memory is different from long-term storage.

3. How is the primacy effect usually explained? How is the recency effect usually explained?

4. What does it mean to say that working memory holds 7 plus-or-minus 2 "chunks"? What is a chunk?

5. What evidence suggests that operation span is a better measure of working memory than the more standard digit-span measure?

6. How does the rehearsal loop manage to hold on to information with only occasional involvement by the central executive?

7. What is the difference between maintenance rehearsal and relational (or elaborative) rehearsal?

8. What does it mean to say, "It doesn't matter if you *intend* to memorize; all that matters for

memory is how exactly you engage the material you encounter"?

9. What is deep processing, and what impact does it have on memory?

10. What does it mean to say, "The creation of memory connections often occurs at the time of learning, but the main benefit of those connections comes later, at the time of memory retrieval"?

11. In what ways is deep and elaborate processing superior to deep processing on its own?

12. Why do mnemonic strategies help memory? What are the limitations of mnemonic use?

13. What's the evidence that there's a clear linkage between how well you understand material when you first meet it, and how fully you'll recall that information later on?

14. Explain why memorizing involves a contribution from the memorizer, both in terms of what the memorizer *does* while memorizing, and also in terms of what the memorizer *knows* prior to the memorizing.

THINK ABOUT IT

1. Imagine that, based on what you've read in this chapter, you were asked to write a "training pamphlet" advising students how to study more effectively, so that they would remember what they studied more fully and more accurately. What would you write in the pamphlet?

DEMONSTRATIONS & APPLYING COGNITIVE PSYCHOLOGY ESSAYS

For demonstrations of key concepts in cognitive psychology, take a look at the Online Demonstrations. To explore more of the practical applications of cognitive psychology in themed essays, visit the online reader.

Online Demonstrations

- Demonstration 6.1: Primacy and Recency Effects
- Demonstration 6.2: Chunking
- Demonstration 6.3: The Articulatory Rehearsal Loop
- Demonstration 6.4: Sound-Based Coding
- Demonstration 6.5: Remembering Things You Hadn't Noticed
- Demonstration 6.6: The Effects of Unattended Exposure
- Demonstration 6.7: Depth of Processing

Online Applying Cognitive Psychology Essays

- Cognitive Psychology and Technology: "My Phone Remembers for Me"
- Cognitive Psychology and Health: Prospective Memory
- Cognitive Psychology and the Law: The Video-Recorder View

ZAPS COGNITION LABS

Go to ZAPS online cognition labs to conduct hands-on experiments on key concepts.

INQUIZITIVE

It's time to complete your study experience! Go to InQuizitive to practice actively with this chapter's concepts and get personalized feedback along the way.

Answer: Actually, none of the images shown in Figure 6.10 depict the Apple logo. The bottom-middle image has the bite and the dimple in the right positions, but it shows the stem pointing the wrong way. The bottom-left image shows the stem and bite correctly, but it's missing the dimple!

chapter 7

The Many Types of Memory

what if... We first met the patient H.M. in Chapter 1. H.M. was in his 20s when he had brain surgery intended to control his epilepsy, and, as we've discussed, this surgery had an unexpected and horrible consequence: H.M. lost the ability to form new memories. If asked what he did last week, or yesterday, or even an hour ago, H.M. had no idea. He couldn't recognize the faces of medical staff he'd seen day after day. He could read and reread a book without realizing he'd read the same book many times before.

A related pattern of memory loss occurs among patients who suffer from Korsakoff's syndrome. We'll say more about this syndrome later in the chapter, but for now let's highlight a paradox. These patients, like H.M., are profoundly amnesic; they're completely unable to recall the events of their own lives. But these patients (and H.M. as well) all seem to have "unconscious" memories—memories they don't know they have.

We reveal these unconscious memories if we test Korsakoff's patients *indirectly*. For example, if we ask them, "Which of these melodies did you hear an hour ago?" they'll answer randomly—confirming their amnesia. But if we ask them, "Which of these melodies do you prefer?" they're likely to choose the ones that, in fact, they heard an hour ago—indicating that they do somehow remember (and are influenced by) the earlier experience. If we ask them, "Have you ever seen a puzzle like this one before?" they'll say no. But if we ask them to solve the puzzle, their speed will be much faster the second time—even though they insist it's the *first* time they've seen the puzzle. Their speed will be even faster the third time they solve the puzzle and the fourth, although again and again they'll claim they're seeing the puzzle for the very first time. Likewise, they'll fail if we ask them, "I showed you some words a few minutes ago; can you tell me which of those words began 'CHE . . .'?" But, alternatively, we can ask them, "What's the first word that comes to mind that starts 'CHE . . .'?" With this question, they're likely to respond with the word they'd seen earlier—a word that they ostensibly could not remember.

preview of chapter themes

- Learning does not simply place information in memory; instead, learning prepares you to retrieve the information in a particular way. As a result, learning that is good preparation for one sort of retrieval may be inadequate for other sorts of retrieval.

- In general, retrieval is more likely to succeed if your perspective is the same during learning and during retrieval, just as we would expect if learning establishes retrieval paths that help you later when you "travel" the same path in your effort toward locating the target material.

- Some experiences seem to produce unconscious memories. Consideration of these "implicit memory" effects will help us understand the various ways in which memory influences you and will also help us see where the feeling of familiarity comes from.

- Finally, an examination of amnesia confirms a central theme of the chapter—namely, that we cannot speak of "good" or "bad" memory in general. Instead, we need to evaluate memory by considering how, and for what purposes, the memory will be used.

These observations invite the claim that there are different types of memory—including a type that's massively disrupted in these amnesic patients, and one that is apparently intact (also see **Figure 7.1**). But how many types of memory are there? How does each one function? Is it possible that processes or strategies that create one type of memory might be less useful for some other type? These questions will be central to this chapter.

FIGURE 7.1 MIRROR DRAWING

(Panel A) In a mirror-drawing task, participants must draw a precisely defined shape—they might be asked, for example, to trace a line between the inner and outer star. The trick, though, is that the participants can see the figure (and their own hand) only in the mirror. (Panel B) Performance is usually poor at first but gradually gets better. Remarkably, the same pattern of improvement is observed with amnesic patients, even though on each attempt they insist that they're performing this task for the very first time.

Learning as Preparation for Retrieval

Putting information into long-term memory helps you only if you can retrieve that information later on. Otherwise, it would be like putting money into a savings account without the option of ever making withdrawals, or like writing books that could never be read. But let's emphasize that there are different ways to retrieve information from memory. You can try to *recall* the information ("What was the name of your sixth-grade teacher?") or to *recognize* it ("Was the name perhaps Miller?"). If you try to recall the information, a variety of cues may or may not be available ("Did the name perhaps begin with an *M*? Did it perhaps rhyme with 'tiller'"?).

In Chapter 6, we largely ignored these variations in retrieval. We talked as if material was well established in memory or was not, with little regard for how the material would be retrieved from memory. There's reason to believe, however, that we can't ignore these variations in retrieval, and in this chapter we'll examine the interaction between how a bit of information was learned and how it is retrieved later.

The Crucial Role of Retrieval Paths

In Chapter 6, we argued that when you're learning, you're making connections between the newly acquired material and other information already in your memory. Later on, these connections serve as *retrieval paths*: When you want to locate information in memory, you travel on these paths, moving from one memory to the next until you reach the target material.

These claims have an important implication. To see this, bear in mind that retrieval paths—like any paths—have a starting point and an ending point: The path leads you from Point A to Point B. That's useful if you want to move from A to B, but what if you're trying to reach B from somewhere else? What if you're trying to reach Point B, but at the moment you happen to be nowhere close to Point A? In that case, the path linking A and B may not help you.

As an analogy, imagine that you're trying to reach Chicago from somewhere to the west. For this purpose, what you need is some highway coming in from the west. It won't help that you've constructed a wonderful road coming into Chicago from the *east*. That road might be valuable in other circumstances, but it's not the path you need to get from where you are right now to where you're heading.

Do retrieval paths in memory work the same way? If so, we might find cases in which your learning is excellent preparation for one sort of retrieval but useless for other types of retrieval—as if you've built a road coming in from one direction but now need a road from another direction. Do the research data show this pattern?

Context-Dependent Learning

Consider classic studies on **context-dependent learning** (Eich, 1980; Overton, 1985). In one study, Godden and Baddeley (1975) asked scuba divers to learn various materials. Some of the divers learned the material while sitting on dry land; others learned while underwater, hearing the material via a special communication set. Within each group, half of the divers were then tested while above water, and half were tested below (see **Figure 7.2**).

Underwater, the world has a different look, feel, and sound, and this context could easily influence what thoughts come to mind for the divers in the study. Imagine, for example, that a diver is feeling cold while underwater. This context will probably lead him to think "cold-related" thoughts, and with these thoughts in his mind during the learning episode, the diver is likely to form memory connections between these thoughts and the materials he's trying to learn.

Let's now imagine that this diver is back underwater at the time of the memory test. Most likely he'll again feel cold, which may once more lead him to "cold-related" thoughts. These thoughts, in turn, are now connected (we've proposed) to the target materials, and that gives us what we want: The cold triggers certain thoughts, and because of the connections formed during learning, those thoughts trigger the target memories.

Of course, if the diver is tested for the same memory materials *on land*, he might have other links, other memory connections, that will lead to the target memories. Even so, on land the diver will be at a disadvantage because the "cold-related" thoughts aren't triggered—so there will be no benefit from the memory connections that are now in place, linking those thoughts to the sought-after memories.

FIGURE 7.2 THE DESIGN OF A CONTEXT-DEPENDENT LEARNING EXPERIMENT

Half of the participants (deep-sea divers) learned the test material while underwater; half learned while on land. Then, within each group, half were tested while underwater; half were tested on land. We expect a retrieval advantage if the learning and test circumstances match. Therefore, we expect better performance in the top left and bottom right cells.

		Test while	
		On land	Underwater
Learn while	On land	Learning and test circumstances match	*CHANGE* of circumstances between learning and test
	Underwater	*CHANGE* of circumstances between learning and test	Learning and test circumstances match

By this logic, we should expect that divers who learn material while underwater will remember the material best if they're again underwater at the time of the test. This setting will enable them to use the connections they established earlier. In terms of our previous analogy, they've built certain highways, and we've put the divers into a situation in which they can use what they've built. And the opposite is true for divers who learned while on land; they should do best if tested on land. That is exactly what the data show (see **Figure 7.3**).

Similar results have been obtained in other studies, including studies designed to mimic the learning situation of a college student. In one experiment, research participants read a two-page article similar to the sorts of readings they might encounter in their college courses. Half the participants read the article in a quiet setting; half read it in noisy circumstances. When later given a short-answer test, those who read the article in quiet did best if tested in quiet—67% correct answers, compared to 54% correct if tested in a noisy environment. Those who read the article in a noisy environment did better if tested in a noisy environment—62% correct, compared to 46%. (For related results, see, among others, Grant et al., 1998; Smith & Vela, 2001.)

In another study, Smith et al. (1978) reported the same pattern if learning and testing took place in different rooms—with the rooms differing in appearance, sounds, and scent. In this study, though, there was an important twist: In one version of the procedure, the participants learned materials in one room and were tested in a different room. Just before testing, however, the participants were urged to think about the room in which they had learned—what it looked like and how it made them feel. When tested, these participants performed as well as those for whom there was no room change (Smith, 1979). What matters, therefore, is not the *physical* context but the *psychological* context. As a result, you can get the benefits of context-dependent learning through a strategy of **context reinstatement**—re-creating

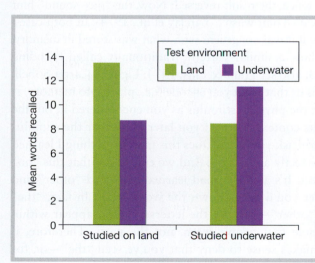

FIGURE 7.3 CONTEXT-DEPENDENT LEARNING

Scuba divers learned materials either while on land or while underwater. Then, they were tested while on land or underwater. Performance was best if the divers' circumstances at the time of the test were matched to those in place during learning. (AFTER GODDEN & BADDELEY, 1975)

TEST YOURSELF

1. What does context-dependent learning tell us about the nature of retrieval paths?
2. In what ways is a retrieval path like an "ordinary" path (e.g., a path or highway leading to a particular city)?

the thoughts and feelings of the learning episode even if you're in a different place at the time of recall. That's because what matters for memory retrieval is the mental context, not the physical environment itself.

Encoding Specificity

In the scuba-diving experiment, notice that the *content* of the divers' memory must have been shaped somehow by the context in which the learning took place. Otherwise, if the context actually left no trace in memory, why would a *return* to the context matter?

Using our analogy once again, we might say that your memory contains both the information you were focusing on during learning *and* the highways you've built, leading toward that information. These highways—the memory connections—can of course guide your search for the target information; that's what we've been emphasizing so far. But it turns out that the connections can do more: They can also change the *meaning* of what is remembered, because "memory plus *this* set of connections" often has a different meaning from "memory plus *that* set of connections." This change in meaning, in turn, can have profound consequences for how you remember the past.

In an early experiment exploring this point, participants read target words (e.g., "piano") in one of two contexts: "The man lifted the piano" or "The man tuned the piano." In each case, the sentence led the participants to think about the target word in a particular way, and it was this thought that was encoded into memory. In other words, what was placed in memory wasn't just the word "piano." Instead, what was recorded in memory was the idea of "piano as something heavy" or "piano as musical instrument."

This difference in memory content became clear when participants were later asked to recall the target words. If they had earlier seen the "lifted" sentence, they were likely to recall the target word if given the cue "something heavy." The hint "something with a nice sound" was much less effective. But if participants had seen the "tuned" sentence, the result reversed: Now, the "nice sound" hint was effective, but the "heavy" hint wasn't (Barclay et al., 1974). In both cases, the cue was effective only if it was congruent with what was stored in memory.

Other experiments show a similar pattern, traditionally called **encoding specificity** (Tulving, 1983; also see Hunt & Ellis, 1974; Light & Carter-Sobell, 1970). This label reminds us that what you encode (i.e., place into memory) is indeed specific—not just the physical stimulus as you encountered it, but the stimulus together with its context. Then, if you later encounter the stimulus *in some other context*, you ask yourself, "Does this match anything I learned previously?" and you correctly answer no. And we emphasize that this "no" response is indeed correct. It's as if you had learned the word "other" and were later asked whether you'd been shown the word "the." In fact, "the" does appear as part of "other"—because the letters *t h e* do appear within "other." But it's the whole that people learn, not the parts. Therefore, if you've seen "other," it makes sense to deny that you've seen "the"—or, for

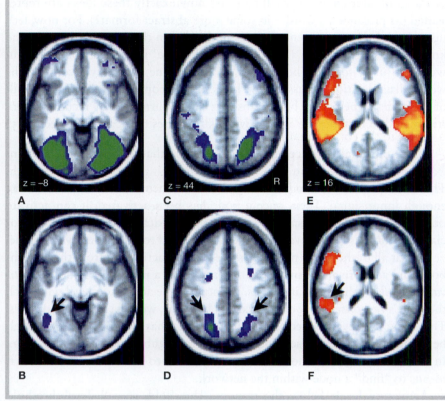

FIGURE 7.4
REMEMBERING
"RE-CREATES" AN
EARLIER EXPERIENCE

The text argues that what goes into your memory is a record of the material you've encountered *and also* a record of the connections you established during learning. On this basis, it makes sense that the brain areas activated when you're remembering a target overlap considerably with the brain areas that were activated when you first encountered the target. Here, the top panels show brain activation while viewing one picture (A), another picture (C), or while hearing a particular sound (E). The bottom panels show brain activation while *remembering* the same targets. (AFTER WHEELER ET AL., 2000)

that matter, "he" or "her"—even though all these letter combinations are contained within "other."

Learning a list of words works in the same way. The word "piano" was contained in what the research participants learned, just as "the" is contained in "other." What was learned, however, wasn't just this word. Instead, what was learned was the broader, integrated experience: the word as the perceiver understood it. Therefore, "piano as musical instrument" *isn't* what participants learned if they saw the "lifted" sentence, so they were correct in asserting that this item wasn't on the earlier list (also see **Figure 7.4**).

The Memory Network

In Chapter 6, we introduced the idea that memory acquisition—and, more broadly, *learning*—involves the creation (or strengthening) of memory connections. In this chapter, we've built on this idea, arguing that the connections serve as retrieval paths guiding you toward the information you seek. But what are these connections? How do they work? And who (or what) is traveling on these "paths"?

TEST YOURSELF

3. What is encoding specificity? How is it demonstrated?

According to many theorists, memory is best thought of as a vast *network* of ideas. In later chapters, we'll consider how exactly these ideas are represented (as pictures? as words? in some more abstract format?). For now, let's just think of these representations as **nodes** within the network, just like the knots in a fisherman's net. (In fact, the word "node" is derived from the Latin word for knot, *nodus*.) These nodes are tied to one another via connections we'll call **associations** or **associative links**. Some people find it helpful to think of the nodes as being like light bulbs that can be turned on by incoming electricity, and to imagine the associative links as wires that carry the electricity.

Spreading Activation

Theorists speak of a node becoming *activated* when it has received a strong enough input signal. Then, once a node has been activated, it can activate other nodes: Energy will spread out from the just-activated node via its associations, and this will activate the nodes connected to the just-activated node.

To put all of this more precisely, nodes receive activation from their neighbors, and as more and more activation arrives at a particular node, the *activation level* for that node increases. Eventually, the activation level will reach the node's *response threshold*. Once this happens, we say that the node *fires*. This firing has several effects, including the fact that the node will now itself be a source of activation, sending energy to its neighbors and activating them. In addition, firing of the node will draw attention to that node; this is what it means to "find" a node within the network.

Activation levels below the response threshold, so-called **subthreshold activation**, also play an important role. Activation is assumed to accumulate, so that two subthreshold inputs may add together, in a process of **summation**, and bring the node to threshold. Likewise, if a node has been partially activated recently, it is in effect already "warmed up," so that even a weak input will now be sufficient to bring it to threshold.

These claims mesh well with points we raised in Chapter 2, when we considered how neurons communicate with one another. Neurons receive activation from other neurons; once a neuron reaches its threshold, it fires, sending activation to other neurons. All of this is precisely parallel to the suggestions we're describing here.

Our current discussion also parallels claims offered in Chapter 4, when we described how a network of detectors might function in object recognition. In other words, the network linking *memories* to one another will resemble the networks linking *detectors* to one another (e.g., Figure 4.9). Detectors, like memory nodes, receive their activation from other detectors; they can accumulate activation from different inputs, and once activated to threshold levels, they fire.

Returning to long-term storage, however, the key idea is that activation travels from node to node via associative links. As each node becomes activated and fires, it serves as a source for further activation, spreading onward through the network. This process, known as **spreading activation**, enables us to deal with an obvious issue: How does one navigate through the maze of associations? If you start a search at one node, how do you choose where to go from there? The answer is that in most cases you don't "choose" at all. Instead, activation spreads out from its starting point in all directions simultaneously, flowing through whatever connections are in place.

Retrieval Cues

This sketch of the memory network leaves a great deal unspecified, but even so it allows us to explain some well-established results. For example, why do hints help you to remember? Why, for example, do you draw a blank if asked, "What's the capital of South Dakota?" but then remember if given the cue "Is it perhaps a man's name?" Here's one likely explanation. Mention of South Dakota will activate nodes in memory that represent your knowledge about this state. Activation will then spread outward from these nodes, eventually reaching nodes that represent the capital city's name. It's possible, though, that there's only a weak connection between the SOUTH DAKOTA nodes and the nodes representing PIERRE. Maybe you're not very familiar with South Dakota, or maybe you haven't thought about this state's capital for some time. In either case, this weak connection will do a poor job of carrying the activation, with the result that only a trickle of activation will flow into the PIERRE nodes, and so these nodes won't reach threshold and therefore won't be "found."

Things will go differently, though, if a hint is available. If you're told, "South Dakota's capital is also a man's name," this will activate the MAN's NAME node. As a result, activation will spread out from this source at the same time that activation is spreading out from the SOUTH DAKOTA nodes. Therefore, the nodes for PIERRE will now receive activation from two sources simultaneously, and this will probably be enough to lift the nodes' activation to threshold levels. In this way, question-plus-hint accomplishes more than the question by itself (see **Figure 7.5**). (We should probably mention, though, that most people who live in Pierre pronounce it "pier"—like the thing you fish off of—and not like the man's name. The rest of the country, however, does not know this.)

Semantic Priming

The explanation we've just offered rests on a key assumption—namely, the *summation of subthreshold activation*. In other words, we relied on the idea that the insufficient activation received from one source can add to the insufficient activation received from another source. Either source of activation on its own wouldn't be enough, but the two can combine to activate the target nodes.

Can we document this summation more directly? In a **lexical-decision task**, research participants are shown a series of letter sequences on a computer screen. Some of the sequences spell words; other sequences aren't words (e.g., "blar, plome"). The participants' task is to hit a "yes" button if the sequence spells a word and a "no" button otherwise. Presumably, they perform this task by "looking up" these letter strings in their "mental dictionary," and

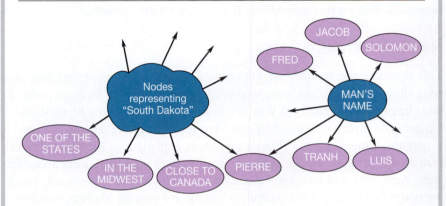

FIGURE 7.5 ACTIVATION OF A NODE FROM TWO SOURCES

A participant is asked, "What is the capital of South Dakota?" This activates the SOUTH DAKOTA nodes, and activation spreads from there to all of the associated nodes. However, it's possible that the connection between SOUTH DAKOTA and PIERRE is weak, so PIERRE may not receive enough activation to reach threshold. Things will go differently, though, if the participant is also given the hint "South Dakota's capital is also a man's name." Now, the PIERRE node will receive activation from two sources: the SOUTH DAKOTA nodes and the MAN'S NAME nodes. With this double input, it's more likely that the PIERRE node will reach threshold. This is why the hint ("man's name") makes the memory search easier.

base their response on whether or not they find the string in the dictionary. We can therefore use participants' speed of response as an index of how quickly they can locate the word in their memories.

In a series of classic studies, Meyer and Schvaneveldt (1971; Meyer et al., 1974) presented participants with *pairs* of letter strings, and participants had to respond "yes" if both strings were words and "no" otherwise. For example, participants would say "yes" in response to "chair, bread" but "no" in response to "house, fime." Also, if both strings were words, sometimes the words were semantically related in an obvious way (e.g., "nurse, doctor") and sometimes they weren't ("cake, shoe"). Of interest was how this relationship between the words would influence performance.

Consider a trial in which participants see a related pair, like "bread, butter." To choose a response, they first need to "look up" the word "bread" in memory. This means they'll search for, and presumably activate, the relevant node, and in this way they'll decide that, yes, this string is a legitimate word. Then, they're ready for the second word. But in this sequence, the node for BREAD (the first word in the pair) has just been activated. This will, we've hypothesized, trigger a spread of activation outward from this node, bringing activation to other, nearby nodes. These nearby nodes will surely include BUTTER, since the association between "bread" and "butter" is a strong one.

Therefore, once the BREAD node (from the first word) is activated, some activation should also spread to the BUTTER node.

From this base, think about what happens when participants turn their attention to the second word in the pair. To select a response, they must locate "butter" in memory. If they find this word (i.e., find the relevant node), then they know that this string, too, is a word, and they can hit the "yes" button. But the process of activating the BUTTER node has already begun, thanks to the (subthreshold) activation this node just received from BREAD. This should accelerate the process of bringing this node to threshold (since it's already partway there), and so it will require less time to activate. As a result, we expect quicker responses to "butter" in this context, compared to a context in which "butter" was preceded by some unrelated word.

Our prediction, therefore, is that trials with related words will produce **semantic priming**. The term "priming" indicates that a specific prior event (in this case, presentation of the first word in the pair) will produce a state of readiness (and, therefore, faster responding) later on. There are various forms of priming (in Chapter 4, we discussed *repetition* priming). In the procedure we're considering here, the priming results from the fact that the two words in the pair are related in meaning—therefore, this is *semantic* priming.

The results confirm these predictions. Participants' lexical-decision responses were faster if the stimulus words were related (see **Figure 7.6**), just as we would expect on the model we're developing.

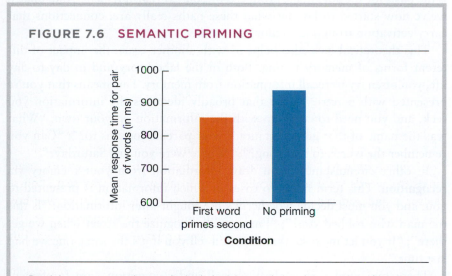

FIGURE 7.6   SEMANTIC PRIMING

Participants were given a lexical-decision task involving pairs of words. In some pairs, the words were semantically related (and so the first word in the pair primed the second); in other pairs, the words were unrelated (and so there was no priming). Responses to the second word were reliably faster if the word had been primed—providing clear evidence of the importance of subthreshold activation. (AFTER MEYER & SCHVANEVELDT, 1971)

4. What is subthreshold activation of a memory node? What role does subthreshold activation play in explaining why retrieval hints are often helpful?

5. How does semantic priming illustrate the effectiveness of sub-threshold activation?

Before moving on, though, we should mention that this process of spreading activation—with one node activating nearby nodes—is not the whole story for memory search. As one complication, people have some control over the *starting points* for their memory searches, relying on the mechanisms of executive control (Chapters 5 and 6). In addition, evidence suggests that once the spreading activation has begun, people have the option of "shutting down" some of this spread if they're convinced that the wrong nodes are being activated (e.g., Anderson & Bell, 2001; Johnson & Anderson, 2004). Even so, spreading activation is a crucial mechanism. It plays a central role in retrieval, and it helps us understand why memory connections are so important and so helpful.

Different Forms of Memory Testing

Let's pause to review. In Chapter 6, we argued that learning involves the creation or strengthening of connections. This is why memory is promoted by understanding (because understanding consists, in large part, of seeing how new material is connected to other things you know). We also proposed that these connections later serve as retrieval paths, guiding your search through the vast warehouse that is memory. In this chapter, we've explored an important implication of this idea: that (like all paths) the paths through memory have both a starting point and an end point. Therefore, retrieval paths will be helpful only if you're at the appropriate starting point; this, we've proposed, is the basis for the advantage produced by *context reinstatement*. And, finally, we've now started to lay out what these paths really are: connections that carry activation from one memory to another.

This theoretical base also helps us with another issue: the impact of different forms of memory testing. Both in the laboratory and in day-to-day life, you often try to **recall** information from memory. This means that you're presented with a retrieval cue that broadly identifies the information you seek, and you need to come up with the information on your own: "What was the name of that great restaurant your parents took us to?"; "Can you remember the words to that song?"; "Where were you last Saturday?"

In other circumstances, you draw information from your memory via **recognition**. This term refers to cases in which information is presented to you, and you must decide whether it's the sought-after information: "Is this the man who robbed you?"; "I'm sure I'll recognize the street when we get there"; "If you let me taste that wine, I'll tell you if it's the same one we had last time."

These two modes of retrieval—recall and recognition—are fundamentally different from each other. Recall—by definition—involves a situation in which you have to come up with the sought-after information on your own. Recall therefore requires memory search, because you need to locate the information within memory. As a result, recall depends heavily on the memory connections we've been emphasizing so far.

Recognition, in contrast, often depends on a sense of **familiarity**. Imagine, for example, that you're taking a recognition test, and the fifth word on the test is "butler." In response to this word, you might find yourself thinking, "I don't recall seeing this word on the list, but this word feels really familiar, so I guess I must have seen it recently. Therefore, it must have been on the list." In this situation, you know *that* this test word feels familiar, but you're not sure *why* it feels familiar; in other words, you can't specify the *source* of the familiarity. Even so, even without **source memory**, you make a sensible inference about where the familiarity came from: You attribute the familiarity to the earlier encounter, and thanks to this **attribution** you'll probably respond "yes" on the recognition test.

Familiarity and Source Memory

But what sort of remembering is involved when some word (or face, or idea) feels familiar to you? Let's be clear, first, that familiarity is distinct from source memory. We know this because the two types of memory are independent of each other—so it's possible for an event to be familiar without any source memory, and possible to have source memory without familiarity. As an illustration, think about the common experience in which you're watching a movie and realize that one of the actors is familiar, but (with considerable frustration) you can't recall where you've seen that actor before. Or you're walking down the street and see a familiar face, but immediately find yourself asking, "Where do I know that woman from? Does she work at the grocery store I shop in? Is she the driver of the bus I often take?" You're at a loss to answer these questions; all you know is that the face is familiar.

In cases like these, you can't "place" the memory; you can't identify the context in which the face was last encountered. But you're certain the face is familiar, even though you don't know why—a clear example of familiarity without source memory.

Here's the opposite case: In Chapter 2 we discussed Capgras syndrome. Someone with this syndrome might have a detailed, accurate memory of (for example) what his father looks like, and probably remembers where and when he last saw his father. Even so, when his father is in view, his face looks hauntingly unfamiliar. This is a situation with source memory but no familiarity. (For further evidence—and a patient who, after surgery, has intact source memory but disrupted familiarity—see Bowles et al., 2007; also see Yonelinas & Jacoby, 2012.)

We can also document the difference between source memory and familiarity another way. In many studies, research participants have been asked, during a recognition test, to make a **"remember/know" distinction**. This involves pressing one button (to indicate "remember") if they actually recall the episode of encountering a particular item, and pressing a different button ("know") if they don't recall the encounter but just have a broad feeling that the item must have been on the earlier list. With one response, participants

"THEY LOOK SO FAMILIAR . . . BUT WHERE DO I KNOW THEM FROM?!?"

The photos here show successful TV or film actors. The odds are good that for some of them you'll immediately register that the faces seem familiar but won't be sure why. You know you've seen these actors in some movie or show, but which one? (We provide the actors' names at the chapter's end.)

TEST YOURSELF

6. Define "recognition" and "recall."
7. What evidence indicates that source memory and familiarity are distinct from each other?

are indicating that they have a source memory; with the other, they're indicating an *absence* of source memory. Basically, a participant using the "know" response is saying, "This item seems familiar, so I know it was on the earlier list even though I don't remember the experience of seeing it" (Gardiner, 1988; Hicks & Marsh, 1999; Jacoby et al., 1998; for some complications, though, see Umanath & Coane, 2020; Williams & Lindsay, 2019).

Using fMRI scans, researchers have shown that "remember" and "know" judgments depend on different brain areas. The scans show heightened activity in the hippocampus when participants indicate that they "remember" a particular test item, suggesting that this brain structure is crucial for source memory. In contrast, "know" responses are associated with activity in a different area—the anterior parahippocampus, with the implication that this brain site is crucial for familiarity. (See Aggleton & Brown, 2006; Diana et al., 2007; Montaldi et al., 2006; Rugg & Curran, 2007; Wagner et al., 2005.)

Familiarity and source memory can also be distinguished during learning. If certain brain areas (e.g., the rhinal cortex) are especially active during learning, then the stimulus is likely to seem familiar later on (see **Figure 7.7A**). In contrast, if other brain areas (e.g., the hippocampal region) are particularly active during learning, there's a high probability that the person will indicate source memory for that stimulus when tested later (**Figure 7.7B**). (See, e.g., Davachi & Dobbins, 2008; Davachi et al., 2003; Ranganath et al., 2003.)

We still need to ask, though, what's going on in these various brain areas to create the relevant memories. Activity in the hippocampus is probably helping to create the memory connections we've been discussing all along, and it's these connections that promote source memory. But what about familiarity? What "record" does it leave in memory? The answer to this question leads us to a very different sort of memory.

FIGURE 7.7 FAMILIARITY VERSUS SOURCE MEMORY

Subsequent familiarity effects

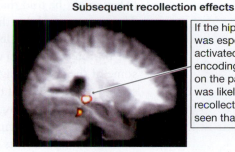

If the rhinal cortex was especially activated during encoding, then the stimulus was likely to seem familiar when viewed later on.

Subsequent recollection effects

If the hippocampus was especially activated during encoding, then later on the participant was likely to recollect having seen that stimulus.

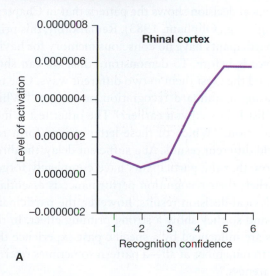

Rhinal cortex

Level of activation

0.0000008
0.0000006
0.0000004
0.0000002
0.0000000
−0.0000002

Recognition confidence
1 2 3 4 5 6

A

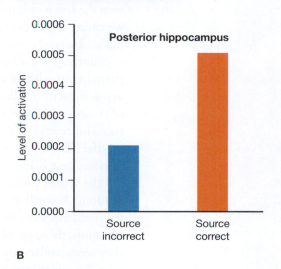

Posterior hippocampus

Level of activation

0.0006
0.0005
0.0004
0.0003
0.0002
0.0001
0.0000

Source incorrect   Source correct

B

In this study, researchers tracked participants' brain activity during encoding and then analyzed the data according to what happened later, when the time came for retrieval.   (AFTER RANGANATH ET AL., 2003)

Implicit Memory

How can we find out if someone remembers a previous event? The obvious path is to ask her—"How did the job interview go?"; "Have you ever been to a Beyoncé concert?"; "Is this the book you told me about?" But at the start of this chapter, we talked about a different approach: We can expose someone to an event, then later reexpose her to the same event and assess whether her response to the second encounter is different from the first. Specifically, we can ask whether the first encounter somehow *primed* the person—got her ready— for the second exposure. If so, it would seem that the person must retain some record of the first encounter—she must have some sort of memory.

Memory without Awareness

In a number of studies, participants have been asked to read through a list of words, with no indication that their memories would be tested later on. (They might be told that they're merely checking the list for spelling errors.) Then, sometime later, the participants are given a lexical-decision task: They are shown a series of letter strings and, for each, must indicate (by pressing one button or another) whether the string is a word or not. Crucially, though, some of the letter strings in the lexical-decision task are duplicates of words seen in the first part of the experiment (i.e., they were on the list participants had checked for spelling), enabling us to ask whether the first exposure somehow primed the participants for the second encounter.

In these experiments, lexical decisions are quicker if the person has recently seen the test word; that is, lexical decision shows the pattern that in Chapter 4 we called "repetition priming" (e.g., Oliphant, 1983). Remarkably, this priming is observed even when participants have no conscious memory for having encountered the stimulus words before. To demonstrate this, we can show participants a list of words and then test them in two different ways. One test assesses memory directly, using a standard recognition procedure: "Which of these words were on the list I showed you earlier?" The other test is indirect and relies on lexical decision: "Which of these letter strings form real words?" These two tests yield different results. At a sufficient delay, the direct memory test is likely to show that the participants have completely forgotten the words presented earlier; their recognition performance is essentially random. According to the lexical-decision results, however, the participants still remember the words—and so they show a strong priming effect. In this situation, then, participants are influenced by a specific past experience that they seem (consciously) not to remember at all—a pattern sometimes referred to as "memory without awareness."

A different example draws on a task called **word-stem completion**. In this task, participants are given three or four letters and must produce a word with this beginning. If, for example, they're given *cla-*, then "clam" or "clatter" would be acceptable responses, and the question of interest for us is which of these responses the participants produce. It turns out that people are more likely to offer a specific word if they've encountered it recently; once again, this priming effect is observed even if participants, when tested directly, show no conscious memory of their recent encounter with that word (Graf et al., 1982).

Results like these lead psychologists to distinguish two types of memory. **Explicit memories** are those usually revealed by **direct memory testing**—testing that urges participants to remember the past. Recall is a direct memory test; so is a standard recognition test. **Implicit memories**, however, are typically revealed by **indirect memory testing** and are often manifested as priming effects. In this form of testing, participants' current behavior is demonstrably influenced by a prior event, but they may be unaware of this. Lexical decision, word-stem completion, and many other tasks provide indirect means of assessing memory. (See, for example, Mulligan & Besken, 2013; for a different perspective on these data, though, see Cabeza & Moscovitch, 2012.)

How exactly is implicit memory different from explicit memory? We'll say more about this question before we're done; but first we need to say more about how implicit memory *feels* from the rememberer's point of view. This will lead us back into our discussion of familiarity and source memory.

False Fame

In a classic study, Jacoby et al. (1989) presented participants with a list of names to read out loud. The participants were told nothing about a memory test; they thought the experiment was concerned with how they pronounced the names. Sometime later, in the second step of the procedure, the participants were shown a new list of names and were asked to rate each person on this list according to how famous each one was. The list included some real, very famous people; some real but not-so-famous people; and some fictitious names that the experimenters had invented. The fictitious names, though, were of two types: Some had occurred on the prior ("pronunciation") list, and some were simply new names. A comparison between those two types will indicate how the prior familiarization (during the pronunciation task) influenced the participants' judgments of fame.

For some participants, the "famous" list was presented right after the "pronunciation" list; for other participants, there was a 24-hour delay between these two steps. To see how this delay matters, imagine that you're a participant in the immediate-testing condition: When you see one of the fictitious-but-familiar names, you might decide, "This name sounds familiar, but that's because I just saw it on the previous list." In this situation, you have a feeling that the (familiar) name is distinctive, but you also know *why* it's distinctive—because you remember your earlier encounter with the name. In other words, you have both a sense of familiarity *and* a source memory, so there's nothing here to persuade you that the name belongs to someone famous, and you respond accordingly. But now imagine that you're a participant in the other condition, with the 24-hour delay. Because of the delay, you may not recall seeing that particular name in the pronunciation task. But the broad sense of familiarity remains anyway, so in this setting you might say, "This name rings a bell, and I have no idea why. I guess this must be a famous person." And this is, in fact, the pattern of the data: When the two lists are presented one day apart, participants are likely to rate the made-up names as being famous.

Apparently, the participants in this study noted (correctly) that some of the names did "ring a bell" and so did trigger a certain feeling of familiarity. The false judgments of fame, however, come from the way participants *interpreted* this feeling and what conclusions they drew from it. Basically, participants in the 24-hour-delay condition forgot the real source of the familiarity (appearance on a recently viewed list) and instead filled in a bogus source ("Maybe I saw this person in a movie?"). And it's easy to see why they made this misattribution. After all, the experiment was described to them as being about fame, and other names on the list were actually those of famous people. From the participants' point of view, therefore, it was reasonable to infer in this setting that any name that "rings a bell" belongs to a famous person.

We need to be clear, though, that this misattribution is possible only because the feeling of familiarity produced by these names was relatively vague and therefore open to interpretation. The suggestion, then, is that implicit memories may leave people with only a broad sense that a stimulus is somehow distinctive—that it "rings a bell" or "strikes a chord." What happens after this depends on how they interpret that feeling. (For more on "false fame," see Buchli, 2019.)

Implicit Memory and the "Illusion of Truth"

How broad is this potential for *mis*interpreting an implicit memory? Participants in one study heard a series of statements and had to judge how interesting each statement was (Begg et al., 1992). As an example, one sentence was "The average person in Switzerland eats about 25 pounds of cheese each year." (This is false; the average in 1992, when the experiment was done, was closer to 18 pounds.) Another was "Henry Ford forgot to put a reverse gear in his first automobile." (This is true, and it must have been embarrassing the first time he parked the car facing a wall.)

After hearing these sentences, the participants were presented with some more sentences, but now they had to judge the credibility of these sentences, rating them on a scale from *certainly true* to *certainly false*. However, some of the sentences in this "truth test" were repeats from the earlier presentation, and the question of interest is how sentence credibility is influenced by sentence familiarity.

In this study (and many others), sentences heard before were more likely to be accepted as true. That is, familiarity increased credibility—a pattern known as the **illusion of truth**. (See Begg et al., 1985; Brown & Halliday, 1990; Moons et al., 2009; Cornielle et al. 2020.) What's going on here? At the time of the "truth" test, participants were of course still able to remember that they'd earlier rated a bunch of sentences for how interesting they were. But, thanks to a short delay, they no longer remembered all of the specific sentences they'd seen in that earlier step of the procedure. In other words, they no longer had a (conscious) explicit memory for many of these sentences. They did, however, still have an implicit memory for these specific sentences. This memory left them, though, only with a sense that the sentence seemed vaguely familiar, and with no clear recollection of where that familiarity was coming from. This apparently led them to thoughts along the lines of "I'm sure I've heard that somewhere before; I guess it must be true."

The relevance of this result to the political arena or to advertising should be clear. A newspaper headline might inquire, "Is Mayor Wilson a crook?" Or the headline might declare, "Known liar claims Wilson is a crook!" In either case, the assertion that Wilson is a crook would become familiar, and this familiarity can, by itself, increase the likelihood that you'll later believe in Wilson's dishonesty. Political mudslinging does, in fact, produce nasty effects.

(For related findings, including the other effects of political misinformation, see Ecker et al., 2014; Unkelbach et al., 2019.)

Attributing Implicit Memory to the Wrong Source

A different example involves the legal system. In an early study by Brown et al. (1977), research participants witnessed a staged crime. Two or three days later, they were shown "mug shots" of individuals who supposedly had participated in the crime. But as it turns out, the people in these photos were different from the actual "criminals"—no mug shots were shown for the truly "guilty" individuals. Finally, after four or five more days, the participants were shown a lineup and were asked to select the individuals seen in Step 1—namely, the original crime (see **Figure 7.8**).

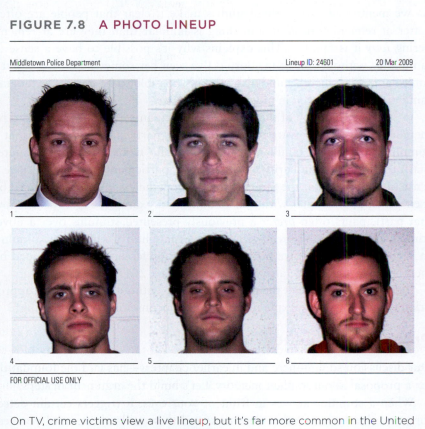

FIGURE 7.8   A PHOTO LINEUP

Middletown Police Department   Lineup ID: 24601   20 Mar 2009

1 _____   2 _____   3 _____

4 _____   5 _____   6 _____

FOR OFFICIAL USE ONLY

On TV, crime victims view a live lineup, but it's far more common in the United States for the victim (or witness) to see a "photo lineup" like this one. Unfortunately, victims sometimes pick the wrong person, and this error is more likely to occur if the suspect is familiar to the victim for some reason other than the crime. The error is unlikely, though, if the face is *very* familiar, because in that case the witness will have both a feeling of familiarity and an accurate source memory. ("Number 2 looks familiar, but that's because I see him at the gym all the time.")

TEST YOURSELF

8. What is the difference between implicit and explicit memory? Which of these is said to be "memory without awareness"?

9. What is the role of implicit memory in explaining the false fame effect?

The data in this study show a pattern known as **source confusion**. The participants correctly realized that one of the faces in the lineup looked familiar, but they were confused about the source of the familiarity. They falsely believed they had seen the person's face in the original "crime," when, in truth, they'd seen that face only in a subsequent photograph. In fact, the likelihood of this error was quite high, with 29% of the participants (falsely) selecting from the lineup an individual they had seen only in the mug shots. (Also see Davis et al., 2008; Kersten & Earles, 2017. For examples of similar errors in real-life criminal investigations, see Garrett, 2011. For a broader discussion of eyewitness errors, see Reisberg, 2014.)

Theoretical Treatments of Implicit Memory

As we mentioned earlier, these studies make it clear that people are often better at remembering *that* something is familiar than they are at remembering *why* it is familiar. This explains why it's possible to have a sense of familiarity without source memory ("I've seen her somewhere before, but I can't figure out where!") and also why it's possible to be *correct* in judging familiarity but *mistaken* in judging source.

In addition, in many of these studies, participants are being influenced by memories they aren't aware of. In some cases, participants do realize that a stimulus is somehow familiar, but they have no memory of the encounter that produced the familiarity. In other cases, participants don't even have a sense of familiarity for the target stimulus; nonetheless, they're influenced by their previous encounter with that stimulus. For example, experiments show that participants often *prefer* a previously presented stimulus over a novel stimulus, even though they have no sense of familiarity with either stimulus. In such cases, people have no idea that their preference is being guided by memory (Murphy, 2001; also see Montoya et al., 2017).

It does seem, then, that the phrase "memory without awareness" is appropriate. But how can we explain this form of unconscious "remembering"?

Processing Fluency

Our discussion so far—here and in earlier chapters—has laid the foundation for a proposal about implicit memory. Let's build the argument in steps.

When a stimulus arrives in front of your eyes, it triggers certain detectors, and these trigger other detectors, and these still others, until you recognize the object. ("Oh, it's my stuffed bear, Blueberry.") We can think of this sequence as involving a "flow" of activation that moves from detector to detector. We could, if we wished, keep track of this flow and in this way identify the "path" that the activation traveled through the network. Let's refer to this path as a **processing pathway**—the sequence of detectors, and the connections *between* detectors, that the activation flows through in recognizing a specific stimulus.

Cryptoplagiarism

In 1970, (former Beatle) George Harrison released the song "My Sweet Lord." It turns out, though, that the song is virtually identical to one released years before that—"He's So Fine," by the Chiffons—and in 1976 Harrison was found guilty of copyright infringement. (You can find both recordings on YouTube, and you'll instantly see that they're really the same song.) In his conclusion to the court proceedings, the judge wrote, "Did Harrison deliberately use the music of 'He's So Fine'? I do not believe he did so deliberately. Nevertheless, it is clear that 'My Sweet Lord' is the very same song as 'He's So Fine.' . . . This is, under the law, infringement of copyright, and is no less so even though subconsciously accomplished" (*Bright Tunes Music Corp. v. Harrisongs Music, Ltd.*, 420 F. Supp. 177—Dist. Court, SD New York 1976).

How can we understand the judge's remarks? Can there be "subconscious" plagiarism? The answer is yes, and the pattern at issue is sometimes referred to as "cryptoplagiarism"—inadvertent copying that is entirely unwitting and uncontrollable, and usually copying that comes with the strong sense that you're the inventor of the idea, even though you've taken the idea from someone else.

In one study, participants sat in groups and were asked to generate words in particular categories— for example, names of sports or musical instruments (Brown & Murphy, 1989; also Marsh et al., 1999). Later, the same participants were asked to recall the words they (and not others in the group) had generated, and also to generate new entries in the same categories. In this setting, participants often "borrowed" others' contributions—sometimes (mis)remembering others' words as though they had themselves produced them, sometimes offering words as "new" when, in fact, they'd been mentioned by someone else in the initial session.

This pattern fits well with the chapter's discussion of implicit memory. The participants in this study (and others) had lost any explicit memory of the earlier episode in which they encountered someone else's ideas. Even so, an implicit memory remained and emerged as a priming effect. Specifically, because of the priming, participants were more likely to produce those words when asked— with no realization that their production had been influenced by a prior episode.

Likewise, imagine talking with a friend about your options for an upcoming writing assignment. Your friend suggests a topic, but after a moment's thought you reject the suggestion, convinced that the topic is too challenging. A few days later, you're again trying to choose a topic, and (because of the priming) your friend's suggestion comes to mind. Thanks to the earlier conversation with your friend, though, you now have the advantage of some "warm-up" in considering this topic, and that helps you to think through how you might develop the idea. As a result, you decide that the topic isn't so challenging after all, and you go forward with the topic—all with no conscious recollection of your initial conversation with your friend. So you may not realize that the idea "came to you" because of a priming effect, and you may be entirely unaware that the idea seemed workable only because of the "warm-up" provided by the early conversation. The outcome: You'll present the idea as though it's entirely your own, giving your friend none of the credit she deserves.

We don't know if this is what happened with George Harrison. Even so, the judge's conclusion in that case seems entirely plausible, and there's no question that inadvertent, unconscious plagiarism is a real phenomenon.

In the same way, we've proposed in this chapter that *remembering* often involves the activation of a node, and this node triggers other nearby nodes so that they become activated; they trigger still other nodes, leading eventually to the information you seek in memory. So here, too, we can speak of a processing pathway—the sequence of nodes, and connections between nodes, that the activation flows through during memory retrieval.

We've also said that the use of a processing pathway *strengthens* that pathway. This is because the baseline activation level of nodes or detectors increases if the nodes or detectors have been used frequently in the past, or if they've been used recently. Likewise, connections (between detectors or nodes) grow stronger with use. For example, by thinking about the link between, say, "Katherine" and "Los Angeles," you can strengthen the connection between the corresponding nodes, and this will help you remember that your friend Katherine lives in LA.

Now, let's put the pieces together. Use of a processing pathway strengthens the pathway. As a result, the pathway will be a bit more efficient, a bit faster, the next time you use it. Theorists describe this fact by saying that use of a pathway increases the pathway's **processing fluency**—that is, the speed and ease with which the pathway will carry activation.

In many cases, this is all the theory we need to explain implicit memory effects. Consider implicit memory's effect on lexical decision. In this procedure, you first are shown a list of words, including, let's say, the word "bubble." Then, we ask you to do the lexical-decision task, and we find that you're faster for words (like "bubble") that had been included in the earlier list. This increase in speed provides evidence for implicit memory, and the explanation is straightforward. When we show you "bubble" early in the experiment, you read the word, and this involves activation flowing through the appropriate processing pathway for this word. This warms up the pathway, and as a result the path's functioning will be more fluent the next time you use it. Of course, when "bubble" shows up later as part of the lexical-decision task, it's handled by the same (now, more fluent) pathway, and so the word is processed more rapidly—exactly the outcome that we're trying to explain.

For other implicit-memory effects, though, we need a further assumption—namely, that people are *sensitive* to the degree of processing fluency. That is, just as people can tell whether they've lifted a heavy carton or a lightweight one, or whether they've answered an easy question ("What's 2 + 2?") or a harder one ("What's 17 × 19?"), people also have a broad sense of when they have perceived easily and when they have perceived only by expending more effort. They likewise know when a sequence of thoughts was particularly fluent and when the sequence was labored.

This fluency, however, is perceived in an odd way. For example, when a stimulus is easy to perceive, you don't experience something like "That stimulus sure was easy to recognize!" Instead, you merely register a vague sense of specialness. You feel that the stimulus "rings a bell." No matter how it is described, though, this sense of specialness has a simple cause—namely, the detection of fluency, created by practice.

People also seem to notice *discrepancies* between how easy (or hard) it was to carry out some mental step and how easy (or hard) they expected it to be (Wänke & Hansen, 2015; Whittlesea, 2002). In other words, a stimulus is registered as distinctive, or "rings a bell," when you detect a difference between experience and expectations. To see how this matters, imagine that a friend unexpectedly gets a haircut (or gets new eyeglasses, or adds or removes some facial hair). When you see your friend, you realize immediately that *something* has changed, but you're not sure what. You're likely to ask puzzled questions ("Are those new glasses?") and get a scornful answer. ("No, you've seen these glasses a hundred times over the last year.") Eventually your friend tells you what the change is—pointing out that you failed to notice that he'd shaved off his mustache (or some such).

What's going on here? You obviously can still recognize your friend, but your recognition is less fluent than in the past because of the change in your friend's appearance, and you notice this change—but then are at a loss to explain it (see **Figure 7.9**).

We still need one more step in our hypothesis, but it's a step we've already introduced: When a stimulus feels special (because of a change in fluency or a discrepancy between the fluency expected and the fluency experienced), you often want to know why. Thus, the vague feeling of specialness (again, produced by fluency) can trigger an attribution process, as you ask, "Why did that stimulus stand out?"

In many circumstances, you'll answer this question correctly, and so the specialness will be (accurately) interpreted as *familiarity* and attributed to the correct

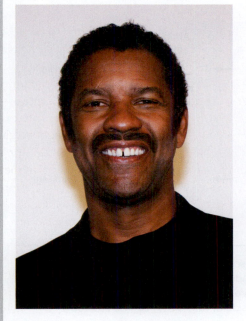

FIGURE 7.9   CHANGES IN APPEARANCE

The text emphasizes our sensitivity to increases in fluency, but we can also detect decreases. For example, in viewing a picture of someone whose face you know, you might notice that something is new in his appearance, but you might be unsure about what exactly the change involves. In this setting, the change in appearance has disrupted your well-practiced steps of perceiving an otherwise familiar face, so your perception of the face is *less* fluent than it's been in the past. This lack of fluency is what gives you the "something is new" feeling. But then the attribution step fails: You can't identify what produced this feeling (so you end up offering various weak hypotheses, such as "Is that a new haircut?" when, in fact, it's a mustache and goatee that are new). This case provides the mirror image of the cases we've been considering, in which familiarity leads to an *increase* in fluency, so that something "rings a bell" but you can't say why. In the picture shown here, you probably recognize Denzel Washington, and you probably also realize that something is "off" in the picture. Can you figure out what it is? (We've actually made several changes to Denzel's appearance; can you spot them all?)

source. ("That woman seems distinctive, and I know why: It's the woman I saw yesterday in the dentist's office.") In other situations, though, things don't go so smoothly, and—as we have seen—people sometimes misinterpret their own processing fluency, falling prey to the errors and illusions we have been discussing.

The Nature of Familiarity

All of these points provide us—at last—with a proposal for what "familiarity" is, and the proposal is surprisingly complex. You might think that familiarity is simply a feeling that's produced more or less directly when you encounter a stimulus you've met before. But the research findings we've been discussing point toward a different proposal—namely, that "familiarity" is more like a *conclusion that you draw* rather than a *feeling triggered by a stimulus*. Specifically, the evidence suggests that a stimulus will seem familiar whenever the following list of requirements is met: First, you have encountered the stimulus before. Second, because of that prior encounter (and the "practice" it provided), your processing of that stimulus is now faster and more efficient; there is, in other words, an increase in processing fluency. Third, you detect that increased fluency, and this leads you to register the stimulus as somehow distinctive or special. Fourth, you try to figure out *why* the stimulus seems special, and you reach a particular conclusion—namely, that the stimulus has this distinctive quality *because* it's a stimulus you've met before in some prior episode (see **Figure 7.10**).

FIGURE 7.10 THE CHAIN OF EVENTS LEADING TO THE SENSE OF "FAMILIARITY"

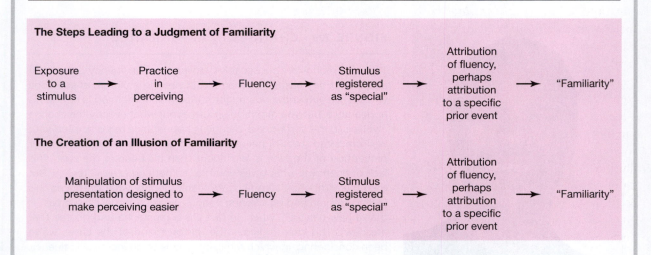

In the top line, practice in perceiving leads to fluency, and if the person attributes the fluency to some specific prior event, the stimulus will "feel familiar." The bottom line, however, indicates that fluency can be created in other ways: by presenting the stimulus more clearly or for a longer exposure. Once this fluency is detected, though, it can lead to steps identical to those in the top row. In this way, an "illusion of familiarity" can be created.

Let's be clear, though, that none of these steps happens consciously—you're not aware of seeking an interpretation or trying to explain why a stimulus feels distinctive. All you experience consciously is the end product of all these steps: the sense that a stimulus feels familiar. Moreover, this conclusion about a stimulus isn't one you draw carelessly; instead, you're likely to arrive at this conclusion only when you have supporting information. Thus, imagine that you encounter a stimulus that "rings a bell." You're likely to decide the stimulus is familiar if, perhaps, you also have an (explicit) source memory, so that you can recall where and when you last encountered that stimulus. You're also likely to decide a stimulus is familiar if the surrounding circumstances support it. For example, if you're asked, "Which of these words were on the list you saw earlier?" the question itself gives you a cue that some of the words were recently encountered, and so you're more likely to attribute fluency to that encounter.

The fact remains, though, that judgments like these sometimes go astray, which is why we need this complicated theory. We've considered cases in which a stimulus is objectively familiar (you've seen it recently) but doesn't *feel* familiar—just as our theory predicts. In these cases, you detect the fluency but attribute it to some other source. ("That melody is lovely" rather than "The melody is familiar.") In other words, you go through all of the steps shown in the top of Figure 7.10 except for the last two: You don't attribute the fluency to a specific prior event, and so you don't experience a sense of familiarity.

We can also find the opposite sort of case—in which a stimulus is not familiar (i.e., you've *not* seen it recently) but feels familiar anyhow—and this, too, fits with the theory. This sort of *illusion of familiarity* can be produced if the processing of a completely novel stimulus is more fluent than you expected—perhaps because (without telling you) we've sharpened the focus of a computer display or presented the stimulus for a few milliseconds longer than other stimuli you're inspecting (e.g., Whittlesea, 2002; Whittlesea et al., 1990; for other fluency-based illusions, see Lanska & Westerman, 2018). Cases like these can lead to the situation shown in the bottom half of Figure 7.10. And as our theory predicts, these situations do produce an illusion: Your processing of the stimulus is unexpectedly fluent; you seek an attribution for this fluency, and you're fooled into thinking the stimulus is familiar—so you say you've seen the stimulus before, when in fact you haven't. This illusion is a powerful confirmation that the sense of familiarity does rest on processes like the ones we've described. (For more on fluency, see Besken & Mulligan, 2014; Griffin et al., 2012; Hertwig et al., 2008; Lanska et al., 2013; Oppenheimer, 2008; Tsai & Thomas, 2011. For a glimpse of what fluency amounts to in the nervous system, see Knowlton & Foerde, 2008.)

The Hierarchy of Memory Types

There's no question, then, that we're sometimes influenced by the past without being aware of that influence, and so (for example) we respond differently to familiar stimuli than we do to novel stimuli, even if we have no subjective feeling of familiarity. On this basis, it seems that our conscious recollection seriously underestimates what's in our memories, and, in fact, research has documented many ways in which unconscious memories influence what we do, think, and feel.

In addition, the data are telling us that there are two different kinds of memory: one type ("explicit") is conscious and deliberate, the other ("implicit") is typically unconscious and automatic. These two broad categories can then be further subdivided, as shown in **Figure 7.11**. Explicit memories can be subdivided into episodic memories (memory for specific events) and semantic memory (more general knowledge). Episodic and semantic memories do interact in many ways (e.g., Renoult et al., 2019; also see McRae & Jones, 2012; Weidemann et al., 2019), but they are still distinguishable—in their contents, their functioning, and their biological basis.

Implicit memory, in turn, is often divided into four subcategories, as shown in the figure. Our emphasis here has been on one of the subtypes— priming—largely because of its role in producing the feeling of familiarity. However, the other subtypes of implicit memory are also important and can

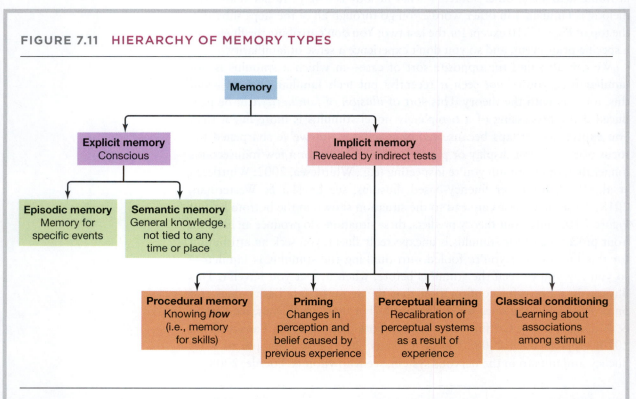

FIGURE 7.11   HIERARCHY OF MEMORY TYPES

In our discussion, we've distinguished two types of memory—explicit and implicit. However, there are reasons to believe that each of these categories must be subdivided further, as shown here. Evidence for these subdivisions includes functional evidence (the various types of memory follow different rules) and biological evidence (the types depend on different aspects of brain functioning).

be distinguished both in terms of their functioning (i.e., they follow some-what different rules) and in their biological underpinnings.

Some of the best evidence for these distinctions, though, comes from the clinic, not the laboratory. In other words, we can learn a great deal about these various types of memory by considering individuals who have suffered different forms of brain damage. Let's look at some of that evidence.

Amnesia

As we have discussed, a variety of injuries or illnesses can lead to a loss of memory, or **amnesia**. Some forms of amnesia are *retrograde*, meaning that they disrupt memory for things learned *prior to* the event that initiated the amnesia (see **Figure 7.12**). **Retrograde amnesia** is often caused by blows to the head; the afflicted person is unable to recall events that occurred just before the blow. Other forms of amnesia have the reverse effect, causing disruption of memory for experiences *after* the onset of amnesia; these are cases of **anterograde amnesia**.

Disrupted Episodic Memory, but Spared Semantic Memory

Studies of amnesia can teach us many things. For example, do we need all the distinctions shown in Figure 7.11? Consider the case of Clive Wearing, whom we met in the opening to Chapter 6. (You can find more detail about Wearing's case in an extraordinary book by his wife—see Wearing, 2011.) Wearing's episodic memory is massively disrupted, but his memory for generic information, as well as his deep love for his wife, seem to be entirely

TEST YOURSELF

10. What is processing fluency, and how does it influence us?
11. In what sense is familiarity more like *a conclusion that you draw*, rather than a *feeling triggered by a stimulus*?

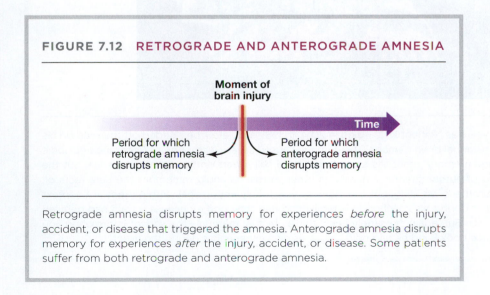

FIGURE 7.12 RETROGRADE AND ANTEROGRADE AMNESIA

Retrograde amnesia disrupts memory for experiences *before* the injury, accident, or disease that triggered the amnesia. Anterograde amnesia disrupts memory for experiences *after* the injury, accident, or disease. Some patients suffer from both retrograde and anterograde amnesia.

intact. Other patients show the reverse pattern—disrupted semantic memory but preserved episodic knowledge. One patient, for example, suffered damage (from encephalitis) to the front portion of her temporal lobes. As a consequence, she lost her memory of many common words, famous people, and even the fundamental traits of animate and inanimate objects. She still had detailed memories, though, for her wedding and honeymoon, her father's illness and death, and other past episodes (Schacter, 1996; also see Cabeza & Nyberg, 2000).

These cases (and other evidence too; see **Figure 7.13**) provide the *double dissociation* that demands a distinction between episodic and semantic memory. It's observations like these that force us to the various distinctions shown in Figure 7.11.

FIGURE 7.13 **SEMANTIC MEMORY WITHOUT EPISODIC MEMORY**

Kent Cochrane—known for years as "Patient K.C."—died in 2014. In 1981, at age 30, he skidded off the road on his motorcycle and suffered substantial brain damage. The damage caused severe disruption of Cochrane's episodic memory but left his semantic memory intact. As a result, he could still report on the events of his life, but the reports were entirely devoid of autobiographical quality. In other words, he could remember the bare facts of, say, what happened at his brother's wedding, but the memory was totally impersonal, with no recall of context or emotion. He also knew that during his childhood his family had fled their home because a train had derailed nearby, spilling toxic chemicals. But, again, he simply knew this as factual material—the sort of information you might pick up from a reference book—and he had no recall of his own experiences during the event.

Anterograde Amnesia

We've mentioned the patient known as H.M. several times. His memory loss was the result of brain surgery in 1953, and over the next 55 years (until his death in 2008) H.M. participated in a vast number of studies. Some people suggest he was the most-studied individual in the history of psychology (for a review of H.M.'s case, see Corkin, 2013; Milner, 1966, 1970; also O'Kane et al., 2004; Skotko et al., 2004, 2008).

After his surgery, H.M. was still able to recall events that took place *before* the surgery—and so his amnesia was largely anterograde, not retrograde. But the amnesia was severe. Episodes he experienced after the surgery, people he had met, stories he had heard—all seemed to leave no lasting record, as though nothing new could get into his long-term storage.

A similar amnesia has been found in patients who have been longtime alcoholics. The problem isn't the alcohol itself; the problem instead is that alcoholics often have inadequate diets and so are vulnerable to problems caused by various forms of malnutrition. One of these problems is the disorder we mentioned at the start of this chapter, the disorder known as **Korsakoff's syndrome** (Rao et al., 1986; Ritchie, 1985).

Patients suffering from Korsakoff's syndrome seem similar to H.M. in many ways. They typically have no problem remembering events that took place before the onset of alcoholism. They can also maintain current topics in mind as long as there's no interruption. New information, though, if displaced from the mind, seems to be lost forever. Korsakoff's patients who have been in the hospital for decades will casually mention that they arrived only a week ago; if asked the name of the current president or events in the news, they unhesitatingly give answers appropriate for two or three decades earlier, whenever the disorder began (Marslen-Wilson & Teuber, 1975; Seltzer & Benson, 1974).

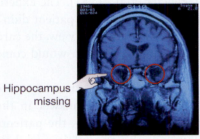 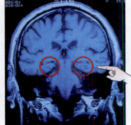

A Anterior   **B** Posterior

H.M.'S BRAIN

H.M.'s contribution to our science continued after his death—with careful postmortem examination of his brain. These MRI scans have revealed that H.M.'s surgery destroyed part of his hippocampus (the anterior portion—i.e., the portion closer to the front of the head; Panel A) but not the posterior portion (closer to the rear of the head; Panel B).

Anterograde Amnesia: What Kind of Memory Is Disrupted?

At the chapter's beginning, we mentioned other evidence that complicates this portrait of anterograde amnesia, and it's evidence that brings us back to the distinction between implicit and explicit memory. As it turns out, some of this evidence has been available for a long time. In 1911, the Swiss psychologist Édouard Claparède (1911–1951) reported the following incident. He was introduced to a young woman suffering from Korsakoff's amnesia, and he reached out to shake her hand. However, Claparède had secretly positioned a pin in his own hand so that when they clasped hands the patient received a painful pinprick. (Modern investigators would regard this experiment as a cruel and unacceptable violation of a patient's rights, but ethical standards were much, much lower in 1911.) The next day, Claparède returned and reached out to shake hands with the patient. Not surprisingly, she gave no indication that she recognized Claparède or remembered anything about the prior encounter. (This confirms the diagnosis of amnesia.) But just before their hands touched, the patient abruptly pulled back and refused to shake hands with Claparède. He asked her why, and after some confusion the patient said vaguely, "Sometimes pins are hidden in people's hands."

What was going on here? On the one side, this patient seemed to have no memory of the prior encounter with Claparède. She certainly didn't mention it in explaining her refusal to shake hands, and when questioned closely about the earlier encounter, she showed no knowledge of it. But, on the other side, she obviously remembered something about the painful pinprick she'd gotten the previous day. We see this clearly in her behavior.

A related pattern occurs with other Korsakoff's patients. In one of the early demonstrations of this point, researchers used a deck of cards like those used in popular trivia games. Each card contained a question and some possible answers, in multiple-choice format (Schacter et al., 1981). The experimenter showed each card to a Korsakoff's patient, and if the patient didn't know the answer, he was told it. Then, outside of the patient's view, the card was replaced in the deck, guaranteeing that the same question would come up again in a few minutes.

When the question did come up again, the patients in this study were likely to get it right—and so apparently had learned the answer in the previous encounter. Consistent with their diagnosis, though, the patients had no recollection of the learning: They were unable to explain *why* their answers were correct. They didn't say, "I know this bit of trivia because the same question came up just five minutes ago." Instead, patients were likely to say things like "I read about it somewhere" or "My sister once told me about it."

Many studies show similar results. In setting after setting, Korsakoff's patients are unable to recall episodes they've experienced; they seem to have no explicit memory. But if they're tested indirectly, we see clear indications of memory—and so these patients seem to have intact implicit memories.

(See, e.g., Graf & Schacter, 1985; Moscovitch, 1982; Schacter, 1996; Schacter & Tulving, 1982; Squire & McKee, 1993.)

Can There Be Explicit Memory without Implicit?

We can also find patients with the reverse pattern—intact explicit memory, but impaired implicit. One study compared a patient who had suffered brain damage to the hippocampus but not the amygdala with a second patient who had the opposite pattern: damage to the amygdala but not the hippocampus (Bechara et al., 1995). These patients were exposed to a series of trials in which a particular stimulus (a blue light) was reliably followed by a loud boat horn, while other stimuli (green, yellow, or red lights) were not followed by the horn. Later on, the patients were exposed to the blue light on its own, and their bodily arousal was measured; would they show a fright reaction in response to this stimulus? In addition, the patients were asked directly, "Which color was followed by the horn?"

The patient with damage to the hippocampus did show a fear reaction to the blue light; indeed, his results on this point look just like results for control participants (i.e., people without brain damage; see **Figure 7.14**). However, when asked directly, this patient couldn't recall which of the lights had been associated with the boat horn.

The patient with damage to the amygdala showed the opposite pattern. She was able to report that it was only the blue light that was associated with the horn, demonstrating fully intact explicit memory. When presented with the blue light, however, she showed no fear response.

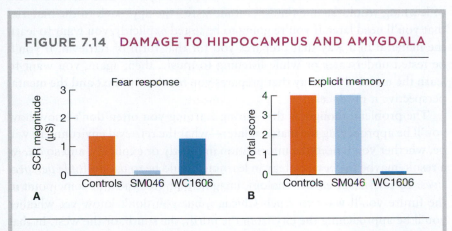

FIGURE 7.14   DAMAGE TO HIPPOCAMPUS AND AMYGDALA

Panel A shows results for a test probing implicit memory via a fear response; Panel B shows results for a test probing explicit memory. Patient SM046 had suffered damage to the amygdala and shows little evidence of implicit memory (i.e., no fear response—indexed by the *skin conductance response*, or SCR) but a normal level of explicit memory. Patient WC1606 had suffered damage to the hippocampus and shows the opposite pattern: massively disrupted explicit memory but a normal fear response.   (AFTER BECHARA ET AL., 1995)

Optimal Learning

Let's put these amnesia findings into the broader context of the chapter's main themes. Throughout the chapter, we've suggested that we often can't make claims about learning or memory acquisition without some reference to how the learning will be used later on. For example, whether it's better to learn underwater or on land depends on where you will be tested. Whether it's better to learn while listening to jazz or while sitting in a quiet room depends on the acoustic background of the memory test environment.

These ideas are echoed in the neuropsychology data. Specifically, it would be misleading to say that brain damage (whether from Korsakoff's syndrome or some other source) ruins someone's ability to create new memories. Instead, brain damage is likely to disrupt some types of learning but not others, and how this matters for the person depends on how the newly learned material will be accessed. Thus, someone who suffers hippocampal damage will probably appear normal on an indirect memory test but seem amnesic on a direct test, while someone who suffers amygdala damage will probably show the reverse pattern.

These points are important for our theorizing about memory, but they also have a practical implication. Right now, you are reading this material and presumably want to remember it later on. You're also encountering new material in other settings (perhaps in other classes you're taking), and surely you want to remember that as well. How should you study all of this information if you want the best chances of retaining it for later use?

At one level, the message from this chapter might be that the ideal form of learning would be one that's "in tune with" the approach to the material that you'll need later. If you're going to be tested explicitly, you want to learn the material in a way that prepares you for that form of retrieval. If you'll be tested underwater or while listening to music, then, again, you want to learn the material in a way that prepares you for that context and the mental perspective it produces.

The problem, though, is that during learning you often don't know how you'll be approaching the material later—what the retrieval environment will be, whether you'll need the information implicitly or explicitly, and so on. As a result, maybe the best strategy in learning would be to use *multiple perspectives*. To revisit our earlier analogy, imagine that you know at some point in the future you'll want to reach Chicago, but you don't know yet whether you'll be approaching the city from the north, the south, or the west. In that case, your best bet might be to build multiple highways, so that you can reach your goal from any direction. Memory works the same way. If you initially think about a topic in different ways and in relation to many other ideas, then you'll establish many paths leading to the target material—and so you'll be able to access that material from many different perspectives. The practical message from this chapter, then, is that this multiperspective approach may provide the optimal learning strategy.

TEST YOURSELF

12. Define "retrograde" and "anterograde" amnesia.
13. What type(s) of memory are disrupted in patients suffering from Korsakoff's syndrome?

"truthiness"

Stephen Colbert invented the word "truthiness" in 2005. This playful term refers to the degree to which some statement seems likely to be true based only on the intuitions of the reader (or hearer), without any consideration of evidence or logic. With an obvious dose of sarcasm, Colbert commented, "I'm no fan of dictionaries or reference books telling us what is or isn't true." Instead, he suggested, "try looking it up in your gut." That's truthiness: "truth that comes from the gut, not books." (Quotes from Newman et al., 2012.)

For political persuasion, truthiness is a good thing: Voters are more likely to accept claims that are high in truthiness. But for purposes of rational debate, truthiness is a problem. We don't want people to be seduced by false claims just because those claims happen to have a lot of truthiness. Instead, for rational debate, we surely want our assessment to be guided by the evidence.

It's alarming, then, that many aspects of the Internet, and social media in particular, are perfectly positioned for promoting truthiness. Let's start with the fact that the Internet often allows vivid multimedia displays: a message plus an accompanying picture or video. How does this matter? In one study, participants had to make judgments about whether statements were true or false (Newman et al., 2012; Newman et al., 2015; also see Derksen et al., 2020). In one version of the procedure, the statements named a famous person and said either "This person is alive" or "This person is dead." Half of the time, the statements were presented on their own; half of the time, the statements were presented with a picture of the person. In a subsequent study, participants had to judge broad claims like "Giraffes are the only mammals that cannot jump," again presented for half of the participants with a picture (of a giraffe) and, for the other half, without.

In this study, the picture provided no information. (Seeing a photo of a giraffe tells you nothing about the animal's leaping ability.) Even so, the photos enhanced truthiness. Statements, no matter what they said, were more likely to be judged true if accompanied by a suitable photograph.

In addition, let's bear in mind that you can choose what you're going to look at on the Internet. This means that you'll often obtain information from an interest group you've selected, or from a connection on WhatsApp. In these cases, the information is coming from someone you're more likely to trust, and this point on its own can add to the truthiness of a claim.

Let's also note that if a claim or report goes viral on the Web, you're likely to encounter that claim over and over. Likewise, in an interest group on the Web or a YouTube channel you've chosen, you're likely to interact with people who share your interests and views, and who therefore offer sentiments similar to your own. (This pattern is sometimes called the "Internet echo chamber," a term referring to the way that interrelated and confirming statements are "echoed" around the interest group.)

CAN GIRAFFES JUMP?

Various experts tell us that, in fact, giraffes can jump—although they can't jump high, and they can't jump far. (You can find examples of giraffe jumping on YouTube!) As this photo shows, though, they can get themselves into some peculiar positions. No matter what the facts, however, merely seeing a picture of a giraffe makes people more likely to accept the claim that "Giraffes are the only mammals that cannot jump." The picture adds no information, but it increases the "truthiness" of the claim.

This repeated exposure (because the content has gone viral or because of the "echo chamber") will make you more and more fluent in thinking about the ideas you've now encountered, and this fluency has many effects. For example, the chapter discusses the "illusion of truth"—a pattern in which fluently processed sentences seem more credible. This is a case in which repeated exposure increases truthiness.

Likewise, viral content often involves a specific example—perhaps an example of some politician saying something outrageous, or an example of a member of some group acting in a way you don't like. If you encounter multiple reports of this example, this will probably lead you to an overestimate of how common this sort of example is, and also a biased judgment for how "typical" the example is for its category. (For more on this sort of "frequency judgment," see Chapter 12.) These points provide yet another route through which the Internet "echo chamber" can shape truthiness.

Reliance on truthiness is troubling. Facts do matter. Logic matters. A photograph, or frequent mention on the Internet, does not make something true. It therefore has to be a concern that the Internet provides many ways to amplify truthiness, independent of what the evidence actually shows.

For more on this topic:

Derksen, D. G., Giroux, M. E., Connolly, D. A., Newman, E. J., & Bernstein, D. M. (2020). Truthiness and law: Non probative photos bias perceived credibility in forensic contexts. *Applied Cognitive Psychology, 34*(6), 1335–1344.

Kozyreva, A., Lewandowsky, S., & Hertwig, R. (2020). Citizens versus the internet: Confronting digital challenges with cognitive tools. *Psychological Science in the Public Interest, 21*(3), 103–156.

Nadarevic, L., Reber, R., Helmecke, A. J., & Köse, D. (2020). Perceived truth of statements and simulated social media postings: An experimental investigation of source credibility, repeated exposure, and presentation format. *Cognitive Research: Principles and Implications, 5*(56).

Newman, E. J., Garry, M., Bernstein, D. M., Kantner, J., & Lindsay, D. S. (2012). Nonprobative photographs (or words) inflate truthiness. *Psychonomic Bulletin & Review, 19*, 969–974.

Newman, E. J., Garry, M., Unkelbach, C., Bernstein, D. M., Lindsay, D. S., & Nash, R. A. (2015). Truthiness and falseness of trivia claims depend on judgmental contexts. *Journal of Experimental Psychology: Learning, Memory & Cognition, 41*(5), 1337–1348.

Smelter, T. J., & Calvillo, D. P. (2020). Pictures and repeated exposure increase perceived accuracy of news headlines. *Applied Cognitive Psychology, 34*(5), 1061–1071.

chapter review

SUMMARY

- In general, the chances that someone will remember an earlier event are greatest if the physical and mental circumstances in place during memory retrieval match those in place during learning. This is reflected in the phenomenon of context-dependent learning.

- A similar pattern is reflected in the phenomenon of "encoding specificity." This term refers to the idea that people usually learn more than the specific material to be remembered itself; they also learn that material within its associated context.

- All these results arise from the fact that learning establishes connections among memories, and these connections serve as retrieval paths. Like any path, these lead from some starting point to some target. To use a given path, therefore, you must return to the appropriate starting point. In the same way, if there is a connection between two memories, then activating the first memory is likely to call the second to mind. But if the first memory isn't activated, this connection, no matter how well established, will not help in locating the second memory—just as a large highway approaching Chicago from the south won't be helpful if you're trying to reach Chicago from the north.

- This emphasis on memory connections fits well with a conceptualization of memory as a vast network, with individual nodes joined to one another via connections or associations. An individual node becomes activated when it receives enough of an input signal to raise its activation level to its response threshold. Once activated, the node sends activation out through its connections to all the nodes connected to it.

- Hints are effective because they enable the target node to receive activation from two sources simultaneously—from nodes representing the main cue or question, and also from nodes representing the hint.

- Activating one node does seem to prime nearby nodes through the process of spreading activation. This is evident in studies of semantic priming in lexical-decision tasks.

- Some learning strategies are effective as preparation for some sorts of memory tests but ineffective for other sorts of tests. Some strategies, for example, are effective at establishing source memory rather than familiarity; other strategies do the reverse.

- Different forms of learning also play a role in producing implicit and explicit memories. Implicit memories are those that influence you even when you have no awareness that you're being influenced by a previous event. In many cases, implicit-memory effects take the form of priming—for example, in a lexical-decision task or word-stem completion. But implicit memories can also influence you in other ways, producing a number of memory-based illusions.

- Implicit memory can be understood as the consequence of increased processing fluency, produced by experience in a particular task with a particular stimulus. The fluency is sometimes detected and registered as a sense of "specialness" attached to a stimulus. Often, this specialness is attributed to some cause, but this attribution can be inaccurate.

- Implicit memory is also important in understanding the pattern of symptoms in anterograde amnesia. Amnesic patients perform badly on tests requiring explicit memory and may not even recall events that happened just minutes earlier. However, they often perform at near-normal levels on tests involving implicit memory. This disparity underscores the fact that we cannot speak in general about good and bad memories, good and poor learning. Instead, learning and memory must be matched to a particular task and a particular form of test; learning and memory that are excellent for some tasks may be poor for others.

KEY TERMS

context-dependent learning (p. 230)

context reinstatement (p. 231)

encoding specificity (p. 232)

nodes (p. 234)

associations or associative links (p. 234)

subthreshold activation (p. 234)

summation (p. 234)

spreading activation (p. 234)

lexical-decision task (p. 235)

semantic priming (p. 237)

recall (p. 238)

recognition (p. 238)

familiarity (p. 239)

source memory (p. 239)

attribution (p. 239)

"remember/know" distinction (p. 239)

word-stem completion (p. 242)

explicit memory (p. 242)

direct memory testing (p. 242)

implicit memory (p. 242)

indirect memory testing (p. 242)

illusion of truth (p. 244)

source confusion (p. 246)

processing pathway (p. 246)

processing fluency (p. 248)

amnesia (p. 253)

retrograde amnesia (p. 253)

anterograde amnesia (p. 253)

Korsakoff's syndrome (p. 255)

TEST YOURSELF AGAIN

1. What does context-dependent learning tell us about the nature of retrieval paths?

2. In what ways is a retrieval path like an "ordinary" path (e.g., a path or highway leading to a particular city)?

3. What is encoding specificity? How is it demonstrated?

4. What is subthreshold activation of a memory node? What role does subthreshold activation play in explaining why retrieval hints are often helpful?

5. How does semantic priming illustrate the effectiveness of subthreshold activation?

6. Define "recognition" and "recall."

7. What evidence indicates that source memory and familiarity are distinct from each other?

8. What is the difference between implicit and explicit memory? Which of these is said to be "memory without awareness"?

9. What is the role of implicit memory in explaining the false fame effect?

10. What is processing fluency, and how does it influence us?

11. In what sense is familiarity more like *a conclusion that you draw*, rather than *a feeling triggered by a stimulus*?

12. Define "retrograde" and "anterograde" amnesia.

13. What type(s) of memory are disrupted in patients suffering from Korsakoff's syndrome?

THINK ABOUT IT

1. Some people describe the eerie sensation of "déjà vu"—a feeling in which a place or face seems familiar, even though they're quite certain they've never been in this place, or seen this face, before. Can you generate a hypothesis about the roots of déjà vu, drawing on the material in the chapter?

DEMONSTRATIONS & APPLYING COGNITIVE PSYCHOLOGY ESSAYS

For demonstrations of key concepts in cognitive psychology, take a look at the Online Demonstrations. To explore more of the practical applications of cognitive psychology in themed essays, visit the online reader.

Online Demonstrations

- Demonstration 7.1: Retrieval Paths and Connections
- Demonstration 7.2: Encoding Specificity
- Demonstration 7.3: Spreading Activation in Memory Search
- Demonstration 7.4: Semantic Priming
- Demonstration 7.5: Studying for Different Types of Tests
- Demonstration 7.6: Priming From Implicit Memory
- Demonstration 7.7: Unconscious "Motor Memories"

Online Applying Cognitive Psychology Essays

- Cognitive Psychology and Education: Familiarity Can Be Treacherous
- Cognitive Psychology and Health: Memory under Anesthesia
- Cognitive Psychology and the Law: The Cognitive Interview
- Cognitive Psychology and the Law: In-Court Identifications

ZAPS COGNITION LABS

Go to ZAPS online cognition labs to conduct hands-on experiments on key concepts.

INQUIZITIVE

It's time to complete your study experience! Go to InQuizitive to practice actively with this chapter's concepts and get personalized feedback along the way.

The performers who appear on p. 240 are (*left to right*) Danielle Brooks, Chris Elliot, Hunter Schafer, Randall Park, and Olivia Coleman.

chapter **8**

Remembering
Complex Events

what if... What were you doing on March 19, 2011? What did you have for lunch that day? What was the weather like? These seem like odd questions; why should you remember these details from a decade ago? But imagine if you *could* remember those details—and similar details for every other day in your life. In other words, what would life be like if you had a "super memory"—so that, essentially, you never forgot anything?

People certainly differ in how, and how well, they remember the past (e.g., Berntsen et al., 2019; Palombo et al., 2018; Rubin, 2020; Unsworth, 2019). But, at the extreme, some people seem to have virtually perfect memories for their lives. These people show a pattern called "highly superior autobiographical recall" (HSAM). One of these individuals, for example, claims that she can recall every day of her life over the last four decades. "Starting on February 5, 1980, I remember everything. That was a Tuesday."

If asked about a randomly selected date—say, February 10, 2013—people with HSAM can remember where they were that day, what time they woke up, and what shoes they wore. Their performance is just as good if they're asked about October 7, 2008, or December 19, 2007. And when checked, their memories turn out to be uniformly accurate.

These individuals are remarkable in how much they remember, but they're quite normal in other ways. For example, their extraordinary memory capacity hasn't made them amazing geniuses or incredible scholars. Even though they have an exceptional capacity for remembering their own lives, they have no advantage in remembering other sorts of content or performing other mental tasks. This point has been documented with careful testing, but it is also evident in the fact that researchers weren't aware such people existed until just a decade or so ago (e.g., Parker et al., 2006). Apparently, these individuals, even with their incredible memory capacity, are ordinary enough in other ways so that we didn't spot them until recently (McGaugh & LePort, 2014.)

Humans have been trying for centuries to improve their memories, but it seems that a "perfect" memory may provide less of an advantage than you might think. We'll return to this point, and what it implies about memory functioning, later in the chapter.

preview of chapter themes

- Outside the lab, you often try to remember materials that are related in some way to other things you know or have experienced. Over and over, we will see that this other knowledge—the knowledge you bring to a situation— helps you to remember by promoting retrieval, but it can also promote error.

- The memory errors produced by prior knowledge tend to be quite systematic: You often recall the past as more "normal," more in line with your expectations, than it actually was.

- Even acknowledging the memory errors, our overall assessment of memory can be quite positive. This is because memories are accurate most of the time, and the errors that do occur can be understood as the by-products of mechanisms that generally serve us well.

- Finally, we will consider three factors that play an important role in shaping memory outside of the laboratory: *involvement with an event, emotion,* and *the passage of time*. These factors require some additional principles as part of our overall theory, but they also confirm the power of more general principles—principles hinging, for example, on the role of memory connections.

Memory Errors, Memory Gaps

Where did you spend last summer? What country did you grow up in? Where were you five minutes ago? These are easy questions, and you effortlessly retrieve this information from memory the moment you need it. If we want to understand how memory functions, therefore, we need to understand how you locate these bits of information (and thousands of others just like them) so readily.

But we also need to account for some other observations. Sometimes, when you try to remember an episode, you draw a blank. On other occasions, you recall something, but with no certainty that you're correct: "I think her nickname was Dink, but I'm not sure." And sometimes, when you recall a past episode, it turns out that your memory is mistaken. Perhaps a few details were different from the way you recall them. Or perhaps your memory is completely wrong, misrepresenting large elements of the original episode. Worse, in some cases you can remember entire events that never happened at all! In this chapter, we'll consider how, and how often, these errors arise. Let's start with some examples.

Memory Errors: Some Initial Examples

In 1992, an El Al cargo plane lost power in two of its engines just after taking off from Amsterdam's Schiphol Airport. A few minutes later, the plane crashed into an 11-story apartment building in Amsterdam's Bijlmermeer neighborhood. The building collapsed and burst into flames; 43 people were killed, including the plane's entire crew.

Ten months later, researchers questioned 193 Dutch people about the crash, asking them in particular, "Did you see the television film of the moment the plane hit the apartment building?" More than half of the participants (107 of them) reported seeing the film, even though there was no such film. No camera had recorded the crash; no film (or any reenactment) was shown on television. The participants seemed to be remembering something that never took place (Crombag et al., 1996).

In a follow-up study, investigators surveyed another 93 people about the plane crash. These people were also asked whether they'd seen the (nonexistent) TV film, and then they were asked detailed questions about exactly what the film had shown: Was the plane burning when it crashed, or did it catch fire a moment later? In the film, did they see the plane come down vertically with no forward speed, or did it hit the building while still moving horizontally at a considerable speed?

Two thirds of these participants reported seeing the film, and most of them were able to provide details about what they had seen. When asked about the plane's speed, for example, only 23% said that they couldn't remember. The others gave various responses, presumably based on their "memory" of the (nonexistent) film.

Other studies have produced similar results. There was no video footage of the 1997 car crash in which Princess Diana was killed, but 44% of the British participants in one study recalled seeing the footage (Ost et al., 2002). More than a third of the participants questioned about a nightclub bombing in Bali recalled seeing a (nonexistent) video, and nearly all these participants reported details about what they'd seen in the video (Wilson & French, 2006).

It turns out that more persistent questioning can lead some of these people to admit they actually don't remember seeing the video. Even with persistent questioning, though, many participants continue to insist that they did see the video—and they offer additional information about exactly what they saw in the film (e.g., Patihis & Loftus, 2015; Smeets et al., 2006). Also, in all these studies, let's emphasize that participants are thinking back to an emotional and much-discussed event; the researchers aren't asking them to recall a minor occurrence.

Is memory more accurate when the questions come after a shorter delay? In a study by Brewer and Treyens (1981), participants were asked to wait briefly in the experimenter's office prior to the procedure's start. After 35 seconds, participants were taken out of this office and told that there actually was no experimental procedure. Instead, the study was concerned with their memory for the room in which they'd just been sitting.

Participants' descriptions of the office were powerfully influenced by their prior beliefs. Surely, most participants would expect an academic office to contain shelves filled with books. In this particular office, though, no books were in view (see **Figure 8.1**). Even so, almost one third of the participants (9 of 30) reported seeing books in the office. Their recall, in other words, was governed by their expectations, not by reality.

How could this happen? How could so many Dutch participants be wrong in their recall of the plane crash? How could intelligent, alert college students fail to remember what they'd seen in an office just moments earlier?

TEST YOURSELF

1. What is the evidence that in some circumstances many people will misremember significant events they have experienced?
2. What is the evidence that in some circumstances people will even misremember *recent* events?

FIGURE 8.1 THE OFFICE USED IN THE BREWER AND TREYENS STUDY

No books were in view in this office, but many participants, biased by their expectations of what should be in an academic office, remembered seeing books.

(AFTER BREWER & TREYENS, 1981)

Memory Errors: A Hypothesis

In Chapters 6 and 7, we emphasized the importance of the memory connections that link each bit of knowledge in your memory to other bits. Sometimes these connections tie together similar episodes, so that a trip to the beach ends up being connected in memory to your recollection of other trips. Sometimes the connections tie an episode to certain ideas—ideas, perhaps, that were part of your *understanding* of the episode, or ideas that were triggered by some element within the episode.

But it's not just separate episodes and ideas that are linked in this way. Even for a single episode, its elements are stored separately from one another and are linked by connections. In fact, the storage is "modality-specific," with the bits representing what you *saw* being stored in brain areas devoted to visual processing, the bits representing what you *heard* being stored in brain areas specialized for auditory processing, and so on (e.g., Nyberg et al., 2000; Wheeler et al., 2000; also see Chapter 7, Figure 7.4, p. 233).

With all these connections in place—element to element, episode to episode, episode to related ideas—information ends up being stored in memory in a system that resembles a vast spiderweb, with each bit of information connected by many threads to other bits elsewhere in the web. This was the idea that in Chapter 7 we described as a huge *network* of interconnected *nodes*.

As we've discussed, these connections play a crucial role in memory retrieval. Imagine that you're trying to recall the restaurant you ate at during your beach trip. You'll start by activating nodes in memory that represent some aspect of the trip—perhaps your memory of the rainy weather. Activation will then flow outward from there, through the connections you've established, and this will energize nodes representing other aspects of the trip. The flow of activation can then continue from there, eventually reaching the nodes you seek. In this way, the connections serve as *retrieval paths*, guiding your search through memory.

Obviously, then, memory connections are a good thing; without them, you might never locate the information you're seeking. But the connections can also create problems. As you add more and more links between the bits of *this* episode and the bits of *that* episode, you're gradually knitting these two episodes together. As a result, you may lose track of the "boundary" between the episodes. More precisely, you're likely to lose track of which bits of information were contained within which event. In this way, you become vulnerable to what we might think of as "transplant" errors, in which a bit of information encountered in one context is transplanted into another context.

In the same way, as your memory for an episode becomes more and more interwoven with other thoughts you've had about the event, it may become difficult to keep track of which elements are linked to the episode because they were actually *part of* the episode itself, and which are linked merely because they were *associated with* the episode in your thoughts. This, too, can produce transplant errors, in which elements that were part of your thinking get misremembered as if they were actually part of the original experience.

Understanding Both Helps and Hurts Memory

It seems, then, that memory connections both help and hurt recollection. They *help* because the connections, serving as retrieval paths, enable you to locate information in memory. But connections can *hurt* because they sometimes make it difficult to see where the remembered episode stops and other, related knowledge begins. As a result, the connections encourage **intrusion errors**—errors in which other knowledge intrudes into the remembered event.

To see how these points play out, consider an early study by Owens et al. (1979). In this study, half of the participants read the following passage:

Nancy arrived at the cocktail party. She looked around the room to see who was there. She went to talk with her professor. She felt she had to talk to him but was a little nervous about just what to say. A group of people started to play charades. Nancy went over and had some refreshments. The hors d'oeuvres were good, but she wasn't interested in talking to the rest of the people at the party. After a while she decided she'd had enough and left the party.

Other participants read the same passage, but with a prologue that set the stage:

Nancy woke up feeling sick again, and she wondered if she really was pregnant. How would she tell the professor she had been seeing? And the money was another problem.

TABLE 8.1 NUMBER OF PROPOSITIONS REMEMBERED BY PARTICIPANTS

STUDIED PROPOSITIONS (THOSE IN STORY)		INFERRED PROPOSITIONS (THOSE NOT IN STORY)	
Theme Condition	Neutral Condition	Theme Condition	Neutral Condition
29.2	20.2	15.2	3.7

In the Theme condition, a brief prologue set the stage for the passage that was to be remembered.   (AFTER OWENS ET AL., 1979)

All participants were then given a recall test in which they were asked to remember the sentences as exactly as they could. As you can see in **Table 8.1**, participants who had read the prologue (the Theme condition) recalled more of the original story (i.e., they remembered more of the propositions actually contained within the story). This is what we should expect, based on the claims in Chapter 6: The prologue provided a meaningful context for the remainder of the story, and this helped understanding. Understanding, in turn, promoted recall.

At the same time, the story's prologue also led participants to include elements in their recall that weren't mentioned in the original episode. In fact, participants who had seen the prologue made *four times* as many intrusion errors as did participants who hadn't seen the prologue. For example, they might include in their recall something like "The professor had gotten Nancy pregnant." This idea isn't part of the story but is certainly implied, so it will probably be part of participants' understanding of the story. It's then this understanding (including the imported element) that is remembered.

The DRM Paradigm

Similar effects, with memory connections *helping* and *hurting* memory, can be demonstrated with simple word lists. In many experiments, participants have been presented with lists like this one: "bed, rest, awake, tired, dream, wake, snooze, blanket, doze, slumber, snore, nap, peace, yawn, drowsy." Immediately after hearing this list, participants are asked to recall as many of the words as they can.

The words in this list are obviously related. They're all associated with sleep, and the presence of this theme makes the words easy to remember. It turns out, though, that the theme word "sleep" is not itself included in the list. Nonetheless, research participants spontaneously make the connection between the list and the theme word, and this connection leads to frequent memory errors. In one study, for example, participants recalled 65% of the words that actually were on the list, but they (mistakenly) also "recalled" seeing the theme word 50% of the time. In other words, false recall of the theme word was almost as frequent as accurate recall of the words actually presented (Roediger & McDermott, 1995)!

This procedure is referred to as the **DRM paradigm,** terminology that honors the investigators who developed it (James Deese, Henry Roediger III, and Kathleen McDermott). The procedure yields errors even if participants are put on their guard before the procedure begins—that is, told about the nature of the lists and the frequency with which they produce errors. Even with this warning, the errors remain (Gallo et al., 1997; McDermott & Roediger, 1998; Roediger & McDermott, 2000). Apparently, the mechanisms leading to these errors are so automatic that people can't inhibit them.

Schematic Knowledge

Imagine that you go to a restaurant with a friend. Of course, you've been in restaurants before, and you have some commonsense knowledge about what normally happens here. You'll be seated; someone will bring menus; you'll order, then eat; eventually, you'll pay and leave. Knowledge like this is often referred to with the Greek word **schema.** Schemas, or schemata, summarize the broad pattern of what's normal in a situation—and so your kitchen schema tells you that a kitchen is likely to have a stove but no piano; your dentist's office schema tells you that there are likely to be magazines in the waiting room, that you'll probably get a new toothbrush when you leave, and so on.

Schemas help you in many ways. In a restaurant, for example, you're not puzzled when someone keeps filling your water glass or when someone else drops by to ask, "How is everything?" Your schema tells you that these are normal occurrences in a restaurant, and you instantly understand how they fit into the broader framework.

Schemas also help when the time comes to *recall* how an event unfolded. This is because there are often gaps in your recollection—either because you didn't notice certain things in the first place, or because you've gradually forgotten some aspects of the experience. (We'll say more about forgetting later in the chapter.) In either case, you can rely on your schemas to fill in these gaps. So, in thinking back to your dinner at Chez Pierre, you might not remember anything about the menus. Nonetheless, you can be reasonably sure that there were menus and that they were given to you early on and taken away after you placed your order. On this basis, you're likely to include menus within your "recall" of the dinner, even if you have no memory of seeing the menus for this particular meal. In other words, you'll supplement what you actually remember with a plausible reconstruction based on your schematic knowledge. And in most cases this after-the-fact reconstruction will be correct, since schemas do, after all, describe what happens most of the time.

Evidence for Schematic Knowledge
Clearly, then, schematic knowledge helps you, by guiding your understanding and enabling you to reconstruct things you can't remember. But schematic knowledge can sometimes hurt you, by promoting errors in perception and

memory. Moreover, the *types* of errors produced by schemas are quite predictable. As an example, imagine that you visit a dentist's office, and this one (atypically) happens not to have any magazines in the waiting room. You'll probably forget this detail after a while, and if so, what will happen when you later try to recall your trip to the dentist? If you rely on schematic knowledge, you'll "remember" that there were magazines (since, after all, there usually are some scattered around the waiting room). In this way, your schema-based recollection will make this dentist's office seem more typical, more ordinary, than it actually was.

Here's the same point in more general terms. We've already said that schemas tell you what's typical in a setting. Therefore, if you rely on schematic knowledge to fill gaps in your recollection, you'll fill those gaps with *what's normally in place* in that sort of situation. As a result, any reliance on schemas will make the world seem more "normal" than it really is and will make the past seem more "regular" than it actually was.

This tendency toward "regularizing" the past has been documented in many settings. The classic demonstration, however, comes from studies published long ago by British psychologist Frederic Bartlett. Bartlett presented his participants with a story taken from the folklore of Native Americans (Bartlett, 1932). When tested later, the participants did reasonably well in recalling the gist of the story, but they made many errors in recalling the particulars, and the pattern of errors was quite systematic: The details omitted tended to be ones that made little sense to Bartlett's British participants. Likewise, aspects of the story that were unfamiliar were often changed into aspects that were more familiar; steps of the story that seemed inexplicable were supplemented to make the story seem more logical.

Overall, then, the participants' memories seem to have "cleaned up" the story they had read—making it more coherent (from their perspective), more sensible. This is exactly what we would expect if the memory errors derived from the participants' attempts to understand the story and, with that, their efforts toward fitting the story into a schematic frame. Elements that fit within the frame remained in their memories (or could be reconstructed later). Elements that didn't fit dropped out of memory or were changed.

In the same spirit, consider the Brewer and Treyens study mentioned at the start of this chapter—the study in which participants remembered seeing shelves full of books, even though there were none. This error was produced by schematic knowledge. During the event itself (while the participants were sitting in the office), schematic knowledge told the participants that academic offices usually contain many books, and this knowledge biased what the participants paid attention to. (If you're already certain that the shelves contain books, why should you spend time looking at the shelves? This would only confirm something you already know—see Võ & Henderson, 2009.) Then, when the time came to recall the office, participants used their schema to reconstruct what the office *must have* contained—a desk, a chair, and of course lots of books. In this way, the memory for the actual office was eclipsed by generic knowledge about what a "normal" academic office contains.

Likewise, think back to the misremembered plane crash and the related studies of people remembering videos of other prominent events, even though there were no videos of these events. Here, too, the memory errors distort reality by making the past seem more regular, more typical, than it really was. After all, people often hear about major news events via a television broadcast or Internet or social media coverage, and these reports usually include vivid video footage. So here, too, the past as remembered seems to have been assimilated into the pattern of the ordinary. The event as it unfolded was unusual, but the event *as remembered* becomes typical of its kind—just as we would expect if understanding and remembering were guided by our knowledge of the way things generally unfold.

The Cost of Memory Errors

There's a "good news, bad news" quality to our discussion so far. On the positive side, memory connections serve as retrieval paths, allowing you to locate information in storage. The connections also enrich your understanding, because they tie each of your memories into a context provided by other things you know. In addition, links to schematic knowledge enable you to supplement your perception and recollection with well-informed (and usually accurate) inference.

On the negative side, though, the same connections can undermine memory accuracy, and memory errors are troubling. As we've discussed in other contexts, you rely on memory in many aspects of life, and it's unsettling that the memories you rely on may be *wrong*—misrepresenting how the past unfolded.

Eyewitness Errors

In fact, we can easily find circumstances in which memory errors are deeply consequential. For example, errors in eyewitness testimony (e.g., identifying the wrong person as the culprit or misreporting how an event unfolded) can potentially send an innocent person to jail and therefore allow the actual perpetrator to go free.

How often do eyewitnesses make mistakes? One answer comes from U.S. court cases in which DNA evidence, not available at the time of the trial, shows that the courts had convicted people who were, in truth, not guilty. There are hundreds of these exonerations, and the exonerees had (on average) spent more than a dozen years in jail for crimes they didn't commit. Many of them were on death row, awaiting execution.

When closely examined, these cases yield a clear message. Some of these men and women were convicted because of dishonest informants; some because analyses of forensic evidence had been botched. But by far the most common concern is eyewitness errors. In fact, according to most analyses, eyewitness errors contributed to at least three quarters of these false convictions—more than all other causes combined (e.g., Garrett, 2011; Reisberg, 2014).

TEST YOURSELF

3. What is the evidence that your *understanding* of an episode can produce intrusion errors?
4. What is the DRM paradigm, and what results does this procedure produce?
5. What is schematic knowledge, and what evidence tells us that schematic knowledge can help us—and also can undermine our memory accuracy?

EXONERATION OF THE INNOCENT

Guy Miles spent more than 18 years in prison for an armed robbery he did not commit. He is one of the hundreds of people who were convicted in U.S. courts but then proven innocent by DNA evidence. Mistaken eyewitness evidence accounts for more of these false convictions than all other causes combined. Note in addition that these false convictions typically involve a "double error"—with someone innocent doing time in jail, and the guilty person walking around free.

Planting False Memories

An enormous amount of research has examined eyewitness memory—the sort of memory that police rely on when investigating crimes. In one early study, Loftus and Palmer (1974) showed participants a series of pictures depicting an automobile collision. Later, participants were asked questions about the collision, but the questions were phrased in different ways for different groups. Some participants were asked, "How fast were the cars going when they hit each other?" A different group was asked, "How fast were the cars going when they smashed into each other?"

This small difference in wording had a substantial influence: Participants in the "hit" group (on average) estimated the speed to have been 34 miles per hour; those in the "smashed" group estimated 41 miles per hour—20% higher (see **Figure 8.2**). But what is critical comes next: One week later, the participants were asked in a perfectly neutral way whether they had seen any broken glass in the pictures. Participants who had initially been asked the "hit" question tended to remember that no glass was visible; participants who had been asked the "smashed" question, though, often (mistakenly) remembered seeing glass. It seems, therefore, that the change of just one word within the initial question can have a significant effect—in this case, more than doubling the likelihood of memory error.

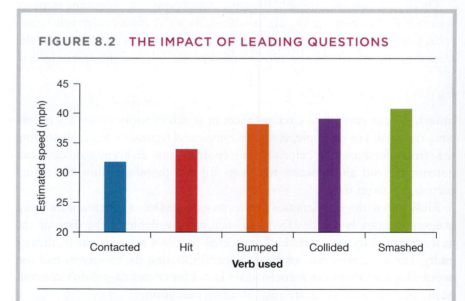

FIGURE 8.2 THE IMPACT OF LEADING QUESTIONS

Witnesses who were asked how fast the cars were going when they "hit" each other reported (on average) a speed of 34 miles per hour. Other witnesses, asked how fast the cars were going when they "smashed" into each other, gave estimates 20% higher. When all participants were later asked whether they'd seen broken glass at the scene, participants who'd been asked the "smashed" question were more likely to say yes—even though there was no broken glass.   (AFTER LOFTUS & PALMER, 1974)

In other studies, participants have been asked questions that contain overt misinformation about an event. For example, they might be asked, "How fast was the car going when it raced by the barn?" when, in truth, no barn was in view. In still other studies, participants are exposed to descriptions of the target event allegedly written by "other witnesses." They might be told, for example, "Here's how someone else recalled the crime; does this match what you recall?" Of course, the "other witness" descriptions contained some misinformation, enabling researchers to determine if participants "pick up" the false leads (e.g., Paterson & Kemp, 2006; also Edelson et al. , 2011). In other studies, researchers ask questions that require the participants themselves to *make up* some bit of misinformation. For example, participants could be asked, "In the video, was the man bleeding from his knee or from his elbow after the fall?" Even though it was clear in the video that the man wasn't bleeding at all, participants are forced to choose one of the two options (e.g., Chrobak & Zaragoza, 2008; Zaragoza et al., 2001).

These procedures are all variations on the same theme. In each case, the participant experiences an event and then is exposed to a misleading suggestion about how the event unfolded. Then some time is allowed to pass. At the end of this interval, the participant's memory is tested. And in each of these variations, the outcome is the same: A substantial number of participants—in some studies, more than one third—end up incorporating the false suggestion into their memory of the original event.

Of course, some attempts at manipulating memory are more successful, some less so. It's easier, for example, to plant *plausible* memories rather than implausible ones. (However, memories for implausible events can also be planted—see Hyman, 2000; Li et al., 2020; Mazzoni et al., 2001; Pezdek et al., 2006; Scoboria et al., 2006; Thomas & Loftus, 2002.) Errors are also more likely if the post-event information *supplements* what the person remembers, in comparison to *contradicting* what the person would otherwise remember. It's apparently easier, therefore, to "add to" a memory than it is to "replace" a memory (Chrobak & Zaragoza, 2013). False memories are also more easily planted if the research participants don't just *hear* about the false event but, instead, are urged to *imagine* how the suggested event unfolded. In one study, participants were given a list of possible childhood events (going to the emergency room late at night; winning a stuffed animal at a carnival; getting in trouble for calling 911) and were asked to "picture each event as clearly and completely" as they could. This simple exercise was enough to increase participants' confidence that the event had really occurred (Garry et al., 1996; also Mazzoni & Memon, 2003; Sharman & Barnier, 2008; Shidlovski et al., 2014).

Even with these variations, let's emphasize the consistency of the findings. We can use subtle procedures (with slightly leading questions) to plant false information in someone's memory, or we can use a more blatant procedure (requiring that the person make up the bogus facts). We can use pictures, movies, or live events as the to-be-remembered materials. In all cases, it's remarkably easy to alter someone's memory, with the result that the past as the person remembers it can differ markedly from the past as it really was. This is a widespread pattern, with numerous implications for how we think about the past and how we think about our *reliance* on our own memories. (For more on research in this domain, see Carpenter & Schacter, 2017; Cochran et al., 2016; Loftus, 2017; Rich & Zaragoza, 2016. For research documenting similar memory errors in *children*, see, e.g., Brown & Lamb, 2018; Reisberg, 2014.)

Are There Limits on the Misinformation Effect?

The studies just described reflect the **misinformation effect**—a term referring to memory errors that result from misinformation received after an event was experienced. What sorts of memory errors can be planted in this way?

We've mentioned studies in which participants remember broken glass when really there was none or remember a barn when there was no barn in view. Similar procedures have altered how *people* are remembered—and so, with just a few "suggestions" from the experimenter, participants remember clean-shaven men as bearded, young people as old, and fat people as thin (e.g., Christiaansen et al., 1983; Frenda et al., 2011). Likewise, researchers have led participants to remember seeing that someone had a prominent tattoo when, in truth, there was none (Eisen et al., 2017).

In these studies, just one word ("hit" vs. "smashed") can be enough to alter someone's recollection. What happens, though, if we ramp up our efforts to plant false memories? Can we create larger-scale errors? In one study, college students were told that the investigators were trying to learn how different people remember the same experience. The students were then given a list of events that (they were told) had been reported by their parents; the students were asked to recall these events as well as they could, so that the investigators could compare the students' recall with their parents' (Hyman et al., 1995).

Some of the events on the list actually had been reported by the participants' parents. Other events were bogus—made up by the experimenters. One of the bogus events was an overnight hospitalization for a high fever; in a different experiment, the bogus event was attending a wedding reception and accidentally spilling a bowlful of punch on the bride's family.

In an initial interview, more than 80% of the genuine events (i.e., the events actually reported by the students' parents) were recalled, but none of the students recalled the bogus events. However, repeated attempts at recall changed this pattern. By a third interview, 25% of the participants were able to remember the embarrassment of spilling the punch, and many were able to supply the details of this (entirely fictitious) episode. Other studies have shown similar results. Participants have been led to recall details of particular birthday parties that, in truth, they never had (Hyman et al., 1995); or an incident of being lost in a shopping mall even though this event never took place; or a (fictitious) event in which they were the victim of a vicious animal attack (Loftus, 2003, 2004; also see, e.g., Chrobak & Zaragoza, 2008; Geraerts et al., 2009; Laney & Loftus, 2010; also see **Figure 8.3**).

FIGURE 8.3 THE BALLOON RIDE THAT NEVER WAS

A

B

In one study, participants were shown a faked photo (Panel B) created from a real childhood snapshot (Panel A). With this prompt, many participants were led to a vivid, detailed recollection of the balloon ride—even though it never occurred (Wade et al., 2002)!

False Memories, False Confessions

How far off track can memory go? One study explored the limits, using multiple techniques to encourage false memories (Shaw & Porter, 2015). The interviewer repeatedly asked participants to recall an event that (supposedly) she had learned about from their parents. She assured participants that she had detailed information about the (fictitious) event, and she applied social pressure with comments like "Most people are able to retrieve lost memories if they try hard enough." She offered smiles and encouraging nods whenever participants showed signs of remembering the (bogus) target events; if participants couldn't recall the target events, she showed signs of disappointment. She also encouraged participants to use a memory retrieval technique (guided imagery) that is known to foster false memories.

With these (and other) factors in play, the researchers persuaded many of their participants that just a few years earlier the participants had committed a crime that led to police contact. In fact, many participants were able to remember an episode in which they had assaulted another person with a weapon and then been detained by the police. This felony never happened, but many participants "recalled" it anyhow. Their memories were in many cases rich with detail, and on many measures indistinguishable from memories known to be accurate.

A substantial number of people have vivid, elaborate memories for an episode in which they were abducted by space aliens. They report the aliens' medical examination of their human captive; in some cases, they describe being impregnated by the aliens. Some people regard these reports as proof that our planet has been visited by extraterrestrials. Most scientists, however, regard these reports as false—as "memories" for an event that never happened. On this interpretation, the abduction reports illustrate how *wrong* our memories can sometimes be.

Let's be clear, though, that this study used many forms of influence and encouragement. It takes a lot to pull memory this far off track! There has also been debate over just how many of the participants in this study truly developed false memories. Even so, the results show that it's possible for a large number of people to have memories that are emotionally powerful, deeply consequential, and utterly false. (For discussion of Shaw and Porter's study, see Wade et al., 2017; Shaw, 2018; also see Otgaar, Bücken, et al., 2019.)

Avoiding Memory Errors

Evidence is clear that people do make mistakes—at times, large mistakes—in remembering the past. But let's not lose track of the fact that people usually *don't* make mistakes. In other words, you generally can trust your memory, because more often than not your recollection is detailed, long-lasting, and *correct*. (For confirmation of this point, see Diamond et al., 2020.)

This mixed pattern, though, demands a question: Is there some way to figure out when you've made a memory mistake and when you haven't? Is there a way to decide which memories you can rely on and which ones you can't?

Memory Confidence

In evaluating memories, people rely heavily on expressions of *certainty* or *confidence*. Specifically, people tend to trust memories that are expressed with confidence. ("I distinctly remember her yellow jacket; I'm sure of it.")

Psychology students sometimes get teased by their peers: "Why are you taking psych courses? It's all a matter of common sense!" The same sentiment can arise when psychologists testify in court cases, trying to help judges and juries understand how someone's memory can be mistaken. In the past, some judges have refused this testimony, asserting that the judge and jury already know everything they need to know about memory—that the expert would offer no information (using the legal jargon) "beyond the ken of the average juror."

How should we think about these notions? Each of us, of course, has had a lifetime of experience working with and relying on our memories; that experience has surely taught us a lot about how memory functions. Even so, it's easy to find widespread beliefs about memory that are incorrect. Often, these beliefs start with a kernel of truth but understate the actual facts. For example, everyone knows that memories are sometimes inaccurate; people talk about their memories "playing tricks" on them. However, most people are astonished to learn how common memory errors are and how large the errors can be. Therefore, in relying on common sense, people (including judges and juries) might trust memory more than they should.

For example, in one study, college students were surveyed about their perceptions of various risks (Wilson & Brekke, 1994). These students were largely unconcerned about the risk of someone biasing their memory with leading questions; they regarded this risk as roughly equivalent to the risk of someday being kidnapped by space aliens. In contrast, studies make it plain that just a word or two of leading can produce memory errors in roughly one third of the people questioned. Surely, the danger of extraterrestrial abduction is much lower than this.

Other commonsense beliefs are flatly wrong. For example, some people have the view that certain types of events are essentially immune to forgetting. They speak about those events as somehow "burned into the brain" and say things like "I'll never forget the events of 9/11" or ". . . the day I got married" or ". . . what he looked like when he pulled the trigger." However, the "burned into the brain" idea is wrong, and investigators often document large-scale errors in these singular, significant memories.

Additional examples are easy to find. These include the widely held view that someone's degree of certainty is a good index of whether their memory is accurate (this is true, but only in a narrow set of circumstances); the common belief that our memories function just as a video recorder functions (not at all true); or the belief that hypnosis can enable someone to recover long-lost memories (utterly false).

In fact, let's note an irony here. Commonsense beliefs about memory (or about psychology in general) are sometimes sensible and sometimes not. If scientific research corrects a mistaken commonsense belief, then obviously we've learned something. But if the research turns out to *confirm* common sense, then here too we've learned something—because we've learned that this is one of the times when common sense is on track. On that basis, we shouldn't scoff at results that "merely" confirm common sense, because these results can be just as informative as results that truly surprise us.

They're more cautious about memories that are hesitant. ("I think she was wearing yellow, but I'm not certain.")

Evidence suggests, though, that a person's degree of certainty is an uneven indicator of whether a memory is trustworthy. On the positive side, there are circumstances in which certainty and memory accuracy are highly correlated (e.g., Wixted et al., 2015; Wixted & Wells, 2017). On the negative side, though, we can easily find exceptions to this pattern—including memories that are expressed with total certainty ("I'll never forget that day; I remember it as though it were yesterday") but turn out to be entirely mistaken. In fact, we can find circumstances in which there's no correspondence at all between how certain someone says she is, in recalling the past, and how accurate that recollection is likely to be. As a result, if we try to categorize memories as correct or incorrect based on someone's confidence, we'll often get it wrong. (For some of the evidence, see Hirst et al., 2009; Reisberg, 2014; Wells & Quinlivan, 2009.)

How can this be? One reason is that a person's confidence in a memory is often influenced by factors that have no impact on memory accuracy. When these factors are present, confidence can be artificially inflated, and with no change in the accuracy level, any connection between confidence and accuracy is strained or even shattered.

Participants in one study witnessed a (simulated) crime and later were asked if they could identify the culprit from a group of pictures. Some of the participants were then given feedback—"Good, you identified the suspect"; others weren't. The feedback couldn't possibly influence the accuracy of the identification, because the feedback arrived only after the identification had occurred. But the feedback did have a large impact on how confident participants said they'd been when making their lineup selection (see **Figure 8.4**), and so the linkage between confidence and accuracy was essentially eliminated (Wells & Bradfield, 1998; Charman et al., 2011; also see Douglass & Pavletic, 2012; Semmler & Brewer, 2006; Wright & Skagerberg, 2007).

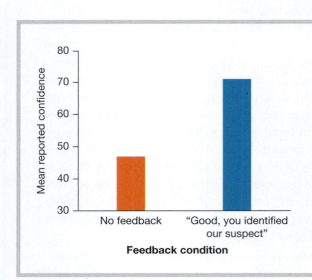

FIGURE 8.4 CONFIDENCE MALLEABILITY

In one study, participants first tried to identify a culprit from a police lineup and then indicated (on a scale of 0 to 100) how confident they had been in their selection. Some participants received no feedback about their choice; others received feedback after making their selection but before indicating their confidence level. The feedback couldn't possibly influence accuracy (because the selection had already been made), but it dramatically increased confidence. (AFTER WELLS & BRADFIELD, 1998)

How alarmed should we be about all these points? There's no question that large memory errors occur, and likewise no argument that in some circumstances a person's level of certainty about their memory tells us little. It's also plain that there are settings in which various factors can make the likelihood of memory error quite high. Putting these pieces together—and here naming just one implication of these facts—there are certainly legal cases in which there are substantial concerns about the memory-based evidence.

Overall, though, no one really knows just how often people make these deeply consequential errors. (For a glimpse of debate over this issue, see Becker-Blease & Freyd, 2017; Brewin et al., 2020; Lindsay & Hyman, 2017; McNally, 2017; Nash et al., 2017; Otgaar et al., 2017; Scoboria & Mazzoni, 2017.) Even so, there is no doubt that memory errors can lead to tragic problems—whether we are considering an error made by an eyewitness to a crime or an error made by a patient in reporting to his doctor when his symptoms began. As a result, researchers continue to pour effort into studies seeking ways to decrease the risk of error and to detect errors when they occur. In this fashion, cognitive psychologists are making a substantial contribution to the legal system, the practice of medicine, and more. (For examples of this effort toward improving memory reports, see Brandon et al., 2019; Dickinson et al., 2019; Wells et al., 2020.)

Memory Errors Are Unavoidable

We've been discussing memory errors, but we should emphasize that these errors are not a sign that our memories are somehow flawed or deficient. Instead, in ways we've already suggested, memory errors may simply be the price humans pay in order to gain enormous benefits. For example, we've argued that some memory errors arise because the various episodes in your memory are densely interconnected with one another; it's these interconnections that allow elements to be transplanted from one remembered episode to another. But we've also noted that these connections have a purpose: They're the retrieval paths that make memory search possible. Therefore, to avoid the errors, you would need to restrict the connections; but if you did that, you would lose the ability to locate your own memories within long-term storage.

The memory connections that lead to error also help you in other ways. Our environment, after all, is in many ways predictable, and it's enormously useful for you to exploit that predictability. There's little point, for example, in scrutinizing a kitchen to make sure there's a stove in the room, because in the vast majority of cases there is. So why take the time to confirm the obvious? Likewise, there's little point in taking special note that, yes, this restaurant does have menus and, yes, people in the restaurant are eating and not having their cars repaired. These, too, are obvious points, and it would be a waste of effort to give them special notice.

On these grounds, reliance on schematic knowledge is a good thing. Schemas guide your attention to what's informative in a situation, rather than what's self-evident (e.g., Gordon, 2006), and they guide your inferences at the time of recall. If this use of schemas sometimes leads you astray, that's a small price to pay for the gain in efficiency that schemas allow.

In the same way, the blurring together of episodes may be a blessing, not a problem. Think, for example, about all the times when you've been with a particular friend. These episodes are related to one another in an obvious way, and so they're likely to become interconnected in your memory. This will cause difficulties if you want to remember which episode is which and whether you had a particular conversation in this episode or that one. But rather than lamenting this, maybe we should *celebrate* what's going on here. Because of the "blurring together," all the episodes will merge in your memory, so that what resides in memory is one integrated package, containing all of your knowledge about your friend. As a result, rather than complaining about memory confusion, we should rejoice over the memory *integration* and "cross-referencing."

In all of these ways, our overall assessment of memory can be upbeat. We have, to be sure, discussed a range of memory errors, and, again, some of the errors lead to awful consequences. At the same time, though, these errors are a product of mechanisms that otherwise help you—to locate your memories within storage, to be efficient in your contact with the world, and to form general knowledge. Thus, even with the errors, it seems that human memory functions in a way that serves us extraordinarily well. (For a related discussion of the benefits of memory "problems," with a focus on forgetting, see Fawcett & Hulbert, 2020.)

TEST YOURSELF

8. What factors seem to *undermine* the relationship between your degree of certainty in a memory and the likelihood that the memory is accurate?
9. Explain why the mechanisms that produce memory *errors* may actually be mechanisms that help us in important ways.

Forgetting

We've been discussing the errors people sometimes make in recalling the past, but of course there's another way your memory can let you down: Sometimes you *forget*. You try to recall what was on the shopping list, or the name of an acquaintance, or what happened last week, and you simply draw a blank. Why does this happen? Are there things you can do to diminish forgetting?

The Causes of Forgetting

Let's start with one of the more prominent examples of "forgetting"—which turns out not to be forgetting at all. Imagine meeting someone at a party, being told his name, and moments later realizing you don't have a clue what his name is—even though you just heard it. This common (and embarrassing) experience is not the result of ultra-rapid forgetting. Instead, it stems from a failure in acquisition. You were exposed to the name but barely paid attention to it and, as a result, never learned it in the first place.

What about "real" cases of forgetting—cases in which you once knew the information but no longer do? For these cases, one of the best predictors of forgetting (not surprisingly) is the **retention interval**—the amount of time that elapses between the initial learning and the subsequent retrieval. As this interval grows, you're likely to forget more and more of the earlier event (see **Figure 8.5**).

FIGURE 8.5 FORGETTING CURVE

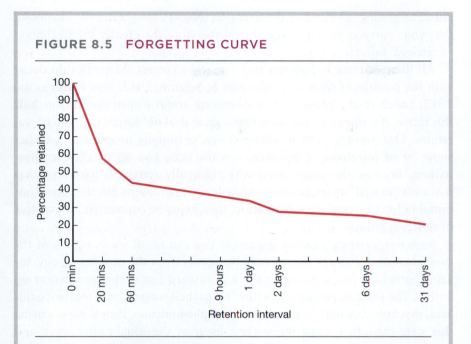

The figure shows retention after various intervals since learning. The data shown here are from classic work by Hermann Ebbinghaus, so the pattern is often referred to as an "Ebbinghaus forgetting curve." The actual speed of forgetting (i.e., how "steep" the "drop-off" is) depends on how well learned the material was at the start. Across most situations, though, the pattern is the same—with the forgetting being rapid at first but then slowing down. Mathematically, this pattern is best described by an equation framed in terms of "exponential decay."

One explanation for this pattern comes from the **decay theory of forgetting**, which proposes rather directly that memories fade or erode with the passage of time. Maybe this is because the relevant brain cells die off. Or maybe the connections among memories need to be constantly refreshed—and if they're not refreshed, the connections gradually weaken.

A different possibility is that new learning somehow interferes with older learning. This view is referred to as **interference theory**, and according to this view, the passage of time isn't the direct cause of forgetting. Instead, the passage of time creates the opportunity for new learning, and it is the new learning that disrupts the older memories.

A third hypothesis blames **retrieval failure**. The idea here is that the "forgotten memory" is still in long-term storage, but the person trying to retrieve the memory simply cannot locate it. This proposal rests on the notion that retrieval from memory is far from guaranteed, and we argued in Chapter 7 that retrieval is more likely if your perspective at the time of retrieval matches the perspective in place at the time of learning. If we now assume that your perspective is likely to change as time goes by, we can make a prediction about forgetting: The greater the retention interval, the greater the likelihood that your perspective has changed, and therefore the greater the likelihood of retrieval failure.

All three of these hypotheses turn out to be correct. Memories do decay with the passage of time (e.g., Altmann & Schunn, 2012; also Hardt et al., 2013; Sadeh et al., 2016), so any theorizing about forgetting must include this factor. But there's no question that a great deal of "forgetting" is retrieval failure. This point is evident whenever you're initially unable to remember some bit of information, but then, a while later, you do recall that information. Because the information was eventually retrieved, we know that it wasn't "erased" from memory through either decay or interference. Your initial failure to recall the information, then, must be counted as an example of retrieval failure.

Sometimes retrieval failure is *partial*: You can recall some aspects of the desired content, but not all. An example comes from the maddening circumstance in which you're trying to think of a word but simply can't come up with it. The word is, people say, on the "tip of their tongue," and following this lead, psychologists refer to this as the **TOT phenomenon**. People experiencing this state can often recall the starting letter of the sought-after word and approximately what it sounds like. So, for example, a person might remember "it's something like *Sanskrit*" in trying to remember "scrimshaw" or "something like *secant*" in trying to remember "sextant" (Brown, 1991; James & Burke, 2000; Schwartz & Metcalfe, 2011; Stasenko & Gollan, 2019).

What about interference? In one early study, Baddeley and Hitch (1977) asked rugby players to recall the names of the other teams they had played against over the course of a season. The key here is that not all players made it to all games (because of illness, injuries, or schedule conflicts). This fact enables us to compare players for whom "two games back" means two weeks ago, to players for whom "two games back" means four weeks ago. In this way, we can look at the effects of retention interval (two weeks vs. four) with the number of intervening games held constant. Likewise, we can compare players for whom the game a month ago was "three games back" to players for whom a month ago means "one game back." Now, we have the retention interval held constant, and we can look at the effects of intervening events. In this setting, Baddeley and Hitch reported that the mere passage of time accounts for very little; what really matters is the number of intervening events (see **Figure 8.6**). This is just what we would expect if interference, and not decay, is the major contributor to forgetting.

But *why* does memory interference occur? In many cases, newly arriving information gets interwoven with older information, producing a risk of confusion about which bits are old (i.e., the event you're trying to remember) and which bits are new (i.e., information that you picked up after the event). In addition, in some cases, new information seems literally to replace old information—much as you no longer save the rough draft of one of your papers once the final draft is done. In this situation, the new information isn't woven into the older memory; instead, it erases it.

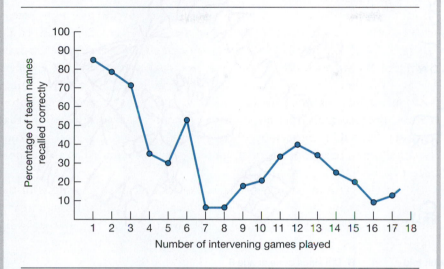

FIGURE 8.6 FORGETTING FROM INTERFERING EVENTS

Members of a rugby team were asked to recall the names of teams they had played against. Overall, the broad pattern of the data shows that memory performance was powerfully influenced by the number of games that intervened between the game to be recalled and the attempt to remember. This pattern fits with an interference view of forgetting. (AFTER BADDELEY & HITCH, 1977)

Undoing Forgetting

Is there any way to *undo* forgetting and to recover seemingly lost memories? One option, often discussed, is hypnosis. The idea is that under hypnosis a person can "return" to an earlier event and remember virtually everything about the event, including aspects the person didn't even notice or think about at the time.

The reality, however, is otherwise. Hypnotized participants often do give detailed reports of the target event, but not because they remember more; instead, they're just willing to *say* more in order to comply with the hypnotist's instructions. As a result, their "memories" are a mix of recollection, guesses, and inferences—and, of course, the hypnotized individual cannot tell which of these are which (Lynn et al., 2020; Mazzoni & Lynn, 2007).

On the positive side, though, there are procedures that can diminish forgetting, including a procedure dubbed the Cognitive Interview. This procedure was designed to help police in their investigations and, specifically, is aimed at maximizing the quantity and accuracy of information obtained from eyewitnesses to crimes. (For broad discussion, see Dickinson et al., 2019.) The cognitive interview has several elements, including an effort toward *context reinstatement*—steps that put witnesses back into the mindset they were in at the time of the crime. (For more on context reinstatement, see Chapter 7.) In

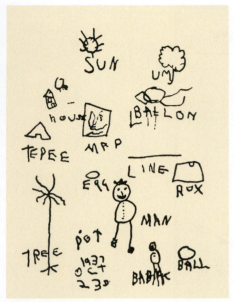

A Drawings done by hypnotized adult told that he was 6 years old

B Drawings done at age 6

HYPNOTIC AGE REGRESSION

In one study, participants were asked to draw a picture while mentally "regressed" to age 6. At first glance, their drawings (see Panel A for an example) looked remarkably childlike. But when compared to the participants' own drawings made at that age (see Panel B for an example), it's clear that the hypnotized adults' drawings were much more sophisticated. They represent an adult's conception of what a childish drawing is, rather than being the real thing.

addition, we know that retrieval of memories from long-term storage is more likely if a suitable cue is provided. The Cognitive Interview therefore offers a diverse set of retrieval cues with the idea that the more cues provided, the greater the chance of finding one that triggers the target memory.

The Cognitive Interview is quite successful, both in the laboratory and in real crime investigations, producing more complete recollection without compromising accuracy. This success adds to the argument that much of what we call "forgetting" can be attributed to retrieval failure, and it can be undone simply by providing more support for retrieval.

Also, rather than *undoing* forgetting, perhaps we can *avoid* forgetting. The key here is simply to "revisit" a memory periodically. Each "visit" seems to refresh the memory, with the result that forgetting is much less likely. Researchers have examined this effect in several contexts, including one that's pragmatically quite important: Students often have to take exams, and confronting the material on an exam is, of course, an occasion in which students "revisit" what they've learned. These revisits, we've just suggested, should slow forgetting, and on this basis taking an exam can actually help students to hang on to the material they've learned. Several studies have confirmed this "testing effect": Students have better long-term retention for materials they were tested on, compared to materials they merely reread or somehow reviewed on their own.

(See, among others, Halamish & Bjork, 2011; Healy et al., 2017; Karpicke, 2012; McDaniel et al., 2007; McDermott, 2021; Thomas et al., 2020.)

Related effects emerge if students are simply asked questions periodically that require a brief revisit to materials they've encountered (Brown et al., 2014). In fact, that's the reason why the textbook you're reading right now includes Test Yourself questions. Answering those questions will actually help readers to remember what they've read!

Autobiographical Memory

We've now discussed many studies in which participants were asked to remember simple stimuli like word lists or short sentences. But we've also considered memories for more complex materials. In some of the studies we've mentioned, the research participants were actually involved in the remembered episode, and not just external witnesses (e.g., the false memory that they had committed a felony). We've also looked at studies that involved memories for emotional events (e.g., the plane crash discussed at the chapter's start) and memory over the very long term (e.g., memories for childhood events "planted" in adult participants).

Do these factors—involvement in the remembered event, emotion, and long delay—affect how or how well someone remembers? These factors are surely relevant to the sorts of remembering people do outside the laboratory, and all three are central for **autobiographical memory**—the memory that each of us has for the episodes and events of our lives. Let's explore how each of these factors influences what we remember.

Memory and the Self

Having some involvement in an event (as opposed to passively witnessing it) turns out to have a large effect on memory, because, overall, information relevant to the self is better remembered than information that's not self-relevant (e.g., Constable et al., 2019; Symons & Johnson, 1997; Westmacott & Moscovitch, 2003). This effect emerges in many forms, including an advantage in remembering adjectives that apply to you relative to adjectives that don't, better memory for names of places you have visited relative to names of places you've never been, and so on (see **Figure 8.7**).

But here, too, we can find memory errors, in part because your "memory" for your own life is (just like other memories) a mix of genuine recall and some amount of schema-based reconstruction. For example, consider the fact that most adults believe that in many regards they've been reasonably consistent, reasonably stable, over their lifetimes. This belief (in essence, people's schematic knowledge *about themselves*) creates a bias in how they remember the past. Specifically, this belief leads people to misremember some of their past attitudes, their past likes and dislikes, in a fashion that makes the past look more like the present than it really was (Conway & Ross, 1984; Devitt & Schacter, 2018; Holmberg & Homes, 1994).

TEST YOURSELF

10. Explain the mechanisms hypothesized by each of the three major theories of forgetting: decay, interference, and retrieval failure.

11. What techniques or procedures seem *in*effective as a means of "undoing" forgetting? What techniques or procedures seem to diminish or avoid forgetting?

FIGURE 8.7   SELF-REFERENCING AND THE BRAIN

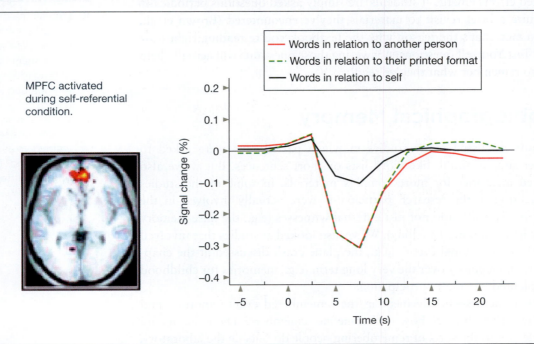

MPFC activated during self-referential condition.

Legend:
- Words in relation to another person
- Words in relation to their printed format
- Words in relation to self

y-axis: Signal change (%)
x-axis: Time (s)

You are more likely to remember words that refer to *you*, in comparison to words in other categories. Here, participants were asked to judge adjectives in three conditions: answering questions like "Does this word describe the president?" or "Is this word printed in capital letters?" or "Does this word describe you?" Data from fMRI recordings showed a distinctive pattern of processing when the words were "self-referential." Specifically, self-referential processing is associated with activity in the medial prefrontal cortex (MPFC). This extra processing is part of the reason why self-referential words are better remembered.   (AFTER KELLEY ET AL., 2002)

As an example, how did you feel about your mother when you were a young child? In answering this question, people tend to "project" their current views into the past. This point shows up in the fact that any changes in your *current* appraisal of Mom (so that you now end up thinking of her in warmer terms than you used to, or perhaps in colder terms) tend to produce corresponding changes in your recall of how you felt about her in the past—a clear instance of autobiographical memories being reconstructed based on current views (Patihis et al., 2019).

Memory and Emotion

Another factor central to autobiographical memory is *emotion*. Many of your life experiences are of course emotional, making you feel happy, or sad, or angry, or afraid, and in general emotion helps you to remember. One reason is emotion's impact on memory **consolidation**—the process through which memories are biologically "cemented in place." (See Hardt et al., 2010; Wang & Morris, 2010; although also see Dewar et al., 2010.)

Whenever you experience an event or gain new knowledge, your memory for this new content is initially quite fragile. Over the next few hours, though, various biological processes stabilize this memory and put it into a more enduring form. This process—consolidation—takes place "behind the scenes," without you thinking about it, but it's crucial. If the consolidation is interrupted for some reason (e.g., because of extreme fatigue or injury), no memory is established and recall later will be impossible. (That's because there's no information in memory for you to retrieve; you can't read text off a blank page!)

A number of factors can promote consolidation. For example, evidence is increasing that key steps of consolidation take place in times of quiet rest and also while you're asleep—and so a good night's rest actually helps you, later on, to remember things you learned while awake the day before. (See Ackermann & Rasch, 2014; Giuditta, 2014; Paller et al., 2021; Rasch & Born, 2013; Tononi & Cirelli, 2013; Wamsley, 2019.)

In addition, and crucially for our purposes here, emotion enhances consolidation. Specifically, emotional events trigger a response in the amygdala, and the amygdala in turn increases activity in the hippocampus, and the hippocampus, we know, is crucial for getting memories established. (See Chapter 7. For reviews of emotion's biological effects on memory, see Buchanan, 2007; Ford & Kensinger, 2019; Hoscheidt et al., 2010; Joëls et al., 2011; Yonelinas & Ritchey, 2015.)

Emotion also shapes memory through other mechanisms. An event that's emotional is likely to be important to you, virtually guaranteeing that you'll pay close attention as the event unfolds, and we know that attention and thoughtful processing help memory. In addition, you tend to mull over emotional events in the minutes (or hours) following the event, and this is tantamount to memory rehearsal. For these reasons, it's not surprising that emotional events are well remembered (Reisberg & Heuer, 2004; Talmi, 2013).

Let's note, though, that emotion doesn't just influence *how well* you remember; it also influences *what* you remember. Specifically, in many settings, emotion seems to produce a "narrowing" of attention, so that all of your attention will be focused on just a few aspects of the scene. This narrowing makes it likely that these attended aspects will be firmly placed into memory, but it also implies that the rest of the event, excluded from the narrowed focus, won't be remembered later (e.g., Gable & Harmon-Jones, 2008; Reisberg & Heuer, 2004).

What exactly you'll focus on, though, may depend on the specific emotion. Different emotions lead you to set different *goals*: If you're afraid, your goal is to escape; if you're angry, your goal is to deal with the person or issue that's made you angry; if you're happy, your goal may be to relax and enjoy! In each case, you're likely to pay attention to aspects of the scene directly relevant to your goal, and this will color how you remember the emotional event. (See Fredrickson, 2000; Harmon-Jones et al., 2013; Huntsinger, 2012, 2013; Kaplan et al., 2012; Levine & Edelstein, 2009; for discussion of emotion's impact at the time of memory retrieval, see Kensinger & Ford, 2020.)

Flashbulb Memories

One group of emotional memories seems special. These are the so-called **flashbulb memories**—memories of extraordinary clarity, typically for highly emotional events, retained despite the passage of many years. When Brown and Kulik (1977) introduced the term "flashbulb memory," they pointed to the memories people had of the moment in 1963 when they first heard that President John Kennedy had been assassinated. In the Brown and Kulik study, people interviewed more than a decade after that event remembered it "as though it were yesterday," and many participants were certain they'd never forget that awful day. Moreover, participants' recollection was quite detailed—with people remembering where they were at the time, what they were doing, and whom they were with. Indeed, many participants were able to recall the clothing worn by people around them, the exact words uttered, and the like.

Many other events have produced flashbulb memories. For example, most Americans (at least those old enough) can clearly recall where they were when they heard about the attack on the World Trade Center in 2001; many people vividly remember what they were doing in 2009 when they heard that Michael Jackson had died; many Italians have clear memories of their country's victory in the 2006 World Cup, or the Pope's resignation in 2013 (Curci et al., 2015); and so on.

The events that trigger a flashbulb memory, though, may differ from country to country. One study, for example, indicated that people in China often report flashbulb memories for social or international events. People in the United States, in contrast, are more likely to report flashbulb memories for political or terrorism events (Schmidt & Qiao, 2019; for more on cultural differences in memory, see Anakwah et al., 2020).

Flashbulb memories can also involve personal events: Many women remember the onset of their menstrual cycle (Pillemer et al., 1987). People can have flashbulb memories of a particular accident or illness (Lanciano et al., 2018) or for receiving a troubling medical diagnosis (May & Dein, 2020), but also for a positive event, like getting accepted into a college or a fraternity (Kraha & Boals, 2014).

Remarkably, though, these vivid, high-confidence memories can contain substantial errors. Thus, when people say, "I'll never forget that day . . ." they're sometimes *wrong*. For example, Hirst et al. (2009) interviewed more than 3,000 people soon after the September 11 attack on the World Trade Center, asking how they first heard about the attack; who brought them the news; and what they were doing at the time. When these individuals were reinterviewed a year later, more than a third (37%) provided a substantially different account. Even so, the participants were strongly confident in their recollection (rating their degree of certainty, on a 1-to-5 scale, at an average of 4.4; also see Hirst & Phelps, 2016; Hirst et al., 2015; Rubin & Talarico, 2007; Schmidt, 2012).

Why do some flashbulb memories turn out to be mistaken, while others seem entirely accurate? The answer involves several factors, including how, how often, and with whom someone discussed the flashbulb event. In many cases, this discussion may encourage people to "polish" their reports—so that

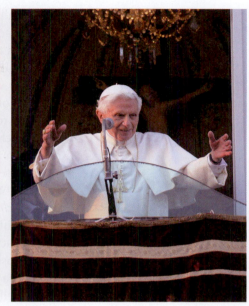

FLASHBULB MEMORIES

People often have especially clear and long-lasting memories for events like first hearing about the attack on the World Trade Center in September 2001, or the news of Michael Jackson's death in 2009, or the Pope's resignation in 2013. These memories—called "flashbulb memories"—are vivid and compelling, but they are not always accurate.

they're offering their audience a "better," more interesting narrative. After a few occasions of telling and retelling this version of the event, the new version may replace the original memory. (For more on these issues, see Luminet & Curci, 2009; Tinti et al., 2009; Tinti et al., 2014.)

Notice, then, that an understanding of flashbulb memories requires us to pay attention to the *social aspects* of remembering. In many cases, of course, people "share" memories with one another (and so, for example, I tell you about my vacation, and you tell me about yours). Likewise, in the aftermath of an important event, people often compare their recollections. ("Did you see how he ran when the alarm sounded!?") In each of these cases, people often alter their account to allow for a better conversation. They may, for example, leave out mundane bits or add bits to impress their listeners. These adjustments, in turn, will often alter the way the event is later remembered.

In addition, people sometimes "pick up" new information in these conversations—if, for example, someone who was present for the same event noticed a detail that you missed. Often, this new information will be absorbed into other witnesses' memory—a pattern sometimes referred to as "co-witness contamination." The term "contamination," though, seems harsh, because sometimes conversations about the past can improve memory (Vredeveldt et al., 2019). Even so, sometimes a witness to an event will make a *mistake* in recalling what happened, and after conversation, other witnesses may absorb this mistaken bit into their own recollection (Hope et al., 2013).

Overall, then, conversations can sometimes have a positive impact on the accuracy of someone's eventual report, and sometimes a negative impact. How this dynamic plays out will depend both on what each person remembers and on other factors—including each person's expectations about what the other will likely remember, and also patterns of social interaction. As an example of these complexities, in one study, long-married couples were asked together to recall their wedding day. Husbands and wives certainly influenced each others' recall, but with an asymmetry—with women influencing men more than the reverse (Grysman et al., 2020; for more discussion of the social aspects of remembering, see Choi et al., 2017; Masswood et al., 2019; Roediger & Abel, 2015; Yamashiro & Hirst, 2020; for more on social influence on *children's memory*, see Fivush, 2019.)

Returning to flashbulb memories, though, let's not lose track of the fact that the accuracy of these memories is uneven. Some flashbulb memories are marvelously accurate; others are filled with error. Therefore, the common-sense idea that these memories are somehow "burned into the brain" and always reliable is surely mistaken. Apparently, memory errors can occur even in the midst of our strongest, most vivid recollections.

Traumatic Memories

Flashbulb memories usually concern events that were strongly emotional. Sadly, though, we can also find cases in which people experience truly extreme emotion, and this leads us to ask: How are *traumatic* events remembered? If someone has witnessed wartime atrocities, can we count on the accuracy of their testimony in a war-crimes trial? If someone suffers through the horrors of a sexual assault, will the painful memory eventually fade?

Most traumatic events are well remembered for many years. In fact, victims of atrocities often seem plagued by a cruel enhancement of memory, leaving them with extra-vivid and long-lived recollections of the terrible event (e.g., Alexander et al., 2005; Goodman et al., 2003; Peace & Porter, 2004; Porter & Peace, 2007; Thomsen & Berntsen, 2009). As a result, people who have experienced trauma sometimes complain about having "too much" memory and wish they remembered *less*.

This enhanced memory can be understood in terms of a mechanism we've already mentioned: consolidation. This process is promoted by the conditions that accompany bodily arousal, including the extreme arousal typically present in a traumatic event (Buchanan & Adolphs, 2004; Hamann, 2001; McGaugh, 2015). But this doesn't mean that traumatic events are always well remembered. There are, in fact, cases in which people who've suffered through extreme events have little or no recall of their experience (e.g., Arrigo & Pezdek, 1997). We can also sometimes document substantial errors in someone's recall of a traumatic event (Paz-Alonso & Goodman, 2008).

What factors are producing this mixed pattern? In some cases, traumatic events are accompanied by sleep deprivation, head injuries, or substance abuse, each of which can disrupt memory (McNally, 2003). In other cases, the memory-promoting effects of arousal are offset by the complex memory effects of *stress*. The key here is that the experience of stress sets off a cascade of biological reactions. These reactions produce changes throughout the body, and these changes have multiple effects on memory. First, stress seems to enhance memory for materials that are directly relevant to the source of the stress. But, second, stress has the opposite effect—undermining memory—for other aspects of the event, and also for the details of the event (Shields et al., 2017). As a result, the person will certainly remember the broad outline of what happened—but *only* the broad outline. (Also see Goldfarb et al., 2019.)

One line of evidence for these points comes from a study of soldiers who were undergoing survival training. As part of the training, the soldiers were deprived of sleep and food, and they went through a realistic simulation of a prisoner-of-war interrogation. One day later, the soldiers were asked to identify their interrogator from a lineup. Despite the extensive (40-minute) face-to-face encounter with the interrogator and the relatively short (one-day) retention interval, many soldiers picked the wrong person from the lineup. Indeed, soldiers who had experienced an especially stressful interrogation picked the wrong person in the lineup 68% of the time. (See Morgan et al., 2004; also see Deffenbacher et al., 2004; Hope et al., 2012; Valentine & Mesout, 2008.)

Finally, we note that some authors suggest that traumatic memories are distinctive in other ways—with a claim that these memories tend to be "fragmented" (lacking a coherent structure) and also a claim that traumatic memories emphasize sensory qualities of an event rather than the narrative itself (e.g., Bisby et al., 2020). However, the evidence on these points is mixed, and it is far from clear whether traumatic memories differ from other memories in these ways (Reisberg & Heuer, 2020; Taylor et al., 2020).

Repression and "Recovered" Memories

A further claim about traumatic memories is controversial: Some authors argue that people can sometimes defend themselves against extremely painful memories by pushing these memories out of awareness. Some writers suggest that the painful memories are "repressed" or "suppressed"; others use the term "dissociation" to describe this self-protective mechanism. No matter what terms we use, the idea is that these painful memories (including, in many cases, memories for childhood abuse) aren't erased; instead, the memories are "buried." As a result, these memories won't be consciously available, but they will still exist in a person's long-term storage and in suitable circumstances can be "recovered"—that is, made conscious again. (For indications of how widely endorsed these claims are, see Dodier et al., 2019; Otgaar, Howe, et al., 2019.)

Most memory researchers, however, are skeptical about this proposal. As one consideration, painful events—including events that seem likely candidates for repression—seem typically to be well remembered, and this is the opposite of what we would expect if a self-protective mechanism was in place. (We mentioned some examples in our discussion of how trauma promotes memory; for further evidence, see Bidrose & Goodman, 2000; Goldfarb et al., 2019; Malmquist, 1986; Quas et al., 1999.) In addition, some of the abuse memories reported as "recovered" may, in fact, have been remembered all along, and so they provide no evidence of repression or dissociation. In these cases, the memories had appeared to be "lost" because the person refused to discuss these memories for many years; "recovery" of these memories simply reflects the fact that the person is at last willing to talk about them. This sort of "recovery" can be extremely consequential—emotionally and legally—but doesn't tell us anything about how memory works.

Sometimes, though, memories do seem to be genuinely lost for a while and then recovered. But this pattern may not reveal the operation (and, eventually, the "lifting") of repression or dissociation. Instead, this pattern may be the result of retrieval failure—a mechanism that can "hide" memories for periods of time, only to have them reemerge once a suitable retrieval cue is available. Here, too, the recovery may be of enormous importance for the person who is finally remembering the long-lost episodes; but again, this merely confirms the role of an already-documented memory mechanism, with no need for theorizing about repression.

In addition, we need to acknowledge the possibility that at least some recovered memories may, in fact, be false memories. After all, we know that false memories occur and that they're more likely when someone is recalling the distant past than when one is trying to remember recent events. It's also relevant that many recovered memories emerge only with the assistance of a therapist who is genuinely convinced that a client's psychological problems stem from long-forgotten episodes of childhood abuse. Even if therapists scrupulously avoid leading questions, their expectations might still lead them to shape their clients' memory in other ways—for example, by giving signs of interest or concern if the clients hit on the "right" line of exploration, by spending more time on topics related to the alleged memories, and so on. In these ways, the climate within a therapeutic session could guide the client toward finding exactly the "memories" the therapist expects to find.

Overall, then, we need to be cautious about the claim that some sort of self-protection mechanism can "hide" painful memories from view, with the possibility of recovering those memories later. There are often other explanations available for cases of apparent memory "recovery." And here—as in all cases—the accuracy of someone's recollection cannot be taken for granted. Even so, at least some of these now-voiced memories are sure to be correct and can provide evidence for terrible crimes. We therefore cannot dismiss claims of recovered memory, but we need to examine each of these claims with considerable care. (For discussions of this difficult—and sometimes angrily debated—issue, see, among others, Brewin, 2020; Dalenberg et al., 2012; Geraerts et al., 2009; Küpper et al., 2014; Loftus, 2017; Ost, 2013; Otgaar et al., 2021; Patihis et al., 2014; Pezdek & Blandon-Gitlin, 2017; Wang et al., 2019; Wessel et al., 2020.)

Long, Long-Term Remembering

In the laboratory, a researcher might ask you to recall a word list you read just minutes ago or a film you saw a week ago. Away from the lab, however, people routinely try to remember events from years—perhaps decades—back. These longer *retention intervals* are generally associated with a greater amount of forgetting, but, impressively, memories from long ago can sometimes turn out to be entirely accurate.

In an early study, Bahrick et al. (1975; also Bahrick, 1984; Bahrick & Hall, 1991) tracked down the graduates of a particular high school—people who had graduated in the previous year, and the year before, and the year before that, and ultimately people who had graduated 50 years earlier. These alumni were shown photographs from their own year's high school yearbook, and for each photo they were given a group of names and had to choose the name of the person shown in the picture. The data for this "name-matching" task show remarkably little forgetting; performance was approximately 90% correct if tested 3 months after graduation, the same after 7 years, and the same after 14 years. In some versions of the test, performance was still excellent after 34 years (see **Figure 8.8**).

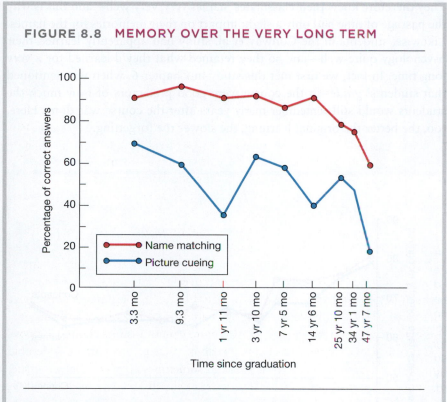

FIGURE 8.8 **MEMORY OVER THE VERY LONG TERM**

When people were tested for how well they remembered names and faces of their high school classmates, their memory was remarkably long-lasting. In the name-matching task, participants were given a group of names and had to choose the right one. In the picture-cueing task, participants had to come up with the names on their own. In both tasks, the data show a sharp drop-off after 47 years, but it is unclear whether this reflects an erosion of memory or a more general drop-off in performance caused by the normal process of aging. (AFTER BAHRICK ET AL., 1975)

As a different example, what about the material you're learning right now? Five years from now, will you still remember what you've learned? How about a decade from now? Conway et al. (1991, 1992) explored these questions, testing students' retention of a cognitive psychology course taken years earlier. The results echo the pattern we've already seen. Some forgetting of names and specific concepts was observed during the first 3 years after the course. After the third year, however, performance stabilized, so that students tested after 10 years still remembered a fair amount—in fact, just as much as students tested after 3 years (see **Figure 8.9**).

In an earlier section, we argued that the retention interval is crucial for memory and that memory gets worse as time goes by. The data now in front of us, though, indicate that *how much* the interval matters—that is, how quickly memories "fade"—may depend on how well established the memories were in the first place. The high school students in the Bahrick et al. study had seen their classmates day after day for (perhaps) several years. They therefore knew their classmates' names very, very well—and this is why the passage of time had only a slight impact on their memories for the names. Likewise, students in the Conway et al. study had apparently learned their psychology quite well—and so they retained what they'd learned for a very long time. In fact, we first met this study in Chapter 6, when we mentioned that students' *grades* in the course were good predictors of how much the students would still remember many years after the course was done. Here, too, the better the original learning, the slower the forgetting.

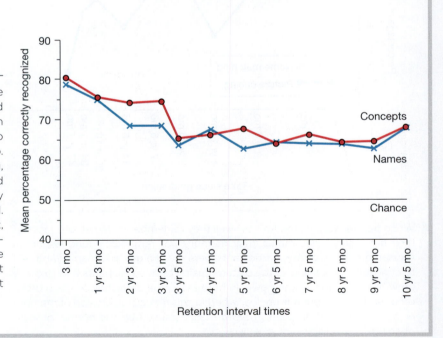

FIGURE 8.9 LONG-TERM RETENTION OF COURSE MATERIALS

Participants in this study were quizzed about material they had learned in a college course taken as recently as three months ago or as far back as a decade ago. The data showed some forgetting, but then performance leveled off; memory seemed remarkably stable from three years onward. Note that in a recognition task, memory is probed with "familiar-or-not" questions, so someone with no memory, responding at random, would get 50% right just by chance.

(AFTER CONWAY, ET AL., 1991)

We can maintain our claim, therefore, that the passage of time is the enemy of memory: Longer retention intervals produce lower levels of recall. However, if the material is very well learned at the start, and also if you periodically "revisit" the material, you can dramatically diminish the impact of the passing years.

How General Are the Principles of Memory?

There is certainly more to be said about autobiographical memory. For example, it can't be surprising that people tend to remember significant turning points in their lives and often use these turning points as a means of organizing their autobiographical recall (Enz & Talarico, 2015; Rubin & Umanath, 2015). Perhaps related, there are also memory patterns associated with someone's *age*. Specifically, some people insist they can remember events from very early in life (e.g., events before their first birthday; Akhtar et al., 2018), but there is reason to believe many of these early memories may be *fictions*. Evidence suggests, in fact, that most people recall very little from their first three years (e.g., Akers et al., 2014; Bauer et al., 2019; Morrison & Conway, 2010). In contrast, people generally have clear and detailed memories of their late adolescence and early adulthood, a pattern known as the "reminiscence bump." (See **Figure 8.10**; Conway & Haque, 1999; Conway et al., 2005; Dickson et al., 2011; Koppel & Rubin, 2016; Rathbone et al.,

TEST YOURSELF

12. What is memory consolidation?
13. What is a flashbulb memory? Are flashbulb memories distinctive in how accurate they seem to be?

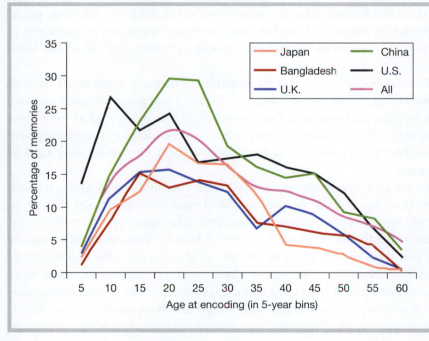

FIGURE 8.10 THE LIFESPAN RETRIEVAL CURVE

Most people have few memories of their early childhood (roughly from birth to age 3 or 4); this pattern is referred to as "childhood amnesia." In contrast, the period from age 10 to 30 is well remembered, producing a pattern called the "reminiscence bump." This "bump" has been observed in multiple studies and in diverse cultures; events from this time in young adulthood are often remembered in more detail (although perhaps less *accurately*) than more recent events.

2008; Rathbone et al., 2017.) As a result, for many Americans, the last years of high school and the years they spend in college are likely to be the most memorable periods of their lives.

But in terms of the broader themes of this chapter, where does our brief survey of autobiographical memory leave us? In many ways, this form of memory is similar to other sorts of remembering. Autobiographical memories can last for years and years, but so can memories that don't refer directly to your own life. Autobiographical remembering is far more likely if the person occasionally revisits the target memories; these rehearsals dramatically reduce forgetting. But the same is true in non-autobiographical remembering.

Autobiographical memory is also open to error, just as other forms of remembering are. We saw this in cases of flashbulb memories that turn out to be false. We've also seen that misinformation and leading questions can plant false autobiographical memories—about birthday parties that never happened and trips to the hospital that never took place (also see Brown & Marsh, 2008). Misinformation can even reshape memories for traumatic events, just as it can alter memories for trivial episodes in the laboratory (Morgan et al., 2013; Paz-Alonso & Goodman, 2008).

These facts strengthen a claim that has been emerging in our discussion over the last three chapters: Certain principles seem to apply to memory in general, no matter what is being remembered. All memories depend on connections. The connections promote retrieval. The connections also facilitate interference, because they allow one memory to blur into another. The connections can fade with the passage of time, producing memory gaps, and the gaps are likely to be filled via reconstruction based on generic knowledge. All these things seem to be true whether we're talking about relatively recent memories or memories from long ago, emotional memories or memories of calm events, memories for complex episodes or memories for simple word lists.

But this doesn't mean that all principles of memory apply to all types of remembering. As we saw in Chapter 7, the rules that govern implicit memory may be different from those that govern explicit memory. And as we've now seen, some of the factors that play a large role in shaping autobiographical remembering (e.g., the role of emotion) may be irrelevant to other sorts of memory.

In the end, therefore, our overall theory of memory is going to need more than one level of description. We'll need some principles that apply to only certain types of memory (e.g., principles specifically aimed at emotional remembering). But we'll also need broader principles, reflecting the fact that some themes apply to memory of all sorts (e.g., the importance of memory connections). As the last three chapters have shown, these more general principles have moved us forward considerably in our understanding of memory in many different domains and have enabled us to illuminate many aspects of learning, of memory retrieval, and of the sources of memory error.

medical histories

In obvious ways, your ability to remember depends on your health, because if you're ill, your brain won't function at its best, and that will likely produce problems in memory. It's less obvious, though, that the opposite is also true—because there are settings in which your health depends on your memory.

When doctors diagnose someone with a contagious disease—whether it's measles or something deadly, like the Ebola virus or (more recently) COVID-19—they want to move quickly to locate others who may have been infected. That way, they can treat (and perhaps quarantine) other infected individuals as soon as possible. But how do they find these people? Often, they rely on "contact tracing." They ask the already-diagnosed patient: Where have you been in the last few days? Who else was present? Did you touch these other individuals? Questions like these plainly depend on patients *remembering* where they've been, who else was there, and what they did. In this way, the likelihood of containing the contagion depends on memory.

Here's a different example: Every year, there are outbreaks of illness arising from people eating contaminated food, and when there is such an outbreak, investigators scramble to track down the source of the infection. Public health investigators will want to know what foods each of the affected patients has been eating, what restaurants they've patronized, and so on. In this way, investigators can locate the common element among the infected individuals. Then, once they've identified the source of the infection, they can recall the contaminated food or demand that a restaurant bring its procedures up to a healthy standard. But, of course, here too we rely on memory—with people remembering what and where they've recently eaten.

Another example is more routine: You visit your doctor with some medical complaint. The office visit begins with someone taking a "history": How has your health been lately? When did your current complaint begin? Are there circumstances in which the complaint is better or worse? These questions will guide the doctor's diagnosis and treatment plan, and once more we're relying on your memory.

It cannot be a surprise, though, that in each of these settings memory is far from reliable. When doctors are trying to track an infection or seeking the source of food poisoning, they're likely to ask about mundane events—how you spent an ordinary Tuesday, or what you had for lunch the day before yesterday. In other words, they're asking about events that were part of your ordinary routine, events that were in no way exciting or distinctive; and events like these are, in general, difficult to remember.

What about medical histories? One early study (Cohen & Java, 1995) asked people to keep a health diary for three months, recording medically significant events such as symptoms, injuries, medications, and visits to health professionals. When asked to recall these events later, research participants

recalled only half of the events they'd recorded into the diaries. In another study (Eze-Nliam et al., 2012), patients admitted to a hospital's cardiology service were asked about their previous medical conditions; their responses were then compared to the actual medical record. The data showed many discrepancies—with regard to reports of prior illnesses such as bronchitis or pneumonia, and even with regard to whether patients reported a prior heart attack.

Can we improve matters? One study (Brewer et al., 2005) explored the benefits of specific memory cues. Researchers questioned patients infected with sexually-transmitted diseases, asking the patients to recall their sexual and/or injection partners. The patients were first asked simply to list their partners; then they were further questioned, prompted with cues that (among other points) named specific places where the patient might have met someone. The data indicated that 72% of the sexual/injection partners were listed only with this additional cueing.

The text discusses another option—the Cognitive Interview (CI), a protocol initially developed for police interviewing crime witnesses. One study, though, was modeled after the questioning that authorities might do in an investigation of food poisoning (Fisher & Quigley, 1992). Participants in this study selected and ate a variety of foods from a smorgasbord. Later, participants were asked to recall what they had eaten. Participants questioned with the CI were, a week later, able to recall twice as many foods as those questioned with the procedure ordinarily used in public health investigations.

Another study simulated epidemiological research (Mosser & Evans, 2019). Participants were invited to imagine that they had a contagious disease, and, motivated by this thought, were asked to list everyone they had interacted with in the last three days. Participants were also asked more specific questions, including a request that they list any individuals they might have shared saliva with via a shared cigarette or drink. Participants questioned with the CI remembered 35% more of their contacts overall, but the CI provided no reliable advantage in remembering "droplet-transmitted contacts"—perhaps because the latter type of contact is on its own quite memorable.

Plainly, then, limitations on memory can be obstacles for health care—but it seems that we can draw on available research to improve memories in ways that can improve the practice of medicine.

For more on this topic . . .

Brewer, D. D., Potterat, J. J., Muth, S. Q., Malone, P. Z., Montoya, P., Green, D. L., Rogers, H. L., & Cox, P. A. (2005). Randomized trial of supplementary interviewing techniques to enhance recall of sexual partners in contact interviews. *Sexually Transmitted Diseases*, *32*(3), 189–193.

Cohen, G., & Java, R. (1995). Memory for medical history: Accuracy of recall. *Applied Cognitive Psychology*, *9*(4), 273–288.

Eze-Nliam, C., Cain, K., Bond, K., Forlenza, K., Jankowski, R., Magyar-Russell, G., Yenokyan, G., & Ziegelstein, R. C. (2012). Discrepancies between the medical record and the reports of patients with acute coronary syndrome regarding important aspects of the medical history. *BMC Health Services Research*, *12*, article 78.

Fisher, R. P., & Quigley, K. L. (1992). Applying cognitive theory in public health investigations: Enhancing food recall with the cognitive interview. In J. M. Tanur (Ed.), *Questions about questions: Inquiries into the cognitive bases of surveys* (pp. 154–169). New York, NY: Russell Sage Foundation.

Garry, M., Hope, L., Zajac, R., Verrall, A. J., & Robertson, J. M. (2020). Contact tracing: A memory task with consequences for public health. *Perspectives on Psychological Science*, *16*(1), 175–187.

Mosser, A. E., & Evans, J. R. (2019). From the police station to the hospital bed: Using the cognitive interview to enhance epidemiologic interview. In J. J. Dickinson, N. Schreiber Compo, R. N. Carol, B. L. Schwartz, & M. R. McCauley (Eds.), *Evidence-based investigative interviewing* (pp. 93–115). New York, NY: Routledge.

chapter review

SUMMARY

• Memory is usually accurate, but errors do occur and can be quite significant. In general, these errors are produced by the connections that link memories to one another and link memories for specific episodes to other, more general knowledge. These connections help you because they serve as retrieval paths. But the connections can also "knit" separate memories together, making it difficult to keep track of which elements belong in which memory.

• Some memory errors arise from your understanding of an episode. The understanding promotes memory for the episode's gist but also encourages memory errors. A similar pattern emerges in the DRM paradigm, in which a word related to other words on a list is (incorrectly) recalled as being part of the list. Closely related effects arise from schematic knowledge. This knowledge helps you understand an episode, but at the same time a reliance on schematic knowledge can lead you to remember an episode as being more "regular," more "normal," than it actually was.

• Memory errors can also arise through the misinformation effect, in which people are exposed to some (false) suggestion about a previous event. Such suggestions can easily change the details of how an event is remembered and can, in some cases, plant memories for entire episodes that never occurred at all.

• People often seem genuinely unable to distinguish their accurate memories from their inaccurate ones. This is because false memories can sometimes be recalled with just as much detail, emotion, and confidence as historically accurate memories. The absence of a consistent connection between memory accuracy and memory confidence contrasts with the commonsense belief that you should rely on someone's degree of certainty in assessing their memory. The problem in this commonsense belief lies in the fact that confidence is influenced by factors (such as feedback) that have no impact on accuracy, and this influence can undermine the linkage between accuracy and confidence.

• While memory errors are easily documented, cases of accurate remembering can also be observed, and they are probably more numerous than cases involving memory error. Memory errors are more likely, though, in recalling distant events rather than recent ones. One reason is decay of the relevant memories; another reason is retrieval failure. Retrieval failure can be either complete or partial; the tip-of-the-tongue phenomenon provides a clear example of partial retrieval failure. Perhaps the most important source of forgetting, though, is interference.

• People have sought various ways of undoing forgetting, including hypnosis and certain drugs. These approaches, however, seem ineffective. Forgetting can be diminished, though, through procedures that provide a rich variety of retrieval cues, and it can be avoided through occasional revisits to the target material.

• Although memory errors are troubling, they may be the price you pay in order to obtain other advantages. For example, many errors result from the dense network of connections that link your various memories. These connections sometimes make it difficult to recall which elements occurred in which setting, but the same connections serve as retrieval paths—and without those connections, you might have great difficulty in locating your memories in long-term storage.

• Autobiographical memory is influenced by the same principles as any other form of memory, but it is also shaped by its own set of factors. For example, episodes connected to the self are, in general, better remembered—a pattern known as the "self-reference effect."

• Autobiographical memories are often emotional, and this has multiple effects on memory. Emotion seems to promote memory consolidation, but it may also produce a pattern of memory narrowing. Some emotional events give rise to very clear, long-lasting flashbulb memories. Despite their subjective clarity, these memories can contain errors and in some cases can be entirely inaccurate. At the extreme of emotion, trauma has mixed effects on memory. Some traumatic events are not remembered, but most traumatic events seem to be remembered for a long time and in great detail.

• Some events can be recalled even after many years have passed. In some cases, this is because the knowledge was learned very well in the first place. In other cases, occasional rehearsals preserve a memory for a very long time.

KEY TERMS

intrusion errors (p. 269)
DRM paradigm (p. 271)
schema (p. 271)
misinformation effect (p. 276)
retention interval (p. 282)
decay theory of forgetting (p. 283)
interference theory (p. 283)

retrieval failure (p. 283)
TOT phenomenon (p. 284)
autobiographical memory (p. 287)
consolidation (p. 288)
flashbulb memories (p. 290)

TEST YOURSELF AGAIN

1. What is the evidence that in some circumstances many people will misremember significant events they have experienced?

2. What is the evidence that in some circumstances people will even misremember *recent* events?

3. What is the evidence that your *understanding* of an episode can produce intrusion errors?

4. What is the DRM paradigm, and what results does this procedure produce?

5. What is schematic knowledge, and what evidence tells us that schematic knowledge can help us—and also can undermine our memory accuracy?

6. What is the misinformation effect? Describe three different procedures that can produce this effect.

7. Some people insist that our memories are consistently accurate in remembering the gist, or overall content, of an event; when we make memory errors, they claim, we make mistakes only about the details within an event. What evidence allows us to *reject* this claim?

8. What factors seem to *undermine* the relationship between your degree of certainty in a memory and the likelihood that the memory is accurate?

9. Explain why the mechanisms that produce memory *errors* may actually be mechanisms that help us in important ways.

10. Explain the mechanisms hypothesized by each of the three major theories of forgetting: decay, interference, and retrieval failure.

11. What techniques or procedures seem *in*effective as a means of "undoing" forgetting? What techniques or procedures seem to diminish or avoid forgetting?

12. What is memory consolidation?

13. What is a flashbulb memory? Are flashbulb memories distinctive in how accurate they seem to be?

THINK ABOUT IT

1. You sometimes hear people say things like, "I wish I had a better memory." What does this mean? If you could somehow improve your memory, what would your "ideal" be? What would you change in order to give yourself the best possible memory? Then, in light of the points in the chapter, are there steps you could take that actually might give you a better memory (however you've chosen to define "better")? What would those steps be?

DEMONSTRATIONS & APPLYING COGNITIVE PSYCHOLOGY ESSAYS

For demonstrations of key concepts in cognitive psychology, take a look at the Online Demonstrations. To explore more of the practical applications of cognitive psychology in themed essays, visit the online reader.

Online Demonstrations

- Demonstration 8.1: Associations and Memory Error
- Demonstration 8.2: Memory Accuracy and Confidence
- Demonstration 8.3: The Tip-of-the-Tongue Effect
- Demonstration 8.4: Memory for Words
- Demonstration 8.5: Childhood Amnesia

Online Applying Cognitive Psychology Essays

- Cognitive Psychology and Education: Remembering for the Long Term
- Cognitive Psychology and Technology: Which Is Better: Memory or a Videorecording?
- Cognitive Psychology and the Law: Jurors' Memory

ZAPS COGNITION LABS

Go to ZAPS online cognition labs to conduct hands-on experiments on key concepts.

INQUIZITIVE

It's time to complete your study experience! Go to InQuizitive to practice actively with this chapter's concepts and get personalized feedback along the way.

Knowledge

In Parts 2 and 3, we saw case after case in which your interactions with the world are guided by knowledge. In perceiving, for example, you make inferences guided by knowledge about the world's regular patterns. In attending, you anticipate inputs guided by your knowledge about what's likely to occur. In learning, you connect new information to things you already know.

But what is knowledge? How is it represented in the mind? How do you locate knowledge in memory when you need it? We've already taken steps toward answering these questions—by arguing that knowledge is represented in the mind by means of a network of interconnected nodes. In this section, we'll expand this proposal in important ways. In Chapter 9, we'll describe the basic building blocks of knowledge—individual concepts. We'll consider several hypotheses about how concepts are represented in the mind, and we'll see that each hypothesis captures part of the truth. Along the way, we'll see that knowledge about individual concepts depends on linkages to other, related concepts. For example, you can't know what a "dog" is without also understanding what an "animal" is, what a "living thing" is, and so on. As a result, connections among ideas will be crucial here, just as they were in previous chapters.

Chapters 10 and 11 then focus on two special types of knowledge: knowledge about language and knowledge about visual images. In Chapter 10, we'll see that your knowledge of language is highly creative, allowing you to produce new words and new sentences that no one has ever used before. But at the same time, the creativity is constrained, so there are some words, and some sequences of words, that seem unacceptable to virtually any language user. In order to understand these facts, we'll consider the possibility that language knowledge involves abstract rules that are, in some way, honored by every user of the language. In Chapter 11, we'll see that mental images involve representations that are distinct from those involved in other forms of knowledge, but we'll also consider ways in which memory for visual appearances is governed by the same principles as other forms of knowledge.

Concepts and
Generic Knowledge

chapter **9**

what if... In Chapter 8, we mentioned people who have superior autobiographical recall. It's remarkable how much these individuals can remember—but some people, it turns out, remember even more. One might say that these people have "perfect memories," but this terminology would be misleading.

We begin with a work of fiction. In a wonderful short story titled "Funes the Memorious," the Argentine writer Jorge Luis Borges describes a character—Funes—who never forgets anything. But rather than being proud of this capacity, Funes is immensely distressed by his memorial prowess: "My memory, sir, is like a garbage heap" (p. 152).

Among other problems, Funes complains that he cannot think in general terms. He remembers so much about how individuals *differ* that he has a hard time focusing on what they might *have in common*: "Not only was it difficult for him to comprehend that the generic symbol *dog* embraces so many unlike individuals of diverse size and form; it bothered him that the dog at 3:14 (seen from the side) should have the same name as the dog at 3:15 (seen from the front)" (Borges, 1964, p. 153).

Funes is a fictional character, but consider the actual case of Solomon Shereshevsky (Luria, 1968). Shereshevsky, like Funes, never forgot anything. After hearing a lengthy speech, he could repeat it back word for word. If shown a complex mathematical formula (even one that had no meaning for him), he could reproduce it perfectly months later. He effortlessly memorized poems written in languages he didn't understand. And Shereshevsky's flawless retention wasn't the result of some deliberate trick or strategy. Just the opposite: Shereshevsky seemed to have no choice about his level of recall.

Like Funes, Shereshevsky wasn't well served by his extraordinary memory. He had difficulty, for example, recognizing faces because he was distracted by the *changes* in a face from one view to the next. And, like Funes, Shereshevsky couldn't get past the detail of his own recollections in order to think about his experiences in abstract terms.

There are, of course, settings in which you want to remember the specific episodes of your life. But the problems suffered by Funes and Shereshevsky remind us that there are sometimes disadvantages for this type of particularized recall. In many settings, you want to set aside the details of this or that episode and, instead, weave your experiences together so that you can pool information received from various sources.

- Basic concepts—like "chair" and "dog"—are the building blocks of all knowledge. However, attempts at *defining* these concepts usually fail because we easily find exceptions to any definition that might be proposed.

- This leads to a suggestion that knowledge of these concepts is cast in terms of *probabilities*—so that a creature that has wings and feathers, and that flies and lays eggs, is *probably* a bird.

- Many results are consistent with this probabilistic idea and show that the more a test case resembles the "prototype" for a category, the more likely people are to judge the case as being in that category.

- Other results, however, indicate that conceptual knowledge includes other beliefs—beliefs that link a concept to other concepts and also specify why the concept is as it is.

- These beliefs may be represented in the mind as propositions encoded in a network structure. Alternatively, they may be represented in a distributed form in a connectionist network.

- We are driven, therefore, to a multipart theory of concepts. Your conceptual knowledge likely includes a prototype for each category and also a set of remembered exemplars. But you also seem to have a broad set of beliefs about each concept—beliefs about why the concept takes the form it does, and you rely on these beliefs in a wide range of judgments about the concept.

This enables you to create a more complete, more integrated type of knowledge—one that allows you to think about dogs in general rather than focusing on *this* view of *that* dog; or one that helps you remember what your friend generally looks like rather than what he looked like, say, yesterday at 1:42 in the afternoon. This more general type of knowledge is surely drawn from day-to-day experience, but it is somehow abstracted away from that experience. What is this more general type of knowledge?

Understanding Concepts

I, Dan Reisberg, have a dog named Milo. (This is true; you can see Milo in **Figure 9.1**.) You've probably never heard about Milo before, but you already know a lot about him. You know that he's likely to bark and chase cats, but unlikely to climb trees or hibernate through the winter. You know that he has fur and not feathers. You might consider playing fetch with him, but you surely wouldn't challenge him to a game of chess. You know he probably lives in my house and likely wasn't around 25 years ago. And so on. In sum, merely by knowing that Milo is a pet dog, you know a lot.

Conversely, if you learn some new fact about Milo, you may assume the same is true for other dogs. If you learn, for example, that he's been ill because of drinking stagnant water in the park, you might become more concerned about what your own pet is drinking.

Examples like these remind us how powerful our basic concepts and categories are. Concepts (like "dog") allow you to apply your general knowledge to new cases you encounter (like Milo). Likewise, your concepts enable you

FIGURE 9.1 **WHY IS CATEGORIZATION SO IMPORTANT?**

If you decide that Milo is a dog, then you instantly know a great deal about him (e.g., that he's likely to enjoy walks and is unlikely to climb trees). Notice, then, that categorization enables you to apply your general knowledge to new cases. And if you learn something new about Milo (e.g., that he's at risk for a particular virus), you're likely to assume the same is true for other dogs. In this way, categorization also enables you to draw broad conclusions from specific experiences.

to draw broad conclusions from your experience (so that things you learn about Milo can be applied to other dogs you meet, and maybe to other pets, or even other animals).

But what exactly does it mean to know and understand a concept? How is this knowledge represented in the mind? Let's begin with a simple hypothesis: that understanding a concept is like knowing a dictionary definition. If someone knows what a "dog" is, therefore, or a "taxi," they can offer something like a definition for these terms—and likewise for all the other concepts in each person's knowledge base. As we'll see, though, this hypothesis quickly runs into problems, so we'll need to turn to a more complicated proposal.

Definitions: What Is a "Dog"?

You know perfectly well what a dog is, and you used this knowledge in thinking about Milo. But what is this knowledge? What does the knowledge involve? One possibility is that you know something akin to a dictionary definition—something like: "A dog is a creature that (a) is an animal, (b) has four legs, (c) barks, (d) wags its tail." You could then use this definition in straightforward ways: If you were asked whether Milo truly is a dog, you could use the definition as a checklist, scrutinizing him for the various defining features. When told that Milo is an animal, you would know that you hadn't learned anything new, because this information is already contained within the definition. If you were asked what dogs, cats, and horses have in common, you could scan your definition of each one looking for common elements.

THE HUNT FOR DEFINITIONS

It is remarkably difficult to define even very familiar terms. For example, what is a "dog"? Most people include "has fur" in the definition, but what about the hairless Chihuahua? Many people include "communicates by barking" in the definition, but what about the Basenji (one of which is shown here)—a breed of dog that makes a noise sometimes described as a "yodel," but doesn't bark?

This proposal is correct in some cases, and so, for example, you certainly know definitions for concepts like "triangle" and "even number." But what about more commonplace concepts? The concern here was brought to light by the 20th-century philosopher Ludwig Wittgenstein, who argued (e.g., Wittgenstein, 1953) that simple terms we all use every day actually don't have definitions. For example, consider the word "shoe." You might define "shoe" as an item of apparel made out of leather, designed to be worn on the foot. But what about wooden shoes? What about a shoe designed by a master shoemaker, intended only for display? What about a shoe filled with cement, which therefore can't be worn? Similarly, a definition for "dog" might specify "has four legs," but what about a dog that has lost a limb in some accident? We might include "communicates by barking" as part of the definition of dog, but what about the African Basenji, which doesn't bark?

Family Resemblance

It seems, then, we can't say things like "A dog is a creature that has fur and four legs and barks." That's because we easily find exceptions to this rule (a hairless Chihuahua; a three-legged dog; the barkless Basenji). But surely we *can* say, "Dogs *usually* are creatures that have fur, four legs, and bark, and a creature without these features is *unlikely to be* a dog." This phrasing preserves what's good about definitions—the fact that they do name relevant features, shared by most members of the category. But this phrasing also allows a degree of uncertainty, some number of exceptions to the rule.

In a similar spirit, Wittgenstein proposed that members of a category have a **family resemblance** to one another. To understand this term, think about an actual family—your own, perhaps. There are probably no "defining features" for your family—features that every family member has. Nonetheless, there are features that are common in the family, and so, if we consider family members two or three at a time, we can usually find shared attributes. For example, you, your brother, and your mother might all have the family's beautiful red hair and the same wide lips; as a result, you three look alike to some extent. Your sister, however, doesn't have these features. She's still recognizable as a member of the family, though, because (like you and your father) she has the family's typical eye shape and the family's distinctive chin. In this way, the common features in the family depend on what "subgroup" you're considering—hair color shared for *these* family members; eye shape shared by *those* family members; and so on.

One way to think about this pattern is by imagining the "ideal" for each family—someone who has *all* of the family's features. (In our example, this would be a wide-lipped redhead with the right eye and chin shapes.) In many families, this person may not exist, so perhaps there's nobody who has every one of the family's distinctive features—and so no one who looks like the "perfect Jones" (or the "perfect Martinez" or the "perfect Goldberg"). Nonetheless, each member of the family shares at least some features with this ideal—and therefore has some features in common with other family members. This feature overlap is why the family members resemble one another, and it's how we manage to recognize these individuals as all belonging to the same family.

Wittgenstein proposed that ordinary categories like "dog" or "game" or "furniture" work in the same way. There may be no features that are shared by all dogs or all games. Even so, we can identify "characteristic features" for each category—features that many (perhaps most) category members have. These are the features that enable you to recognize that a dog is a dog, a shoe is a shoe, and so on.

Prototypes and Typicality Effects

How should psychologists think about Wittgenstein's proposal? Let's begin with the idea that definitions essentially set "boundaries" for a category. If a test case has certain attributes, then it's "inside" the boundaries. If a test case doesn't have the defining attributes, then it's "outside" the boundaries—and so not in the category. The notion of family resemblance, though, suggests a different approach: Perhaps we can identify a category by specifying its "center," rather than the boundaries. Just as we spoke earlier about the "ideal" family member, perhaps the concept of "tree" is represented in the mind by a **prototype**—that is, a depiction of the "ideal" tree, and all judgments about

TYPICALITY IN FAMILIES

In the Smith family, many (but not all) of the brothers have dark hair, so dark hair is typical for the family (i.e., is found in *many* family members) but doesn't define the family (i.e., is not found in *all* family members). Likewise, wearing glasses is typical for the family but isn't a defining feature; so is having a mustache and a big nose. Many concepts have the same character—with many features shared among the instances of the concept, but no features shared by all of the instances.

trees are made with reference to this ideal. Likewise for "bird" or "house" or any other concept in your repertoire—in each case, the concept is represented by the appropriate prototype. (For classic statements of this proposal, see Rosch, 1973, 1978; Rosch & Mervis, 1975.)

Prototypes and Graded Membership

In most cases, the prototype for a category will be an average of the various category members you've encountered. So, for example, the prototype coffee cup will be the average shape of the cups you've seen and the average size of the cups you've seen. Likewise, the prototype bedroom will be the average size of bedrooms you've seen and will contain the furnishings and decorations that you've most often seen. (Notice, then, that different people, each with their own experiences, will have slightly different prototypes.)

But how do you use a prototype in your interactions with the world? Imagine that you're trying to decide whether it's okay to pour coffee into the object you see sitting on the shelf. Is the object a coffee cup or not? In making this decision, you might compare the object with the relevant prototype in your memory. If there's enormous similarity, the object before you probably is in the category; if there's little similarity, you'll look for something else to pour your coffee into.

The proposal, then, is that judgments about category membership depend on resemblance to the prototype. Let's emphasize, though, that resemblance is a *matter of degree*. After all, some coffee cups do resemble the prototype closely, while others have less in common with this ideal. In technical terms, we'd say that category members differ in their **typicality**—that is, how much they resemble the prototype.

Now let's put these points together: If membership depends on resemblance, and resemblance is a matter of degree, then membership in a category

CATEGORIES HAVE PROTOTYPES

As the text describes, people seem to have a prototype in their minds for a category like "dog." For many people, the German shepherd shown here is close to that prototype, and the other dogs depicted are more distant from the prototype.

isn't a "yes" or "no" decision; instead, it's a matter of "more" or "less." In other words, categories have (what's called) **graded membership**, such that objects close to the prototype (high in typicality) are "better" members of the category than objects farther from the prototype. Or, to put the idea in crude terms, some cups are "cuppier" than others, some books "bookier" than others, and so on for all the other categories you can think of.

Testing the Prototype Notion

Many studies confirm the graded-membership idea. For example, in classic studies using a **sentence verification task**, research participants were presented with a series of sentences, and their job was to indicate (by pressing the appropriate button) whether each sentence was true or false. In this procedure, participants' responses were slower for sentences like "A penguin is a bird" than for sentences like "A robin is a bird"; slower for "An Afghan hound is a dog" than for "A German shepherd is a dog" (Smith et al., 1974).

Why should this be? According to a prototype perspective, participants choose their response ("true" or "false") by comparing the thing mentioned (e.g., penguin) to their prototype for that category (i.e., their bird prototype). When there is close similarity between the test case and the prototype, participants can make their decisions quickly; in contrast, judgments about items distant from the prototype take more time. And given the results, it seems that penguins and Afghan hounds are more distant from their respective prototypes than are robins and German shepherds.

Other evidence can be understood in similar terms. For example, in a **production task** we simply ask people to name as many birds or dogs as they can. According to a prototype view, they'll do this task by first locating their bird or dog prototype in memory and then asking themselves what resembles this prototype. In essence, they'll start with the center of the category (the prototype) and work their way outward from there. So birds close to the prototype should be mentioned first; birds farther from the prototype, later on.

By this logic, the first birds mentioned in the production task should be the birds that yielded fast response times in the verification task; that's because what matters in both tasks is proximity to the prototype. Likewise, the birds mentioned later in production should have yielded slower response times in verification. This is exactly what happens (Mervis et al., 1976).

In fact, this outcome sets the pattern of evidence for prototype theory. Over and over, in category after category, members of a category that are "privileged" on one task (e.g., they yield the fastest response times) turn out also to be privileged on other tasks (e.g., they're most likely to be mentioned). As another illustration of this pattern, consider the data from **rating tasks**. In these tasks, participants are given instructions like these: "We all know that some birds are 'birdier' than others, some dogs are 'doggier' than others, and so on. I'm going to present you with a list of birds or of dogs, and I want you to rate each one on the basis of how 'birdy' or 'doggy' it is" (Rosch, 1975; also Malt & Smith, 1984).

TABLE 9.1 PARTICIPANTS' TYPICALITY RATINGS FOR THE CATEGORY "FRUIT" AND THE CATEGORY "BIRD"

Fruit	Rating	Bird	Rating
Apple	6.25	Robin	6.89
Peach	5.81	Bluebird	6.42
Pear	5.25	Seagull	6.26
Grape	5.13	Swallow	6.16
Strawberry	5.00	Falcon	5.74
Lemon	4.86	Mockingbird	5.47
Blueberry	4.56	Starling	5.16
Watermelon	4.06	Owl	5.00
Raisin	3.75	Vulture	4.84
Fig	3.38	Sandpiper	4.47
Coconut	3.06	Chicken	3.95
Pomegranate	2.50	Flamingo	3.37
Avocado	2.38	Albatross	3.32
Pumpkin	2.31	Penguin	2.63
Olive	2.25	Bat	1.53

Ratings were made on a 7-point scale, with 7 corresponding to the highest typicality. Note also that the least "birdy" of the birds isn't a bird at all!

(AFTER MALT & SMITH, 1984)

People are easily able to make these judgments, and quite consistently they rate items as being very "birdy" or "doggy" when these instances are close to the prototype (as determined in the other tasks). They rate items as being less "birdy" or "doggy" when these are farther from the prototype. This finding suggests that once again, people perform the task by comparing the test item to the prototype (see **Table 9.1**).

Basic-Level Categories

It does seem, then, that certain category members are "privileged," and this privilege shows up in a wide range of tasks. It turns out, also, that certain *types of category* are privileged—in their structure and the way they're used. For example, imagine that we show you a picture like the one in **Figure 9.2** and ask, "What is this?" You're likely to answer "a chair" and unlikely to offer a more specific response ("upholstered armchair") or a more general one ("an item of furniture"). Likewise, we might ask, "How do people get to work?" In responding, you're unlikely to say, "Some people drive Fords;

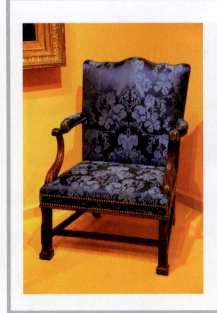

FIGURE 9.2 BASIC VERSUS SUPERORDINATE LABELING

What is this? The odds are good that you would answer, "It's a chair," using the basic-level description rather than the more general label ("It's a piece of furniture") or a more specific description ("It's an upholstered armchair")—even though these other descriptions would certainly be correct.

some drive Toyotas." Instead, your answer is likely to use more general terms, such as "cars," "trains," and "buses."

In keeping with these observations, researchers propose that there is a "natural" level of categorization, neither too specific nor too general, that people tend to use in their conversations and their reasoning. The special status of this **basic-level categorization** can be demonstrated in many ways. Basic-level categories are usually represented in our language via a single word, while more specific categories are identified with a phrase. Thus, "chair" is a basic-level category, and so is "apple." The more specific (subordinate) categories of "lawn chair" or "kitchen chair" aren't basic level; neither is "Granny Smith apple" or "Golden Delicious apple."

We've already suggested that if you're asked to identify an object, you're likely to use the basic-level term. In addition, if asked to explain what members of a category have in common with one another, you have an easy time with basic-level categories ("What do all chairs have in common?") but some difficulty with more inclusive (superordinate) categories ("What does all furniture have in common?"). In these (and other) ways, basic-level categories do seem to reflect a natural way to categorize the objects in our world. (For more on basic-level categories, see Murphy, 2016; Pansky & Koriat, 2004; Rogers & Patterson, 2007; Rosch et al., 1976.)

Exemplars

Let's return, though, to our main agenda. As we've seen, some members of a category are "better" than others, and the better members are recognized more readily, mentioned more often, judged to be more typical, and so on.

TEST YOURSELF

3. Why is graded membership a consequence of representing the category in terms of a prototype?
4. What tasks show us that concept judgments often rely on prototypes and typicality?
5. Give an example of a basic-level category, and then name some of the subcategories within this basic-level grouping.

FIGURE 9.3 TYPICALITY AND ATTRACTIVENESS

Typicality influences many judgments about category members, including attractiveness. Which of these pictures shows the most attractive-looking fish? Which one shows the least attractive-looking? In several studies, participants' ratings of attractiveness have been closely related to (other participants') ratings of typicality—so that people seem to find more-typical category members to be more attractive (e.g., Halberstadt & Rhodes, 2003).

(For yet another way you're influenced by typicality, see **Figure 9.3**.) All of this fits well with the idea that conceptual knowledge is represented via a prototype and that we categorize by making comparisons to that prototype. It turns out, though, that your knowledge about "birds" and "fruits" and "shoes" and so on also includes another element.

Analogies from Remembered Exemplars

Imagine that we place a wooden object in front of you and ask, "Is this a chair?" According to the prototype view, you'll answer by calling up your chair prototype from memory and comparing the object to that prototype. If the resemblance is great, you'll announce, "Yes, this is a chair."

But you might make this decision in a different way. You might notice that the object is very similar to an object in your Uncle Jiang's living room, and you know that Uncle Jiang's object is a chair. (After all, you've seen him sitting in the thing, reading his newspaper; you've heard him refer to the thing as "my chair," and so on.) These points allow an easy inference: If the new object resembles Jiang's, and if Jiang's object is a chair, then it's a safe bet that the new object is a chair, too.

The idea here is that in some cases categorization can rely on knowledge about specific category members (e.g., "Jiang's chair") rather than the prototype (e.g., the ideal chair). This process is referred to as **exemplar-based reasoning**, with an exemplar being defined as a specific remembered instance—in essence, an example.

A Combination of Exemplars and Prototypes

There are, in fact, good reasons for you to rely on prototypes *and* on exemplars in your thinking about categories. Prototypes provide an economical representation of what's typical for a category, and there are many circumstances in which this quick summary is useful. But exemplars, for their part, provide information that's lost from the prototype—including information about the variability within the category.

To see how this matters, consider the fact that people routinely "tune" their concepts to match the circumstances. For example, they think about birds differently when considering tropical birds than when thinking about North American birds; they think about gifts differently when considering gifts for a student rather than gifts for a faculty member (Barsalou, 1988; Barsalou & Sewell, 1985). In fact, people can adjust their categories in fairly precise ways: not just "gift," but "gift for a 4-year-old" or "gift for a 4-year-old who recently broke her wrist" or "gift for a 4-year-old who likes sports but recently broke her wrist." This pliability in concepts is easy to understand if people are relying on exemplars; after all, different settings, or different perspectives, would trigger different memories and so bring different exemplars to mind.

It's useful, then, that conceptual knowledge includes prototypes *and* exemplars, because each has its own advantages. However, the mix of exemplar and prototype knowledge may vary from person to person and from concept to concept. One person might have extensive knowledge about individual horses, so she has many exemplars in memory; the same person might have only general information (a prototype, perhaps) about snowmobiles. Some other person might show the reverse pattern. And for all people, the pattern of knowledge might depend on the size of the category and how easily confused the category memories are with one another—with exemplars being used when the individuals are more distinct. (For discussion, see Murphy, 2016; Smith et al., 2016; Thibeault et al., 2018. For discussion of the *neural basis* for exemplar storage, see Ashby & Rosedahl, 2017; also see **Figure 9.4**.)

Overall, though, it cannot be surprising that people can draw on either prototypes or exemplars when thinking about concepts. The reason is that the two types of information are used in essentially the same way. In either case, an object before your eyes triggers some representation in memory (either a representation of a specific instance, according to exemplar theory,

FIGURE 9.4 DISTINCTIONS WITHIN CATEGORIES

The chapter suggests that you have knowledge of both exemplars and prototypes. As a further complication, you also have special knowledge about distinctive individuals within a category. Thus, you know that Kermit has many froggy properties (he's green, he eats flies, he hops) but also has unusual properties that make him a rather unusual frog (since, after all, he can talk, he can sing, and he's in love with a pig).

TEST YOURSELF

6. What is *similar* in the processes of categorizing via a prototype and the processes of categorizing via an exemplar? What is *different* between these two types of processes?

or the prototype, according to prototype theory). In either case, you assess the resemblance between this conceptual knowledge, supplied by memory, and the novel object before you: "Does this object resemble my sister's couch?" If so, the object is a couch. "Does the object resemble my prototype for a soup bowl?" If so, it's probably a soup bowl.

Given these similarities, it seems plausible that we might merge the prototype and exemplar proposals, with each of us on any particular occasion relying on whichever sort of information (exemplar or prototype) comes to mind more readily.

The Difficulties with Categorizing via Resemblance

It seems, then, that your understanding of basic concepts includes at least two types of knowledge: a prototype for the concept, and also some number of exemplars for that concept. It turns out, though, that we need more theory than this, because of a complication in *how you use* prototypes or exemplars.

The Differences between Typicality and Categorization

One of the key ideas in our discussion so far is that you make decisions about category membership by making comparisons to a prototype or an exemplar. If, for example, you think that Mike closely resembles your prototype for "bully," you will probably decide that he is a bully. But if he seems totally different from your prototype, you'll likely draw the opposite conclusion.

Likewise for occasions in which you're trying to decide if a particular plant is a "weed"—again, comparing it to the relevant prototype—or whether a particular event is a "tragedy."

This perspective clearly implies that judgments of typicality and judgments of category membership should go hand in hand. Close resemblance to what's typical for the category? Probably in the category. No resemblance to what's typical? Probably not in the category. Despite these claims, though, judgments of typicality often seem entirely separate from judgments of category membership. For example, robins seem for most people to be closer to the typical bird than penguins are; even so, most of us are certain that both robins and penguins are birds. Likewise, Moby Dick was definitely not a typical whale, but he certainly was a whale; Abraham Lincoln wasn't a typical American, but he was an American. These observations suggest that there's some basis for judging category membership that's not tied to typicality, and we need to specify what that basis is. As an approach to this issue, let's think through an example. Consider a lemon. Paint the lemon with red and white stripes. Is it still a lemon? Most people say that it is. Now, inject the lemon with sugar water, so it has a sweet taste. Then, run over the lemon with a truck, so that it's flat as a pancake. What have we got at this point? Do we have a striped, artificially sweet, flattened lemon? Or do we have a non-lemon? Most people still accept this poor, abused fruit as a lemon; but consider what this judgment involves. We've taken steps to make this object more and more distant from the prototype and also very different from any specific lemon you've ever encountered (and therefore very different from any remembered exemplars). But this seems not to shake your faith that the object remains a lemon. To be sure, we have a not-easily-recognized lemon, an exceptional lemon, but it's still a lemon. Apparently, something can be a lemon with virtually no resemblance to other lemons.

TYPICALITY?

Greta Thunberg is certainly not a typical teenager. (How many teens have addressed the United Nations? How many have had the courage to say "How dare you?" to world leaders who were failing to take climate change seriously?) But even though she's not a typical teen, she is undeniably a teen. Sometimes, therefore, category membership does not depend on typicality. (And, ironically, this is one of the few cases in which category membership *does* depend on a definition: A teen is someone at least 13 years old, but not yet 20.)

Related points emerge in research with children. In one early study, preschool children were asked what makes something a "coffeepot," a "raccoon," and so on (Keil, 1986). As a way of probing their beliefs, the children were asked whether it would be possible to turn a toaster into a coffeepot. Children realized that we'd have to widen the holes in the top of the toaster and fix things so that the water wouldn't leak out of the bottom. We'd also need to design a place to put the coffee grounds. But the children saw no obstacles to these manipulations and were quite certain that with these adjustments in place, we would have created an acceptable coffeepot.

Things were different, though, when the children were asked a parallel question—whether one could, with suitable adjustments, turn a skunk into a raccoon. The children understood that we could dye the skunk's fur, teach it to climb trees, and, in general, teach it to behave in a raccoon like fashion. Even with these adjustments, the children steadfastly denied that we would have created a raccoon. A skunk that looks, sounds, and acts just like a raccoon might be a very peculiar skunk, but it would be a skunk nonetheless. (For other evidence suggesting that people reason differently about *naturally occurring items* like raccoons and *manufactured items* like coffeepots, see Estes, 2003; German & Barrett, 2005; Levin et al., 2001. Also see "The Diversity of Concepts" section on p. 327.)

What lies behind all these judgments? If people are asked why the abused lemon still counts as a lemon, they're likely to mention that it grew on a lemon tree, is genetically a lemon, and is still made up of (mostly) the "right stuff." It's these "deep" features that matter, not the lemon's current properties. And so, too, for raccoons: In the children's view, being a raccoon isn't merely a function of having the relevant features; instead, according to the children, the key to being a raccoon involves (among other things) having a raccoon mommy and a raccoon daddy. In this way, a raccoon, just like a lemon, is defined in ways that refer to deep properties and not to mere appearances.

Notice, though, that these claims about an object's deep properties depend on a web of other beliefs—beliefs that are, in each case, "tuned" to the category being considered. Thus, you're more likely to think that a creature is a raccoon if you're told that it has raccoons as parents, but this is true only because you have some ideas about how a creature comes to be a raccoon— ideas that are linked to your broader understanding of biological categories and inheritance. It's this understanding that tells you that parentage is relevant here. If this point isn't clear, consider as a contrasting case the steps you'd go through in deciding whether Judy really is a doctor. In this case, you're unlikely to worry about whether Judy has a doctor mommy and a doctor daddy, because your beliefs tell you, of course, that for this category parentage doesn't matter.

As a different example, think about the category "counterfeit money." A counterfeit bill, if skillfully produced, will have a nearly perfect resemblance to the prototype for legitimate money. Despite this resemblance, you understand that a counterfeit bill isn't in the category of legitimate money,

A SPANIEL, NOT A WOLF, IN SHEEP'S CLOTHING?

Both of these creatures resemble the prototype for sheep, and both resemble many sheep exemplars you've seen (or perhaps read about). But are they really sheep?

so here, too, your categorization doesn't depend on typicality. Instead, your categorization depends on a web of other beliefs, including beliefs about circumstances of printing. A $20 bill is legitimate, you believe, only if it was printed with the approval of, and under the supervision of, the relevant government agencies. And once again, these beliefs arise only because you have a broader understanding of what money is and how government regulations apply to monetary systems. In other words, you consider circumstances of printing only because your understanding tells you that the circumstances are relevant here, and you won't consider circumstances of printing in a wide range of other cases. If asked, for example, whether a copy of the Lord's Prayer is "counterfeit," your beliefs tell you that the Lord's Prayer is the Lord's Prayer no matter where (or by whom) it was printed. Instead, what's crucial for the prayer's "authenticity" is simply whether the words are the correct words.

The Complexity of Similarity

Let's pause to review. There's no question that judgments about categories are often influenced by typicality. That's why we need to include prototypes and exemplars in our theorizing. Sometimes, though, category judgments are *independent* of typicality: You judge some candidates to be category members even though they don't resemble the prototype at all (think about Moby Dick or the abused lemon). You judge some candidates not to be in the category even though they do resemble the prototype (think about counterfeit money or the disguised skunk).

We need to ask, therefore, how you think about categories when you're not guided by typicality. The answer, it seems, is that you focus on attributes that you believe are essential for each category. Your judgments about what's essential, however, depend, on your *beliefs* about that category. Therefore, you consider parentage when thinking about a category (like skunk or raccoon) for which you believe biological inheritance is important. You consider circumstances of printing when you're concerned with a category (like counterfeit money) that's shaped by your beliefs about economic systems. And so on.

Here's another way to make the same general point: In order to use a prototype or an exemplar, you need to make a judgment of *resemblance*—how much does Mike resemble your prototype for "bully"? How much does the Tesla Model X (with a base price in the vicinity of $100,000) resemble your idea of "dream car"? These questions, though, lead to a new and broader concern: How do you judge resemblance? How do you decide whether two things resemble each other? The obvious suggestion is that objects resemble each other if they share properties, and the more properties shared, the greater the resemblance. Therefore, we can say there's some resemblance between an apple and a tennis ball because they share a shape (round) and a size (about 3 or 4 inches in diameter). The resemblance is limited, though, because there are many properties that these objects don't share (color, "furry" surface, and so on).

It turns out, though, that this idea of "resemblance from shared properties" won't work. To see why, consider plums and lawn mowers; how much do these two things resemble each other? Common sense says they don't resemble each other at all, but we'll reach the opposite conclusion if we simply count "shared properties" (Murphy & Medin, 1985). After all, both weigh less than a ton, both are found on Earth, both have a detectable odor, both are used by people, both can be dropped, both cost less than a thousand dollars, both are bigger than a grain of sand, both are unlikely birthday presents for your infant daughter, both contain carbon molecules, both cast a shadow on a sunny day. And on and on and on. With a little creativity, you could probably count thousands of properties shared by these two objects—but that doesn't change the basic assessment that there's not a close resemblance here. (For discussion, see Goldstone & Son, 2012; Goodman, 1972; Markman & Gentner, 2001; Medin et al., 1993.)

The solution to this puzzle, though, seems easy: Resemblance *does* depend on shared properties, but—more precisely—it depends on whether the objects share *important, essential* properties. On this basis, you regard plums and lawn mowers as different from each other because the features they share are trivial or inconsequential. But this idea leads to yet another question: How do you decide which features to ignore when assessing similarity and which features to consider? How do you decide, in comparing a plum and a lawn mower, which features are relevant and which ones aren't?

These questions bring us back to familiar territory, because your decisions about which features are important depend on your *beliefs about the concept in question*. Thus, in judging the resemblance between plums and lawn mowers, you were unimpressed that they share the feature "cost less than a thousand dollars." That's because you believe cost is irrelevant for these categories. (If a super deluxe lawn mower cost a million dollars, it would still be a lawn mower, wouldn't it?) Likewise, you don't perceive plums to be similar to lawn mowers even though both weigh less than a ton, because you know this attribute, too, is irrelevant for these categories.

To recap: In using a prototype or exemplar, you need to make a judgment of resemblance. Specifically, you need to decide how much some candidate object resembles the prototype or exemplar. Judgments of resemblance, in turn, depend on your being able to focus on the features that are essential, so that you're not misled by trivial features. And, finally, decisions about what's essential (cost or weight or whatever) vary from category to category, and they vary in particular according to your beliefs about that category. Thus, *cost* isn't essential for plums and lawn mowers, but it is a central attribute for other categories (e.g., the category "luxury item"). Likewise, having a particular weight isn't essential for plums or lawn mowers, but it is prominent for other categories. (Does a sumo wrestler resemble a hippopotamus? Here you might be swayed by weight.)

We've already said that you're influenced by background beliefs when considering oddball cases like the mutilated lemon. The bottom line here, though, is that you're also influenced by your beliefs in ordinary cases, because, to put the matter simply, your background beliefs provide crucial guidance whenever you're thinking about resemblance.

The Broader Role of Conceptual Knowledge

Overall, then, our proposal so far involves four broad claims. First, you are influenced by *typicality* in many settings—and so "typical" members of a category are privileged in a wide range of tasks. Second, these typicality effects reveal a substantial role for *prototypes* and *exemplars* in your thinking about categories and concepts. But, third, your use of prototypes and exemplars rests on judgments of *resemblance*; and, fourth, to make these judgments, you have to draw on other knowledge. This other knowledge tells you what attributes are crucial for judging resemblance and what attributes can be ignored. It's this other knowledge that tells you that the abused lemon still resembles other lemons *in the ways that matter*, and that a counterfeit dollar bill doesn't resemble real money *in the ways that matter*. And likewise for all of the more-familiar concepts that you use all the time: You know that a penguin is a bird, for example (even if it's not a typical bird), because your knowledge tells you that it resembles the prototype in the ways that matter. And you know that a bat isn't a bird (even though it has wings and flies) because your knowledge tells you it *doesn't* resemble the prototype in the ways that matter.

Category Knowledge Guides Your Thinking about New Cases

It turns out, in addition, that your background knowledge about your various concepts influences you in other ways. Imagine, for example, that you're at a party, and you see one of the party guests jump fully clothed into a pool.

TEST YOURSELF

7. Give an example in which something is definitely a category member even though it has little resemblance to the prototype for the category.
8. In judging similarity, why is it not enough simply to count all of the properties that two objects have in common?

BLUE GNU

In judging resemblance or in categorizing an object, you focus on the features that (you believe) are important for an object of that type, and you ignore nonessential features. Imagine that you encounter a creature and wonder what it is. Perhaps you reason, "This creature reminds me of the animal I saw in the zoo yesterday. The sign at the zoo indicated that the animal was a gnu, so this must be one, too. Of course, the gnu in the zoo was a different color and slightly smaller. But I bet that doesn't matter. Despite the new blue hue, this is a zoo gnu, too." Notice that in drawing this conclusion you've decided that color isn't a critical feature, so you categorize despite the contrast on this dimension. But you know that color does matter for other categories—and so, for example, you know that something's off if a jeweler tries to sell you a green ruby or a red emerald. Thus, in case after case, the features that you consider depend on the specific category.

Odds are good that you would decide this person belongs in the category "drunk," but why? Jumping into a pool in this way surely isn't part of the *definition* of being drunk, and it's unlikely to be part of the *prototype* (Medin & Ortony, 1989). But each of us has certain beliefs about how drunks behave, and this set of beliefs enables us to think through what being drunk will or will not cause someone to do. On this basis we would decide that, yes, someone who jumped into the pool fully clothed probably was drunk.

Similarly, imagine that you're looking for an entirely new way to build airplanes. Could your new plane perhaps be made out of wood? Could it be made out of ceramic? How about making it out of whipped cream? You immediately reject this last option, because you know that a plane's function depends on its aerodynamic properties, and those depend on the plane's shape. Whipped cream wouldn't hold its shape, so it isn't a candidate for airplane construction. This is an easy conclusion to draw—but only because your "airplane" concept contains some ideas about why airplanes are as they are.

Your various beliefs also affect how quickly you learn new concepts. Imagine that you're given a group of objects and must decide whether each belongs in Category A or Category B. Category A, you're told, includes objects that are metal, have a regular surface, are of medium size, and are easy to grasp. Category B, in contrast, includes objects that aren't made of metal, have irregular surfaces, and are small and hard to grasp. This sorting task would be difficult—unless we give you another piece of information: namely, that Category A includes objects that could serve as substitutes for a hammer. With this clue, you immediately draw on your other knowledge about hammers, including your understanding of what a hammer is and how it's

used. This understanding enables you to see why Category A's features aren't an arbitrary hodgepodge; instead, the features form a coherent package. And once you see this point, learning the experimenter's task (distinguishing Category A from Category B) is easy. (See Medin, 1989; Wattenmaker et al., 1986. For related findings, see Heit & Bott, 2000; Kaplan & Murphy, 2000; Rehder & Ross, 2001.)

Category Knowledge Guides Your Inferences

At the chapter's start, we noted that your categories enable you to extend your knowledge in important ways. Having learned that Milo is a dog, you can apply your other dog-knowledge, and so you immediately know many things about Milo. Likewise, if you learn some new fact about Milo, you're likely to infer that this fact applies to other dogs as well.

There are, however, some limits on the inferences you'll consider, and this is another arena in which we see the effect of typicality. In an early study, participants, when told a new fact about robins, were willing to infer that the new fact would also be true for ducks. If they were told a new fact about ducks, however, they wouldn't extrapolate to robins (Rips, 1975). Apparently, people were willing to make inferences from the typical case to the whole category, but not from an atypical case to the category.

But, in addition, your inferences are also guided by your broad set of beliefs—beliefs that tell you, among other things, how categories are related to each other. For example, if told that grass contains a certain chemical, people are willing to believe that cows have the same chemical inside them. This

You have concepts for *things* ("chair," "book," "kitchen"), concepts for *actions* ("running," "hiding," "dancing"), and concepts for *animals* ("cat," "cow," "dragon"). But you also have concepts that apply to *people.* You understand what a "nurse" is, and a "toddler," and a "nerd" or a "jock." You also have concepts for various religious, racial, and ethnic groups ("Jew," "Muslim," "African American," "Italian"), various political groups ("radical," "ultra conservative"), and many others as well.

In many ways, concepts representing your ideas about people have the same profile as any other concepts: It's difficult to find a rigid definition for most of these groups, because we can usually find individuals who are in the group even though they don't quite fit the definition. You also have a cluster of interwoven beliefs about these groups—beliefs that link your ideas about the group to many other ideas. You also have a prototype in mind for the group, but here we typically use a different term: You have a *stereotype* for the group.

How are stereotypes different from prototypes? Prototypes are a summary of your experience—and so your prototype for "dog" can be thought of as an average of all the dogs you've seen. Stereotypes, in contrast, are often acquired through social channels—with friends or family, or perhaps public figures, shaping your ideas about what "lawyers" are like, or "Canadians," or "Italians." In addition, stereotypes often include an emotional or evaluative dimension, with the result that there are groups you're afraid of, groups you respect, groups you sneer at.

Let's acknowledge, though, that stereotypes can serve the same cognitive function as prototypes. In both cases, these representations provide an efficient means of organizing large quantities of information (and so serve the same function as *schemas,* which we described in Chapter 8). But, of course, a reliance on stereotypes can lead to a list of toxic problems—racism, sexism, homophobia, prejudice against anyone wearing a hijab, and more.

Many factors fuel these ugly tendencies, including the fact that people often act as if all members of the stereotyped group were alike. They assume, for example, that a tall African American individual is probably a talented basketball player, and that a Semitic-looking young man wearing a headscarf is likely to be a terrorist. These assumptions are, of course, indefensible because humans in any group differ from one another, and there's no justification for jumping to conclusions about someone just because you've decided they're a member of a particular group.

This kind of assumption, though, is widespread enough so that social psychologists give it a name: the *outgroup homogeneity effect.* This term refers to the fact that most people are convinced that their "ingroup" (the group they themselves belong to) is remarkably varied, while "outgroups" (groups they don't belong to) are quite homogeneous. In other words, no matter who you count as "they" and who you count as "we," you're likely to agree that "*they* all think and act alike; *we,* however, are wonderfully diverse."

In combating prejudice, then, it's important to realize that this assumption of homogeneity isn't just wrong; it can also have ugly consequences. There may be intellectual efficiency in thinking about women, or the elderly, or politicians as if these groups were uniform, but in doing so you fail to respect the differences from one person to the next—and may end up with beliefs, feelings, or actions that are impossible to justify and often deeply harmful.

inference isn't guided by typicality; it's guided instead by beliefs about cause and effect, and (of course) by the knowledge that cows *eat* grass (Medin et al., 2003; also see Heit, 2000; Heit & Feeney, 2005; Rehder & Hastie, 2004).

The Diversity of Concepts

The notion that people are guided by their *beliefs* about categories has yet another implication: People may think about different concepts in different ways. For example, most people believe that *natural kinds* (groups of objects that exist naturally in the world, such as bushes or alligators or stones or mountains) are as they are because of forces of nature that are consistent across the years. As a result, the properties of these objects are relatively stable. Thus, there are certain properties that a bush must have in order to survive as a bush; certain properties that a stone must have because of its chemical composition. Things are different, though, for *artifacts* (objects made by human beings). If we wished to make a table with 15 legs rather than 4, or one made of gold, we could do this. The design of tables is up to us; and the same is true for most artifacts.

This observation leads to the proposal that people will reason differently about natural kinds and artifacts—because they have different beliefs about why categories of either sort are as they are. We've already seen one result consistent with this idea: the finding that children agree that toasters could be turned into coffeepots but not that skunks could be turned into raccoons. Plainly, the children had different ideas about artifacts (like toasters) than they had about animate objects (like skunks). Other results confirm this pattern. In general, people tend to assume more stability and more homogeneity when reasoning about natural kinds than when reasoning about artifacts (Atran, 1990; Coley et al., 1997; Rehder & Hastie, 2004).

The diversity of concepts, as well as the role of beliefs, is also evident in another context. Many concepts can be characterized in terms of their features (e.g., the features that most dogs have, the features that chairs usually have, and so on; after Markman & Rein, 2013). Other concepts, though, are characterized by a *goal*; examples include categories like "diet food" or "exercise equipment" (Barsalou, 1983, 1985). Your understanding of these concepts depends on your understanding of the goal (e.g., "losing weight") and some cause-and-effect beliefs about the elements or steps that would help you achieve that goal. Similar points apply to *relational categories* ("rivalry," "hunting") and *event categories* ("visits," "dates," "shopping trips"); here, too, you're influenced by a web of beliefs about how various elements (the predator and the prey; the shopper and the store) are related to each other.

Concepts and the Brain

The contrasts among different types of concepts are also reflected in neuroscience evidence. For example, fMRI scans show that different brain sites are activated when people are thinking about living things as opposed to when thinking about nonliving things (e.g., Chao et al., 2002). Within the domain of nonliving things, different sites are activated when people are thinking about manufactured objects such as tools rather than natural objects such as rocks (Gerlach et al., 2002; Kellenbach et al., 2003).

Apparently, different types of concepts are represented in different brain areas, and this point is confirmed by observations of people who have suffered brain damage. In some cases, these people lose the ability to name certain objects—a pattern termed **anomia**—or to answer simple questions about these objects ("Does a whale have legs?"). Often, the problem is specific to certain categories, such that some patients lose the ability to name living things but not nonliving things; other patients show the reverse pattern. (See Mahon & Caramazza, 2009; Mahon & Hickok, 2016. For broader discussion, see Peru & Avesani, 2008; Phillips et al., 2002; Rips et al., 2012.) Sometimes the disruption caused by brain damage is even more specific, with some patients losing the ability to answer questions about fruits and vegetables but still being able to answer questions about other objects, living or nonliving (see **Figure 9.5**).

Why does the brain separate things in this way? One proposal emphasizes the types of information that are essential for different concepts. In this view, the recognition of living things may depend on perceptual properties (especially visual properties) that enable us to identify horses or trees or other animate objects. In contrast, the recognition of nonliving things may depend on their functional properties (Warrington & McCarthy, 1983, 1987; for an alternative conception, though, see Caramazza & Shelton, 1998).

Embodied Concepts

As an interesting complication, though, brain scans also show that *sensory* and *motor* areas in the brain are activated when people are thinking about certain concepts (Mahon & Caramazza, 2009; Mahon & Hickok, 2016; McRae & Jones, 2012). For example, when someone is thinking about the concept "kick," we can observe activation in brain areas that (in other circumstances) control the movement of the legs; when someone is thinking about rainbows, we can detect activation in brain areas ordinarily involved in color vision. Findings like these suggest that conceptual knowledge is intertwined with knowledge about what particular objects look like (or sound like or feel like) and also with knowledge about how one might interact with the object.

Some theorists go a step further and argue for a position referred to as "embodied" or "grounded cognition." The proposal is that the body's sensory and action systems play an essential role in all our cognitive processes; it's inevitable, then, that our concepts will include representations of perceptual properties and motor sequences associated with each concept. (See Barsalou, 2008, 2016; Chrysikou et al., 2017; Pulvermüller, 2013. For a glimpse of the debate over this perspective, see Witt et al., 2020. For a discussion of how this approach might handle *abstract* concepts, see Borghi et al., 2017.)

FIGURE 9.5 DIFFERENT BRAIN SITES SUPPORT DIFFERENT CATEGORIES

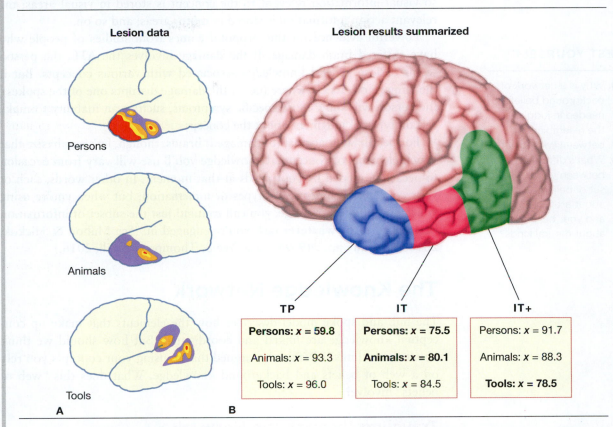

Lesion data

Persons

Animals

Tools

A

Lesion results summarized

TP

| Persons: x = 59.8 |
| Animals: x = 93.3 |
| Tools: x = 96.0 |

IT

| Persons: x = 75.5 |
| Animals: x = 80.1 |
| Tools: x = 84.5 |

IT+

| Persons: x = 91.7 |
| Animals: x = 88.3 |
| Tools: x = 78.5 |

B

Brain damage often causes anomia—an inability to name common objects. But the specific loss depends on where exactly the brain damage has occurred. Panel A summarizes lesion data for patients who had difficulty naming persons (top), animals (middle), or tools (bottom). The colors indicate the percentage of patients with damage at each site: red, most patients; purple, few. Panel B offers a different summary of the data: Patients with damage in the brain's temporal pole (TP, shown in blue) had difficulty naming persons (only 59.8% correct) but were easily able to name animals and tools. Patients with damage in the inferotemporal region (IT, shown in red) had difficulty naming persons and animals but did somewhat better naming tools. Finally, patients with damage in the lateral occipital region (IT+) had difficulty naming tools but did reasonably well naming animals and persons.

(AFTER DAMASIO, ET AL., 1996)

Notice, though, that the data here fit well with a theme we've seen throughout this chapter—namely, that conceptual knowledge has many elements. These include a prototype, exemplars, a set of beliefs about the concept (including why the concept is as it is), and (we now add) representations of perceptual properties and actions associated with the concept. How is this diverse set of elements represented and organized in the brain? One influential perspective is the **hub and spoke model** (Patterson & Lambon Ralph, 2016; Lambon Ralph et al., 2017). According to this model, a "hub," supported by tissue in the anterior temporal lobes (ATL), connects and integrates information from many other brain areas. This other information (the "spokes") is represented in more-specialized brain regions—and so visual information relevant to the concept is stored in visual areas; the relevant action information is stored in motor areas; and so on.

Powerful evidence for this proposal comes from studies of people who have suffered brain damage. If the damage involves the ATL, the person seems to lose general knowledge associated with various concepts. But if the damage occurs elsewhere (i.e., if the damage disrupts one of the spokes), the person will show more specific symptoms, such as an inability to make certain types of judgment about the concept.

For people with normal (undamaged) brains, though, let's emphasize that which elements of conceptual knowledge you'll use will vary from occasion to occasion, guided by your needs at that moment. In other words, each of your concepts includes many types of information; but when you're using your conceptual knowledge, you call to mind just the subset of information that's needed for whatever task you're engaged in. (See Mahon & Hickok, 2016, especially pp. 949–950; also Yee & Thompson-Schill, 2016.)

The Knowledge Network

The hub and spoke model describes how the elements that make up conceptual knowledge are linked and coordinated. But how should we think about these "links"? We've also argued that in using your concepts you rely on a web of beliefs and background knowledge. What does this "web of beliefs" involve?

Traveling through the Network to Retrieve Knowledge

In earlier chapters, we explored the idea that information in long-term memory is represented by means of a network, with associative links connecting nodes to one another. Let's now carry this proposal one step further. The associative links don't just tie together the various bits of knowledge; they also help *represent* the knowledge. For example, you know that George Washington was an American president. This simple idea can be represented as an associative link between a node representing WASHINGTON and a node representing PRESIDENT. In other words, the link itself is a constituent of the knowledge.

On this view, how do you retrieve knowledge from the network, so that you can use what you know? Presumably, the retrieval relies on processes we've described in other chapters—with activation spreading from one node to the next. This spread of activation is quick but does take time, and the farther the activation must travel, the more time needed. This leads to a prediction—that you'll need less time to retrieve knowledge involving closely related ideas, and more time to retrieve knowledge about more distant ideas.

TEST YOURSELF

9. Why is a network of background beliefs needed in judging the resemblance between two objects?
10. What's different between your set of beliefs about artifacts and your beliefs about natural kinds?

Collins and Quillian (1969) tested this prediction many years ago, using the *sentence verification task* described earlier in this chapter. Their participants were shown sentences such as "A robin is a bird" or "Cats have claws" or "Cats have hearts." Mixed together with these obviously true sentences were various false sentences (e.g., "A cat is a bird"), and in response to each sentence, participants had to hit a "true" or "false" button as quickly as they could.

Participants presumably perform this task by "traveling" through the network, seeking a connection between nodes. When the participant finds the connection from, say, the ROBIN node to the BIRDS node, this confirms that there's an associative path linking these nodes, which tells the participant that the sentence about these two concepts is true. This travel should require little time if the two nodes are directly linked by an association, as ROBIN and BIRDS probably are (see **Figure 9.6**). In this case, we'd expect participants to answer "true" rather quickly. The travel will require more time, however, if the two nodes are connected only indirectly (e.g., ROBIN and ANIMALS), so that we'd expect slower responses to sentences that require a "two-step" connection than to sentences that require a single connection.

Collins and Quillian also argued that there's no point in storing in memory the fact that cats have hearts *and* the fact that dogs have hearts *and* the

---

FIGURE 9.6 HYPOTHETICAL MEMORY STRUCTURE FOR KNOWLEDGE ABOUT ANIMALS

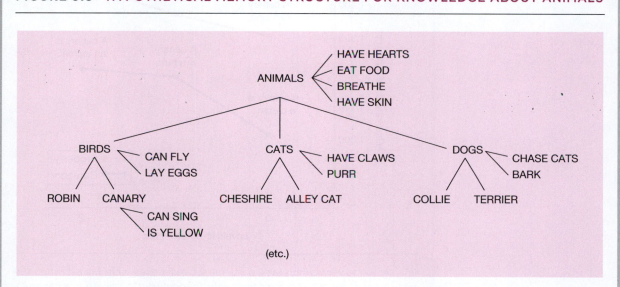

Collins and Quillian proposed that the memory system avoids redundant storage of connections between CATS and HAVE HEARTS, and between DOGS and HAVE HEARTS, and so on for all the other animals. Instead, HAVE HEARTS is stored as a property of all animals. To confirm that cats have hearts, therefore, you must traverse two links: from CATS to ANIMALS, and from ANIMALS to HAVE HEARTS. (AFTER COLLINS & QUILLIAN, 1969)

fact that squirrels have hearts. Instead, they proposed, it would be more efficient just to store the fact that these various creatures are animals, and then the separate fact that animals have hearts. As a result, the property "has a heart" would be associated with the ANIMALS node rather than the nodes for each individual animal, and the same is true for all the other properties of animals, as shown in the figure. According to this logic, we should expect relatively slow responses to sentences like "Cats have hearts," since, to choose a response, a participant must locate the linkage from CAT to ANIMALS and then a second linkage from ANIMALS to HAVE HEARTS. We would expect a quicker response to "Cats have claws," because here there would be a direct connection between CAT and the node representing this property. (Why a direct connection? All cats have claws, but some other animals don't, so this information couldn't be entered at the higher level.)

As **Figure 9.7** shows, these predictions are borne out. Responses to sentences like "A canary is a canary" take approximately 1 second (1,000 ms).

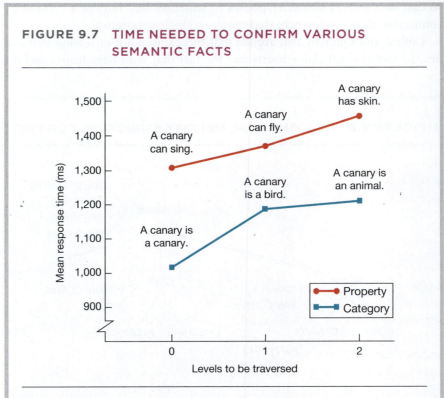

FIGURE 9.7   TIME NEEDED TO CONFIRM VARIOUS SEMANTIC FACTS

In a sentence verification task, participants' responses were fastest when the test required them to traverse zero links in memory ("A canary is a canary"), slower when the necessary ideas were separated by one link, and slower still if the ideas were separated by two links. Responses were also slower if participants had to take the additional step of traversing the link from a category label ("bird") to the node representing a property of the category (CAN FLY).

(AFTER COLLINS & QUILLIAN, 1969)

This is presumably the time it takes just to read the sentence and to move your finger on the response button. Sentences like "A canary can sing" require an additional step of traversing one link in memory and yield slower responses. Sentences like "A canary can fly" require the traversing of two links, from CANARY to BIRDS and then from BIRDS to CAN FLY, so they are correspondingly slower.

Other data, however, add some complications. For example, we saw earlier in the chapter that verifications are faster if a sentence involves creatures close to the prototype—so that responses are faster to, say, "A canary is a bird" than to "An ostrich is a bird." This difference isn't reflected in Figure 9.7, nor is it explained by the layout in Figure 9.6. Clearly, then, the Collins and Quillian view is incomplete.

In addition, the principle of "nonredundancy" proposed by Collins and Quillian doesn't always hold. For example, the property of "having feathers" should, on their view, be associated with the BIRDS node rather than (redundantly) with the ROBIN node, the PIGEON node, and so on. This fits with the fact that responses are relatively slow to sentences like "Sparrows have feathers." However, it turns out that participants respond rather quickly to a sentence like "Peacocks have feathers." This is because in observing peacocks, you often think about their prominent tail feathers (Conrad, 1972). Therefore, even though it is informationally redundant, a strong association between PEACOCK and HAS FEATHERS is likely to be established.

Even with these complications, we can often predict the speed of knowledge access by counting the number of nodes participants must traverse in answering a question. This observation powerfully confirms the claim that associative links play a pivotal role in knowledge representation. (For more recent exploration about how distance within the memory network influences search time, see Kumar et al., 2019.)

Propositional Networks

To represent the full fabric of your knowledge, however, we need more than simple associations. After all, we need somehow to represent the contrast between "Sam has a dog" and "Sam is a dog." If all we had is an association between SAM and DOG, we wouldn't be able to tell these two ideas apart.

One widely endorsed proposal solves this problem with a focus on **propositions**, defined as the smallest units of knowledge that can be either true or false (Anderson, 1976, 1980, 1993; Anderson & Bower, 1973). For example, "Children love candy" is a proposition, but "Children" is not; "Susan likes blue cars" is a proposition, but "blue cars" is not. Propositions are easily represented as sentences, but this is just a convenience. They can also be represented in various nonlinguistic forms, including a structure of nodes and linkages, and that's exactly what Anderson's model does.

Figure 9.8 provides an example. Here, each ellipse identifies a single proposition. Associations connect the ellipse to ideas that are the proposition's constituents, and the associations are labeled to specify the constituent's role

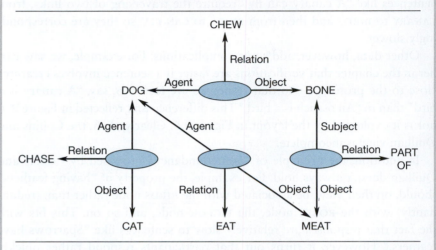

FIGURE 9.8 NETWORK REPRESENTATIONS OF SOME OF YOUR KNOWLEDGE ABOUT DOGS

Your understanding of dogs—what they are, what they're likely to do—is represented by an interconnected network of propositions, with each proposition being indicated by an ellipse. Labels on the arrows indicate each node's role within the proposition. (AFTER ANDERSON, 1980)

within that proposition. This enables us to distinguish, say, the proposition "Dogs chase cats" (shown in the figure) from the proposition "Cats chase dogs" (not shown).

This model shares many claims with the network theorizing we discussed in earlier chapters. Nodes are connected by associative links. Some of these links are stronger than others. The strength of a link depends on how frequently and recently it has been used. Once a node is activated, the process of spreading activation causes nearby nodes to become activated as well. The model is distinctive, however, in its attempt to represent knowledge in terms of propositions, and the promise of this approach has attracted the support of many researchers. (For discussion, see Salvucci, 2017; for some alternative models, see Flusberg & McClelland, 2017; Kieras, 2017. For more on how this network can store information, see **Figure 9.9**.)

Distributed Processing

In the model just described, individual ideas are represented with *local representations* (a term we first met in Chapter 4). Each node represents one idea so that when that node is activated, you're thinking about that idea, and when you're thinking about that idea, that node is activated. **Connectionist networks**, in contrast, take a different approach. They rely on *distributed representations* (again, a term we met in Chapter 4) in which each idea is

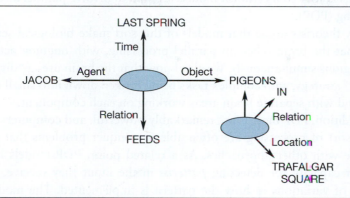

In order to represent episodes, the propositional network includes time and location nodes. This fragment of a network represents two propositions: the proposition that Jacob fed pigeons last spring, and the proposition that the pigeons are in Trafalgar Square. Notice that no time node is associated with the proposition about pigeons being in Trafalgar Square. Therefore, what's represented is that the feeding of the pigeons took place last spring but that the pigeons are always in the square.

represented, not by a certain set of nodes, but instead by a pattern of activation across the network. To take a simple case, the concept "birthday" might be represented by a pattern in which nodes B, F, H, N, P, and R are firing, whereas the concept "computer" might be represented by a pattern in which nodes C, G, H, M, O, and S are firing. Note that node H is part of both of these patterns and probably part of the pattern for other concepts as well. Therefore, we can't attach any meaning or interpretation to this node by itself; we can only learn what's being represented by looking at many nodes simultaneously to find out what pattern of activation exists across the entire network. (For more on local and distributed representations, see Chapter 4; also see the related discussion of neural coding in Chapter 2.)

This reliance on distributed representation has important consequences for how a connectionist network functions. Imagine being asked what sort of computer you use. For you to respond, the idea "computer" needs to trigger the idea "MacBook" (or "Dell" or whatever it is you have). In a distributed network, this means that the many nodes representing the concept "computer" have to manage collectively to activate the many nodes representing "MacBook." To continue our simple illustration, node C has to trigger node L at the same time that node G triggers node A, and so on, leading ultimately to the activation of the L-A-F-J-T-R combination that, let's say, represents "MacBook." In short, a network using distributed representations must use processes that are similarly distributed, so that one widespread activation pattern can evoke a different (but equally widespread) pattern. In addition, the steps bringing this about must all occur simultaneously—in parallel—with each other, so that one entire representation can smoothly trigger the next. This is why connectionist models are said to involve **parallel distributed processing** (PDP).

Many theorists argue that models of this sort make biological sense. We know that the brain relies on parallel processing, with ongoing activity in many regions simultaneously. We also know that the brain uses a "divide and conquer" strategy, with complex tasks being broken down into small components, and with separate brain areas working on each component.

In addition, PDP models are remarkably powerful, and computers relying on this sort of processing are often able to conquer problems that seemed insoluble with other approaches. As a related point, PDP models have an excellent capacity for detecting *patterns* in the input they receive, despite a range of variations in how the pattern is implemented. The models can therefore recognize a variety of different sentences as all having the same structure, and a variety of game positions as all inviting the same next move. As a result, these models are impressively able to generalize what they have "learned" to new, never-seen-before variations on the pattern. (For a broad view of what connectionism can accomplish, see Flusberg & McClelland, 2017; Hoffman et al., 2018.)

Concepts: Putting the Pieces Together

We have now covered a lot of ground—discussing both individual concepts and also how these concepts might be woven together, via the network, to form larger patterns of knowledge. We've also talked about how the network itself might be set up—with knowledge perhaps represented by propositions, or perhaps via a connectionist network. But where does all of this leave us?

You might think there's nothing glorious or complicated about knowing what a dog is, or a lemon, or a fish. Your use of these concepts is effortless, and so is your use of thousands of other concepts. No one over the age of 4 takes special pride in knowing what an odd number is, nor do people find it challenging to make the elementary sorts of judgments we've considered throughout this chapter.

As we've seen, though, human conceptual knowledge is impressively complex. At the very least, this knowledge contains several parts. We've suggested that people have a prototype for most of their concepts as well as a set of remembered exemplars, and that people use these various elements for a range of judgments about the relevant category. People also seem to have a set of beliefs about each concept they hold, and (among other things) these beliefs reflect the individuals' understanding of cause-and-effect relationships—for example, why drunks act as they do, or how a chemical found in grass might be transmitted to cows. These beliefs are woven into a broader network that stores all the information in your memory, and that

TEST YOURSELF

11. What does it mean to say that knowledge can be represented via network connections?
12. What is a propositional network?
13. Why do distributed representations require distributed processing?

network influences how you categorize items and also how you reason about the objects in your world.

Apparently, then, even our simplest concepts require a multifaceted representation in our minds, and it is this richness, presumably, that makes human conceptual knowledge extremely powerful and flexible—and so easy to use in a remarkable range of circumstances.

COGNITIVE PSYCHOLOGY AND THE LAW

defining legal concepts

In many court cases, the judge's or jury's task lies in categorizing someone's actions. A jury might need to decide, for example, whether a defendant's actions fall into the category of "sexual harassment." (If the defendant was offensive in some way, but his actions don't fit the legal definition of "harassment," then he isn't guilty of harassment.) Or, as a different example, a jury might be certain that the defendant caused someone's death, but they still need to decide whether the crime should be categorized as "first-degree murder" or "second-degree"—a categorization with large implications for the likely punishment.

To help with this categorization, laws define each crime in precise terms. For example, there is a careful definition of "robbery," a precise definition of "trespassing" or "first-degree murder," and so on. Even with these definitions, though, the courts often encounter ambiguous cases—cases in which it's not at all clear whether a person has committed a crime, or what crime they've committed. At the least, this reminds us how difficult it is to find satisfactory, broadly useful definitions for concepts—a point that has been important throughout Chapter 9. But we also need to ask: How do courts proceed when they encounter one of these ambiguous cases?

We've seen that people have prototypes in mind for their various concepts, and so, in day-to-day life, they often assess a new case by asking how closely it resembles that prototype. It turns out that jurors do the same in making legal judgments. As a result, they're more likely to convict someone if the trial facts fit with their prototype for the crime—if the facts fit the jurors' idea of, say, a "typical bank robbery" or a "typical hit-and-run violation." Put differently, a "typical" crime with weak evidence is more likely to lead to a conviction than an unusual crime with similarly weak evidence. Of course, this is legally nonsensical: Jury decisions should depend only on the evidence and the legal definition of the crime. The jurors' ideas about what's typical should play no role at all—especially when we acknowledge that these ideas are shaped more by TV crime shows than by actual crime statistics. Nonetheless, the prototypes do influence the jury, and so legal judgments (like concept use in general) are plainly shaped by typicality.

Moreover, concept users often seem to have a set of beliefs in mind about why a concept is as it is, and they use these beliefs in reasoning about the concept. The chapter used the example of someone jumping into a pool fully

STALKING

Being stalked is frightening and can be dangerous. But "stalking"—as a crime—is difficult to define, and it is often difficult to decide whether a specific act (or series of acts) counts as stalking. The U.S. Department of Justice, however, suggests this (somewhat complicated) definition. Do you think the definition is adequate? Stalking, according to the Justice Department, is " a course of conduct directed at a specific person that involves repeated (two or more occasions) visual or physical proximity, nonconsensual communication, or verbal, written, or implied threats, or a combination thereof, that would cause a reasonable person fear."

clothed. You're likely to categorize this person as a "drunk," not because the person fits your definition for being drunk or even fits your prototype, but because you have a set of beliefs about how drunks are likely to act. Based on those beliefs, you decide that drunkenness is the most plausible explanation for the behavior you just observed, and you categorize accordingly.

Similar categorization strategies are evident in the courtroom. Consider the crime of stalking. This crime is difficult to define in a crisp way; in fact, it's defined in different ways in different states. Usually, though, the definition includes the idea that the stalker intended to force some sort of relationship with the victim—perhaps a relationship involving intimacy or a relationship in which the victim feels fear. Often, however, there's no direct evidence of this intention, so the jury needs to infer the intention either from the defendant's behaviors or from the context.

In making these inferences, jurors rely on their "theory" of stalking—their beliefs about how and why one individual might stalk another. This helps us understand why juries are more likely to convict someone of stalking if, for example, the defendant was a former intimate of the person being "stalked." Apparently, jurors are guided by their ideas about how former (but now rejected) lovers behave—even if these ideas have nothing to do with the legal definition of stalking.

How should we think about these points? On one side, we want jurors to be guided by the law, and not by their (perhaps idiosyncratic, perhaps uninformed) intuitions about the crime at issue in a trial. On the other side, the U.S. legal system relies on the good sense and good judgment of juries—so plainly we want jurors to use their judgment. How best to balance these points isn't clear, but the tension between these points might be inevitable, given what we know about human concepts and human categorization.

For more on this topic . . .

Dunlap, E. E., Lynch, K. R., Jewell, J. A., Wasarhaley, N. E., & Golding, J. M. (2015). Participant gender, stalking myth acceptance, and gender role stereotyping in perceptions of intimate partner stalking: A structural equation modeling approach. *Psychology, Crime & Law, 21*(3), 234–253.

Huntley, J. E., & Costanzo, M. (2003). Sexual harassment stories: Testing a story-mediated model of juror decision-making in civil litigation. *Law and Human Behavior, 27*(1), 29–51.

McKimmie, B. M., Masser, B. M., & Bongiorno, R. (2014). What counts as rape? The effect of offense prototypes, victim stereotypes, and participant gender on how the complainant and defendant are perceived. *Journal of Interpersonal Violence, 29*(12), 2273–2303.

Strub, T., & McKimmie, B. M. (2015). Sugar and spice and all things nice: The role of gender stereotypes in jurors' perceptions of criminal defendants. *Psychiatry, Psychology and Law, 23*(4), 487–498.

chapter review

SUMMARY

- People cannot provide definitions for most of the concepts they use, and so, apparently, knowing a concept and being able to use it competently do not require knowing a definition. However, when trying to define a term, people usually mention properties that are in fact closely associated with the concept. One proposal, therefore, is that your knowledge specifies what is typical for each concept, rather than naming properties that are truly definitive for the concept. Concepts based on typicality will have a family resemblance structure, with different category members sharing features but with no features being shared by the entire group.

- Concepts may be represented in the mind via prototypes, with each prototype representing what is most typical for that category. This implies that categories will have graded membership, and many research results are consistent with this prediction. The results converge in identifying some category members as "better" members of the category. This is reflected in sentence verification tasks, production tasks, explicit judgments of typicality, and so on.

- In addition, basic-level categories seem to be the ones we learn earliest and use most often. Basic-level categories (e.g., "chair") are more homogeneous than their broader, superordinate categories ("furniture") and much broader than their subordinate categories ("armchair"). They are also usually represented by a single word.

- Category knowledge also includes some number of specific exemplars, and category judgments can be made by drawing analogies to these remembered exemplars. The exemplar model can explain your ability to view categories from a new perspective. Even so, prototypes provide an efficient summary of what is typical for the category. Perhaps it's not surprising, therefore, that your conceptual knowledge includes exemplars and prototypes.

- Sometimes categorization doesn't depend at all on whether the test case resembles a prototype or a category exemplar. This is evident with some weird cases (a mutilated lemon), but it's also evident with more mundane categories ("raccoon"). In these examples, categorization seems to depend on knowledge about a category's essential properties.

- Knowledge about essential properties is not just a supplement to categorization via resemblance. Instead, knowledge about essential properties may be a *prerequisite* for judgments of resemblance. With this knowledge, you're able to assess resemblance with regard to just those properties that truly matter for the category and not be misled by irrelevant or accidental properties.

- The properties that are essential for a category vary from one category to the next. The identification of these properties seems to depend on beliefs held about the category, including causal beliefs that specify why the category features are as they are. These beliefs describe the category not in isolation but in relation to various other concepts.

- Researchers have proposed that knowledge is stored within the same memory network that we've discussed in earlier chapters. Searching through this network seems to resemble travel in the sense that greater travel distances (more connections to be traversed) require more time.

- To store all of knowledge, the network may need more than simple associations. One proposal is that the network stores propositions, with different nodes each playing the appropriate role within the proposition.

- A different proposal is that knowledge is contained in memory via distributed representations. These representations require distributed processes.

KEY TERMS

family resemblance (p. 311)
prototype (p. 311)
typicality (p. 312)
graded membership (p. 313)
sentence verification task (p. 313)
production task (p. 313)
rating task (p. 313)

basic-level categorization (p. 315)
exemplar-based reasoning (p. 317)
anomia (p. 328)
hub and spoke model (p. 329)
propositions (p. 333)
connectionist networks (p. 334)
parallel distributed processing (PDP) (p. 336)

TEST YOURSELF AGAIN

1. Consider the word "chair." Name some attributes that might plausibly be included in a definition for this word. But, then, can you describe objects that you would count as chairs even though they don't have one or more of these attributes?

2. What does it mean to say that there is a "family resemblance" among the various animals that we call "dogs"?

3. Why is graded membership a consequence of representing the category in terms of a prototype?

4. What tasks show us that concept judgments often rely on prototypes and typicality?

5. Give an example of a basic-level category, and then name some of the subcategories within this basic-level grouping.

6. What is *similar* in the processes of categorizing via a prototype and the processes of categorizing via an exemplar? What is *different* between these two types of processes?

7. Give an example in which something is definitely a category member even though it has little resemblance to the prototype for the category.

8. In judging similarity, why is it not enough simply to count all of the properties that two objects have in common?

9. Why is a network of background beliefs needed in judging the resemblance between two objects?

10. What's different between your set of beliefs about artifacts and your beliefs about natural kinds?

11. What does it mean to say that knowledge can be represented via network connections?

12. What is a propositional network?

13. Why do distributed representations require distributed processing?

THINK ABOUT IT

1. You easily understand the following sentence: "At most colleges and universities, a large number of students receive financial aid." But how do you manage to understand the sentence? How is the concept of "financial aid" represented in your mind? Do you have a prototype (perhaps for "student on financial aid")? Do you have some number of exemplars? A network of beliefs? Can you specify what these beliefs involve? What other concepts do you need to understand in order to understand "financial aid"?

DEMONSTRATIONS & APPLYING COGNITIVE PSYCHOLOGY ESSAYS

For demonstrations of key concepts in cognitive psychology, take a look at the Online Demonstrations. To explore more of the practical applications of cognitive psychology in themed essays, visit the online reader.

Online Demonstrations

- Demonstration 9.1: The Concept of "Scientist"
- Demonstration 9.2: Assessing Typicality
- Demonstration 9.3: Basic-Level Categories
- Demonstration 9.4: The Search for Definitions

Online Applying Cognitive Psychology Essays

- Cognitive Psychology and Education: Learning New Concepts
- Cognitive Psychology and Technology: "Smart Phones, Smart Toilets"
- Cognitive Psychology and Health: Diagnosis of Mental Disorders

ZAPS COGNITION LABS

Go to ZAPS online cognition labs to conduct hands-on experiments on key concepts.

INQUIZITIVE

It's time to complete your study experience! Go to InQuizitive to practice actively with this chapter's concepts and get personalized feedback along the way.

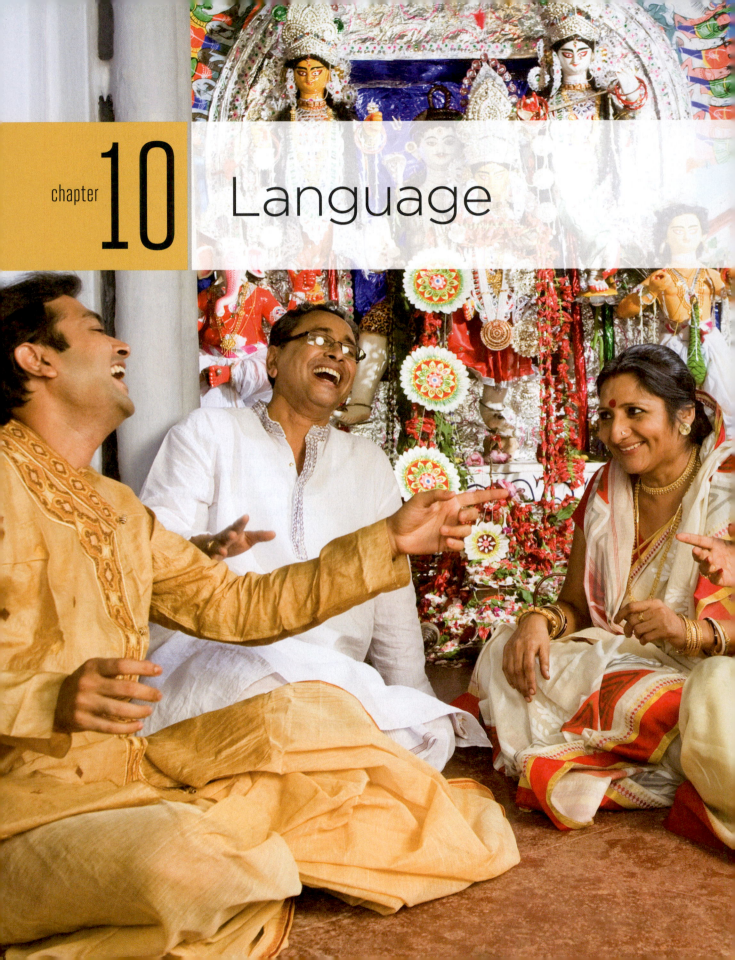

chapter 10

Language

what if... On January 8, 2011, Congresswoman Gabby Giffords was meeting with citizens outside a grocery store near Tucson, Arizona. A man ran up to the crowd and began shooting. Six people were killed; Giffords was among the others who were wounded. A bullet had passed through her head, traveling the length of her brain's left side and causing extensive damage.

As a result of her brain injury, Giffords has suffered from many profound difficulties, including a disorder termed "aphasia"—a loss of the ability to produce and understand ordinary language.

In the years since the shooting, though, Giffords has shown a wonderful degree of recovery. Just five months after the injury, an aide announced that her ability to comprehend language had returned to a level that was "close to normal, if not normal." Her progress was slower for language production. Consider an interview she gave in early 2014. Giffords had, on the third anniversary of her shooting, decided to celebrate life by skydiving. In a subsequent TV interview, she described the experience: "Oh, wonderful sky. Gorgeous mountain. Blue skies. I like a lot. A lot of fun. Peaceful, so peaceful."

Giffords's recovery is remarkable, but—sadly—not typical. The outcome for patients with aphasia is highly variable, and many recover far less of their language ability than Giffords has. Her case is typical, though, in other ways. Different brain areas control the comprehension and the production of speech, so it's common for one of these capacities to be spared while the other is damaged, and the prospects for recovery are generally better for language comprehension than for production. And like Giffords, many patients with aphasia retain the ability to *sing* even if they've lost the ability to *speak*—a clear indication that these seemingly similar activities are controlled by different processes.

Giffords also shares with other patients the profound frustration of aphasia. This condition is, after all, a disorder of *language*, not a disorder of *thought*. As a result, patients with aphasia can think normally but complain (often with great difficulty) that they feel "trapped" in their own heads, unable to express what they're thinking. They are sometimes forced to grunt and point in hopes of conveying their meaning; in other cases, their speech is so slurred that others cannot understand them, so they are caught in a situation of trying again and again to express themselves—but often without success.

- Language can be understood as having a hierarchical structure—with units at each level being assembled to form the larger units at the next level.

- At each level in the hierarchy, we can combine and recombine units, but the combinations seem to be governed by various types of rules. The rules provide an explanation of why some combinations of elements are rare and others seem prohibited outright. Within the boundaries created by these rules, though, language is *generative*, allowing any user of the language to create a virtually unlimited number of new forms (new sound combinations, new words, new phrases).

- A different set of principles describes how, moment by moment, people interpret the sentences they encounter; in this process, people are guided by many factors, including syntax, semantics, and contextual information.

- In interpreting sentences, people seem to use a "compile as you go" strategy, trying to figure out the role of each

- word the moment it arrives. This approach is efficient but can lead to error.

- A further layer of complexity involves the processes needed to understand conversation. Here, people are guided by prosodic information and the pragmatic rules that govern language use. They also rely on "common ground"—assumptions and beliefs shared by the conversational partners—to fill in bits that are not overtly expressed in the conversation.

- Our extraordinary skill in using language is made possible in part by the fact that large portions of the brain are specialized for language use, making it clear that we are, in a literal sense, a "linguistic species."

- Finally, language surely influences our thoughts, but in an indirect fashion: Language is one of many ways to draw our attention to this or that aspect of the environment. This shapes our experience, which in turn shapes our cognition.

To understand the extent of this frustration, bear in mind that we use language to share our ideas with one another, and our feelings and our needs. Without language, cooperative endeavors would be a thousand times more difficult. Without language, the acquisition of knowledge would be enormously impaired. Plainly, then, language capacity is crucial for us all, and in this chapter we'll consider the nature of this extraordinary and uniquely human skill.

The Organization of Language

Language use involves a special type of translation. I might, for example, want to tell you about a happy event in my life, and so I need to translate my ideas about the event into sounds that I can utter. You, in turn, detect those sounds and need to convert them into some sort of comprehension. How does this translation—from ideas to sounds, and then back to ideas—take place?

The answer lies in the fact that language use relies on well-defined patterns—patterns in how individual words are used, patterns in how words are put together into phrases. I follow those patterns when I express my ideas, and the same patterns guide you in figuring out what I just said. In essence, then, we're both using the same "rule book," with the result that (most of the time) you can understand my messages, and I yours.

But where does this "rule book" come from? And what's in the book? More concretely, what are the patterns of English (or whatever language you speak) that—apparently—we all know and use? As a step toward tackling these issues, let's note that language has a hierarchical structure, as depicted in **Figure 10.1**. At the highest level of the structure (not shown in the figure) are the ideas intended by the speaker, or the ideas that the listener derives from the input. These ideas are typically expressed in **sentences**—coherent sequences of words that express the speaker's intended meaning. Sentences, in turn, are composed of phrases, which are composed of words. Words are composed of **morphemes**, the smallest language units that carry meaning. Some morphemes, like "umpire" or "talk," are units that can stand alone, and they usually refer to particular objects, ideas, or actions. Other morphemes get "bound" onto these "free" morphemes and add information crucial for interpretation. Examples of bound morphemes in Figure 10.1 are the past-tense morpheme "ed" and the plural morpheme "s." Then, finally, in spoken language, morphemes are conveyed by sounds called **phonemes**, defined as the smallest units of sound that serve to distinguish words in a language.

Language is also organized in another way: Within each of these levels, people can combine and recombine the units to produce novel utterances—assembling phonemes into brand-new morphemes or assembling words into brand-new phrases. Crucially, though, not all combinations are possible—so

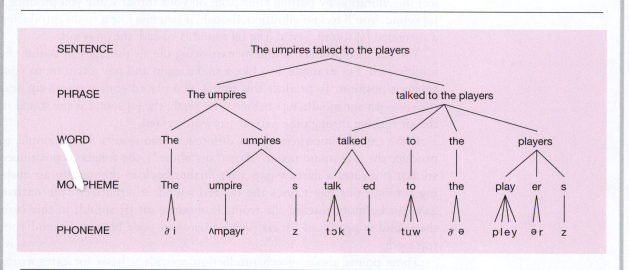

FIGURE 10.1   THE HIERARCHY OF LINGUISTIC UNITS

It is useful to think of language as having a hierarchical structure. At the top of the hierarchy, there are sentences. These are composed of phrases, which are themselves composed of words. The words are composed of morphemes, and when the morphemes are pronounced, the units of sound are called "phonemes." In describing phonemes, the symbols correspond to the actual sounds produced, independent of how these sounds are expressed in ordinary writing.

that a new breakfast cereal, for example, might be called "Klof" but would probably seem strange to English speakers if it were called "Ngof." Likewise, someone might utter the novel sentence "I admired the lurking octopi" but almost certainly wouldn't say, "Octopi admired the I lurking." What lies behind these points? Why are some sequences acceptable—even if strange—while others seem awkward or even unacceptable? The answers to these questions are crucial for any understanding of what language *is*.

Phonology

Let's use the hierarchy in Figure 10.1 as a way to organize our examination of language. We'll start at the bottom of the hierarchy—with the sounds of speech.

The Production of Speech

In ordinary breathing, air flows quietly out of the lungs and up through the nose and mouth (see **Figure 10.2**). There will be some sort of sound, though, if this airflow is interrupted or altered, and this fact is crucial for vocal communication.

For example, within the larynx there are two flaps of muscular tissue called the "vocal folds." (These structures are also called the "vocal cords," although they're not cords at all.) These folds can be rapidly opened and closed, producing a buzzing sort of vibration known as **voicing**. You can feel this vibration by putting your palm on your throat while you produce a [z] sound. You'll feel no vibration, though, if you hiss like a snake, producing a sustained [s] sound. Try it! The [z] sound is voiced; the [s] is not.

You can also produce sound by narrowing the air passageway within the mouth itself. For example, hiss like a snake again and pay attention to your tongue's position. To produce this sound, you placed your tongue's tip near the roof of your mouth, just behind your teeth; the [s] sound is the sound of the air rushing through the narrow gap you created.

If the gap is somewhere else, a different sound results. For example, to produce the [sh] sound (as in "shoot" or "shine"), the tongue is positioned so that it creates a narrow gap a bit farther back in the mouth; air rushing through this gap causes the desired sound. Alternatively, the narrow gap can be more toward the front. Pronounce an [f] sound; in this case, the sound is produced by air rushing between your bottom lip and your top teeth.

These points about speech production provide a basis for categorizing speech sounds. We can distinguish sounds, first, according to how the airflow is restricted; this is referred to as **manner of production**. Thus, air is allowed to move through the nose for some speech sounds but not others. Similarly, for some speech sounds, the flow of air is fully stopped for a moment (e.g., [p], [b], and [t]). For other sounds, the air passage is restricted, but air continues to flow (e.g., [f], [z], and [r]).

FIGURE 10.2   THE HUMAN VOCAL TRACT

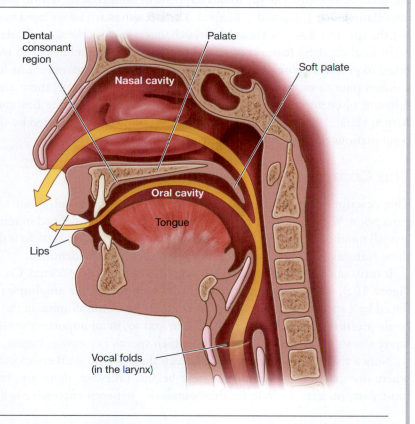

Speech is produced by airflow from the lungs that passes through the larynx and from there through the oral and nasal cavities. Different vowels are created by movements of the lips and tongue that change the size and shape of the oral cavity. Consonants are produced by movements that temporarily obstruct the airflow through the vocal tract.

Second, we can distinguish between sounds that are voiced—produced with the vocal folds vibrating—and those that are not. The sounds of [v], [z], and [n] (to name a few) are voiced; [f], [s], [t], and [k] are unvoiced. (You can confirm this by running the hand-on-throat test while producing each of these sounds.) Finally, sounds can be categorized according to where the airflow is restricted; this is referred to as **place of articulation**. For example, you close your lips to produce "bilabial" sounds like [p] and [b]; you place your top teeth close to your bottom lip to produce "labiodental" sounds like [f] and [v]; and you place your tongue just behind your upper teeth to produce "alveolar" sounds like [t] and [d].

These points allow us to describe any speech sound in terms of a few simple features. For example, what are the features of a [p] sound? First, we specify the manner of production: This sound is produced with air moving through the mouth (not the nose) and with a full interruption to the flow of air. Second, voicing: The [p] sound happens to be unvoiced. Third, place of articulation: The [p] sound is bilabial. These features are all we need to identify the [p], and if any of these features changes, so does the sound's identity.

In English, these features of sound production are combined and recombined to produce 40 or so different phonemes. Other languages use as few as a dozen phonemes; still others use many more. (For example, there are 141 different phonemes in the language of Khoisan, spoken by the Bushmen of Africa; Halle, 1990.) In all cases, though, the phonemes are created by simple combinations of the features just described.

The Complexity of Speech Perception

This description of speech sounds invites a simple proposal about speech *perception*. We've just said that each speech sound can be defined in terms of a small number of features. Perhaps, then, all a perceiver needs to do is detect these features, and with this done, the speech sounds are identified.

It turns out, though, that speech perception is more complicated. Consider **Figure 10.3**, which shows the moment-by-moment sound amplitudes produced by a speaker uttering a brief greeting. It's these amplitudes, in the form of air-pressure changes, that reach the ear, and so, in an important sense, the figure shows the pattern of input with which speech perception begins.

Notice that within this stream of speech there are no markers to indicate where one phoneme ends and the next begins. Likewise, there are, for the most part, no gaps to indicate the boundaries between successive syllables

FIGURE 10.3   THE ACTUAL PATTERN OF SPEECH

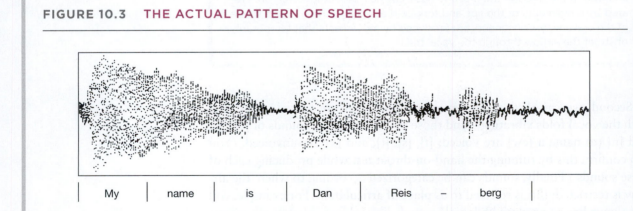

| My | name | is | Dan | Reis | – | berg | |

Shown here are the moment-by-moment sound amplitudes produced by the author uttering a greeting. Notice that there is no gap between the sounds carrying the word "my" and the sounds carrying "name." Nor is there a gap between the sounds carrying "name" and the sounds carrying "is." Therefore, the listener needs to figure out where one sound stops and the next begins, a process known as speech segmentation.

or successive words. Therefore, as your first step toward phoneme identification, you need to "slice" this stream into the appropriate segments—a step known as **speech segmentation**.

For many people, this pattern comes as a surprise. Most of us are convinced that there are brief pauses between words in the speech we hear, and it's these pauses, we assume, that mark the word boundaries. But this perception turns out to be an illusion, and we are "hearing" pauses that aren't actually there. This is evident when we "hear" the pauses in the "wrong places" and segment the speech stream in a way the speaker didn't intend (see **Figure 10.4**). The illusion is also revealed when we physically measure

---

FIGURE 10.4   AMBIGUITY IN SEGMENTATION

*"Boy, he must think we're pretty stupid
to fall for that again."*

Almost every child has heard the story of Chicken Little. No one believed this poor chicken when he announced, "The sky is falling!" It turns out, though, that the acoustic signal—the actual sounds produced—would have been the same if Chicken Little had exclaimed, "This guy is falling!" The difference between these utterances ("The sky . . ." vs. "This guy . . .") isn't in the input. Instead, the difference lies in how the listener segments the sounds.

---

the speech stream (as we did in order to create Figure 10.3) or when we listen to speech we can't understand—for example, speech in a foreign language. In the latter circumstance, we lack the skill needed to segment the stream, so we're unable to "supply" the word boundaries. As a consequence, we hear what is really there: a continuous, uninterrupted flow of sound. That is why speech in a foreign language often sounds so fast.

Speech perception is further complicated by a phenomenon known as **coarticulation** (Liberman, 1970; also Daniloff & Hammarberg, 1973). This term refers to the fact that in producing speech, you don't utter one phoneme at a time. Instead, the phonemes overlap, so that while you're producing the [s] sound in "soup," for example, your mouth is getting ready to say the vowel. While uttering the vowel, you're already starting to move your tongue, lips, and teeth into position for producing the [p].

This overlap helps to make speech production more fluent. But the overlap also has consequences for the sounds produced, and so the [s] you produce while getting ready for one upcoming vowel is actually different from the [s] you produce while getting ready for a different vowel. As a result, we can't point to a specific acoustical pattern and say, "This is the pattern of an [s] sound." Instead, the acoustical pattern is different in different contexts. Speech perception therefore has to "read past" these context differences in order to identify the phonemes produced.

Aids to Speech Perception

The need for segmentation in a continuous speech stream, the variations caused by coarticulation, and also the variations from speaker to speaker all make speech perception rather complex. Nonetheless, you manage to perceive speech accurately and easily. How do you do it?

Part of the answer lies in the fact that the speech you encounter, day by day, is surprisingly limited in its range. Each of us knows tens of thousands of words, but most of these words are rarely used. In fact, one early count suggested that the 50 most commonly used words in English make up roughly half of the words you actually hear (Miller, 1951; also see Brysbaert et al. 2018; Jesse, 2021).

In addition, the perception of speech shares a crucial attribute with other types of perception: a reliance on knowledge and expectations that supplement the input and guide your interpretation. In other words, speech perception (like perception in other domains) weaves together "bottom-up" and "top-down" processes—processes that, on the one side, are driven by the input itself, and on the other side, depend on the broader pattern of what you know.

The contribution of top-down processes is evident, for example, in the **phonemic restoration effect**. To demonstrate this effect, researchers start by recording a bit of speech, and then they modify what they've recorded. For example, they might remove the [s] sound in the middle of "legislatures" and replace the [s] with a brief burst of noise. This now-degraded stimulus can then be presented to participants, embedded in a sentence such as

The state governors met with their respective legi*latures.

When asked about this stimulus, participants insist that they heard the complete word, "legislatures," accompanied by a burst of noise (Repp, 1992; Samuel, 1987, 1991). It seems, then, that they use the context to figure out what the word must have been, but then insist that they actually heard the word. In fact, participants are often inaccurate if asked when exactly they heard the noise burst. They can't tell whether they heard the noise during the second syllable of "legislatures" (so that it blotted out the missing [s], forcing them to *infer* the missing sound) or at some other point (so that they were able to *hear* the missing [s] with no interference). Apparently, the top-down process literally changes what participants hear—leaving them with no way to distinguish what was heard from what was inferred.

How much does the context in which we hear a word help us? Pollack and Pickett (1964) recorded a number of naturally occurring conversations, and, from these recordings, they spliced out individual words and presented them in isolation to their research participants. With no context to guide them, participants were able to identify only half of the words. If restored to their original context, though, the same stimuli were easy to identify. Apparently, the benefits of context are considerable. (For more recent discussion, see Signoret et al., 2018.)

Categorical Perception

Speech perception also benefits from a pattern called **categorical perception**. This term refers to the fact that people are much better at hearing the differences *between* categories of sounds than they are at hearing the variations *within* a category of sounds. In other words, you're very sensitive to the differences between, say, a [g] sound and a [k], or the differences between a [d] and a [t]. But you're surprisingly insensitive to differences within each of these categories, so you have a hard time distinguishing, say, one [p] sound from another, somewhat different [p] sound. And, of course, this pattern is precisely what you want, because it enables you to hear the differences that matter without hearing (and being distracted by) inconsequential variations within the category.

Demonstrations of categorical perception generally rely on a series of stimuli, created by computer. The first stimulus in the series might be a [ba] sound. Another stimulus might be a [ba] that has been distorted a tiny bit, to make it a little bit closer to a [pa] sound. A third stimulus might be a [ba] that has been distorted a bit more, so that it's a notch closer to a [pa], and so on. In this way we create a series of stimuli, each slightly different from the one before, ranging from a clear [ba] at one extreme, through a series of "compromise" sounds, until at the other extreme we reach a clear [pa] sound.

CATEGORICAL PERCEPTION IN OTHER SPECIES

The pattern of categorical perception isn't limited to language—or to humans. A similar pattern, for example, with much greater sensitivity to between-category differences than to within-category variations, has been documented in the hearing of the chinchilla.

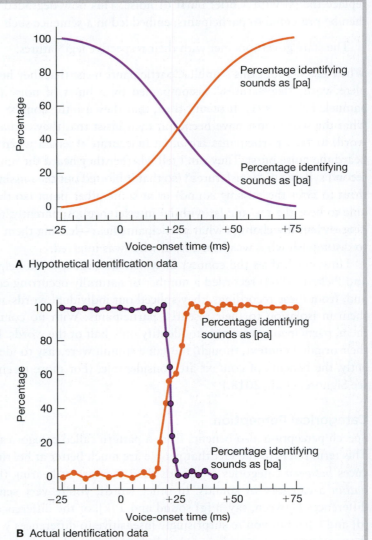

A Hypothetical identification data

B Actual identification data

FIGURE 10.5   CATEGORICAL PERCEPTION

With computer speech, we can produce a variety of compromises between a [pa] sound and a [ba] sound, differing only in when the voicing begins (i.e., the voice-onset time, or VOT). Panel A shows a plausible hypothesis about how these sounds will be perceived: As the sound becomes less and less like an ordinary [ba], people should be less and less likely to perceive it as a [ba]. Panel B, however, shows the actual data: Research participants seem indifferent to small variations in the [ba] sound, and they categorize a sound with a 10 ms or 15 ms VOT in essentially the same way that they categorize a sound with a 0 VOT. The categorizations also show an abrupt categorical boundary between [pa] and [ba], although there is no corresponding abrupt change in the stimuli themselves.

(AFTER LISKER & ABRAMSON, 1970)

How do people perceive these various sounds? **Figure 10.5A** shows the pattern we might expect. After all, our stimuli are gradually shading from a clear [ba] to a clear [pa]. Therefore, as we move through the series, we might expect people to be less and less likely to identify each stimulus as a [ba], and correspondingly more and more likely to identify each as a [pa]. The actual data, however, shown in **Figure 10.5B**, don't fit with this prediction. Even though the stimuli are gradually changing from one extreme to another, participants "hear" an abrupt shift, so that roughly half the stimuli are reliably categorized as [ba] and half are reliably categorized as [pa]. Moreover, participants seem indifferent to the differences *within* each category. Across the first dozen stimuli, the syllables are becoming less and less [ba]-like, but this is not reflected in how the listeners identify the sounds. Likewise, across the last dozen stimuli, the syllables are becoming more and more [pa]-like, but again, this trend has little effect. What listeners seem to hear is either a [pa] or a [ba], with no gradations inside of either category. (For early demonstrations, see Liberman et al., 1957; Lisker & Abramson, 1970; for reviews, see Handel, 1989; Yeni-Komshian, 1993.)

It seems, then, that your perceptual apparatus is "tuned" to provide just the information you need. After all, you want to know whether someone advised you to "take a path" or "take a bath." You certainly care whether a friend said, "You're the best" or "You're the pest." Plainly, the difference between [b] and [p] matters to you, and this difference is clearly marked in your perception. In contrast, you usually don't care how exactly the speaker pronounced "path" or "best"—that's not information that matters for getting the meaning of these utterances. And here too, your perception serves you well by largely ignoring these "subphonemic" variations. (For more on the broad issue of speech perception, see Mattys, 2012.)

Combining Phonemes

English relies on just a few dozen phonemes, but these sounds can be combined and recombined to produce thousands of different morphemes, which can themselves be combined to create word after word. As we mentioned earlier, though, there are rules governing these combinations, and users of the language respect these rules. In English, for example, certain sounds (such as the final sound in "going" or "flying") can occur at the end of a word but not at the beginning. Other combinations seem prohibited outright. For example, the sequence "tlof" seems anomalous to English speakers; very few words in English contain the "tl" combination within a single syllable. These limits, however, are simply facts about English; they are not at all a limit on what human ears can hear or human tongues can produce, and other languages routinely use combinations that for English speakers seem unspeakable. For example, the fish known as the axolotl takes its name from the Nahuatl language.

There are also rules governing the adjustments that occur when certain phonemes are uttered one after another. For example, consider the "s" ending that marks the English plural—as in "books," "cats," and "tapes." In these cases, the plural is pronounced as an [s]. In other contexts, though, the plural ending is pronounced differently. Say these words out loud: "bags," "duds," "pills." If you listen carefully, you'll realize that these words actually end with a [z] sound, not an [s].

English speakers all seem to know the rule that governs this distinction. (The rule hinges on whether the base noun ends with a voiced or an unvoiced sound; for classic statements of this rule, see Chomsky & Halle, 1968; Halle, 1990.) Moreover, they obey this rule even with novel, made-up cases. For example, I have one wug, and now I acquire another. Now, I have two . . . what? Without hesitation, people pronounce "wugs" using the [z] ending—in accord with the standard pattern. Even young children pronounce "wugs"

TEST YOURSELF

2. Define "voicing," "manner of production," and "place of articulation."
3. What is speech segmentation, and why is it an important step in speech perception?
4. What is categorical perception?

COGNITION outside the lab

"Read My Lips"

In 1988, presidential candidate George H. W. Bush uttered the memorable instruction "Read my lips," and then he slowly enunciated "No . . . new . . . taxes." Bush intended the initial phrase to mean something like "Note what I'm saying. You can count on it," and other speakers have adopted this idiom, using the words "read my lips" to emphasize their message.

Aside from this locution, though, what is lip-reading, and who uses it? The basic idea, of course, is that lip-reading is a means of understanding speech based on visual cues, including (but not limited to) movement of the lips. Bear in mind, though, that many speech sounds are created by movements hidden inside of the mouth and throat; as a result, the set of cues available to vision is limited. Even so, skilled lip-readers (relying on a mix of visual cues, context, and knowledge of the language) can glean much of the content of the speech that they see.

However, we need to set aside the idea that lip-reading is used only when the auditory signal is weak. Instead, lip-reading is an integral part of ordinary speech perception. Of course, you often don't *need* lip-reading; if you did, you'd never be able to use the telephone or understand an interview on the radio. But even so, you rely on lip-reading in many settings—even if the signal reaching your ears is perfectly clear.

Powerful evidence comes from the McGurk effect, first described in a 1976 paper entitled "Hearing Lips and Seeing Voices" (McGurk & MacDonald, 1976). In this effect, the audio track plainly conveys the sound of someone saying one sound (perhaps "ba"), but the carefully synchronized video shows someone uttering a different sound ("va"). If you listen to the recording with eyes closed, you consistently hear one sound; if

you listen while watching the video, you unmistakably hear the other sound. (Try it. There are many versions of this effect available on YouTube.) It seems, then, that you have no choice about using the lip cues, and when those cues are available to you, they can change what you "hear."

A different sort of evidence comes from settings in which the input is easy to hear, but difficult to understand. Consider the case of someone who's had a year or two of training in a new language—maybe someone who took two years of French in high school. This person now travels to Paris and is able to communicate well enough in face-to-face conversation, but they become hopelessly lost when trying to communicate in a phone call.

Can we document this pattern in the laboratory? In one study, participants tried to understand someone speaking in a language that the participants knew, but were not fluent in. (This is, of course, the situation of the French novice trying to get by in Paris.) In a second study, participants heard English-language material that was clearly spoken but difficult to understand, because the prose was quite dense. (They were listening to a complex excerpt from the writings of the philosopher Immanuel Kant.) In both of these cases, participants were able to "hear" more if they could both see and hear the speaker, in comparison to a condition in which there was no visual input.

You shouldn't be embarrassed, therefore, if you dread making a phone call in a language that's not your native tongue. Whether you're using your second language or your first, lip-reading is a normal part of speech perception, and at least part of what you "hear" is actually coming to you through your eyes.

with a [z], and so, it seems, they too have internalized—and obey—the relevant principles (Berko, 1958).

Morphemes and Words

A typical college graduate in the United States knows between 75,000 and 100,000 different words. These counts have been available for many years (e.g., Oldfield, 1963; Zechmeister et al., 1995), and there's no reason to think they're changing. For each word, the speaker knows the word's *sound* (the sequence of phonemes that make up the word) and its *orthography* (the sequence of letters that spell the word). The speaker also knows how to use the word within various phrases, governed by the rules of syntax (see **Figure 10.6**). Finally, speakers know the meaning of a word; they have a *semantic representation* for the word to go with the *phonological representation*.

Building New Words

Estimates of vocabulary size, however, need to be interpreted with caution, because the size of someone's vocabulary is subject to change. One reason is that new words are created all the time. For example, discussions on social media often include offers of "merch" and references to "sponcon." We're all listening to "podcasts," a word derived from an Apple device—the iPod— that didn't exist prior to 2001. Likewise, changes in diet have put words like "vegan" and "paleo" into common use. Everyone's now taking "selfies," although it was only in 2012 that *Time* magazine listed "selfie" as one of the year's top ten "buzzwords" (itself a term invented just a few decades back).

Often, new words are created by combining or adjusting existing words (and so "sponcon" refers to "sponsored content"; "paleo" is a shortened form of "Paleolithic"). In addition, once these new entries are in the language, they can be combined with other elements—usually by adding

FIGURE 10.6 **KNOWING A WORD**

(1)	She can place the books on the table.
(2)	* She can place on the table.
(3)	* She can sleep the books on the table
(4)	She can sleep on the table.

Part of what it means to "know a word" is knowing how to use a word. For example, a verb like "place" requires an object—so that Sentence 1 (with an object) sounds fine, but Sentence 2 is anomalous. Other words have other requirements. "Sleep," for example, does not take an object—so Sentence 3 is anomalous, but Sentence 4 is fine.

the appropriate morphemes. Imagine that you've just heard the word "mansplain" for the first time. You know instantly that someone who does this activity is a "mansplainer" and that the activity itself is "mansplaining," and you understand someone who says, "I was so annoyed when he mansplained the joke."

Once again, therefore, note the **generativity** of language—that is, the capacity to create an endless series of new combinations, all built from a small set of fundamental units. Someone who "knows English," therefore (or someone who knows *any* language), hasn't just memorized the vocabulary of the language and some set of phrases. Instead, people who "know English" know how to create new forms within the language: They know how to combine morphemes to create new words, how to "adjust" phonemes when they're put together into novel combinations, and so on. This knowledge isn't conscious—and so most English speakers could not articulate the principles governing the sequence of morphemes within a word, or why they pronounce "wugs" with a [z] sound rather than an [s]. Nonetheless, speakers honor these principles in their day-by-day use of the language and their day-to-day creation of novel words.

Syntax

The potential for producing new forms is even more remarkable when we consider the upper levels in the language hierarchy—the levels of *phrases* and *sentences*. This point becomes obvious when we ask: If you have 60,000 words in your vocabulary, or 80,000, how many sentences can you build from those words?

Sentences range in length from the very brief ("Go!" or "I do") to the absurdly long. Most sentences, though, contain 20 words or fewer. With this length limit, it has been estimated that there are 100,000,000,000,000,000,000 possible sentences in English (Pinker, 1994). If you could read these sentences at the insane rate of 1,000 per second, you'd still need over 30,000 *centuries* to read through this list! (In fact, this estimate may be too low. In a 1960 publication, Miller et al. estimated that the number of possible sentences is actually 10^{30}—billions of times larger than the estimate we're using here.)

Once again, though, there are limits on which combinations (i.e., which sequences of words) are acceptable and which ones are not. For example, in English you could say "The boy hit the ball" but not "The boy hit ball the." Likewise, you could say "The moose squashed the car" but not "The moose squashed the" or just "Squashed the car." Virtually any speaker of the language would agree that these errant sequences have something wrong in them, but what exactly is the problem with these "bad" strings? The answer lies in the rules of **syntax**—rules that govern the structure of a phrase or sentence.

TEST YOURSELF

5. Why is it difficult to give an exact count of the number of words in someone's vocabulary?

You might think that the rules of syntax depend on *meaning*, so that meaningful sequences are accepted as "sentences" while meaning-*less* sequences are rejected as nonsentences. This suggestion, though, is wrong. As one concern, many nonsentences do seem meaningful, and no one's confused when Sesame Street's Cookie Monster insists, "Me want cookie." Likewise, viewers understood the monster's wistful comment in the 1935 movie *Bride of Frankenstein*: "Alone, bad; friend, good."

In addition, consider these two sentences:

'Twas brillig, and the slithy toves did gyre and gimble in the wabe.

Colorless green ideas sleep furiously.

(The first of these is from Lewis Carroll's famous poem "Jabberwocky"; the second was penned by the linguist Noam Chomsky.) These sentences are, of course, without meaning: Colorless things aren't green; ideas don't sleep; toves aren't slithy. Nonetheless, speakers of English, after a moment's reflection, regard these sequences as grammatically acceptable in a way that "Furiously sleep ideas green colorless" is not. It seems, therefore, that we need principles of syntax that are separate from considerations of semantics or sensibility.

SYNTAX AND MORPHEMES IN "JABBERWOCKY"

In the poem "Jabberwocky," Lewis Carroll relies on proper syntax and appropriate use of morphemes to create gibberish that is wonderfully Englishlike: "He left it dead, and with its head / He went galumphing back."

Phrase Structure

The rules of syntax have many functions. For a start, they specify which elements must appear in a phrase and (for many languages) govern the sequence of those elements. **Phrase-structure rules** also define the overall organization of the sentence—and therefore determine how the various elements are linked to one another.

One way to depict phrase-structure rules is with a **tree structure** like the one shown in **Figure 10.7**. You can read the structure from top to bottom, and as you move from one level to the next, you can see that each element (e.g., a noun phrase or a verb phrase) has been "expanded" in a way that's governed by the phrase-structure rules.

Prescriptive Rules, Descriptive Rules

We need to be clear, though, about what sort of rules we're discussing. Let's begin with the fact that most of us were taught, at some stage of our education, how to talk and write "properly." We were taught never to say "ain't." Many of us were scolded for starting a sentence with "And" or "But." Warnings like these are the result of **prescriptive rules**—rules describing how something (in this case: language) is "supposed to be." Language that doesn't follow these rules, it's claimed, is "improper" or maybe even "bad."

You should, however, be skeptical about these prescriptive rules. After all, languages change with the passage of time, and what's "proper" in one

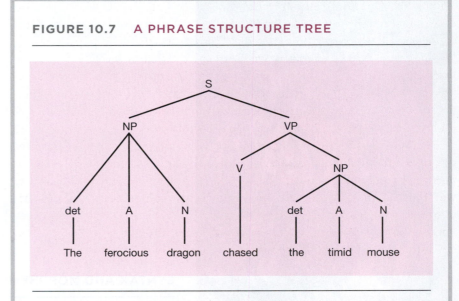

FIGURE 10.7   A PHRASE STRUCTURE TREE

The diagram shows that the overall sentence (S) consists of a noun phrase (NP) plus a verb phrase (VP). The noun phrase is composed of a determiner (det) followed by an adjective (A) and a noun (N). The verb phrase is composed of a verb (V) followed by a noun phrase (NP).

period is often different from what seems right at other times. In the 1600s, for example, people used the pronouns "thou" and "ye," but those words are gone from modern usage. Likewise, not so long ago people were careful to distinguish "who" and "whom," and also "me" and "I." But these distinctions are fading fast, and for most of us it sounds stiff, formal, and old-fashioned to ask, "With whom are you going?" Similarly, when you get home this evening, your roommate might call from a back room: "Who's there?" Few people would reply, "It is I." Instead, almost all of us would think it's fine to say, "It's me!"

Similarly, recent discussions of gender identity have led many people to use "they" to refer to just one person. In this way, speakers avoid using the pronouns "he" or "she," pronouns that indicate someone's gender. As it turns out, though, this shift in usage has been under way for years, independent of gender politics, with people often using "they" to refer to one person. (As an illustration, and no matter how you think about gender issues, you're probably okay with sentences like this one: "Each person has to make their own decision about what level of risk they'll tolerate." Here, the words "they" and "their" are referring back to "each person"—referring to the *single individual* who is making this decision. It seems, then, that "they" and "their" are being used here as singular nouns, not plurals.)

Changes like these make it difficult to justify prescriptive rules, because, again, what's considered "proper" shifts as the years ago by. In essence, then, any insistence on prescriptive rules seems to rest on the idea that the English spoken, say, a generation or two ago was proper and correct, and that the English spoken either before or after this "golden age" is somehow inferior. It's hard to think of any basis for this claim, so it seems instead that the prescriptive rules reflect only the preferences of a particular group at a particular time—and there's no reason why our usage should be governed by their preferences. In addition, it's not surprising that the groups that set these rules are usually groups with high prestige or social standing (Labov, 2007). When people strive to follow prescriptive rules, then, it's often because they hope to join (or, at least, be associated with) these elite groups.

Phrase-structure rules, in contrast, are not prescriptive; they are **descriptive rules**—that is, rules characterizing the language as it's ordinarily used by fluent speakers and listeners. There are, after all, strong regularities in the way English is used, and the rules we're discussing here describe these patterns. No value judgment is offered about whether these patterns constitute "proper" or "good" English. These patterns simply describe how English is structured—or perhaps we should say, *what English is.*

The Function of Phrase Structure

No one claims that language users are consciously aware of phrase-structure rules. Instead, the idea is that people have somehow internalized these rules and obey them in their use of, and also their judgments about, language.

If, for example, a sequence of words lacks an element that should, according to the rules, be in place, you'll probably think there's a mistake in the

"THEY" AS A SINGULAR PRONOUN

"No one really knows why they are alive until they know what they'd die for."

Recent discussions of gender identity have encouraged people to use "they" as a singular pronoun, rather than "he" or "she." In this fashion, people avoid language that specifies someone's gender. It turns out, though, this usage of "they"—as a singular pronoun—has been in place for many years, as exemplified by this well-known quotation from Martin Luther King Jr.

sequence. Likewise, you'll balk at sequences of words that include elements that (according to the rules) shouldn't be there, or elements that should be in a different position within the string. These points enable us to explain why you think sequences like these need some sort of repair: "His argument emphasized in modern society" or "Susan appeared cat in the door."

Perhaps more important, phrase-structure rules help you *understand* the sentences you encounter. For example, the NP + VP sequence, defined by the phrase-structure rules, typically divides a sentence into the "doer" (the NP) and some information about that doer (the VP). Likewise, the V + NP sequence usually indicates the action described by the sentence and then the recipient of that action. In this way, the phrase structure of a sentence provides an initial "road map" that's useful in understanding the sentence. To take a simple case, it's the phrase structure that tells us who's doing what when we hear "The boy chased the girl." Without syntax (e.g., if our sentences were merely lists of words, such as "boy, girl, chased"), we'd have no way to know who was the chaser and who (if anyone) was chaste. (Also see **Figure 10.8**.)

Sometimes, though, two different phrase structures can lead to the same sequence of words, and if you encounter one of these sequences, you may not know which structure was intended. How will this affect you? We've just suggested that phrase structures guide interpretation, and so, with multiple phrase structures available, there should be more than one way to interpret the sentence. This turns out to be correct—often, with comical consequences (see **Figure 10.9**).

Sentence Parsing

A sentence's phrase structure, we've said, conveys crucial information about who did what to whom. Once you know the phrase structure, therefore, you're well on your way to understanding the sentence. But how do you figure out the phrase structure in the first place? This would be an easy question if sentences were uniform in their structure: "The boy hit the ball." "The girl drove the car." "The elephant trampled the geraniums." But, of course,

TEST YOURSELF

6. What evidence tells us that the rules of syntax can be separated from considerations of whether or not a string of words has meaning?

7. What are phrase-structure rules, and what does it mean that these rules are "descriptive," not "prescriptive"?

The large tomato made a satisfying splat when it hit the floor.

A

The large tomato made a satisfying splat when it hit the floor.

B

FIGURE 10.8   PHRASE STRUCTURE ORGANIZATION AIDS THE READER

Panel A shows a sentence written so that the breaks between lines correspond to breaks between phrases; this makes reading easier because the sentence has been visually "pre-organized." In Panel B, the sentence has been rewritten so that the visual breaks don't correspond to the boundaries between phrases. Reading is now slower and more difficult.

FIGURE 10.9   PHRASE STRUCTURE AMBIGUITY

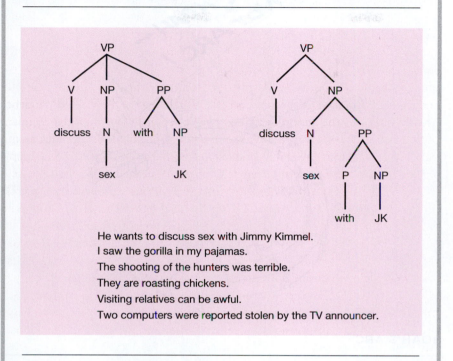

He wants to discuss sex with Jimmy Kimmel.
I saw the gorilla in my pajamas.
The shooting of the hunters was terrible.
They are roasting chickens.
Visiting relatives can be awful.
Two computers were reported stolen by the TV announcer.

Often, the words of a sentence are compatible with more than one phrase structure; in such cases, the sentence will be ambiguous. Therefore, you can understand the first sentence here either as describing *a discussion with Kimmel* or as describing *sex with Kimmel*; both analyses of the verb phrase are shown. Can you find both interpretations for the remaining sentences?

sentences are more variable than this, and such variation makes identification of a sentence's phrase structure much more difficult.

How, therefore, do you **parse** a sentence—that is, figure out each word's syntactic role? It seems plausible that you'd wait until the sentence's end, and only then go to work on figuring out the structure. With this strategy, your comprehension might be slowed a little (because you're waiting for the sentence's end), but you'd avoid errors, because your interpretation could be guided by full information about the sentence's content.

It turns out, though, that people don't use this wait-for-all-the-information strategy. Instead, they parse sentences as they hear them, trying to figure out the role of each word the moment it arrives (e.g., Tanenhaus & Trueswell, 2006). This approach is efficient (since there's no waiting) but, as we'll see, can lead to errors.

NOAH'S ARC

Sometimes linguistic ambiguity involves the interpretation of a phrase's organization. Sometimes, though, the ambiguity involves the interpretation of a single word. Sometimes the ambiguity is evident in spoken language but not in written language.

Garden Paths

Even simple sentences can be ambiguous if you're open-minded (or perverse) enough:

> Mary had a little lamb. (But I was quite hungry, so I had the lamb and also a bowl of soup.)

> Time flies like an arrow. (But fruit flies, in contrast, like a banana.)

Temporary ambiguity is also common inside a sentence. More precisely, the early part of a sentence is often open to multiple interpretations, but then the later part of the sentence clears things up. Consider this example:

> The old man the ships.

In this sentence, most people read the initial three words as a noun phrase: "the old man." However, this interpretation leaves the sentence with no verb, so a different interpretation is needed, with the subject of the sentence being "the old" and with "man" being the verb. (Who mans the ships? It is the old, not the young. The old man the ships.) Likewise:

The secretary applauded for his efforts was soon promoted.

Here, people tend to read "applauded" as the sentence's main verb, but it isn't. Instead, this sentence is just a shorthand way of answering the question, "Which secretary was soon promoted?" (Answer: "The one who was applauded for his efforts.")

These examples are referred to as **garden-path sentences**: You're initially led to one interpretation (you are, as they say, "led down the garden path"), but this interpretation turns out to be wrong. So you need to reject your first interpretation and find an alternative. Here are two more examples:

Fat people eat accumulates.

Because he ran the second mile went quickly.

Garden-path sentences highlight the risk attached to the strategy of interpreting a sentence as it arrives: The information you need in order to understand these sentences arrives only late in the sequence, and so, to avoid an interpretive dead end, you'd be better off remaining neutral about the sentence's meaning until you've gathered enough information. That way, you'd know that "the old man" couldn't be the sentence's subject, that "applauded" couldn't be the sentence's main verb, and so on. But this isn't what you do. Instead, you commit yourself fairly early to one interpretation and then try to "fit" subsequent words, as they arrive, into that interpretation. This strategy is often effective, but it does lead to the "double-take" reaction when late-arriving information forces you to abandon your initial interpretation.

Syntax and Knowledge as Guides to Parsing

What is it that leads you down the garden path? Why do you initially choose one interpretation of a sentence, one parsing, rather than another? Many cues are relevant, because many types of information influence parsing. For one, people usually seek the simplest phrase structure that will accommodate the words heard so far. This strategy is fine if the sentence structure is indeed simple; the strategy produces problems, though, with more complex sentences. To see how this plays out, consider the earlier sentence, "The secretary applauded for his efforts was soon promoted." As you read "The secretary applauded," you had the option of interpreting this as a noun phrase plus the beginning of a separate clause modifying "secretary." This is the correct interpretation, and it's required by the way the sentence ends. However, you ignored this possibility, at least initially, and went instead with a simpler interpretation—of a noun phrase plus verb, with no idea of a separate embedded clause.

People also tend to assume that they'll be hearing (or reading) *active-voice* sentences rather than *passive-voice* sentences, so they generally interpret a sentence's initial noun phrase as the "doer" of the action and not the recipient. As it happens, most of the sentences you encounter are active, not passive, so this assumption is usually correct (for early research, see Slobin, 1966; Svartvik, 1966). However, this assumption can slow you down when you do encounter a passive sentence. Of course, this assumption added to your difficulties with the "secretary" sentence: The embedded clause there is in the passive voice (the secretary was applauded by someone else); your tendency to assume active voice, therefore, works against the correct interpretation of this sentence. (For description of the settings in which the passive voice is *useful,* though, see Ferreira, 2021.)

Not surprisingly, parsing is also influenced by the function words that appear in a sentence and by various morphemes that signal syntactic role (Bever, 1970). For example, people easily grasp the structure of "He gliply rivitched the flidget." That's because the "-ly" morpheme indicates that "glip" is an adverb; the "-ed" identifies "rivitch" as a verb; and "the" signals that "flidget" is a noun—all excellent cues to the sentence structure. This factor, too, is relevant to the "secretary" sentence, which included none of the helpful function words. Notice that we didn't say, "The secretary who was applauded . . ."; if we had said that, the chance of misunderstanding would have been greatly reduced.

Parsing is also guided by background knowledge, and in general people try to parse sentences in a way that makes sense to them. So, for example, readers are unlikely to misread the headline *Drunk Gets Six Months in Violin Case* (Gibson, 2006; Pinker, 1994; Sedivy et al., 1999). And this point, too, matters for the "secretary" sentence: Your background knowledge tells you that women secretaries are more common than men, and this added to your confusion in figuring out who was applauding and who was applauded. (Also see **Figure 10.10.**)

With all these factors stacked against you, it's no wonder you were (temporarily) confused about "the secretary." Indeed, with all these factors in place, garden-path sentences can sometimes be enormously difficult to comprehend. For example, spend a moment puzzling over this (fully grammatical) sequence:

The horse raced past the barn fell.

(If you get stuck with this sentence, try adding the words "that was" just before "raced.")

Prosody

We've now described several strategies that you use in parsing the sentences you encounter. The role of these strategies is obvious when the strategies mislead you, as they do with garden-path sentences. Bear in mind, though,

TEST YOURSELF

8. What's the evidence that *multiple factors* play a role in guiding how you parse a sentence?
9. What is a garden-path sentence?

FIGURE 10.10 N400 BRAIN WAVE

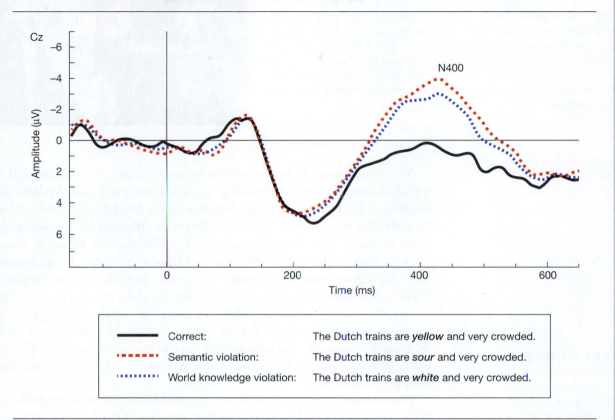

Correct:	The Dutch trains are *yellow* and very crowded.
Semantic violation:	The Dutch trains are *sour* and very crowded.
World knowledge violation:	The Dutch trains are *white* and very crowded.

In parsing a sentence, you rely on your (nonlinguistic) knowledge about the world. This point is evident in a study of electrical activity in the brain while people were hearing different types of sentences. Some of the sentences were sensible and true ("The Dutch trains are yellow and very crowded"). Other sentences contained a semantic anomaly ("The Dutch trains are sour and very crowded"), and this peculiarity produced the N400 brain wave. The key, though, is that a virtually identical N400 was produced in a third condition in which sentences were perfectly sensible but false: "The Dutch trains are white and very crowded." (The falsity was immediately obvious to the Dutch participants in this study.) Apparently, world knowledge (including knowledge about train color) is a part of sentence processing from a very early stage. (FIG. AFTER HAGOORT, P., HALD, L., BASTIAANSEN, M., & PETERSSON, K. M. (2004). INTEGRATION OF WORD MEANING AND WORD KNOWLEDGE IN LANGUAGE COMPREHENSION *SCIENCE, 304*(5669), 438-441 © 2004 AAAS. REPRINTED WITH PERMISSION FROM AAAS.)

that the same strategies are used for *all* sentences and usually do lead to the correct parsing.

It turns out, however, that our catalogue of strategies isn't complete, because you also make use of other factors. Your interpretation of sentences is guided, for example, by the *context* in which you encounter sentences, including the conversational context and the **extralinguistic context**—the physical and social setting in which you hear or see sentences.

Prosody • **365**

LANGUAGE DIFFERENCES IN PROSODY

Prosody cues don't just *accompany* language. Instead, they are *part of* a language. This is evident in the fact that many aspects of prosody differ from one language to another—and so, when you communicate with someone less familiar with your own language, you often need to shift your vocabulary, your syntax, and also your pattern of pauses and pitch. Here, a Spanish journalist converses with Saharawi refugees, whose native language is Hassānīya.

TEST YOURSELF

10. What is prosody?
11. Why are printed versions of garden-path sentences more likely to puzzle you, compared to spoken versions of the same sentences?

Your understanding is also guided by another cue: the rise and fall of speech intonation and the pattern of pauses. These pitch and rhythm cues, together called **prosody**, actually communicate a great deal of information. Prosody can, for example, direct the listener's attention by specifying the focus or theme of a sentence (Jackendoff, 1972; also see Kraus & Slater, 2016). Consider the simple sentence "Sol sipped the soda." Now, imagine how you'd pronounce this sentence in response to each of these questions: "Was it Sue who sipped the soda?"; "Did Sol gulp the soda?"; or "Did Sol sip the soup?" You'd probably say the same words ("Sol sipped the soda") in response to each of these queries, but you'd adjust the prosody in order to highlight the information crucial for each question. (Try it. Imagine answering each question, and pay attention to how you shift your pronunciation.)

Prosody can also clarify a sentence that would otherwise be entirely confusing (Beach, 1991). This is why *printed versions* of garden-path sentences are more likely to puzzle you—because in print, prosody provides no information. Imagine, therefore, that you *heard* the sentence "The horse raced past the barn fell." The speaker would probably pause momentarily between "horse" and "raced," and again between "barn" and "fell," making it likely that you'd understand the sentence with no problem.

Pragmatics

What does it mean to "know a language"—to "know English," for example? It should be clear by now that the answer has many parts. Any competent language user needs somehow to know (and obey) a rich set of rules about how (and whether) elements can be combined. Language users rely on a further set of principles whenever they perceive and understand linguistic inputs. Some of these principles are rooted in syntax; others depend on semantics; still others depend on prosody. All these factors then seem to interact, so that your understanding of the sentences you hear (or see in print) is guided by all these principles at the same time.

These points, however, still *understate* the complexity of language use and, with that, the complexity of the knowledge someone must have in order to use a language. This point becomes clear when we consider language use at levels beyond the hierarchy shown in Figure 10.1—for example, when we consider language as it's used in ordinary conversation. As an illustration, imagine that someone asks you, "Do you know the time?" You'll understand this as a request that you report what time it actually is—even though the question, understood literally, is a yes/no question about the extent of your temporal knowledge.

Once again, though, this is a setting in which we encounter *rules*— **pragmatic rules**, rules that govern how people actually use language. Years ago, philosopher Paul Grice described these rules in terms of a series of "maxims" that speakers follow and listeners count on (Grice, 1989). The "maxim of relation," for example, says that speakers should say things that are relevant to the conversation. For example, imagine that someone asks, "What happened to the roast beef?" and gets a reply, "The dog sure looks happy." Here, your assumption of relevance will most likely lead you to infer that the dog must have stolen the meat. Likewise, the "maxim of quantity" specifies that a speaker shouldn't be more informative than is necessary. On this point, imagine that you ask someone, "What color are your eyes?" and he responds, "My left eye is blue." The extra detail here invites you to assume that the speaker specified "left eye" for a reason—and so you'll probably infer that the person's right eye is some other color. In these ways, listeners count on speakers to be cooperative and collaborative, and speakers proceed knowing that listeners make these assumptions. (For more on the collaborative nature of conversation, see Andor, 2011; Clark, 1996; Davis & Friedman, 2007; Holtgraves, 2002; Noveck & Reboul, 2008; Noveck & Sperber, 2005).

Conversations and Common Ground

The maxims just described apply specifically to language use; they are, in effect, part of your "language knowledge." But your ability to use language also depends on knowledge separate from language itself. This knowledge is seamlessly interwoven with your knowledge of phonemes, morphemes, and syntax—a point that once again calls attention to the complexity of language use.

We saw one example way back in Chapter 1, when we noted the importance of background knowledge in your understanding of a simple story. (It was the story that began, "Betsy wanted to bring Jacob a present . . ."; see pp. 5–6.) In order to understand that story, you needed to draw on your knowledge about gift-giving, piggy banks, and more. Without that knowledge, the story would have been incomprehensible.

The same point can be made about conversations. Consider, for example, this bit of dialogue (after Pinker, 1994; also see Gernsbacher & Kaschak, 2013; Graesser & Forsyth, 2013; Zwaan, 2016):

Woman: I'm leaving you.

Man: Who is he?

TEST YOURSELF

12. "What happened to the roast beef?" "The dog sure looks happy." Explain what happened in this conversational exchange, and how the exchange will be understood.

You easily provide the soap-opera script that lies behind this exchange, but you do so by drawing on a fabric of additional knowledge—in this case, knowledge about the vicissitudes of romance.

Examples like these are easy to find, because speakers routinely skip past points they regard as obvious and count on the listener to fill in the bits that aren't overtly expressed. And the filling-in usually goes smoothly, thanks to the fact that people in a conversation are likely to have similar beliefs and make similar assumptions. In other words, the filling-in is successful because the participants in the conversation draw on their **common ground**—beliefs shared by the conversational partners. (For early statements of this point, see Clark, 1996; Holtgraves, 2002.)

Often, early stages of a conversation serve to *establish* common ground—with speakers reminding each other of shared beliefs, settling on what terms they'll use, and specifying names so that, later in the conversation, they'll know who's meant by the pronouns "he" or "she" or "they." Finding common ground, however, can be difficult if the conversational participants have different backgrounds or different views about the nature of their conversation; and in the absence of common ground, miscommunication is common. This point highlights the danger of misunderstanding when (for example) a physician is talking with a patient or a police officer is interrogating a suspect. In the former situation, the misunderstanding can leave the patient confused and ill-informed, potentially causing health problems down the road. In the latter situation, the miscommunication may actually be deliberate, so that the suspect does not realize what the police officer knows or what the officer intends to do (e.g., Luke & Alceste, 2020).

Questions about common ground are also relevant to a concern that is common on many university campuses—accusations of sexual assault. In some (but certainly not all) of these cases, the sexual partners genuinely misunderstood each other—with one partner convinced that consent was given, and the other partner convinced that there had been a clear statement of refusal. This catastrophic misunderstanding is made more likely by the fact that much of the communication around intimacy is nonverbal, and also the fact that refusal is often framed in gentle terms, perhaps because the refuser fears the outcome of a more direct refusal. But the risk of misunderstanding is also encouraged by a lack of common ground—with the two partners in the conversation often having different beliefs and perspectives, including beliefs rooted in gender stereotypes and myths about sexual intentions and sexual behavior. (For discussion, see Davis & Loftus, 2015; Lee et al., 2020; Reisberg & Heuer, 2020.)

The Biological Roots of Language

Each of us uses language all the time—to learn, to instruct, to persuade, to express affection. We use language both for idle chitchat and for deeply consequential conversations. We use this tool as easily as we breathe; we spend far more effort in choosing our clothes in the morning than we do in choosing the words we will speak. But these observations must not hide the facts that language is a remarkably complicated tool and that we are all exquisitely skilled in its use.

How is all of this possible? How is it that ordinary human beings—including young children—manage the extraordinary task of mastering and using language? According to many authors, the answer lies in the fact that humans are equipped with sophisticated neural machinery specialized for language use. Let's take a quick look at this machinery.

Aphasias

As we described at the chapter's start, damage to specific parts of the brain can cause a disruption of language known as aphasia. (We first met this form of brain damage in Chapter 2.) Damage to the brain's left frontal lobe, especially a region known as **Broca's area** (see **Figure 10.11**), usually produces a pattern of symptoms known as **nonfluent aphasia**. People with this disorder

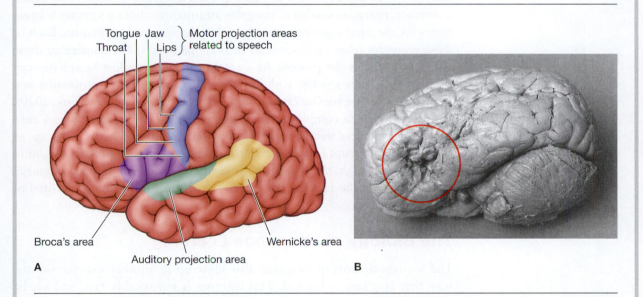

FIGURE 10.11   SOME OF THE BRAIN AREAS CRUCIAL FOR THE PERCEPTION AND PRODUCTION OF LANGUAGE

Tongue Jaw } Motor projection areas
Throat   Lips } related to speech

Broca's area

Auditory projection area

A

Wernicke's area

B

Panel A shows some of the many brain regions that are crucial in supporting the comprehension and production of language. For most individuals, most of these regions are in the left cerebral hemisphere (as shown here). Broca's area (named after the physician Paul Broca) is heavily involved in language production; Wernicke's area (named after the physician Karl Wernicke) plays a crucial role in language comprehension. Panel B shows a photograph of the actual brain of Broca's patient "Tan." Because of his brain damage, this patient was no longer able to say anything other than the syllable "Tan"—leading to the nickname that's often used for him. This pattern (along with observations gained through Tan's autopsy) led Broca to propose that a specific brain region is crucial for speech.

can understand language they hear but cannot write or speak. In extreme cases, a patient with this disorder cannot utter any words at all. In less severe cases, only a part of the patient's vocabulary is lost, but the patient's speech becomes labored and fragmented. One early study quoted a patient with aphasia as saying, "Here . . . head . . . operation . . . here . . . speech . . . none . . . talking . . . what . . . illness" (Luria, 1966, p. 406).

Different symptoms are associated with damage to a brain site known as **Wernicke's area** (again see Figure 10.11). Patients with this sort of damage usually suffer from a pattern known as **fluent aphasia**. These patients can talk freely, but they say very little. One patient, for example, uttered, "I was over the other one, and then after they had been in the department, I was in this one" (Geschwind, 1970, p. 904). Or another patient: "Oh, I'm taking the word the wrong way to say, all of the barbers here whenever they stop you it's going around and around, if you know what I mean, that is tying and tying for repucer, repucuration, well, we were trying the best that we could while another time it was with the beds over there the same thing" (Gardner, 1974, p. 68).

This distinction between fluent and nonfluent aphasia, however, captures the data only in the broadest sense. One reason lies in the fact that—as we've seen—language use involves the coordination of many different processes. These include processes needed to "look up" word meanings in your "mental dictionary," processes needed to figure out the structural relationships within a sentence, processes needed to integrate information about a sentence's structure with the meanings of the words within the sentence, and so on. Each of these processes relies on its own set of brain pathways, and damage to those pathways disrupts the process. As a result, the language loss in aphasia can sometimes be quite specific, with impairment just to a specific processing step (for a broad review, see Gazzaniga et al., 2019; also Fedorenko & Blank, 2020).

Even with these complexities, the point here is that humans have a considerable amount of neural tissue that is specialized for language. Damage to this tissue can disrupt language understanding, language production, or both. In all cases, though, the data make it clear that our skill in using language rests in part on the fact that we have a lot of neural apparatus devoted to precisely this task.

The Biology of Language Learning

The biological roots of language also show up in another manner—in the way that language is learned. This learning is remarkably fast, and so, by 3 or 4 years of age, almost every child is able to converse at a reasonable level. Moreover, this learning can proceed in an astonishingly wide range of environments. Children who talk a lot with adults learn language, and so do children who talk very little with adults. How should we think about this? The answer may lie in highly sophisticated learning capacities that have specifically evolved for language learning. Support for this notion comes from many sources, including observations of **specific-language impairment (SLI)**. Children with this disorder have normal intelligence but, even so, are slow to learn language and, throughout their lives, have difficulty in understanding and producing many sentences. They also perform poorly on tasks designed to test linguistic knowledge. They have difficulty, for example, completing passages like this one: "I like to blife. Tomorrow I will blife. Yesterday I did the same thing. Yesterday I _____." Most 4-year-olds know that the answer is "Yesterday I blifed." But adults with SLI cannot do this task—apparently having failed to learn the simple principle involved in forming the past tense of regular verbs (Bishop & Norbury, 2008; van der Lely & Pinker, 2014).

Sign Language

The human capacity for language is also evident in another way: the fact that children learn language even if their communication with adults is strictly limited. Evidence on this point comes from children who are born deaf and have no opportunity to learn sign language. (In some cases, this is because their caretakers don't know how to sign; in other cases, it's because the caretakers choose not to teach signing.) Even in these extreme cases, language emerges: Children in this situation *invent* their own gestural language (called "home sign") and teach the language to the people in their surroundings (Goldin-Meadow, 2003, 2017; Senghas et al., 2006).

Most users of sign language, however, don't rely on "home sign." Instead, they use one of the conventional sign languages (such as American Sign Language, or ASL), learned through communication with other signers. No matter which sign language we examine, though, it's clear that sign languages are truly languages—with all the richness and complexity of oral languages. Indeed, sign languages show most of the fundamental properties of language that we have discussed in this chapter—with a hierarchical organization like the one depicted in Figure 10.1, a complex grammar, and so on.

The Active Nature of Language Learning

To understand language learning, though, we need to acknowledge the obvious fact that children who grow up in Paris learn to speak French; children who grow up in Beijing learn to speak Mandarin. It's plain, therefore, that

SIGN LANGUAGE

Across the globe, humans speak many different languages—English, Hindi, Mandarin, Quechua, to name just a few. Many humans, though, communicate through sign language. Actually, there are multiple sign languages, and so, for example, American Sign Language (ASL) is quite different from South African Sign Language or Danish Sign Language.

language learning depends on the child picking up information from his or her environment. But what learning mechanisms are involved here?

Part of the answer rests on the fact that children are exquisitely sensitive to patterns and regularities in what they hear, as though each child were an astute statistician, keeping track of the frequency-of-occurrence of this form or that. (For an example in young infants, see Aslin et al., 1998; Marcus et al., 1999; Saffran, 2003; Xu & Garcia, 2008.) Children also seem to derive broad principles from what they hear. Consider, for example, how English-speaking children learn to form the past tense. Initially, they proceed in a word-by-word fashion, so they memorize that the past tense of "play" is "played," the past tense of "climb" is "climbed," and so on. By age 3 or so, however, children seem to realize that they don't have to memorize each word's past tense as a separate vocabulary item. Instead, they realize they can produce the past tense by manipulating morphemes—that is, by adding the "-ed" ending onto a word. This is, of course, an important discovery for children, because this principle enables them to generate the past tense for new verbs, ones they've never encountered before.

However, children over-rely on this pattern, and their speech at this age contains **overregularization errors**: They say things like "Yesterday we goed" or "Yesterday I runned." The same thing happens with other morphemes, so that children of this age also overgeneralize their use of the plural ending—they say things like "I have two foots" or "I lost three tooths" (Marcus et al., 1992).

It seems, then, that children are keenly sensitive to patterns in the language that they're learning, and they're able to figure out the principles that govern these patterns. In addition, language learning relies on a theme that has been in view throughout this chapter: Language has many elements (syntax, semantics, phonology, prosody, etc.), and these elements interact in ordinary language use (so that you rely on a sentence's syntactic form to figure out its meaning; you rely on semantic cues in deciphering the syntax). In the same way, language learning relies on all these elements in an interacting fashion. For example, children rely on prosody (the rise and fall of pitch, the pattern of timing) as clues to syntax, and adults speaking to children helpfully exaggerate these prosodic signals, easing the children's interpretive burden. Children also rely on their vocabulary, listening for words they already know as clues helping them to process more complex strings. Likewise, children rely on their knowledge of semantic relationships as a basis for figuring out syntax. In this way, the very complexity of language is both a burden for the child (because there's so much to learn in "learning a language") and an aid (because the child can use each element as a source of information in trying to figure out the other elements).

Animal Language

We've suggested that humans are biologically prepared for language learning, and this claim has many implications. Among other points, if language learning is somehow tied to human biology, then we might expect *not* to find language capacity in other species. Of course, many species do have sophisticated communication systems—including the songs and clicks of whales, the dances of honeybees, and the various alarm calls of monkeys. These naturally occurring systems, however, are limited—with small vocabularies and little (or perhaps nothing) that corresponds to the rules of syntax that are evident in human language. These other species certainly have nothing that resembles our capacity to produce or understand an unending variety of new sentences.

Perhaps, though, these naturally occurring systems understate what animals can do. Perhaps animals can do more if only we help them a bit. To explore this issue, researchers have tried to train animals to use more sophisticated forms of communication. Some researchers have tried to train dolphins to communicate with humans; one project involved an African gray parrot; other projects have focused on primates—asking what a chimpanzee, gorilla, or bonobo might be capable of. The results from these studies are impressive, but it's notable that the greatest success involves animals that are quite similar to humans genetically (e.g., Savage-Rumbaugh & Fields, 2000; Savage-Rumbaugh & Lewin, 1994). For example, Kanzi, a male bonobo, seems to understand icons on a keyboard as *symbols* that refer to other ideas, and he also has some mastery of syntax—so he responds differently and (usually) appropriately, using stuffed animals, to the instructions "Make the doggie bite the snake" or "Make the snake bite the doggie."

Kanzi's abilities, though, after an enormous amount of careful training, are way below those of the average 3- or 4-year-old human who has received no explicit language training. (For example, as impressive as Kanzi is, he hasn't mastered the distinction between present, past, and future tense, although every human child effortlessly learns this basic aspect of language.) Therefore, it seems that other species (especially those closely related to us) can learn the rudiments of language, but nothing in their performance undercuts the amazing differences between human language capacity and that in other organisms.

"Wolf Children"

It does seem, then, that human biology gives us a fabulous start on language learning. To turn this "start" into "language capacity," however, we also need a communicative partner.

In 1920, villagers in India discovered a wolf mother in her den together with four cubs. Two were baby wolves, but two were human children, subsequently named Kamala and Amala. No one knows how they got there or why the wolf adopted them. Roger Brown (1958) tells us what these children were like:

> Kamala was about eight years old and Amala was only one and one-half. They were thoroughly wolfish in appearance and behavior: Hard callus had developed on their knees and palms from going on all fours. Their teeth were sharp edged. They moved their nostrils sniffing food.

COMMUNICATION AMONG VERVET MONKEYS

Animals of many species communicate with one another. For example, Vervet monkeys give alarm calls when they spot a nearby predator. But they have distinct alarm calls for different types of predator—so their call when they see a leopard is different from their call when they see an eagle or a python. The fact remains, though, that no naturally occurring animal communication system comes close to human language in richness or complexity.

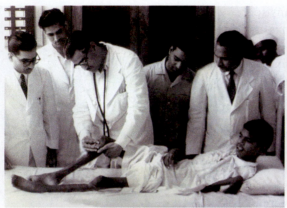
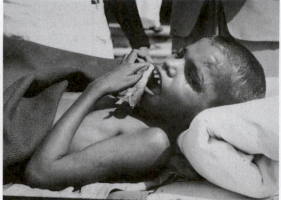

A MODERN WILD BOY

Ramu, a young boy discovered in India in 1976, appears to have been raised by wolves. He was deformed—apparently from lying in cramped positions, as in a den. He couldn't walk, and he drank by lapping with his tongue. His favorite food was raw meat, which he seemed to be able to smell at a distance. After he was found, he lived at the home for destitute children run by Mother Teresa in Lucknow, Uttar Pradesh. He learned to bathe and dress himself but never learned to speak. He continued to prefer raw meat and would often sneak out to prey upon fowl in the neighbor's chicken coop. Ramu died at the age of about 10 in February 1985.

Eating and drinking were accomplished by lowering their mouths to the plate. They ate raw meat. . . . At night they prowled and sometimes howled. They shunned other children but followed the dog and cat. They slept rolled up together on the floor. . . . Amala died within a year but Kamala lived to be eighteen. . . . In time, Kamala learned to walk erect, to wear clothing, and even to speak a few words. (p. 100)

The outcome was similar for the 30 or so other wild children for whom researchers have evidence. None could be rehabilitated to use language normally, although some (like Kamala) did learn to speak a few words. Of course, the data from these wild children are difficult to interpret, partly because we don't know why the children were abandoned in the first place. (Is it possible that these children were abandoned because their human parents detected some birth defect? If so, these children may have been impaired in their functioning from the start.) Nonetheless, the consistency of these findings underscores an important point: Language learning may depend on both a human genome and a human environment.

Language and Thought

Virtually every human knows and uses a language. But it's also important that people use *different* languages. Some of us speak English, others German, and still others Abkhaz or Choctaw or Kanuri or Quanzhou; some of us use some form of sign language. How do these differences matter? Is it possible

TEST YOURSELF

13. What is aphasia?
14. What are overregularization errors?
15. What do we learn from the fact that so-called wolf children never gain full language proficiency?

Many people believe that the native peoples of the far north (including the Inuit) have an enormous number of terms for various forms of snow and are correspondingly skilled in discriminating types of snow. It turns out, though, that the initial claim (the number of terms for snow) is wrong; the Inuit have roughly the same number of snow terms as do people living further south. (For debate about this issue, though, see Robson, 2012.) In addition, if the Inuit people are more skilled in discriminating snow types, is this because of the language that they speak? Or is it because their day-to-day lives require that they stay alert to the differences among snow types? (AFTER ROBERSON ET AL., 2000)

that people who speak different languages end up being different in their thought processes?

Linguistic Relativity

The notion that language shapes thought is generally attributed to the anthropologist Benjamin Lee Whorf and is often referred to as the Whorfian hypothesis. Whorf (e.g., 1956) argued that the language you speak forces you into certain modes of thought. He claimed, therefore, that people who speak different languages inevitably *think* differently—a claim of **linguistic relativity**.

To test this claim, one line of work has examined how people perceive colors, building on the fact that some languages have many terms for colors (red, orange, mauve, puce, salmon, ocher, etc.) and others have few (see **Figure 10.12**). Do these differences among languages affect perception? Evidence suggests, in fact, that people who speak languages with a richer color vocabulary are able to make finer and more sharply defined distinctions among the various hues (Özgen, 2004; Roberson et al., 2000; Winawer et al., 2007).

Other studies have focused on the fact that some languages emphasize absolute directions (terms like the English words "east" or "west" that are defined independently of which way the speaker is facing at the moment). Other languages emphasize relative directions (words like "right" or "left" that do depend on which way the speaker is facing). Research suggests that these language differences can lead to corresponding differences in how people remember—and perhaps how they perceive—position (Majid et al., 2004; Pederson et al., 1998).

Languages also differ in how they describe events. In English, we tend to use active-voice sentences that name the agent of the action, even if the action was accidental ("Sam made a mistake"). It sounds awkward or evasive to describe these events in other terms ("Mistakes were made"). In other languages, including Japanese and Spanish, it's common *not* to mention the

FIGURE 10.12 COLORS IN DIFFERENT LANGUAGES

English naming

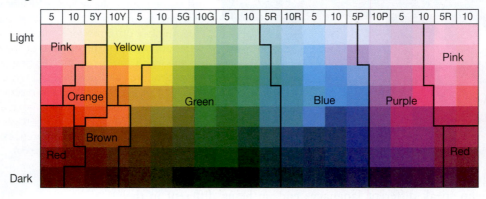

Berinmo naming

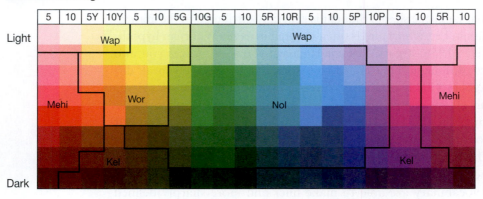

The Berinmo people, living in Papua New Guinea, have only five words for describing colors, and so, for example, they use a single word ("nol") to describe colors that English speakers call "green" and colors we call "blue." (The letters and numbers in these panels refer to a system often used for classifying colors.) These differences, from one language to the next, have an impact on how people perceive and remember colors. This effect is best understood in terms of attention: Language can draw our attention to some aspect of the world and in this way can shape our experience and, therefore, our cognition. (AFTER ROBERSON ET AL., 2000)

agent for an accidental event, and this in turn can shape memory: After viewing videos of accidental events, Japanese and Spanish speakers are less likely than English speakers to remember the person who triggered the accident (Boroditsky, 2011).

How should we think about all these results? Whorf's notion was that language has a direct impact on cognition, so that the categories recognized by your language become the categories used in your thought. In this view, language has a unique effect on cognition (because no other factor shapes cognition in this way), and as a result, language's influence is irreversible: Once your language has led you to think in certain ways, you will forever think in those ways. From this perspective, then, there are literally some ideas that, say, a Japanese speaker can contemplate but an English speaker cannot, and vice versa—and likewise, say, for a Hopi or a French speaker, or for someone who uses sign.

A different possibility is more modest—and more plausible: The language you hear often guides what you pay attention to, and what you pay attention to shapes your thinking. In this view, language does have an influence, but the influence is indirect: The influence works *via* the mechanisms of attention. Why is this distinction (direct effect vs. indirect effect) important? The key is that other factors can also guide your attention, with the result that in many settings these factors will erase any effects that language might have. Put differently, the idea here is that your language might bias your attention in one way, but other factors will bias your attention in the opposite way—canceling out language's impact. On this basis, the effects of language on cognition might easily be reversible, and certainly not as fundamental as Whorf proposed.

To see how this point plays out, let's look at a concrete case. We've mentioned that when English speakers describe an event, our language usually requires that we name (and so pay attention to) the actor who caused the event; when Spanish speakers describe the same event, their language doesn't have this requirement, and so it doesn't force them to think about the actor. In this way, the structure of each language influences what each person will pay attention to, and the data tell us that this difference in focus has consequences for thinking and for memory.

But we could, if we wished, simply give the Spanish speakers an instruction: "Pay attention to the actor." Or we could make sure that the actor is wearing a brightly colored coat, using a perceptual cue to guide attention. These simple steps can (and often do) offset the bias created by language.

The logic is similar for the effect of language on color perception. If you're a speaker of Berinmo (a language spoken in New Guinea), your language makes no distinction between "green" and "blue," so it never leads you to think about these as separate categories. If you're an English speaker, your language does make this distinction, and this can draw your attention to what all green objects have in common and what all blue objects have in common. If your attention is drawn to this point again and again, you'll gain familiarity with the distinction and eventually become better at making the distinction. Once more, therefore, language does matter—but it matters because of language's impact on attention. (For another example, exploring how the impact of grammatical *gender* is dependent on the context and the task, see Samuel et al., 2019.)

These points do not in any way undermine the claim that language can shape thought. It can. As one more example, research suggests that using *nouns* to describe a specific event can call your attention to the action that defines the event, while using the corresponding *verb* calls attention to the actors. This is likely the reason why, in one study, Israeli citizens expressed less anger when asked whether they would support the "division of Jerusalem," compared to other citizens asked whether they would support "dividing Jerusalem" (Idan et al., 2018).

Similarly, language can shape thought by placing an idea within one framework rather than another. In one study, participants read a paragraph about a city dealing with a high crime rate. Half the participants read that "crime is a wild beast preying on" the city; others read that "crime is a virus infecting" the city. This choice of metaphor had a powerful effect: If they'd read about crime-as-beast, few participants (only 26%) thought that social reform was needed; most (74%) thought that increased enforcement was the better path forward. But if they'd read about crime-as-virus, the number of participants inclined toward social reform almost doubled (to 44%); now only 56% opted for increased enforcement (Thibodeau & Boroditsky, 2011).

Undeniably, then, language (whether it's the specific choice of words or a particular metaphor) influences how and what we think. What is at issue, though, is *how* language has its effect. If (as Whorf claimed) language directly and uniquely shapes thought, then the effects of language on cognition will be systematic and permanent. But the evidence favors an alternative view— that it's your *experience* that shapes thought. Your experience, of course, depends on what you pay attention to, and language often guides attention. But language is just one of the factors guiding what you pay attention to, and on this basis, the effects of language will often be offset by other influences. (For more on these issues, see Lupyan et al., 2020.)

To recap: More than a half-century ago, Whorf argued for a strong claim—that the language people speak has a lifelong impact, determining what people can or cannot think, what ideas they can or cannot consider. There is an element of truth here, because language can and does shape cognition. But language's impact is neither profound nor permanent, and there is no reason to accept Whorf's ambitious proposal.

Bilingualism

There's one more—and intriguing—way that language is said to influence cognition. It comes from cases in which someone knows more than one language.

Children raised in bilingual homes generally learn both languages quickly and well (Kovelman et al., 2008). Early in language development, bilingual children do tend to have smaller vocabularies than monolingual children, but bilingual children soon catch up on this dimension (Bialystok et al., 2009). These findings surprise many people, on the expectation that bilingual children would become confused—blurring together their languages and getting mixed up about which words and which rules belong in each language. But this confusion seems not to occur.

In fact, researchers have explored the possibility that children raised bilingually develop specific skills that help them avoid confusing their two languages—so that they develop a skill of (say) turning off their French-based habits in *this* setting so that they can speak uncompromised English, and then turning off their English-based habits in *that* setting so that they can speak fluent French. This skill would obviously support language learning, but some researchers proposed that the same skill would also help bilingual children in other settings. The idea was that bilinguals might, in general, end up better at switching between competing tasks or avoiding various types of distraction.

Some early findings seemed to confirm this bilingual advantage, but these findings have not held up in more recent studies. (For glimpses of the evidence, see Bialystok & Grundy, 2018; Goldsmith & Morton, 2018; Gunnerud et al., 2020; Hartanto & Yang, 2019, 2020; Lehtonen et al., 2018; Nichols et al., 2020.) At best, this advantage seems to emerge only with certain tasks or in certain age groups (perhaps in children, but not adults). Further research is needed in this domain, but in the meantime, bilingualism provides another arena in which scholars continue to explore the ways in which language may shape cognition.

TEST YOURSELF

16. What does it mean to say that language's effects on cognition are *indirect* and *reversible*?

COGNITIVE PSYCHOLOGY AND TECHNOLOGY

the "vocabulary" of texting?

For roughly 100 years, the telegraph was the principal way people communicated across great distances. Sending messages by telegraph was, however, rather expensive, with the price dependent on the number of words. People therefore developed a style of communication, sometimes called "telegraphese," that used as few words as possible.

Now, in the 21st century, a different form of communication has become prominent—texting, and here, too, there is a corresponding style of communication. Texting very rapidly led to a series of widely used abbreviations: LOL. TMI. G2G. ROFL. IMO. Even the activity of texting gained its own abbreviation, and so people often communicate with a "DM."

People sometimes refer to these abbreviations as the "vocabulary" of texting, but is this the right label? The answer has to be tentative because the way people text, and the platforms used for texting, are constantly changing. As a result, anything we say here could soon be out of date. Even so, we can offer a few points that may help to illustrate what "words" are and what "language" is.

The abbreviation TMI is particularly useful—efficiently capturing in three letters a notion that might otherwise require many words: "This is more information than I want, perhaps because it's private, or just something I'd really prefer not to think about, and so I wish you hadn't expressed what you just expressed." Unpacked in this way, this abbreviation isn't itself a word to be used within some language; it is instead the expression of a rather complex proposition!

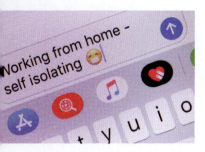

LANGUAGE EVOLUTION

The chapter notes that languages evolve as time goes by. The same is true for emojis. New technology has an effect (so that animated emojis are now common), and the broader world also has an impact—leading, for example, to emojis responding to the COVID-19 pandemic.

But could TMI *become* a word? (And, again, this is an issue for which anything that's written here could soon be out of date; perhaps TMI is already a word.) One option is that TMI could become a verb: "I'm so tired of him TMI-ing." "I can't believe he TMI-ed me again." "The moment she's had a couple of beers, she's likely to TMI." You have no difficulty understanding these sentences, and this reminds us of the fact that languages are dynamic—routinely adding new forms. Notice also the role of function morphemes. The chapter notes that words like "singing" and "walked" each have two parts—a content morpheme and then a function morpheme tagged onto it. The advantage of this separation becomes clear when we realize that the function morphemes are separate units that can freely be combined with other content morphemes. The moment "TMI" becomes a verb, therefore, it can be modified with the "ing" or "ed" ending, allowing a speaker (or a texter) to talk about this activity as ongoing (TMI-ing) or in the past tense (TMI-ed).

What about emojis? These pictures are a prominent part of texting, as people add images of smiley faces, clapping hands, and various vegetables onto their messages. So far, these emojis seem to function as free standing propositions—and so you probably have no trouble decoding emojis that convey messages like "I'm disappointed but relieved," "You did a great job," or "Okay, got it." It's easy to imagine, though, that the heart emoji or the fire emoji might become a word on its own and used in broader sentences. (You've surely seen the bumper stickers already: "I ♥ my cat," or some such.) This sort of "lexicalization," though, seems less likely for, say, the emoji of a face with tears of joy.

Finally, there's also been some discussion of what the use of texting might do to the broader language. Some critics have worried that the popularity of texting may erode people's ability to spell properly; this seems, however, more an issue of language "evolution" rather than language "erosion." Other people have suggested that texting may help people who might be dyslexic; little research so far explores this issue. Perhaps most important, we need to bear in mind that people who text will also continue to *talk to each other*, aside from their communication via smartphone or tablet. If so, it seems unlikely that texting will cut deeply into the complexity and power of human language.

For more on this topic . . .

Grace, A., Kemp, N., Martin, F. H., & Parrila, R. (2013). Undergraduates' text messaging language and literacy skills. *Reading and Writing, 27*, 855–873.

Kemp, N., & Clayton, J. (2017). University students vary their use of textese in digital messages to suit the recipient. *Journal of Research in Reading, 40*(S1), S141–S157.

Tagg, C. (2015). *Exploring digital communication: Language in action.* New York, NY: Routledge.

Verheijen, L. (2013). The effects of text messaging and instant messaging on literacy. *English Studies, 94*(5), 582–602.

Wood, C., Kemp, N., & Plester, B. (2014). *Text messaging and literacy: The evidence.* New York, NY: Routledge.

chapter review

SUMMARY

- All speech is built up from a few dozen phonemes, although the selection of phonemes varies from language to language. Phonemes, in turn, are built up from a small number of production features: voicing, place of articulation, and manner of production. Phonemes can be combined to form more complex sounds, but combinations are constrained by a number of rules.

- Speech perception is more than a matter of detecting the relevant features in the input sound stream. Perceivers also need to deal with speaker-to-speaker variation in how sounds are produced; they also need to segment the stream of speech and cope with coarticulation. The process of speech perception is helped enormously by context, but we also have the impressive skill of categorical perception, which makes us keenly sensitive to differences between categories of speech sounds but insensitive to distinctions within each category.

- People know many thousands of words, and for each one they know the sound of the word, its syntactic role, and its semantic representation. Our understanding of words is also generative, enabling us to create limitless numbers of new words. Some new words are wholly made up (e.g., "geek"), but many new words are shortened versions of existing words ("paleo diet") or combinations of existing morphemes ("sponcon").

- The rules of syntax govern whether a sequence of words is grammatical. One set of rules governs phrase structure, and the word groups identified by these rules do correspond to natural groupings of words. Phrase-structure rules also guide interpretation. Like all the rules discussed in this chapter, though, phrase-structure rules are descriptive, not prescriptive.

- To understand a sentence, a listener or reader needs to parse the sentence, determining each word's syntactic role. Evidence suggests that people parse a sentence as they see or hear each word, and this approach sometimes leads them into parsing errors that must be repaired later; this outcome is revealed by garden-path sentences. Parsing is guided by syntax, semantics, and the extralinguistic context.

- In understanding conversation, perceivers rely on pragmatic rules. Perceivers also make inferences to fill in bits that are left unspoken in the conversation, relying on the common ground that they share with their conversational partner.

- The biological roots of language are revealed in many ways. The study of aphasia makes it clear that some areas of the brain are specialized for learning and using language. The rapid learning of language also supports the biological basis for language.

- Children are extremely sensitive to patterns in the language that they hear. Children also seem to derive general principles that enable them to create new forms; this is evident in children's overregularization errors. Children can also use their understanding of one aspect of language (e.g., phonology or vocabulary) to help learn about other aspects (e.g., syntax).

- There has been considerable discussion about the ways in which thought might be shaped by the language one speaks. Language certainly guides and influences your thoughts, and the way a thought is formulated into words can have an effect on how you think about the thought's content. In addition, language can call your attention to a category or to a distinction, which makes it likely that you will have experience in thinking about the category or distinction. This experience, in turn, can promote fluency in these thoughts. However, these effects are not unique to language (because other factors can also draw your attention to the category), nor are they irreversible. As a result, there is no evidence that language can shape what you *can* think.

- Research shows that children raised in bilingual homes learn both languages as quickly and as well as monolingual children learning their single language. In fact, bilingual children seem to develop an impressive ability to switch between languages, although the evidence is not clear on whether this ability helps them in other settings that require control of mental processes.

KEY TERMS

sentence (p. 345)
morpheme (p. 345)
phoneme (p. 345)
voicing (p. 346)
manner of production (p. 346)
place of articulation (p. 347)
speech segmentation (p. 349)
coarticulation (p. 350)
phonemic restoration effect (p. 350)
categorical perception (p. 351)
generativity (p. 356)
syntax (p. 356)
phrase-structure rules (p. 358)
tree structure (p. 358)
prescriptive rules (p. 358)

descriptive rules (p. 359)
parse (p. 361)
garden-path sentence (p. 363)
extralinguistic context (p. 365)
prosody (p. 366)
pragmatic rules (p. 367)
common ground (p. 368)
Broca's area (p. 369)
nonfluent aphasia (p. 369)
Wernicke's area (p. 370)
fluent aphasia (p. 370)
specific-language impairment (SLI) (p. 370)
overregularization error (p. 372)
linguistic relativity (p. 375)

TEST YOURSELF AGAIN

1. What are morphemes? What are phonemes?

2. Define "voicing," "manner of production," and "place of articulation."

3. What is speech segmentation, and why is it an important step in speech perception?

4. What is categorical perception?

5. Why is it difficult to give an exact count of the number of words in someone's vocabulary?

6. What evidence tells us that the rules of syntax can be separated from considerations of whether or not a string of words has meaning?

7. What are phrase-structure rules, and what does it mean that these rules are "descriptive," not "prescriptive"?

8. What's the evidence that *multiple factors* play a role in guiding how you parse a sentence?

9. What is a garden-path sentence?

10. What is prosody?

11. Why are printed versions of garden-path sentences more likely to puzzle you, compared to spoken versions of the same sentences?

12. "What happened to the roast beef?" "The dog sure looks happy." Explain what happened in this conversational exchange, and how the exchange will be understood.

13. What is aphasia?

14. What are overregularization errors?

15. What do we learn from the fact that so-called wolf children never gain full language proficiency?

16. What does it mean to say that language's effects on cognition are *indirect* and *reversible*?

THINK ABOUT IT

1. There is no question that some languages capture, in a single word, ideas that in other languages can only be described with a long phrase. One example is the German word "Schadenfreude," which translates as "a feeling of joy that comes from learning about another person's troubles." Do you think this difference matters for cognition—so that people who know this word can think more efficiently, or more effectively, than people who don't know this word? If so, how is this different from the hypothesis offered years ago by Whorf?

DEMONSTRATIONS & APPLYING COGNITIVE PSYCHOLOGY ESSAYS

For demonstrations of key concepts in cognitive psychology, take a look at the Online Demonstrations. To explore more of the practical applications of cognitive psychology in themed essays, visit the online reader.

Online Demonstrations

- Demonstration 10.1: Phonemes and Subphonemes
- Demonstration 10.2: The Speed of Speech
- Demonstration 10.3: Coarticulation
- Demonstration 10.4: The Most Common Words
- Demonstration 10.5: Patterns in Language
- Demonstration 10.6: Ambiguity
- Demonstration 10.7: Language Use in Jokes

Online Applying Cognitive Psychology Essays

- Cognitive Psychology and Education: Writing
- Cognitive Psychology and Health: Dyslexia
- Cognitive Psychology and the Law: Remembering Conversations
- Cognitive Psychology and the Law: Jury Instructions

ZAPS COGNITION LABS

Go to ZAPS online cognition labs to conduct hands-on experiments on key concepts.

INQUIZITIVE

It's time to complete your study experience! Go to InQuizitive to practice actively with this chapter's concepts and get personalized feedback along the way.

chapter 11

Visual Knowledge

what if... Researchers use many approaches to study *dreams*. The obvious path, though, is simply to ask people about the content of their dreams. For example, consider this exchange. E is the experimenter; S is the person reporting on a dream she'd had about a cancer clinic (Kerr, 1983, p. 276).

S: I was in a room that looked similar to my instant banker at work, but it was a big machine with lots of buttons, like a car machine.

E: Like an instant banker machine?

S: Right, at [name of bank]. And I don't know why I was there, but I guess there was a screen and there were other buttons you could push, you could look in and see how different cancer patients are doing.

E: Was this visual, could you see anything?

S: I couldn't, but I stood by the screen and I knew that *others* could see what was going on through all the little panels.

. . .

S: I guess I imagined the board with the buttons. Maybe because I imagined them in my mind, it was not that I could really see them with my eyes, but I know what that board looks like, and the only reason I know what it looks like is by touch, and I could remember where the buttons were without touching them on the boards.

. . .

E: Okay. Where did the events in this experience seem to be taking place? What were the settings?

S: It seemed to be a large room that was oblong in shape, and there seemed to be an X-ray machine's work. I felt like it was in an office building where I worked.

E: And you mentioned something before about the bank?

S: Uh huh, it looked like the bank where I do my instant banking (E: Okay.), except it was larger and more oblong.

E: And is that more like where you worked?

S: No, where I do work, the room is smaller, just large enough for that little instant banker machine.

. . . .

- In important ways, mental images are picture-like, representing in a direct way the spatial layout of the represented scene. It's not surprising, therefore, that there is considerable overlap between imagery and perception—in how each functions and in their neural bases.

- In addition to visual imagery, people use spatial imagery, which may be represented in the mind in terms of movements or perhaps in some abstract format.

- Although they are picture-like, images (visual or spatial) are not pictures; instead, images seem to be organized in a way that pictures are not.

- Even though images in working memory provide a distinctive form of representation, information about appearances in long-term memory may not be distinctive. In fact, long-term memory for sensory information seems to obey all the principles we described in earlier chapters for verbal or symbolic memories.

This dream report seems in most ways unremarkable—other people, describing their own dreams, offer reports that are similar. What is remarkable, though, is that this report was offered by someone who had been blind since birth.

The dreamer's blindness helps us understand some aspects of this report (e.g., she says that she only knew what the board looked like *by touch*). Close reading also reveals the absence of any "visual" properties in the dream: There are no mentions of colors or visible textures on surfaces. But how should we think about other aspects of the dream? How could she know "what that board *looks like*"? What was it, in the dream, that told her the room was large and oblong?

Questions like these also raise a broader issue: How much of your mental life is shaped by vision? With that, what does it mean for a dream or any other mental content to be "visual"? To approach these issues, let's start with the sort of visual imagery that most sighted people have all the time.

Visual Imagery

You have knowledge of many different types. You know what a fish is, but you also know what a fish looks like and what fish smells like when it's cooking. You know what a guitar is, but you also know what one sounds like. Likewise, people describe their *thoughts* in a variety of ways: Sometimes, they claim, their thoughts seem to be formulated in words. Sometimes their thoughts seem more abstract—a sequence of ideas that lack concrete form. But sometimes, people claim, their thoughts involve a sequence of *pictures* or *sounds* or other sensory impressions.

What can we say about this variety? How are sights or sounds or smells represented in the mind? In this chapter, we'll focus largely on *visual* knowledge and *visual* thoughts (and, for now, our focus will be on sighted individuals, not the blind). As we proceed, though, you should keep an eye on how the questions we're asking might be applied to other forms of nonverbal knowledge.

The Mind's Eye

How many windows are there in your house or apartment? Who has a broader mouth, relative to the shape of her face: Taylor Swift or Ariana Grande? For most people, questions like these seem to elicit "mental pictures." You know what Swift and Grande look like, and you call a "picture" of each woman before your "mind's eye" in order to make the comparison. Likewise, you call to mind a "map" of your apartment and count the windows by inspecting this map. Many people even trace the map in the air when they're counting the windows, moving their finger around to follow the imagined map's contours.

Various practical problems also seem to evoke images. There you are in a store, trying on a new sweater. Will it look good with your blue pants? To decide, you'll probably try to visualize the blue of the pants, using your "mind's eye" to consider how they'll look with the sweater. Similarly, if a friend asks you, "Was David in class yesterday?" you might try to answer by visualizing what the room looked like during the class; is David "visible" in your image?

These examples illustrate the common, everyday use of visual images—as a basis for making decisions, as an aid to remembering. But surely there's no tiny eye somewhere deep in your brain; the phrase "mind's eye" therefore cannot be taken literally. Likewise, mental "pictures" cannot be actual pictures; with no eye deep inside the brain, who or what would inspect such pictures? In light of these puzzles, what *are* images?

Introspections about Images

People have written about imagery (and the "mind's eye") for hundreds of years. The first systematic research, though, was conducted in the late 1800s by Francis Galton. Galton was Charles Darwin's cousin, but he was also extraordinary on his own. Among other achievements, he devised the first weather map, developed a system for analyzing fingerprints in criminal investigations, and invented the silent dog whistle.[1]

Galton was particularly interested in how people differ from one another, and as part of his inquiry he explored the nature of visual imagery. His method was straightforward: He asked various people simply to describe their images and rate them for vividness (Galton, 1883). In other words, he asked his research participants to *introspect*, or "look within"

---

1. We should acknowledge the darker elements of Galton's intellectual work. Galton played a major role, for example, in launching the eugenics movement—a movement that has had a succession of horrific consequences, including many racist policies.

(a method that we first met in Chapter 1), and to report on their own mental contents.

The **self-report data** that Galton obtained fit well with common sense. Many of his participants reported that they could "inspect" their images much as they would inspect a picture, and their descriptions made it clear that they were "viewing" their images from a certain position and a certain distance—just as they'd look at an actual scene from a specific viewing perspective. They also reported that they could "read off" from the image details of color and texture. All of this implies a mode of representation that is, in many ways, picture-like—and this is, of course, consistent with our informal manner of describing mental images as "pictures in the head," to be inspected with the "mind's eye."

There was, however, another side of these early data, because many of Galton's participants actually seemed *incapable* of forming a visual image. They had no difficulty thinking about the scenes Galton named for them, but they insisted that in no sense were they "seeing" these scenes. When they described their "images," their reports were completely devoid of visual qualities—with no mention of color or size or viewing perspective.

These observations suggest that people differ in their capacity for visual imagery— so that some people are "visualizers" and others are not. But, if so, what consequences does this have? What tasks can visualizers do that "non-visualizers" cannot (or vice versa)?

Before we can answer these questions, though, we need to address a methodological concern raised by Galton's data, and it's a concern that might have occurred to you right at the start of this chapter, when we talked about dreams in someone who was blind. When a blind person says a room "looked similar" to her bank machine, what does that mean? Surely this person intends something different from what a sighted person would mean when saying the same words. For that matter, blind people routinely talk about "watching TV" or "taking a look at something," and they know that a star "appears" as a small spot in the night sky (Kerr & Domhoff, 2004). These phrases are surely metaphorical when used by the blind, and obviously the subjective experience of someone blind "watching TV" is different from the experience of someone with full vision.

Points like these remind us that there's a "translation step" involved whenever people describe their inner experience with some sort of verbal report, and there's no guarantee that everyone translates in the same way. Returning to Galton's study, it's possible that all of his participants had the *same* imagery skill but varied in how they described their experience (i.e., in how they translated the experience into words). Maybe some were cautious, so they kept their descriptions brief and undetailed; others were more extravagant and took pleasure in providing elaborate reports. In this way, Galton's data might reveal differences in how people *talk about* their imagery, not differences in imagery itself.

To address this concern, we need a more objective means of assessing imagery—one that doesn't rely on the subjectivity inherent in self-reports.

With this more objective approach, we could assess the differences, from one individual to the next, suggested by Galton's data. In fact, with this more objective approach we could hope to find out exactly what images *are*. Let's look at the data, and then, from that base, we'll return to the intriguing differences in imagery experience from one person to the next. This framework will also enable us to address the puzzle we met at the chapter's start: the imagery experience of the blind.

TEST YOURSELF

1. What is the concern about self-report data, and Galton's data in particular?

Chronometric Studies of Imagery

Imagery researchers are keenly sensitive to the concerns we've just described, so they rarely ask participants to *describe* their images. Instead, imagery experiments require people to *do something* with their images—usually, make a judgment based on the image. Researchers can then examine how rapidly people make these judgments, and these measurements can be used to test hypotheses. In other words, many studies are **chronometric** ("time-measuring") **studies**.

Mental Images as "Picture-like"

Consider what would happen if you were asked to *write a paragraph* describing a cat. Most likely you'd mention the distinctive features of cats—their whiskers, their claws, and so on. Your paragraph probably wouldn't include the fact that cats have heads, since this is obvious and not worth mentioning. But now consider what would happen if we ask you to *draw a picture* of a cat. In this format, the cat's head would be rather prominent, simply because the head is relatively large and up front. Claws and whiskers might be less prominent, because these features are small and would take up little space in your drawing.

The point here is that the pattern of *what information is included*, as well as what information is prominent, depends on the mode of presentation. For a description, features that are prominent will be those that are distinctive and strongly associated with the object being described. For a *depiction*, in contrast, size and position will determine what's prominent and what's not.

Against this backdrop, we can ask what information is available in a visual image. Is it the pictorially prominent features, which would imply a depictive mode of representation, or is it the verbally prominent ones, implying a descriptive mode? In an early study by Kosslyn (1976), research participants were asked to form a series of mental images and to answer yes/no questions about each. For example, they were instructed to form a mental image of a cat and then asked: "Does the cat have a head? Does the cat have claws?" Participants responded to these questions quickly, but—crucially—responses to the head question were quicker than those to the claws question. This difference suggests that information readily available in the image follows the rules for pictures, not paragraphs. For comparison, though, a different group of participants was instructed merely to think about cats (with no mention of imagery). These participants, when asked the same questions, gave quicker responses about the claws than about the head—the reverse pattern of the first group. It seems, therefore, that people have the option of thinking about cats via imagery and also the option of thinking about cats without imagery; as the mode of representation changes, so does the pattern of information availability.

In a different experiment, participants were asked to memorize the fictional map shown in **Figure 11.1** and, in particular, to memorize the locations of the various landmarks: the well, the straw hut, and so on (Kosslyn et al., 1978). The experimenters made sure participants had the map memorized by asking them to draw a replica of it from memory; once they could do this, the main experiment began. Participants were asked to form an image of the

FIGURE 11.1   FICTIONAL ISLAND USED IN IMAGE-SCANNING EXPERIMENTS

Participants in the study first memorized this map, including the various landmarks (the hut, the well, the patch of grass, and so on). They then formed a mental image of the map for the scanning procedure.

(AFTER KOSSLYN, 1983)

FIGURE 11.2   SCANNING TIMES IN VISUAL IMAGERY

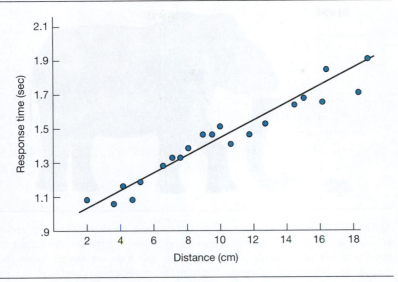

Participants had to "scan" from one point on their mental image to another point; they pressed a button to indicate when their "mind's eye" had arrived at its destination. Response times were closely related to the "distance" participants had to scan across on the image.   (AFTER KOSSLYN, 1983)

island and to point their "mind's eye" at a specific landmark—let's say, the well. Another landmark was then mentioned, perhaps the hut, and participants were asked to imagine a black speck moving in a straight line from the first landmark to the second. When the speck "reached" the target, participants pressed a button, stopping a clock. This action provided a measure of how long the participants needed to "scan" from the well to the hut. The same was done for the well and the tree, and the hut and the patch of grass, so that the researchers ended up with scanning times for each of the various pairs of landmarks.

Figure 11.2 shows the results. The data from this **image-scanning procedure** reveal that participants scan across their images at a constant rate, so that doubling the scanning "distance" doubles the time required for the scan, and tripling the distance triples the time required.

Similar results emerge if participants are given a task that requires them to "zoom in" on their images (e.g., a task that requires them to inspect the image for some small detail) or a task that requires them to "zoom out" (e.g., a task that requires a more global judgment). In these studies, response times are directly proportional to the amount of zoom required, suggesting once again that "travel" in the imaged world resembles travel in the actual world, at least with regard to timing (**Figure 11.3**).

FIGURE 11.3   ZOOMING IN ON MENTAL PICTURES

Just as it takes time to "scan across" a mental image, it also takes time to "zoom in" on one. As a result, participants respond slowly if they're instructed to imagine a mouse standing with an elephant and then are asked: "Does the mouse have whiskers?" To answer this question, participants need a bit of time (which we can measure) to zoom in on the mouse, in order to bring the whiskers "into view." Responses were faster if participants were initially asked to imagine the mouse standing next to a paper clip. For this image, participants started with a "close-up" view, so no zooming was needed to "see" the whiskers.

Mental Rotation

Whether you're scanning across a mental image, therefore, or zooming in on one, "traveling" a greater "distance" requires more time. This is the same relationship we would observe if we asked research participants to move their eyes across an actual map (rather than an image of one) or literally to zoom in on a real picture. In these cases, too, traveling a greater distance would require more time. All of this points toward the similarity between mental images and actual out-in-the-world pictures.

Other results, though, suggest that mental images may be more like "mental sculptures" rather than "mental pictures." In a series of classic experiments by Shepard, Cooper, and Metzler, participants were asked to decide whether pairs like the one in **Figure 11.4A** showed two different shapes or just one shape viewed from two different perspectives (Cooper & Shepard, 1973; Shepard & Cooper, 1982; Shepard & Metzler, 1971). In other words, is it possible to "rotate" the form shown on the left in Figure 11.4A so that it will end up looking just like the form on the right? What about the two shapes shown in **Figure 11.4B** or the two in **11.4C**?

To perform this **mental rotation task,** participants seem first to imagine one of the forms rotating into alignment with the other. Then, once the forms are

FIGURE 11.4   STIMULI FOR A MENTAL ROTATION
EXPERIMENT

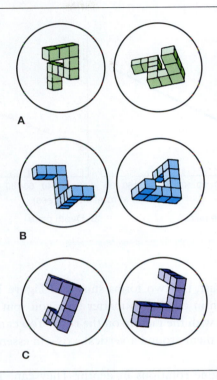

Participants had to judge whether the two stimuli shown in Panel A are the
same as each other but viewed from different perspectives, and likewise for
the pairs shown in Panels B and C. Participants seem to make these judgments by imagining one of the forms rotating until its position matches that
of the other form.   (FIG. AFTER SHEPARD, R. N., & METZLER, J. (1971). MENTAL ROTATION
OF THREE-DIMENSIONAL OBJECTS. *SCIENCE, 171*(3972) 701–703. © 1971 AAAS. REPRINTED WITH
PERMISSION FROM AAAS.)

oriented in the same way, participants can make their judgment. This step of
imagined rotation takes some time, and the amount of time depends on how
much rotation is needed. **Figure 11.5** shows the data pattern, with response
times clearly influenced by how far apart the two forms were in their initial
orientations. Once again, therefore, imagined "movement" resembles actual
movement: The farther you have to imagine a form rotating, the longer the
evaluation takes.

Notice, though, that if you were to cut out the left-hand drawing in
Figure 11.4A and spin it around while leaving it flat on the table, you
could align it with the drawing on the right. The relevant rotation, therefore,
is one that leaves the pictures within the two-dimensional plane in which they

FIGURE 11.5   DATA
FROM A MENTAL
ROTATION EXPERIMENT

Panel A shows data from stimulus pairs requiring mental rotation in two dimensions, so that
the imaged forms stay within the
imagined picture plane. Panel B
shows data from pairs requiring
an imagined rotation in depth.
The data are similar, indicating
that participants can imagine
three-dimensional rotations as
easily as they can imagine two-
dimensional rotations.

(AFTER SHEPARD & METZLER, 1971)

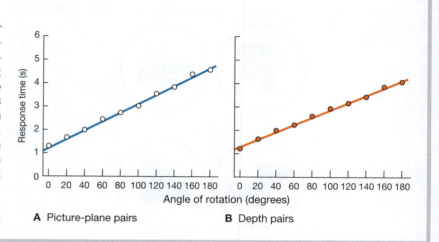

A Picture-plane pairs   **B** Depth pairs

are drawn. In contrast, the two forms shown in Figure 11.4B are identical
except for a rotation in depth. No matter how you spin the *picture* on the
left, it won't line up with the picture on the right. You can align these forms,
but only if you spin them around a vertical axis—in essence, lifting them off
the page.

Can people imagine rotations in depth? They can. The accuracy level
with these rotations is around 95%, and the response-time data resemble
those obtained with picture-plane rotation (compare Figures 11.5A and
11.5B). Apparently, participants have no difficulty representing three-
dimensional forms and three-dimensional movement in their images. (For
more on mental rotation, including differences between men and women in
how well they do this task, see Boone & Hegarty, 2017; Voyer et al., 2020;
also see **Figure 11.6**.)

The Concern about Demand Character

In both mental rotation and mental scanning, then, the farther the imagined
"travel," the longer it takes. But do these results reflect the basic nature of
imagery? Or is there another way to interpret the data? Participants in these
studies obviously know that movement through the world takes time and
that moving a longer distance takes more time. Perhaps, therefore, participants simply control the timing of their responses in order to re-create this
"normal" pattern.

This proposal can be fleshed out in a variety of ways, but to phrase things
strongly, maybe participants in these studies aren't imagining rotations or
scanning across an image at all. Instead, maybe they're thinking, "The experimenter just asked me to scan a long way, and I'd like to make it look like I'm

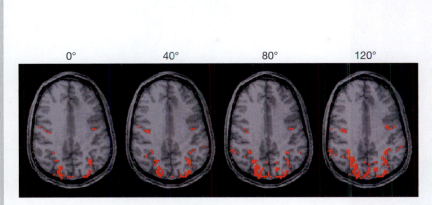

FIGURE 11.6 BRAIN ACTIVITY IN MENTAL ROTATION

As the text describes, it takes more time to imagine something rotating, say, 80 degrees than it does to imagine it moving 40 degrees. Related data come from brain scans—with more brain activity needed for a 40-degree rotation than for no rotation at all, and even more activity needed for an 80-degree or a 120-degree rotation.

(AFTER CARPENTER ET AL., 1999)

obeying. I know that a long scan takes a long time, so let me wait a moment before hitting the response button."

Why should participants act in this way? One reason is that research participants usually want to be helpful, and they do all they can to give the experimenter "good" data. As a result, they're very sensitive to the **demand character** of the experiment—that is, cues that might signal how they're "supposed to" behave in that situation. (For early discussion of how demand character might influence imagery experiments, see Intons-Peterson, 1983, 1999; Intons-Peterson & White, 1981).

A different possibility is that this sort of "simulation" is, in fact, what imagery is really all about. Perhaps whenever people try to "imagine" something, they draw on their knowledge about how an event in the world would actually unfold, and they do their best to simulate this event. In this case, a longer scan or a greater rotation requires more time, not because there really is some "travel" involved but because people know that these manipulations should take more time and do their best to simulate the process (Pylyshyn, 1981).

As it turns out, though, we can set aside these concerns, enabling us to conclude that the scanning and rotation data are as they are, not through simulation, but *because of how images represent spatial layout*. Several lines of evidence support this claim, including data we will turn to, later in the chapter, examining the neural bases for imagery. But we can also tackle concerns about demand character directly. In several studies, experimenters have asked participants to make judgments about spatial layout but have taken care never to mention that imagery might be relevant to the task (e.g., Finke & Pinker, 1982). This procedure avoids any suggestion to participants that they should simulate some sort of "mental travel." Even so, participants in these procedures spontaneously form images and scan across them, and

TEST YOURSELF

2. What is a chronometric study?
3. Why do image-scanning studies indicate that images *depict* a scene rather than *describe* the scene?
4. What does it mean to say that an experiment's results might be influenced by demand character?

There is, of course, no "box" trapping this mime. Instead, the mime is simulating what would happen if he were trapped in a box. In the same way, researchers have asked whether study participants, guided by an experiment's demand character, are simply simulating (re-creating?) how they'd act if they were looking at a picture.

their responses show the standard pattern: longer response times observed with longer scans. Apparently, this result emerges whenever participants are using visual imagery—whether the result is encouraged by the experimenters' instructions or not.

Imagery and Perception

If—as it seems—images do resemble pictures, then are the mental processes used to inspect images similar to those used to inspect stimuli? More broadly, what is the relation between imaging and perceiving?

Let's hypothesize that there's some overlap between imaging and perceiving—that there are, in other words, certain mental processes that are involved in both activities. On this basis, we should expect interference if participants try to do both of these activities at once, on the idea that if these processes are occupied with imaging, then they're not available for perceiving. This prediction is correct: Participants are less successful in detecting dim visual stimuli if they're simultaneously trying to hold a visual image before their "mind's eye." They're likewise less successful in detecting faint sounds if they're simultaneously trying to form an auditory image before their "mind's ear" (Segal & Fusella, 1970, 1971; also see Farah & Smith, 1983).

What happens, though, if participants are contemplating a mental image *related to* the stimulus they're trying to perceive? Can visualizing a possible input "pave the way" for perception? Farah (1985) had participants visualize a form (either an *H* or a *T*). A moment later, either an *H* or a *T* was actually presented—but at a low contrast, making the letter difficult to perceive. With this setup, perception was facilitated if participants had just been visualizing the target form, and the effect was quite specific: Visualizing an *H* made it easier to perceive an *H*; visualizing a *T* made it easier to perceive a *T*. This result provides further confirmation that visualizing and perceiving draw on similar mechanisms, so that one of these activities can prime the other. (Also see Pearson, 2014; Pearson et al., 2015.)

Visual Imagery and the Brain

The overlap between imaging and perceiving is also clear in biological evidence, because it turns out that many of the brain structures required for vision are also crucial for imagery. We know that vision relies heavily on tissue located in the occipital cortex (and so these brain areas are highly activated whenever you're examining a visual stimulus; see Chapter 2). Activity levels are also high in these areas when participants are visualizing a stimulus before their "mind's eye" (Dijkstra et al., 2019; Pearson, 2019; Thompson & Kosslyn, 2000; see Figure 2.9, p. 44).

The biological parallels between imagery and perception can be documented even at a fine grain. For example, Areas V1 and V2 in the cortex are involved in the earliest stages of visual perception, responding to specific low-level features of the input. It's striking, therefore, that the same brain areas are particularly active whenever participants are maintaining highly detailed images, and that the amount of brain tissue showing activation increases as participants imagine larger and larger objects (Behrmann, 2000; Kosslyn & Thompson, 2003; Pearson et al., 2015). In a similar way, certain areas in the brain are highly sensitive to motion in ordinary visual perception, and it turns out that the same brain areas are particularly activated when participants are asked to *imagine* movement patterns (Goebel et al., 1998). Likewise, brain areas that are especially active during the perception of faces are also highly activated when people are imagining faces (O'Craven & Kanwisher, 2000; also see **Figure 11.7**).

In fact, these various parallels have enabled researchers to develop techniques for "decoding" patterns of brain activation in people who are holding visual images (e.g., Albers et al., 2013; Kay et al., 2008; Pearson, 2014; Schlegel et al., 2013; Thirion et al., 2006). The idea here sounds like mind reading, but it's entirely real. Research participants are first shown various pictures, so that the researchers can document the pattern of brain activity associated with viewing each picture. The participants are then asked to create and maintain a visual image while the investigators record brain activity. The activity (an fMRI pattern) is then subjected to mathematical analysis, allowing computers to compare the activation patterns while *visualizing* with the activation patterns while *seeing*. With impressive accuracy, this comparison enables the researchers to figure out just what each participant was imagining at that moment—in essence, using brain data to read the participant's thoughts.

TEST YOURSELF

5. What's the evidence that visual imagery relies on some of the same mental processes as actual vision?

FIGURE 11.7   IMAGERY FOR FACES AND PLACES IN THE BRAIN

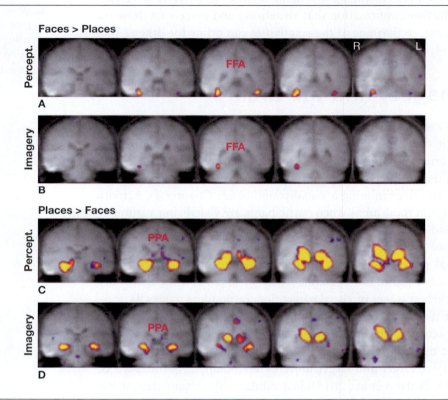

The successive brain pictures in each row show different "slices" through the brain, moving from the front to the back. To analyze the data, researchers initially compared brain activity in two conditions: when participants were viewing *faces* and when they were viewing *places* (scenes). Next, the researchers compared brain activity in two more conditions: when the participants were *visualizing* faces or places. The row marked A shows brain sites that were more activated when participants were viewing *faces* than *places*; not surprisingly, activity levels are high in the fusiform face area (FFA). The row marked B shows brain sites that were more activated when participants were *visualizing faces* than when they were visualizing places. The key here is that rows A and B look rather similar: The pattern of brain activation is roughly the same in the perception and imagery conditions. The bottom two rows show the brain sites that were more activated when participants were viewing (row C) or visualizing (row D) *places*, with considerable activity in the parahippocampal place area (PPA). Again, the activity pattern is quite similar for the perception and imagery conditions.

Visual Imagery and Brain Disruption

Further evidence comes from *transcranial magnetic stimulation* (TMS), a technique we first described in Chapter 2. TMS creates a series of strong magnetic pulses at a specific location on the scalp; doing so causes a (temporary!) disruption in the brain region directly below this scalp area (Helmuth, 2001). In this way, it's possible to disrupt Area V1 in an otherwise normal brain. (Area V1, recall, is the brain area where axons from the visual system first reach the occipital cortex; see Chapter 3.) Not surprisingly, using TMS in this way causes problems in vision, but it also causes parallel problems in visual imagery, providing a powerful argument that Area V1 is important both for the processing of visual information and for the creation of visual images (Kosslyn et al., 1999).

Still more evidence comes from studies of brain damage, and here, too, we find parallels between visual perception and visual imagery. For example, in some patients brain damage has disrupted the ability to perceive color; in most cases, these patients also lose the ability to imagine scenes in color. Like-wise, patients who, because of brain damage, have lost the ability to perceive fine detail seem also to lose the ability to visualize fine detail; and so on. (See Farah et al., 1992; Kosslyn, 1994; however, we'll add some complications to this point later in the chapter.)

Brain damage also causes parallels in how people *pay attention* to visual inputs and to visual images. In one case, a patient had suffered a stroke and, as a result, had developed the "neglect syndrome" we described in Chapter 5. If this patient was shown a picture, he seemed to see only the right side of it; if asked to read a word, he read only the right half. The same pattern was evident in the patient's imagery. In one test, he was urged to visualize a familiar plaza in his city and to list the buildings "in view" in the image. If the patient imagined himself standing at the northern edge of the plaza, he listed all the buildings on the plaza's western side (i.e., on his right), but none on the eastern. If the patient imagined himself standing on the southern edge of the plaza, he listed all the sights on the plaza's eastern side, but none on the western. In both cases, he neglected half of the imaged scene, just as he did with perceived scenes (Bisiach & Luzzatti, 1978; Bisiach et al., 1979).

Spatial Images and Visual Images

We are building an impressive case for a close relationship between imagery and perception. Indeed, the evidence so far implies that we can truly speak of imagery as being *visual* imagery, drawing on the same mechanisms and having many of the same traits as actual vision. Other results, however, add some complications.

Early in the chapter, we discussed dreams in people who have been blind since birth, and more broadly, many studies have examined imagery in the blind. These procedures need to be adapted in important ways—so that, for example, the stimuli to be imaged are initially presented as sculptures to be explored with the hands, rather than as pictures to be examined visually. Once this is done, however, experiments parallel to those we've described can be carried out with the blind—procedures examining how the blind scan across an image, for example, or how they imagine a form in rotation. What are the results? In tests involving mental scanning, blind individuals produce response times proportional to the "distance" traveled in the image—exactly the result we've already seen with sighted people. In tests requiring mental rotation, response times with blind research participants are proportional to

NEGLECT SYNDROME IN VISUAL IMAGERY

Because of brain damage, a patient had developed the pattern (first discussed in Chapter 2) of unilateral neglect—so he paid attention only to the right half of the visual world. He showed the same pattern in his visual images. When asked to imagine himself standing at the southern edge of the Piazza del Duomo and to describe all he could "see" in his image, he only listed buildings on the piazza's eastern side. When he imagined himself standing at the northern edge of the piazza, he only listed buildings on the western side. In both cases, he neglected the left half of the (visualized) piazza.

the amount of "rotation" needed, just as with participants who have normal vision. In fact, in procedure after procedure, people blind since birth produce results just like those from people who can see. The blind, in other words, seem to have normal imagery. (For a sampling of the data, see Carpenter & Eisenberg, 1978; Giudice et al., 2011; Kerr, 1983; Marmor & Zabeck, 1976; Paivio & Okovita, 1971; Zimler & Keenan, 1983. For an overview of imagery in the blind—including the ways in which visually impaired individuals differ from one another—see Heller & Gentaz, 2014.)

What's going on here? It seems unlikely that people blind since birth are using a sense of what things "look like" to perform these tasks. Presumably, therefore, they have some other way of thinking about spatial layout and spatial relations. This "spatial imagery" might be represented in the mind in terms of a series of imagined movements, so that it's body imagery or motion imagery rather than visual imagery. Alternatively, perhaps spatial imagery isn't tied to any sensory modality, but is instead part of our broader cognition about spatial arrangements and layout.

One way or another, though, it looks like we need to distinguish between *visual* and *spatial* imagery. Blind individuals presumably use spatial imagery to carry out the tasks we've been discussing in this chapter; it seems plausible that sighted people can use either visual or spatial imagery to carry out these tasks.

This distinction between visual and spatial imagery is confirmed by neuroscience evidence. We've already noted the cases in which brain damage seems to produce similar patterns of disruption in seeing and imaging—patients who (because of brain damage) have lost their color vision and also the ability to imagine scenes in color; patients who have lost their ability to perceive motion and also the ability to imagine movement. But there are exceptions to this pattern—that is, cases in which brain damage causes problems in imagery but not in perception, or vice versa. (See, e.g., Bartolomeo et al., 1998; Behrmann, 2000; Goldenberg et al., 1995; Logie & Della Salla, 2005; Servos & Goodale, 1995.)

What should we make of this uneven pattern—with brain damage sometimes causing similar problems in imagery and in perception, and sometimes not? The answer lies in the fact that *visual* imagery relies on brain areas also needed for vision, with the result that damage to these areas disrupts both imagery and vision. *Spatial* imagery, in contrast, relies on different brain areas, and so damage to visual areas won't interfere with this form of imagery, and damage to brain sites needed for this imagery won't interfere with vision (see **Figure 11.8**).

Likewise, consider patient L.H. He suffered brain damage in an automobile accident and, afterward, had enormous difficulty in tasks requiring judgments about visual appearance—for example, judgments about *color* (Farah et al., 1988). L.H. performed well, though, on tasks like image scanning or mental rotation, tasks that require spatial manipulations or memory for spatial positions. To make sense of L.H.'s profile, it seems once again crucial to distinguish between visual tasks (for which he's impaired) and spatial ones (for which he's not) and, correspondingly, between visual imagery and spatial imagery.

Individual Differences in Imagery

Various lines of evidence, therefore, suggest there are at least two types of imagery—one visual and one spatial—and, presumably, most people have the capacity for both types: They can "visualize" and they can "spatialize." But this invites a new question: When do people use one type of imagery, and when do they use the other?

To some extent, the answer depends on the task. For example, to think about *colors*, you need to imagine exactly what something *looks like*; it won't be enough just to think about shapes or spatial positions. In this case, therefore, you'll need visual imagery, not spatial. Or, as a reverse case, think about tasks that require complex navigation—perhaps navigation through a building or across an entire city. For tasks like these, visualizing the relevant layout may be difficult and would include a lot of detail irrelevant to the navigation. In this setting, spatial imagery, not visual, may be a better option (Hegarty & Stull, 2012).

TEST YOURSELF

6. What do we learn from the fact that some forms of brain damage have *similar* effects on a person's ability to see and the person's ability to perform many imagery tasks?

7. What do we learn from the fact that some forms of brain damage have *different* effects on a person's ability to see and the person's ability to perform many imagery tasks?

FIGURE 11.8 **BRAIN AREAS CRUCIAL FOR VISUAL AND SPATIAL TASKS**

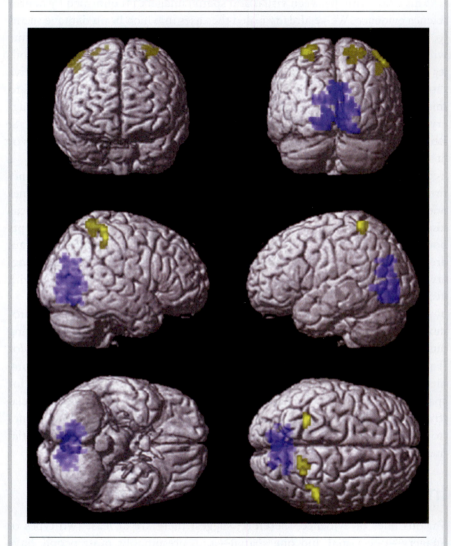

In one condition of this study, participants had to visualize a particular target in a particular location. In the other condition, participants had to imagine a rotation of a target (Thompson et al., 2009). The authors refer to these conditions as Spatial Location and Spatial Transformation, but the distinction at issue parallels the distinction made in the text between visual and spatial tasks. The two types of tasks clearly relied on distinct brain regions, providing further evidence that we must distinguish between visual and spatial imagery. The blue areas in the figure indicate brain regions associated with the more "visual" task; the yellow areas indicate brain regions associated with the more "spatial" task.

In other cases, either form of imagery will get the job done. For an image-scanning task, for example, you can think about what a speck would *look like* as it zooms across an imagined scene, or you can think about what it would *feel like* to move your finger across the scene. In these cases, the choice between visual and spatial imagery will depend on other factors, including your preferences and perhaps the exact instructions you receive.

The choice between these forms of imagery will also be influenced by each individual's ability levels. Some people may be poor visualizers but good "spatializers," and they would surely rely on spatial imagery, not visual, in most tasks. For other people, this pattern might be reversed.

With this context, think back to Galton's data, mentioned early in this chapter. If we take those data at face value, they imply that people differ markedly in their conscious experience of imaging. People with vivid imagery report that their images are truly picture-like: in color, quite detailed, and with the depicted objects viewed from a particular distance and a particular viewing angle. People without vivid imagery, in contrast, say none of these things. Their images, they report, are not at all picture-like, and it's meaningless to ask them whether an image is in color or in black and white; their image, they say, simply isn't the sort of thing that could be in color or in black and white. Likewise, it's meaningless to ask whether their image is viewed from a particular distance or angle; their image is abstract in a way that makes these points inapplicable. In no sense, then, do these "non-imagers" feel like they're "seeing" with the "mind's eye." From their perspective, these figures of speech are (at best) loosely metaphorical. This stands in clear contrast to the reports offered by vivid imagers; for them, mental seeing really does seem like actual seeing.

Roughly 10% of the population will, in this way, "declare themselves entirely deficient in the power of seeing mental pictures" (Galton, 1883, p. 110). As William James (1890) put it, they "have no visual images at all worthy of the name" (p. 57). Note the dates here; we've known for more than a century that some people lack the capacity for visualization. Even so, this pattern was largely unknown to medical doctors and not discussed at all in the medical literature; as a result, the pattern was described in 2015 as newly "discovered" (e.g., Zimmer, 2010, 2015) and given a new name: aphantasia. (Despite the media reports, the scholars who suggested this label certainly knew the relevant history, including Galton's important contribution; Zeman et al., 2015, 2016.)

What should we make of this? Do members of our species really differ in whether they're capable of experiencing visual images? To explore this issue, a number of studies have compared "vivid imagers" and "non-imagers" on tasks that depend on mental imagery, with the obvious prediction that people with vivid imagery will do better in these tasks. The key, though, is that when people describe their images as "vivid," they seem to be reporting how much their image experience is *like seeing*—their self-report, in other words, provides an assessment of *visual* imagery. To document the benefits of this imagery, therefore, we need to focus on tasks that truly require visual imagery (i.e., tasks that cannot be performed perfectly well with *spatial* imagery).

Consider, for example, tasks that require people to make a judgment about what an imagined object would look like—for example, what its color would look like or whether a small gap in the object would be "visible" in the image. People with vivid imagery do perform better on these tasks—presumably, because their vivid images enable them to "see" exactly what the imagined objects look like. (See, e.g., Cui, et al., 2007; Keogh & Pearson, 2011; Kozhevnikov et al., 2005; Pearson et al., 2011. For more on procedures that assess "color imagery," see Wantz et al., 2015.)

Imagery differences from one person to the next are also reflected in patterns of brain activation. In one study, participants self-reported how vivid their imagery was, rating specific images on a scale that ranged from "perfectly clear and vivid as normal vision" (a score of 1) to "no image; you just know you are thinking of the object" (a score of 5). Then, while in an fMRI scanner, the participants were instructed to visualize a specific scene (e.g., someone climbing up some stairs). The results, shown in **Figure 11.9**, indicate a clear relationship between self-reported vividness and degree of activation in the brain's visual cortex (Cui et al., 2007).

FIGURE 11.9   BRAIN ACTIVATION REFLECTS IMAGERY VIVIDNESS

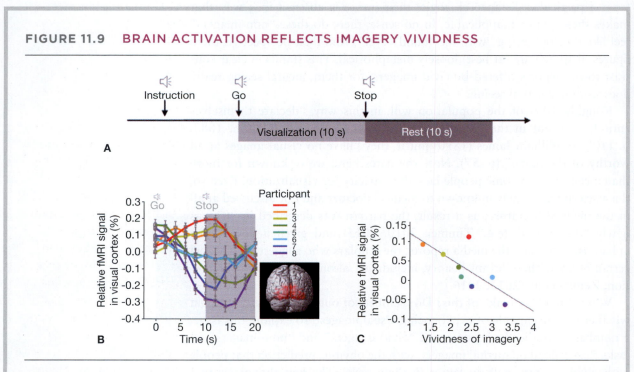

(Panel A) Participants began to visualize when they heard the "go" signal and stopped when they heard the "stop" signal. The fMRI signal being measured focused on early visual cortex (Brodmann's areas 17 and 18); the relevant brain areas are highlighted in Panel B. In Panel C, *low* scores of self-reported vividness indicate vivid imagery; a score of 5 would indicate a self-report that the person was experiencing no visual image at all.

Life without Vision

If you're someone who experiences vivid visual imagery, you may find it bizarre that other people never have this experience. After all, "mental pictures" are probably a prominent part of your mental life, and you use imagery even when there's no need. For example, when reading a novel, you likely form mental pictures of what the characters look like—and when you see the movie based on the book, you may be annoyed because the performers don't look like they "should"!

What would it be like, though, to lack this capacity? We can gain some understanding by considering people blind from birth—people with no vision and no capacity for visualization. Specifically, you might explore a remarkable series of YouTube videos starring Tommy Edison. With wonderful humor and fabulous openness, Edison answers questions he's received about what it's like to be blind.

Some of the questions people send to Edison seem odd: Do blind people turn on the lights when they're home alone? (No.) Can he tell when people are staring at him? (No.) Would it bother him if he had a houseguest who walked around naked? (No, although he thinks the idea is strange, and he hopes they don't sit on the furniture.)

In answering other questions, though, Edison makes it clear that he has a limited understanding of the visual world. For example, he doesn't understand what *color* is all about. When people tell him that both the sky and ice are blue, that's a puzzle. "Same color means two completely different things? I don't get it."

Edison can, however, imagine things. In one video, he's asked to imagine a soda bottle. "I think about the shape of it. . . . I think about the plastic;

I think about the cap; those things on the bottom so it doesn't fall down—the five things there. . . ." He then explains, "I couldn't imagine a bottle of soda on the table because I'd have to be touching it to know it was there. I see the shape through my hands." Describing another object, he says, "Of course, I imagine it, but I just don't do it the way you do. . . . To 'visualize' something for me is to remember what it feels like."

Tommy Edison does understand the larger-scale spatial world. He's worked as a radio disk jockey—and so he commuted to the station and moved around the studio. These achievements required an accurate grasp of where things were relative to each other and relative to him, and he plainly had that spatial understanding.

Edison's spatial sense is also evident in his ability to *draw*. He does find it odd to "put a three-dimensional thing onto a flat piece of paper." Even so, he can draw objects—for example, a car—combining what he's learned from multiple experiences, all knit together by an overall sense of the parts' positions relative to one another. It's interesting that his drawings also preserve a "vantage" point: He draws the cat with two legs, "because, from where I'm sitting, that's all I can see of the kitty."

People with rich visual imagery probably can't understand what Edison's internal experience is like. Nonetheless, his descriptions powerfully remind us of how much can be achieved without vision or visualizing, and therefore may help us understand what these capacities provide for us. Above all, Edison's candid reports give us a wonderful portrait of experiences and a mental life different from the ones most of us enjoy. Visit him on YouTube!

How Does Vivid Imagery Matter?

It appears, then, that people really do differ in the nature of their imagery experience. Most people report detailed, colorful visual images and claim that these images are a routine part of their inner experience. But other people (including the author of this book!) insist they have no visual images—for example, they can't close their eyes and call to mind a picture of their best friend's face; they seem unable to call up an image of a scene they've seen countless times. As we mentioned before, for them, concepts like "mental pictures" or the "mind's eye" are strained metaphors.

How do these differences in experience influence people outside the laboratory, away from experimenters' tasks? What can people "with imagery" do that people "without imagery" cannot? The evidence suggests a several-part answer. One study, for example, indicated a link between imagery prowess and career choice, with visual imagers being more likely to succeed in the arts, while people with spatial imagery seem better suited to careers in science or engineering (Kozhevnikov et al., 2005, but also see **Figure 11.10**). Visual imagery also seems to play a role in autobiographical memory, with "non-imagers" less likely to feel as if they can "relive" their memories (Greenberg

---

FIGURE 11.10 "MY MIND'S EYE IS BLIND"

People with rich visual imagery are astonished to hear that many other people seem to have no visualization skill at all. Remarkably, though, people with "aphantasia" can still work in jobs that involve visual materials—and this includes some of the world's best animators. For example, Glen Keane (shown here), the Oscar-winning creator of Pocahontas and many other Disney characters, reports that he has no visual images at all. Likewise for Ed Catmull, former president of Pixar and Walt Disney Animation Studios. Catmull has commented, "my mind's eye is blind." As an illustration, he recalls that he once tried to perform Tibetan meditation and was told to picture a sphere in front of him. "I went home, closed my eyes. . . . I couldn't see a thing," even though, "for an entire week I kept trying to visualize this sphere."

& Knowlton, 2014; Hobson et al., 2000; also see Butler et al., 2016; Rubin & Umanath, 2015).

There may also be a linkage between vivid visual imagery and some aspects of emotion and even mental health (Pearson et al., 2015). There is, for example, some indication that people with more vivid imagery tend to experience stronger emotions (Blouin-Hudon & Pychyl, 2015). Perhaps related, people diagnosed with phobias sometimes experience troubling images—such as vivid images of snakes for someone with *ophidiophobia* (fear of snakes), or images of spiders for someone with *arachnophobia* (fear of spiders). It seems plausible that future therapies will embrace these findings, seeking somehow to disrupt or defuse these troubling images.

Let's emphasize, though, that more research is needed to explore the consequences of vivid imagery—or to explore the consequences of being a non-imager. In the meantime, the data do suggest that this aspect of someone's inner experience may have far-reaching effects.

Spatial Skills

What about spatial imagery? What do we know about how people differ in their spatial skills? To tackle this issue, we need to distinguish different types of spatial skills. One type is often measured by the mental-folding task (Shepard & Feng, 1972). In this task, people are shown six connected squares representing an unfolded and flattened cube. The test taker is asked to imagine refolding the squares to form a cube, and then has to decide whether the two "arrow tips" would meet in the now-created cube (see **Figure 11.11**).

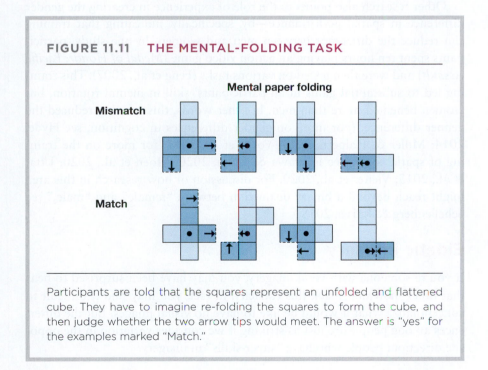

FIGURE 11.11   **THE MENTAL-FOLDING TASK**

Participants are told that the squares represent an unfolded and flattened cube. They have to imagine re-folding the squares to form the cube, and then judge whether the two arrow tips would meet. The answer is "yes" for the examples marked "Match."

People differ markedly in their ability to do this task, but it turns out that people successful in mental folding are not particularly skilled in tasks like mental rotation (see p. 392). Apparently, these tasks—even though both depend on some type of spatial reasoning—involve different mechanisms (e.g., Harris et al., 2013; Milivojevic et al., 2003). Moreover, research indicates that mental rotation relies heavily on right-hemisphere mechanisms; mental folding draws heavily on both hemispheres (Milivojevic et al., 2003).

These tasks also differ in another way. Mental rotation shows a robust gender difference (with men being faster and more accurate than women; e.g., Voyer, 2011; Voyer et al., 2020). There's little difference, though, in men's and women's performance on mental folding (Harris et al., 2013).

In fact, men have an advantage in a variety of spatial-reasoning tasks. What produces this gender difference? Some authors suggest an influence of men's and women's hormones (for discussion, see Castro-Alonso & Jansen, 2019; Hyde, 2014), but there's no question that differences in strategy and experience are also important. Consider, for example, the task of learning your way around in a new environment, so that you'll be able to navigate in that environment later on. Many studies show an advantage for men on this task, but why? The answer may depend on how men and women explore the environment at the start, with men traveling longer distances without changing course and making fewer returns to previously visited locations (Munion et al., 2019). It seems, then, the gender difference in this task may not reflect some deep contrast between men's and women's biology; instead, the gender difference may simply derive from differing exploratory habits.

Other research also points to the role of experience in creating the gender difference in spatial performance—by, specifically, indicating that training can reduce the difference between men and women. In one study, participants spent ten hours playing an action video game (*Medal of Honor: Pacific Assault*) and were then tested on various tasks (Feng et al., 2007). This training led to substantial gains in all participants' skill in mental rotation, but women benefited more than men. In other words, this training reduced the gender difference. (For more on gender differences in cognition, see Hyde, 2014; Miller & Halpern, 2014; Voyer et al., 2017; for more on the training of spatial skills, see Ishikawa & Zhou, 2020; Moen et al., 2020; Uttal et al., 2013; Vieites et al., 2020. For discussion of how research in this area might reach beyond a binary distinction between "female" and "male," see Schellenberg & Kaiser, 2018.)

Eidetic Imagery

If you're someone with vivid imagery, you may have been surprised to hear that other individuals lack this capacity. In fact, you may find it difficult to conceptualize what it would be like to have no visual images. But the differences among people are just as striking if we consider variation in the opposite direction: people who have "super-skills" in imagery.

TEST YOURSELF

8. What evidence is there that there are different types of spatial skill?

9. What evidence suggests that the gender difference in spatial skill is heavily influenced by (and may be due to) experience and training?

There is a lot of folklore associated with the idea of "photographic memory," but this term needs to be defined carefully. Some people have fabulously detailed memories, but without any "photographic" quality. These people use careful rehearsal, or complex, well-practiced mnemonics, to remember facts and faces—and so they can recall the value of pi to a hundred decimal places, or the names of a hundred people they've just met. These memories, however, aren't in any way "visual," and imagery isn't necessary for these memorization strategies.

Other people, in contrast, do seem to have exquisitely detailed imagery that can truly be described as "photographic." Researchers refer to this type of imagery as **eidetic imagery**, and people with this skill are called "eidetikers." This form of imagery is sometimes found in people who have been diagnosed as autistic: They can briefly glance at a complex scene and then draw incredibly detailed reproductions of the scene, as though they really had taken a "photograph" when first viewing it. (See Chapter 14.) But similar capacities can be documented with no link to autism. For example, in one early study Stromeyer (1982) described a woman who could recall poetry written in a language she didn't understand, even years after she'd seen the poem; she was also able to recall complicated random dot patterns after viewing them only briefly. Similarly, Haber (1969; Haber & Haber, 1988) showed a picture like the one in **Figure 11.12** to a 10-year-old eidetiker for just 30 seconds. After the picture was taken away, the boy was unexpectedly asked detail questions: "How many stripes were there on the cat's back? How many leaves on the front flower?" The child was able to give completely accurate answers, as though his memory had perfectly preserved the picture's content.

We know relatively little about this form of imagery. We do know that the capacity is rare. We know that some people who claim to have this capacity do not: They often do have fabulous memories, but they rely on mnemonics, not on some special form of imagery. But beyond these obvious points, this remains a truly intriguing phenomenon in need of further research.

Images Are Not Pictures

Let's return, though, to more ordinary forms of imagery. At many points in this chapter, we've referred to mental images as "mental pictures," and that terminology does seem appropriate in many ways: Visual images do depict a scene in a way that seems quite pictorial. In other regards, though, this comparison may be misleading.

We've already mentioned that mental images can represent three-dimensional figures, and so they may be more like mental sculptures than mental pictures. We've also distinguished visual images and spatial images, and we've seen that *some* images are like pictures to be explored with the mind's eye, and other images are not. But on top of these points, there's a further complication. To introduce this issue, let's review some points we raised

TEST YOURSELF

10. What evidence confirms that people do actually differ in the vividness of their visual images?
11. What is eidetic imagery?

FIGURE 11.12   EIDETIC IMAGERY

Eidetic imagery is vastly more detailed than ordinary imagery. In one study (Haber, 1969), a 10-year-old was shown a picture like this one for 30 seconds. After the picture was taken away, the boy was unexpectedly asked detail questions: "How many stripes were there on the cat's back? How many leaves on the front flower?" The child was able to give completely accurate answers, as though his memory had perfectly preserved the picture's content.

in Chapter 3 and, with them, an example we met there. **Figure 11.13A** shows the figure known as the Necker cube (see also Figure 3.11). The drawing of this cube—the stimulus itself—is ambiguous: It can be understood as a depiction of a cube viewed from above (and a bit to the side) or as a depiction of a cube viewed from below (and a bit to the side). The picture itself, in other words, doesn't specify which of these two cubes it shows, and so the picture is neutral with regard to interpretation—and fully compatible with either interpretation.

Unlike the picture, though, your *perception* of the cube is not neutral, is not indeterminate with regard to depth. Instead, at any moment in time you perceive the cube as having one arrangement in depth or another. Your perception, in other words, specifies a configuration in depth, a specification

FIGURE 11.13   THE NECKER CUBE AND THE DUCK/RABBIT

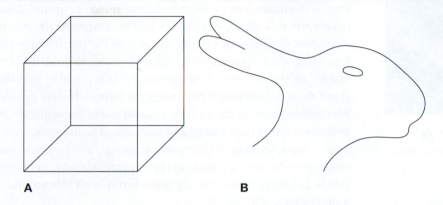

(Panel A) The cube can be perceived as if viewed from above or below. The drawing, in other words, is neutral with regard to interpretation. However, your *perception* of the drawing isn't neutral, and so you perceive the cube as having one interpretation or the other. (Panel B) This figure can be perceived either as a duck looking left or as a rabbit looking right. The picture itself is ambiguous, specifying neither duck nor rabbit. When people view the picture, they can easily find both interpretations. When people view a mental image of this figure, however, the form seems to lose its ambiguity.

that in this case supplements an ambiguous drawing in order to create an unambiguous perception.

As we discussed in Chapter 3, the configuration in depth is just one of the ways that perception goes beyond the information given in a stimulus. Your perception of a stimulus also specifies a figure/ground organization, the form's orientation (e.g., identifying the form's "top"), and so on. These specifications serve to organize the form and have a powerful impact on its subjective appearance—and with that, what the form is seen to resemble and what the form will evoke in memory.

The point, then, is that your **percepts** (i.e., your mental representations of the stimuli you're perceiving) are in some ways similar to pictures, but in other ways different. Like pictures, percepts are *depictions*, representing key aspects of the three-dimensional layout of the world. Percepts, in other words, are not descriptions of a stimulus; instead, percepts (just like pictures) show directly what a stimulus looks like. At the same time, percepts are in some ways different from pictures: They are *organized* depictions and therefore unambiguous in a way that pictures are not.

What about visual images? Are they like pictures—neutral with regard to organization and open to different interpretations? Or are they organized in the way percepts seem to be, and so, in a sense, already interpreted? One line of evidence comes from studies of ambiguous figures. Participants were first shown a series of practice stimuli to make sure that they understood what it

meant to reinterpret an ambiguous figure (Chambers & Reisberg, 1985). They were then shown a drawing of one more ambiguous figure—the duck/rabbit, shown in **Figure 11.13B**. Then, after this figure had been removed from view, they were instructed to form a mental image of it and asked if they could reinterpret this image, just as they had reinterpreted the practice figures.

Across several experiments, not one of the participants succeeded in reinterpreting their images: They reliably failed to find the duck in a "rabbit image" or the rabbit in a "duck image." Is it possible that they didn't understand their task or didn't remember the figure? To rule out these possibilities, participants were given a blank piece of paper immediately after their failure at reinterpreting their image and were asked to draw the figure based on their image. Now, looking at their own drawings, all the participants were able to reinterpret the configuration in the appropriate way. In other words, we have 100% failure in reinterpreting these forms with images and 100% success a moment later with drawings.

Apparently, therefore, what participants "see" in their image (even if it's a *visual* image, not a spatial one) isn't a "picture"—neutral with regard to interpretation and open to new interpretations. Instead, images are inherently organized, just as percepts are. As such, images are unambiguous and strongly resistant to reinterpretation. (For more on these issues, see Peterson et al., 1992; Thompson et al., 2008.)

Images and Pictures: An Interim Summary

Images, both visual and spatial, provide a distinctive way of representing the world—and so *visualizing* a robot, for example, is quite different from thinking about the word "robot" or merely contemplating the idea "robot." As one key difference, images are, without question, like pictures in the fact that images show exactly what a form looks like. Visualizing a robot, therefore, will highlight the robot's appearance in your thoughts and make it much more likely that you'll be reminded of other forms having a similar appearance. Thinking about the robot without an image might not highlight appearance and so will probably call different ideas to mind. Creating an image will also make some attributes of a form more prominent and others less so (e.g., the cat's head rather than its whiskers). This, too, can influence what further ideas the image calls to mind—and so, again, putting your thoughts into imagery can literally shape the flow and sequence of your ideas.

At the same time, we've highlighted ways in which images are *not* picture-like. The duck/rabbit example reminds us that images are inherently organized in a way that pictures are not, and this organization can influence the sequence of your thoughts—with your understanding of the image (e.g., where its "top" and "front" are; its figure/ground organization) guiding which discoveries will, and which will not, easily flow from the image.

Where does all this leave us? Images have a great deal in common with pictures, but they are also different from pictures. As a result, the common phrase "mental pictures" is misleading, and it would be more accurate to say that mental images are picture-like. We also need to keep track of the contrast between visual images and spatial images. As we have seen, this contrast shows up in many aspects of the data, and it must be part of our theorizing if we're going to explain what imagery is, how it is supported by the brain, and how it functions in shaping our thoughts.

Long-Term Visual Memory

So far, our discussion has focused on "active" images—images that you're currently contemplating, images presumably held in working memory. What about visual information in long-term memory? For example, if you wish to form an image of an elephant, you need to draw on your knowledge of what an elephant looks like in order to create the active image. What is this knowledge, and how is it represented in long-term storage?

Image Information in Long-Term Memory

In earlier chapters, we suggested that your various concepts—for example, your concept of "president" or "animal" or "Trafalgar Square"—are represented by some number of nodes in long-term memory. Perhaps we can adapt this proposal to account for long-term storage of visual information.

One possibility is that nodes in long-term memory represent entire, relatively complete pictures. In other words, to form a mental image of, say, an elephant, you would activate the ELEPHANT PICTURE nodes; to scrutinize an image of your father's face, you would activate the FATHER'S FACE nodes. However, evidence speaks against this idea (e.g., Kosslyn, 1980, 1983). Instead, images seem to be stored in memory in a piece-by-piece fashion. To form an image, therefore, you first have to activate the nodes specifying the "image frame," which depicts the form's global shape. Then, elaborations can be added to this frame, if you wish, to create a full and detailed image.

In support of this claim, images containing *more parts* take longer to create, just as we would expect if images are formed on a piece-by-piece basis (see **Figure 11.14**). In addition, images containing *more detail* take longer

TEST YOURSELF

12. Images are certainly picture-*like*, but what evidence points to a distinction between mental images and actual out-in-the-world pictures?

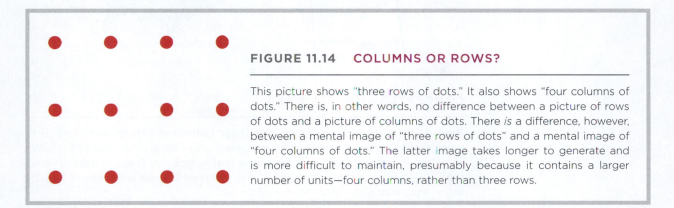

FIGURE 11.14   COLUMNS OR ROWS?

This picture shows "three rows of dots." It also shows "four columns of dots." There is, in other words, no difference between a picture of rows of dots and a picture of columns of dots. There *is* a difference, however, between a mental image of "three rows of dots" and a mental image of "four columns of dots." The latter image takes longer to generate and is more difficult to maintain, presumably because it contains a larger number of units—four columns, rather than three rows.

to create, in accord with this hypothesis. We also know that imagers have some degree of control over how complete and detailed their images will be, so that (depending on the task, the imagers' preferences, etc.) images can be quite sketchy or quite elaborate (Reisberg, 1996). This variation is easily explained if imagers first create an image frame and only then add as much detail as they want. (For discussion of the neural basis for this frame-then-details sequence, see Pearson et al., 2015.)

Verbal Coding of Visual Materials

In some cases, though, visual information is represented in long-term storage in another way: via a verbal label. This point is relevant to issues we met in Chapter 10, concerning the interplay between language and thought. Specifically, evidence tells us that individuals with large color vocabularies have better color memories, probably because they're remembering the verbal label for the color rather than the color itself.

A related point was made in a classic study by Carmichael et al. (1932). Their research participants were shown pictures like those in the center column of **Figure 11.15**. Half of the participants were shown the top form and told, "This is a picture of eyeglasses." The other half were told, "This is a picture of a barbell." Later, the participants were asked to reproduce these pictures as carefully as they could, and those who had understood the

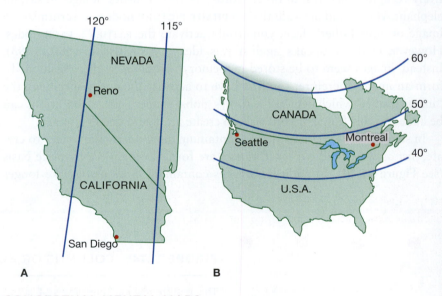

CONCEPTUAL MENTAL MAPS

Research participants tend to judge San Diego to be west of Reno and Montreal to be north of Seattle. But these judgments are wrong. (Panel A) A map of California and Nevada with lines of longitude shows that in fact San Diego is east of Reno. (Panel B) A map of the United States and southern Canada with lines of latitude shows that Seattle is slightly north of Montreal.

FIGURE 11.15 THE INFLUENCE OF VERBAL LABELS ON VISUAL MEMORY

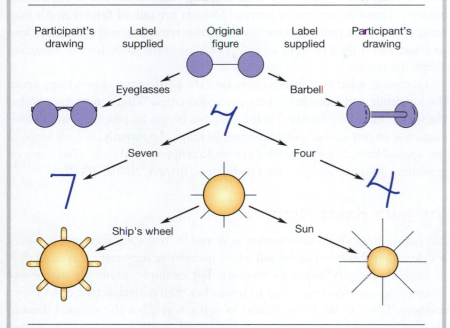

Participants were shown the figures in the middle column. If the top figure was presented with the label "eyeglasses," participants were later likely to reproduce the figure as shown on the left. If the figure was presented with the label "barbell," they were likely to reproduce it as shown on the right. (And so on for the other figures.) One interpretation of these data is that participants were remembering the verbal label and not the drawing itself.

(AFTER CARMICHAEL ET AL., 1932)

picture as eyeglasses produced drawings that resembled eyeglasses; those who understood the picture as weights distorted their drawings appropriately. This is, again, what one would expect if the participants had memorized the description rather than the picture itself and were re-creating the picture on the basis of this description. (For a related finding, showing that how we perceive and remember *faces* is biased by verbal labels, see Eberhardt et al., 2003.)

A similar message emerges from tasks that require participants to reason about spatial position. In one study, participants were asked: "Which is farther north: Seattle or Montreal? Which is farther west: Reno, Nevada; or San Diego, California?" Many participants responded that Montreal is farther north and that San Diego is farther west, but both responses are wrong. Seattle, for example, is roughly 200 miles farther north than Montreal is (Stevens & Coupe, 1978).

These errors arise because participants seem to be reasoning this way: "Montreal is in Canada; Seattle is in the United States. Canada is north of the United States. Therefore, Montreal must be farther north than Seattle." This kind of reasoning makes sense and will often bring you to the correct answer. (That's because most parts of Canada are indeed farther north than most parts of the United States.) Even so, this reasoning will sometimes lead to error, and it does so in this case. (The logic is the same for the Reno/San Diego question.)

Of course, what is of interest here isn't the participants' knowledge about the longitude and latitude of these particular cities. What's important is that the sort of reasoning revealed in these studies hinges on propositional knowledge, not on any sort of mental images or maps. Apparently, at least some of our spatial knowledge relies on a symbolic/propositional code. (For more on reasoning about geography, see Friedman & Brown, 2000a, 2000b.)

Imagery Helps Memory

No matter how visual information is stored in long-term memory, however, it's clear that this information influences memory in important ways and that, in general, imagery improves memory. For example, materials that evoke imagery are considerably easier to remember than materials that don't evoke imagery. This can be demonstrated in many ways, but the original demonstration involved a two-step procedure. First, participants were presented with a list of nouns and asked to rate each noun, on a scale from 1 to 7, for how readily it evoked an image (Paivio, 1969; Paivio, Yuille, & Madigan, 1968). Examples of words receiving high ratings were "church," with an average rating of 6.63, and "elephant," rated at 6.83. Words receiving lower ratings included "context" (2.13) and "virtue" (3.33).

As a second step, the researchers asked whether these imagery ratings, generated by one group of participants, could be used to predict memory performance with a new group of participants. The new participants were asked to memorize lists of words, and the data reliably indicated that these participants learned high-imagery words more readily than low-imagery words (Paivio, 1969; Paivio, Smythe, & Yuille, 1968).

As a related point, it's clear that memory can be enormously aided by the use of imagery mnemonics. In one study, some participants were asked to learn pairs of words by rehearsing each pair silently. Other participants were instructed to make up a sentence for each pair of words, linking the words in some sensible way. Still other participants were told to form a mental image for each pair of words, with the image combining the words in some interaction. The results showed poorest recall performance by the rehearsal group and intermediate performance by the group that generated the sentences. Both of these groups, though, did much worse than the imagery group (Bower & Winzenz, 1970; for further discussion of mnemonic techniques, see Chapter 6).

In order to be helpful, though, imagery mnemonics need to do more than depict the objects side by side. These mnemonics are helpful only if they show the objects to be remembered *interacting* in some way. (For the classic demonstration of this point, see Wollen et al., 1972.) This isn't surprising: As we saw in Chapter 6, memory is improved in general if you can find ways to organize the material; interacting images provide one way of achieving this organization.

Imagery can also help you memorize materials that aren't in any strict sense "visual"—including materials concerned with issues of *timing* and *sequence*. Let's say that you want to learn several facts about Marta, with some of the facts concerned with Marta's past and some with her future. Perhaps you want to remember that a week ago Marta was in a great mood, that two months ago she bought a new car, and that next month she'll be flying to London. To learn these various facts, you might imagine them arranged in a line—with past events off to the left and future events, in proper sequence, arrayed to the right.

Do people use this strategy? One study examined patients with neglect syndrome. As we mentioned in Chapter 5, these patients attend only to the right side of space and consistently overlook stimuli on their left. We then saw in this chapter (p. 400) that these patients show a corresponding pattern in their *imagery*, consistently overlooking objects that might be depicted on the left in an image. How will all of this matter if these patients are using the mnemonic strategy just described? If they're imagining events on a timeline, they'll probably overlook events on the left—that is, past events. And that's the pattern of the results: Patients with left spatial neglect have a harder time remembering *past* facts about Marta (in the example we sketched) and an easier time remembering future facts. As the study's authors put it, these patients seem to neglect the "left side" of time—just as we would expect if they're using the strategy we've outlined (Saj et al., 2014).

Dual Coding

There's no question, then, that imagery improves memory, with at least two mechanisms contributing. First, we've just suggested that imagery provides a way of organizing materials, and of course organization helps memory. But, second, imageable materials (such as high-imagery words) will be doubly represented in memory: The word itself will be remembered, and so will the corresponding picture. This pattern is referred to as **dual coding**, and it has a significant advantage: When the time comes to retrieve these memories, either record—the verbal or the image—will provide the information you seek. This gives you a double chance of locating the information you need, thereby easing the process of memory search.

Of course, framing things in this way builds on the idea that you have (at least) two types of information in long-term storage: memories that represent the content of symbolic (and perhaps verbal) materials, and memories that represent imagery-based materials. Paivio (1971), the source of the dual-coding proposal, argued that these two types of memory differ from each other in important ways—including the information that they contain and the ways they're accessed. Access to symbolic memories, he suggested, is easiest if the cue provided is a word, as in: "Do you know the word 'squirrel'?" Access to an image-based memory, in contrast, is easiest if one begins with a picture: "Do you recognize this pictured creature?"

Memory for Pictures

Even with these differences, symbolic and visual memories are alike in many ways, and so many of the claims we made in Chapters 6, 7, and 8 apply with equal force to both memory types. Recall of both types, for example, is dependent on memory connections; priming effects can be observed with both types of memory; encoding specificity is observed in both domains; and so on.

Likewise, visual memory (like memory in general) is heavily influenced by schema-based, generic knowledge—knowledge about how events unfold in general. Chapter 8 described how these knowledge effects influence memory for sentences and stories, but similar effects can be demonstrated with pictures. In an early study, Friedman (1979) showed participants pictures of scenes such as a typical kitchen or a typical barnyard. The pictures also contained some unexpected objects—the kitchen picture, for example, included some items rarely found in a kitchen, such as a fireplace. Participants later took a recognition test in which they had to discriminate between pictures they'd actually seen and altered versions of these pictures in which something had been changed.

Participants' memories were plainly influenced by their broader knowledge of what "should be" included in these scenes. Thus, in some of the test pictures, one of the ordinary, expected objects in the scene had been changed—for example, participants might be shown a kitchen picture in which a different kind of stove appeared in place of the original stove, or one in which a radio replaced the toaster on the counter. Participants rarely noticed these changes and tended (incorrectly) to respond that this new picture was "old"—that is, it had been seen before. This outcome is sensible on schema grounds: Both the original and the altered pictures were fully consistent with the kitchen schema, so both would be compatible with a schema-based memory.

However, participants almost always noticed changes to the unexpected objects in the scene. If the originally viewed kitchen had a fireplace and the test picture did not, participants consistently detected this alteration. Again, this outcome is predictable on schema grounds: The fireplace didn't fit with the kitchen schema and so was likely to be noted in memory. In fact, Friedman recorded participants' eye movements during the original presentations of the pictures. Her data showed that participants tended to look twice as long at the unexpected objects as they did at the expected ones; clearly, these objects did catch the participants' attention.

A different line of evidence also shows schema effects in picture memory. Recall our claim that in understanding a story, people place the story within a schematic frame. As we saw in Chapter 8, this can often lead to intrusion errors, as people import their own expectations and understanding into the story and therefore end up remembering the story as including more than it actually did.

A similar pattern can be demonstrated with picture memory, in a phenomenon known as **boundary extension**. (See Intraub & Bodamer, 1993; Intraub & Dickinson, 2008. Also see Hale et al., 2016; McDunn et al., 2014; Munger & Multhaup, 2016.) In one of the early demonstrations of this pattern, participants were shown the top panel in **Figure 11.16** and then were later asked to sketch what they had seen (Intraub & Richardson, 1989). Two of the participants' drawings are shown at the bottom of Figure 11.16, and the boundary extension is clear: Participants remember the scene as less of a close-up view than it actually was, and they correspondingly remember the scene as containing more of the backdrop than it did. This effect is observed whether participants initially see a few pictures or many, whether they are tested immediately or after a delay, and even when they are explicitly warned about boundary extension and urged to avoid this effect.

Intraub has argued that this boundary extension arises from the way in which people perceive these pictures in the first place. People understand a picture, she claims, by means of a perceptual schema. This schema places the picture in a larger context, informing the perceiver about the real-world scene only partially revealed by the picture. Intraub suggests that this leads people to a series of expectations about what they might see if they could somehow look beyond the picture's edges, and these expectations become part of the experience of viewing the picture. It's then the *experience* that is

FIGURE 11.16
BOUNDARY EXTENSION IN PICTURE MEMORY

Participants were initially shown the photograph at the top of this picture. The two panels below show the scene as drawn from memory by two different participants. They clearly recalled the scene as a wide-angle shot, revealing more of the background than the photograph actually did.

(AFTER INTRAUB & RICHARDSON, 1989)

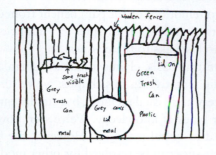

TEST YOURSELF

13. What evidence suggests that visual information is often stored in long-term memory via a representation that's not really "visual"?

14. What's the evidence that imagery can help you to memorize?

remembered—and so your memory includes both the picture itself and also your understanding of what you'd see if you explored further, leading to the boundary extension that reliably emerges in the data.

It seems, therefore, that picture memory generally follows the same rules, and is influenced by the same factors, as memory for verbal materials. Schema effects can be found in both domains. Similarly, participants show primacy and recency effects when they learn a series of pictures (Tabachnick & Brotsky, 1976), just as they do when they learn a series of words (Chapter 6). Spread of activation can be demonstrated with nonverbal materials (Kroll & Potter, 1984), just as it can be with verbal materials (Chapter 9). In short, there's considerable commonality between picture memory and memory of other sorts, confirming our suggestion of a memory system that holds diverse contents but with a uniform set of operating principles.

The Diversity of Knowledge

When you're thinking about an image—that is, holding the image in working memory—there's no question that you're considering a distinctive form of mental representation. Images in working memory contain different information than other representations do; they require a set of operations (like scanning, or rotation, or zooming) that are irrelevant to other sorts of memory contents. Therefore, our theorizing about active images has to be different from our theorizing about other forms of representation.

The situation changes, however, when we turn to long-term memory and consider your long-term retention for what a circus clown looks like or your recollection of what an earlier-viewed picture contained. These image-based memories seem to be stored in the same memory system as every other memory—and so they're influenced by exactly the same principles.

It appears, then, that your memory contains diverse contents (verbal memories, abstract memories, memories for sight and sounds and tastes), but there's just one set of rules applicable to everything that's in storage. However, we should attach a caution to this claim. In this chapter, we've focused on visual memories, and one might ask whether similar conclusions would emerge with other categories of knowledge. For example, do memories for smells benefit from rehearsal, show schema effects, and the like? Do memories for emotions or for pain benefit from deep processing? Do they show the effects we called (in Chapter 7) "implicit memory" effects? Relatively little research speaks to these issues.

On this basis, claims about the singularity of long-term memory should remain tentative. In this chapter, we've surveyed what is known about visual imagery and visual memory, but similar questions still need to be asked about other types of knowledge. We've seen how things stand on these issues with regard to visual materials. However, the field awaits additional data before these issues can be resolved for other modalities.

visualization and pain relief

Many practitioners report that visualization techniques can produce dramatic pain relief. The Arthritis Foundation website, for example, invites readers to "Imagine waking up one morning with joints so stiff and achy you can barely move them. Instead of reaching for the nearest bottle of pain relievers, you close your eyes, breathe deeply and visualize your pain as a glowing orb floating serenely away from your body. This scenario might sound too out-there to possibly work. Yet guided imagery . . . is a well-recognized and scientifically validated way to relieve pain, stress, anxiety and depression."

Other websites also offer endorsements. The Harvard Women's Health Watch site offers advice for people who suffer from backache, fibromyalgia, arthritis, or other chronic pain. The site suggests that "meditation with guided imagery, which often involves imagining yourself in a restful environment, may reduce your need for pain medication."

Does visualization provide pain relief? And, if it does, what's the mechanism? The results are mixed with regard to the first question, but even so, some studies do yield positive outcomes. For example, a 2015 article gathered together the results of seven different studies that had tried guided imagery as a treatment for pain in arthritis and other rheumatic diseases (Giacobbi et al., 2015). All seven of the studies indicated a benefit from imagery. Another research project asked patients to listen to a guided imagery audio recording two weeks before and then three weeks after surgery for a total knee replacement (Jacobson et al., 2016). The study found faster recovery (measured as gait velocity) in the guided imagery group.

There's certainly room for debate, though, about *how* visualization helps when it does seem to help. It's likely that many mechanisms are in play, all at the same time. First, if someone is paying close attention to a visual image, then they're not paying attention to the pain, and this by itself may be helpful. In essence, the visualization is, in this situation, helping someone simply by distracting them away from the pain. Second, visualization techniques often help people to relax—with slower breathing and decreased stress. The relaxation may provide direct relief from pain and may also diminish the medical problem that led to the pain in the first place. Third, visualization instructions may create a placebo effect. After all, we know that medical outcomes can sometimes be improved by giving the patient an inert pill (e.g., a sugar pill), as long as the patient *believes* the pill is potent medicine. In such cases, it's the belief, not the pill, that's having a medical effect.

You might take the position, though, that there's little reason to care which of these mechanisms is operative. No matter what the mechanism, there's a potential for a medical benefit; and in an era in which people are deeply

PAIN RELIEF IN CHILDBIRTH

Many parents hope (or, in some cases, need) to minimize the use of pain medication during childbirth. In this setting, alternative means of reducing pain—including visualization techniques—can be enormously valuable.

concerned about the overuse of pain medications (especially opiates), we should welcome these medication-free approaches.

There's one issue, however, for which the debate about mechanism might matter: If visualization provides pain relief through distraction or relaxation, then it doesn't matter exactly what the person visualizes—as long as the visualization has a calming effect. The person might therefore visualize strolling on a beach, or relaxing in a hammock, or drifting down a river in a canoe. Likewise, if there's a placebo effect in play, the imaged content is again irrelevant, as long as the person believes the image will be helpful.

Let's be clear, though, that some practitioners (including one that we've already quoted) argue that the content of your visualization does matter, and they offer very specific advice about what should be visualized in order to gain pain relief. We've mentioned the advice that you should "visualize your pain as a glowing orb floating serenely away from your body." In preparation for childbirth, some birth coaches encourage the woman to visualize her cervix gradually opening wide—and the coaches sometimes provide medical drawings of a cervix to facilitate the visualization. People diagnosed with cancer sometimes visualize their tumor shrinking or a healing light shining on their body. Indeed, you can find assertions on the Internet along the lines of "if we visualize our healthy cells multiplying and cancerous cells dissolving and disappearing, our body may be able to act out those mental images."

You should, however, be skeptical about these specific suggestions. There is, first, no reason to think that visualization actually diminishes a cancerous tumor. More positively, the other suggestions (relaxing your cervix or visualizing the orb) may work; but if they do, it's for the reasons we've already discussed. In other words, these specific forms of visualizing are just one way to keep yourself calm, reduce stress, and distract yourself away from pain. It's fine, therefore, if you instead choose your own content for your visualization—whether it's a beach stroll, or relaxing in a friend's arms, or lying in the grass and watching the clouds. In all cases, this visualization may help you to cope with, and maybe even escape, your pain.

For more on this topic . . .

Arthritis Foundation. (n.d.). *Guided imagery for arthritis pain*. https://www
.arthritis.org/living-with-arthritis/treatments/natural/other-therapies
/mind-body-pain-relief/guided-imagery.php

Giacobbi, P. R., Jr., Stabler, M. E., Stewart, J., Jaeschke, A.-M., Siebert, J. L., &
Kelley, G. A. (2015). Guided imagery for arthritis and other rheumatic dis-
eases: A systematic review of randomized control trials. *Pain Management
Nursing, 16*(5), 792–803.

Harvard Women's Health Watch. (2015, April). *6 ways to use your mind to
control pain*. Harvard Health Publishing, Harvard Medical School. https://
www.health.harvard.edu/mind-and-mood/6-ways-to-use-your-mind-to
-control-pain

Jacobson, A. F., Umberger, W. A., Palmieri, P. A., Alexander, T. S., Myerscough, R. P., Draucker, C. B., Steudte-Schmiedgen, S., & Kirschbaum, C. (2016). Guided imagery for total knee replacement: A randomized, placebo-controlled pilot study. *Journal of Alternative and Complementary Medicine, 22*(7), 563–575.

Posadzki, P., Lewandowski, W., Terry, R., Ernst, E., & Stearns, A. (2012). Guided imagery for non-musculoskeletal pain: A systematic review of randomized clinical trials. *Journal of Pain and Symptom Management, 44*(1), 95–104.

Verkuilen (2018, June 19). *The power of the mind can help heal cancer: The science behind guided imagery: How does it work?* Thrive Global Community. https://thriveglobal.com/stories/the-science-behind-guided-imagery-how-does-it-work/

chapter review

SUMMARY

- People differ enormously in how they describe their imagery experience, particularly the vividness of that experience. However, concerns about how we should interpret these self-reports have led investigators to seek more objective ways of studying mental imagery.

- Chronometric studies indicate that the pattern of what information is more available and what is less available in an image closely matches the pattern of what is available in an actual picture. Likewise, the times needed to scan across an image, to zoom in on an image to examine detail, or to imagine the form rotating, all correspond closely to the times needed for these operations with actual pictures. These results emerge even when the experimenter makes no mention of imagery, ruling out an account of these data in terms of the experiment's demand character.

- In many settings, visual imagery seems to involve mechanisms that overlap with those used for visual perception. This is reflected in the fact that imaging one thing can make it difficult to perceive something else, or that imaging the appropriate target can prime a subsequent perception. Further evidence comes from neuroimaging and studies of brain damage; this evidence confirms the considerable overlap between the biological basis for imagery and that for perception.

- Not all imagery, however, is visual, so that we need to distinguish between *visual* and *spatial* imagery. This proposal is confirmed by studies of individuals with brain damage, some of whom seem to lose the capacity for visual imagery but retain their capacity for spatial imagery. This proposal may also help us understand the pattern of individual differences in imagery ability, with some individuals being particularly skilled in visual imagery and some in spatial.

- Evidence suggests that there are different types of spatial ability. One type, needed for the mental rotation task, relies heavily on mechanisms in the brain's right hemisphere and shows a robust gender difference (with men faster than women); another type, measured by mental folding, shows neither of these patterns. The gender differences themselves are heavily influenced by training and experience.

- Just as some individuals seem to have little or no visual imagery, other individuals—called "eidetikers"—seem to have fabulously detailed, photographic imagery. There's no question that this astonishingly vivid imagery exists in some people, but the mechanisms behind it remain unknown.

- Even when imagery is visual, mental images are picture-like; they aren't actually pictures. Unlike pictures, mental images seem to be accompanied by a perceptual reference frame that guides the interpretation of the images and also influences what can be discovered about the images.

- To create a mental image, you draw on information stored in long-term memory. Using this information, the imager first constructs a frame for the image and then can elaborate the frame as needed. Also, at least some information about visual appearance or spatial arrangement is stored in long-term memory in terms of verbal labels or conceptual frameworks. For example, information about the locations of cities may be stored in terms of propositions ("Montreal is in Canada; Canada is north of the United States") rather than being stored in some sort of mental map.

- Imagery helps people to remember, so word lists are more readily recalled if the words are easily imaged; similarly, instructions to form images help people to memorize. These benefits may be the result of dual coding: storing information in both a verbal format and a format that encodes appearances; this approach doubles the chances of recalling the material later on.

● Memory for pictures follows most of the same rules as any other form of memory; for example, it is influenced by schematic knowledge. It is unclear, though, what other categories of memory there might be. In each case, other kinds of memory are likely to have some properties that are distinctive and also many properties that are shared with memories of other sorts.

KEY TERMS

self-report data (p. 388)
chronometric studies (p. 389)
image-scanning procedure (p. 391)
mental rotation task (p. 392)
demand character (p. 395)

eidetic imagery (p. 409)
percepts (p. 411)
dual coding (p. 417)
boundary extension (p. 419)

TEST YOURSELF AGAIN

1. What is the concern about self-report data, and Galton's data in particular?

2. What is a chronometric study?

3. Why do image-scanning studies indicate that images *depict* a scene rather than *describe* the scene?

4. What does it mean to say that an experiment's results might be influenced by demand character?

5. What's the evidence that visual imagery relies on some of the same mental processes as actual vision?

6. What do we learn from the fact that some forms of brain damage have *similar* effects on a person's ability to see and the person's ability to perform many imagery tasks?

7. What do we learn from the fact that some forms of brain damage have *different* effects on a person's ability to see and the person's ability to perform many imagery tasks?

8. What evidence is there that there are different types of spatial skill?

9. What evidence suggests that the gender difference in spatial skill is heavily influenced by (and may be due to) experience and training?

10. What evidence confirms that people do actually differ in the vividness of their visual images?

11. What is eidetic imagery?

12. Images are certainly picture-*like,* but what evidence points to a distinction between mental images and actual out-in-the-world pictures?

13. What evidence suggests that visual information is often stored in long-term memory via a representation that's not really "visual"?

14. What's the evidence that imagery can help you to memorize?

THINK ABOUT IT

1. People differ markedly in their skill of recognizing previously viewed faces. (Want to know how you measure up? Point an Internet browser at the Cambridge Face Memory Test.) Is it plausible that these differences are linked to the person's skill in forming visual images? How might you test this?

2. Often, a movie is based on a popular book, and you sometimes hear people say things like this: "The movie was hard to watch because the main figure in the story didn't look at all like I'd imagined her, based on the book." Is it plausible that people who most often say this are the people with the clearest, most vivid imagery? How might you test this?

DEMONSTRATIONS & APPLYING COGNITIVE PSYCHOLOGY ESSAYS

For demonstrations of key concepts in cognitive psychology, take a look at the Online Demonstrations. To explore more of the practical applications of cognitive psychology in themed essays, visit the online reader.

Online Demonstrations

- Demonstration 11.1: The Paper Folding Test
- Demonstration 11.2: Imagery Vividness
- Demonstration 11.3: Imaged Synthesis
- Demonstration 11.4: Mnemonic Strategies
- Demonstration 11.5: Auditory Imagery

Online Applying Cognitive Psychology Essays

- Cognitive Psychology and Education: Using Imagery
- Cognitive Psychology and Technology: Cellphone Pictures
- Cognitive Psychology and the Law: Lineups

ZAPS COGNITION LABS

Go to ZAPS online cognition labs to conduct hands-on experiments on key concepts.

INQUIZITIVE

It's time to complete your study experience! Go to InQuizitive to practice actively with this chapter's concepts and get personalized feedback along the way.

part 5

Thinking

The capacity for *thought* is surely a central part of what makes us human, and we rely on this capacity all the time. We draw conclusions; we make choices; we solve problems. But how do we achieve these things? How do we think? How *well* do we think? In this section, we'll see that human thinking is often flawed, and we'll encounter examples of bad judgment, improper reasoning, and highly inefficient problem solving. In some cases, this poor performance comes from laziness—with people not bothering to think things through. In other cases, people *choose* not to think things through, because they've decided in advance what conclusion they prefer, whether the conclusion is justified by the facts or not. But in many other settings, people try to be reasonable yet rely on strategies that can sometimes lead to error. People use these strategies, though, because they're efficient—inviting the suggestion that the errors may be the price people pay for efficient thinking.

It's also clear, though, that people often rise above all of these limitations, and so end up thinking carefully and well. This point will drive us toward a multilayered conception of thinking, because we'll need to describe both the shortcuts that people use and also the more careful strategies that people often turn to. In addition, we'll need to tackle the obvious questions of *why* and *when* people rely on one sort of thinking or the other. What are the circumstances that lead to efficient-but-risky thinking, and what are the triggers for slower-but-better thinking?

It's also important that people seem to differ in their thinking. Some people are wonderfully logical; others seem foolish. Some people are creative problem solvers; others are stymied by even simple problems. Some people seem fabulously intelligent; others seem less so. In this section, we'll examine these differences as well.

Finally, one other set of issues will arise in this section: How much of thought is conscious? Are there benefits associated with conscious thought, as opposed to unconscious thought? We will tackle these questions in the book's final chapter.

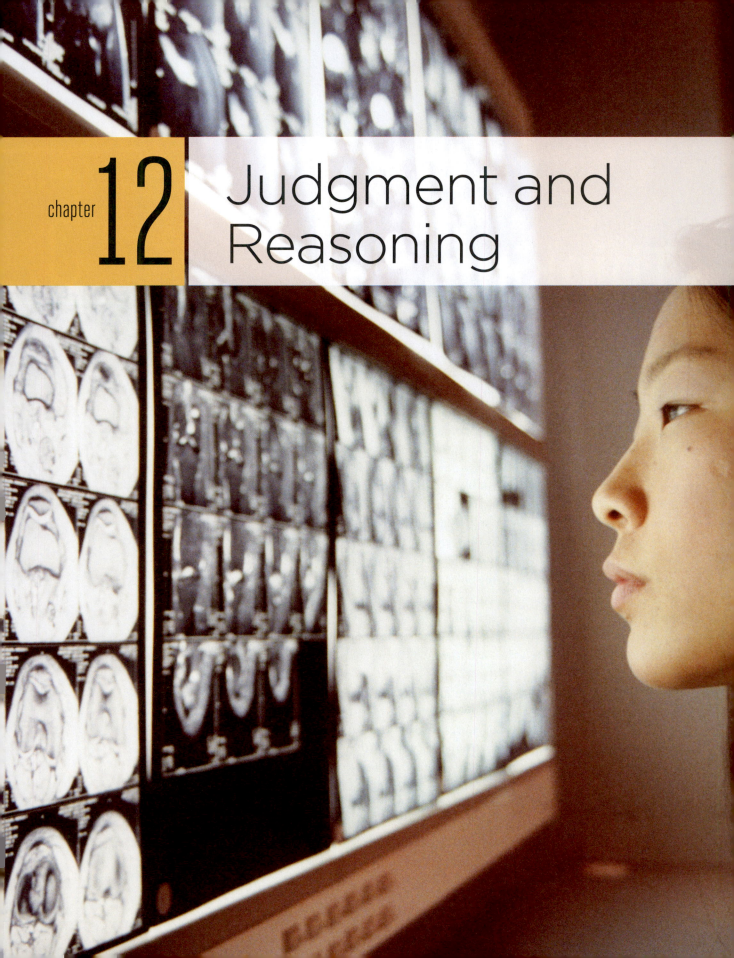

chapter **12**

Judgment and
Reasoning

what if... The activity we call "thinking" involves many processes, and this point blocks us from asking in a general way: "What would happen if you lost the ability to think?" We can, however, ask what would happen if you lost *this* aspect of thinking or *that* aspect—and the answers are often surprising.

Many of us regard *emotion* as a force that disrupts thinking. We say things like "I was so angry I couldn't think straight" or "I knew I'd regret the choice, but at that moment I was listening more to my heart than to my head." These sentiments capture important truths, but they overstate the separation between "heart" and "head," because emotion turns out to play a huge role in our ordinary thinking. We see this if we ask: "What if someone loses *the capacity for ordinary emotion*?" Consider Elliot, a patient whose case is discussed in detail by Antonio Damasio (1994). Elliot had undergone surgery to remove a brain tumor, and the surgery seemed to have little impact on his intellect; his IQ was just as high after the operation as it was before. But after the operation, Elliot became hopelessly indecisive. In scheduling an appointment, he needed 30 minutes, staring at his calendar, to decide which of two days would be better for him. He needed so much time to choose where he'd eat lunch that he was likely to miss lunchtime. Even the simplest of decisions—whether to use a blue pen or a black one for office paperwork—was paralyzing for him.

Because of damage to a brain region called the "orbitofrontal cortex" (see **Figure 12.1**), Elliot seemed to have lost emotions; Damasio reports that he "never saw a tinge of emotion" in his hours of conversation with Elliot. When tested in the laboratory, Elliot showed no bodily response at all if shown pictures depicting tragedy or aggression; he didn't react to sexual images, or gruesome pictures of wounds, or any other images that for most people cause a powerful emotional response.

But why did Elliot's lack of emotion lead to paralysis in his decision making? Part of the answer lies in the fact that decisions often involve an element of risk ("Will this dinner taste as good as the menu description implies?"). To evaluate these risks, people rely heavily on emotion—and so, if thinking about the dinner fills you with joyful anticipation, you'll judge the risk to be low (Slovic & Peters, 2010). Or, as a contrasting case, if thinking about a terrorist attack fills you with dread, you'll likely judge the risk of an attack to be high. But these processes were

- In a wide range of circumstances, people use cognitive shortcuts, or "heuristics," to make judgments. These heuristics are efficient and often lead to sensible conclusions, but sometimes they can lead to error.

- People use heuristics even when they're highly motivated to be accurate, and trained experts often rely on the same heuristics. Therefore, expert judgments are also vulnerable to error.

- In some circumstances, people step away from heuristic use ("Type 1" thinking) and rely instead on more sophisticated ("Type 2") forms of reasoning—and so they judge covariation accurately, are sensitive to base rates, and so on.

- Evidence suggests that Type 2 reasoning is likely to come into play only if the circumstances are right and only if the case being judged contains the appropriate triggers for this form of reasoning.

- The quality of people's thinking is also uneven within the broad domain of deduction. For example, people show a pattern of "confirmation bias" and so are more sensitive to, and more accepting of, evidence that supports their beliefs than they are of evidence that challenges their beliefs.

- Errors in logical reasoning follow patterns that suggest people are guided by principles other than those of logic. Contrary to the principles of formal logic, people's reasoning is heavily influenced by the *content* of what they're reasoning about.

- People seem not to base their decisions on utility calculations; this is evident in the fact that many factors (including a decision's frame) have a strong impact on decisions even though these factors don't change utilities in any way. People seem instead to make decisions that they feel they can justify, so they are influenced by factors that make one choice or another seem more compelling.

- Another factor influencing decision making is emotion. However, people are often inaccurate in predicting their future emotions, with the result that they work hard to avoid regret that they wouldn't have felt anyhow, and they spend money for things that provide only short-term pleasure.

unavailable for (never-emotional) Elliot, with disastrous consequences for his decision making.

There are, of course, occasions in which emotion can disrupt thinking. But, apparently, there are also settings in which emotion *is needed for* productive thinking. We'll need to address this point before we're through.

Judgment

People sometimes hold beliefs because they're echoing claims they've heard from others. Or they hold beliefs that represent the way they *want* the world to be. But it's surely true that people often seek to draw conclusions from evidence they encounter, often evidence provided by life experiences. This form of thinking is called "judgment," so let's ask how—and how well—do people make judgments.

Experience is, of course, an extraordinary teacher, and you're likely to believe the sports coach who, after many seasons, tells you which game strategies work and which ones don't. Likewise, you trust the police detective who asserts that over the years he's learned how to tell whether a suspect is lying.

But we can easily find cases in which people *don't* learn from experience: "He's getting married *again*? Why does he think this one will last longer than the last four?"; "It doesn't matter how many polite New Yorkers she meets; she's still convinced that everyone from that city is rude."

FIGURE 12.1 ORBITOFRONTAL CORTEX

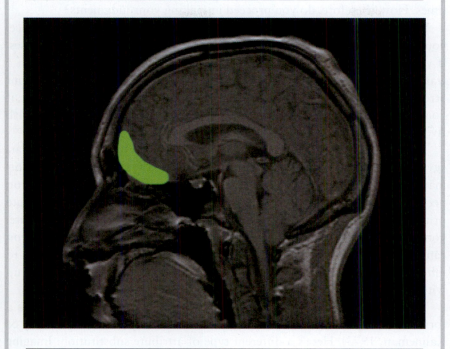

The area highlighted in green is the orbitofrontal cortex—the portion of the brain just behind the eyeballs. Many researchers argue that this brain region plays a crucial role in the processes through which we detect and interpret our emotions.

What's going on here? Why do people sometimes draw accurate conclusions from their experience, and sometimes not?

Attribute Substitution

Let's start with the *information* you use when drawing a conclusion from experience. Imagine that you're shopping for a car and trying to decide if European cars are reliable. Surely, you'd want to know how often these cars need repair—how frequent are the problems? As a different case, imagine that you're trying to choose an efficient route for your morning drive to work. Here you might want to ask: When you've gone down 4th Avenue, how often were you late? How often were you late when you stayed on Front Street?

Examples like these remind us that judgments often begin with a **frequency estimate**—an assessment of how often various events have occurred in the past. For many judgments you make in day-to-day life, though, you don't have direct access to frequency information. You're unlikely to know the exact count of how many VW's break down, in comparison to how many Hondas. You probably don't have a detailed list of your various commute times. How, therefore, do you proceed in making your judgments?

Let's pursue the decision about commuting routes. In making your choice, you're likely to do a quick scan through memory, looking for relevant cases. If you can immediately think of three occasions when you got caught in a traffic snarl on 4th Avenue and can't think of similar occasions on Front Street, you'll probably decide that Front Street is the better bet. In contrast, if you can recall two horrible traffic jams on Front Street but only one on 4th Avenue, you'll draw the opposite conclusion.

The strategy you're using here is known as **attribute substitution**—a strategy in which you rely on easily assessed information as a proxy for the information you really need. In this judgment about traffic, the information you need is *frequency* (how often you've been late when you've taken one route or the other), but you don't have access to this information. As a substitute, you base your judgment on *availability*—how easily and how quickly you can come up with relevant examples. The logic is this: "Examples leap to mind? Must be a common, often-experienced event. A struggle to come up with examples? Must be a rare event."

This strategy—relying on *availability* as a substitute for *frequency*—is a form of attribute substitution known as the **availability heuristic** (Tversky & Kahneman, 1973). Here's a different type of attribute substitution: Imagine that you're applying for a job. You hope that the employer will examine your credentials carefully and make a thoughtful judgment about whether you'd be a good hire. It's likely, though, that the employer will rely on a faster, easier strategy. Specifically, he may barely glance at your résumé and, instead, ask himself how much you resemble other people he's hired who have worked out well. Do you have the same mannerisms or the same look as Joan, an employee he's very happy with? If so, you're likely to get the job. Or do you remind him of Jane, an employee he had to fire after just two months? If so, you'll still be looking at the job ads tomorrow.

In this case, the person who's interviewing you needs to judge a *probability* (namely, the probability that you'd work out well if hired) and instead relies on *resemblance* to known cases. This substitution is referred to as the **representativeness heuristic**.

The Availability Heuristic

People rely on heuristics like availability and representativeness in a wide range of settings, and so, if we understand these strategies, we understand how a great deal of thinking proceeds. (See **Table 12.1** for a comparison of two strategies, and also two other forms of attribute substitution.)

In general, the term **heuristic** describes an efficient strategy that usually leads to the right answer. The key word, however, is "usually," because heuristics allow errors; that's the price you pay in order to gain efficiency. The

TABLE 12.1   DIFFERENT TYPES OF ATTRIBUTE SUBSTITUTION

You want to judge . . .	Instead you rely on . . .	This usually works because . . .	But this strategy can lead to error because . . .
Frequency of occurrence in the world	"Availability heuristic"—how easily can you think of cases?	Events that are frequent in the world are likely to be more available in memory.	Many factors *other than* frequency in the world can influence availability from memory!
Probability of an event being in a category or having certain properties	"Representativeness heuristic"—how much resemblance is there between that event and other events in the category?	Many categories are homogeneous enough so that the category members do resemble one another.	Many categories are not homogeneous!
Risks and potential benefits associated with an outcome	"Affect heuristic"—how does thinking about the outcome make you feel?	Substantial dangers are often deeply frightening! Positive outcomes often lead you to feel good.	Often, the level of emotion associated with an outcome is influenced by factors having little connection to the likelihood of the outcome.
Estimates of value	"Effort heuristic"—how much effort did you have to spend to gain the outcome?	Often, it takes more work to obtain things of higher value.	Often, value is independent of effort—consider what you can buy with $20 *earned* vs. $20 *found on the street*.

availability and representativeness heuristics both fit this profile. In each case, you're relying on an attribute (availability or resemblance) that's easy to assess, and that's the source of the efficiency. And in each case, the attribute is correlated with the target dimension, so that it can serve as a reasonable proxy for the target: Events or objects that are frequent in the world are, in most cases, likely to be easily available in memory, so generally you'll be fine if you rely on availability as an index for frequency. And many categories are homogeneous enough so that members of the category do resemble one another; that's why you can often rely on resemblance as a means of judging probability of category membership.

Nonetheless, these strategies can lead to error. To take a simple case, ask yourself: "Are there more words in the dictionary beginning with the letter *R* ('rose,' 'rock,' 'rabbit') or more words with an *R* in the third position ('tarp,' 'bare,' 'throw')?" Most people insist that there are more words beginning with *R* (Tversky & Kahneman, 1973, 1974), but the reverse is true, by a wide margin.

Why do people get this wrong? The answer lies in availability. If you search your memory for words starting with *R*, many will come to mind. (Try it: How many *R*-words can you name in 10 seconds?) But if you search your memory for words with an *R* in the third position, fewer will come up. (Again, try this for 10 seconds.) This difference, favoring the words beginning with *R*, arises because your memory is organized roughly like a dictionary, with words that share a starting sound all grouped together. As a result, it's easy to search memory using "starting letter" as your cue; a search based on "*R* in third position" is more difficult. In this way, the organization of memory creates a bias in what's easily available, and this bias in availability leads to an error in frequency judgment.

The Range of Availability Effects

How often are people influenced by availability? Let's start with the fact that people regularly overestimate the frequency of events that are, in actuality, quite rare (Lichtenstein et al., 1978). This probably plays a part in people's willingness to buy lottery tickets; they overestimate the likelihood of winning. Likewise, physicians often overestimate the likelihood of encountering a rare disease and, in the process, fail to pursue

ABUSE OF THE AVAILABILITY HEURISTIC?

Imagine a diabolical college professor who wants to improve student evaluations of his teaching. A possible strategy is suggested by a study in which students were asked to list ways a particular course could be improved (Fox, 2006). Students were then asked for an overall rating of how good the course was. Students in one group were asked to list just two potential improvements to the course. These students had an easy time generating this short list, and guided by the availability heuristic, they seemed to reason this way: "It sure was easy to come up with possible improvements for the course. I guess, therefore, that the course must have many flaws and so isn't very good." As a result, they gave the course lower ratings than students who were asked to do a more difficult task—come up with ten potential improvements for the course. Students in the latter group ended up with much more evidence in their view for the course's problems, but that's not what mattered. Instead, these students seemed to be thinking: "It was hard to produce this list. I guess, therefore, the course doesn't have many flaws; if it did, I'd have had an easier time thinking of improvements. So I'll give the course a high rating." Of course, no professor would ever think about exploiting this pattern to manipulate student evaluations. . . .

other, more appropriate, diagnoses (e.g., Elstein et al., 1986; Obrecht et al., 2009).

What's the role of availability here? The answer lies in the fact that you're likely to notice and think about rare events, especially rare *emotional* events. As a result, these events are well recorded in memory, and this will make these events easily available to you. As a consequence, if you rely on the availability heuristic, you'll overestimate the frequency of these distinctive events and, correspondingly, overestimate the likelihood of similar events happening in the future.

Here's a different example. Participants in one study were asked to think about episodes in their lives in which they'd acted in an assertive manner (Schwarz et al., 1991; also see Raghubir & Menon, 2005). Half of the participants were asked to recall 6 episodes; half were asked to recall 12 episodes. Then, all the participants were asked some general questions, including how assertive overall they thought they were.

Participants had an easy time coming up with 6 episodes, and so, using the availability heuristic, they concluded, "Those cases came quickly to mind; therefore, there must be a large number of these episodes; therefore, I must be an assertive person." In contrast, participants who were asked for 12 episodes had some difficulty generating the longer list, so they concluded, "If these cases are so difficult to recall, I guess the episodes can't be typical for how I act."

Consistent with these suggestions, participants who were asked to recall fewer episodes judged themselves to be more assertive. Notice, ironically, that the participants who tried to recall more episodes actually ended up with more evidence in view for their own assertiveness. But it's not the quantity of evidence that matters. Instead, what matters is the ease of coming up with the episodes. Participants who were asked for a dozen episodes had a hard time with the task *because they'd been asked to do something difficult*—namely, to come up with a lot of cases. But the participants seemed not to realize this. They reacted only to the fact that the examples were difficult to generate, and using the availability heuristic, they concluded that being assertive was relatively infrequent in their past.

The Representativeness Heuristic

Similar points can be made about the representativeness heuristic. Just like availability, this strategy often leads to the correct conclusion. But here, too, the strategy can sometimes lead you astray.

How does the representativeness heuristic work? Let's start with the fact that many of the categories you encounter are relatively homogeneous. The category "birds," for example, is reasonably uniform with regard to the traits of *having wings*, *having feathers*, and so on. Virtually every member of the category has these traits, and so, in these regards, each member of the category resembles most of the others. Likewise, the category "motels" is homogeneous with regard to traits like *has beds in each room* and *has an*

HOW IMPORTANT IS YOUR COUNTRY?

How large a contribution has your home country made to world history? Chances are good that you can easily think of examples in which your nation did make a difference, and so these examples are readily available to you. This point helps us understand why people overestimate their country's importance and—on average—estimate the contribution as being ten times greater than it actually was (Zaromb et al., 2018). Shown here is part of the opening ceremony for the 2010 World Cup soccer tournament.

office, and so, again, in these regards each member of the category resembles the others.

The representativeness heuristic capitalizes on this homogeneity. We expect each individual to resemble the other individuals in the category (i.e., we expect each individual to be *representative* of the category overall). As a result, we can use resemblance as a basis for judging the likelihood of category membership. So if a creature resembles other birds you've seen, you conclude that the creature probably is a bird. We first met this approach in Chapter 9, when we were discussing simple categories like "dog" and "fruit." But the same approach can be used more broadly—and this is the heart of the representativeness strategy. Thus, if a job candidate resembles successful hires you've made, you conclude that the person will probably be a successful hire; if someone you meet at a party resembles engineers you've known, you assume that the person is likely to be an engineer.

Once again, though, use of this heuristic can lead to error. Imagine tossing a coin over and over, and let's say that it lands heads up six times in a row. Many people believe that on the next toss the coin is more likely to come up tails. They reason that if the coin is fair, then any series of tosses should contain roughly equal numbers of heads and tails. If no tails have appeared for a while, then some are "overdue" to make up the balance.

This pattern of thinking is called the "gambler's fallacy." To see that it is a fallacy, bear in mind that a coin has no "memory," so the coin has no way of knowing how long it has been since the last tails. Therefore, the likelihood of a tails occurring on any particular toss must be independent of what happened on previous tosses; there's no way that the previous tosses could possibly influence the next one. As a result, the probability of a tails on toss number 7 is .50, just as it was on the first toss—and on every toss.

What produces the gambler's fallacy? The explanation lies in the assumption of category homogeneity. We know that in the long run, a fair coin will produce equal numbers of heads and tails. Therefore, the category of "all tosses" has this property. Our assumption of homogeneity, though, leads us to expect that any "representative" of the category will also have this property—that is, any sequence of tosses will also show the 50-50 split. But this isn't true: Some sequences of tosses are 75% heads; some are 5% heads. It's only when we combine these sequences that the 50-50 split emerges. (For a different perspective on the gambler's fallacy, see Farmer et al., 2017.)

Reasoning from a Single Case to the Entire Population

The assumption of homogeneity can also lead to a different error, one that's in view whenever people try to persuade each other with a "man who" argument. To understand this term (proposed by Nisbett & Ross, 1980), imagine that you're shopping for a new cell phone. You've read various consumer magazines and decided, based on their test data, that you'll buy a Smacko brand phone. You report this to a friend, who is aghast. "Smacko? You must be crazy. Why, I know a guy who bought a Smacko, and the case fell apart two weeks after he got it. Then, the wire for the headphones went. Then, the charger failed. How could you possibly buy a Smacko?"

What should you make of this argument? The consumer magazines tested many phones and reported that, say, 2% of all Smackos have repair problems. In your friend's "data," 100% of the Smackos (one out of one) broke. It seems silly to let this "sample of one" outweigh the much larger sample tested by the magazine; but even so, your friend probably thinks he's offering a persuasive argument. What guides your friend's thinking? He must be assuming that the category will resemble the instance. Only in that case would reasoning from a single instance be appropriate.

If you listen to conversations around you, you'll regularly hear "man who" (or "woman who") arguments. "What do you mean, cigarette smoking causes cancer?! I have an aunt who smoked for 50 years, and she runs in marathons!" Often, these arguments seem persuasive. But they have force only by virtue of the representativeness heuristic and your assumption of category homogeneity.

Detecting Covariation

It cannot be surprising that people often rely on mental shortcuts. After all, you don't have unlimited time, and many of the judgments you make, day by day, are far from life-changing. It's unsettling, though, that people use the same shortcuts when making deeply consequential judgments. And to make things worse, the errors caused by the heuristics can trigger other sorts of errors, including errors in judgments of **covariation**. This term has a technical meaning, but for our purposes we can define it this way: X and Y "covary" if X tends to be on the scene whenever Y is, and if X tends to be absent whenever Y is absent. For example, exercise and stamina covary: People who do the first tend to have a lot of the second. Years of education and annual salary also covary (and so people with more education tend to earn more), but the covariation is weaker than that between exercise and stamina. Notice, then, that covariation can be strong or weak, and it can also be negative or positive. Exercise and stamina, for example, covary positively (as exercise increases, so does stamina). Exercise and risk of heart attacks covary negatively (because exercise strengthens the heart muscle, decreasing the risk).

TEST YOURSELF

1. What is attribute substitution?
2. In the availability heuristic, what is the information you need, and what attribute do you use as a substitute?
3. In the representativeness heuristic, what is the information you need, and what attribute do you use as a substitute?
4. What is a "man who" argument? Why are "man who" arguments often misleading?

Covariation is important for many reasons—including the fact that it's what you need to consider when checking on a belief about cause and effect. For example, do you feel better on days when you eat a good breakfast? If so, then the presence or absence of a good breakfast in the morning should covary with how you feel as the day wears on. Similarly: Are you more likely to fall in love with someone tall? Does your car start more easily if you pump the gas pedal? These, too, are questions that hinge on covariation, leading us to ask: How accurately do people judge covariation?

Illusions of Covariation

People routinely "detect" covariation even where there is none. For example, many people are convinced there's a relationship between someone's astrological sign (e.g., whether the person is, say, a Libra or a Virgo) and their personality, yet no serious study has documented this covariation. Likewise, many people believe they can predict the weather by paying attention to their arthritis pain ("My knee always acts up when a storm is coming"). This belief, too, turns out to be groundless. Other examples concern social stereotypes (e.g., the idea that being "moody" covaries with gender), superstitions (e.g., the idea that Friday the 13th brings bad luck), and more. (For some of the evidence, see King & Koehler, 2000; Redelmeier & Tversky, 1996; Shaklee & Mims, 1982.)

What causes these illusions? Part of the problem, of course, involves situations in which someone deliberately ignores the facts, perhaps because the person feels well served by a particular belief, and so has no wish to check on the belief. But, in addition, people who are trying to respect the evidence sometimes consider only a subset of the facts, and it's often a subset skewed by their prior expectations. This virtually guarantees mistaken judgments, since even if the judgment process were 100% fair, a biased input would lead to a biased output.

Specifically, when judging covariation, your selection of evidence is often guided by **confirmation bias**—a tendency to be more alert to evidence that *confirms* your beliefs rather than to evidence that might *challenge* them. We'll say more about confirmation bias later, but for now let's note how confirmation bias can distort the assessment of covariation. Let's say, for example, that you have the belief that big dogs tend to be vicious. With this belief, you're more likely to notice big dogs that are, in fact, vicious and little dogs that are friendly. As a result, a biased sample of dogs is available to you, in the dogs you perceive and the dogs you remember. Therefore, if you try to estimate covariation between dog size and temperament, you'll get it wrong. This isn't because you're ignoring the facts. The problem instead lies in your "data"; if the data are biased, so will be your judgment.

Base Rates

Assessment of covariation is also pulled off track by another problem: neglect of **base-rate information**—information about how frequently something occurs in general. Imagine that we're testing a new drug in the hope that it will cure the common cold. Here, we're trying to find out if taking the drug covaries with a better medical outcome, and let's say that our study tells us that 70% of patients taking the drug recover from their illness within 48 hours. This result is uninterpretable on its own, because we need the base rate: We need to know how often *in general* people recover from their colds in the same time span. If it turns out that the overall recovery rate within 48 hours is 70%, then our new drug is having no effect whatsoever.

Similarly, do good-luck charms help? Let's say that you wear your lucky socks whenever your favorite team plays, and the team has won 85% of its games. Here, too, we need to ask about base rates: How many games has your team won over the last few years? Perhaps the team has won 90% over-all. In that case, your socks may actually be a jinx.

Despite the importance of base rates, people often ignore them. In a clas-sic study, Kahneman and Tversky (1973) asked participants this question: If someone is chosen at random from a group of 70 lawyers and 30 engineers, what is his profession likely to be? Participants understood perfectly well that the probability of this person being a lawyer is .70. Apparently, in some set-tings people are appropriately sensitive to base-rate information.

Other participants did a similar task, but they were given the same base rates *and also* brief descriptions of certain individuals. Based on this informa-tion, they were asked whether each individual was more likely to be a lawyer or an engineer. These descriptions provided **diagnostic information**—infor-mation about the particular case—and some of the descriptions had been crafted (based on common stereotypes) to suggest that the person was a law-yer; some suggested engineer; some were relatively neutral.

We've already seen that people are responsive to base-rate information if this is the only information they have. Plainly, then, people understand that the base rates are relevant to their judgment. And, of course, people also under-stand the value of the diagnostic information: If you're told that someone has no math skills, loves debate, and goes to work in reasonably formal clothing, surely you realize that this tips the scales toward "lawyer," and not "engineer."

When given *both* types of information, therefore, we should expect that the participants will combine these inputs as well as they can. If both the base rate and the diagnostic information favor the lawyer response, partici-pants should offer this response with confidence. If the base rate indicates one response and the diagnostic information the other response, participants should temper their estimates accordingly.

However, this isn't what participants did. When provided with both types of information, they relied only on the descriptive information about the individual. In fact, when given both the base rate and the diagnostic informa-tion, participants' responses were the same if the base rates were as already described (70 lawyers, 30 engineers) or if the base rates were reversed (30 lawyers, 70 engineers). This reversal had no impact on participants' judgments, confirming that they were indeed ignoring the base rates.

What produces this neglect of base rates? The answer, in part, is attribute substitution. When asked whether a particular person—Quinn, let's say—is

TEST YOURSELF

5. What is a base rate? Why is base-rate information important?

a lawyer or an engineer, people seem to turn this question about category membership into a question about resemblance. (In other words, they rely on the representativeness heuristic.) Therefore, to ask whether Quinn *is* a lawyer, they ask themselves how much Quinn *resembles* (their idea of) a lawyer. This substitution is (as we've discussed) often helpful, but the strategy provides no role for base rates—and this guarantees that people will routinely ignore base rates. Consistent with this claim, base-rate neglect is widespread and can be observed both in laboratory tasks and in many real-world judgments. (For some indications, though, of when people *do* take base rates into account, see Griffin et al., 2012; Pennycook et al., 2014.)

Dual-Process Models

It's troubling that we can document judgment errors even when—as far as we can tell—people are genuinely trying to evaluate the evidence. We can even document these errors among experts—financial managers making large investments (e.g., Hilton, 2003; Kahneman, 2011); physicians diagnosing cancer (but ignoring base rates; Eddy, 1982; also see Koehler et al, 2002); surgeons evaluating the risk of postsurgical side effects (Garcia-Retamero et al., 2020). The errors occur even when people are strongly motivated to be careful, with clear instructions and financial rewards offered for good performance (Arkes, 1991; Hertwig & Ortmann, 2003).

Could it be, then, that human judgment is fundamentally flawed? If so, this might explain why people are so ready to believe in telepathy and a variety of bogus cures (Gilovich, 1991; King & Koehler, 2000). Indeed, it might help us understand why, in 2020, many people had crazy ideas about COVID-19 (including the belief that the disease was spread by 5G cell towers, or the belief that you could cure the disease by ingesting bleach). Similarly, maybe these flaws in human judgment help us see why racism, neglect of poverty, and denial of climate change are so widespread; maybe all of these problems are the tragic result of people's inability to understand facts and to draw decent conclusions.

Before we make these claims, however, let's acknowledge another side to our story: Sometimes human judgment rises above the heuristics we've described so far. People often rely on availability in judging frequency, but sometimes they seek other (more accurate) bases for their judgments. Likewise, people often rely on the representativeness heuristic, and so (among other concerns) they draw conclusions from "man who" stories. But in other settings people are keenly sensitive to sample size, and they draw no conclusions if their sample is small or possibly biased. (For an early statement of this point, see Nisbett et al., 1983; for more recent discussion, see Kahneman, 2011.) How can we make sense of this mixed pattern?

Ways of Thinking: Type 1, Type 2

A number of authors have proposed that people have two distinct ways of thinking. One type of thinking is fast and easy; the heuristics we've described fall into this category. The other type is slower and more effortful, but also more accurate.

Researchers have offered various versions of this **dual-process model**, and different theorists use different terminology (Evans, 2012a, 2012b; Kahneman, 2011; Pretz, 2008; Shafir & LeBoeuf, 2002; also Fischhoff & Broomell, 2020). We'll rely on rather neutral terms (initially proposed by Stanovich & West, 2000; Stanovich, 2012), so we'll use **Type 1** as the label for the fast, easy sort of thinking and **Type 2** as the label for the slower, more effortful thinking. (Also see **Figure 12.2**.)

When do people use one type of thinking or the other? One hypothesis is that people *choose* when to rely on each system; presumably, they shift to the more accurate Type 2 when making judgments that really matter. As we've discussed, however, people rely on Type 1 heuristics even when incentives are offered for accuracy, even when making important professional judgments, even when making medical diagnoses that may literally be matters of life and death. Surely people would choose to use Type 2 in these cases if they could, yet they still rely on Type 1 and fall into error. On these grounds, it's difficult to argue that using Type 2 is a matter of deliberate choice.

Instead, evidence suggests that Type 2 is likely to come into play only if it's triggered by certain cues and only if the circumstances are right. We've suggested, for example, that Type 2 judgments are slower than Type 1, and so it's not surprising that heuristic-based judgments (and, thus, heuristic-based *errors*) are more likely when judgments are made under time pressure (Finucane et al., 2000). We've also said that Type 2 judgments require *effort*,

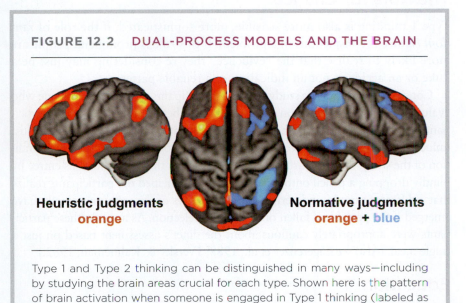

FIGURE 12.2   DUAL-PROCESS MODELS AND THE BRAIN

Heuristic judgments
orange

Normative judgments
orange + blue

Type 1 and Type 2 thinking can be distinguished in many ways—including by studying the brain areas crucial for each type. Shown here is the pattern of brain activation when someone is engaged in Type 1 thinking (labeled as "heuristic" in the figure, and then the pattern when someone is engaged in Type 2 thinking (labeled as "normative" in the figure).

so this form of thinking is more likely if the person can focus attention on the judgment being made (De Neys, 2006; Ferreira et al., 2006).

Triggers for Skilled Intuition

Before we move on, though, let's acknowledge that Type 1 thinking can on its own sometimes be quite sophisticated. For example, we've already said that people typically ignore base rates—and, as a result, misinterpret the evidence they encounter. But *sensitivity* to base rates can also be demonstrated, even in cases involving Type 1 thinking (e.g., Pennycook et al., 2014). This mixed pattern is attributable, in part, to how the base rates are presented. Base-rate neglect is more likely if the relevant information is cast in terms of probabilities or proportions: "There is a .01 chance that people like Mary will have this disease"; "Only 5% of the people in this group are lawyers." But base-rate information can also be conveyed in terms of *frequencies*, and it turns out that people are more likely to use the base rates if they're conveyed in this way. For example, people are more alert to a base rate phrased as "12 out of every 1,000 cases" than they are to the same information cast as a percentage (1.2%) or a probability (.012). (See Gigerenzer & Hoffrage, 1995; also Brase, 2008; Cosmides & Tooby, 1996.) It seems, then, that much depends on how the problem is presented, with some presentations being more "user friendly" than others. (For more on the circumstances in which Type 1 thinking can be sophisticated, see De Neys & Pennycook, 2019; Gigerenzer & Gaissmaier, 2011; Kahneman & Klein, 2009; Oaksford & Hall, 2016.)

The Role for Chance

Type 1 thinking is also more sensible, more sophisticated, if the role of *random chance* is conspicuous in a problem. If this role is prominent, people are more likely to realize that the "evidence" they're considering may just be a fluke or an accident, not an indication of a reliable pattern.

Consider, for example, a study in which participants read about someone who evaluated a restaurant based on just one meal (Nisbett et al., 1983). Many participants saw no problem here; they didn't realize that (perhaps) the diner was just unlucky and happened to have chosen the menu's worst option. In another condition of the study, though, participants were told that the diner chose his entrée by blindly dropping a pencil onto the menu. This cue helped the participants realize that a different sample, and perhaps different views of the restaurant, might have emerged if the pencil had fallen on a different selection. As a result, these participants were appropriately cautious about the diner's assessment based on just a single meal. (Also see Gigerenzer et al., 1988; Tversky & Kahneman, 1982.)

Education

Other studies show that the quality of a person's thinking can be shaped by *education*. In one early study, Fong, Krantz, & Nisbett (1986) conducted a telephone survey of "opinions about sports," calling students who were taking an undergraduate course in statistics. Half of the students were contacted during the first week of the semester; half were contacted during the last week.

In their course, these students had learned about the importance of sample size. They'd been reminded that accidents do happen, but that accidents don't keep happening over and over. A pattern visible in a larger sample of data is therefore unlikely to be the result of some accident; hence, larger samples are more reliable, more trustworthy, than small samples.

This classroom training had a broad impact. In the phone interview (which was—as far as the students knew—not in any way connected to their course), one of the questions involved a comparison between how well a baseball player did in his first year and how well he did in the rest of his career. This is essentially a question about sample size (with the first year being just a sample of the player's overall performance). Did the students realize that sample size was relevant here? For those contacted early in the term, only 16% gave answers that showed any consideration of sample size. For those contacted later, the number of answers influenced by sample size more than doubled (to 37%).

It seems, then, that how well people think about evidence can be improved, and the improvement applies to problems in new domains and new contexts. Training in statistics, it appears, can have widespread benefits. (For more on education effects, see Bunge & Leib, 2020; Gigerenzer et al., 2008; Klauer & Phye, 2008.)

The Cognitive Reflection Test

Another relevant factor involves someone's thinking habits. Specifically, in order to avoid judgment errors, you sometimes need to resist the obvious answer to a question and spend just a moment thinking about why that obvious answer might be *wrong*. People differ in how consistently they proceed in this (cautious, sensible) fashion, and this tendency is measured by the Cognitive Reflection Test (CRT; **Figure 12.3**). For each question on this

---

FIGURE 12.3   THE COGNITIVE REFLECTION TEST (CRT)

(1) A bat and a ball cost $1.10 in total. The bat costs $1.00 more than the ball. How much does the ball cost? _____ cents

(2) If it takes 5 machines 5 minutes to make 5 widgets, how long would it take 100 machines to make 100 widgets? _____ minutes

(3) In a lake, there is a patch of lily pads. Every day, the patch doubles in size. If it takes 48 days for the patch to cover the entire lake, how long would it take for the patch to cover half of the lake? _____ days

TEST YOURSELF

6. What are the differences between Type 1 and Type 2 thinking?
7. What are some of the factors that can, in some settings, encourage (or perhaps allow) Type 2 thinking?

test, there's an obvious answer that turns out to be incorrect. To do well on the test, therefore, you need to step past this answer and give the question a bit more thought; if you do, the correct answer is readily available (Frederick, 2005; also see Thomson & Oppenheimer, 2016; Toplak et al., 2014.)

People who do well on the CRT are less likely to make the errors we've described in this chapter. In fact, people with higher CRT scores tend to have better scientific understanding, and they even seem more analytic in their moral decisions (Baron et al., 2015; Pennycook et al., 2016; Travers et al., 2016; but also see Patel et al, 2019). Let's be clear, though, that no one is immune to the errors we've been discussing; nonetheless, the risk of error does seem lower in people who score well on the CRT.

Confirmation and Disconfirmation

In this chapter so far, we've been looking at thinking that requires **induction**—the process through which you make forecasts about new cases, based on cases you've already observed. Just as important, though, is **deduction**—a process in which you start with claims or assertions that you count as "given" and ask what follows from these premises. For example, perhaps you're already convinced that red wine gives you headaches or that relationships based on physical attraction rarely last. You might want to ask: What follows from this? What implications do these claims have for your other beliefs or actions?

"MY PARENTS DIED. THEIR PARENTS DIED. THEIR PARENTS DIED... IT RUNS IN THE FAMILY."

DRAWING CONCLUSIONS FROM EVIDENCE

We rely on induction in many settings. Sometimes we misread the pattern. Sometimes we detect the pattern but draw the wrong conclusions.

Deduction has many functions, including the fact that it helps keep your beliefs in touch with reality. After all, if deduction leads you to a prediction based on your beliefs and the prediction turns out to be *wrong*, this indicates that something is off track in your beliefs—and so claims you thought were solidly established may not be so solid after all.

Does human reasoning respect this principle? If you encounter evidence confirming your beliefs, does this strengthen your convictions? If evidence challenging your beliefs should come your way, do you adjust?

Confirmation Bias

It seems sensible that in evaluating any belief, you'd want to take a balanced approach: You'd surely consider any evidence favoring the belief, but you'd need to weigh that against evidence that might challenge the belief. And, in fact, evidence that challenges you can be especially valuable; many authors argue that this type of evidence is more informative than evidence that seems to support you. (For the classic statement of this position, see Popper, 1934.)

There's a substantial gap, however, between these suggestions about what people *should* do and what they actually do. Specifically, people routinely display a pattern we've already mentioned, *confirmation bias*: a greater sensitivity to confirming evidence and a tendency to neglect disconfirming evidence. Confirmation bias can take many different forms (see **Figure 12.4**).

FIGURE 12.4   CONFIRMATION BIAS

Confirmation bias takes many forms:

- First, when people are assessing a belief or a hypothesis, they're more likely to seek evidence that might confirm the belief than evidence that might disconfirm it.

- Second, when disconfirming evidence is made available to them, people often fail to use it in adjusting their beliefs.

- Third, when people encounter confirming evidence, they take it at face value; when they encounter disconfirming evidence, they reinterpret the evidence to diminish its impact.

- Fourth, people often show better memory for confirming evidence than for disconfirming evidence, and, if they do recall the latter, they remember it in a distorted form that robs the evidence of its force.

- Finally, people often fail to consider alternative hypotheses that might explain the available data just as well as their current hypothesis does.

"Confirmation bias" is a blanket term that refers to many specific effects. We've listed some of these effects here.

What all the forms have in common, though, is the tendency to protect your beliefs from challenge. (See, among others, Gilovich, 1991; Kassin et al., 2012; Schulz-Hardt et al., 2000.)

In an early demonstration of confirmation bias, Wason (1966, 1968) presented research participants with a series of numbers, such as "2, 4, 6." The participants were told that this trio of numbers followed a specific rule, and their task was to figure out the rule. Participants were allowed to propose their own trios of numbers ("Does '8, 10, 12' follow the rule?"), and in each case the experimenter responded appropriately ("Yes, it follows the rule" or "No, it doesn't"). Then, once participants were satisfied that they had discovered the rule, they announced their "discovery."

The rule was actually quite simple: The three numbers had to be in ascending order, and so "1, 3, 5" follows the rule, but "6, 4, 2" does not, and neither does "10, 10, 10." Despite this simplicity, participants had difficulty discovering the rule, often requiring many minutes. This was largely due to the type of information they requested as they tried to evaluate their hypotheses: To an overwhelming extent, they sought to *confirm* the rules they had proposed; requests for disconfirmation were relatively rare. And it's noteworthy that those few participants who did seek out disconfirmation for their hypotheses were more likely to discover the rule. It seems, then, that confirmation bias was strongly present in this experiment and interfered with performance.

Reinterpreting Disconfirming Evidence

Here's a different manifestation of confirmation bias. When people encounter information confirming their beliefs, they're likely to take the evidence at face value, accepting it without challenge or question. In contrast, when people encounter evidence inconsistent with their beliefs, they're often skeptical and scrutinize this new evidence with care, seeking flaws or ambiguities.

One study examined gamblers who bet on professional football games (Gilovich, 1983; Gilovich & Douglas, 1986). These people firmly believed they had good strategies for picking winners, and their faith in these strategies was undiminished by a series of losing bets. Why is this? It's because the gamblers didn't understand their losses as "losses." Instead, they remembered them as flukes or oddball coincidences: "I was right. New York was going to win if it hadn't been for that crazy injury to their running back"; "I was correct in picking St. Louis. They would have won except for that goofy bounce the ball took after the kickoff." In this way, winning bets were remembered as wins; losing bets were remembered as "near wins." No wonder, then, that the gamblers maintained their views despite the contrary evidence provided by their empty wallets.

Belief Perseverance

Even when disconfirming evidence is undeniable, people still cling to their beliefs—a pattern called **belief perseverance**. Participants in one study were asked to read a series of suicide notes; their task was to figure out which notes were authentic, collected by police, and which were fake, written by other students as an exercise. As participants offered their judgments, they received feedback about how well they were doing—that is, how accurate they were in detecting the authentic notes. The trick, though, was that the feedback had nothing to do with the participants' actual judgments. By prearrangement, some participants were told that they were performing at a level well above average in this task; other participants were told the opposite—that they were performing at a level far below average (Ross et al., 1975; also Ross & Anderson, 1982).

Later on, participants were debriefed. They were told that the feedback they had received was bogus and had nothing to do with their performance. They were even shown the experimenter's instruction sheet, which had assigned them in advance to the *success* or *failure* group. They were then asked a variety of additional questions, including some for which they had to assess their own "social sensitivity." Specifically, they were asked to rate their actual ability, as they perceived it, in tasks like the suicide-note task.

Let's emphasize that participants were making these judgments about themselves after they'd been told clearly that the feedback they'd received was randomly determined and had no credibility whatsoever. Nonetheless, participants who had received the "above average" feedback continued to think of their social sensitivity as being above average, and likewise their ability to judge suicide notes. Those who had received the "below average" feedback showed the opposite pattern. All participants, in other words, persevered in their beliefs even when the basis for the belief had been completely discredited.

Imagine yourself as one of the participants, and let's say that we've told you that you're performing rather poorly at the suicide-note task. As you digest this new "information" about yourself, you'll probably wonder, "Could this be true? Am I less sensitive than I think I am?" To check on this possibility, you might search through your memory, looking for evidence that will help you evaluate this suggestion.

What sort of evidence will you seek? This is where confirmation bias comes into play. Because of this bias, chances are good that you'll check on the researcher's information by seeking other episodes in your memory that might confirm your lack of social perception. As a result, you'll soon have two sources of evidence for your social insensitivity: the (bogus) feedback provided by the researcher, and the supporting information you came up with yourself, thanks to your (selective) memory search. So even if the researcher discredits the information he provided, you still have the information you provided yourself, and on this basis you might maintain your belief.

Of course, in this experiment, participants could be led either to an enhanced estimate of their own social sensitivity or to a diminished estimate, depending on which false information they were given in the first place. Presumably, this is because the range of episodes in participants' memories is

The Dangers of Fake News and Misinformation

People have all sorts of false beliefs. Some of these beliefs cause little harm, but others have serious consequences. For example, some people believe that vaccines cause autism (they don't), and guided by this (mistaken) belief, they create a substantial health risk by not vaccinating their children. During the 2020 COVID-19 pandemic, some people were convinced that wearing masks did nothing to prevent spread of the disease—or, worse, caused harm. (Some people were convinced, for example, that masks somehow increased infection risk.) As a result, many people refused to wear masks—and therefore contributed to the devastating spread of the virus. Or, as yet another example, many people continue to deny the threat of climate change despite the overwhelming scientific evidence, and so they vote against policies that might diminish the threat.

Why do people believe in these false claims? Part of the explanation involves public figures who promote these false beliefs and label any challenges to their claims as "fake news." This

derision of (supposedly) fake news is, of course, one more version of the broad pattern of *confirmation bias*. As the chapter describes, this term refers to the various ways in which people seek out—and accept without question—information that's consistent with their views, but greet disconfirming information with harsh skepticism. This bias can protect all sorts of beliefs—even foolish ones—from appropriate fact-checking.

The heuristics we've discussed are also relevant. People sometimes point to a city that's experiencing freezing temperatures and use this as a "refutation" of claims about global warming. This type of argument is akin to the "man who" stories fostered by the representativeness heuristic, in which people draw broad conclusions from a single (and atypical) case. (In this instance, the "refutation" also rests on a misunderstanding of the difference between the day-to-day patterns that define "weather" and the larger pattern that defines "climate.")

Likewise, think about this claim: "Who cares that 97% of the scientists agree about climate

CO$_2$ IS NOT A POLLUTANT

Confirmation bias can take many forms. In one form, people rely on assertions that might be sensible in some other context, but, in order to "support" their position, they use the assertions in a fashion that's entirely misleading. It is true, for example, that CO$_2$ is desirable and useful in many settings (as one example, dissolved CO$_2$ is the source of the bubbles in soda and beer). But it's also true that excess CO$_2$ in the atmosphere is playing a central role in altering our climate and endangering us all.

change? Scientists are often wrong. After all, scientists used to think the sun orbited around the Earth." This sounds suspiciously like the availability heuristic at work—using one salient case as a basis for what is surely a misleading claim about the frequency of scientific error.

It's also relevant that many people get their information from the Internet—and, of course, evidence that's extreme or even inflammatory is likely to go viral. These extreme cases can then (via the availability heuristic) influence judgments of what's typical and can invite overgeneralization (via the representativeness heuristic). And if a report is echoed over and over in social media, a different form of attribute substitution comes into play, along the lines of "everyone's saying it, so I guess it must be true."

The Internet also helps people implement confirmation bias. Bear in mind that this bias shapes what information you seek; and if you're looking for evidence to confirm your doubts about climate change, or to document the concerns about vaccination, or even to sustain your belief that ESP exists, it's easy to locate some website with the content you're after. Confirmation bias also makes it likely that you will accept this information, confirming your beliefs, even if the information is coming from a dubious source.

In addition, some news sources try to offer "balanced" presentations, providing information on both sides of an issue. Often, though, this "balance" doesn't represent the actual distribution of the evidence. A speaker discussing the threat of climate change is representing the position held by the huge majority of experts; a speaker denying climate change is drawn from the very few professionals who hold a nonstandard view.

What is the impact of this sort of "balanced" presentation? Research suggests that this format encourages people to give comparable weight to both sides of the issue—that is, equal weight to the view that represents almost every scientist, as well as the view that comes from a tiny minority. The result? People end up believing there's far more disagreement among the experts than there actually is; and with this (illusory!) disagreement now in view, people conclude there's no reason to pay attention to what the experts are saying (Koehler, 2016).

The message here is a troubling one. As we said at the start, some false beliefs do little harm. But for many issues, the dangers inherent in false beliefs are enormous, and they provide powerful reason to care deeply about the judgment and reasoning errors described in this chapter.

What's the path forward? Research psychologists are starting to pay more and more attention to strategies that might "debias" people—that is, undo some of the errors already in place (e.g., Lewandowsky et al., 2017; Lewandowsky et al. 2012). And, of course, we should all be alert to, and make use of, websites that provide "fact-checking" services—politifact.com, factcheck.org, snopes .com, and others. Steps like these seem urgent once we acknowledge that false beliefs and reasoning errors can threaten our political systems, our lives, and our planet.

TEST YOURSELF

8. What is confirmation bias? What are some of the specific forms that confirmation bias can take?

9. What is the role of confirmation bias in producing belief perseverance?

wide: In some previous episodes they've been sensitive, and in some they haven't been. Therefore, if they search through their memories seeking to confirm the hypothesis that they've been sensitive in the past, they'll find confirming evidence. If they search through memory seeking to confirm the opposite hypothesis, this too will be possible. In short, they can confirm either hypothesis via a suitably selective memory search. This outcome highlights the dangers built into a selective search of the evidence and, more broadly, the danger associated with confirmation bias. (For a different perspective, see O'Rear & Radvansky, 2020. For other studies showing that people hang on to beliefs even when the *basis* for the belief has been destroyed, see Chan et al., 2017; Ecker & Ang, 2019, Rich & Zaragoza, 2016; Walter & Tukachinsky, 2020.)

Logic

In displaying confirmation bias, people sometimes seem to defy logic. "If my gambling strategy is good, then I'll win my next bet. But I lose the bet. Therefore, my strategy is good." How should we think about this? In general, do people fail to understand—or perhaps ignore—the rules of *logic*?

Reasoning about Syllogisms

Over the years, a number of theorists have proposed that human thought does follow the rules of logic, and so, when people make reasoning errors, the problem must lie elsewhere: carelessness, perhaps, or a misinterpretation of the problem. (For classic statements of this view, see Boole, 1854; Mill,

HOW LOGICAL ARE WE?

Errors in logic are extraordinarily common—in adults and in children, and even when we are contemplating very simple logical arguments.

1874; Piaget, 1952.) It turns out, however, that errors in logical reasoning happen all the time. If people are careless or misread problems, they do so rather frequently. This is evident, for example, in studies using **categorical syllogisms**—a type of logical argument that begins with two assertions (the problem's **premises**), each containing a statement about a category, as shown in **Figure 12.5**. The syllogism can then be completed with a conclusion that may or may not follow from these premises. The cases shown in the figure are all **valid syllogisms**—that is, the conclusion *does* follow from the premises stated. In contrast, here is an example of an **invalid syllogism**:

All P are M.

All S are M.

Therefore, all S are P.

To see that this is invalid, try translating it into concrete terms, such as "All plumbers are mortal" and "All secretaries are mortal." Both of these are surely true, but it doesn't follow from this that "All secretaries are plumbers."

Research participants who are asked to reason about syllogisms do remarkably poorly, with error rates often as high as 70% to 90%. (Early data were reported by Chapman & Chapman, 1959; also see Khemlani & Johnson-Laird, 2012.) And the errors aren't random (as they might be, if people were just being careless). Instead, patterns in the errors indicate that people approach these exercises with consistent strategies; the problem, of course, is that these strategies often have no basis in logic.

For example, people often show a pattern called **belief bias**: If a syllogism's conclusion happens to be something people believe to be true anyhow, they're likely to judge the conclusion as following logically from the premises. Conversely, if the conclusion happens to be something they believe to be false, they're likely to reject the conclusion as invalid (Evans, 2012b; Stephens et al., 2019; Trippas et al., 2017).

This strategy at first appears reasonable. Why wouldn't you endorse conclusions you believe to be true, based on the totality of your knowledge,

All M are B.
All D are M.
  Therefore, all D are B.

All X are Y.
Some A are X.
  Therefore, some A are Y.

Some A are not B.
All A are G.
  Therefore, some G are not B.

FIGURE 12.5   EXAMPLES OF CATEGORICAL SYLLOGISMS

All of the syllogisms shown here are valid—that is, if the two premises are true, then the conclusion must be true.

and reject claims you believe to be false? Let's be clear, though, that there's a problem here: When people show the belief-bias pattern, they're failing to distinguish between good arguments (those that are truly persuasive) and bad ones. As a result, they'll endorse an illogical argument if it happens to lead to conclusions they like, and they'll reject a logical argument if it leads to conclusions they have doubts about.

The Four-Card Task

Similar conclusions derive from research on reasoning about **conditional statements**. These are statements of the "If X, then Y" format, with the first statement providing a *condition* under which the second statement is guaranteed to be true.

Often, psychologists study conditional reasoning with the **selection task** (sometimes called the **four-card task**). In this task, participants are shown four playing cards, as in **Figure 12.6** (after Wason, 1966, 1968). The participants are told that each card has a number on one side and a letter on the other. Their task is to evaluate this rule: "If a card has a vowel on one side, it must have an even number on the other side." Which cards must be turned over to put this rule to the test?

In many studies, roughly a third of the participants turn over just the "A" card to check for an even number. In addition, many turn over both the "A" and the "6." However, just a handful of participants give the correct answer—turning over the "A" and the "7." Plainly, performance is atrocious

---

FIGURE 12.6   THE FOUR-CARD TASK

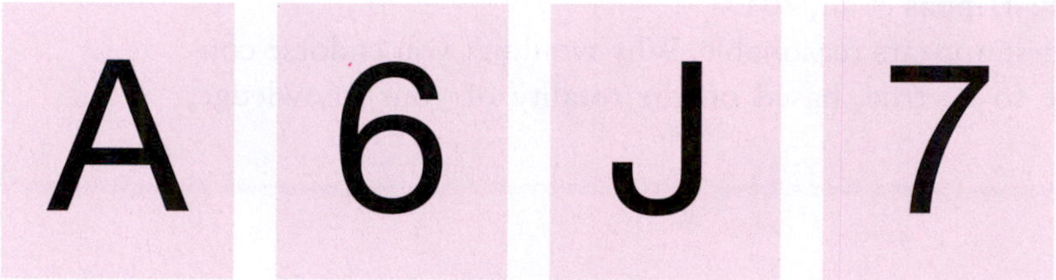

A 6 J 7

Which cards would you turn over to test this rule: "If a card has a vowel on one side, it must have an even number on the other side"? If we turn over the "A" card and find an even number, that's consistent with the rule. But if we turn it over and find an odd number, that's inconsistent. Therefore, by turning over the "A," we'll discover whether this card is consistent with the rule or not. In other words, there's something to be learned by turning over this card. What about the "J"? The rule makes no claims about what's on the flip side of a consonant card, so no matter what we find on the other side, it won't challenge the rule. Therefore, there's nothing to be learned by turning over this card; we already know (without flipping it over) that it's consistent with the rule. By similar reasoning, we'll learn nothing by turning over the "6"; no matter what we find, it satisfies the rule. Finally, if we turn over the "7" and a consonant is on the other side, this fits with the rule. If there's a vowel on the other side, this doesn't fit. Therefore, we do want to turn over this card, because there's a chance that we might find something informative.

---

in this problem, with more than 90% of participants giving wrong answers. (See Figure 12.6 for an explanation of the right answer.)

Performance is much better, though, with some variations of the four-card task. For example, Griggs and Cox (1982) asked their participants to test rules like this one: "If a person is drinking beer, then the person must be at least 21 years old." As in the other studies, participants were shown four cards and asked which cards they would need to turn over to test the rule (see **Figure 12.7**). In this version, participants did quite well: 73% (correctly) selected the card labeled "Drinking a beer" and also the card labeled "16 years of age." They did not select "Drinking a Coke" or "22 years of age."

It seems, then, that how well you think depends on what you're thinking about. The problems posed in Figures 12.6 and 12.7 have the same logical structure, but they yield very different performances. (For discussion, see Ragni et al., 2018; for more on logical reasoning, see Oaksford & Chater, 2020.) This point draws our attention to the parallels between studies of logical reasoning and our earlier discussion of how people make judgments about the evidence they encounter. In both domains (inductive judgments and deductive reasoning) it's easy to document errors in people's thinking. But in both domains we can also document higher-quality thinking, and this more sophisticated thinking can be encouraged by the "right" circumstances. Specifically, in our discussion of judgment, we listed several factors that can trigger better thinking. Now, in our discussion of logic, we've seen that a problem's *content* can sometimes trigger more accurate reasoning. Thus, the quality of thinking is certainly uneven—but with the right triggers (and, it turns out, proper education), it can be improved.

TEST YOURSELF

10. What is belief bias? Why is belief bias a problem in logical reasoning?

11. What is the four-card (or selection) task? How well do people perform in this task?

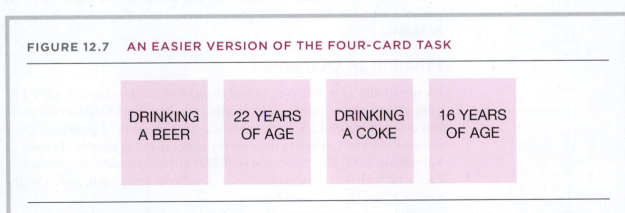

FIGURE 12.7   AN EASIER VERSION OF THE FOUR-CARD TASK

| DRINKING A BEER | 22 YEARS OF AGE | DRINKING A COKE | 16 YEARS OF AGE |

Participants do reasonably well with this version of the four-card task. Here, each card shows a person's age on one side and what the person is drinking on the other side. The participants' task is to select the cards that would have to be turned over in order to test the following rule: "If a person is drinking beer, then the person must be at least 21 years old."

Decision Making

We turn now to a different type of thinking: the thinking that underlies *choices*. Choices, big and small, fill your life, whether you're choosing what courses to take next semester, how to spend your next vacation, or whether to stay with your current partner. How do you make any of these decisions?

Costs and Benefits

Each of us has our own values—things we prize, or conversely, things we hope to avoid. Likewise, each of us has a series of goals—things we hope to accomplish, things we hope to see. The obvious suggestion, then, is that we use these values and goals in making decisions. In choosing courses for next semester, for example, you'll choose classes that are interesting (something you value) and also those that help fill the requirements for your major (one of your goals). In choosing a medical treatment, you hope to avoid pain and also to retain your physical capacities as long as possible.

To put this a bit more formally, each decision will have certain costs attached to it (consequences that will carry you farther from your goals) as well as benefits (consequences moving you toward your goals and providing things you value). In deciding, you weigh the costs against the benefits and seek a path that will minimize the former and maximize the latter. When you have several options, you choose the one that provides the best balance of benefits and costs.

Economists cast these ideas in terms of **utility maximization**. The word "utility" refers to the value that you place on a particular outcome. Some people gain utility from eating in fancy restaurants; others gain utility from watching their savings accumulate in a bank account; still others, from giving their money to charity. No matter how you gain utility, the proposal is that you try to make decisions that will bring you as much utility as possible. (See von Neumann & Morgenstern, 1947; also see Speekenbrink & Shanks, 2012.)

Framing of Outcomes

It's remarkably easy, however, to find cases in which decisions are guided by principles that have little to do with utility maximization. Consider the problem posed in **Figure 12.8**. In this choice, a huge majority of people—72%—choose Program A, selecting the sure bet rather than the gamble (Tversky & Kahneman, 1987; also Willemsen et al., 2011). Now consider the problem in **Figure 12.9**. Here, a large majority—78%—choose Program B, preferring the gamble rather than the sure bet.

These two problems are objectively identical: 200 people saved out of 600 is the same as 400 dead out of 600. Nonetheless, the change in how the problem is phrased—that is, the **framing** of the decision—has an enormous impact, turning a 3-to-1 preference (72% to 28%) in one direction into a 4-to-1 preference (78% to 22%) in the opposite direction.

FIGURE 12.8 THE DISEASE PROBLEM: POSITIVE FRAME

Imagine that the United States is preparing for the outbreak of an unusual disease, which is expected to kill 600 people. Two alternative programs to combat the disease have been proposed. Assume that the exact scientific estimates of the consequences of the programs are as follows:

If Program A is adopted, 200 people will be saved.

If Program B is adopted, there is a one-third probability that 600 people will be saved, and a two-thirds probability that no people will be saved.

Which program would you prefer? There is clearly no right answer to this question; one could defend selecting the "risky" choice (Program B) or the less rewarding but less risky choice (Program A). The clear majority of respondents, however, lean toward Program A, with 72% choosing it over Program B. Note that this problem is "positively" framed in terms of lives "saved." (FROM TVERSKY, A., & KAHNEMAN, D. (1981). THE FRAMING OF DECISIONS AND THE PSYCHOLOGY OF CHOICE. *SCIENCE, 211*(4481), 453–458 © 1981 AAAS. REPRINTED WITH PERMISSION.)

FIGURE 12.9 THE DISEASE PROBLEM: NEGATIVE FRAME

Imagine that the United States is preparing for the outbreak of an unusual disease, which is expected to kill 600 people. Two alternative programs to combat the disease have been proposed. Assume that the exact scientific estimates of the consequences of the programs are as follows:

If Program A is adopted, 400 people will die.

If Program B is adopted, there is a one-third probability that nobody will die, and a two-thirds probability that 600 people will die.

Which program would you prefer? This problem is identical in content to the one shown in Figure 12.8: 400 dead out of 600 people is the same as 200 saved out of 600. Nonetheless, respondents react to the problem shown here rather differently than they do to the one in Figure 12.8. In the "lives saved" version, 72% choose Program A. In the "will die" version, 78% choose Program B. Essentially, by changing the phrasing we reverse the pattern of respondents' preferences. (FROM TVERSKY, A., & KAHNEMAN, D. (1981). THE FRAMING OF DECISIONS AND THE PSYCHOLOGY OF CHOICE. *SCIENCE, 211*(4481), 453–458 © 1981 AAAS. REPRINTED WITH PERMISSION.)

We should emphasize that there's nothing wrong with participants' individual choices. In either Figure 12.8 or Figure 12.9, there's no "right answer," and you can persuasively defend either the decision to avoid risk (by selecting Program A) or the decision to gamble (by choosing Program B). The problem lies in the contradiction created by choosing Program A in one context and Program B in the other context. In fact, if a single participant is given both frames on slightly different occasions, she's quite likely to contradict herself. For that matter, if you wanted to manipulate someone's evaluation of these programs (e.g., if you wanted to manipulate voters or shoppers), then framing effects provide an effective way to do this.

Related effects are easy to demonstrate. When participants are given the first problem in **Figure 12.10**, almost three quarters of them (72%) choose Option A—the sure gain of $100. Participants contemplating the second problem generally choose Option B, with 64% going for this choice (Tversky & Kahneman, 1987). Note, though, that the problems are once again identical. Both pose the question of whether you'd rather end up with a certain $400 or with an even chance of ending up with either $300 or $500. Despite this equivalence, participants treat these problems very differently, preferring the sure thing in one case and the gamble in the other.

In fact, there's a reliable pattern in these data. If the frame casts a choice in terms of *losses*, decision makers tend to be **risk seeking**—that is, they prefer to gamble, presumably attracted by the idea that maybe they'll avoid the loss.

FIGURE 12.10   **FRAMING EFFECTS IN MONETARY CHOICES**

Problem 1

Assume yourself richer by $300 than you are today. You have to choose between:
A. a sure gain of $100
B. 50% chance to gain $200 and 50% chance to gain nothing

Problem 2

Assume yourself richer by $500 than you are today. You have to choose between:
A. a sure loss of $100
B. 50% chance to lose nothing and 50% chance to lose $200

These two problems are identical. In both cases, the first option leaves you with $400, while the second option leaves you with an even chance between $300 and $500. Despite this equivalence between the two problems, respondents prefer the first option in Problem 1 (72% select this option) and the second option in Problem 2 (64% select this option). Once again, by changing the frames we reverse the pattern of preferences.

So, for example, when the disease problem is cast in terms of people dying (Figure 12.9), people choose Program B, apparently focused on the hope that with this program there may be no loss of life. Likewise, Problem 2 in Figure 12.10 casts the options in terms of financial losses, and this, too, triggers risk seeking: People reliably choose the 50-50 gamble over the sure loss. (This pattern—a willingness to take risks—is especially strong when people contemplate *large* losses; Harinck et al., 2007; but also see Yechiam et al., 2019.)

In contrast, if the frame casts a choice in terms of gains, decision makers are likely to show **risk aversion**: They refuse to gamble, choosing instead to hold tight to what they already have. Thus, Figure 12.8 casts the disease problem in terms of gains (the number of people saved), and this leads people to prefer the risk-free choice (Program A) over the gamble offered by Program B. (And likewise for Problem 1 in Figure 12.10.)

Again, there's nothing wrong with either of these strategies by itself: If someone prefers to be risk seeking, this is fine; if someone prefers to be risk averse, this is okay too. The problem arises when people flip-flop between these strategies, depending on how the problem is framed. (For more on framing, see Usher et al., 2019.)

Framing of Questions and Evidence

Related effects emerge with changes in how a *question* is framed. For example, imagine that you're on a jury in a messy divorce case; the parents are battling over who will get custody of their only child. The two parents have the attributes listed in **Figure 12.11**. To which parent will you award sole custody of the child?

Research participants who are asked this question tend to favor Parent B by a wide margin. After all, this parent does have a close relationship with the child and has a good income. Note, though, that we asked to which parent you would *award* custody. Results are different if we ask participants to which parent they would *deny* custody. In this case, 55% of the participants choose to deny custody to Parent B (and so, by default, award custody to Parent A). In other words, the decision is simply reversed: With the "award" question, most participants award custody to Parent B. With the "deny" question, the majority deny custody to Parent B—and so give custody to Parent A (Shafir, 1993; Shafir et al., 1993).

People are also influenced by how *evidence* is framed. For example, they rate a basketball player more highly if the player has made 75% of his free throws, compared to their ratings of a player who has missed 25% of his free throws. They're more likely to endorse a medical treatment with a "50% success rate" than one with a "50% failure rate." And so on. (See Levin & Gaeth, 1988; Levin et al., 1988; also Dunning & Parpal, 1989.)

Opt-In versus Opt-Out

A related pattern again hinges on how a decision is presented. Let's start with the fact that more than 100,000 people in the United States are waiting for medically necessary organ transplants. You can help these people by agreeing

FIGURE 12.11   THE INFLUENCE OF HOW A QUESTION IS FRAMED

Imagine that you serve on the jury of an only-child sole-custody case following a relatively messy divorce. The facts of the case are complicated by ambiguous economic, social, and emotional considerations, and you decide to base your decision entirely on the following few observations. To which parent would you award sole custody of the child?

Parent A   average income
average health
average working hours
reasonable rapport with the child
relatively stable social life

Parent B   above-average income
very close relationship with the child
extremely active social life
lots of work-related travel
minor health problems

When asked the question shown here, 64% of the research participants decided to award sole custody to Parent B. Other participants, however, were asked a different question: "To which parent would you deny sole custody?" Asked this question, 55% of the participants chose to deny sole custody to Parent B (and so, by default, to award custody to Parent A). Thus, with the "award" question, a majority votes for granting custody to Parent B; with the "deny" question, a majority votes for granting custody to Parent A.

to be an organ donor; then, when you die, organs from your body might help as many as 50 different people.

In light of these facts, it's discouraging that relatively few Americans agree to be organ donors, and the reason may lie in the way the decision to donate is framed. In the United States, decisions about organ donation are "opt-in" decisions: The potential donor has to say explicitly that they wish to be a donor; otherwise, the assumption is that the person will not be an organ donor. Other countries use the reverse system: Unless people say explicitly that they don't want to be donors ("opt-out"), the assumption is that they will be donors.

How much does this contrast matter? In Germany, which relies on an opt-in system like the one used in the United States, only 12% of German citizens have agreed to be organ donors. Neighboring Austria, with a reasonably similar culture, uses an opt-out system, and here 99% of the citizens agree to be donors. (We might add, though, that in recent years German lawmakers have been discussing whether to shift to an opt-out system for organ donation, and it is possible that Germany's rules may have shifted by the time this book is published. For research in this domain, see Davidai et al., 2012; Johnson & Goldstein, 2003; Thaler, 2009.)

Similar patterns have been observed with other decisions—for example, the decision to participate in "green energy" programs, or the step of signing up for a plan that will make an automatic monthly contribution to your pension fund (Sunstein, 2016). In each case, there's a sharp contrast between the number of people who say they're in favor of these programs and the number of people who actually participate. And in each case, part of the reason for non-participation is the reliance on an opt-in system.

This pattern has broad implications for public policy, and some public figures suggest that governments should design programs that "nudge" people to sign up for green energy, to save for their retirement, and so on. (See Thaler & Sunstein, 2009; Sunstein, 2016; although, for discussion, see Bruzzone, 2008; Randhawa et al., 2010.) But, in addition, the contrast between opt-in and opt-out decisions reminds us that our choices are governed not just by what's at stake, but also by how the decision is framed.

Maximizing Utility versus Seeing Reasons

In case after case, then, people are powerfully influenced by changes in how a decision is framed, even though, on most accounts, these changes have no impact on the utility you'd receive from the various options. To explain these findings, one possibility is that people are trying to use (something like) utility calculations when making decisions but aren't very good at it. As a result, they're pulled off track by distractions, including how the decision is framed. A different possibility, though, is more radical. Perhaps we're not guided by utilities at all. Instead, suppose our goal is simply to make decisions that we feel good about, decisions that we think are reasonable and justified. This view of decision making is called **reason-based choice** (Shafir et al., 1993; also Redelmeier & Shafir, 1995). To see how this account plays out, let's go back to the divorce/custody case described in Figure 12.11. Half of the participants in this study were asked to which parent they would *award* custody. These participants therefore asked themselves: "What would justify giving custody to one parent or another?" and this drew their attention to each parent's positive traits. As a result, they were swayed by Parent B's above-average income and close relationship with the child. Other participants were asked to which parent they would *deny* custody, and this led them to ask: "What would justify this denial?" This approach drew attention to the parents' negative attributes—especially, Parent B's heavy travel schedule and health problems.

In both cases, then, the participants relied on *justification* in making their decision. As it turns out, though, the shift in framing caused a change in the factors relevant to that justification, and this is why the shift in framing reversed the pattern of decisions. (For a different example, see **Figure 12.12**.)

Emotion

Still another factor needs to be included in our theorizing, because people's decisions are powerfully influenced by *emotion*. (See, among others, Kahneman, 2003; Loewenstein et al., 2001; Slovic et al., 2002; Weber & Johnson, 2009.)

ENDOWMENT EFFECT

What produces the contrast between opt-in and opt-out decisions? Part of the answer is the "endowment effect"— the tendency to put a higher value on your current status and possessions simply because they are currently your own. In an early demonstration of this effect, one group of participants was given a coffee mug and then given the opportunity to sell it. A different group of participants was given cash and then the opportunity to buy the coffee mug. The first group set a value on the mug that was twice as high as the value set by the second group; apparently, the simple fact of already possessing the mug doubled its value. (See Kahneman et al., 1990; also see Carmon & Ariely, 2000; Morewedge & Giblin, 2015; Smitizsky et al., 2021.)

FIGURE 12.12 THE COST OF TOO MANY OPTIONS

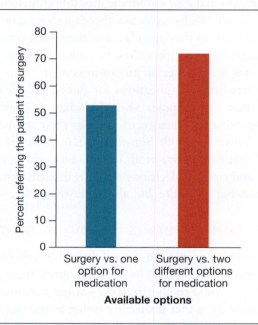

Practicing physicians were given a description of a patient and were asked to choose a treatment. For one group of physicians, the choices offered were surgery and a specific medication. For a second group, the choices included surgery, the same medication, and a different medication. When doctors were choosing between one drug and surgery, many thought the drug was worth a try, and only 53% referred the patient for surgery. When the doctors had three choices, though, they found it difficult to justify choosing either drug over the other; each had its advantages and disadvantages. And with no good reasons for choosing either drug, the physicians chose neither, and so most—72%—opted for surgery instead. This outcome makes little sense from a utility perspective, but it's easy to understand if we assume that the doctors were looking for *reasons* for their decisions and took action only when they could justify the action. (AFTER REDELMEIER & SHAFIR, 1995)

We mentioned the importance of emotion early in the chapter, when we saw that Elliot, unable to feel emotion, seems unable to make decisions. But what is the linkage between emotion and decision making? At the chapter's start, we pointed out that many decisions involve an element of risk. (Should you try out a new, experimental drug? Should we rely more on nuclear power? Should you sign up for the new professor's course, even though you don't know much about her?) In cases like these, we suggested, people seem to assess the risk in emotional terms. For example, they ask themselves how much dread they experience when thinking about a nuclear accident, and they use that dread as an indicator of risk (Fischhoff et al., 1978; Slovic et al.,

2002; also Pachur et al., 2012; in Table 12.1, we referred to this strategy as the "affect heuristic").

But there are other ways that emotion can influence decisions. Here, we start with the fact that—of course—*memories* can cause a strong bodily reaction. In remembering a scary movie, you again become tense and your palms might sweat. In remembering a romantic encounter, you again become aroused. In the same way, *anticipated events* can also produce bodily arousal, and Damasio (1994) suggests that you use these sensations—he calls them **somatic markers**— as a way of evaluating your options. So, in making a choice, you literally rely on your "gut feelings" to assess your options—an approach that pulls you toward options that trigger positive feelings and away from ones that trigger negative feelings. (For discussion of the neural mechanisms that enable people to use these somatic markers, see Coricelli et al., 2007; Damasio, 1994; Dunn et al., 2010; Jones et al., 2012; Naqvi et al., 2006; also **Figure 12.13**.)

Predicting Emotions

Here's another way emotion shapes decision making: Many decisions depend on a *forecast* of future emotions. Imagine that you're choosing between two apartments you might rent for next year. One is cheaper and larger but faces a noisy street. Will you get used to the noise, so that soon it won't bother you? If so, then you should take the apartment. Or will the noise grow increasingly obnoxious as the weeks pass? If so, you should pay the extra money for the other apartment. Plainly, your decision here depends on a prediction about the future—about how your likes and dislikes will change as time goes by.

Research suggests, though, that **affective forecasting**—your predictions for your own emotions—is often inaccurate. In many studies, people have been asked how they would feel after a significant event; the events at issue include "breaking up with a romantic partner, losing an election, receiving a gift, learning they have a serious illness, failure to secure a promotion, scoring well on an exam," and so on (Gilbert & Ebert, 2002, p. 503; Kermer et al., 2006; see also **Figure 12.14**). People can usually predict whether their reaction will be positive or negative—and so they realize that scoring well on an exam will make them feel good and that a romantic breakup will make them feel bad. But people consistently overestimate how long these feelings will last—apparently underestimating their ability to adjust to changes in fortune, and also underestimating how easily they'll find excuses and rationalizations for their own mistakes. (For evidence, though, that people aren't awful all the time in predicting their own emotions, see Doré et al., 2016.)

As a related matter, people generally believe that their *current* feelings will last longer than they actually will—so they seem to be convinced that things that bother them now will continue to bother them in the future, and that things that please them now will continue to bring pleasure in the future. In both directions, people underestimate their own ability to adapt; as a result, they work to avoid things that they'd soon get used to anyhow and spend money for things that provide only short-term pleasure. (For data, see Hsee

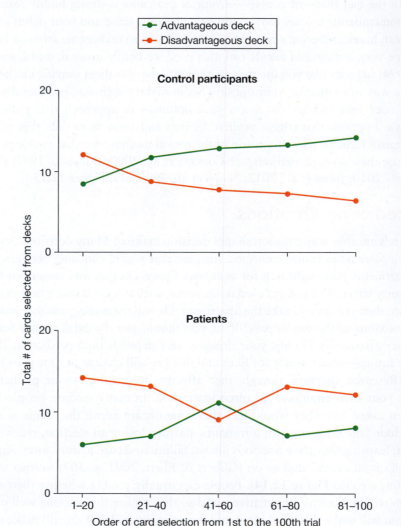

FIGURE 12.13   EMOTION AND DECISION MAKING

Control participants

Patients

Total # of cards selected from decks

Order of card selection from 1st to the 100th trial

- ● Advantageous deck
- ● Disadvantageous deck

In this study, participants had to choose cards from one of two decks. One deck (the "disadvantageous" one) offered large payoffs but also large penalties; so, in the long run, it was better to choose from the other ("advantageous") deck, which provided smaller payoffs but also smaller penalties. Control participants—people with no brain damage—quickly learned about the decks and were soon making most of their choices from the advantageous deck (and so earned more overall). Participants with damage to the orbitofrontal cortex, in contrast, continued to favor the risky deck. Because of their brain damage, they were unable to use the somatic markers normally associated with risk—so they failed to heed the "gut feeling" that could have warned them against a dangerous choice.

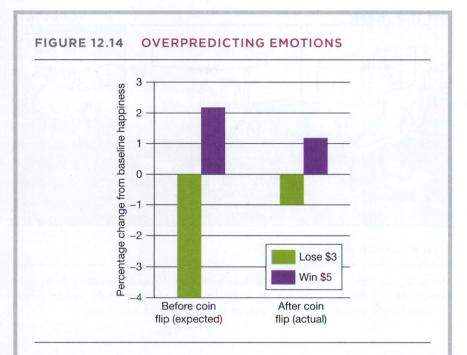

FIGURE 12.14   OVERPREDICTING EMOTIONS

People are often inaccurate in predicting their own emotions. Here, people sensibly predicted that they'd be unhappy if a gamble caused a $3 loss, but the sadness they actually experienced after the coin flip (right side of the figure) was much less than the sadness they'd predicted before the coin flip (left side of the figure). Likewise, people knew they'd be happy if they won $5, but the happiness they experienced was less than the happiness they'd predicted.   (AFTER KERMER ET AL., 2006)

& Hastie, 2005; Sevdalis & Harvey, 2007; Wilson et al., 2000; also see Frank et al., 2021.)

Research on Happiness

Earlier in this chapter, we saw that people often make errors in judgment and reasoning. It now appears that people also lack skill in decision making. Framing effects leave them open to manipulation and self-contradiction, and errors in affective forecasting guarantee that people will often take steps to avoid regrets that in reality they wouldn't have felt, and pay for expensive toys that they'll soon lose interest in.

Some investigators draw strong conclusions from these findings. One author has suggested that, because of the ordinary functioning of memory and reasoning, people are unlikely to move efficiently toward happiness; the best they can do is "stumble on happiness" (Gilbert, 2006). Perhaps they would be better off, he argues, if someone else made their choices for them. In a similar vein, another author asserts that people are "predictably irrational" in their decision making and we're stuck with that (Ariely, 2009). Yet another

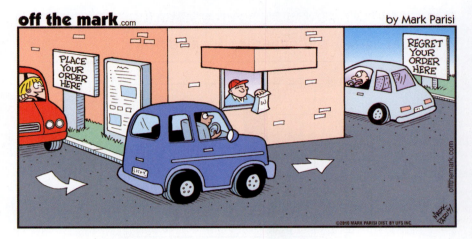

off the mark.com   by Mark Parisi

THE ROLE OF REGRET

In making decisions, people are powerfully motivated to avoid decisions they might regret later. It turns out, though, that when decisions work out badly, people generally experience far less regret over their choice than they'd anticipated.

TEST YOURSELF

12. What does it mean to say that decision making is heavily influenced by how a decision is "framed"?
13. In what circumstances are people risk averse? When are they risk seeking?
14. What is affective forecasting, and how accurate are people in this type of forecasting?

author notes that we all like to have choices but argues that our world often offers us *too many* choices, and this actually makes us less happy—a pattern he calls the "paradox of choice" (Schwartz, 2003).

Plainly, these are issues that demand scrutiny, with implications for how each of us lives and also, perhaps, implications that might guide government policies or business practices, helping people to become happy (Layard, 2010; Thaler & Sunstein, 2009). In fact, the broad study of "subjective well-being"—what it is, what promotes it—has become an active and exciting area of research. In this way, the study of *how* people make decisions has led to important questions—and, perhaps, some helpful answers—regarding how they *should* make decisions. In the meantime, the research highlights some traps to avoid and suggests that each of us should be more careful in making the choices that shape our lives.

COGNITIVE PSYCHOLOGY AND THE LAW

pretrial publicity

If a crime is particularly horrid, or if it involves famous people, then reports of the crime will be splashed across the news. Even if the crime isn't "newsworthy," reports may still circulate on Facebook or Twitter, as people share their views about the crime, the defendant, and the upcoming trial. Some of the comments may be inflammatory (if, for example, people are expressing their outrage about the crime). Some may contain false information. Some may reveal information that the courts need to keep out of a jury's view.

But all of this—whether on the front page of the local news or on someone's Twitter feed—is permitted, thanks to the protections the United States gives to free speech and a free press.

It's also crucial, though, that we protect a defendant's right to a fair trial, and so we need to ask what impact this pretrial publicity might have on citizens who are asked to sit on the jury. In thinking this through, let's start with the fact that pretrial publicity is rarely neutral or balanced. Instead, content analyses show that for criminal trials this publicity rather consistently emphasizes the police and prosecution perspective. How will this affect any jurors who have been exposed to this publicity? One concern here is confirmation bias. As the chapter discusses, this bias takes many forms, including a tendency to accept evidence favoring your views at face value but to subject evidence challenging your views to special scrutiny, seeking flaws or weaknesses in these unwelcome facts. This tendency can easily be documented in trials. In one study, participants were first exposed to a newspaper article that created a bias about a particular murder trial (Hope et al., 2004). These research-participant "jurors" were then presented with the trial evidence and had to evaluate how persuasive each bit of evidence was. The results showed a clear effect of the newspaper article: Evidence consistent with the (biased) pretrial publicity was seen as more compelling; evidence inconsistent with the publicity was seen as less compelling. Worse, this effect then fed on itself. Each bit of evidence that the "jurors" heard was filtered through their confirmation bias, so the evidence seemed particularly persuasive if it favored the view they held already. This led the jurors to be more confident that their view was, in fact, correct. (After all, the evidence—as they interpreted it—did seem to favor that view.) This now-stronger view, in turn, amplified the confirmation bias, which colored how the "jurors" interpreted the next bit of evidence. Around and around we go—with confirmation bias coloring how the evidence is interpreted, which strengthens the belief held by the "jurors," which creates more confirmation bias, which colors how later evidence is interpreted, which further strengthens the belief.

In this study, the pretrial publicity had a powerful effect on the "jury's" verdict, but we need to be clear that the publicity didn't influence the verdict directly. In fact, the odds are good that the "jurors" weren't thinking of the publicity at all when they voted "guilty" or "not guilty." Instead, their verdicts were based (as they should be) on the jurors' evaluation of the trial evidence. The problem, though, is that this evaluation was itself powerfully shaped by the pretrial publicity, via the mechanisms we've just described.

In light of these results, we might worry that the courts' protections against juror bias may not be adequate. In some trials, for example, jurors are merely asked: "Can you set aside any personal beliefs or knowledge you have obtained outside the court and decide this case solely on the evidence you hear from the witness stand?" This question is surely not a sufficient safeguard, because effects like confirmation bias work automatically and

"KNOCK-KNOCK"

In 2012, Trayvon Martin was shot and killed by George Zimmerman. The case received an enormous amount of publicity and pretrial protest. Then, when it was time to select jurors for Zimmerman's trial, his attorney surprised everyone by telling a knock-knock joke. "Knock knock." "Who's there?" "George Zimmerman." "George Zimmerman who?" "Ah, good. You're on the jury." The joke was bizarre, but the attorney's point was clear: He was trying to find jurors who didn't know who Zimmerman was—that is, jurors who hadn't been following, and perhaps been influenced by, the pretrial publicity. In the end, Zimmerman claimed self-defense and was acquitted, although Trayvon was carrying no weapon—just a cell phone, a cigarette lighter, and a bag of Skittles.

unconsciously. Jurors therefore have no way to know how, whether, or to what extent their thinking is shaped by this bias. As a related point, jurors might promise, at the trial's outset, to base their verdict only on what they heard during the trial; then, in the jury room, they might do all they can to honor this promise. As we've now seen, though, that's no protection at all. In the study we described, the "jury's" ultimate decision was based on the evidence, but that doesn't change the fact that the decision was based on the evidence *as viewed through the lens provided by pretrial publicity*.

Clearly, then, the courts need a more potent means of avoiding these influences. One option is to exclude jurors who have been exposed to pretrial publicity, but that idea brings its own problems. Jurors are supposed to be representative of the broader community. Imagine, then, that a crime has been widely publicized and discussed, and we allow people onto the jury only if they've been aware of none of this discussion. In that case, our jury might end up consisting of a group of people who never follow the news and never pay attention to what's going on in their surroundings. There's certainly a concern here that this would not be a "normal", fair, or representative jury.

A different possibility is that we might move the trial's location away from the community in which the crime had been publicized. But this, too, is complicated, and might not work at all if a crime has received national publicity.

Plainly, then, there is some complexity here. It seems certain that we will continue to protect free speech and a free press. But we need to be alert to the conflict that can sometimes emerge between these principles and a defendant's right to a fair and unbiased trial.

For more on this topic . . .

Devine, D. J. (2012). *Jury decision making: The state of the science*. New York: New York University Press.

Devine, D. J., Buddenbaum, J., Houp, S., Studebaker, N., & Stolle, D. P. (2009). Strength of evidence, extraevidentiary influence and the liberation hypothesis: Data from the field. *Law and Human Behavior*, 33, 136–148.

Hope, L., Memon, A., & McGeorge, P. (2004). Understanding pretrial publicity: Predecisional distortion of evidence by mock jurors. *Journal of Experimental Psychology: Applied*, 10(2), 111–119.

Steblay, N. M., Besirevic, J., Fulero, S. M., & Jimenez-Lorente, B. (1999). The effects of pretrial publicity on juror verdicts: A meta-analytic review. *Law and Human Behavior*, 23(2), 219–235.

Studebaker, C. A., & Penrod, S. D. (2005). Pretrial publicity and its influence on juror decision making. In N. Brewer & K. D. Williams (Eds.), *Psychology and law: An empirical perspective* (pp. 254–275). New York, NY: Guilford Press.

chapter review

SUMMARY

● Induction often relies on attribute substitution—so that, for example, people estimate frequency by relying on availability. Thus, they judge an observation to be frequent if they can easily think of many examples of that observation. The more available an observation is, the greater the frequency is judged to be.

● Judgments based on the availability heuristic are often accurate, but they do risk error. The risk derives from the fact that many factors influence availability, including the pattern of what's easily retrievable from memory and bias in what you notice in your experiences.

● People also use the representativeness heuristic, relying on the assumption that categories are relatively homogeneous, so that any case drawn from the category will be representative of the entire group. Because of this assumption, people expect a relatively small sample of evidence to have all the properties that are associated with the entire category; an example is the gambler's fallacy. Similarly, people seem insensitive to the importance of sample size, so they believe that a small sample of observations is just as informative as a large sample. In the extreme, people are willing to draw conclusions from just a single observation, as in "man who" arguments.

● People are likely to make errors in judging covariation. In particular, their beliefs and expectations sometimes lead them to perceive illusory covariations. The errors are often attributable to the fact that confirmation bias causes people to notice and remember a biased sample of the evidence, which leads to inaccurate covariation judgments.

● People often seem insensitive to base rates. Again, this can be demonstrated both in novices evaluating unfamiliar materials and in experts making judgments in their professional domains.

● Use of heuristics is widespread, and so are the corresponding errors. However, we can also find cases in which people rely on more sophisticated judgment strategies, and thus are alert to sample size and sample bias, and do consider base rates. This has led many theorists to propose dual-process models of thinking. One process (Type 1) relies on fast, effortless shortcuts; another process (Type 2) is slower and more effortful but is less likely to lead to error.

● Type 1 thinking is more likely when people are pressed for time or distracted. However, Type 1 thinking can be observed even in the absence of time pressure or distraction, and even when the matter being judged is both familiar and highly consequential.

● Better-quality thinking seems more likely when the data are described in terms of frequencies rather than probabilities and also when the data are easily coded in statistical terms (with *chance* playing a prominent role in shaping the sample). Type 2 thinking is also more likely if people bring to a situation background knowledge that helps them to code the data and to understand the cause-and-effect role of sample bias or base rates. Training in statistics also makes Type 2 thinking more likely, leading us to the optimistic view that judging is a *skill* that can be improved through suitable education.

● Reasoning often shows a pattern of confirmation bias. People tend to seek evidence that might confirm their beliefs rather than evidence that might challenge their beliefs. When evidence challenging a belief is in view, it tends to be underused or reinterpreted. One manifestation of confirmation bias is belief perseverance, a pattern in which people continue to believe a claim even after the basis for it has been thoroughly discredited.

- People's performance with logic problems such as categorical syllogisms or problems involving conditional statements is often quite poor. The errors aren't the product of carelessness and often derive from belief bias.

- How well people reason depends on what they're reasoning about. This is evident in the four-card task, in which some versions of the task yield reasonably good performance, even though other versions yield enormous numbers of errors.

- According to many economists, people make decisions by calculating the expected utility of each of their options. Evidence suggests, however, that decisions are often influenced by factors that have nothing to do with utility—for example, how the question is framed or how the possible outcomes are described. If the outcomes are described as potential gains, decision makers tend to be risk averse; if outcomes are described as potential losses, decision makers tend to be risk seeking.

- Some investigators have proposed that people's goal in making decisions is not to maximize utility but, instead, to make decisions that they think are reasonable or justified. When people cannot justify a decision, they sometimes decide *not* to decide.

- Decisions are also clearly influenced by emotion. This influence is evident in decision makers' efforts toward avoiding regret; it is also evident in decision makers' reliance on their own bodily sensations as a cue for evaluating various options. Decision makers are surprisingly inept, however, at predicting their own future reactions. This is true both for predictions of regret and for predictions of future enjoyment or future annoyance.

KEY TERMS

TEST YOURSELF AGAIN

1. What is attribute substitution?

2. In the availability heuristic, what is the information you need, and what attribute do you use as a substitute?

3. In the representativeness heuristic, what is the information you need, and what attribute do you use as a substitute?

4. What is a "man who" argument? Why are "man who" arguments often misleading?

5. What is a base rate? Why is base-rate information important?

6. What are the differences between Type 1 and Type 2 thinking?

7. What are some of the factors that can, in some settings, encourage (or perhaps allow) Type 2 thinking?

8. What is confirmation bias? What are some of the specific forms that confirmation bias can take?

9. What is the role of confirmation bias in producing belief perseverance?

10. What is belief bias? Why is belief bias a problem in logical reasoning?

11. What is the four-card (or selection) task? How well do people perform in this task?

12. What does it mean to say that decision making is heavily influenced by how a decision is "framed"?

13. In what circumstances are people risk averse? When are they risk seeking?

14. What is affective forecasting, and how accurate are people in this type of forecasting?

THINK ABOUT IT

1. Science is usually concerned with *what is*. Scientists typically leave it to others (philosophers, social theorists, policy makers) to decide *what should be*. In the domain of decision making, though, many psychologists do make policy recommendations—for "opt-out" procedures rather than "opt-in," or for specific decision-making practices that (according to research) will make people happier. Should scientists take these steps? Or should the highly subjective realm of "what is valuable, what is desirable" be kept separate from the realm of objective scientific study?

DEMONSTRATIONS & APPLYING COGNITIVE PSYCHOLOGY ESSAYS

For demonstrations of key concepts in cognitive psychology, take a look at the Online Demonstrations. To explore more of the practical applications of cognitive psychology in themed essays, visit the online reader.

Online Demonstrations

- Demonstration 12.1: Sample Size
- Demonstration 12.2: Relying on the Representativeness Heuristic
- Demonstration 12.3: "Man Who" Arguments
- Demonstration 12.4: Applying Base Rates
- Demonstration 12.5: Frequencies versus Percentages
- Demonstration 12.6: Cognitive Reflection
- Demonstration 12.7: The Effect of Content on Reasoning
- Demonstration 12.8: Wealth versus Changes in Wealth
- Demonstration 12.9: Probabilities versus Decision Weights
- Demonstration 12.10: Framing Questions
- Demonstration 12.11: Mental Accounting
- Demonstration 12.12: Seeking Reasons

Online Applying Cognitive Psychology Essays

- Cognitive Psychology and Education: Making People Smarter
- Cognitive Psychology and Technology: Who Makes Better Decisions: Humans or Machines?
- Cognitive Psychology and Health: Informed Consent
- Cognitive Psychology and the Law: Confirmation Bias in Police Investigations

ZAPS COGNITION LABS

Go to ZAPS online cognition labs to conduct hands-on experiments on key concepts.

INQUIZITIVE

It's time to complete your study experience! Go to InQuizitive to practice actively with this chapter's concepts and get personalized feedback along the way.

chapter **13**

Problem Solving and Creativity

what if... In many ways, humans are remarkably alike. We all have one nose, a heart with four chambers, a liver with three lobes. And to a large extent we all have the same brains—and so the structures inside your skull are virtually identical to the ones inside mine. It's no surprise, then, that throughout this book we've been able to discuss truths that apply to all of us—the ways in which we all pay attention, the ways in which we all learn and remember.

But people also differ—in their personalities, their values, and their cognition. We've occasionally mentioned these differences, but the time has come to focus on these differences directly. In this chapter, we'll focus on how people differ in their ability to solve problems they encounter, and with this, how they differ in their *creativity*. Then, in Chapter 14, we'll turn to the ways in which people differ in their *intelligence*. After all, every one of us knows people who seem amazingly smart and also people who seem relatively slow. What do these differences amount to?

Let's begin with creativity. What can psychology say about the creativity of Wolfgang Mozart, who composed more than 600 musical works (symphonies, concertos, operas, and more) by the time of his early death at age 35? What can we say about Ursula K. Le Guin, an immensely popular American author who wrote 21 novels (including works of science fiction), 12 children's books, 5 volumes of poetry, and more? What about Steve Jobs, who revolutionized the way people use computers, or Marie Curie, the first woman to win a Nobel Prize (actually, she won *two* Nobel prizes)?

History suggests we'll need a variety of accounts to describe these creative giants. For example, consider Thomas Edison—arguably one of the world's greatest inventors. Edison is best known for inventing the first practical light bulb, but he also invented devices crucial for power generation, sound recording, and motion pictures. One hallmark of Edison's work, though, was an extraordinary amount of testing. In his efforts toward finding a plant-based substitute for rubber, for example, Edison reportedly tested over 17,000 plant samples, until he found one that gave him what he needed. In developing the light bulb, Edison explored at least 6,000 designs before he found one that worked. Edison summed up his own career by commenting that "genius is one percent inspiration and ninety-nine percent perspiration."

- Often, people solve problems by using heuristics. In other cases, people solve problems by drawing analogies based on problems they've solved in the past.

- Training can draw someone's attention to a problem's deep structure, promoting analogy use and helping the person divide a problem into subproblems. Experts also benefit from highly cross-referenced knowledge in their domain of expertise.

- Problem solving is often stymied by how the person approaches the problem, and that leads to questions

about how people find new and creative approaches to problems.

- When closely examined, creative approaches seem to be the result of the same processes that are evident in "ordinary" problem solving—processes hinging on analogies, heuristics, and the like. As a result, we can say that the creative *product* is often extraordinary, but the creative *process* may not be.

The pattern seems entirely different, though, for other geniuses. Leonardo da Vinci, for example, was an inventor, painter, sculptor, architect, musician, and mathematician. He was also a productive scientist and made important contributions to the study of anatomy, geology, and paleontology. His extraordinary output was guided by his extensive training (he became an apprentice to a leading Florentine artist at age 17 and remained in training for several years), but there is no indication of the sort of tenacious trial and error that seemed crucial for Edison.

How should we think about either of these cases? And what is the relationship between their accomplishments (some authors call it "Big-C Creativity," after Simonton & Damian, 2013) and the ("little-c") creativity many of us aspire to in daily life when, when, for example, we hope to find a creative way to begin a conversation or repair a damaged friendship?

General Problem-Solving Methods

People solve problems all the time. Some problems are pragmatic ("I want to go to the store, but Tom borrowed my car. How can I get there?"). Others are social ("I really want Amy to notice me; how should I arrange it?"). Others are academic ("I'm trying to prove this theorem. How can I do it, starting from these axioms?"). What these situations share, though, is the need to figure out some path toward a goal—a configuration that defines what we call **problem solving**. How do people solve problems?

Problem Solving as Search

Researchers often compare problem solving to a process of *search*, as though you were navigating through a maze, seeking a forward path (see Newell & Simon, 1972; also Bassok & Novick, 2012; Mayer, 2012). To make this point concrete, consider the Hobbits and Orcs problem in **Figure 13.1**. For this problem, you have choices for the various moves you can make (transporting

FIGURE 13.1 THE HOBBITS AND ORCS PROBLEM

This problem has been used in studies of problem solving. Can you solve it?

creatures back and forth), but you're limited by the size of the boat and the requirement that Hobbits can never be outnumbered (lest they be eaten). This situation leaves you with a set of options shown graphically in **Figure 13.2**. The figure shows the moves available early in the solution and depicts the options as a tree, with each step leading to more branches. All the branches together form the **problem space**—that is, the set of all states that can be reached in solving the problem.

FIGURE 13.2 THE PROBLEM SPACE FOR HOBBITS AND ORCS

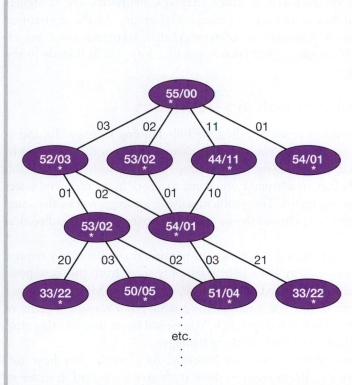

etc.

Each circle shows a possible problem state. The state 54/01, for example, indicates that five Hobbits and four Orcs are on the east bank; there are no Hobbits, but one Orc, on the west bank. The star shows the position of the boat. The numbers alongside each line indicate the number of creatures in the boat during each river crossing. The move 02, for example, transports no Hobbits, but two Orcs. The problem states shown here are all the "legal" states. (Other states and other moves would result in some of the Hobbits being eaten.) Thus, there are four legal moves one can make, starting from the initial state. From these, there are four possible moves one can make, but these lead to just two problem states (53/02 and 54/01). From these two states, there are four new states that can be reached, and so on. We have here illustrated the initial moves that can be made in solving this problem; the shortest path to the problem's solution involves 11 moves.

To solve this problem, one strategy would be to trace through the entire problem space, exploring each branch in turn. This would be like exploring every corridor in a maze, an approach that might guarantee that you'd eventually find the solution. For most problems, however, this approach would be hopeless. Consider the game of chess. In chess, which move is best at any point in the game depends on what your opponent will be able to do in response to your move, and then what you'll do next. To make sure you're choosing the best move, therefore, you need to think ahead through a few cycles of play, so that you can select as your current move the one that will lead to the best sequence.

Let's imagine, therefore, that you decide to look ahead just three cycles of play—three of your moves and three of your opponent's. Early in the game (before the pieces have spread out a bit), your options are limited. Once the game is under way, however, some calculation indicates that there will be roughly 700 million possibilities for how the game could unfold over three cycles of play. This number immediately rules out the option of considering every possibility. If you could evaluate 10 sequences per second, you'd still need more than 2 years, on a 24/7 schedule, to evaluate the full set of options for each move. And, of course, there's nothing special here about chess, because most real-life problems offer so many options that you couldn't possibly explore every one.

Plainly, then, you somehow need to narrow your search through a problem space, and, specifically, what you need is a problem-solving **heuristic**. As we've discussed in other chapters, heuristics are strategies that are efficient but at the cost of occasional errors. In the domain of problem solving, a heuristic is a strategy that narrows your search through the problem space—but (you hope) in a way that still leads to the problem's solution.

General Problem-Solving Heuristics

One commonly used heuristic is called the **hill-climbing strategy**. To understand this term, imagine that you're hiking through the woods and trying to figure out which trail leads to the mountaintop. You obviously need to climb uphill to reach the top, so whenever you come to a fork in the trail, you select the path that's going uphill. The problem-solving strategy works the same way: At each point, you choose the option that moves you in the direction of your goal.

This strategy is of limited use, however, because many problems require that you briefly move *away* from your goal; only then, from this new position, can the problem be solved. For instance, if you want Mingus to notice you more, it might help if you go away for a while; that way, he'll be more likely to notice you when you come back. You would never discover this ploy, though, if you relied on the hill-climbing strategy.

Even so, people often rely on this heuristic. As a result, they have difficulties whenever a problem requires them to "move backward in order to

I want to take my son to nursery school. What's the difference between what I have and what I want? One of distance. What changes distance? My automobile. My automobile won't work. What is needed to make it work? A new battery. What has new batteries? An auto repair shop.

I want the repair shop to put in a new battery; but the shop doesn't know I need one. What is the difficulty? One of communication. What allows communication? A telephone . . .

One commonly used problem-solving heuristic is means-end analysis. In this strategy, you compare your current status to your desired status and ask: "What means do I have to make these more alike?" Among other benefits, this strategy helps you to break a problem into small subproblems.

(AFTER NEWELL & SIMON, 1972, P. 416)

go forward." Often, at these points, people drop their current plan and seek some other solution to the problem: "This must be the wrong strategy; I'm going the wrong way." (See, e.g., Jeffries et al., 1977; Thomas, 1974.)

Fortunately, people have other heuristics available to them. For example, people often rely on **means-end analysis**. In this strategy, you compare your current state to the goal state and you ask: "What means do I have to make these more alike?" **Figure 13.3** offers a commonsense example.

Pictures and Diagrams

People have other options in their mental toolkit. For example, it's often helpful to translate a problem into some sort of mental image or even a picture. Consider the problem in **Figure 13.4**. Most people try an algebraic

Solomon is proud of his 26-volume encyclopedia, placed neatly, with the volumes in alphabetical order, on his bookshelf. Solomon doesn't realize, though, that there's a bookworm sitting on the front cover of the A volume. The bookworm begins chewing his way through the pages on the shortest possible path toward the back cover of the Z volume.

Each volume is 3 inches thick (including pages and covers), so that the entire set of volumes requires 78 inches of bookshelf. The bookworm chews through the pages and covers at a steady rate of ¾ of an inch per month. How long will it take before the bookworm reaches the back cover of the Z volume?

FIGURE 13.4   THE BOOKWORM PROBLEM

People who try an algebraic solution to this problem often end up with the wrong answer.

TEST YOURSELF

1. What does it mean to say that a problem-solving heuristic allows you to trim the size of the problem space?
2. What is means-end analysis?

solution to this problem (width of each volume multiplied by the number of volumes, divided by the worm's eating rate) and end up with the wrong answer. People generally get this problem right, though, if they start by visualizing the arrangement. Now, they can see the actual positions of the worm's starting point and end point, and this takes them to the correct answer. (See **Figure 13.5.**)

Drawing on Experience

Where do these points leave us with regard to the questions with which we began—and, in particular, the ways in which people differ from one another in their mental abilities? There's actually little difference from one person to the next in the use of strategies like hill climbing or means-end analysis—most people can and do use these strategies. People do differ, of course, in their drawing ability and in their imagery prowess (see Chapter 11), but these points are relevant only for some problems. Where, then, do the broader differences in problem-solving skill arise?

Problem Solving via Analogy

Sometimes a problem reminds you of other problems you've solved in the past, so you can rely on past experience in tackling the current challenge. In other words, you solve the current problem by means of an analogy with other, already solved, problems.

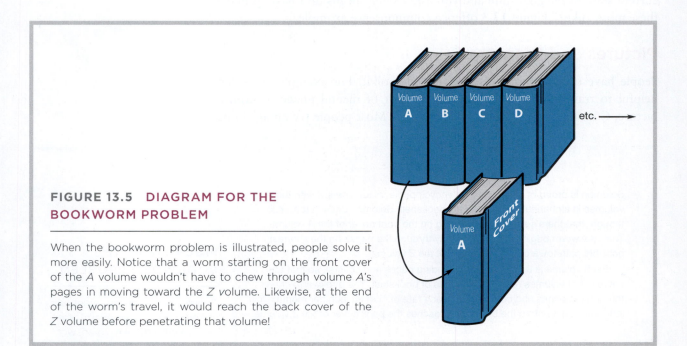

FIGURE 13.5   DIAGRAM FOR THE BOOKWORM PROBLEM

When the bookworm problem is illustrated, people solve it more easily. Notice that a worm starting on the front cover of the *A* volume wouldn't have to chew through volume *A*'s pages in moving toward the *Z* volume. Likewise, at the end of the worm's travel, it would reach the back cover of the *Z* volume before penetrating that volume!

It's easy to show that analogies are helpful (Chan et al., 2012; Gentner & Smith, 2012; Holyoak, 2012), but it's also plain that people under-use analogies. Consider the tumor problem (see **Figure 13.6A**). This problem is difficult, but people generally solve it if they use an analogy. Gick and Holyoak (1980) first had their participants read about a related situation (see **Figure 13.6B**) and then presented them with the tumor problem. When participants were encouraged to use this hint, 75% were able to solve the tumor problem. Without the hint, only 10% solved the problem.

FIGURE 13.6   THE TUMOR PROBLEM

Suppose you are a doctor faced with a patient who has a malignant tumor in his stomach. To operate on the patient is impossible, but unless the tumor is destroyed the patient will die. A kind of ray, at a sufficiently high intensity, can destroy the tumor. Unfortunately, at this intensity the healthy tissue that the rays pass through on the way to the tumor will also be destroyed. At lower intensities the rays are harmless to healthy tissue but will not affect the tumor. How can the rays be used to destroy the tumor without injuring the healthy tissue?

A

A dictator ruled a country from a strong fortress, and a rebel general, hoping to liberate the country, vowed to capture the fortress. The general knew that an attack by his entire army would capture the fortress, but he also knew that the dictator had planted mines on each of the many roads leading to the fortress. The mines were set so that small groups of soldiers could pass over them safely, since the dictator needed to move his own troops to and from the fortress. However, any large force would detonate the mines, blowing them up and also destroying the neighboring villages.

   The general knew, therefore, that he couldn't just march his army up one of the roads to the fortress. Instead, he devised a simple plan. He divided his army into small groups and dispatched each group to the head of a different road. When all were ready, he gave the signal and each group marched up a different road to the fortress, with all the groups arriving at the fortress at the same time. In this way, the general captured the fortress and overthrew the dictator.

B

The tumor problem, designed by Duncker (1945) and presented in Panel A, has been studied extensively. Can you solve it? One solution is to aim multiple low-intensity rays at the tumor, each from a different angle. The rays will meet at the site of the tumor and so, at just that location, will sum to full strength. People are much more likely to solve this problem if they're encouraged to use the hint provided by the problem shown in Panel B.

Gick and Holyoak also had another group of participants read the "general and fortress" story, but these participants weren't told that this story was relevant to the tumor problem. Only 30% of this group solved the tumor problem (see **Figure 13.7**). (Also see Kubricht et al., 2017.) It seems, then, that people don't use this (obviously helpful) analogy unless they're specifically told to do so. Why is this? One reason lies in how people search through memory when seeking an analogy. In solving the tumor problem, people seem to ask themselves: "What else do I know about tumors?" This search will help them remember other situations in which they thought about tumors, but it won't lead them to the "general and fortress" problem. This (potential) analogue will therefore lie dormant in memory and provide no help.

To locate helpful analogies in memory, therefore, you need to look beyond the superficial features of the problem and think instead about the principles governing the problem—focusing on the problem's "deep structure." As a related point, you'll be able to use an analogy only if you figure out how to map the prior case onto the problem now being solved—only if you realize, for example, that converging groups of soldiers correspond to converging rays and that a fortress-to-be-captured corresponds to a tumor-to-be-destroyed. This **mapping** process can be difficult (Holyoak, 2012; Reed, 2017), and failures to figure out the mapping are another reason people regularly fail to find and use analogies.

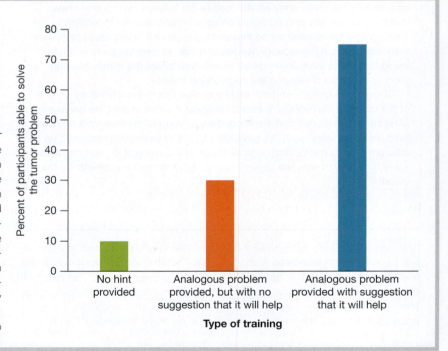

FIGURE 13.7 THE IMPORTANCE OF ANALOGIES IN SOLVING PROBLEMS

Participants rarely solved the tumor problem if they were given no hints. However, if they were given an analogous problem (the general and fortress) and encouraged to use this problem as a guide, most did solve the tumor problem. Surprisingly, though, participants often failed to make use of the analogy unless they were specifically encouraged to do so.

(AFTER GICK & HOLYOAK, 1980)

Strategies to Make Analogy Use More Likely

Perhaps, then, we have our first suggestion about why people differ in their problem-solving ability. Perhaps the people who are better problem solvers are those who make better use of analogies—plausibly, because they pay attention to a problem's deep structure rather than its superficial traits.

Consistent with these claims, it turns out that we can *improve* problem solving by encouraging people to pay attention to the problems' underlying dynamic—and, specifically, the *relationships* involved in a problem. For example, Goldwater and Jamrozik (2019) found that participants were more likely to think of analogies if the participants had a "relational mindset" during their initial learning—so that, from the start, participants thought about the cases they were learning in terms of their underlying structure. To create this mindset, participants were simply given appropriate labels: "This is an example of a *trade-off*" or (for a different case) "This is an example of a *positive feedback loop.*"

Note, though, that these labels had to be in place when the (potential) analogues were first learned. The data showed no benefit from inducing a "relational mindset" later on, when the time came to hunt for analogies. It seems, then, that efforts toward encouraging analogy use should focus on the examples being placed into memory, cases that can later serve as analogies. There seems to be less payoff from steps that might shape how people hunt for analogies when they're in the midst of problem solving. (For related data, see Catrambone et al., 2006; Kurtz & Loewenstein, 2007.)

Expert Problem Solvers

How far can we go with these points? Can these simple ideas explain the difference between ordinary problem solvers and genuine experts? To some extent, they can.

We've suggested, for example, that it's helpful to think about problems in terms of their deep structure, and this is, it seems, the way experts think about problems. In one early study, participants were asked to categorize simple physics problems (Chi et al., 1981). Novices tended to place together all the problems involving river currents, all the problems involving springs, and so on, in each case focusing on the surface form of the problem. In contrast, experts (PhD students in physics) ignored these details of the problems and, instead, sorted according to the physical principles relevant to the problems' solution. (For more on expertise, see Ericsson & Towne, 2012.)

We've also claimed that attention to a problem's deep structure promotes analogy use, so if experts are more attentive to this structure, they should be more likely to use analogies. And they are (e.g., Bassok & Novick, 2012), both in laboratory settings and in their work: Christensen and Schunn (2005) recorded work meetings of a group of engineers trying to create new products for the medical world. As the engineers discussed their options, analogy use was frequent—with an analogy being offered in the discussion every 5 minutes!

Setting Subgoals

Experts also have other advantages. For example, it's often helpful to break a problem into subproblems so that the overall challenge can be tackled part by part rather than all at once. This, too, is a technique that experts often use.

Classic evidence on this point comes from studies of chess experts (de Groot, 1965, 1966; also see Chase & Simon, 1973). The data show that these experts are particularly skilled in organizing a chess game—in seeing the structure of the game, understanding its parts, and perceiving how the parts are related to one another. This skill can be revealed in many ways, including how chess masters remember board positions. In one procedure, chess masters were able to remember the positions of 20 pieces after viewing the board for just 5 seconds; average players remembered many fewer (see **Figure 13.8**). In addition, there was a pattern to the experts' recollection: In recalling the layout of the board, the experts would place four or five pieces in their proper positions, then pause, then recall another group, then pause, and so on. In each case, the group of pieces was one that made "tactical sense"—for example, the pieces involved in a "forked" attack, a chain of mutually defending pieces, and the like. (For data with other forms of expertise, see Tuffiash et al., 2007; also see Sala & Gobet, 2017.)

It seems, then, that the masters—experts in chess—memorize the board in terms of higher-order units, defined by their strategic function within the

---

FIGURE 13.8   EXPERTS REMEMBERING PATTERNS

A Actual position

B Typical master player's performance

C Typical average player's performance

Experienced chess players who viewed the pattern in Panel A for 5 seconds were easily able to memorize it (Panel B); average players could not (Panel C), and performance from outright novices was even worse. This is because the experts were able to organize the pattern into meaningful chunks, thereby lightening their memory load. Cross-hatched squares indicate memory errors.   (FIG. 8.15 FROM BOOTZIN, R. R. (1979). *PSYCHOLOGY TODAY: AN INTRODUCTION.* NEW YORK, NY: MCGRAW HILL EDUCATION. © 1979 MCGRAW-HILL EDUCATION. REPRINTED WITH PERMISSION.)

game. This perception of higher-order units helps to organize the experts' thinking. By focusing on these units and how they're related to one another, the experts keep track of broad strategies without getting bogged down in the details. Likewise, these units set subgoals for the experts. Having perceived a group of pieces as a coordinated attack, an expert sets the subgoal of preparing for the attack. Having perceived another group of pieces as the early development of a pin (a situation in which a player cannot move without exposing a more valuable piece to an attack), the expert creates the subgoal of avoiding the pin.

Experts also have other advantages, including the simple fact that they know much more about their domains of expertise than novices do, and they often have already-assembled routines that they can use for many tasks (Logan, 2018). Experts also organize their knowledge more effectively than novices do. In particular, studies indicate that experts' knowledge is heavily cross-referenced, so that each bit of information has associations to many other bits (e.g., Bédard & Chi, 1992; Bransford et al., 1999; Reed, 2017). As a result, experts have better access to what they know. It's clear, therefore, that there are multiple factors separating novices from experts, but these factors all hinge on the processes we've already discussed—with an emphasis on analogies, subproblems, and memory search. Apparently, then, we can use our theorizing so far to describe how people (in particular, novices and experts) differ from one another.

TEST YOURSELF

3. Why do people seem to under-use analogies in solving problems?
4. What are some of the advantages that expert problem solvers have, compared to those who are not experts?

Defining the Problem

Experts, we've said, define problems in their area of expertise in terms of the problems' underlying structure. As a result, the experts are more likely to break a problem into meaningful parts, more likely to realize what other problems are analogous to the current problem, and so more likely to benefit from analogies.

Clearly, then, there are better and worse ways to define a problem—ways that will lead to a solution and ways that will obstruct it. But what does it mean to "define" a problem? And what determines how people define the problems they encounter?

Ill-Defined and Well-Defined Problems

For many problems, the goal and the options for solving the problems are clearly stated at the start: Get all the Hobbits to the other side of the river, using the boat. Solve the math problem, using the axioms stated. Many problems, though, are rather different. For example, we all hope for peace in the world, but what will this goal involve? There will be no fighting, of course, but what other traits will the goal have? Will the nations currently on the map still be in place? How will disputes be settled? It's also unclear what steps should be tried in an effort toward reaching this goal. Would diplomatic negotiations work? Or would economic measures be more effective?

Problems like this one are said to be **ill-defined**, with no clear statement at the outset of how the goal should be characterized or what operations might serve to reach that goal. Other examples of ill-defined problems include "having a good time while on vacation" and "saving money for college."

When confronting ill-defined problems, your best bet is often to create subgoals, because many ill-defined problems have reasonably well-defined parts, and by solving each of these you can move toward solving the overall problem. A different strategy is to add some structure to the problem by including extra constraints or extra assumptions. In this way, the problem becomes well-defined instead of ill-defined—perhaps with a narrower set of options in how you might approach it, but even so, with a plausible set of operations to try.

Functional Fixedness

Even for well-defined problems, there's often more than one way to understand them. Consider the problem in **Figure 13.9**. To solve it, you need to cease thinking of the box as a container and instead think of it as a

FIGURE 13.9   THE CANDLE PROBLEM

You are given the objects shown: a candle, a book of matches, and a box of tacks. Your task is to find a way to attach the candle to the wall of the room, at eye level, so that it will burn properly and illuminate the room.

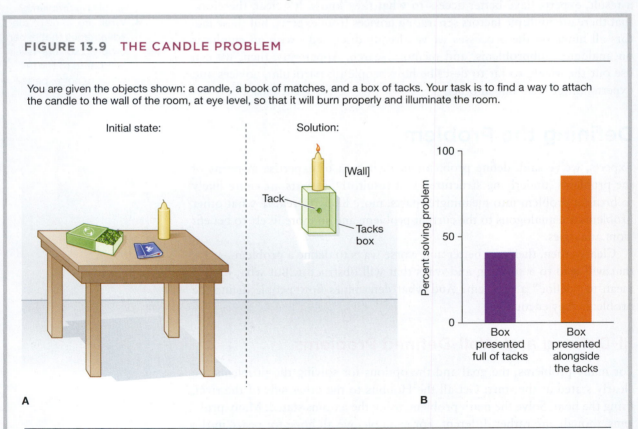

Initial state:

Solution:

[Wall]

Tack

Tacks box

A

B

What makes this problem difficult is the tendency to think of the box of tacks as a box—that is, as a container. The problem is readily solved, though, once you think of the box as a potential platform. However, this approach is less likely if the box is presented initially *full of tacks*. This presentation emphasizes the usual function of the box (as a container), making it less likely that participants will think of an alternative function for it.

potential platform. Thus, your chances of solving the problem depend on how you represent the box in your thoughts, and we can show this by *encouraging* one representation or another. In a classic study, participants were given the equipment shown in Figure 13.9A: some matches, a box of tacks, and a candle. This configuration (implicitly) underscored the box's conventional function. As a result, the configuration increased **functional fixedness**—the tendency to be rigid in how one thinks about an object's function. With fixedness in place, the problem was rarely solved (Duncker, 1945; Fleck & Weisberg, 2004).

Other participants were given the same tools, but configured differently. They were given some matches, a pile of tacks, the box (now empty), and a candle. In this setting, the participants were less likely to think of the box as a container for the tacks, and so less likely to think of the box *as a container*. As a result, they were more likely to solve the problem (Duncker, 1945). (Also see **Figure 13.10**; for more on fixedness, see McCaffrey, 2012.)

FIGURE 13.10 THE TWO-STRING PROBLEM

You enter a room in which two strings are hanging from the ceiling and a pair of pliers is lying on a table. Your task is to tie the two strings together. Unfortunately, though, the strings are positioned far enough apart so that you can't grab one string and hold on to it while reaching for the other. How can you tie them together?

The two-string problem is difficult—because of functional fixedness. The trick here is not to think of the pliers in terms of their usual function—squeezing or pulling. Instead, the trick is to think of them as a weight. The solution to the puzzle is to tie the pliers to one string and push the pliers away from the other string. While this pendulum is in motion, go and grab the second string. Then, when the pendulum swings back toward you, grab it and you're all set.

Einstellung

A related obstacle to problem solving arises when people start work on a problem and, because of their early steps, get locked into a particular line of thinking. In this case, too, people can end up victims of their own assumptions, rigidly following a path that no longer serves them well.

Some investigators describe this rigidity as a **problem-solving set**—the collection of beliefs and assumptions a person makes about a problem. Other investigators use the term *Einstellung*, the German word for "attitude," to describe the problem solver's beliefs, habits, and preferred strategies.

A classic demonstration of Einstellung involves the water jar problem, illustrated in **Figure 13.11**. Most participants find the solution, and once they do so, we give them some new problems. Crucially, though, all of the problems in the series can be solved in the same way, using the "formula" shown in the figure.

FIGURE 13.11 **THE WATER JAR PROBLEM**

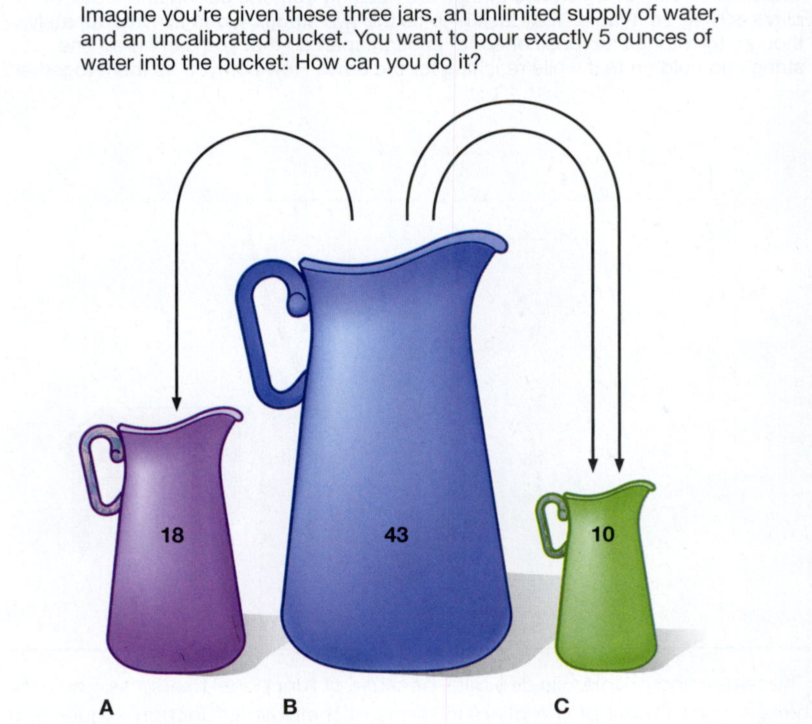

Imagine you're given these three jars, an unlimited supply of water, and an uncalibrated bucket. You want to pour exactly 5 ounces of water into the bucket: How can you do it?

A — 18   B — 43   C — 10

The solution is shown here, and it can be summarized by formula B − A − 2C. Once participants have solved a couple of problems, though, each of which can be solved in the same way, they seem to grow blind to other solution paths.

After solving several problems with this design, participants are given one more problem: Jar A holds 18 ounces; Jar B holds 48 ounces; Jar C holds 4 ounces. The goal is 22 ounces. Participants generally solve this problem in the same way they've solved the previous problems, failing to see that a more direct route to the goal is possible—by filling A, filling C, and combining them (18 + 4). Their prior success in using the same procedure over and over renders them blind to the more efficient alternative (Luchins, 1942; Luchins & Luchins, 1950a, 1950b).

Let's be clear that, in a way, participants are doing something sensible here: Once they've discovered a strategy that "gets the job done," they might as well use that strategy, with no reason to hunt for an alternative plan. It's unsettling, though, that this mechanization of problem solving can interfere with subsequent performance.

"Thinking outside the Box"

Another example of a problem-solving set involves the nine-dot problem (see **Figure 13.12**). People routinely fail to solve this problem, because—according to some interpretations—they (mistakenly) assume that the lines they draw need to stay inside the "square" defined by the dots. In fact, this problem is probably the source of the cliché "You need to think outside the box."

Ironically, though, this cliché may be misleading. In one study, participants were told explicitly that to solve the problem their lines would need to go outside the square. The hint provided little benefit, and most participants

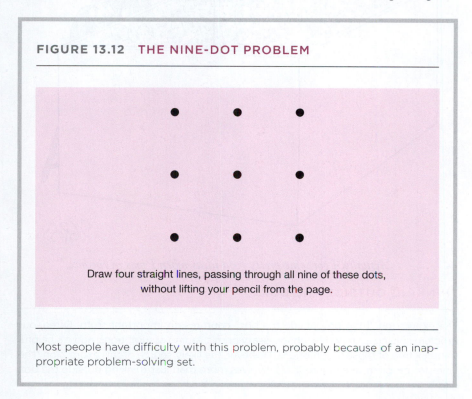

FIGURE 13.12   THE NINE-DOT PROBLEM

Draw four straight lines, passing through all nine of these dots, without lifting your pencil from the page.

Most people have difficulty with this problem, probably because of an inappropriate problem-solving set.

still failed to find the solution (Weisberg & Alba, 1981). Apparently, beliefs about "the box" aren't the obstacle. Even when we eliminate these beliefs, performance remains poor.

Nonetheless, the expression "think outside the box" does get the broad idea right, because to solve this problem people do need to jettison their initial approach. Specifically, most people assume that the lines they draw must begin and end on dots. People also have the idea that they'll need to maximize the number of dots "canceled" with each move; as a result, they seek solutions in which each line cancels a full row or column of dots. It turns out, though, that these assumptions are wrong; and so, guided by these mistaken beliefs, people find this problem quite hard. (See Kershaw & Ohlsson, 2004; MacGregor et al., 2001; also Öllinger et al., 2013.)

It's clear, then, that in the nine-dot problem and many other problems as well, people are victims of their own problem-solving set; to find the solution, they need to change that set. This phrasing, however, makes it sound like a set is a bad thing, blocking the discovery of a solution. Let's emphasize, though, that sets also provide a benefit. This is because (as we mentioned earlier) most problems offer a huge number of options as you seek the solution—an enormous number of moves you might try or approaches you might consider. A problem-solving set helps you, therefore, by narrowing your options, which in turn eases the search for a solution. Thus, in solving the nine-dot problem,

"Actually, I got some pretty good ideas when I was in the box."

THINKING OUTSIDE THE BOX

The expression "thinking outside the box" captures an important truth: Often, our problem solving is limited by unnecessary or misleading assumptions, and it's helpful to break free of those assumptions. However, the likely source of this expression (the nine-dot problem; see Figure 13.12) involves more than just thinking outside the box (i.e., the square formed by the dots).

you didn't waste any time wondering whether you should try drawing the lines while holding the pencil between your toes or whether the problem was hard because you were sitting down while you worked on it instead of standing up. These are foolish ideas, so you brushed past them. But what identifies them as foolish? It's your problem-solving set, which tells you, among other things, which options are plausible, which ones are physically possible, and so on.

In this way, a set can blind you to important options and thus be an obstacle. But a set can also blind you to a wide range of futile strategies, and this is a good thing: It enables you to focus, much more productively, on options that are likely to work out. Indeed, without a set, you might be so distracted by silly notions that even the simplest problem would become insoluble.

Creativity

There is no question, though, that efforts toward a problem solution can sometimes be hindered by someone's set, and this observation points us toward another way in which people differ. Some people are remarkably flexible in their approaches to problems; they seem easily able to "think outside the box." Other people, in contrast, seem far too ready to rely on routine, so they're more vulnerable to the obstacles we've just described.

How should we think about these differences? Why do some people reliably produce novel and unexpected solutions, while other people offer only familiar solutions? This is, in effect, a question of why some people are *creative* and others aren't—a question that forces us to ask: What is creativity?

Case Studies of Creativity

One approach to this issue focuses on people like the ones we mentioned at the chapter's start—a group of individuals that includes artists like Pablo Picasso and Johann Sebastian Bach, or scientists like Charles Darwin and Marie Curie. By studying these giants, perhaps we can draw hints about the nature of creativity when it arises, on a much smaller scale, in day-to-day life.

Research suggests, in fact, that highly creative people like Bach and Curie do have certain things in common, and we can think of these elements as "prerequisites" for creativity (e.g., Hennessey & Amabile, 2010). These individuals, first of all, generally have great knowledge and skills in their domain. This point can't be surprising: If you don't know the basics of chemistry, you can't be a creative chemist. If you're not a skilled storyteller, you can't be a great novelist.

In fact, this need for knowledge and skill may explain why creativity is typically "domain-specific." In other words, someone who's a creative poet may not be a creative cook; someone who's a creative musician may not be a creative writer. But we shouldn't put this point too strongly, because people are often creative in a broad "category" of activities (Carson et al., 2005; Kaufman & Baer, 2004). Some people, for example, are creative in performance

TEST YOURSELF

5. Why are problem-solving sets often a problem? But why are problem-solving sets also useful?
6. What is functional fixedness?

(and so they're creative in dance and dramatic performance). Other people might be creative in expressing themselves (and so creative both in their writing and in their humor); others might be creative in science (and so creative scientists, creative inventors, and perhaps even creative cooks).

Other prerequisites for creativity, though, are not tied to specific domains. For example, to be creative you need certain personality traits: a willingness to take risks, a willingness to ignore criticism, an ability to tolerate ambiguous findings or situations, and an inclination not to "follow the crowd." In addition, highly creative people tend to be motivated by the pleasure of their work rather than by the promise of external rewards. With this, highly creative people tend to work extremely hard on their endeavors and to produce a lot of their product, whether these products are poems, paintings, or scientific papers. Finally, highly creative people have generally been "in the right place at the right time"—that is, in environments that allowed them freedom, provided them with the appropriate supports, and offered them problems "ripe" for solution with the resources available.

Notice that these last observations highlight the contribution of factors outside the person, as well as the person's own capacities and skills. The external environment, for example, is the source of crucial knowledge and resources, and it often defines the problem itself. This is why many authors have suggested that we need a "sociocultural approach" to creativity—one that considers the social and historical context, as well as the processes unfolding inside the creative individual's mind (e.g., Sawyer, 2006).

We still need to ask, however: What does go on in a creative mind? If a person has all the prerequisites just listed, what happens next to produce the creative step forward? The answer involves multiple elements (e.g., Dygert & Jarosz, 2020), and we may need to separate different subtypes of creativity (e.g., Dietrich, 2019). Even so, it will be instructive to examine a proposal offered years ago by Wallas (1926). His notion fits well with some common-sense ideas about creativity, and his framework continues to guide much of the modern research. Nonetheless, the evidence forces us to question several of Wallas's claims.

The Moment of Illumination

According to Wallas, creative thought proceeds through four stages. In the first stage, **preparation**, the problem solver gathers information and does some work on the problem, but with little progress. In the second stage, **incubation**, the problem solver sets the problem aside and seems not to be working on it. Wallas argued, though, that the problem solver continues to work on the problem unconsciously during this stage, so actually the problem's solution is continuing to develop, unseen. This development leads to the third stage, **illumination**, in which a key insight or new idea emerges, paving the way for the fourth stage, **verification**, in which the person confirms that the new idea really does lead to a solution and works out the details.

Historical evidence suggests, however, that many creative discoveries don't include the steps Wallas described—or if they do, they include these steps in a complex, back-and-forth sequence (Weisberg, 1986). Likewise, the moment of illumination celebrated in Wallas's proposal may be more myth than reality. When we examine creative discoveries in science or art, we usually find that the new ideas emerged, not from some glorious leap forward, but instead from a succession of "mini-insights," each moving the process along in some small way (Klein, 2013; Sawyer, 2006).

And when people do have the "Aha!" experience that, for Wallas, signified illumination, what does this involve? Metcalfe (1986; Metcalfe & Wiebe, 1987) gave her participants a series of "insight problems" like those shown in **Figure 13.13A**. As participants worked on each problem, they rated their progress by using a judgment of "warmth" ("I'm getting warmer . . . , I'm getting warmer . . ."), and these ratings did capture the "moment of insight." Initially, the participants didn't have a clue how to proceed and gave warmth

FIGURE 13.13 INSIGHT PROBLEMS

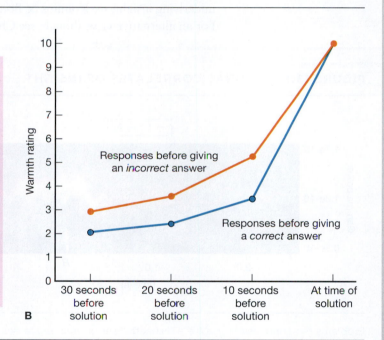

Problem 1
A stranger approached a museum curator and offered him an ancient bronze coin. The coin had an authentic appearance and was marked with the date 544 B.C. The curator had happily made acquisitions from suspicious sources before, but this time he promptly called the police and had the stranger arrested. Why?

Problem 2
A landscape gardener is given instructions to plant four special trees so that each one is exactly the same distance from each of the others. How should the trees be arranged?

A

B

As participants worked on these problems, they were asked to judge their progress by using an assessment of "warmth" ("I'm getting warmer . . . , I'm getting warmer . . . , I'm getting hot!"). To solve Problem 1, you need to realize that no one in the year 544 B.C. knew that it was 544 B.C.; that is, no one could have known that Christ would be born 544 years later. For Problem 2, the gardener needs to plant one of the trees at the top of a tall mound and then plant the other trees around the base of the mound, with the three together forming an equilateral triangle and with the fourth forming a triangle-based pyramid (i.e., a tetrahedron). (AFTER METCALFE, 1986) ratings of 1 or 2; then, abruptly, they saw a way forward and their warmth ratings shot up to the top of the scale.

To understand this pattern, though, we need to look separately at participants who subsequently announced the correct solution to the problem and those who announced an *incorrect* solution. Remarkably, the pattern is the same for both groups (see **Figure 13.13B**). In other words, some participants abruptly announced that they were getting "hot" and, moments later, solved the problem. Other participants made the same announcement and, moments later, slammed into a dead end.

It seems, therefore, that when you say "Aha!" it means only that you've discovered a new approach, one that you've not yet considered. This is important, because often a new approach is just what you need. But there's nothing magical about the "moment of illumination." This moment doesn't signal that you've at last discovered a path leading to the solution. Instead, it means only that you've discovered something new to try, with no guarantee that this "something new" will be helpful. (For more on procedures that can *promote* "Aha!" moments, see Patrick et al., 2015; also Patrick & Ahmed, 2014. For more on the insight process overall, see Bassok & Novick, 2012; Laukkonen et al., 2020; Smith & Ward, 2012; van Steenburgh et al., 2012. For discussion of neural mechanisms underlying insight, see Kounios & Beeman, 2014, 2015, and also **Figure 13.14**. For an alternative view, though, see Chuderski & Jastrzębski, 2018.)

FIGURE 13.14   NEURAL CORRELATES OF INSIGHT

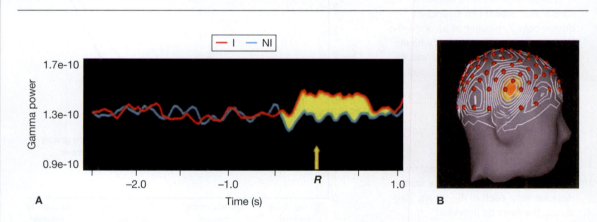

Problems requiring insight involve a distinctive set of brain processes. In Panel A, the letter *R* and the yellow arrow indicate the moment at which the research participant announced that he or she had figured out the problem solution, either for a problem requiring some insight (red line, keyed "I") or for a problem not requiring a special insight (blue line, keyed "NI"). To make the difference between these lines easily visible, the difference is shaded in yellow. The time axis shows the time relative to the participants' announcement that they'd found the problem's solution. The measure of "gamma power" is derived from EEG procedures, and it represents the square of the voltage measured in brain waves. Panel B shows the spatial focus of this distinctive brain process—called "gamma-band activity." The red dots in Panel B show where the EEG electrodes were placed.

Incubation

What about Wallas's second stage, incubation? His claim here fits well with a common experience: You're working on a problem but getting nowhere with it. You give up and turn to other matters. Sometime later, when you're thinking about something altogether different, the problem's solution pops into your thoughts. What has happened? According to Wallas, your time away from the problem allowed incubation to proceed—unconscious work on the problem that led to considerable progress.

Systematic studies, however, tell us that this pattern is (at best) unreliable. In these studies, participants are given a problem to solve. Some participants work on the problem continuously; some are interrupted for a while. The prediction, based on Wallas's proposal, is that we'll observe better performance in the latter group—the group that can benefit from incubation.

The data, however, are mixed. Some studies do show that time away from a problem helps in finding the problem's solution, but many studies find no effect. (See Baird et al., 2012; Dodds et al., 2007, 2012; Gilhooly et al., 2012; Hélie & Sun, 2010; Sio et al., 2017.) The explanation for this mixed pattern isn't clear. Some researchers argue that incubation is disrupted if you're under pressure to solve the problem. Other authors suggest that time away from a problem is more helpful if you're *asleep* during this interval (Sanders et al., 2019; for more on the relationship between sleep and problem solving, see Lewis et al., 2018). Still other authors suggest a benefit from incubation is more likely if the circumstances allow your thoughts to "wander" during the incubation period. (For reviews of this literature, see Baird et al., 2012; Gilhooly et al., 2012; Kounios & Beeman, 2015.)

Why should "mind wandering" be relevant here? In Chapter 7 we described the process of *spreading activation* through which one memory can activate related memories. It seems likely that when you're carefully working on a problem, you try to direct this flow of activation—and perhaps end up directing it in unproductive ways. When you simply allow your thoughts to wander, though, the activation can flow wherever the memory connections take it, and this may lead to new ideas being activated. (See, among others, Gable et al., 2019; Kounios & Beeman, 2015; Radel et al., 2015; for some complications, though, see Seli et al., 2018.) This process provides no guarantee that *helpful* or *productive* ideas will come to mind, only that *more* (and perhaps unanticipated) ideas will be activated. In this way, incubation is like illumination—a source of new possibilities that may or may not pay off.

In some cases, however, there's a more mundane explanation of incubation effects. Your early efforts with a problem may have been tiring or frustrating, and the interruption simply provides an opportunity for the frustration or fatigue to dissipate. Likewise, your early efforts with a problem may have been dominated by a particular approach, a particular set. If you put the problem aside for a while, it's possible you'll forget about (or lose interest in) these earlier tactics, freeing you to explore other, more productive avenues. (See Smith & Beda, 2020a, 2020b; Storm & Patel, 2014; Vul & Pashler, 2007.)

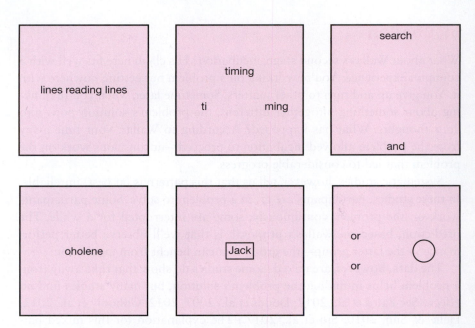

AN INCUBATION BENEFIT FROM SIMPLE FORGETTING

Shown here are the problems used in a study of incubation. Each panel refers to a familiar word or phrase; participants had to figure out what the word or phrase was. Clues were given for each problem, but for many of the problems the clues were designed to be misleading. Control participants had a minute to work on each puzzle; other participants worked on each puzzle for 30 seconds, then were interrupted, and later returned to the puzzle for an additional 30 seconds. This interruption did improve performance, so that problem solution was more likely for the incubation group. Crucially, though, the researchers tested participants' memory for the misleading clues, and they found that the incubation participants were less likely to remember the clues. The researchers argued that this forgetting is what created the incubation advantage: After the interruption, participants were no longer misled by the bad clues, and their performance improved accordingly. (The solutions to these puzzles appear at the end of the chapter.) (AFTER SMITH & BLANKENSHIP, 1991)

With all of these proposals in view, it remains unclear why time away from a problem sometimes helps and sometimes doesn't. We know that if you're stymied by a problem, it sometimes is a good idea to walk away from it for a while. But sometimes your best bet is just to keep plugging away, doggedly trying to move forward. For now, research provides less guidance than we'd like in choosing which of these is the better plan.

The Nature of Creativity

Where does this discussion leave us with regard to our overarching question—the question of how people differ in their cognitive abilities? In discussing *expertise*, we saw that experts in a domain have a stack of advantages: a tendency to think about problems in terms of their structure rather than their surface form, a broad knowledge base deriving from their experience

"Sleep on it."

The history of ideas contains many reports of insights emerging at unexpected times and in unexpected places. One often-mentioned example involves Archimedes, who allegedly made a crucial discovery (how to measure the volume of a complex shape) while settling into a bathtub. (According to some reports, Archimedes leapt out of the bath and raced home naked, crying "Eureka! Eureka!") Another example involves the mathematician Henri Poincaré. He'd been working on a problem with little success and decided he needed a break. He therefore joined a geological expedition, but just as he was stepping onto the bus, the solution came to him in a flash. Or, as one more instance, the poet Samuel Coleridge composed one of his most famous works in bed—during an opium-influenced dream.

There is room for skepticism about each of these accounts, but even so, these reports invite us to ask whether problem solving is indeed fostered by a bed, a bath, or a bus. Some of the data are intriguing: In one study, people were presented with puzzles in the evening, with each puzzle associated with a distinct sound. Then, overnight, half of the sounds were presented to the people while they were asleep. In the morning, people solved 32% of the puzzles for which they'd heard these overnight cues, but only 20% of the remaining (uncued) puzzles (Sanders et al., 2019).

What's going on here? We know that people who are sound asleep are still somewhat sensitive to signals in their environment. (The classic example is the sleeping mother who is reliably awakened by the sound of her baby's crying, but not by other noises.) More, we know that environmental

THE MANY BENEFITS OF SLEEP

A night's sleep provides many benefits—and may actally be a spur to creative problem solving.

cues are sometimes incorporated into a person's dreams. And, finally, we know that dreams often combine ideas in novel ways. These novel combinations will often be bizarre, but they can sometimes be productive—and that may be the source of the benefit in the sound-cue experiment (Lewis et al., 2018). In essence, your dreams may randomly jumble a problem's elements into new patterns or may toss these elements together with other ideas. For some problems, these novel combinations may be exactly what you need in your search for a solution.

When you're stuck on a problem, people sometimes suggest—on commonsense grounds—that you should "sleep on it," and that the problem will "look different in the morning." It seems there may be some truth to this idea. Sleep, of course, has benefits for your physical and mental health, but the evidence suggests it can sometimes also help in solving intellectual puzzles.

in a field, heavily cross-referenced memories, and so on. Now, in discussing *creativity*, we've seen a similar pattern: Highly creative people tend to have certain personality traits (e.g., a willingness to take risks), a lot of knowledge, intense motivation, and some amount of luck. But what mental processes do they rely on? When we examine Darwin's notebooks or Picasso's early sketches, we discover that these creative giants relied on analogies, hints, heuristics, and a lot of hard work, just as the rest of us do (Gruber, 1981; Sawyer, 2006; Weisberg, 1986). In some cases, creativity may even depend on blind trial and error (e.g., Klein, 2013; Simonton, 2011); with this sort of process, the great artist or great inventor is simply someone who's highly discriminating—and thus able to discern which of the randomly produced products actually have value.

Creative people also rely heavily on memory search—tackling a problem by drawing on things they already know. But, as one more element of creativity, people differ in *how* or *how well* they search through memory. As one proposal, some authors emphasize a skill of **convergent thinking**—an ability to spot ways in which seemingly distinct ideas might be interconnected. This ability is sometimes measured through the Remote Associates Test (Mednick, 1962; Mednick & Mednick, 1967; also Smith et al., 2013; also Cushen & Wiley, 2018; see **Figure 13.15**). In this test, you're given a trio of words, and you need to find one more word that fits with each of the three. For example, you might be given the trio *cross, rain,* and *tie*; the correct answer is *bow* (as in *crossbow, rainbow,* and *bowtie*).

FIGURE 13.15   CREATIVITY AS THE ABILITY TO FIND NEW CONNECTIONS

For each trio of words, think of a fourth word that is related to each of the first three. For example, for the trio "snow, down, out," the answer would be "fall" ("snowfall"; "downfall"; "fallout").

1.	off	top	tail
2.	ache	sweet	burn
3.	dark	shot	sun
4.	arm	coal	peach
5.	tug	gravy	show

Mednick argued that creativity involves the ability to find new connections among ideas. This ability is measured in the Remote Associates Test, for which some sample items are shown here. (The solutions are given at the end of the chapter.)   (AFTER MEDNICK & MEDNICK, 1967)

Other authors emphasize the skill of **divergent thinking**—an ability to move your thoughts in novel, unanticipated directions. (See Guilford, 1967, 1979; also see Beaty et al., 2014; Hass, 2017; Vartanian et al., 2009; see **Figure 13.16**.) Here, there's no "right answer." Instead, success in divergent thinking is reflected in an ability to come up with a large number of new ideas—ideas that can then be evaluated to see if they're of any value.

As a related matter, people also differ in how much their current thinking breaks away from their past thoughts—a measure called "forward flow." Research suggests that this measure is associated with creativity both in the arts (e.g., in performance majors) and in business (e.g., in entrepreneurs; Gray et al., 2019). And—importantly—all three of the abilities we've mentioned (divergent thinking, convergent thinking, forward flow) seem distinct from one another (Dygert & Jarosz, 2020), opening the prospect that there are actually different ways to be creative (also see Dietrick, 2019).

Putting all of these pieces together, what is it that allowed Darwin or Picasso, Martha Graham or Georgia O'Keeffe, to achieve their monumental creativity? The key may lie in a *combination* of factors. Many of us are smart or particularly skillful in memory search; many of us are willing to take risks and to ignore criticism; many of us live in a cultural setting that might

TEST YOURSELF

7. Define each of the stages proposed by Wallas—preparation, incubation, illumination, and verification.
8. What does research tell us about whether incubation truly helps problem solving?
9. What does research tell us is really going on in the "Aha!" moment of illumination?

FIGURE 13.16 CREATIVITY AS DIVERGENT THINKING

Tests of divergent thinking require you to think of new uses for simple objects or new ways to think about familiar ideas. How many different uses can you think of for a brick?

As a paperweight.
As the shadow-caster in a sundial (if positioned appropriately).
As a means of writing messages on a sidewalk.
As a stepladder (if you want to grab something just slightly out of reach).
As a nutcracker.
As a pendulum useful for solving the two-string problem.

Choose five names, at random, from the telephone directory. In how many different ways could these names be classified?

According to the number of syllables.
According to whether there is an even or odd number of vowels.
According to whether their third letter is in the last third of the alphabet.
According to whether they rhyme with things that are edible.

Guilford (1967, 1979) argued that creativity lies in the ability to take an idea in a new, unprecedented direction. Among its other items, his test of creativity asks people to think of new uses for a familiar object. Some possible responses are listed here.

support a new discovery. Some of us are skilled in convergent thinking, or divergent. Some of us have better ability to examine and combine ideas, a notion we discussed in Chapter 6 under the label "working memory capacity." (For more on the link between this capacity and creativity, see Chuderski & Jastrzębski, 2018.) What may distinguish creative geniuses, though, is that they are the special people who have *all* of these ingredients—the right intellectual tools, the right personality characteristics, the good fortune to be living in the right context, and so on. It's a rare individual who has all of these elements, and it's probably the combination of all these elements that provides the recipe for extraordinary creativity.

brainstorming

Students often ask: Is there some sort of training that can promote creativity? Is there some strategy one can use, in approaching a problem, to increase the chances of hitting on a creative solution? The chapter offers some suggestions: Sometimes sleep helps. Sometimes a period of time away from a problem helps you find a solution. Sometimes it helps to reflect on your assumptions, with the hope of figuring out if you've been trapped by an unproductive set. And sometimes it helps to adopt (what's called) a "counterfactual mindset," in which you try to think about things that almost happened or didn't happen (Markman et al., 2007; Wong et al., 2009).

Other strategies, though, seem less helpful. For example, some people believe that "brainstorming" with a group of others is productive. The idea here is that you get together with a group and freely spout out ideas, encouraging one another to voice whatever notions come to mind, carefully avoiding any criticism that might inhibit the flow of thought. Evidence suggests, however, that this procedure doesn't produce better ideas. Indeed, the outcome is better if the members of the group each work on their own and combine their

BRAINSTORMING

Many people believe that creative problem solving is fostered by "brainstorming" with a group of others. The notion is that members of the group freely spout out ideas, carefully avoiding any criticism.

proposals only later. Why is this? One concern is that being in a group can inhibit some people, no matter how encouraging (or forgiving) the tone of the conversation. Another concern is that paying attention to others' ideas can distract you from coming up with your own notions.

The base idea of brainstorming, though—just letting the ideas flow—may be sensible (even if there's no reason to think you're better off doing this with a group). After all, in our discussion of incubation we saw that the benefit (when there is one) may come simply from trying out new approaches; that's why mind wandering during the incubation period may be useful. In our discussion of sleep effects, we made a similar point: Sleep (and, more specifically, dreaming) may randomly toss the elements of a problem into new combinations, and every once in a while the novel combination is just what you need. Likewise, a technique called "creative cognition" emphasizes the importance of open-mindedness (Finke, 2016; Ward et al., 1995): People are given a dozen or so elements to work with, are encouraged to make a *random* selection from this group, and then are urged to be playful in how the elements are combined. People are told to "avoid making your object correspond to a familiar object, and don't worry what it might be used for." Evidence suggests that this approach is often productive.

At the chapter's start, we considered the contrast between Thomas Edison and Leonardo da Vinci. Edison insisted that his success depended on trying idea after idea until he found one that worked. And if he didn't find what he was after, he still counted that as a success: "I have not failed. I've just found 10,000 ways that won't work." Maybe, then, for those of us who are not da Vinci or Mozart or Alvin Ailey, Edison's approach may be the right one. Try and try and try, as open-mindedly as you can, not being limited by assumptions. Then scrutinize your output with care. Maybe one of the things you've tried will be the key!

For more on this topic:

Finke, R. (2016). *Creative imagery: Discoveries and inventions in visualization.* New York, NY: Psychology Press.

Kounios, J., & Beeman, M. (2015). *The eureka factor: Aha moments, creative insight, and the brain.* New York, NY: Random House.

Markman, K. D., Lindberg, M. J., Kray, L. J., & Galinsky, A. D. (2007). Implications of counterfactual structure for creative generation and analytical problem solving. *Personality and Social Psychology Bulletin, 33*(3), 312–324.

Wong, E. M., Galinsky, A. D., & Kray, L. J. (2009). The counterfactual mind-set: A decade of research. In K.D. Markman, W. M. P. Klein, & J. A. Suhr (Eds.), *Handbook of imagination and mental stimulation* (pp. 161–174). New York, NY: Taylor & Francis.

chapter review

SUMMARY

• Problem solving is often likened to a process of search in which you seek a path leading from a starting point to the goal. In many problems, though, there are too many paths to allow examination of each, and this is why problem-solving heuristics are crucial. Heuristics applicable to a wide range of problems include hill climbing and means-end analysis.

• Visual images and diagrams also aid problem solving, and so do analogies to earlier-solved problems. Nonetheless, analogies seem to be underused by many problem solvers, possibly because problem solvers search their memory with an emphasis on a problem's superficial features rather than its underlying dynamic. Analogy use can be promoted, therefore, by instructions or contexts that encourage people to focus on a problem's deeper structure.

• Experts in an area generally pay more attention to a problem's underlying structure than to its surface form, an approach that helps the experts to find and use analogies. Focusing on the problem's underlying structure also helps the experts to break the problem into subproblems.

• The likelihood of solving a problem is enormously influenced by how the person perceives or defines the problem. The problem definition can include unnoticed assumptions about the form the solution must take, assumptions about the use or function of elements contained within the problem, and assumptions about what types of procedures one should try in solving the problem. The approach to a problem is also sometimes shaped by Einstellung—a pattern in which the problem solver continues to use a particular approach to a problem, failing to realize that more efficient approaches are available. All of these forms of problem-solving sets are usually helpful, because they guide the problem solver away from pointless lines of attack on the problem. But the problem-solving set can also be an obstacle—if, for example, the solution requires a change in the set. As a result, problem-solving sets in the form of functional fixedness can be significant obstacles to problem solution.

• Investigators who are interested in creativity have often relied on detailed case studies of famous creative individuals. These case studies have identified certain shared traits that seem to be "prerequisites" for great creativity. The case studies also suggest a need for a sociocultural approach to creativity.

• Some scholars suggest that creative problem solving proceeds through four stages: preparation, incubation, illumination, and verification. However, other researchers are skeptical about these four stages, and careful studies of creativity have provided little evidence to suggest that creativity involves special or exotic processes. For example, incubation is often mentioned as a form of unconscious problem solving, but some studies indicate that the benefits of incubation, when they occur, can be understood in simpler terms: recovery from fatigue or the forgetting of unfruitful earlier approaches. In the same way, the moment of illumination seems to indicate only that the problem solver has located a new approach to a problem; in many cases, this new approach ultimately leads to a dead end.

• Creative individuals may be distinctive, however, in their capacity for either *convergent* or *divergent thinking*. Convergent thinking refers to the ability to spot ways in which distinct ideas might be connected. Divergent thinking refers to the ability to move one's thoughts in novel, unanticipated directions.

• In light of all these data, though, many authors have suggested that creativity may simply be the extraordinary product that results from an assembly of ordinary elements—elements that include cognitive processes (memory search through spreading activation, heuristics, etc.) and also emotional and personality characteristics that foster the processes and circumstances needed for creativity.

KEY TERMS

problem solving (p. 474)
problem space (p. 475)
hill-climbing strategy (p. 476)
means-end analysis (p. 477)
mapping (p. 480)
ill-defined problems (p. 484)
functional fixedness (p. 485)
problem-solving set (p. 486)

Einstellung (p. 486)
preparation (p. 490)
incubation (p. 490)
illumination (p. 490)
verification (p. 490)
convergent thinking (p. 496)
divergent thinking (p. 497)

TEST YOURSELF AGAIN

1. What does it mean to say that a problem-solving heuristic allows you to trim the size of the problem space?

2. What is means-end analysis?

3. Why do people seem to under-use analogies in solving problems?

4. What are some of the advantages that expert problem solvers have, compared to those who are not experts?

5. Why are problem-solving sets often a problem? But why are problem-solving sets also useful?

6. What is functional fixedness?

7. Define each of the stages proposed by Wallas—preparation, incubation, illumination, and verification.

8. What does research tell us about whether incubation truly helps problem solving?

9. What does research tell us is really going on in the "Aha!" moment of illumination?

THINK ABOUT IT

1. In this chapter, we've deliberately mentioned individuals regarded as creative in the sciences (Charles Darwin, Marie Curie) and individuals creative in the arts (Pablo Picasso, Martha Graham). Do the principles we've discussed apply equally to both of these domains? What attributes or processes do you think are the *same* in scientific and artistic creativity? What attributes or processes do you think are *different*?

DEMONSTRATIONS & APPLYING COGNITIVE PSYCHOLOGY ESSAYS

For demonstrations of key concepts in cognitive psychology, take a look at the Online Demonstrations. To explore more of the practical applications of cognitive psychology in themed essays, visit the online reader.

Online Demonstrations

- Demonstration 13.1: Analogies
- Demonstration 13.2: Verbalization and Problem Solving
- Demonstration 13.3: Incubation
- Demonstration 13.4: Remote Associates

Online Applying Cognitive Psychology Essays

- Cognitive Psychology and Technology: Computer Creativity
- Cognitive Psychology and Health: Expert Systems in Medicine
- Cognitive Psychology and the Law: Legal Creativity

ZAPS COGNITION LABS

Go to ZAPS online cognition labs to conduct hands-on experiments on key concepts.

INQUIZITIVE

It's time to complete your study experience! Go to InQuizitive to practice actively with this chapter's concepts and get personalized feedback along the way.

The solutions to the puzzles on **p. 494** are: *reading between the lines, split-second timing, search high and low, hole in one, Jack in the Box,* and *double or nothing.*

The solutions to the puzzles on **p. 495** are: *spin (spinoff, topspin, tailspin), heart (heartache, sweetheart, heartburn), glasses (dark glasses, shot glasses, sunglasses), pit (armpit, coal pit, peach pit), boat (tugboat, gravy boat, showboat).*

chapter 14 Intelligence

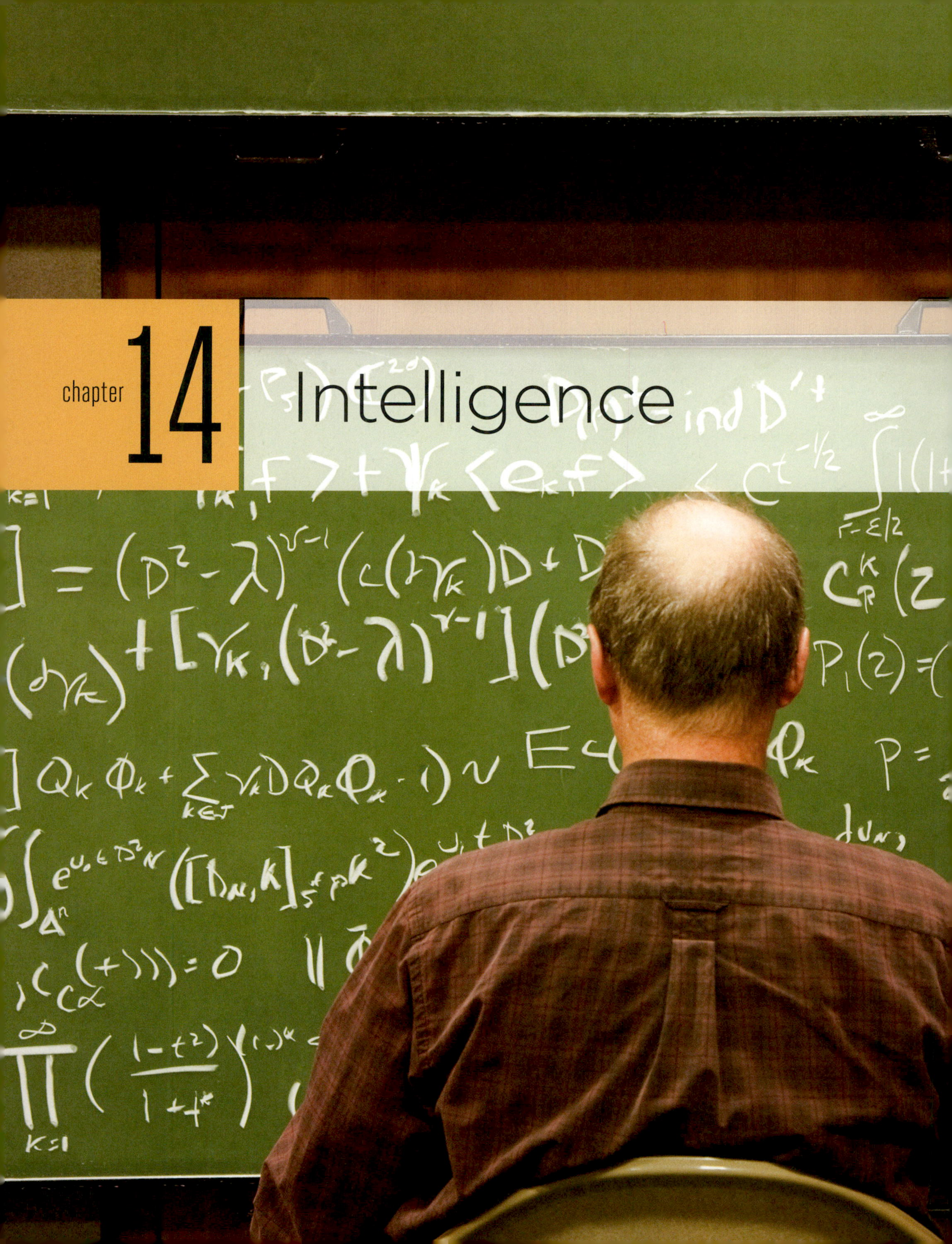

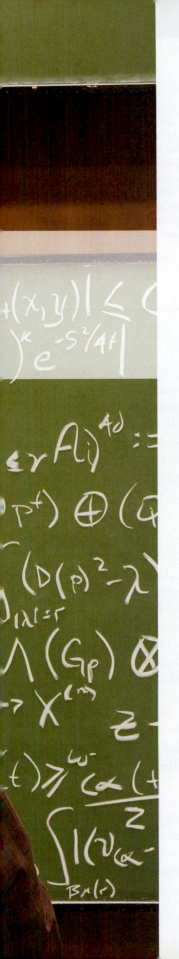

what if...

Researchers have developed a variety of tests for measuring intelligence, and as we'll see, there are powerful reasons to take these tests seriously—they do measure something important. But people with extremely *low* scores often have amazing abilities, and a consideration of these individuals provides insights into what intelligence is and when intelligence is needed.

Consider Stephen Wiltshire. His IQ score has been measured at 52, a score often interpreted as indicating profound disability. But it seems wrong to count Stephen as "disabled." Among his other attributes, Stephen is a gifted artist and has a near-perfect visual memory. He has been called the "Living Camera," and it's easy to see why: After a 30-minute helicopter ride over London, he was able to draw (from memory) an exquisitely detailed aerial view of the city. He's done the same for Rome, New York City, and Tokyo. The resulting drawings are so large (more than 15 ft across) and so precise that Stephen needs many days to finish each one—and, again, bear in mind that this is many days of drawing based on just a few minutes of view.

When carefully checked, Stephen's drawings turn out to be fabulously accurate, with an exact correspondence between his artwork and the actual view. Stephen creates an error-free reproduction of building positions and sizes, and he's even correct in drawing the number of windows in each building, the number of columns on each building's façade, and more. (For more on cases like this, see Treffert, 2014.)

People like Stephen are termed "autistic savants." This condition is rare, and scholars estimate that worldwide there may only be 100 autistic savants at a level of talent like Stephen's. Rare or not, the achievements of these individuals provide a compelling reminder that there can sometimes be a huge separation between being intelligent and having some incredible talent. But, in that case, what is intelligence? When is it helpful (or even needed), and—conversely—what tasks seem not to require the capacities measured by intelligence tests?

preview of chapter themes

- Measures of intelligence turn out to be reliable and valid, and so, if we know someone's score on an intelligence test, we can predict that person's performance in a wide range of settings (both academic and otherwise).

- The data suggest that we can truly speak of "intelligence-in-general"—intelligence that applies to a wide range of tasks. General intelligence may be a result of mental speed or the result of better executive control, with some people being better able to control their own thoughts.

- Genetic and environmental factors both matter for intelligence, but, crucially, these factors interact in producing a person's level of intelligence.

- There has been much discussion about how *groups* differ in their average level of performance. For example, American Whites and American Blacks differ in the average scores for each group, and part of the explanation lies in the differing levels of nutrition, health care, and education available to large segments of these groups. In addition, social stereotypes play an enormous role in how individuals are trained and encouraged, as well as in the expectations that individuals hold for their own performance.

What Is Intelligence?

We all admire people who seem wonderfully intelligent, and we express concerns about (and try to help) those we consider intellectually dull. But what is "intelligence"? Is there a way to measure it? And should we be focused on *intelligence* (singular) or *intelligences* (plural)? In other words, is there such a thing as "intelligence-in-general," so that someone who has this resource will be better off in all mental endeavors? Or should we instead talk about different types of intelligence, so that someone might be "smart" in some domains but less so in others?

Measuring Intelligence

People disagree about how the word "intelligence" should be defined. Remarkably, though, early efforts toward measuring intelligence proceeded without a clear definition. Instead, Alfred Binet (1857–1911) and his colleagues began with a simple idea—namely, that intelligence is a capacity that matters for many aspects of cognitive functioning. They therefore created a test that included a range of tasks: repeating a string of digits, understanding a story, doing arithmetic, and so on. Performance was then assessed with a composite score, summing across these various tasks.

In its original form, the test score was computed as a ratio between someone's "mental age" (the level of development reflected in test performance) and their chronological age. (The ratio was then multiplied by 100 to get the final score.) This ratio—or *quotient*—was the source of the test's name: The test evaluated a person's "intelligence quotient," or IQ.

Modern forms of the test no longer calculate this ratio, but they're still called "IQ tests." One commonly used test is the Wechsler Adult Intelligence Scale, or WAIS (Wechsler, 2003). Like Binet's original test, this test relies on numerous subtests. There are tests that assess general knowledge, vocabulary, and comprehension (see **Figure 14.1A**), and also a perceptual-reasoning scale

FIGURE 14.1 INTELLIGENCE TEST ITEMS

- Vocabulary
  Presents a series of words of increasing difficulty; asks for a definition of each word: "What is a lute?" or "What does solitude mean?"
- Comprehension
  Asks the test-taker to explain why certain social practices are followed or the meaning of common proverbs: "What does it mean to say, 'Don't judge a book by its cover'?"
- Similarities
  Presents pairs of objects and asks how the items in each pair are alike: "In what ways are an airplane and a car alike?"
- Information
  Asks whether the test-taker knows various bits of information, with each bit being something that is widely known in our culture: "Who is the president of Russia?"

A Sample questions from verbal scale of the WAIS

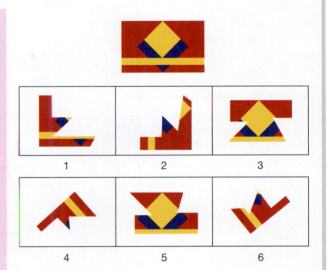

B WAIS visual puzzle

Panel A shows questions used in some of the verbal subtests of the Wechsler Adult Intelligence Scale (WAIS). Panel B shows a sample item used in the perceptual-reasoning portion of the WAIS; the task is to assemble some of the parts to form the pattern shown.

that includes puzzles like the one in **Figure 14.1B**. Separate subtests assess working memory and speed of intellectual processing.

Other intelligence tests have different formats. The Raven's Progressive Matrices test (**Figure 14.2**; Raven & Raven, 2008) hinges entirely on a person's ability to analyze figures and detect patterns. This test presents the test-taker with a series of grids (these are the "matrices"), and he or she must select an option that completes the pattern in each grid. This test is designed to minimize influence from verbal skills or background knowledge. (For yet another means of testing intelligence, and also a recent overview, see Revelle et al., 2020.)

Reliability and Validity

Whenever we design a test—to assess intelligence, personality, or anything else—we need to determine whether the test is *reliable* and *valid*. **Reliability** refers to how consistent a measure is, and one aspect of reliability is *consistency from one occasion to another*: If we give you a test, wait a while, and then give it again, do we get the same outcome? The issue here is **test-retest reliability**.

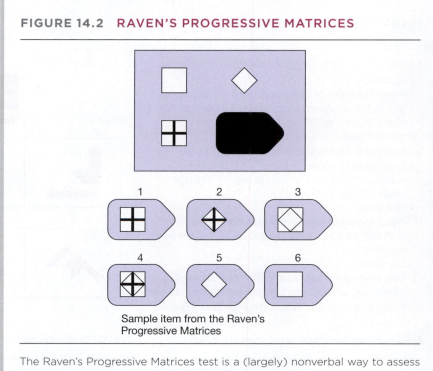

FIGURE 14.2   RAVEN'S PROGRESSIVE MATRICES

Sample item from the Raven's
Progressive Matrices

The Raven's Progressive Matrices test is a (largely) nonverbal way to assess IQ. The figure shows an easy item from the test; the task is to identify the figure that completes the pattern. The test items get harder and harder as the test progresses.

Intelligence tests have strong test-retest reliability. There is, for example, a high correlation between measurements of someone's IQ at age 6 and measurements of IQ when they're 18. For that matter, if we know someone's IQ at age 11, we can accurately predict what their IQ will be at age 80. (See, e.g., Deary, 2014; Deary et al., 2013.)

It's important, though, that IQ scores can change—especially if there's a substantial change in the person's environment. (We'll return to this point later in the chapter; also see Ramsden et al., 2011.) Nonetheless, if the environment is reasonably stable, the data show remarkable constancy in IQ scores, over spans as long as 70 or 80 years.

What about the validity of the IQ test? In general, the term **validity** refers to whether a test actually measures what it is intended to measure, and one way to approach this issue is via an assessment of **predictive validity**. The logic behind this assessment is straightforward. If intelligence tests truly measure what they're supposed to, then someone's score on the test should allow us to predict how well that person will do in settings that require intelligence. And here, too, the results are impressive, with studies showing (for example) a reasonable correlation between a person's IQ and measures of academic performance, such as grade point average. (See Arneson et al., 2011; Deary, 2012; Kuncel et al., 2004.)

IQ scores are also correlated with performance outside of the academic world. For example, an IQ score is a strong predictor of how someone will perform on the job, although—sensibly—the data indicate that IQ matters more for some jobs than for others (Sackett et al., 2008; Schmidt & Hunter, 2004). Jobs of low complexity require relatively little intelligence, so the correlation between IQ and job performance is small (although still positive) for such jobs—for example, a correlation of .20 between IQ and performance on an assembly line. As jobs become more complex, intelligence matters more, so the correlation between IQ and performance gets stronger (Gottfredson, 1997). For example, we find correlations between .50 and .60 when we look at IQ scores and people's success as accountants or shop managers.

IQ scores are also correlated with other life outcomes. People with higher IQ's tend to end up with higher-prestige careers and are less likely to suffer various life problems (e.g., they are less likely to become pregnant as teens). Higher-IQ people even live longer—although with a complicated pattern of cause-and-effect. (For more on this point, see the essay "IQ and Life Expectancy" on page 527.) Among other considerations, higher-IQ individuals are less likely to die in automobile accidents (see **Table 14.1**) and less likely to have difficulty following doctors' instructions. (See Deary et al., 2010; Gottfredson, 2004; Murray et al., 2012.)

Let's emphasize, though, that no matter what the setting, IQ scores are never a perfect predictor of life outcomes. This cannot be a surprise, because of course other factors matter in all of these domains. For example, how well you'll do in school also depends on your motivation, whether you stay healthy, whether your friends encourage you to study or instead go to parties, and dozens of other factors. Some of these factors can be controlled by the individual, but many cannot (including the quality of instruction you receive, the availability of needed resources, and more).

All of these points make it inevitable that intelligence levels won't be a perfect predictor of your academic achievement. More bluntly, these points make it inevitable that some high-IQ people will perform poorly in school, while some low-IQ people will excel.

TABLE 14.1   THE RELATION BETWEEN IQ
AND HIGHWAY DEATHS

IQ	Death rate per 100,000 drivers
>115	51.3
100–115	51.5
85–99	92.2
80–84	146.7

Note: From Holden, C. (2003). The practical benefits of general intelligence. *Science, 299*(5604), 192–193.

TEST YOURSELF

1. What does it mean to assess a measurement's reliability and its validity?
2. What evidence tells us that IQ tests do have predictive validity?

Even so, there's no question that there's a strong correlation between IQ and important life outcomes—academic or job performance, longevity, and more. It seems plain, then, that IQ tests do have impressive predictive validity—with the clear implication that these tests are measuring something interesting, important, and consequential.

General versus Specialized Intelligence

If—as it seems—IQ tests are measuring something important, what is this "something"? This question is often framed in terms of two options. One proposal is that the tests measure a singular ability that can apply to any content. The idea here is that your score on an IQ test reveals your *general* intelligence, a capacity that provides an advantage on virtually any mental task. (See Spearman, 1904, 1927; for more recent discussion, see Kaufman et al., 2012.)

In contrast, some authors argue that there's no such thing as being intelligent in a general way. Instead, they claim, each person has a collection of more specific talents—and so you might be "math smart" but not strong with language, or "highly verbal" but not strong with tasks requiring visualization. From this perspective, if we represent your capacities with a single number— an IQ score—this is only a crude summary of what you can do, because it averages together the things you're good at and the things you're not.

Which proposal is correct? One way to find out relies on the fact that, as we've said, many intelligence tests include numerous subtests. It's therefore instructive to compare a person's score on each subtest with their scores on other subtests. In this way, we can ask: If someone does well on one portion of the test, are they likely to do well across the board? If someone does poorly on one subtest, will they do poorly on other subtests as well? If we observe these patterns, this would be an indication that there is some capacity that shapes how well someone does no matter what the specific task might be. In other words, if we observe this sort of consistency from subtest to subtest, this would imply that there is such a thing as intelligence-in-general.

More than a century ago, Charles Spearman developed a statistical procedure that enables us to pursue this issue in a precise, quantitative manner. The procedure is called **factor analysis,** and as the name implies, this procedure looks for common factors—elements that contribute to multiple subtests and therefore link those subtests. Factor analysis confirms that there is a common element shared by all the components of the IQ test. (See Carroll, 1993; Deary, 2012; Johnson et al., 2008; Watkins et al., 2006. For evidence showing the same pattern in a broad set of non-Western countries, see Warne & Burningham, 2019.) Some subtests (e.g., comprehension of a simple story) depend heavily on this general factor; others (e.g., the ability to recall a string of digits) depend less on the factor. Nonetheless, this general factor matters across the board, and that's why scores on all the subtests end up correlated with one another.

Spearman named this common element **general intelligence,** usually abbreviated with the letter *g*. Spearman (1927) argued that people with a high level of *g* will have an advantage in virtually every intellectual endeavor. Conversely, if someone has a low level of *g*, that person will do poorly on a wide range of tasks.

A Hierarchical Model of Intelligence

Other results remind us, though, that *g* isn't the whole story, because people also have more specialized skills. One of these skills involves aptitude for verbal tasks, so that performance on (say) a reading comprehension test depends on how much *g* a person has *and also* on the strength of these verbal skills. A second specialized ability involves quantitative or numerical aptitude, so performance on an arithmetic test depends on how much *g* a person has *and also* the strength of these skills.

Putting these pieces together, we can think of intellectual performance as having a hierarchical structure as shown in **Figure 14.3**. At the top of the hierarchy is *g*, contributing to all tasks. At the next level down are the abilities we just mentioned—linguistic and numerical—and several more, including spatial skill (also shown in the figure), as well as (not shown) an ability to handle fast-paced mental tasks, and an ability to learn new and unfamiliar materials. Then, at the next level are more specific capacities, each useful for a narrow and specialized set of tasks. (See Carroll, 1993; Flanagan et al., 2000; Johnson et al., 2007; McGrew, 2009; Snow, 1994, 1996.)

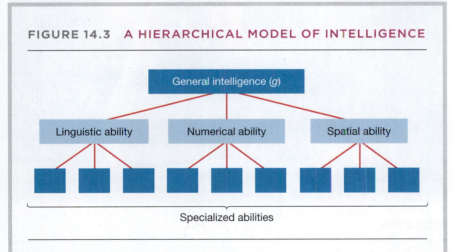

FIGURE 14.3   A HIERARCHICAL MODEL OF INTELLIGENCE

General intelligence (*g*)

Linguistic ability   Numerical ability   Spatial ability

Specialized abilities

Most modern researchers regard intelligence as having a hierarchical structure. General intelligence (*g*) is an ability called on by virtually all mental tasks. At the next level, linguistic, numerical, and spatial abilities are each called on by a range of tasks of a certain type; other abilities at this level include an ability to handle fast-paced tasks and also to memorize new material. At the next level down, more than 80 specialized abilities have been identified, each applicable to a certain type of task.

This hierarchical conception leads to a prediction. If we choose tasks from two different categories—say, a verbal task and one requiring arithmetic—we should still find a correlation in performance, because no matter how different these tasks seem, they do have something in common: They both draw on *g*. If we choose tasks from the *same* category, though—say, two verbal tasks or two quantitative tasks—we should find a *higher* correlation because these tasks have two things in common: They both draw on *g*, and they both draw on the more specialized capacity needed for just that category. The data confirm both of these predictions—moderately strong correlations among all of the IQ test's subtests, and even stronger correlations among subtests in the same category.

It seems, then, that both of the broad hypotheses we introduced earlier are correct. There is some sort of general capacity that is useful for all mental endeavors, but there are also various forms of more specialized intelligence. Each person has some amount of the general capacity and draws on it in all tasks; this is why there's an overall consistency in each person's performance. At the same time, the consistency isn't perfect, because each task also requires

DYSLEXIA

Many people suffer from the disorder called "dyslexia." This disorder should not be understood, however, simply as a problem in reading. Instead, dyslexia is a problem in reading *despite normal intelligence*. In other words, this diagnosis relies on the fact that there's usually an overall consistency in each person's intellectual performance. The person is better at some things, worse at others; but even so the scores tend to resemble one another, because all the scores are shaped by the person's level of *g*. It's only when a person doesn't show this consistency—when, for example, the person's reading scores are markedly out of step with the person's other scores—that a diagnosis of a specific learning disability seems plausible.

more specialized abilities. Each of us has our own profile of strengths and weaknesses for these skills, with the result that there are things we do relatively well and things we do less well.

Fluid and Crystallized Intelligence

It's also important to distinguish between *fluid intelligence* and *crystallized intelligence* (Carroll, 2005; Horn, 1985; Horn & Blankson, 2005). **Fluid intelligence** involves the ability to deal with novel problems. It's the form of intelligence you need when you have no well-practiced routines you can bring to bear on a problem. **Crystallized intelligence,** in contrast, involves your acquired knowledge, including your verbal knowledge and your repertoire of skills—skills useful for dealing with problems similar to those you've already encountered.

Fluid and crystallized intelligence are highly correlated (e.g., if you have a lot of one, you're likely to have a lot of the other). Nonetheless, these two aspects of intelligence differ in important ways. Crystallized intelligence usually increases with age, but fluid intelligence reaches its peak in early adulthood and then declines across the lifespan (see **Figure 14.4**; Horn, 1985; Horn & Noll, 1994; Salthouse, 2004, 2012). Similarly, many factors—including alcohol consumption, fatigue, and depression—cause more impairment in tasks requiring fluid intelligence than in those dependent on crystallized intelligence (Duncan, 1994; Hunt, 1995). Therefore, someone who is tired will probably perform adequately on tests involving familiar routines and familiar facts. The same individual, however, may be markedly impaired if the test requires quick thinking or a novel approach—earmarks of fluid intelligence.

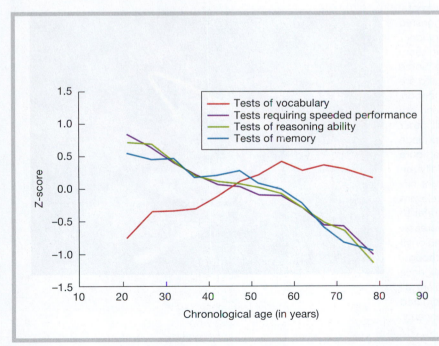

FIGURE 14.4

INTELLIGENCE ACROSS THE LIFESPAN

Tests that involve crystallized intelligence (like tests of vocabulary) often show improvement in test scores across the lifespan, declining only when—at age 70 or so—the person's overall condition starts to deteriorate. In contrast, scores on tests that involve fluid intelligence (like tests requiring speeded performance) peak at age 20 or so and decline thereafter. The "Z-scores" shown here are a common statistical measure used for comparing tests with disparate scoring schemes.

The Building Blocks of Intelligence

It seems, then, that intelligence has many components. However, one component—*g*—is crucial, because this aspect of intelligence is relevant to virtually all mental activities. But what is *g*? What gives a person more *g* or less?

Researchers disagree on this issue. One proposal, though, is simple. Mental processes are quick but do take time, and perhaps the people we consider intelligent are those who are especially fast in these processes. This speed would enable them to perform intellectual tasks more efficiently; it also would give them time for more steps in comparison with those of us who aren't so quick. (See Coyle et al., 2011; Deary, 2012; Schubert & Frischkorn, 2020; Sheppard, 2008.) As a variant of this proposal, some researchers argue that intelligence is created by faster processing, not throughout the brain, but in particular neural pathways — for example, the pathways linking temporal and parietal areas. (See Schubert et al., 2017; for a related idea, see **Figure 14.5**.)

Support for these ideas comes from measures of **inspection time**—the time a person needs to decide, say, which of two lines is longer or which of two tones is higher. These measures correlate around –.30 with intelligence scores. (See Bates & Shieles, 2003; Danthiir et al., 2005; Deary & Derr, 2005; van Ravenzwaaij et al., 2011.) The correlation is negative because lower response times go with higher scores on intelligence tests.

FIGURE 14.5 THE P-FIT MODEL

What is it in the brain that makes intelligence possible? One view is the parieto-frontal integration theory (P-FIT), suggested by Jung & Haier (2007). Their theory identifies a network of brain sites that seem crucial for intellectual performance. Some of the sites are in the parietal lobe and are heavily involved in the control of attention. Other sites are in the frontal lobe and are essential for working memory. Still other important sites are crucial for language processing. (The dark circles in the figure indicate brain areas that are especially relevant in the left hemisphere; the light circles indicate brain areas that are relevant in both hemispheres. The numbers refer to a scheme—so-called Brodmann areas—commonly used for labeling brain regions.) The P-FIT conception emphasizes, though, that what really matters for intelligence is the integration of information from all of these sites—and, thus, the coordinated functioning of many cognitive components.

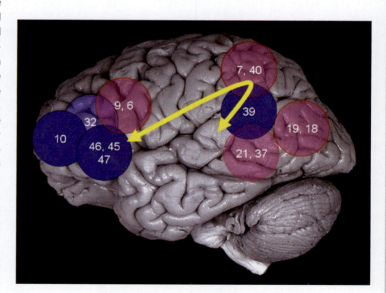

A different proposal about g centers on the notion of *executive control*. We first met this notion in Chapter 5, and then we returned to this idea in Chapter 6, where we saw that *working-memory capacity* (WMC) is actually a measure of executive functioning—that is, a measure of how well people can control the focus of their own attention and direct their own thought processes. We mentioned in Chapter 6 that people with a larger WMC do better on many intellectual tasks, including, we now add, tests specifically designed to measure g. (See, among others, Burgess et al., 2011; Fukuda et al., 2011; Jewsbury et al., 2016; Redick et al., 2016.) Perhaps, therefore, the people we consider intelligent are those who literally have better control of their own thoughts, so they can coordinate their priorities in an appropriate way, override errant impulses, and in general proceed in a deliberate manner when making judgments or solving problems. (For debate on how exactly WMC contributes to intelligence, see Burgoyne et al., 2019; Engle, 2018; Karr et al., 2018; Rey-Mermet et al., 2019; Savi et al., 2019. For discussion of the neural basis for why people differ from one another in their degree of cognitive control, see Schubert et al., 2021.)

As a related proposal, some authors suggest that executive control is important, but not the whole story. On this view, g is actually a measure for the *combined operation* of several different capacities (Kovacs & Conway, 2019). These capacities are distinguishable (and so our theorizing needs to keep them separate), but even so, the capacities overlap in when and how they're used. That's why a single measure (g) emerges in the data; it's a measure of the operation of the full package of overlapping processes.

Plainly, then, there's still disagreement about what g is—and therefore exactly what it is that intelligence tests are measuring. Note, though, that all of these proposals may be correct—and so it's possible that someone with a lot of g is benefiting from swift mental processes *and* a high level of executive control *and* some other processes as well.

Intelligence beyond the IQ Test

We've been focusing on what the IQ test measures, but we also need to consider what it *doesn't* measure. Are there types of intelligence *not* included in conventional intelligence tests?

Practical Intelligence

Some people are "street-smart"—that is, capable of sophisticated reasoning in day-to-day settings—even though they seem to lack the sort of analytical skill needed in a classroom. Psychologist Robert Sternberg has studied this sort of **practical intelligence**, with some of his research focused on whether *teaching* is more effective when instruction is matched to students' abilities (with different forms of instruction for students high in practical ability, students high in analytical ability, and students high in creative ability). Evidence

TEST YOURSELF

3. What's the evidence that something like g—or intelligence-in-general—exists?
4. What's the difference between fluid intelligence and crystallized intelligence?
5. What hypotheses have been proposed for the processes or characteristics that give someone a lot of g?

suggests that "tuning" the curriculum in this way can be helpful. (See Sternberg et al., 2008; Wagner, 2000.)

Measures of Rationality

A different sort of complexity has been highlighted by Keith Stanovich. He reminds us that we all know people who are smart according to their test scores, but who nonetheless ignore facts, who never learn from their mistakes, who make claims that are strongly phrased but utterly baseless, and more. It's people like these who lead us to ask: "How could someone that smart be so stupid?"

In light of such cases (and much other evidence), Stanovich argues that we need separate measures of *intelligence* and *rationality* (Stanovich, 2009; Stanovich et al., 2016). He defines the latter term as the capacity for critically assessing information as it is gathered in the natural environment. Rationality, on this view, includes a number of elements—a willingness to consider evidence contrary to your views; a tendency to "calibrate" the strength of your claims, so that your strength of belief is in line with the strength of the evidence; a willingness to reopen issues if new evidence arrives; and more. Each of these elements, Stanovich proposes, can be measured, with the prospect of developing a "rationality test" that could sit alongside of the already-available intelligence tests.

Other Types of Intelligence

Still other authors highlight a capacity they call **emotional intelligence**—the ability to understand your own emotions and others', as well as the ability to control your emotions when appropriate (Mayer et al., 2008). Tests have been constructed to measure this capacity, and people who score well on these tests are judged to foster a more positive atmosphere in the workplace and to have more leadership potential (Grewal & Salovey, 2005; Lopes et al., 2005). Likewise, college students who score well on these tests are rated by their friends as being more caring and more supportive; they're also less likely to experience conflict with peers (Mayer et al., 2008; also see Pittarello et al., 2018). Evidence suggests that students with greater emotional intelligence also do better academically—perhaps because they are more sophisticated in their emotional appraisal of their academic challenges (MacCann et al., 2020).

Another extension to IQ testing comes from Howard Gardner's **theory of multiple intelligences**. Gardner (1983, 2006) argues for *eight* types of intelligence. Three of these are assessed in standard IQ tests: linguistic intelligence, logical-mathematical intelligence, and spatial intelligence. But Gardner also argues that we should acknowledge musical intelligence, bodily-kinesthetic intelligence (the ability to learn and create complex patterns of movement), interpersonal intelligence (the ability to understand other people), intrapersonal intelligence (the ability to understand ourselves), and naturalistic intelligence (the ability to understand patterns in nature).

Some of Gardner's evidence comes from the study of people with so-called **savant syndrome**—including people like Stephen Wiltshire, mentioned at the start of this chapter. These individuals are profoundly disabled, with IQ scores as low as 40 or 50, but each of them has a stunning level of specialized talent. Some are incredible artists (see **Figure 14.6**). Others are "calendar calculators," able to answer immediately when asked questions like "What day of the week was March 19 in the year 1642?" Still others have remarkable musical skills and can effortlessly memorize lengthy musical works (Hill, 1978; Miller, 1999).

Apparently, then, it's possible to have extreme talent that is separate from intelligence as it's measured on IQ tests. But, overall, how should we think about Gardner's claims? His proposal certainly reminds us that a broad range of human achievements are of enormous value, and surely we should celebrate the skill displayed by an artist at her canvas, a skilled dancer in the ballet, or an empathetic clergyman in a hospital room. These are talents to be acknowledged and, as much as possible, nurtured and developed.

But let's also be clear that Gardner's conception shouldn't be understood as a challenge to conventional intelligence testing. IQ tests were never designed to measure all human talents—so it's no surprise that these tests tell us little about, say, musical intelligence or bodily-kinesthetic intelligence. These other talents are important, but that takes nothing away from the importance of the capacities measured by IQ tests—capacities that (as we've seen) are needed for many aspects of life.

Finally, there's room for debate about whether the capacities showcased by Gardner (or, for that matter, the capacity labeled "emotional intelligence") should be thought of as forms of intelligence. In ordinary conversation, we

FIGURE 14.6 AN "AUTISTIC SAVANT"

We briefly discussed Stephen Wiltshire at the start of this chapter. According to standard intelligence tests, Wiltshire is profoundly disabled, but he has an extraordinary visual memory and is an astounding artist. After a few minutes in a helicopter flying over London, he was able to draw—from memory—a huge, incredibly detailed, highly accurate picture of what he'd seen.

make a distinction between "intelligence" and "talent"—and so, for example, we mean something different if we talk about an "intelligent" athlete in contrast to a "talented" athlete. Likewise, various television shows seek performers with *talent* rather than performers with *intelligence*. Gardner's proposal invites us to step away from this distinction, and the motivation is clear: His use of the term "intelligence" does encourage us to give these other pursuits the esteem they surely deserve. At the same time, his terminology may lead us to ignore distinctions we might otherwise need. (For more on Gardner's claims, see Cowan & Carney, 2006; Deary, 2012; Thioux et al., 2006; Visser et al., 2006; White 2008.)

The Roots of Intelligence

Differences in intelligence, we've suggested, may be the result of variations in mental speed or in the functioning of executive control. But what causes those differences? Why does one person end up with a high level of intelligence, while other people end up with a lower level?

Discussions of these questions are often framed as a choice between two alternatives—"nature versus nurture." In other words, should our explanation emphasize genetics and heredity, or should we focus on learning and the environment? This framing of the issue, however, is misleading: Both types of influence—one rooted in genetics, one rooted in experience—play an important role in shaping intelligence. Moreover, these influences aren't separate; instead, the two types of influence actually *depend* on each other.

We see the impact of genetic influences in the fact that people who resemble each other genetically also resemble each other in their IQ scores. This resemblance is in place even if the individuals grow up in different environments. For example, identical (i.e., monozygotic) twins tend to have highly similar IQ scores even if the twins are reared in different households.

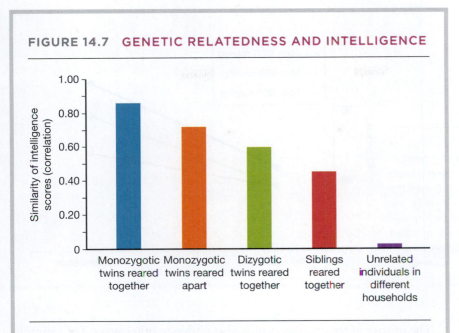

FIGURE 14.7   GENETIC RELATEDNESS AND INTELLIGENCE

Monozygotic twins share 100% of their DNA and tend to resemble each other in intelligence whether they were raised together or not. Dizygotic twins (with 50% overlap in their DNA) show less resemblance, although they resemble each other more than non-twin siblings or randomly selected (unrelated) individuals do.

(See **Figure 14.7**; also see Bouchard et al., 1990; McGue et al., 1993; Plomin & Spinath, 2004.)

There's no question, though, that environmental factors also matter for intelligence. For example, we've known for many years that *living in poverty* impedes intellectual development, and the effect is cumulative: The longer a child remains in such an environment, the greater the harm. This point emerges in the data as a negative correlation between IQ and age. That is, the older the child (the longer she'd been in the impoverished environment), the lower her IQ. (See Asher, 1935; Gordon, 1923; for more recent data, see Heckman, 2006. For discussion of *why* poverty undermines intellectual development, see Nisbett, 2009; Protzko et al., 2013.)

A related—and more optimistic—finding is that *improving* the environment can *increase* IQ. In one study, researchers focused on cases in which the government had removed children from their biological parents because of documented abuse or neglect (Duyme et al., 1999). The researchers compared the children's "pre-adoption IQ" (when the children were living in a high-risk environment) with their IQ in adolescence—after years of living with adoptive families. The data showed substantial improvements in the children's scores, thanks to this environmental change (see **Figure 14.8**). (Also see Diamond & Lee, 2011; Nisbett et al., 2012a, 2012b; Protzko et al., 2013.)

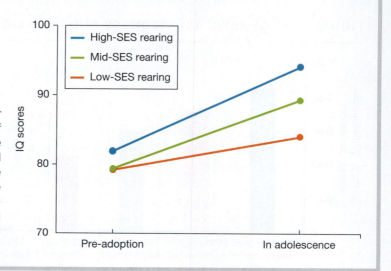

FIGURE 14.8 IQ IMPROVEMENT DUE TO ENVIRONMENTAL CHANGE

Researchers examined the IQ scores of children who were adopted out of horrible environments in which they had been abused or neglected. After the adoption (when the children were in better environments), the children's IQ scores were markedly higher—especially if the children were adopted into a family with higher socioeconomic status (SES).   (AFTER DUYME ET AL., 1999)

The impact of the environment is also visible in other ways. For example, education raises someone's IQ—at a rate that may reach 5 IQ points for every year of schooling (Ritchie & Tucker-Drob, 2018). In addition, studies tell us that around the globe, scores on intelligence tests have been increasing over the last few decades, at a rate of approximately 3 points per decade. This pattern is known as the **Flynn effect**, after James Flynn (1984, 1987, 1999, 2009), the first researcher to document this effect. (See also Daley et al., 2003; Kanaya et al. , 2003; Pietschnig & Voracek, 2015; Trahan et al., 2014; Wai et al., 2012.) This improvement has been observed in relatively affluent nations and also in impoverished nations, and the effect is stronger in measures of fluid intelligence—such as the Raven's Matrices—so it seems to reflect a genuine change in how quickly and flexibly people can think, and not just a worldwide increase in how much information people have.

There's disagreement about the causes of the Flynn effect (e.g., Flynn, 2009; Fox & Mitchum, 2013; Greenfield, 2009; Nisbett et al., 2012a; Pietschnig & Voracek, 2015), and it's likely that several factors contribute. Increased educational opportunity around the world plays a role, and so does improved nutrition and health care worldwide. Regardless of the explanation, though, the Flynn effect cannot be explained genetically. The human genome does change, but not at a speed commensurate with this effect. Therefore, this worldwide improvement becomes part of the evidence documenting that intelligence can indeed be improved by suitable environmental conditions.

We note, though, that there are some indications that the Flynn effect may have slowed or even reversed in recent years (e.g., Bratsberg & Rogeberg, 2018). In addition, evidence suggests that the size of the Flynn effect may vary from group to group, with one study indicating that the effect was larger in the United States for people at the high end of the IQ range, while there was a generation-to-generation *decline* for people at the low end of the range

(Platt et al., 2019). These are potentially important findings, but for present purposes they point to the same conclusion: Intelligence scores are influenced by the environment you live in.

The Interaction among Genetic Factors, Environment, and IQ

Unmistakably, then, genetic factors matter for IQ, and so do environmental factors. But how do we put these pieces together? The key here is that these influences *interact* in crucial ways, and one way to see this interaction is to consider the impact of poverty.

We've already noted that poverty interferes with intellectual development (Hackman & Farah, 2009; Lubinski, 2004; Raizada & Kishiyama, 2010), and if you live in poverty, that's a tragic fact about your environment. But this environmental influence interacts with genetic influences. (See Turkheimer et al., 2003; also Bates et al., 2013; Tucker-Drob et al., 2011.) As an illustration, we've already noted that identical twins tend to have similar IQ scores, and this observation provides powerful evidence that genetic factors play a role. The picture is different, though, if we focus on impoverished families. In these families, the IQ resemblance for identical twins is markedly reduced—indicating that in this setting, genetic factors matter much less for shaping a person's intelligence.

The full explanation of this result is complex. Part of the explanation, though, hinges on the fact that genetic mechanisms enable someone to make full use of the "environmental inputs that support intellectual growth" (Bates et al., 2013, p. 2111). If there is a rich fabric of these inputs, the genetic mechanisms enable the person to gain from them and flourish. But if these inputs are absent, the genetic mechanisms have nothing to work with—so they will likely produce little growth. In other words, the machinery that *could* promote growth is present; but with little input to work on, the machinery can't do its job. (For further discussion of how environmental factors interact with genes, see Cheesman et al., 2020; Taylor et al., 2010; Tucker-Drob & Bates, 2016; Vinkhuyzen et al., 2011.)

Comparisons between Groups

Most research on intelligence—and all of our discussion so far in this chapter—has focused on the differences from one person to the next. There has also been discussion, though, about differences between *groups*, with much of the debate centering on a comparison between American Whites and American Blacks.

We should mention that there's also research comparing other groups, including research comparing the IQ scores of men and women. This research indicates no overall IQ difference between the genders, and, in fact, the evidence indicates that men and women are cognitively similar in more ways than they're different. But there are some differences, and studies tell us that women outperform men on some (but not all) tests of verbal ability, and men

There is an overwhelming consensus in the scientific community that our planet's climate is changing. In fact, there are few scientific claims more firmly established than the claim that our planet is growing warmer. Yet many people, and indeed, many world leaders, seem unconcerned. They deny the basic facts of climate change, or insist (contrary to evidence) that there is no worry here, and (perhaps worst of all) refuse any steps that might address the problem.

How is this possible? How can people remain unpersuaded by the available evidence? The answer has many parts. Some people suggest, as one possibility, that the climate-change deniers are somehow limited in their mental capacities. To put it more bluntly, the suggestion is that the deniers are less intelligent—and so, if we measure their IQ, we'll find that they have lower scores. This explanation is probably correct for some deniers, but it's surely not the whole story, because we can easily find high-IQ individuals who nonetheless deny the reality of climate change. This point is important on its own, but for purposes of the chapter it also reminds us of a key fact: The capacities measured by IQ tests are important and predictive of many life outcomes, but these skills are not enough to ensure a realistic understanding of the evidence you encounter in life.

Could it be that the climate-change deniers have some other, narrower, limitation? Perhaps they're smart overall, but simply do not understand the logic and power of the scientific method. Again, this notion may be correct for some deniers; but, once more, it's certainly not the full explanation. There are various tests designed to measure "science literacy," and we can find many people who do well on this measure but still deny the threat of climate change (e.g., Kahan et al., 2012).

Perhaps the explanation lies in stubborn self-interest: You might choose to look away from the facts if you're making a huge profit from your investment in a coal mine or if you're intensely loyal to some politician who (for whatever reason) denies climate change. (For more on these points, see Hornsey, 2020.) Again, this is surely part of the story; but (as before) we can find climate-change deniers who are high-IQ, literate in science, *and* without any obvious motivation to ignore the evidence.

What other factors, therefore, could be in play here? One study explored this issue by asking *what other beliefs* the deniers have. The results showed that many of the deniers also held other "anti-scientific beliefs" (Lewandowsky et al., 2013). But many also endorsed other baseless claims for which an understanding of science isn't relevant. For example, climate-change deniers are more likely than other people to accept the claim that there never was a U.S. moon landing. (They believe that the videos were instead staged in a film studio.) They're also more likely to believe that the death of England's Princess Diana was the result of an assassination organized by the British royal family. (Both of these claims—about the moon landing and Princess Diana—are widespread, even though there is not a shred of evidence for either of them.)

So now we need to ask: What leads people to accept any of these (false) claims? One prominent factor seems to involve a person's habitual modes of thinking—in essence, how the person generally *uses* their intellectual capacities (e.g., Bronstein et al., 2019; Lantian et al., 2021; Sinclair et al., 2020). Specifically, people are more likely to believe baseless claims if they generally have a thinking style that is less analytic. Put differently, these people are not just open-minded, they're *too* open-minded, and so, without giving the information they encounter much thought, they're willing to accept weak claims, or claims without evidence, and even wildly implausible claims.

Who are the people who seem less inclined toward analytic thinking? Researchers have suggested a number of ways to approach this issue, and one approach relies on the Cognitive Reflection Test (CRT), described in Chapter 12. This test asks whether a person generally tends to grab onto the immediately available answer to a question, or instead pauses to think about the question. People who do worse on the CRT are more likely to believe blatantly inaccurate headlines and are less able to tell the difference between accurate news and "fake news" (Pennycook & Rand,

2019a, 2019b). In many cases, these people are just like everyone else in their intelligence levels, and for many of these issues they're not blinded by bias. The problem instead is that they lack the habit of being thoughtful. They're not inclined to think things through, and in that way we could say that they're "mentally lazy."

Overall, then, the qualities measured by intelligence tests are important, but they're not the only intellectual qualities that matter. In addition, people need to *use* their abilities, and many people don't. It may be this under-use, and not some combination of motivation and self-service, that leads some people to accept fake headlines, endorse crazy conspiracy theories, and deny legitimate science.

There is, we should note, an optimistic side to these findings: We've just suggested that in many cases people believe false claims simply because they fail to think for a moment about whether the claims are accurate or not. If this is right, then perhaps it would be useful just to remind people that they need to pause and think briefly when they encounter new information, asking themselves whether the information is likely to be true. Indeed, in one study this sort of nudge "nearly tripled the level of truth discernment" (Pennycook et al., 2020). Apparently, there is a gain from a simple "stop and think for a moment" reminder— a reminder that might influence what information people accept, and also what information they'll choose to share on social media.

outperform women on some (but not all) tests of spatial ability. (For a broad view of the research, see Deary, 2012; Halpern, 2011; Miller & Halpern, 2013; for more on the gender difference in spatial skills, see Chapter 11. We note in addition that relatively little research has explored these issues with individuals who identify as nonbinary, and this is obviously an area inviting further study.)

There's no question, though, that most of the research in this arena—and the heated debate—has focused on the racial differences. The debate begins with the fact that studies indicate that the average intelligence score of American (and European) Whites is higher than the average score of African Americans (Dickens & Flynn, 2006; Jencks & Phillips, 1998; Rushton, 2012; Rushton & Jensen, 2005). It's enormously important to bear in mind, though, that this is a point about *averages*, and there is, in fact, huge overlap between the full set of scores for American Whites and American Blacks. There are, in other words, American Blacks who outscore the vast majority of Whites, and Whites with scores well below those of most Blacks. Even so, there is a difference between the averages, leading us to ask what's going on here.

Unmistakably, part of the explanation is a pattern of racial bias that infected earlier forms of the IQ tests—bias built into the vocabulary used in the tests, or the tests' assumptions about what facts students would likely know. Indeed, this bias led to a 1979 court ruling in California that prohibited California schools from using IQ tests to evaluate Black children. (For discussion of this history, see Frisby & Henry, 2016.)

More recent forms of the IQ test, though, have taken steps to diminish racial bias, yet the group differences remain. One cause for this difference is economic, because Blacks and Whites in the United States often do not have the same opportunities or access to the same resources. On average, African Americans have lower incomes than Whites and live in less affluent neighborhoods. A higher proportion of Blacks than Whites are exposed to poor nutrition and poor health care, and as we've mentioned, these environmental factors have a substantial impact on IQ (Neisser et al., 1996; Nisbett et al., 2012a).

In fact, a 2020 report suggested that the median net worth of White families living in the United States was roughly ten times larger than the median net worth of Black families; the median income for White households was 60% larger; the number of American Blacks living in poverty was roughly double the number of Whites (Luhby, 2020). On these grounds, some of the difference between Blacks' and Whites' IQ scores isn't a racial difference at all. It is, instead, an economic status difference.

In addition, let's acknowledge that American Blacks are often treated differently from Whites by the people they encounter. They also grow up with different role models than Whites, and they often make different assumptions about what life paths will be open to them. Do these facts matter for intelligence scores? Consider studies of **stereotype threat,** a term that describes the negative impact that social stereotypes, once activated,

HUMAN DIVERSITY

It is important to emphasize that the comparisons among groups—including the comparison between American Blacks and American Whites—are among the *averages* for each group. This point is crucial, because the scores of European American test-takers vary enormously, as do the scores of African American test-takers. In fact, the variation within each group is much, much larger than any between-group variations researchers have detected. As a related point, the overlap between the scores of American Blacks and American Whites is much more impressive than the relatively small difference between the averages. These points carry an important message: We learn little about any individual's abilities simply by knowing their group membership, and it would be wrong (and in most settings, illegal) to use group membership as a basis for making decisions about that individual.

can have on task performance. Concretely, imagine an African American taking an intelligence test. He might become anxious because he knows this is a test on which members of his group are expected to do poorly. This anxiety might be compounded by the thought that poor performance, if it occurs, will only serve to confirm others' prejudices. All of these feelings, in turn, could erode his performance by making it difficult for him to pay attention and do his best work on the test. Moreover, given the thought that poor performance is a distinct possibility, he might decide not to expend enormous effort—if he's likely to do poorly, why struggle against the tide?

We should note in addition that stereotype threat also arises in other settings, and with other groups. In a classic article, Spencer et al. (1999) examined the role of a stereotype threat in shaping women's performance on math tests. The stereotype here is that women have weaker math ability than men, and this stereotype can itself shape performance. In the Spencer et al. study, one group of participants took a math test that (they were told) generally showed a difference between men's and women's performance, and in this setting women did perform less well than men did. Another group, though, took the same test, but was told the test did not produce gender differences. Here, the gender difference was eliminated. Plainly, then, beliefs about the test, and beliefs about one's own performance, can have a powerful impact.

More research is needed to specify how and when stereotype threat influences people—and what steps can be taken to diminish the often toxic effects of these stereotypes. Stereotype threat also reminds us of the need to consider research in light of the historical and social context, since these factors obviously play a role in shaping the stereotypes people have for different racial and cultural groups, different genders, and more. In the meantime, and no matter what groups we're considering, stereotype threat is important for many reasons, including the fact that it draws our attention back to the question of what intelligence is—or, more broadly, what it is that "intellectual tasks" require. One requirement, of course, is a set of cognitive skills and capacities (e.g., mental speed or executive control). A different requirement, however, is a certain perspective toward, and beliefs about, testing and other forms of mental challenge—because, as we've seen, anxiety about failing and fear of confirming others' expectations can undermine performance. These attitudes, in turn, are influenced by social pressures and prejudice, and through this mechanism these external forces can powerfully shape each person's achievements.

What, therefore, is our path forward? As we have seen, intelligence is a predictor of many life outcomes—in the academic world, in the workplace, and beyond. These points add to the (already enormous) urgency of making sure that everyone receives adequate nutrition and health care, as well as appropriate educational opportunities—because we know these factors play an important role in shaping intellectual development. Research also suggests that we may be able to improve intelligence directly—perhaps with targeted training of executive function or with careful instruction to help people develop crystallized intelligence (Au et al., 2015; Chapman & Mudar, 2014; Gamino et al., 2014; Shipstead et al., 2012). But, in addition, this discussion of stereotype threat suggests that we can also move forward by shifting people's expectations, because these too have a powerful influence on intellectual performance. The shift in expectations won't be easy, because these (often racist, often sexist) expectations are held—and reinforced—by many teachers, parents, and even young children; the expectations are built into many social institutions. Nonetheless, given what we know about the linkage between intelligence and success in the workplace, or between intelligence and health, efforts on all of these fronts must be a high priority for all of us.

TEST YOURSELF

7. What evidence makes it clear that *genetic factors* influence someone's level of intelligence? What evidence makes it clear that *environmental factors* influence someone's level of intelligence?

8. What is stereotype threat, and how does it influence performance on an intelligence test?

iq and life expectancy

As the chapter describes, if we know someone's IQ score, we can predict many things about that person's future. IQ scores, in other words, are correlated with many life outcomes, making it plain that IQ tests measure something that matters for many aspects of life.

Some of the surprising correlations, though, concern medical outcomes. To put the matter simply, people with higher IQ live longer. Impressive data come from a survey conducted in 1932, collecting intelligence scores from every child born in Scotland in 1921. Researchers returned to these data decades later and were able to document that IQ scores in these 11-year-old children were good predictors of life expectancy. For example, how many people from this original group were still alive in the 1980s? In other words, how many of these people lived to be at least 60 years old? The answer is 80% for the higher-IQ men in the group, compared to 70% of the lower-IQ men. For women, the contrast is even stronger: Roughly 90% of the higher-IQ women from the original group were still alive at age 60, compared to 76% of the lower-IQ women (Whalley & Deary, 2001.)

Similarly, how many people from this group were still alive in the 1990s? Of the men, slightly more than 50% of the higher-IQ individuals were still alive at that point, compared to 36% of the lower-IQ men. Likewise, roughly 70% of the higher-IQ women in the original group were still alive in the 1990s, compared to 45% of the lower-IQ women.

What lies behind these findings? The answer has many parts, starting with some indirect effects: People with higher IQ scores are likely to end up with more education and better jobs—and therefore greater wealth. This socioeconomic status, in turn, provides a range of health benefits. To put the matter bluntly, people with more money are likely to work in less hazardous occupations and can afford better food, safer cars, housing free of toxins, and on and on—all factors that help keep them healthy and safe. People with less money will have none of these benefits, and often suffer the effects of living in industrialized or congested neighborhoods with questionable air and water quality.

Statistical analyses, however, enable us to look past these socioeconomic effects, and with that step taken, we still find a linkage between IQ and longevity. That's because there are other causal connections in play. For example, evidence suggests that people with higher IQ scores tend to avoid risky behaviors. The chapter mentioned one example: A study conducted in Australia (Holden, 2003) indicated that people with higher IQ scores (above 115) were less likely to die in automobile crashes (5.1 deaths for every 1,000 drivers) compared to people with lower IQ scores (below 85; 14.7 deaths for every 1,000 drivers).

On top of these effects, intelligence levels have yet another impact on health, because higher-IQ individuals are more likely to understand the importance of, and likely to make better use of, medical care. They are likely to seek out medical attention at an earlier stage of an illness. They are more likely to remember and follow a doctor's advice. They are better able to follow instructions about when and how to take medications.

Higher-IQ individuals are also likely to have greater access to health information and more likely to adjust their lives in response to this information. For example, IQ scores are unrelated to whether people smoked cigarettes at some point in their lives. In other words, there's no relationship between IQ and *starting* to smoke. Data show, though, that people with higher IQ scores are more likely to *quit* smoking at some later point—possibly because they have learned of, and take seriously, the health risks involved in smoking.

In short, there are many ways, some direct and some indirect, in which intelligence can help keep you healthy. But the cause-and-effect pattern becomes even more complicated when we acknowledge that the reverse is also true, because being healthy can contribute to your intelligence. Let's start here with the undeniable fact that living in poverty can undermine the development of intelligence—in part because the person receives poorer nutrition and poorer medical care both prenatally and in childhood. The converse,

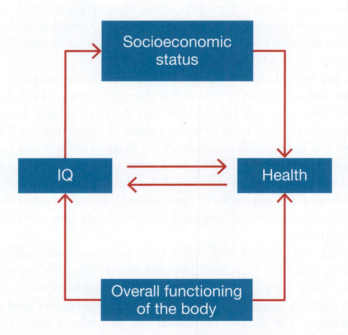

A WEB OF CAUSE-AND-EFFECT RELATIONSHIPS

This figure shows *some* of the cause-and-effect relationships that lead to the statistical correlation between IQ and longevity. In addition, many of the effects are indirect. For example, IQ shapes health via several intermediate steps, including better decisions about lifestyle, better adherence to a doctor's instructions, and more.

of course, is that a *healthy* environment can *promote* the development of intelligence, and this process would certainly contribute to the statistical link between IQ scores and eventual better health.

Notice, then, the "bidirectional" claim: We've already said that lower IQ makes poverty more likely (and the poverty is likely to erode health). We're now saying that poverty, leading to poorer health, makes lower IQ more likely. In other words, cause-and-effect run in both directions—with IQ influencing poverty at the same time that poverty influences IQ.

But there's still a further complication in the cause-and-effect pattern: We've already suggested both that intelligence leads to health and also that being healthy helps you to be intelligent. In addition, it's also likely that to some extent health and IQ scores are both products of the same underlying cause—namely, the overall level of functioning of your body. The idea is that if your body is in general functioning well, then your brain will function well, giving you a higher IQ. But if your body is functioning well, this will also show up in many other measures of your health.

A result consistent with this view involves a surprising correlation: between intelligence and a man's semen quality. Researchers collected data from 425 U.S. army veterans and compared their intelligence scores to three measures of semen quality: the concentration of sperm in the semen, the total count of sperm, and also a measure of mobility by the sperm. The correlations were not strong (the strongest, for sperm count, was $r = .19$), but certainly reliable. The most plausible explanation for this pattern is that we are simply looking at different indicators of the body's overall functioning—with a better level of functioning showing up both in IQ scores and in this rather specific measure of health, namely semen quality (Arden et al., 2009).

In short: Higher IQ contributes to health, and health contributes to higher IQ. And both health and IQ are influenced by other factors—such as the body's overall level of functioning. It's no surprise, then, that IQ and longevity are correlated with each other.

Let's emphasize, though, that none of the correlations we've mentioned here is 1.0 (or even close to it). IQ scores do not set someone's destiny. Many people with low IQ live a long time, attain great wealth, have high-quality semen (if they're men), and more. Many people with high IQ suffer from diseases and engage in risky activities. Even so, these correlations remind us, first, that IQ scores do have powerful predictive value, and second, that there is often considerable complexity in the cause-and-effect relationships that lie behind any of the IQ predictions.

For more on this topic:

Arden, R., Gottfredson, L. S., Miller, G., & Pierce, A. (2009). Intelligence and semen quality are positively correlated. *Intelligence, 37*(3), 277–282.

Batty, G. D., Deary, I. J., & Gottfredson, L. S. (2006). Premorbid (early life) IQ and later mortality risk: Systematic review. *Annals of Epidemiology, 17*(4), 278–288.

Deary, I. J., Weiss, A., & Batty, G. D. (2010). Intelligence and personality as predictors of illness and death: How researchers in differential psychology and chronic disease epidemiology are collaborating to understand and address health inequalities. *Psychological Science in the Public Interest*, *11*(2), 53–79.

Geary, D. C. (2019). The spark of life and the unification of intelligence, health, and aging. *Current Directions in Psychological Science, 28*(3), 223–228

Gottfredson, L. S., & Deary, I. J. (2004). Intelligence predicts health and longevity, but why? *Current Directions in Psychological Science, 13*(1), 1–4.

Holden, C. (2003). The practical benefits of general intelligence. *Science, 299*(5604), 192–193.

Murray, C., Pattie, A., Starr, J. M., & Deary, I. J. (2012). Does cognitive ability predict mortality in the ninth decade? The Lothian birth cohort 1921. *Intelligence, 40*(5), 490–498.

Whalley, L. J., & Deary, I. J. (2001). Longitudinal cohort study of childhood IQ and survival up to age 76. *British Medical Journal, 322*, 1–5.

chapter review

SUMMARY

- Data show that the commonly used measures of intelligence are reliable and valid. The reliability is evident in the fact that a person's IQ score is likely to be roughly the same if tested in childhood and then tested again decades later. The validity is indicated by correlations often observed between IQ scores and performance in tasks that seem to require intelligence. These correlations are well below 1.00, but this simply reminds us that other factors also matter for performance in most domains.

- Most intelligence tests involve numerous subtests, but people who do well on one portion of the test tend to do well across the board. This sort of evidence persuades researchers that there is such a thing as intelligence-in-general—usually referred to as *g*. However, we can also distinguish various forms of more specialized intelligence; therefore, performance on many tasks depends both on a person's level of *g* and on their profile of more specific strengths and weaknesses. This pattern is often summarized in hierarchical models of intelligence.

- We need to distinguish between fluid and crystallized intelligence. Fluid intelligence involves the ability to deal with new and unusual problems. Crystallized intelligence involves acquired knowledge and skills.

- General intelligence, or *g*, is sometimes understood in terms of mental speed, on the idea that people whom we consider smart are literally faster in their intellectual functioning. A different proposal centers on the notion of *working-memory capacity* and *executive control*, with the suggestion that people who are intelligent are literally better able to monitor and direct their own thought processes.

- IQ scores don't assess all of a person's mental capacities. Researchers have also emphasized the importance of practical intelligence, rationality, and emotional intelligence. The theory of multiple intelligences goes further, proposing eight different types of intelligence.

- Genetic differences are part of the reason why people differ in intelligence. This is evident in the fact that people who resemble each other closely in their genetic profile (e.g., identical twins) also tend to resemble each other closely in their IQ scores; this remains true even if the twins were separated at birth and raised separately. It's also true, however, that environmental factors influence intelligence. This is reflected in the fact that various aspects of poverty can undermine intelligence and various forms of enrichment in the environment can improve it. The impact of environment is also evident in the worldwide improvement in IQ scores known as the Flynn effect.

- Crucially, we must understand the interaction between genetic and environmental forces in determining a person's IQ. In simple terms, we can think of the genes as specifying someone's potential, but how that potential will unfold is significantly shaped by the person's environment.

- There has been debate about differences in the average IQ scores of American Blacks and American Whites. The differences can be understood partly in terms of the lower levels of nutrition, medical care, and education that are available for many American Blacks as opposed to Whites. In addition, a large role is played by stereotype threat—a term referring to the negative impact that social stereotypes, once activated, can have on task performance.

KEY TERMS

reliability (p. 507)
test-retest reliability (p. 507)
validity (p. 508)
predictive validity (p. 508)
factor analysis (p. 510)
general intelligence (g) (p. 510)
fluid intelligence (p. 513)
crystallized intelligence (p. 513)

inspection time (p. 514)
practical intelligence (p. 515)
emotional intelligence (p. 516)
theory of multiple intelligences (p. 516)
savant syndrome (p. 517)
Flynn effect (p. 520)
stereotype threat (p. 524)

TEST YOURSELF AGAIN

1. What does it mean to assess a measurement's reliability and its validity?

2. What evidence tells us that IQ tests do have predictive validity?

3. What's the evidence that something like *g*—or intelligence-in-general—exists?

4. What's the difference between fluid intelligence and crystallized intelligence?

5. What hypotheses have been proposed for the processes or characteristics that give someone a lot of *g*?

6. What types of intelligence have been proposed that are separate from the capacities measured by the IQ test?

7. What evidence makes it clear that *genetic factors* influence someone's level of intelligence? What evidence makes it clear that *environmental factors* influence someone's level of intelligence?

8. What is stereotype threat, and how does it influence performance on an intelligence test?

THINK ABOUT IT

1. As the chapter describes, men and women don't differ, on average, in their overall IQ scores. However, men seem to have an advantage in some tasks requiring spatial reasoning, and women seem to have an advantage in some tasks involving verbal reasoning. The chapter suggests, though, that *stereotype threat* is relevant to (at least) some of these gender differences; the chapter uses the example of stereotype threat's impact on women's math performance. What do you believe the stereotypes are for men's cognitive abilities? What do you believe the stereotypes are for women's abilities? What do you think the stereotypes might be for the abilities of non-binary individuals? Can you offer specific suggestions about the circumstances, or the types of intellectual challenges, most likely to elicit stereotype threat in each of these groups?

DEMONSTRATIONS & APPLYING COGNITIVE PSYCHOLOGY ESSAYS

For demonstrations of key concepts in cognitive psychology, take a look at the Online Demonstrations. To explore more of the practical applications of cognitive psychology in themed essays, visit the online reader.

Online Demonstrations

- Demonstration 14.1: Defining Intelligence
- Demonstration 14.2: IQ Testing
- Demonstration 14.3: Different Ways to Be Smart

Online Applying Cognitive Psychology Essays

- Cognitive Psychology and Education: The Goals of Education
- Cognitive Psychology and Technology: The Complexity of Cereal Boxes
- Cognitive Psychology and the Law: Intelligence and the Legal System

ZAPS COGNITION LABS

Go to ZAPS online cognition labs to conduct hands-on experiments on key concepts.

INQUIZITIVE

It's time to complete your study experience! Go to InQuizitive to practice actively with this chapter's concepts and get personalized feedback along the way.

chapter **15**

Conscious Thought, Unconscious Thought

what if... Imagine that your friend René puts a red rose on the table in front of you and asks, "What color is this?" You'd likely be puzzled by this question, but you could still answer, "It's red, obviously." Now, imagine that René asks, "How do you know?" Again, this seems an odd question, but a bit impatiently you'd probably say, "Because I can see it." René, however, is still not satisfied and asks, "But how do you know you can see it?" This question is even odder. After all, how could you *not* know what you're seeing?

This exercise reminds us of the commonsense point that "seeing" involves some sort of "visual awareness." In the same vein, think about the sentence "Linda was looking right at the moose, but she didn't see it." Again, this sentence assumes a linkage between "seeing" and "being aware." That's why the idea that Linda "didn't see" the moose suggests she wasn't aware of its presence.

But what if these commonsense claims are mistaken? Consider patient D.B. He underwent surgery to remove a tumor in his occipital cortex and, with it, a significant amount of brain tissue. As a result, D.B. became partially blind; he was unable to see anything in the left half of the world in front of him. Careful testing, though, revealed a surprising pattern. In one study, D.B. sat in front of a computer screen while a target on the screen's left side moved in some trials and stayed still in others. D.B. insisted he couldn't see the target at all, but when forced to guess, he generally guessed correctly whether the target was moving. Likewise, if asked to reach toward an object off to his left, he insisted he couldn't—but when forced to reach, he generally moved his hand toward the proper location. Later, researchers showed the results of these studies to D.B., and he was bewildered by his own performance, with no idea how his guessing could have been so accurate.

Patient G.Y. showed a similar pattern. He was involved in a traffic accident when he was 8 years old and (like D.B.) suffered damage to the occipital cortex. As a result, G.Y. was blind—he insisted he couldn't see, and he failed to react to visual inputs. Yet, in one study G.Y. was asked to move his arm in a way that matched the motion of a moving target (a point of light). G.Y.'s performance was quite accurate even though he said he couldn't see the target at all. He claimed he only had an "impression" of motion and that he was "aware there was an object moving." But

- Throughout this text, we have discussed processes that provide an unnoticed support structure for cognition. We begin, therefore, by reviewing themes from earlier chapters, in order to ask what sorts of things are accomplished within the "cognitive unconscious."

- Overall, it appears that you can perform a task unconsciously if you arrive at the task with a routine that can be guided by strong habits or powerful cues within the situation. With this constraint, unconscious processes can be remarkably sophisticated.

- Unconscious operations are fast and efficient, but also inflexible. They free you to pay attention to higher-order aspects of a task but leave you ignorant about the sources of your ideas, beliefs, and memories.

- From a biological perspective, we know that most operations of the brain are made possible by highly specialized modules. According to one proposal, these modules can be interrelated by means of workspace neurons, connecting one area of the brain to another and allowing the integration of different processing streams.

- The workspace neurons create a "global workspace," and some scholars argue that this is what makes consciousness possible. The operations of this workspace fit well with many things we know to be true about consciousness.

- However, profound questions remain about how (or whether) the global workspace makes possible the subjective experience that for many theorists is the defining element of consciousness.

it's hard to interpret these remarks, because G.Y. insisted he had no idea what the moving object looked like.

To describe patients like these, Weiskrantz and Warrington coined the term "blind sight" (e.g., Weiskrantz, 1986, 1997). Blind-sight patients are, by any conventional definition, truly blind, but even so they're generally able to "guess" the color of targets that (they insist) they cannot see; they can also "guess" the orientation of lines. Some of these patients can even "guess" the emotional expression of faces that (apparently) they cannot see at all.

Patients with blind sight force us to distinguish between "seeing" and "having visual awareness"—because they apparently can do one but not the other. (For an alternative interpretation of blind sight, though, see Phillips, 2020.) This separation raises questions about just what "seeing" is and why some aspects of seeing can go forward without consciousness. In addition, what might these observations tell us about consciousness itself? If consciousness isn't needed for visual perception, then when is it needed?

The Study of Consciousness

The field of psychology emerged as a separate discipline, distinct from philosophy and biology, in the late 1800s, and in those early years of our field the topic of consciousness was a central concern. In Wilhelm Wundt's laboratory in Germany, researchers sought to understand the "elements" of consciousness; William James, in America, sought to understand the "stream" of consciousness.

The young field of psychology, however, soon rejected this focus on consciousness, arguing that this research was subjective and unscientific. (This rejection was linked to the points we made in Chapter 1—concerned with the problems attached to *introspection* as a research tool.) By the early 20th century, therefore, the topic of consciousness was largely gone from mainstream psychological research (although theorizing about consciousness, without much experimentation, continued). In recent decades, however, researchers have made enormous advances in their understanding of what consciousness is, how it functions, and how the brain makes consciousness possible. In fact, these advances have been woven into the material we've already covered, and so this chapter can do two things at once: describe what's known about consciousness, but also review where we've been for the last 14 chapters.

We should acknowledge at the start, though, that there's still much about consciousness that we don't understand; in fact, there's still disagreement about how consciousness should be defined. We'll return to this conceptual issue later in the chapter. For now, we'll proceed with this rough definition: Consciousness is a state of awareness of sensations or ideas, such that you can reflect on those sensations and ideas, know what it "feels like" to experience these sensations and ideas, and can, in many cases, report to others that you're aware of the sensations and ideas. As we'll see, this definition has certain problems, but it will serve us well enough as an initial guide for discussion.

The Cognitive Unconscious

Activities like perceiving and thinking feel quick and effortless. You instantly recognize the words on this page; you easily remember where you were this morning; you swiftly decide to have Cheddar on your sandwich, not Swiss. As we've seen throughout this book, however, these (and other) intellectual activities are possible only because of an elaborate "support structure"—processes and mechanisms working "behind the scenes." Describing this behind-the-scenes action has been one of the main concerns of this text.

Psychologists refer to this behind-the-scenes activity as the **cognitive unconscious**—the broad set of mental activities, all happening outside of awareness, that make possible your ordinary interactions with the world. The processes that unfold in the cognitive unconscious are sophisticated and powerful, and as we'll see, it's actually quite helpful that a lot of mental work can take place without conscious supervision. At the same time, we'll need to discuss the ways in which the absence of supervision can, in some cases, be a problem for you.

Unconscious Processes, Conscious Products

For many purposes, it's useful to distinguish the *products* created within your mind (beliefs you've formed, conclusions you've reached) from the *processes* that led to these products. This distinction isn't always clear-cut, and in some cases we can quibble about whether a particular mental step counts as "product" or "process." (See, for early discussion, Miller, 1962; Neisser, 1967; Nisbett & Wilson, 1977; Smith & Miller, 1978; White, 1988.) Even so, this distinction allows an important rule of thumb—namely, that you're generally aware of your mental products but unaware of your mental processes.

For example, we saw in Chapter 8 that your memories of the past seamlessly combine genuine recall with some amount of after-the-fact reconstruction. For example, when you "remember" your restaurant dinner last month, you're probably weaving together elements that were actually recorded into memory at the time of the dinner, along with other elements that are just inferences or assumptions. In that earlier chapter, we argued that this weaving together is a good thing, because it enables you to fill in bits that you've forgotten or bits that you didn't notice in the first place. But this weaving together also creates a risk of error: If the dinner you're trying to recall was somehow unusual, then assumptions based on the more typical pattern may be misleading.

Let's be clear, though, about what's conscious here and what's not. Your recollection of the dinner is a mental *product* and is surely something you're aware of. As a result, you can reflect on the dinner if you wish and can describe it if someone asks you. You're unaware, though, of the *process* that brought you this knowledge, so you have no way of telling which bits are supplied by memory retrieval and which bits rest on inference or assumption. And, of course, if you can't determine which bits are which, there's no way for you to reject the inferences or avoid the (entirely unnoticed) assumptions. That's why memory errors are often undetectable: The process that brings you a "memory," it seems, unfolds in the cognitive unconscious, leaving you unable, most of the time, to distinguish genuine recall from (potentially misguided) assumption.

Unconscious Reasoning

The role of the cognitive unconscious is also evident in other settings, and here we meet another layer of complexity—because in many cases people seem to be engaging in a process of unconscious *reasoning*.

In Chapter 7, we discussed a study in which participants convinced themselves that several fictitious names were actually the names of famous people. In this procedure, participants were apparently aware of the fact that some of the names they were reading were distinctive; their conscious experience told them that these names somehow "stood out" from other names on the list. But to make sense of the data from this study, we needed to take a further step and argued that thoughts roughly like these were going through the participants' minds: "That name rings a bell, and I'm not sure why. But the experimenter is asking me about famous names, and there are other famous names on this list in front of me. So I guess that this one must also be the name of some famous person." This surely sounds like something we want to count as "thinking," but the evidence suggests that it's thinking of which the participants were entirely unaware—that is, thinking that took place in their cognitive unconscious.

We can confirm these points in a variety of ways. We can ask participants directly how they made their decisions—and they routinely report nothing like the thoughts we've just hypothesized. But we know that (something like) those thoughts must be in place; otherwise, the data make no sense! We can also warn participants, before starting the experiment, not to reason in this way. Even so, the data show the same illusion of "false fame." Since the reasoning that's involved takes place outside of awareness, there's no way for participants to detect (and avoid) this reasoning, and so no way to avoid the error it produces.

Similarly, imagine that someone is an eyewitness to a crime. The police might show this person a lineup, and let's say that the witness chooses Number 2 as the robber. In Chapter 8, we explored what happens if the witness now gets *feedback* about this identification—if the police say something like, "Good; the person you've chosen is our suspect" or even "You've been a really good witness." In one study, witnesses who received *no* feedback said that when they'd made their lineup selection, their confidence level was (on average) 47%; witnesses who got the feedback, though, expressed much greater confidence: 71%.

Bear in mind here that the feedback arrived only *after* the witnesses had made a lineup selection, and so there's no way the feedback could have altered what (or how much) the witnesses remembered at the time of the selection. Why, then, did the feedback elevate confidence? It seems that the witnesses must have been thinking something like, "The police say I got the right answer, so I guess I can set aside my doubts." Let's emphasize, though, that this feedback doesn't just influence how confident the witnesses are *now*; the feedback also causes the witnesses to adjust their memory for how confident they'd been earlier, when they made their selection—before the feedback was provided! And, of course, witnesses aren't aware of making this adjustment—and so the thought process here is again unconscious.

But the effects of feedback don't stop there. Witnesses who receive this sort of feedback also end up "remembering" that they got a closer, longer, clearer view of the perpetrator, that the lighting was good, and so on (see **Figure 15.1**). Here, the witnesses seem to be thinking something like, "I chose the right person, so I guess I must have gotten a good view after all," and they adjust their memory accordingly. Once more, however, these aren't conscious thoughts, and in this case the witnesses are being misled by some after-the-fact reconstruction.

Interpretation and Inference

In some settings, unconscious thinking can be even more sophisticated. In one early experiment (Nisbett & Schachter, 1966), participants were asked to undergo a series of electric shocks, with each shock slightly more severe than the one before. The question of interest was how far into the series the participants would go. What was the maximum shock they would accept?

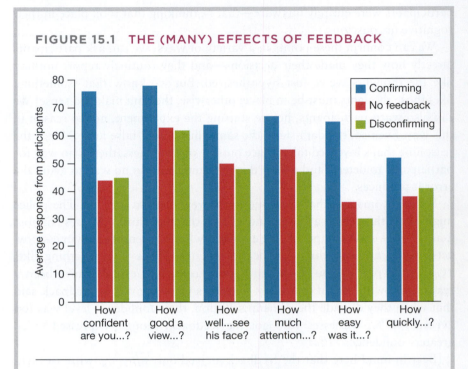

FIGURE 15.1   THE (MANY) EFFECTS OF FEEDBACK

Participants in this study viewed a (videotaped) crime and then attempted to pick the perpetrator's picture out of a lineup. Later, participants received either confirming feedback for their choice ("Good, you identified the actual suspect"), disconfirming feedback ("Actually, the suspect was . . ."), or no feedback. Then, participants were asked further questions about the video. (Confidence was assessed on a 0 to 100 scale, so the numbers shown on the *y*-axis correspond to the actual responses from the research participants. The other questions were answered with a 0 to 10 scale.) Crucially, the feedback arrived well after participants had viewed the crime and after they'd made their ID selection. Therefore, the feedback couldn't possibly have changed the original event ("How good a view did you get?" or "How well did you see his face?"), nor could it have changed the experience of making the identification ("How easy was it for you to choose?"). Nonetheless, the feedback altered the participants' memory for these earlier events. Those who had received confirming feedback now recalled that they'd gotten a better view of the crime, even though all participants got the same view! They also recalled that their ID had been fast and easy, even though their IDs had been no faster than anyone else's.   (AFTER WELLS ET AL., 2003)

Before beginning the series of shocks, some of the participants were given a pill that, they were told, would diminish the pain but would also have several side effects: It would cause trembling in the hands, a jittery stomach, and the like. Actually, none of this was true. The pill was a placebo and had no analgesic properties, nor did it produce any of these side effects. Even so, taking this inert pill was remarkably effective: Participants who took the pill were willing to accept four times as much amperage as control participants.

Why was the placebo so effective? Participants in the *control group* noticed that their hands were shaking, that their stomachs were upset, and so on. (These are, of course, common manifestations of fear—including the fearful anticipation of electric shock.) The participants then used these self-observations as evidence in judging their own states, drawing on what (in Chapter 12) we called "somatic markers." It's as if participants said to themselves, "Oh, look, I'm trembling! I guess I must be scared. Therefore, these shocks must really be bothering me." This led them to terminate the shock series relatively early. Placebo participants, in contrast, attributed the same physical symptoms to the pill. "Oh, look, I'm trembling! That's just what the experimenter said the pill would do. So I guess I can stop worrying about the trembling. Let me look for some other indication of whether the shock is bothering me." As a consequence, these participants were less influenced by their own physical symptoms. In essence, they overruled the evidence of their own anxiety, attributing their internal state to the pill and not the shock. Then, guided by this (mis)attribution, they apparently decided they weren't feeling great distress and so were willing to continue with the experiment. (For related studies, see Nisbett & Wilson, 1977; Wilson, 2002; Wilson & Dunn, 2004.)

Once again, though, let's note that participants' reasoning in this study was entirely unconscious. In fact, the participants were asked, after the procedure, why they had accepted so much shock, and in responding they never mentioned the pill. When asked directly, "During the experiment, did you think about the pill at all?" participants said things like, "No, I was too worried about the shock to think of anything else."

Of course, we know that the participants were mistaken in this claim; the experimental results tell us that. But this takes nothing away from what they were doing intellectually—and unconsciously.

Mistaken Introspections

It does seem useful, then, to distinguish between the (unconscious) processes involved in thought and the (conscious) products that result from these processes. As we've said, this distinction isn't always clear-cut, but it does support a useful rule of thumb about what you're aware of in your mental life and what you're not. Thus, you arrive at a conclusion, but the steps leading to the conclusion are hidden from view. You reach a decision, but again, you're unable to introspect about the processes leading to that decision.

Sometimes, however, the processes of thought do seem to be conscious, and you feel like you can voice the reasons for your decision or the basis for your conclusion, if anyone asks. This surely sounds like a situation in which your thoughts *are* conscious. Remarkably, though, this sense of knowing your own thoughts may, in many cases, be an illusion.

We've just discussed one example of this pattern. In the Nisbett and Schachter (1966) study, participants were asked, right after the study, why they had accepted the electric shock, and the participants firmly denied that they'd been influenced by the pill they'd taken. Instead, they confidently offered other explanations that had nothing to do with the pill. It seems, then, that participants had some beliefs about why they had acted as they did, but their beliefs were *wrong*—systematically ruling out a factor (the pill) that actually was having an enormous impact. (For related evidence, see Bargh, 2005; Custers & Aarts, 2010.)

To put the point more broadly, in many studies the participants think they know why they acted as they did, but they're mistaken. Their self-reports are offered with full confidence, and in many cases the participants insist that they carefully thought about their actions, so that the various causes and influences were, it seems, out in plain view. Nonetheless, from our perspective as researchers, we can see that these introspective reports are wrong—ignoring factors we know to be crucial, highlighting factors we know to be irrelevant.

After-the-Fact Reconstructions

How could these introspections get so far off track? The answer starts with a fact that we've already showcased—namely, that the processes of thought are often unconscious. People seeking to introspect, therefore, have no way to inspect these processes, and so, if they're going to explain their own behavior, they need some other source of information. Often, that other source is likely to be an *after-the-fact reconstruction*. Roughly put, people reason in this fashion: "Why did I act that way? I have no direct information, but maybe I can draw on my broad knowledge about why, in general, people act in certain ways in this situation. From that base, I can make some plausible inferences about why I acted as I did."

These after-the-fact reconstructions will often be correct, because people's beliefs about why they act as they do are generally sensible: "Why am I angry at Gail? She just insulted me, and I know that in general, people tend to get angry when they've been insulted. I bet, therefore, that I'm angry because she insulted me." In cases such as this, an inference based on generic knowledge is likely to be accurate.

DO WE KNOW WHY WE DO WHAT WE DO?

In 2002, rap musician Eminem was sued for copyright infringement for a particular song ("Kill You"). The plaintiff demanded a large sum, because Eminem had made a lot of money from sales of the album on which this song appeared. Eminem's attorneys, however, surveyed people who had bought the album, and they found that fewer than 1% said they'd bought the album for this particular track. Therefore, the attorneys argued, Eminem hadn't profited very much from that song, and so the plaintiffs weren't entitled to much compensation. But should we trust the results of this survey? A study by Kassa et al. (2011) indicated that many people either can't remember, or *misremember*, why they bought a particular CD. This seems a setting, then, in which people really don't know why they did what they did.

In other settings, however, these reconstructions can be totally wrong. They'll go off track, for example, if someone's beliefs about a specific setting happen to be mistaken; in that case, inferences based on those beliefs will obviously be problematic. Likewise, the reconstructions will go off track if the person didn't notice some relevant factor in the setting; here, too, inferences not taking that factor into account will yield mistaken interpretations.

But let's be clear that these after-the-fact reconstructions don't "feel like" inferences. When research participants (or people in general) explain their own behaviors, they're usually convinced that they're simply *remembering* their own mental processes based on some sort of direct inspection of what went on in their own minds. These reconstructions, in other words, feel like genuine "introspections." The evidence we've reviewed, however, suggests that these subjective feelings are mistaken—and so, ironically, this is one more case in which people are conscious of the product and not the process. They're aware of the conclusion ("I acted as I did because . . .") but not aware of the process that led them to the conclusion. So they continue to believe (falsely) that the conclusion rests on an introspection, when it actually rests on an after-the-fact reconstruction. Hand in hand with this, they continue to believe confidently that they know themselves, even though, in reality, their self-perception is (in these cases, at least) focusing on the wrong factors. (For more on this process of "self-interpretation," see Cooney & Gazzaniga, 2003.)

Unconscious Guides to Conscious Thinking

It's plain, though, that in some settings you *are* aware of your own thoughts. Sometimes you make decisions based on a clear, well-articulated "inner dialogue" with yourself. Sometimes you make discoveries based on a visual image that you carefully and consciously scrutinized. Even here, though, there's a role for the cognitive unconscious, because even here a support structure is needed—one that exists at what philosophers have called the "fringe" or the "horizon" of your conscious thoughts (Husserl, 1931; James, 1890).

Evidence for this unnoticed fringe comes from a variety of cases in which your thoughts are influenced by an "unseen hand." For example, in our description of problem solving (Chapter 13), we emphasized the role of a problem-solving *set*—unnoticed assumptions and definitions that guide your search for the problem's solution. Even when the problem solving is conscious and deliberate, even when you "think out loud" about the steps of the problem solution, you're guided by a set. We argued in the earlier chapter that this is generally a good thing, because the set keeps you focused, protecting you from distracting and unproductive lines of thought. But the set can sometimes be an obstacle to problem solving, and the fact that the set is unconscious makes it difficult to overcome the obstacle: It's difficult to alter your assumptions if you're not aware that you're making assumptions!

Similarly, in our discussion of decision making (Chapter 12), we emphasized the importance of a decision's *frame*. You might be completely focused

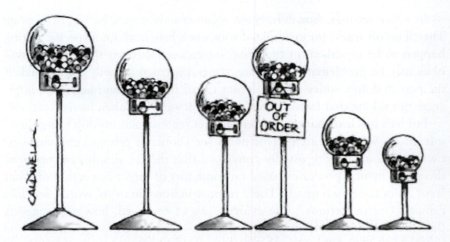

CONSCIOUSNESS IS GUIDED BY UNCONSCIOUS FRAMEWORKS

Language understanding provides another example in which conscious experience is guided by unconscious processes. It's striking, for example, that you often fail to detect the ambiguity you encounter—such as the two ways to interpret "Out of Order." You choose one interpretation ("needs repair") so rapidly that you're generally unaware that another interpretation ("in the wrong position in the series") is even possible.

TEST YOURSELF

1. Give an example in which people are conscious of the "products" created within the mind but not conscious of the "processes" that led to these products.
2. What evidence suggests that unconscious processes can involve sophisticated reasoning?
3. What does it mean to say that sometimes "introspections" are actually just after-the-fact reconstructions?

on the decision and fully aware of your options. Nonetheless, you'll be influenced by the (unnoticed) framing of the decision—the way the options are described and the way the question is posed. You don't think about the framing itself, but it unmistakably colors your thoughts about the decision and plays a large role in determining which option you'll choose.

In these ways, an unnoticed framework can guide your deliberate, conscious thinking—about problems, decisions, and more. In each case, this framework protects you from uncertainty and ambiguity, but it also governs the content and the sequence of your thoughts.

Disruptions of Consciousness

Further evidence for unconscious processes comes from patients who have suffered brain damage. As we saw in Chapter 7, patients suffering from Korsakoff's syndrome seem to have no conscious memory of events they've witnessed or things they've done. If asked directly about these events, the patients insist they have no recollection.

Even so, it would be a mistake to claim these patients have "no memories," because on tests of *implicit* memory these amnesic patients seem quite normal. In other words, they do seem to "remember" if we probe their memories indirectly—not asking them explicitly what they recall, but instead looking for evidence that their current behavior is shaped by specific prior experiences. In these indirect tests, the patients are influenced by memories they don't know they have—and so, apparently, some aspects of remembering can go forward even in the absence of a conscious memory. This is a pattern that Jacoby and Witherspoon (1982) have referred to as "memory without awareness."

Blind Sight

Parallel claims can be made for *perception*. As we said at the chapter's start, the phenomenon of **blind sight** is sometimes observed in patients who have suffered damage to the visual cortex. For all practical purposes, these patients are blind. If asked what they see, they tell us directly that they see nothing. Consistent with this report, they don't react to flashes of bright light, and they hesitate to walk down a corridor, convinced they'll collide with obstacles in their path. Tests reveal, however, that these patients can respond with reasonable accuracy to questions about their visual environment. (See de Gelder, 2010; Rees et al., 2002; Weiskrantz, 1986, 1997.) For example, they can answer questions about the shape and movement of visual targets, and even the emotional expression (sad vs. happy vs. afraid) on faces. If an experimenter requires them to reach toward an object, the patients tend to reach in the right direction and with a hand position (e.g., fingers pinched together or wide open) appropriate for the shape and size of the target. In all cases, though, the patients insist they can't see the targets, and they can offer no explanation for why their "guesses" are consistently accurate. Apparently, these patients are not aware of seeing but, even so, can in some ways "see."

How is this possible? Part of the answer lies in the fact that there may be "islands" of intact tissue within the brain area that's been damaged in these patients. (See Gazzaniga et al., 1994; Radoeva et al., 2008.) In other patients, the explanation rests on the fact that there are several neural pathways carrying information from the eyeballs to the brain. Damage to one of these pathways is the reason that these patients seem (on many measures) to be blind. However, information flow is still possible along other pathways—including a pathway through the superior colliculus in the midbrain (Leh et al., 2006; Tamietto et al., 2010)—and this is what enables these patients to use visual information that they cannot consciously see. One way or the other, though, it's clear that we need to distinguish between "perception" and "conscious perception," because unmistakably it is possible to perceive in the absence of consciousness. (For more data, also showing a sharp distinction between a patient's conscious perception of the world and her ability to gather and use visual information, see **Figure 15.2**; also Goodale & Milner, 2004; Logie & Della Salla, 2005; for a challenge, though, to this conception of blind sight, see Phillips, 2020.)

Subliminal Perception

In the late 1950s, a market researcher named James Vicary allegedly inserted the words "Eat Popcorn" into a single frame of a movie. When the movie was shown in the theater, reports tell us, the brief exposure of this message

FIGURE 15.2   CONSCIOUS SEEING, UNCONSCIOUS SEEING

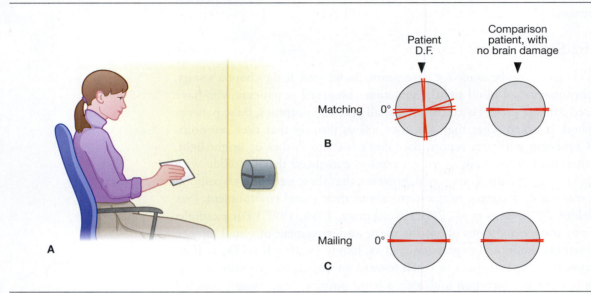

In this study, participants held a card (Panel A) and, in one condition, were asked to hold the card at an angle that matched the orientation of the slot in front of them. In another condition, they were asked to imagine that they were "mailing" the card, placing it into a "mail slot." In the matching task, D.F., a patient diagnosed with visual form agnosia, made many errors (Panel B). In the "mailing" task, in contrast, D.F. performed perfectly (Panel C), consistently matching the card's orientation to the orientation of the slot. It seems, then, that D.F. is (for some purposes) blind, but (for other purposes) is able to see, and she can use what she sees to guide her own actions.

(AFTER GOODALE ET AL., 1991)

wasn't enough for viewers to perceive the message consciously. Even so, the viewers were influenced by the message, and popcorn sales increased by more than 50%.

It turns out, though, that the report of this "Eat Popcorn" experiment was a *hoax*; no experiment was ever done (e.g., Rogers, 1992). However, more recent (and non-fraudulent) research makes it clear that people actually can be influenced by visual inputs they didn't consciously perceive—a pattern referred to as **subliminal perception**. In one line of work, researchers showed participants trios of words (van Gaal et al., 2014; but also see Rabagliati et al., 2018). The first two words were presented very rapidly, and both were followed by a mask that guaranteed that the words weren't consciously perceived. Then a third word was presented—at a longer exposure, with no mask, so that participants were aware of this third word.

The key measure in this study was a brain wave called the "N400." We mentioned this wave in Chapter 10, and there we noted that a larger N400 is observed when participants encounter a sequence of words that violates their expectations. For example, a large N400 will be observed when participants hear the last word in a sequence like, "He drinks his coffee with cream and dog."

In the study of subliminal perception, the conscious presentation of words like "war" produced a larger N400 if this word was preceded by a *subliminal* presentation of a positive word like "happy." The N400 was larger still if the first (and also subliminal) word in the series was "very"—so that the trio was an absurd sequence of "very happy war." In this setting, the (unconscious) prime made the (conscious) presentation of "war" unexpected, leading to the larger N400. Results were different, though, if the first word in the series was "not." Here, the unconscious prime of "not happy" made the (conscious) presentation of "war" less surprising, resulting in a smaller N400.

The results reversed if the second word in this trio was a negative word like "sad." Thus, the subliminal prime "very sad" led to a smaller N400 in response to "war." The subliminal prime "not sad" led to a larger N400 in response to negative words like "war."

It seems, then, that the subliminal words were detected and influencing subsequent perception—creating a context that in some conditions made the word "war" more surprising, and in other conditions less so. The important finding, though, is that participants had somehow combined the successive words, with the result that the phrases "very happy" and "not happy" had opposite effects (and likewise for "very sad" and "not sad"). Apparently, subliminal perception can involve more than the reading of single words; people also seem able (at least in a limited way) to integrate subliminal inputs in a linguistically appropriate fashion. (For complications, though, see Rabagliati et al., 2018.)

Consciousness and Executive Control

Where does all of this discussion leave us? Clearly, a huge range of activities, including complex activities, can be accomplished unconsciously. You can see, you can remember, you can interpret, you can infer—all without any awareness of these activities. So why do you need consciousness at all? What function does it serve? And related to this, what things *can't* you do unconsciously?

The Limits of Unconscious Performance

In tackling these questions, let's start with the fact that your unconscious steps seem, in each of the cases we've discussed, quite sensible. If, for example, the police tell you that the guy you selected from a lineup is indeed their suspect, this suggests that you did, in fact, get a good look at him during the crime. (Otherwise, how were you able to recognize him?) It's not crazy, therefore, that you'd "adjust" your memory for what you saw, because you now know that your view must have been decent. Likewise, imagine that you're making judgments about how famous various people are, and you're looking at a list that includes some unmistakably famous names. If, in this

TEST YOURSELF

4. What is blind sight, and what does it imply about the need for consciousness in perception?
5. What is subliminal perception, and what does it tell us about the need for consciousness in understanding complex stimuli?

setting, one of the other names seems somehow familiar, it again seems sensible that you'd (unconsciously) infer that this name, too, belongs to someone famous.

Over and over, therefore, your unconscious judgments and inferences tend to be fast, efficient, and *reasonable*. In other words, your unconscious judgments and inferences are well tuned to, and appropriately guided by, cues in the situation. This pattern is obviously a good thing, because it means that your unconscious processing won't be foolish. But the pattern provides an important clue about the nature of—and possible limitations on—unconscious processing.

Here's a proposal. Unconscious processing can be complex and sophisticated, but it's strongly guided either by the situation you're in or by prior habit. Therefore, when you (unconsciously) draw a conclusion or make a selection, these steps are likely to be the ones favored by familiarity or by the setting itself. Similarly, when you unconsciously make some response—whether it's an overt action, like reaching for an object that you can't consciously see, or a mental response, like noting the meaning of a word you didn't consciously perceive—you're likely to make a familiar response, one that's well practiced in that situation.

If this proposal is right, then unconscious processing will, to a large extent, be out of your control—governed by habit or by the setting, not by your current plans or desires. And, in fact, this is correct. For example, think about the inferences you make when you fill gaps in what you remember. These inferences are often helpful, but we've discussed how they can lead to errors—in some cases, large and consequential errors. Knowing these facts about memory, however, is no protection at all. Just as you cannot choose to avoid a perceptual illusion, you also cannot choose to avoid memory error, and you cannot "turn off" your inferences even when you want to. The process of making inferences is automatic and effortless, and it's also irresistible (see **Figure 15.3**).

In the same way, the inferences and assumptions that are built into object recognition (Chapter 4) are usually helpful, enabling you to identify objects even if your view is brief or incomplete. Sometimes, though, you want to shut off these inferences, but you can't. For example, if you're proofreading something you've written, you want to be alert to what's actually on the page and not be fooled by your ideas about what *should* be there. Plainly, though, proofreading is hard—and you unconsciously "correct" what's on the page whether you want to or not, with the result that you often fail to see the misspelling or the missng letter. (Also see **Figure 15.4**.)

Similarly, the largely uncontrolled nature of routine makes it easy for you to become a victim of habit, relying on customary patterns even when you hope to avoid them. This is evident, for example, in **action slips**—cases in which you do something different from what you intend. In most cases, these slips involve doing what's *normal* in a situation, rather than what you want to do on that occasion. For example, you're in the car, driving to the store. You intend to turn left at the corner, but, distracted for a

FIGURE 15.3 OUT OF CONTROL

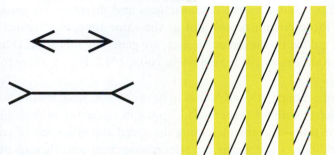

A Müller–Lyer illusion   **B** Poggendorff illusion   **C** Ponzo illusion

The inferences you make in perception and memory are automatic and unconscious—and so they aren't something you can "turn off" when you want to. As a result, any errors produced by these inferences are like the perceptual illusions that shape your reality whether you like it or not. In Panel A, the two horizontals are the same length. In Panel B, the black segments are perfectly aligned, so if you could remove the yellow bars you'd see perfectly straight black lines. In Panel C, the two yellow horizontals are the same length and the same thickness. Knowing these facts, however, doesn't protect you from the illusions. (These illusions are named, by the way, in honor of the people who created them.)

FIGURE 15.4 COUNT THE F'S

FINISHED FILES ARE THE RESULT
OF YEARS OF SCIENTIFIC STUDY
COMBINED WITH THE EXPERIENCE
OF YEARS.

In ordinary reading, you skip over many of the letters on the page and rely on inferences to "fill in" what you've skipped. This process is automatic and essentially uncontrollable—and so it's hard to avoid the skipping even when you want to. Count the appearances here of the letter *F*. For this task, you want to read in a letter-by-letter fashion, but this turns out to be difficult. How many *F*'s are there? Did you find all six?

moment, you turn right, taking the route that you usually take on your way to school (Norman, 1981; Reason, 1990; also see Langer, 1989). This observation is just as we'd expect if routine is forceful, automatic, and uncontrolled.

A Role for Control

The idea, then, is that unconscious processes—in perception, memory, and reasoning—serve as a sophisticated and highly useful set of "mental reflexes." These "reflexes" are guided by the circumstances and therefore are usually appropriate for those circumstances. But at the same time, the "reflexes," because they are guided by the circumstances, are generally inflexible. (For a related view, see Kahneman, 2011; Stanovich, 2009, 2012. For an alternative view, see Hassin, 2013.)

In many regards, though, it's *helpful* not to have control. Since unconscious processes can operate without "supervision," you can run many of these processes at the same time—thereby increasing the speed and efficiency of your mental life. In addition, since you're not supervising these unconscious processes, you're free to devote your attention to other, more pressing matters.

But how do these often-complex processes manage to run without supervision? Part of the answer is biological, and the sequence of events for some unconscious processing (e.g., the steps needed for perception) is likely built into the essential structure of the nervous system. Therefore, no supervision, no attention, was ever required for these steps.

For other sorts of unconscious processing, the answer is different, and it's an answer we first met in Chapter 5. The key idea is that when you're learning a new task, you need to monitor each step so that you'll know when it's time to start the next step. Then, you need to choose what the next step will be and get it started. This combination of monitoring, choosing, and launching does give you close control over how things proceed, but it can also make the performance quite demanding.

After some practice, however, things are different. The steps needed for the task are still there, but you don't think about them one by one. That's because you've stored in memory a complete routine that specifies what all the steps should be and when each step should be initiated. All you need to do is launch the overall routine, and from that point forward you let the familiar sequence unfold. Thus, with no need for monitoring or decisions, you can do the task without paying close attention to it. (For discussion of the neural basis of this shift, see Petersen et al., 1998; also see **Figure 15.5**.)

The Prerequisites for Control

In Chapter 5, we described these changes, made possible by practice, in terms of *executive control*, and that idea is still important here. Unconscious actions (whether rooted in biology or created through practice) go forward without executive control. When you need to direct your own mental processes, though—to rise above habit or to avoid responding to prominent cues in your surroundings—you do need executive control. (For related claims, see Lapate et al., 2014.) But what does executive control involve?

In order to perform its function, executive control needs, first of all, a means of launching desired actions and overriding unwanted actions. In other words, the executive needs an "output" side—things it can do, actions

FIGURE 15.5   ACTIVATED AREAS OF THE BRAIN CHANGE AS TASKS ARE PRACTICED

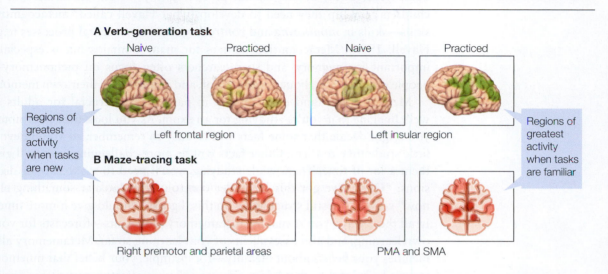

A Verb-generation task

Naive   Practiced   Naive   Practiced

Left frontal region   Left insular region

Regions of greatest activity when tasks are new

Regions of greatest activity when tasks are familiar

B Maze-tracing task

Right premotor and parietal areas   PMA and SMA

Based on PET images, these eight panels show that practicing a task results in a shift of the brain regions that are most active. (A) When confronted with a new ("naive") verb-generation task, areas in the left frontal region, such as the prefrontal cortex, are activated (green areas in the first panel). As the task is practiced, blood flow to these areas decreases (as depicted by the fainter color in the second panel). In contrast, the insular region is less active during naive verb generation. With practice, however, activation in the insula increases, suggesting that practice causes activity in the insula to replace activity previously observed in the frontal regions. (B) An analogous shift in activity is observed elsewhere in the brain during a motor-learning maze-tracing task. Activity in the premotor and parietal areas seen early in the maze task (red areas in the first panel) subsides with practice (fainter red in the second panel), while increases in blood flow are then seen in the primary and supplementary motor areas (PMA and SMA) as a result of practice.

it can initiate. Second, the executive needs some way of representing its goals and subgoals so that they can serve as guides to action; as a related point, the executive needs some way of representing its plan or "agenda" (Duncan et al., 2008; Duncan et al., 2012). Third, on the "input" side, the executive needs to know what's going on in the mind: What bits of information are coming in? How can these bits be integrated with one another? Is there any conflict among the various elements of the arriving information, or conflict between the information and the current goals? Fourth, it also seems plausible that the executive needs to know how easily and how smoothly current processes are unfolding. If the processes are proceeding without difficulties, there's no need to make adjustments; but if the processes are stymied, the executive would probably seek an alternative path toward the goal.

As it turns out, these claims about the prerequisites for control fit well with the traits of conscious experience and also with current claims about the biological basis for consciousness. Before we turn to those claims, though, let's consider a slightly different perspective on issues of mental control.

Metacognition

Some years back, developmental psychologist John Flavell noted that as children grow up they need to develop (what Flavell called) **metacognitive skills**—skills in *monitoring* and *controlling* their own mental processes (e.g., Flavell, 1979). Metacognition matters for many domains but is especially important for memory, and so researchers often focus on **metamemory**—people's knowledge about, awareness of, and control over their own memory.

Metacognition (and metamemory in particular) is crucial for adults as well. Imagine that you're studying for an exam. As you look over your notes, you might decide that some facts will be easy to remember, so you'll devote little study time to them. Other facts will be more challenging, so you'll give them a lot of time. Then, while studying, you'll need to make further decisions: "Okay, I've got this bit under control; I can look at something else now" versus "I'm still struggling with this; I guess I should give it more time." In all these ways, you're making metamemory judgments—forecasts for your own learning, and also assessments of your learning so far. Metamemory also includes your *beliefs* about memory—for example, your belief that mnemonics can be helpful or that "deep processing" is an effective way to memorize (see Chapter 6). Another aspect of metamemory is your ability to *control* your own studying—so that you use your beliefs to guide your own behavior.

There's an obvious link between these claims about metacognition and our broader claims about executive control. In both cases, there's a need for self-monitoring; in both cases, there's a need for self-control and self-direction. In both cases, you're guided by a sense of goals—whether those goals are generated on the spot or derived from your long-standing beliefs about how your own memory functions.

Our emphasis here, however, will be on executive control, largely because it's the more inclusive process—concerned with all sorts of self-monitoring and self-control, not just the monitoring and control of, say, your own memory. Nonetheless, the notion of metacognition (and metamemory in particular) provides further illustration of the ways in which executive control matters for you and how important it is. But how are these points related to consciousness? Let's start with the relevant biology.

The Cognitive Neuroscience of Consciousness

In the last few decades, there has been an avalanche of research on the relationship between consciousness and brain function. Some of this research has focused on cases of brain damage, including the cases of amnesia or blind sight we mentioned earlier. Other research has scrutinized people with normal brains and has asked, roughly, what changes we observe in the brain when someone becomes conscious of a stimulus. (See, among others, Baars & Franklin, 2003; Bogen, 1995; Crick & Koch, 1995; Kim & Blake, 2005; Rees

TEST YOURSELF

6. What sorts of actions can go forward without executive control? When is executive control needed?
7. What is metacognition?

et al., 2002.) In other words, what are the **neural correlates of consciousness** (or, as one author puts it, the *neural signatures* of consciousness—Dehaene, 2014)? As we'll see, consideration of these correlates will lead us directly back to the questions we've just been pondering.

The Many Brain Areas Needed for Consciousness

To explore the neural correlates of consciousness, researchers rely on the recording techniques we described in Chapter 2. Some studies use neuroimaging (PET or fMRI) to assess activity at specific brain locations. Other studies use EEG to track the brain's electrical activity. With all of these methods, researchers can ask how the pattern of brain activity changes when someone shifts attention from one idea to another. Researchers can also track the changes that occur in brain activity when someone first becomes aware of a stimulus that's been in front of their eyes all along.

Research in this arena makes it clear that many different brain areas are crucial for consciousness. In other words, there is no group of neurons or some place in the brain that's the "consciousness center." There is no brain site that functions like a light bulb that "turns on" when you're conscious and then changes brightness when your mental state changes.

It's helpful, though, to distinguish two broad categories of brain sites, corresponding to two aspects of consciousness (for an analogy, see **Figure 15.6**). First, some brain sites are crucial for your overall level of alertness or

---

FIGURE 15.6 TWO SEPARATE ASPECTS OF CONSCIOUSNESS

At any given moment, a radio might be receiving a particular station either dimly or with a clear signal. Likewise, at any given moment the radio might be receiving a rock station, a jazz station, or the news. These two dimensions—the clarity of the signal and the station choice—correspond roughly to the two aspects of consciousness described in the text.

sensitivity, independent of what you're currently sensitive *to*. The difference here is (roughly) the range from being sleepy and dimly aware of a stimulus (or an idea or a memory), at one extreme, and being fully awake, highly alert, and totally focused on a stimulus, at the other extreme. This aspect of consciousness is compromised when someone suffers damage to certain sites in either the thalamus or the *reticular activating system* in the brain stem—a system that controls the overall arousal level of the forebrain and also helps control the cycling between sleep and wakefulness (e.g., Koch, 2008).

Second, a different (and broader) set of brain sites matters for the *content* of consciousness. This content can, of course, vary widely. Sometimes you're thinking about your immediate environment; sometimes you're thinking about past events. Sometimes you're focused on a current task; sometimes you're dreaming about the future. These various contents for consciousness rely on different brain areas—and so cortical structures in the visual system are especially active when you're consciously aware of sights in front of your eyes (or aware of a visual image that you've created); cortical structures in the forebrain are essential when you're thinking about a stimulus that's no longer present in your environment; and so on.

The broad distinction between the *degree of awareness* and the *content of consciousness* is helpful, therefore, when we consider the diversity of brain areas involved in consciousness. (Although, for complications, see Auksztule-wicz et al., 2012; Bayne et al., 2016a, 2016b; Fazekas & Overgaard, 2016.) This distinction is also useful in thinking about *variations* in consciousness, as suggested by **Figure 15.7** (after Laureys, 2005; also Koch, 2008). In dreaming, for example, you're conscious of a richly detailed scene, with its various sights and sounds and events, and so there's a well-defined content, but your sensitivity to the environment is low. In contrast, in the mental state

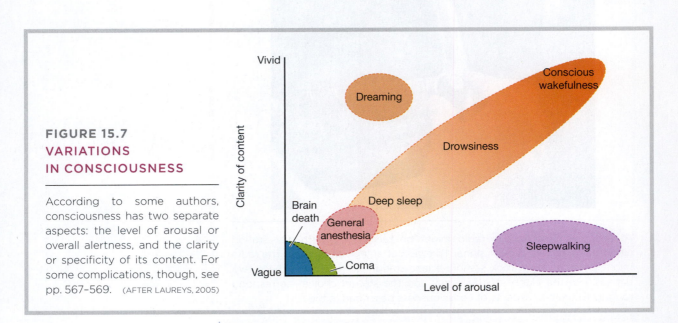

FIGURE 15.7
VARIATIONS IN CONSCIOUSNESS

According to some authors, consciousness has two separate aspects: the level of arousal or overall alertness, and the clarity or specificity of its content. For some complications, though, see pp. 567–569. (AFTER LAUREYS, 2005)

associated with sleepwalking, you're sensitive to certain aspects of the world so that you can, for example, navigate through the environment, but you seem to have no particular thoughts in mind, so the content of your consciousness isn't well defined.

The Neuronal Workspace

What is it in the brain that makes consciousness possible at all? Researchers have offered a variety of proposals, and there is no consensus. (See, for a sampling of views, Lamme & Roelfsema, 2000; Lau & Rosenthal, 2011; Morsella et al., 2016; Tononi et al., 2016.) Many investigators, though, endorse one version or another of the **neuronal workspace hypothesis**. In broad outline, here is the proposal. As we discussed in Chapter 2, different areas within the brain seem highly specialized in their function. The brain areas that make vision possible, for example, are separate from those that support hearing. Even within vision, the various aspects of perception each depend on their own brain sites, with one area specialized for the perception of color, another for the perception of movement, and so on.

We've already said, though, that these various brain sites need somehow to communicate with one another, so that the elements can be assembled into an integrated package. After all, you don't perceive *round + red + moving*; you instead perceive *falling apple*. You don't perceive *rectangular + white + still*; you instead perceive *book page*. In earlier chapters, we referred to this as the "binding problem"—the task of linking together the different aspects of experience in order to create a coherent whole.

We've also said that attention plays a key role in solving the binding problem. For example, a moving stimulus in front of your eyes will trigger a response in one brain area; a red stimulus will trigger a response in another area. In the *absence* of attention, these two neural responses will be independent of each other. However, if you're paying attention to a single stimulus that is red and moving, the neurons in these two systems will fire in synchrony. (See Chapter 3.) When neurons fire in this coordinated way, the brain seems to register the activity as a linkage among the different processing areas. As a result, these attributes are bound together, so that you end up correctly perceiving the stimulus as a unified whole.

This synchronization requires communication, so that neurons in one brain area can influence (and be influenced by) neurons in other, perhaps distant, brain areas. This communication is made possible by "workspace neurons" that literally connect one area of the brain to another. Let's emphasize, though, that the process of carrying information back and forth via the workspace neurons is selective, so that not every bit of neural activity gets linked to every other bit. Instead, various mechanisms create a *competition* among different brain processes, and the "winner" (typically, the most active process) is communicated to other brain areas, while other information is not.

Which elements will "win" in this competition? Again, attention is crucial: When you pay attention to a stimulus, this involves (among other neural steps) activity in the prefrontal cortex that can *amplify* the activity in other neural systems (Dehaene, 2014; Maia & Cleeremans, 2005), and this will shape how the competition plays out. By increasing activity in one area or another, attention ensures that this area wins the competition—and thus ensures that information from this area is broadcast to other brain sites.

Notice, then, that the information flow from each brain area to all the others is *limited*; this point is guaranteed by the competition. At the same time, the information flow is *controllable,* by virtue of what you choose to pay attention to.

With this backdrop, we're ready for our hypothesis. The integrated activity, made possible by the workspace neurons, provides the biological basis for consciousness. The workspace neurons themselves don't carry the *content* of consciousness; the content—the sense of seeing something red, the sense of seeing something moving—is represented in the same neurons that analyzed the perceptual information in the first place. But what the workspace neurons do is glue these bits together, creating a unified experience and promoting the exchange of information from one module to the next. (For specific versions of this hypothesis, see Baars, 2005; Baars & Franklin, 2003; Crick & Koch, 2003; Dehaene, 2014; Dehaene & Changeux, 2011; Maia & Cleeremans, 2005; Roser & Gazzaniga, 2004. For alternatives, see Lamme & Roelfsema, 2000; Lau & Rosenthal, 2011; Morsella & Bargh, 2011; Tononi et al., 2016.)

The Function of the Neuronal Workspace

Let's pause to outline the proposal that's before us. Any idea—whether it's an idea about a stimulus in front of your eyes or an idea drawn from memory—is represented in the brain by means of a widespread pattern of activity, with different parts of the brain each representing just one of the idea's elements. You become *aware of* that idea, though, when these various elements are linked to one another in a single overarching representation made possible by the workspace.

What does this linkage do for you? And how is all this related to our earlier comments about executive control or metacognition? Let's start with some basic facts about conscious experience. It's important, first, that your experience feels unitary and coherent. As we've noted in other contexts, you're not aware of orange and also aware of movement, and roundness, and closeness. Instead, you're aware of a single experience in which the basketball is flying toward you. This integrated coherence is just what the workspace allows: one representation, constructed from the coordinated activity of many processing components (Roser & Gazzaniga, 2004).

Likewise, we emphasized in Chapter 5 that conscious experience is *selective*. In other words, you're conscious of only a narrow slice of the objects and events in your world, so that you might focus on the rose's color but fail to notice its thorns, or a driver might be so absorbed in a phone call that he misses his exit. Moreover, you can typically *choose* what you're going to focus on (so that you might, when picking up the rose, decide to pay attention to those thorns). These observations, too, are easily accommodated by

COGNITION
outside the lab

Mind Wandering

Discussions of consciousness invariably invite questions about *altered states of consciousness*. How should we understand someone's experience when the person is under the influence of some drug or in the midst of a religious experience? There's one altered state, though, that requires neither medication nor meditation; it's the state of mind wandering (Smallwood & Schooler, 2006, 2015).

Virtually everyone has experienced mind wandering. You're sitting at your desk, trying to read, and you suddenly realize that for the last few minutes you've been pointing your eyes at the text but thinking about something altogether different—your plans for the weekend, perhaps, or hopes for a romantic encounter this evening. In these episodes, your thoughts seem largely "unguided"—with each thought passively triggering the next. It does seem right, therefore, to say that your thoughts are "wandering" and not directed toward any particular goal.

When you're mind wandering, you're surely aware of the content of your thoughts (the weekend plans or the encounter). Typically, though, there's a period during which you're not aware that your thoughts were wandering. Of course, at some point you do realize that your thoughts have moved away from your immediate task and—perhaps with some frustration—you re-focus on the text you're trying to read or the lecture you're trying to follow. But a moment earlier, you had wandered "off task" without realizing it.

Some researchers estimate that people spend at least 25% of their waking hours with their thoughts wandering in this fashion. These estimates come from various measures. In an "experience sampling" procedure, researchers interrupt people periodically

and ask: "What are you thinking about *right now*?" In other procedures, researchers can document slips and errors in an assigned task when someone's thoughts have wandered away from the task. In still other studies, researchers can document changes in brain activity when someone's thoughts are wandering. (For an overview of these studies, see Smallwood & Schooler, 2006, 2015.)

Mind wandering can be consequential and, for example, may cause as many automobile accidents as driving while intoxicated. On the positive side, though, there's some suggestion that mind wandering can, at the least, help people to escape boredom and can, more ambitiously, enhance creativity.

People's thoughts wander in all sorts of directions. A great deal of mind wandering, though, involves "mental time travel," with people often thinking about real or possible future events. Mind wandering is also sometimes (although less often) focused on past events, and this past-focus seems especially likely among people who are unhappy.

In light of the costs of mind wandering, though—when driving, listening to an important lecture, or even talking with a friend—is there anything you can do to keep yourself "on task"? Active engagement with the task seems to help. For example, periodic memory tests interwoven into an online lecture help to keep students engaged with the material (Szpunar et al., 2013). More broadly, training in mindfulness—whether a two-week program or just a brief breathing exercise—also turns out to reduce mind wandering (Smallwood & Schooler, 2015). Whether you *want* to avoid mind wandering, though, surely depends on the circumstances, and researchers are just beginning to explore possible benefits of this form of altered consciousness.

the workspace model: The information carried by the workspace neurons is, we've said, governed by a competition (and so is limited) and also shaped by how you focus attention. In this way, the properties of the workspace readily map onto the properties of your experience.

Let's also note that attention both amplifies *and sustains* neural activity. As a result, the workspace, supported by attention, enables you to maintain mental representations in an active state for an extended period. In other words, the workspace makes it possible for you to continue thinking about a stimulus or an idea even after the trigger for that idea has been removed. This point enables us to link the workspace proposal to claims about working memory (Chapter 6) and to the brain areas associated with working memory's function—specifically, the prefrontal cortex, or PFC (Goldman-Rakic, 1987). (For other evidence linking the PFC to conscious awareness, see McIntosh et al., 1999; Miller & Cohen, 2001.) This connection seems appropriate, since working memory is the memory that holds materials you're currently *working on*, which presumably means materials currently within your conscious awareness. (For complications, though, in the linkage between consciousness and working memory, see Soto & Silvanto, 2014.)

The Neuronal Workspace and Executive Control

What is the connection between the neuronal workspace and executive control? Bear in mind that the workspace enables you to assemble into one package the activity going on in different neural systems. This assembly allows you to examine the relationships among various inputs or ideas; it also allows you to produce *new combinations* of ideas and new combinations of operations. In this way, the workspace allows *novelty* in your mental processes, and thus makes it possible for you to rise above habit or routine. The workspace therefore allows you to escape some of the *limits* that seem to characterize unconscious processing.

As a related point, we've already said that unconscious processes are generally inflexible—and so, for example, if there's a conflict between habit and current goals, this has little influence on the process. In contrast, conscious thought *is* guided by a sense of your goals, and it can launch exactly the behavior that will lead to those goals.

How does the workspace support this sensitivity to current goals? By linking the various processing modules, the workspace makes it possible to compare what's going on in one module with what's going on elsewhere in the brain, and this activity enables you to detect conflict—if, for example, two simultaneous stimuli are triggering incompatible responses, or if a stimulus is triggering a response incompatible with your goals. This detection, in turn, enables you to shift processing in one system (again, by adjusting how you pay attention) in light of what's going on in other systems. (For discussion of the brain areas that seem specialized for this sort of "conflict detection," see Botvinick et al., 2004; Dehaene et al., 2003; Mayr, 2004; van Veen & Carter, 2006.)

The neuronal workspace idea also helps us with another puzzle—a shift in consciousness that every one of us experiences every day: the difference between being *awake* and being *asleep*. When you're asleep (and not dreaming), you're not conscious of the passing of time, not conscious of any ongoing stream of thought, and not conscious of many events taking place in your vicinity. This is not, however, because the brain is inactive during sleep; activity in the sleeping brain is, in fact, quite intense. What, then, is the difference between the sleeping brain and the "awake brain"? Evidence suggests that when you're asleep (and not dreaming), communication breaks down among different parts of the cortex, so that the brain's various activities aren't coordinated with one another. The obvious suggestion, then, is that this communication (mediated by the neuronal workspace) is crucial for consciousness, so it makes sense that sleeping people, having temporarily lost this communication, aren't conscious of their state or their circumstances (Massimini et al., 2005). (For a similar account of the loss of consciousness during surgical anesthesia, see Alkire et al., 2008. Also see **Figure 15.8**.)

TEST YOURSELF

8. Cognitive neuroscientists often distinguish "degree of awareness" from the "content of consciousness." What do these two terms mean?
9. What is the neuronal workspace hypothesis? What is the function of the neuronal workspace?

FIGURE 15.8   VARIOUS "NON-CONSCIOUS" STATES

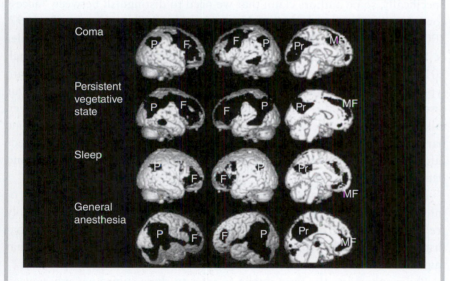

There are many states in which a person suffers an interruption of consciousness. Researchers have therefore asked: What brain sites are compromised in these various states? The dark areas in the figure indicate brain areas that are functioning at a lower level in each state; as can be seen, wide tracts of the brain are involved, including prefrontal tissue (F), parietal tissue (P), and other regions as well. Note that the images in the first and third columns show the brain's right hemisphere (so that the front of the brain is on the right); images in the middle column show the left hemisphere. For more on these states, see pp. 567–569.   (AFTER TSUCHIYA & ADOLPHS, 2007)

The Role of Phenomenal Experience

To recap, therefore, we can draw multiple parallels between the functioning of the neuronal workspace and the traits and capacities of consciousness. We can also link our claims about the workspace to the needs of executive control. The workspace, for example, allows comparisons among the various processing streams, and these comparisons enable the executive to ensure that there are no conflicts, and to choose processes that will move you toward your goals. The workspace also supports the sustained neural activity that enables the executive to keep its goals and plans in view, as you work on some endeavor. The mechanisms involved in the workspace can also amplify certain types of activity, and this allows the executive to take control of mental events—ramping up desired activities and allowing distractions to languish.

Qualia

These suggestions, though, leave a substantial puzzle untouched. In fact, some authors argue that the workspace proposal dodges what philosophers have called the "hard problem" of consciousness (e.g., Chalmers, 1996, 1998). Specifically, some authors claim that we need to distinguish between "access consciousness" and "phenomenal consciousness." (See, e.g., Block, 1997, 2005; Block et al., 2014; Bronfman et al., 2014; Kouider et al., 2010; Paller & Suzuki, 2014. But also see Cohen & Dennett, 2011; Lau & Rosenthal, 2011.) Access consciousness can be defined as someone's sensitivity to certain types of information (and so the person's *access* to that information). Our discussion so far in this chapter has been centered on this access. We've been talking about how the workspace allows a flow of information from one part of the brain to another; we've talked about how the executive needs information about what's going on in the mind in order to set goals and detect possible conflicts.

Phenomenal consciousness, in contrast, isn't about the use or function of information. Instead, this sort of consciousness centers on what it actually *feels like* to have certain experiences—that is, the subjective experience that distinguishes a conscious being from a "zombie" (or robot or computer) that might have access to the same information, but with no "inner experience."

Philosophers use the term **qualia** to refer to these subjective experiences. ("Qualia" is the plural form; the singular is "quale," pronounced KWAH-lee.) As an example, imagine meeting some unfortunate soul who has never tasted chocolate. You could offer this person a detailed and vivid description of what chocolate tastes like. You could compare chocolate's flavor to various other flavors. You might even provide a full account of chocolate's impact on the nervous system (which receptors on the tongue are activated, etc.). What you couldn't do, however, is convey the subjective first-person experience of just what chocolate tastes like. In other words, you could provide this person with lots of information, but not the *quale* of chocolate taste.

There are many questions to ask about qualia. Philosophers have wondered, for example, whether any one of us can truly understand the qualia experienced by other people—a question, in essence, about whether you experience the world in the same way I do (see **Figure 15.9**). Neuroscientists, in contrast, might ask how the nervous system produces qualia: How does biological tissue give rise to subjective states? But a cognitive psychologist might ask: How do qualia matter in shaping mental processes?

Processing Fluency

In truth, we know relatively little about how people are influenced by the subjective experience of consciousness. We've argued in this chapter that the *information content* of consciousness is crucial, but does it matter how this content "feels" from a first-person perspective?

Research provides some hints about these issues—but these are just *hints*, and claims here must be somewhat speculative. Surely, though, this is no

FIGURE 15.9 THE INVERTED SPECTRUM

Does each of us experience the world in the same way? Philosophers sometimes cast this question in terms of the "inverted spectrum" problem. Imagine that your nervous system is somehow "wired differently" from mine. When you perceive red, the color you're experiencing is the color I call "violet." When you perceive blue, the color you're experiencing is the color I call "yellow." Of course, you and I have both learned to call the color of stoplights "red," even though we have very different experiences when looking at a stoplight. We've both learned that mixing yellow and red paints creates orange, even though we have different experiences of this "orange." How, then, would we ever find out if your color experience differs from mine?

surprise: Qualia are, by their nature, undetectable by anyone other than the person who experiences them, so they are obviously difficult to study. It is also possible that some qualia matter deeply in shaping a person's thoughts and actions, while others don't; as a result, research in this arena has to pursue leads wherever we can find them.

Consider, as an illustration, the experience of *processing fluency*. In Chapter 7, we discussed the fact that the steps of perception sometimes proceed swiftly and with little effort but at other times proceed more slowly and with a lot of effort. The same is true for the steps of remembering, or deciding, or any other mental process. In other words, overall, mental processing is sometimes more fluent and sometimes less so, and people seem sensitive to this degree of fluency: They know when their steps have gone easily, and when not.

We've discussed the fact, though, that people don't detect the fluency *as* fluency. They don't have the experience of "Gee, that object sure was easy to perceive." Instead, people simply have a broad sense that their processing was, on this occasion, somehow special—and then they try to figure out *why* the processing was special. So they might decide that the input is one they've met recently (and so the fluency leads to a subjective sense of *familiarity*). Or they might conclude that the name they're considering belongs to someone famous. And so on.

Fluency effects can be demonstrated in many arenas. For example, the confidence expressed in a particular memory is influenced by the fluency of retrieval, apparently based on reasoning along the lines of "That memory came to mind easily; I guess it must be a strong memory and therefore an *accurate* one, so I can be confident that the memory is right." This reasoning is often sensible—but it can be misleading. For example, if you retrieve a memory over and over, the retrieval becomes more fluent because of this "practice," quite independent of how firmly established the memory was at the start. As a result, repeated retrieval increases memory confidence—whether the memory is accurate or not.

Likewise, in Chapter 12 we discussed the *availability heuristic*—the strategy of judging how frequent something is in the world by relying on how easily you can think of relevant examples. For example, are you in general an assertive person? People seem to answer this question by trying to think of events in the past in which they've been assertive, and if the examples come easily to mind, they decide that, yes, they are frequently assertive (Schwarz et al., 1991). So here, too, fluency of retrieval guides your thoughts. (For more on the broad impact of fluency, see, among others, Bernstein et al., 2018; Birch et al., 2017; Dohle & Montoya, 2017; O'Connor & Cheema, 2018; Oppenheimer & Alter, 2014; Schwarz, 2018; Stone & Storm, 2021; Vogel et al., 2020.)

Fluency is certainly different from the more commonly discussed examples of qualia: the raw experience of tasting chocolate, or the experience of itch, or red. Even so, you do notice and react to your own fluency—so this does seem to be an element of your mental life that you're conscious of.

And just as with other qualia, you can experience your own fluency but no one else can, and you can't experience anyone else's fluency. It's also important that we can describe the subjective experience of fluency only in rough terms—talking about someone "resonating" to an input or suggesting that a visual stimulus somehow "rings a bell." To go beyond these descriptions, we need to rely on the fact that each of us knows what fluency feels like, because we've all experienced fluent processing and we've all experienced processing that's not fluent. Each of these points is a trait of qualia, so research on fluency may provide important insights about how and when people are influenced by this entirely personal, entirely subjective, aspect of conscious experience.

Consciousness as Justification for Action

Other evidence hints at a different role for the actual experience of consciousness—a role in promoting, and perhaps allowing, *spontaneous* and *intentional* behavior (Dehaene & Naccache, 2001). To understand this point, consider the blind-sight patients. We've emphasized the fact that these patients are sensitive to visual information, and this tells us something important: Apparently, some aspects of vision can go forward with no conscious awareness and no conscious supervision. But it's also striking that these patients insist that they are blind, and their behaviors are consistent with this self-assessment: They're fearful of walking across a room (lest they bump into something), they fail to react to many stimuli, and so on.

Note the puzzle here. If, as it seems, these patients can see (at least to some extent), why don't they *use* the information that they gain by vision—for example, to guide their reaching or to navigate across the room? The evidence suggests that these patients see enough so that they reach correctly when they do reach. Why, then, don't they reach out on their own? Why do they reach (in the right direction, with the appropriate hand shape) only when the experimenter insists that they try? Is it possible that perceptual information has to be *conscious* before a person puts that information to use? (For further discussion, see Dennett, 1992; Goodale & Milner, 2004; Weiskrantz, 1997.)

Similar questions can be asked about people who suffer from Korsakoff's amnesia. We've emphasized how much these patients do remember, when properly tested (i.e., with tests of implicit memory). But it's also important that people with amnesia don't use this (implicitly) remembered information. For example, amnesic patients will insist that they don't know the route to the hospital cafeteria, so they won't go to the cafeteria on their own. However, if we demand that they *guess* which way to turn to get to the cafeteria, they typically guess correctly. Once again, therefore, we might ask: Why don't the amnesic patients spontaneously use their (implicit) memories? Why do they reveal their knowledge only when we insist that they guess? Is it possible that remembered information has to be conscious before it is put to use? (For similar results, with ordinary college students, with no brain damage, failing to use information that they apparently do remember, see Graf et al., 1982.)

What is going on in all of these cases? Here is one plausible answer. In many situations, you need to take action based on remembered or perceived information. But it's not enough merely to have access to the relevant information. You also need some justification, some reason, to take the information seriously. To make this point concrete, imagine that you're trying to remember a specific event, and some misty thoughts about that event come to mind. You vaguely recall that friends were present; you have a dim idea that food was served. You might hesitate to voice these thoughts, though, because you're not convinced that these thoughts are *memories*. (Maybe they're chance associations or dreams you once had.) As a result, you'll report your memory only if you're satisfied that you are, in fact, remembering. In other words, in order to report on your recollection, you need more than the remembered information. You also need some reason to believe the remembered information is credible.

How do you decide whether to trust your recollection? The answer, perhaps, is conscious experience. In other words, perhaps you'll take action based on some information only if the information "feels right"—that is, if it has the right qualia. If the experience has these qualities, this convinces you that the presented information is more than a chance association, and so you take the information seriously. However, if the conscious presentation is impoverished (as it seems to be in blind sight or in amnesia), you may not trust the information provided by your own eyes or your own memory, so you're paralyzed into inactivity.

In fact, these points can be linked to our earlier claims about the neuronal workspace. Bear in mind that the workspace allows an integration from multiple brain areas, and it's plausible that this integration is essential when you're trying to decide whether to take a memory (or a perception) seriously. The integration enables you to see, among other points, that the information provided by vision is confirmed by touch, that the information gained from your senses is consistent with your other beliefs, and so on. This convergence of cues may play a key role in persuading you that the perception or memory is real, not just a passing thought.

In Shakespeare's play, Macbeth asks himself whether the dagger he sees is real or a hallucination—"a dagger of the mind, a false creation proceeding from a heat-oppressed brain" (act 2, scene 1). He tries to decide by checking the visual information against other cues, asking whether the dagger is "sensible to feeling as to sight." The idea we're discussing here is similar: The confluence of inputs provided by the neuronal workspace may help to provide the richness—and, plausibly, the conscious experience itself—that you use in deciding whether your ideas and perceptions and memories are "false creations" or, instead, are true to reality. And it's only after you decide that they're real that you use them as a basis for action.

TEST YOURSELF

10. What are qualia?
11. What evidence suggests that people are influenced by the quale of processing fluency?

"A DAGGER OF THE MIND"?

In act 2, scene 1, Macbeth asks himself whether he sees a real dagger or "a dagger of the mind, a false creation . . . [of] a heat-oppressed brain." He tries to decide by checking the visual information against other cues. The proposal we're considering is that this is a common pattern—in which you check the credibility of your own thoughts by considering the qualia associated with those thoughts.

Consciousness: What Is Left Unsaid

The cognitive unconscious is remarkably sophisticated—able to recognize objects in the world, to remember, to reason, to draw conclusions. As a result, you often have no direct information about why you decided what you did or acted as you did. We've seen throughout this book, however, that careful research can reveal these processes, leaving us with an understanding of these processes that is both theoretically rich and pragmatically useful.

The fact remains, though, that you *are* aware of some things in your mind, and as we've now seen, researchers have made progress in describing the function of this awareness and its biological underpinnings. There is, however, still a lot that we don't know about consciousness. Our remarks about qualia have been speculative, and debate continues about the completeness (or accuracy) of theorizing about the neuronal workspace. In this chapter, we've also held other issues to the side: Can we specify what it is that changes in conscious experience during meditation or when someone is taking drugs?

And how should we think about an issue of consciousness that emerged in Chapter 11 in our discussion of visual imagery? There, we saw that individuals may *differ* in their conscious experience, with some people apparently enjoying rich, detailed visual images (so that their conscious experience often includes "mental pictures") but with other people insisting they have no mental imagery at all. This is a point in need of investigation—investigation that might illuminate the functional consequences of these differences and also their biological roots.

A different—and immensely difficult—puzzle centers on how the 3 pounds of the human brain make consciousness possible. The brain, after all, is a physical object with a certain mass, a certain temperature (a degree or two warmer than the rest of the body), and a certain volume (a bit less than a half gallon). It occupies a specific position in space. Our conscious thoughts and experiences, in contrast, aren't physical objects and have none of these properties. An idea, for example, doesn't have mass or a specific temperature; a feeling of sadness or fear has neither volume nor a location in space.

How, therefore, is it possible for a physical entity like the brain to give rise to nonphysical thoughts and feelings? Conversely, how can your thoughts and feelings *influence* your brain or your body? Imagine that you want to wave to a friend, and so you do. Your arm, of course, is a physical object with an identifiable mass. To move your arm, therefore, you need some physical force. But your initial idea ("I want to wave to Dan") isn't a physical thing with a mass or a position in space. How, then, could this (nonphysical) idea produce a (physical) force to move your arm?

The puzzles in play here are reflections of a quandary that philosophers refer to as the **mind-body problem**. The term refers to the fact that the mind (and the ideas, thoughts, and feelings it contains) is an entirely different sort of entity from the physical body, and yet the two, somehow, can influence each other. How can this be? The mind-body problem remains a mystery. In this chapter, we've discussed the *correlation* between brain states and conscious states, but we've left untouched the much harder question of how either of these states *causes* changes in the other.

Thus, we leave this chapter acknowledging that our discussion has only tackled part of the problem of consciousness and has left other parts untouched. In fact, it's possible that only some aspects of consciousness can be studied by means of scientific research, while other aspects require other forms of inquiry. Nonetheless, the data we've reviewed in this chapter, as well as the conclusions that flow from these data, provide powerful insights into the nature of consciousness, and these data will certainly inform future discussions of this profound and complex issue. This by itself—the mere fact that research can address these extraordinarily difficult issues—has to be a source of enormous satisfaction for investigators working on these intriguing problems.

"vegetative states"

Questions about consciousness sometimes seem abstract and subjective, with no linkage to careful science and no implications for the practical world. It turns out, though, that discussions of consciousness have important implications for medicine.

In medical settings, patients are sometimes alive but entirely unresponsive—in some cases because of medication, in other cases because of injury or some form of poisoning. But are these patients "conscious"?

Patients in the state we call "coma" show no overt response to lights or sounds or even painful stimuli. They have no detectable sleep-wake cycle; they do not respond to simple commands. Their state is often assessed with the Glasgow Coma Scale, which measures three elements: Does the person open their eyes spontaneously (4 points) or not at all (1 point)? Does the person converse normally (5 points) or make no sounds at all (1 point)? Does the person obey commands (6 points) or not? (The scale also includes specifications for each of the intermediate point values.) The points are added up; a score of 3 or lower indicates a deep coma.

The picture gets complicated, though, when we consider other states that don't fit the standard profile of a coma. (Notice, then, that we may need some finer distinctions than those reflected in **Figure 15.7**.) For example, some patients appear to awaken from a coma and open their eyes, but show only reflex behavior. These patients have what's called the *unresponsive wakefulness syndrome* (UWS; sometimes called a "vegetative state"). The situation is different for patients in a *minimally conscious state* (MCS). They show non-reflex movement and will (for example) track with their eyes a stimulus moving in front of them; they'll follow simple commands like "squeeze my hand." But beyond these (limited) indicators, these patients seem unresponsive to what's going on around them. Still other patients are in the condition called *locked-in syndrome* (LIS). These patients seem to have a normal sleep-wake cycle and can make tiny eye movements, but observers often remain convinced that the LIS patient is unconscious.

It's difficult, though, to assess the consciousness of someone in any of these states, in part because of the limited range of responses these patients can make. Asking them questions about their level of awareness is certainly not an option—they won't (and probably *can't*) respond. How, then, can we find out what (if anything) these patients are feeling, or what (if anything) they're aware of? Powerful cues come from fMRI data. In one case, a patient had suffered brain injury in a traffic accident, and it was unclear whether her condition was best described as LIS (in which case she was probably aware of her surroundings) or UWS. While in an fMRI scanner, the patient was presented with spoken sentences; her brain activity in response to the sentences

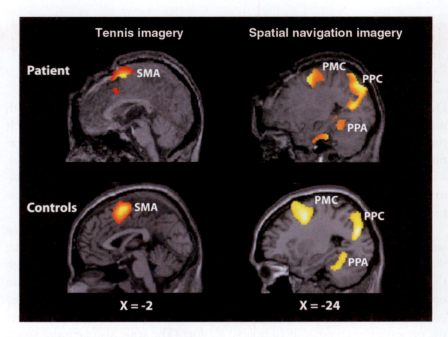

DETECTING CONSCIOUSNESS?

These fMRI scans compare the brain activation in a patient apparently in a vegetative state (after an injury in a traffic accident) with the activation in healthy control patients. The scans indicate that the patient—although otherwise unresponsive—was actually in a locked-in state, and (to some extent) aware. SMA is the supplementary motor area. PPA is the parahippocampal gyrus. PMC is the lateral premotor cortex; PPC is the posterior parietal lobe.

was essentially indistinguishable from that of healthy volunteers. When, as a further step, the sentences contained ambiguous words, there was additional brain activity just as there would be for fully aware individuals hearing these sentences.

As a further exploration, the patient was given verbal instructions—in one condition to imagine that she was playing a game of tennis; in another condition to imagine visiting the rooms in her house. Again, her brain activity was essentially matched to the patterns shown in healthy individuals given the same task—with activity in *motor areas* during the imagined tennis game, and activity in the *parahippocampal place area* during the imagined house tour.

Similar studies have been done with other patients, and in many cases the diagnosis of UWS is confirmed—the patient does not respond in a normal way to either the spoken sentences or the imagery instructions. In other cases, though, patients who had been diagnosed with UWS react as the first patient did—with a strong indication that their state is better understood as the locked-in syndrome, and a strong suggestion that they are (to some extent?) conscious and aware.

Results like these have powerful implications for medical care. For example, when a patient is unconscious, the medical staff, family, and friends often feel free to discuss the patient's status while standing at the patient's bedside—and may say things (including comments about the patient's prognosis) that they would never say if they believed the patient could hear. As a different example, the level of pain medication or anesthesia given to a patient is often adjusted according to the staff's best estimate of what the patient can feel and what the patient is aware of—and these aspects of treatment are likely different for a patient who is unconscious than for one who is locked in but conscious. In these ways, research techniques that *detect* consciousness may lead to different standards of care and treatment for patients in these extreme conditions.

For more on this topic:

Alkire, M. T., Hudetz, A. G., & Tononi, G. (2008). Consciousness and anesthesia. *Science, 322*(5903), 876–880.

Bruno, M.-A., Vanhaudenhuyse, A., Thibaut, A., Moonen, G., & Laureys, S. (2011). From unresponsive wakefulness to minimally conscious PLUS and functional locked-in syndromes: Recent advances in our understanding of disorders of consciousness. *Journal of Neurology, 258*, 1373–1384.

Cruse, D., Chennu, S., Chatelle, C., Bekinschtein, T. A., Fernández-Espejo, D., Pickard, J. D., Laureys, S., & Owen, A. M. (2011). Bedside detection of awareness in the vegetative state: A cohort study. *The Lancet, 378*, 2088–2094.

Owen, A. M., Coleman, M. R., Boly, M., Davis, M. H., Laureys, S., & Pickard, J. D. (2006). Detecting awareness in the vegetative state. *Science, 313*, 1402.

chapter review

SUMMARY

- An enormous amount of cognitive processing happens "behind the scenes," in the cognitive unconscious. In many cases, you're conscious only of the products that result from your mental processes; the processes themselves are unconscious. This is reflected in the fact that you aren't conscious of searching through memory; you're aware only of the results produced by that search. Similarly, you cannot tell when you have truly perceived a word and when you have merely inferred the word's presence.

- Unconscious processing can be rather sophisticated. For example, implicit memory influences you without your being aware that you are remembering at all, and this influence is typically mediated by a complex process through which you attribute a feeling of fluency to a particular cause. Unconscious attributions can also shape how you interpret and react to your own bodily states.

- Even when your thinking is conscious, you're still influenced by unconscious guides that shape and direct your thought. This is evident in the effects of framing in decision making and in the effects of sets in guiding your problem-solving efforts.

- Still further evidence for unconscious achievements comes from the study of blind sight and amnesia. In both cases, patients seem to have knowledge (gained from perception or from memory) but no conscious awareness of that knowledge.

- The cognitive unconscious allows enormous efficiency, but at the cost of flexibility or control. Likewise, the cognitive unconscious keeps you from being distracted by the details of your mental processes, but in some cases there's a cost to your ignorance about how your mental processes unfolded and how you arrived at a particular memory or a particular perception. These trade-offs point the way toward the function of consciousness: Conscious thinking is less efficient but more controllable, and it is also better informed by information about process.

- The neuronal workspace hypothesis begins with the fact that most of the processing in the brain is carried out by separate, specialized modules. When you pay attention to a stimulus, however, the neurons in the various modules are linked by means of workspace neurons. This linkage amplifies and sustains the processing within individual modules, and it allows integration and comparison of the various modules. The integration, it is proposed, is what makes consciousness possible. The integration provides the basis for the unity in your experience; it also enables flexibility and the detection of conflict.

- Several theorists have argued that we must distinguish types of conscious experience. The considerations in this chapter bear more directly on "access consciousness," which is a matter of how information is accessed and used within the mind. The chapter has had less to say about "phenomenal consciousness," which is concerned with the subjective experience of being conscious. Even so, research on mental *fluency* provides an intriguing hint both of how you are guided by qualia and how we can do research on the effects of qualia.

- Consciousness may give you a sense that you have adequate justification for taking an action. This may be why amnesic patients seem unable to take action based on what they (unconsciously) recall and why blind-sight patients seem unable to respond to what they (unconsciously) see.

KEY TERMS

cognitive unconscious (p. 537)
blind sight (p. 545)
subliminal perception (p. 546)
action slips (p. 548)
metacognitive skills (p. 552)

metamemory (p. 552)
neural correlates of consciousness (p. 553)
neuronal workspace hypothesis (p. 555)
qualia (sing. quale) (p. 560)
mind-body problem (p. 566)

TEST YOURSELF AGAIN

1. Give an example in which people are conscious of the "products" created within the mind but not conscious of the "processes" that led to these products.

2. What evidence suggests that unconscious processes can involve sophisticated reasoning?

3. What does it mean to say that sometimes "introspections" are actually just after-the-fact reconstructions?

4. What is blind sight, and what does it imply about the need for consciousness in perception?

5. What is subliminal perception, and what does it tell us about the need for consciousness in understanding complex stimuli?

6. What sorts of actions can go forward without executive control? When is executive control needed?

7. What is metacognition?

8. Cognitive neuroscientists often distinguish "degree of awareness" from the "content of consciousness." What do these two terms mean?

9. What is the neuronal workspace hypothesis? What is the function of the neuronal workspace?

10. What are qualia?

11. What evidence suggests that people are influenced by the quale of processing fluency?

THINK ABOUT IT

1. In light of the evidence and arguments presented in this chapter, could a *computer* ever be conscious? Does a computer need something like "executive control"? (Think about the circumstances or achievements for which humans seem to need executive control; does that help with this question?) Would a computer ever need something like qualia? Explain your responses.

DEMONSTRATIONS & APPLYING COGNITIVE PSYCHOLOGY ESSAYS

For demonstrations of key concepts in cognitive psychology, take a look at the Online Demonstrations. To explore more of the practical applications of cognitive psychology in themed essays, visit the online reader.

Online Demonstrations

- Demonstration 15.1: Practice and the Cognitive Unconscious
- Demonstration 15.2: The Autobiographical Recollection Test
- Demonstration 15.3: Memory for Dreams
- Demonstration 15.4: The Quality of Consciousness

Online Applying Cognitive Psychology Essays

- Cognitive Psychology and Technology: Thermostats Aren't Conscious. What Is?
- Cognitive Psychology and Education: Mindfulness
- Cognitive Psychology and the Law: Unconscious Thinking

ZAPS COGNITION LABS

Go to ZAPS online cognition labs to conduct hands-on experiments on key concepts.

INQUIZITIVE

It's time to complete your study experience! Go to InQuizitive to practice actively with this chapter's concepts and get personalized feedback along the way.

Glossary

"7 plus-or-minus 2" A range often offered as an estimate of the number of items or units able to be contained in *working memory*. (Ch. 6)

acquisition The process of placing new information into *long-term memory*. (Ch. 6)

action potential A brief change in the electrical potential of an *axon*. The action potential is the physical basis of the signal sent from one end of a *neuron* to the other; it usually triggers a further (chemical) signal to other neurons. (Ch. 2)

action slip An error in which a person performs some behavior or makes some response that is different from the behavior or response intended. (Ch. 15)

activation level A measure of the current status for a *node* or *detector*. Activation level is increased if the node or detector receives the appropriate input from its associated nodes or detectors; activation level will be high if input has been received frequently or recently. (Ch. 4)

acuity The ability to see fine detail. (Ch. 3)

affective forecasting The process in which a person predicts how they will feel at some future point about an object or state of affairs. It turns out that people are surprisingly inaccurate in these predictions and, for example, understate their own capacity to adapt to changes. (Ch. 12)

agnosia A disturbance in a person's ability to identify familiar objects. (Ch. 2)

all-or-none law The principle stating that a *neuron* or *detector* either fires completely or does not fire at all; no intermediate responses are possible. (Graded responses are possible, however, by virtue of the fact that a neuron or detector can fire more or less frequently, and for a longer or shorter time.) (Ch. 2)

amnesia A disruption of memory, often due to brain damage. (Ch. 7)

amygdala (pl. amygdalae) An almond-shaped structure in the *limbic system* that plays a central role in emotion and in the evaluation of stimuli. (Ch. 2)

anecdotal evidence A type of evidence that is informally collected and reported; often, a story ("anecdote") about an individual case that happens to have caught someone's attention and happens, at that moment, to strike the person as worth reporting.

anomia A disorder, often arising from specific forms of brain damage, in which the person loses the ability to name certain objects. (Ch. 9)

anterior cingulate cortex (ACC) A brain structure known to play a crucial role in detecting and resolving conflicts among different brain systems.

anterograde amnesia An inability to remember experiences that occurred after the event that triggered the memory disruption. Often contrasted with *retrograde amnesia*. (Ch. 7)

aphasia A disruption to language capacities, often caused by brain damage. See also *fluent aphasia* and *nonfluent aphasia*. (Ch. 2)

apraxia A disturbance in the capacity to initiate or organize voluntary action, often caused by brain damage. (Ch. 2)

Area V1 The site on the *occipital lobe* where axons from the *lateral geniculate nucleus* first reach the cerebral *cortex*. This site is (for one neural pathway) the location at which information about the visual world first reaches the brain. (Ch. 3)

articulatory rehearsal loop One of the low-level assistants hypothesized as being part of the *working-memory system*. This loop draws on *subvocalized* (covert) speech, which serves to create a record in the *phonological buffer*. Materials in this buffer then fade, but they can be refreshed by another cycle of covert speech. (Ch. 6)

association cortex The traditional name for the portion of the human *cortex* outside the motor and sensory projection areas. (Ch. 2)

associations (or associative links) Functional connections that are hypothesized to link *nodes* within a mental network or *detectors* within a detector network; these associations are often hypothesized as the "carriers" of activation from one node or detector to the next. (Ch. 7)

attended channel A stimulus (or group of stimuli) that a person is trying to perceive. Ordinarily, information is understood or remembered from the attended channel. Often contrasted with *unattended channel*. (Ch. 5)

attribute substitution A commonly used strategy in which a person needs one type of information but relies instead on a more accessible form of information.

This strategy works well if the more accessible form of information is well correlated with the desired information. An example is the case in which someone needs information about how frequent an event is in the world and relies instead on how easily they can think of examples of the event. (Ch. 12)

attribution The step of explaining a feeling or event, usually by identifying the factors (or an earlier event) that are the cause of the current feeling or event. This term is often elaborated with the more specific term "causal attribution." (Ch. 7)

autobiographical memory The aspect of memory that records the episodes and events in a person's life. (Ch. 8)

automaticity A state achieved by some tasks and some forms of processing, in which the task can be performed with little or no attention. In many cases, automatized actions can be combined with other activities without interference. Automatized actions are also often difficult to control, leading many psychologists to refer to them as "mental reflexes." (Ch. 5)

automatic tasks Tasks that are well practiced and that do not require flexibility; these tasks usually require little or no attention, and they can be carried out if the person is also busy with some other task. Usually contrasted with *controlled tasks*.

availability heuristic A particular form of *attribute substitution* in which the person needs to judge the frequency of a certain

type of object or the likelihood of a certain type of event. For this purpose, the person is likely to assess the ease with which examples of the object or event come to mind; this "availability" of examples is then used as an index of frequency or likelihood. (Ch. 12)

axon The part of a *neuron* that typically transmits a signal away from the neuron's cell body and carries the signal to another location. (Ch. 2)

baseline level A measurement used as a standard for comparison. The baseline level is typically assessed prior to, or in the absence of, some other specific influence. Then, measures taken once the influence is in place can be compared to the baseline level, in order to ask what impact (if any) the influence had.

base-rate information Information about the broad likelihood of a particular type of event (also referred to as "prior probability"). Often contrasted with *diagnostic information*. (Ch. 12)

basic-level categorization A level of categorization hypothesized as the "natural" and most informative level, neither too specific nor too general. People tend to use basic-level terms (such as "chair," rather than the more general "furniture" or the more specific "armchair") in their ordinary conversation and in their reasoning. (Ch. 9)

behaviorist movement A methodological perspective that dominated American psychology for many years. This perspective emphasized broad principles concerned with how behavior changes in response to different configurations of stimuli (including stimuli that are often called "rewards" and "punishments"). In its early days, behaviorists sought to avoid mentalistic terms (terms that referred to representations or processes inside the mind). (Ch. 1)

belief bias A tendency, within logical reasoning, to endorse a conclusion if the conclusion happens to be something one believes is true anyhow. In displaying this tendency, people seem to ignore both the *premises* of the logical argument and logic itself, and they rely instead on their broader pattern of beliefs about what is true and what is not. (Ch. 12)

belief perseverance A tendency to continue endorsing some assertion or claim, even when the clearly available evidence completely undermines that claim. (Ch. 12)

biased competition theory A proposal that attention functions by shifting neurons' priorities, so that the neurons are more responsive to inputs that have properties associated with the desired or relevant input. (Ch. 5)

bigram detectors Hypothetical units in a recognition system that respond, or fire, whenever a specific letter pair is in view. (Ch. 4)

binding problem The problem of reuniting the various elements of a scene, given that these elements are initially dealt with by different systems in the brain. (Ch. 3)

binocular disparity A *distance cue* based on the differences between the two eyes' views of the world. This difference becomes less pronounced the farther away an object is from the observer. (Ch. 3)

binocular rivalry A pattern that arises when the input to one eye cannot be integrated with the input to the other eye. In this circumstance, the person tends to be aware of only one eye's input at a time.

bipolar cells A type of *neuron* in the eye. Bipolar cells receive their input from the *photoreceptors* and transmit their output to the retinal *ganglion cells*. (Ch. 3)

blind sight A pattern resulting from brain damage, in which the person seems unable to see in part of their field of vision but can often correctly respond to visual inputs when required to do so by an experimenter. (Ch. 15)

bottom-up processing A sequence of events that is governed by the stimulus input itself. Often contrasted with *top-down processing*. (Ch. 4)

boundary extension A tendency for people to remember pictures as being less "zoomed in" (and therefore having wider boundaries) than they actually were. (Ch. 11)

brightness constancy The achievement of perceiving the constant brightness of objects despite changes in the light reaching the eye that result from variations in illumination. (Ch. 3)

Broca's area An area in the left *frontal lobe* of the brain; damage here typically causes *nonfluent aphasia*. (Ch. 10)

catch trials Individual tests ("trials") within a procedure designed to make sure that participants are paying attention and are actually obeying the researcher's instructions. For example, in a *sentence verification task*, researchers routinely draw data only from trials that yielded a "yes" response. However, trials with a "no" response are included as catch trials to make certain that participants are following instructions.

categorical perception The pattern in which speech sounds are heard "merely" as members of a category—the category of [z] sounds, the category of [p] sounds, and so on. Because of categorical perception, perceivers are highly sensitive to the acoustic contrasts that distinguish sounds in different categories; people are much less sensitive to the acoustic contrasts that distinguish sounds within a category. (Ch. 10)

categorical syllogisms A logical argument containing two *premises* and a conclusion, and concerned with the properties of, and relations between, categories. An example is "All trees are plants. All plants require nourishment. Therefore, all trees require nourishment." This is a valid syllogism, since the truth of the premises guarantees the truth of the conclusion. (Ch. 12)

cell body The area of a biological cell containing the nucleus and the metabolic machinery that sustains the cell. (Ch. 2)

center-surround cells A type of *neuron* in the visual system that has a "donut-shaped" *receptive field*. Stimulation in the center of the *receptive field* has one effect on the cell; stimulation in the surrounding ring has the opposite effect. (Ch. 3)

central fissure The separation dividing the *frontal lobes* on each side of the brain from the *parietal lobes*. (Ch. 2)

cerebellum The largest area of the *hindbrain*, crucial for the coordination of bodily movements and balance. (Ch. 2)

cerebral hemisphere One of the two hemispherical brain structures—one on the left side, one on the right—that constitute the major part of the *forebrain* in mammals. (Ch. 2)

change blindness A pattern in which perceivers either do not see or take a long time to see large-scale changes in a visual stimulus. This pattern reveals how little people perceive, even from stimuli in plain view, if they are not specifically attending to the target information. (Ch. 5)

chronometric studies Literally, "time-measuring" studies; generally, studies that measure the amount of time a task takes. Sometimes used as a way of examining the task's components or as a way of examining which brain events are simultaneous with specific mental events. (Ch. 11)

chunks The hypothetical storage units in *working memory*; it is estimated that working memory can hold 7 *plus-or-minus* 2 chunks. However, an unspecified quantity of information can be contained within each chunk, because the content of each chunk depends on how the memorizer has organized the materials to be remembered. (Ch. 6)

clinical neuropsychology The study of brain function that uses, as its main data source, cases in which damage or illness has disrupted the working of some brain structure. (Ch. 1)

coarticulation A trait of speech production in which the way a sound is produced is altered slightly by the immediately preceding and immediately following sounds. Because of this "overlap" in speech production, the acoustic properties of each speech sound vary according to the context in which that sound occurs. (Ch. 10)

coding The system through which one type of information stands for, or represents, a different type of information. In the context of the nervous system, this term refers to the way in which activity in *neurons* manages to stand for, or represent, particular ideas or thoughts. (Ch. 2)

cognitive neuroscience The effort toward understanding humans' mental functioning through close study of the brain and nervous system. (Ch. 1)

cognitive unconscious The broad set of mental activities of which people are completely unaware but that make possible ordinary thinking, remembering, reasoning, and so on. (Ch. 15)

commisure One of the thick bundles of fibers along which information is sent back and forth between the two *cerebral hemispheres*. (Ch. 2)

common ground The set of (usually unspoken) beliefs and assumptions shared by conversational partners. In a conversation, speakers and listeners count on this shared knowledge as a basis for making inferences about points not explicitly mentioned in the conversation, and also as a basis for interpreting elements of the conversation that would otherwise be unclear or ambiguous. (Ch. 10)

computerized axial tomography (CT scan) A *neuroimaging technique* that uses X-rays to construct a precise three-dimensional image of the brain's anatomy. (Ch. 2)

concurrent articulation task The speaking or miming of speech while doing some other task. In many cases, the person is required to say "Tah-Tah-Tah" over and over, or "one, two, three, one, two, three." These procedures occupy the muscles and control mechanisms needed for speech, so they prevent the person from using these resources for *subvocalization*. (Ch. 6)

conditional statements A statement of the format "If X then Y," with the first part (the "if" clause, or antecedent) providing a condition under which the second part (the "then" clause, or consequent) is guaranteed to be true. (Ch. 12)

cones *Photoreceptors* that are able to discriminate hues and that have high *acuity*. Cones are concentrated in the *retina's fovea* and become less frequent in the visual periphery. Often contrasted with *rods*. (Ch. 3)

confirmation bias A family of effects in which people seem more sensitive to evidence that confirms their beliefs than they are to evidence that challenges their beliefs. Thus, if people are given a choice about what sort of information they would like in order to evaluate their beliefs, they request information that's likely to confirm their beliefs. Likewise, if they're presented with both confirming and disconfirming evidence, they're more likely to pay attention to, be influenced by, and remember the confirming evidence, rather than the disconfirming. (Ch. 12)

confound An extra variable contained within an experiment, distinct from the *independent variable*, that could have caused the observed data pattern.

conjunction error An error in perception in which a person correctly perceives what features are present but misperceives how the features are joined, so that (for example) a red circle and a green square might be misperceived as a red square and a green circle. (Ch. 3)

connectionist networks Proposed systems of knowledge representation that rely on *distributed representations*, and that therefore require *parallel distributed processing* to operate on the elements of a representation. (Ch. 9)

consolidation The biological process through which new memories are "cemented in place," acquiring some degree of permanence through the creation of new (or altered) neural connections. (Ch. 8)

context-dependent learning A pattern of data in which materials learned in one setting are well remembered when the person returns to that setting, but are less well remembered in other settings. (Ch. 7)

context reinstatement A procedure in which a person is led to the same mental and emotional state they were in during a previous event; context reinstatement can often promote accurate recollection of that event. (Ch. 7)

contralateral control A pattern in which the left half of the brain controls the right half of the body, and the right half of the brain controls the left half of the body. (Ch. 2)

control condition A situation or condition that does not have, or is not exposed to, the factor the researcher is trying to evaluate. Usually contrasted with *experimental condition*.

controlled tasks Tasks that are novel or that require flexibility in one's approach; these tasks usually require attention, so they cannot be carried out if the person is also busy with some other task. Usually contrasted with *automatic tasks*.

convergent thinking An ability to find ways in which seemingly distinct ideas might be interconnected. Often contrasted with *divergent thinking*. (Ch. 13)

convolutions The wrinkles visible in the cerebral *cortex* that allow the enormous surface area of the human brain to fit into the relatively small volume of the skull. (Ch. 2)

cornea The transparent tissue at the front of each eye that plays an important role in focusing the incoming light. (Ch. 3)

corpus callosum The largest of the *commissures* linking the left and right *cerebral hemispheres*. (Ch. 2)

correlations The tendency for two variables to change together. If one goes up as the other goes up, the correlation is positive; if one goes up as the other goes down, the correlation is negative. A value of +1.00 indicates a perfect positive correlation; a value of −1.00 indicates a perfect negative (or inverse) correlation; a value of 0 indicates that there is no relationship at all between the variables.

cortex The outermost surface of an organ in the body; psychologists are most commonly interested in the brain's cortex and, specifically, the cerebral cortex. (Ch. 2)

counterbalancing A procedural step used to remove the influence of *confounds*. In counterbalancing, the researcher arranges the procedure so that extraneous variables have the same impact on all conditions. For example, the researcher could design the procedure so that the extraneous variables favor the *experimental condition* half the time and favor the *control condition* half the time. With this arrangement in place, the extraneous variable might still influence the overall results (perhaps lifting performance or diminishing it), but, crucially, it cannot influence the difference between the two conditions.

covariation A relationship between two variables such that the presence (or magnitude) of one variable can be predicted from the presence (or magnitude) of the other. Covariation can be positive or negative. If it is positive, then increases in one variable occur when increases in the other occur. If it is negative, then decreases in one neither the research participant nor the person administering the procedure knows whether the participant is in the experimental or the control group, or whether a particular trial (or test session) is in the *experimental condition* or the *control condition.* Among other advantages, this step ensures that there will be no systematic differences between the conditions in how participants are treated or in participants' expectations for the procedure.

double dissociation A pattern of results in which, with some manipulations, one process or structure is influenced more than a second, but then, with other manipulations, the second process or structure is influenced more than the first. With this pattern of results, it is clear that neither structure or process is simply a "weaker" or "more easily manipulated" version of the other. Instead, the data pattern tells us that the two structures are genuinely (and qualitatively) distinct from each other, each governed by its own principles.

DRM paradigm A commonly used experimental design, named after its originators (Deese, Roediger, and McDermott), for eliciting and studying memory errors. In this procedure, a person sees or hears a list of words that are related to a single theme; however, the word that names the theme is not itself included. Nonetheless, people are very likely to remember later that the theme word was presented. (Ch. 8)

dual coding A theory that imageable materials, such as high-imagery words, will be doubly represented in memory: The word itself will be remembered, and so will the corresponding mental image. (Ch. 11)

dual-process model Any model of thinking that claims people have two distinct means of making judgments—one of which is fast, efficient, but prone to error, and one that is slower, more effortful, but also more accurate. (Ch. 12)

early selection hypothesis A proposal that *selective attention* operates at an early stage of processing, so that the unattended inputs receive little analysis. (Ch. 5)

edge enhancement A process created by *lateral inhibition* in which the *neurons* in the visual system give exaggerated responses to edges of surfaces. (Ch. 3)

effect size A statistical measure of how large the difference is between two groups or between two conditions.

eidetic imagery A relatively rare capacity in which the person can retain long-lasting and detailed visual images of scenes that can be scrutinized as if they were still physically present. (Ch. 11)

Einstellung This term is sometimes used interchangeably with the term *problem-solving set,* but is often used more specifically to refer to a rigidity that can grow out of early efforts in solving a series of problems. If these early efforts are successful, the person will likely continue using the same method, even if there is a seemingly-obvious and much more efficient solution available for

subsequent problems in that series. (Ch. 13)

electroencephalogram (EEG) A recording of voltage changes occurring at the scalp that reflect activity in the brain underneath. (Ch. 2)

emotional intelligence The ability to understand one's own and others' emotions and to control one's emotions appropriately. (Ch. 14)

encoding specificity The tendency, when memorizing, to place in memory both the materials to be learned and some amount of their context. As a result, these materials will be recognized as familiar, later on, only if the materials appear again in a similar context. (Ch. 7)

endogenous control of attention A mechanism through which a person chooses (often, on the basis of some meaningful signal) where to focus attention. (Ch. 5)

event-related potentials Changes in an *electroencephalogram (EEG)* in the brief period just before, during, and after an explicitly defined event, usually measured by averaging together many trials in which this event has occurred. (Ch. 2)

excitatory connection A link from one node, or one *detector,* to another, such that activation of one node activates the other. Often contrasted with *inhibitory connection.* (Ch. 4)

executive control The *mental resources* and processes that are used to set goals, choose task priorities, and avoid conflict among competing habits or responses. (Ch. 5)

exemplar-based reasoning Reasoning that draws on knowledge about specific

framing In the context of decision making, a term referring to how the options for a decision (or, in some cases, the decision itself) are described. Often, the framing determines whether the decision is cast in terms of gains or positive attributes (e.g., what you might gain from this or that option), or whether the decision is cast in terms of losses or negative attributes. (Ch. 12)

free recall procedure A method used for testing what research participants remember; participants are given a broad cue ("What happened yesterday?" or "What words were on the list?") and then try to name the relevant items, in any order they choose. It is the flexibility in order that makes this recall "free." (Ch. 6)

frequency One of the central influences on a *detector*'s or *node*'s activation level. Frequency refers to whether the detector or node has been activated often in the past. Often contrasted with *recency*—whether the detector or node has been activated in the recent past. Note that this usage of "frequency" contrasts with the usage of "frequency" within the term "frequency estimate" (someone's assessment of how often an event has occurred in the past or how common an object is in the world).

frequency estimate An essential step in judgment, in which someone makes an assessment of how often they have experienced or encountered a particular object or event. (Ch. 12)

frontal lobes The lobe of the brain in each *cerebral hemisphere*

that includes the prefrontal area and the *primary motor projection area*. (Ch. 2)

functional fixedness A tendency to be rigid in how one thinks about an object's function. This generally involves a strong tendency to think of an object only in terms of its *typical* function. (Ch. 13)

functional magnetic resonance imaging (fMRI scan) A *neuroimaging technique* that uses magnetic fields to construct a detailed three-dimensional representation of the activity levels in different areas of the brain at a particular moment in time. (Ch. 2)

fusiform face area (FFA) A brain area apparently specialized for the perception of faces. (Ch. 2)

ganglion cells A type of *neuron* in the eye. The ganglion cells receive their input from the *bipolar cells*, and then the *axons* of the ganglion cells gather together to form the *optic nerve*, carrying information back to the *lateral geniculate nucleus*. (Ch. 3)

garden-path sentence A *sentence* that initially leads the reader to one understanding of how the sentence's words are related but then requires a change in this understanding to comprehend the full sentence. Examples are "The old man ships" and "The horse raced past the barn fell." (Ch. 10)

general intelligence (g) A mental capacity that is hypothesized as contributing to the performance of virtually any intellectual task. The existence of g is documented by the statistical overlap, usually revealed through *factor*

analysis, among diverse forms of mental testing. (Ch. 14)

generalizability A measure of whether it is legitimate to make claims about people and situations *not* involved in a study based on what was observed within the study.

generativity The trait that enables someone to combine and recombine basic units to create (or "generate") new and more complex entities. Linguistic rules, for example, are generative because they enable a person to combine and recombine a limited set of words to produce a vast number of *sentences*. (Ch. 10)

geons Basic shapes proposed as the building blocks of all complex three-dimensional forms. Geons take the form of cylinders, cones, blocks, and the like, and they are combined to form "geon assemblies." These are then combined to produce entire objects. (Ch. 4)

Gestalt principles A small number of rules that seem to govern how observers organize the visual input, grouping some elements together but perceiving other elements to be independent of one another. (Ch. 3)

glia A type of cell found (along with *neurons*) in the central nervous system. Glial cells have many functions, including the support of neurons, the repair of neural connections in case of damage, and a key role in guiding the initial development of neural connections. A specialized type of glia also provide electrical insulation for some neurons, allowing much faster transmission of neuronal signals. (Ch. 2)

goal neglect A pattern of behavior in which people fail to keep their goal in mind, so that, for example, they rely on habitual responses even if those responses will not move them toward the goal. (Ch. 5)

graded membership The idea that some members of a category are "better" members and therefore are more firmly in the category than other members. (Ch. 9)

heuristic A strategy that is reasonably efficient and works most of the time. In using a heuristic, the person is choosing to accept some risk of error in order to gain efficiency. (Ch. 12)

hill-climbing strategy A commonly used strategy in *problem solving*. If people use this strategy, then whenever their efforts toward solving a problem give them a choice, they will choose the option that carries them closer to the goal. (Ch. 13)

hindbrain One of the three main structures (along with the *forebrain* and the *midbrain*) of the brain; the hindbrain sits atop the spinal cord and includes several structures crucial for controlling key life functions. (Ch. 2)

hippocampus (pl. hippocampi) A structure in the *temporal lobe* that is involved in the creation of *long-term memories* and spatial memory. (Ch. 2)

holistic perception A process in which the ability to identify an object depends on the whole, or the entire configuration, rather than on an inventory of the object's parts. In holistic perception, the parts do play a role—but by virtue of creating the patterns that are critical for recognition. (Ch. 4)

hub and spoke model A proposal for how concepts might be represented in the brain, with tissue in the anterior *temporal lobes* serving as the "hub"—a brain location that connects and integrates information from many other brain areas. The "spokes" represent more specific elements of the concept—with (for example) visual information relevant to the concept stored in visual areas; relevant action information stored in motor areas; and so on. (Ch. 9)

hypothalamus A small structure at the base of the *forebrain* that plays a vital role in the control of motivated behaviors such as eating, drinking, and sexual activity. (Ch. 2)

ill-defined problem A problem for which the goal state is specified only in general terms and the operations available for reaching the goal state are not obvious at the start. (Ch. 13)

illumination The third in a series of stages often hypothesized as crucial for creativity. The first stage is *preparation*; the second, *incubation*. Illumination is the stage in which some new key insight or new idea suddenly comes to mind and is then (on this hypothesis) followed by *verification*. (Ch. 13)

illusion of truth An effect of *implicit memory* in which claims that are familiar end up seeming more plausible. (Ch. 7)

image-scanning procedure An experimental procedure in which participants are instructed to form a specific mental image and then are asked to scan, with their "mind's eye," from one point in the image to another. By timing these scans, the experimenter can determine how long "travel" takes across a mental image. (Ch. 11)

implicit memory A memory revealed by *indirect memory testing* and often manifested as a *priming* effect in which current performance is guided or facilitated by previous experiences. Implicit memories are often accompanied by no conscious realization that one is, in fact, being influenced by specific past experiences. Often contrasted with *explicit memory*. (Ch. 7)

inattentional blindness A pattern in which perceivers seem literally not to see stimuli right in front of their eyes; this pattern is caused by the participants focusing their attention on some other stimulus and not expecting the target to appear. (Ch. 5)

incidental learning Learning that takes place in the absence of any intention to learn and, correspondingly, in the absence of any expectation of a subsequent memory test. Often contrasted with *intentional learning*. (Ch. 6)

incubation The second in a series of stages that are often hypothesized as crucial for creativity. The first stage is *preparation*; the third, *illumination*; the fourth, *verification*. Incubation is hypothesized to involve events that occur when a person puts a problem out of their conscious thoughts but continues nonetheless to work on the problem unconsciously. Many current psychologists are skeptical about this process, and they propose alternative accounts for data that ostensibly document incubation. (Ch. 13)

independent variable The factor that distinguishes the *control* and *experimental conditions*; in most studies, the researcher hopes to learn whether the independent variable has some impact. If it does, this impact will emerge as a contrast between the experimental and the control conditions. In many studies, an independent variable has two "levels"—absent (in the control condition) versus present (in the experimental condition). The independent variable is also sometimes called the "predictor variable" because the study is asking, in effect, whether we can use this variable to predict the study's outcome.

indirect memory testing A form of memory testing in which research participants are not told that their memories are being tested. Instead, they're tested in such a way that previous experiences can influence current behavior. Examples of indirect tests include *word-stem completion*, the *lexical-decision task*, and *tachistoscopic* recognition. Often contrasted with *direct memory testing*. (Ch. 7)

induction A pattern of reasoning in which a person seeks to draw general claims from specific bits of evidence. Often contrasted with *deduction*. (Ch. 12)

inhibitory connection A link from one node, or one *detector*, to another, such that activation of one node decreases the *activation level* of the other. Often contrasted with *excitatory connection*. (Ch. 4)

inspection time The time a person needs to make a simple discrimination between two stimuli; used in some settings as a measure of mental speed, and then used as a way to test the claim that intelligent people literally are capable of faster processing in their brains. (Ch. 14)

integrative agnosia A disorder caused by a specific form of damage to the *parietal lobe*; people with this disorder appear relatively normal in tasks requiring them to detect whether specific features are present in a display, but they are impaired in tasks requiring them to judge how the features are bound together to form complex objects.

intentional learning The acquisition of memories in a setting in which people know that their memory for the information will be tested later. Often contrasted with *incidental learning*. (Ch. 6)

interference theory The hypothesis that materials are lost from memory because of interference from other materials that are also in memory. Interference caused by materials learned prior to the learning episode is called "proactive interference"; interference caused by materials learned after the learning episode is called "retroactive interference." (Ch. 8)

interposition A *monocular distance* cue that relies on the fact that objects farther away are blocked from view by closer objects that happen to be in the viewer's line of sight. (Ch. 3)

inter-rater reliability A measure of agreement among different judges, all called on to evaluate some idea or product or behavior. If this form of *reliability* is high, we know that the evaluations are neither arbitrary nor idiosyncratic.

introspection The process through which one "looks within," to observe and record the contents of one's own mental life. (Ch. 1)

intrusion error A memory error in which a person recalls elements that were not part of the original episode. (Ch. 8)

invalid experiment An experimental procedure that for some reason does not measure what it is intended to measure. Often, this is because the experiment includes a *confound*.

invalid syllogisms A syllogism (such as a *categorical syllogism*, or a syllogism built on a *conditional statement*) in which the conclusion is not logically demanded by the *premises*. (Ch. 12)

inversion effect A pattern typically observed for faces in which the specific face is much more difficult to recognize if the face is presented upside-down; this effect is part of the evidence indicating that face recognition relies on processes different from those involved in other forms of recognition. (Ch. 4)

Korsakoff's syndrome A clinical syndrome characterized primarily by dense *anterograde amnesia*. Korsakoff's syndrome is caused by damage to specific brain regions, and it is often precipitated by a form of malnutrition that is common among long-term alcoholics. (Ch. 7)

lateral fissure The separation dividing the *frontal lobes* on each side of the brain from the *temporal lobes*. (Ch. 2)

lateral geniculate nucleus (LGN) An important way station in the *thalamus* that is the first destination for visual information sent from the eyeball to the brain. (Ch. 3)

lateral inhibition A pattern in which cells, when stimulated, inhibit the activity of neighboring cells. In the visual system, lateral inhibition in the *optic nerve* creates *edge enhancement*. (Ch. 3)

late selection hypothesis A proposal that *selective attention* operates at a late stage of processing, so that the unattended inputs receive considerable analysis. (Ch. 5)

lens The transparent tissue located near the front of each eye that (together with the *cornea*) plays an important role in focusing incoming light. Muscles control the degree of curvature of the lens, allowing the eye to form a sharp image on the *retina*. (Ch. 3)

lesion A specific area of tissue damage. (Ch. 2)

level of processing An assessment of how "deeply" newly learned materials are engaged; *shallow processing* involves thinking only about the material's superficial traits, whereas *deep processing* involves thinking about what the material means. Deep processing is typically associated with a greater probability of remembering the now-processed information. (Ch. 6)

lexical-decision task A test in which participants are shown strings of letters and must indicate, as quickly as possible, whether or not each string of letters is a word in their language. It is proposed that people perform this task by "looking up" these strings in their "mental dictionary." (Ch. 7)

limbic system A set of brain structures including the *amygdala, hippocampus,* and parts of the *thalamus*. The limbic system is believed to be involved in the control of emotional behavior and motivation, and it also plays a key role in learning and memory. (Ch. 2)

limited-capacity system A group of processes in which *mental resources* are limited, so that extra resources supplied to one process must be balanced by a withdrawal of resources somewhere else—with the result that the total resources expended do not exceed the limit of what is available. (Ch. 5)

linear perspective A cue for distance based on the fact that parallel lines seem to converge as they get farther away from the viewer. (Ch. 3)

linguistic relativity The proposal that the language people speak shapes their thought, because the structure and vocabulary of their language create certain ways of thinking about the world. (Ch. 10)

localization of function The research endeavor of determining what specific job is performed by a particular region of the brain. (Ch. 2)

local representation A mode of representation in which information is encoded in a small number of identifiable nodes. Local representations are sometimes spoken of as "one idea per node" or "one content per location." Often contrasted with *distributed representation*. (Ch. 4)

longitudinal fissure The separation dividing the brain's left *cerebral hemisphere* from the right. (Ch. 2)

long-term memory (LTM) The storage system in which we hold all of our knowledge and all of our memories. Long-term memory contains memories that are not currently activated; those that are activated are represented in *working memory*. (Ch. 6)

Mach band A type of illusion in which one perceives a region to be slightly darker if it is adjacent to a bright region, and also perceives a region to be slightly brighter if it is adjacent to a dark region. This illusion, created by *lateral inhibition*, contributes to *edge enhancement*. (Ch. 3)

magnetic resonance imaging (MRI scan) A *neuroimaging technique* that uses magnetic fields (created by radio waves) to construct a detailed three-dimensional representation of brain tissue. Like *CT scans*, MRI scans reveal the brain's anatomy, but they are much more precise than CT scans. (Ch. 2)

maintenance rehearsal A rote, mechanical process in which items are continually cycled through *working memory*, merely by being repeated over and over. Often contrasted with *relational (or elaborative) rehearsal*. (Ch. 6)

manner of production The way in which a speaker momentarily obstructs the flow of air out of the lungs to produce a speech sound. For example, the airflow can be fully stopped for a moment, as in the [t] or [b] sound; or the air can continue to flow, as in the pronunciation of [f] or [v]. (Ch. 10)

mapping The process of figuring out how aspects of one situation or argument correspond to aspects of some other situation or argument; this process is crucial for a problem solver's ability to find and use analogies. (Ch. 13)

mask A visual presentation that is used to interrupt the processing of another visual stimulus. (Ch. 4)

means-end analysis A strategy used in *problem solving* in which the person is guided, step by step, by the difference between the current state and the goal state, and by asking what operations are available for reducing that difference. (Ch. 13)

memory rehearsal Any mental activity that has the effect of maintaining information in *working memory*. Two types of rehearsal are often distinguished: *maintenance rehearsal* and *relational (or elaborative) rehearsal*. (Ch. 6)

mental resources Some process or capacity needed for performance, but in limited supply. (Ch. 5)

mental rotation task An experimental procedure in which participants have to determine whether a shape differs from a target only in its position and orientation or whether the shape has a form different from the shape of the target. (Ch. 11)

metacognitive skills Skills that allow people to monitor and control their own mental processes. (Ch. 15)

metalinguistic judgments Cases in which people are asked to assess or evaluate language, as opposed to using language as they ordinarily would. For example, if asked to assess grammaticality ("Is 'The elephant trampled flowers the' a grammatical sentence?"), people would be making a metalinguistic judgment.

metamemory People's knowledge about, awareness of, and control over their own memory. (Ch. 15)

midbrain One of the three main structures (along with the *forebrain* and the *hindbrain*) of the brain; the midbrain plays an important role in coordinating movements, and it contains structures that serve as "relay" stations for information arriving from the sensory organs. (Ch. 2)

mind-body problem The difficulty in understanding how the mind (a nonphysical entity) and the body (a physical entity) can influence each other, so that physical events can cause mental events, and mental events can cause physical ones. (Ch. 15)

misinformation effect An effect in which reports about an earlier event are influenced by misinformation that the person received after experiencing the event. In the extreme, misinformation can be used to create false memories concerning an entire event that actually never occurred. (Ch. 8)

mnemonic strategies Techniques designed to improve memory accuracy and to make learning easier; in general, mnemonic strategies seek to help memory by imposing an organization on the materials to be learned. (Ch. 6)

modal model A nickname for a specific conception of the "architecture" of memory. In this model, *working memory* serves both as the storage site for material now being contemplated and as the "loading dock" for *long-term memory*. Information can reach working memory through the processes of perception, or it can be drawn from long-term memory. Once in working memory, material can be further processed or can simply be recycled for subsequent use. This model prompted a large quantity of valuable research, but it has now largely been set aside, with modern theorizing offering a very different conception of working memory. (Ch. 6)

monocular distance cues Features of the visual stimulus that indicate distance even if the stimulus is viewed with only one eye. (Ch. 3)

morpheme The smallest language unit that carries meaning. Psycholinguists distinguish content (or "free") morphemes (the primary carriers of meaning) from function (or "bound") morphemes (which specify the relations among words). (Ch. 10)

motion parallax A *distance cue* based on the fact that as an observer moves, the retinal images of nearby objects move more rapidly than do the retinal images of objects farther away. (Ch. 3)

myelin sheath The layer of tissue, formed by specialized *glial* cells, that provides insulation around the *axons* of many *neurons*. There are, however, gaps in this insulation, and the neuronal signal essentially has to "jump" from one gap to the next, dramatically increasing the speed of neurotransmission. (Ch. 2)

N The conventional abbreviation for the total number of participants in a study or, in some circumstances, the total number of participants in a particular condition.

Necker cube One of the classic *reversible (or ambiguous) figures*; the figure is a two-dimensional drawing that can be perceived as a cube viewed from above or as a cube viewed from below. (Ch. 3)

neural correlates of consciousness Events in the nervous system that occur at the same time as, and may be the biological basis of, a specific mental event or state. (Ch. 15)

neural synchrony A pattern of firing by *neurons* in which neurons in one brain area fire at the same time as neurons in another area; the brain seems to use this pattern as an indication that the neurons in different areas are firing in response to the same stimulus. (Ch. 3)

neuroimaging techniques Non-invasive methods for examining either the structure or the activation pattern within a living brain. (Ch. 1, Ch 2.)

neuron An individual cell within the nervous system. (Ch. 2)

neuronal workspace hypothesis A specific claim about how the brain makes conscious experience possible; the proposal is that "workspace neurons" link together the activity of various specialized brain areas, and this linkage makes possible integration and comparison of different types of information. (Ch. 15)

neurotransmitter One of the chemicals released by *neurons* to stimulate adjacent neurons. See also *synapse*. (Ch. 2)

node An individual unit within an associative network. In a scheme using *local representations*, nodes represent single ideas or concepts. In a scheme using *distributed representations*, ideas or concepts are represented by a pattern of activation across a wide number of nodes; the same nodes may also participate in other patterns and therefore in other representations. (Ch. 7)

nonfluent aphasia A disruption of language, caused by brain damage, in which a person loses the ability to speak or write with any fluency. Often contrasted with *fluent aphasia*. (Ch. 10)

occipital lobes The rearmost lobe in each *cerebral hemisphere*, and the one that includes the primary visual projection area. (Ch. 2)

operation span A measure of *working memory*'s capacity. This measure turns out to be predictive of performance in many other tasks, presumably because these tasks all rely on working memory. This measure is also the modern replacement for the (less useful) measure obtained from the *digit-span task*. (Ch. 6)

optic flow The pattern of change in the retinal image in which the image grows larger as the viewer approaches an object and shrinks as the viewer retreats from it. (Ch. 3)

optic nerve The bundle of nerve fibers, formed from the *retina's ganglion cells*, that carries information from the eyeball to the brain. (Ch. 3)

overregularization error In speech production, an error in which a person produces a form that is consistent with a broad pattern, even though that pattern does not apply to the current utterance. Examples would include uttering the word "foots" (applying the general pattern for plurals to the word "foot") or uttering the word "runned" (applying the general pattern for the past tense to the word "run"). Alternatively, in perception or in memory, an error in which someone perceives or remembers a word or event as being closer to the "norm" than it really is. For example, misspelled words are read as though they were spelled correctly; atypical events are misremembered in a way that brings them closer to more-typical events. (Ch. 10)

parallel distributed processing (PDP) A system of handling information in which many steps happen at once (i.e., in parallel) and in which various aspects of the problem or task are represented only in a distributed way. (Ch. 9)

parallel processing A system in which many steps are going on at the same time. Usually contrasted with *serial processing*. (Ch. 3)

parietal lobes The lobe in each *cerebral hemisphere* that lies between the *occipital* and *frontal lobes* and that includes some of the *primary sensory projection areas*, as well as circuits that are crucial for the control of attention. (Ch. 2)

parse To divide an input into its appropriate elements—for example, dividing the stream of incoming speech into its constituent words—or a sequence of words into its constituent phrases. In some settings, parsing also includes the additional step of determining each element's role within the sequence. (Ch. 10)

peer-review process A key step of quality control used in almost all sciences. This process is typically linked to publication in one of the field's specialized journals. Before an article is published, the editor solicits an evaluation of the article from scientists who know the material (the methods, the background) just as well as the paper's authors do. These people are therefore the author's "peers," and their evaluation guides the editor in deciding whether a paper should be published or not. Generally, a paper is published only if the peers find no flaws and no problems; and, in turn, a paper is taken seriously by other scientists only if it is published (and therefore has passed this test).

peg-word system A type of *mnemonic strategy* using words or locations as "pegs" on which to "hang" the materials to be remembered. (Ch. 6)

percepts Internal representations of the world that result from perceiving; percepts are organized depictions. (Ch. 11)

perceptual constancy The achievement of perceiving the constant properties of objects in the world (e.g., their size, shape, and color) despite changes in the sensory information we receive that are caused by changes in our viewing circumstances. (Ch. 3)

perseveration error A pattern of responding in which a person produces the same response over and over, even though the person knows that the task requires a change in response. This pattern is often observed in patients with brain damage in the *frontal lobe*. (Ch. 5)

phoneme A unit of sound that distinguishes one word (or one *morpheme*) from another. For example, the words "peg" and "beg" differ in their initial phoneme—[p] in one case, [b] in the other. Some contrasts in sound, however, do not involve phonemes; these contrasts might indicate the speaker's emphasis or might involve a regional accent, but they do not change the identity of the words being spoken. (These contrasts are sometimes said to be "subphonemic.") (Ch. 10)

phonemic restoration effect A pattern in which people "hear" *phonemes* that actually are not presented but that are highly likely in that context. For example, if one is presented with the word "legislature" but with the [s] sound replaced by a cough, one is likely to hear the [s] sound anyhow. (Ch. 10)

phonological buffer A passive storage system used for holding a representation (essentially an "internal echo") of recently heard or self-produced sounds. (Ch. 6)

photoreceptors Cells on the *retina* that are sensitive to light and that respond (i.e., send a signal to adjacent cells) when they are stimulated by light. (Ch. 3)

phrase-structure rules Constraints that govern what elements must be contained within a phrase and, in many languages, what the sequence of those elements must be. (Ch. 10)

pictorial cues Patterns that can be represented on a flat surface to create the sense of a three-dimensional object or scene. (Ch. 3)

place of articulation The position at which a speaker momentarily obstructs the flow of air out of the lungs to produce a speech sound. For example, the place of articulation for the [b] sound is the lips; the place of articulation for the [d] sound is where the tongue briefly touches the roof of the mouth. (Ch. 10)

population The entire group about which an investigator wants to draw conclusions.

positron emission tomography (PET scan) A *neuroimaging technique* that determines how much glucose (the brain's fuel) is being used by specific areas of the brain at a particular moment in time. (Ch. 2)

postsynaptic membrane The cell membrane of the *neuron* "receiving" information across the *synapse*. Often contrasted with *presynaptic membrane*. (Ch. 2)

practical intelligence The ability to solve everyday problems through skilled reasoning that relies on tacit knowledge acquired through experience. (Ch. 14)

pragmatic rules Principles describing how language is ordinarily used; listeners rely on these principles to guide their interpretation of what they hear. For example, listeners rely on these rules when they interpret the question "Can you pass me the salt?" as a request for the salt, not an inquiry about someone's arm strength. (Ch. 10)

predictive validity An assessment of whether a test measures what it is intended to measure, based on whether the test scores correlate with (i.e., can predict) some other relevant criterion. (Ch. 14)

prefrontal cortex The outer surface (*cortex*) of the frontmost part of the brain (i.e., the frontmost part of the *frontal lobe*). The prefrontal cortex has many functions but is crucial for the planning of complex or novel behaviors, so this brain area is often mentioned as one of the main sites underlying the brain's executive functions. (Ch. 2)

premises The assertions used as the starting point for a logical argument. The premises may or may not be true; logic is concerned instead only with whether a conclusion follows from the premises. (Ch. 12)

preparation In *problem solving*, the first in a series of stages often hypothesized as crucial for creativity. The second stage is *incubation*; the third, *illumination*; the fourth, *verification*. Preparation is the stage in which one begins effortful work on the problem, often with little progress. (Ch. 13)

prescriptive rules Rules describing how things are supposed to be instead of how they are. Often called "normative rules" and contrasted with *descriptive rules*. (Ch. 10)

presynaptic membrane The cell membrane of the *neuron* "sending" information across the *synapse*. Often contrasted with *postsynaptic membrane*. (Ch. 2)

primacy effect An often-observed advantage in remembering the early-presented materials within a sequence of materials. This advantage is generally attributed to the fact that research participants can focus their full attention on these items because, at the beginning of a sequence, the participants are not trying to divide attention between these items and other items in the series. Often contrasted with the *recency effect*. (Ch. 6)

primary motor projection area The strip of tissue, located at the rear of the *frontal lobe*, that is the departure point for nerve cells that send their signals to lower portions of the brain and spinal cord, and that ultimately result in muscle movement. (Ch. 2)

primary sensory projection area The main point of arrival in the *cortex* for information arriving from the eyes, ears, and other sense organs. (Ch. 2)

priming A process through which one input or cue prepares a person for an upcoming input or cue. (Ch. 4)

problem solving A process in which a person begins with a goal and seeks some steps that will lead toward that goal. (Ch. 13)

problem-solving set The starting assumptions that a person uses when trying to solve a new problem. These assumptions are often helpful, because they guide the person away from pointless strategies. But these assumptions can sometimes steer the person away from worthwhile strategies, in which case they can be an obstacle to problem solving. (Ch. 13)

problem space The set of all states that can be reached in solving a problem, as the problem solver moves, by means of the problem's operations, from the problem's initial state toward its goal state. (Ch. 13)

processing fluency The speed or ease of processing involved in recognizing or thinking about a stimulus or idea; usually understood as a reflection of the speed or ease with which activation moves through a *processing pathway*. (Ch. 7)

processing pathway The sequence of *nodes* and connections between nodes through which activation flows when recognizing or thinking about a stimulus or idea. The speed or ease of activation flow is referred to as *processing fluency*. (Ch. 7)

production task An experimental procedure used in studying concepts, in which the participant is asked to name as many examples (e.g., as many fruits) as possible. (Ch. 9)

propositions The smallest unit of knowledge that can be either true or false. Propositions are often expressed via simple *sentences*, but this is merely a convenience; other modes of representation are available. (Ch. 9)

prosody The pattern of pauses and pitch changes that characterize speech production. Prosody can be used (among other functions) to emphasize elements of a spoken *sentence*, to highlight the sentence's intended structure, or to signal the difference between a question and an assertion. (Ch. 10)

prosopagnosia A syndrome in which individuals lose their ability to recognize faces and to make other fine-grained discriminations within a highly familiar category, even though their other visual abilities seem intact. (Ch. 4)

prototype A single "best example," or average, identifying the "center" of a category. (Ch. 9)

qualia (**sing. quale**) The subjective conscious experiences, or "raw feelings," of awareness. Examples include the pain of a headache and the exact flavor of chocolate. (Ch. 15)

r The numerical value used in assessing a *correlation*, varying from −1.00 (a perfect inverse correlation) to +1.00 (a perfect correlation).

r^2 The numerical value calculated by multiplying r by itself (that is, by squaring r). This value tells you how much of the overall variation in one measure can be predicted, based on some second (predictor) measure. Equivalently, this value tells you how much your uncertainty about the first measure is reduced if you also have access to a second measure that predicts the first. If the second measure provides no basis for prediction, then r^2 is zero. If the second measure perfectly predicts the target value, then r^2 is 1.0.

random assignment A procedural step in which participants are assigned randomly (perhaps through a coin toss) to one condition of a study or another. This step ensures that there are no consistent or systematic differences between the participant groups in the two conditions.

random sampling A procedure in which every member of the *population* being studied has an equal chance of being picked for inclusion in the data collection.

rating task A task in which research participants must evaluate some item or category with reference to some dimension, usually expressing their response in terms of some number. For example, they might be asked to evaluate birds for how *typical* they are within the category "birds," using a "1" response to indicate "very typical" and a "7" response to indicate "very atypical." (Ch. 9)

reason-based choice A proposal for how people make decisions. The central idea is that people make a choice when—and only when—they detect what they believe to be a persuasive reason for making that choice. (Ch. 12)

recall The task of memory *retrieval* in which the rememberer must come up with the desired materials, sometimes in response to a cue that names the context in which these materials were earlier encountered (e.g., "Name the pictures you saw earlier"), and sometimes in response to a cue that broadly identifies the sought-after information (e.g., "Name a fruit" or "What is the capital of California?"). Often contrasted with *recognition*. (Ch. 7)

recency One of the central influences on a *detector*'s or *node*'s activation level. Recency refers to whether the detector or node has been activated in the recent past. Often contrasted with *frequency*— whether the detector or node has been activated often in

the past. Note that this usage of "recency" contrasts with the usage of "recency" within the term "recency effect" (a memory advantage for some types of material).

recency effect The tendency to remember materials that occur late in a series. If the series was just presented, the recency effect can be attributed to the fact that the late-arriving items are still in *working memory* (because nothing else has arrived after these items to bump them out of working memory). Often contrasted with the *primacy effect*. (Ch. 6)

receptive field The portion of the visual field to which a cell within the visual system responds. If the appropriately shaped stimulus appears in the appropriate position, the cell's firing rate will change. The firing rate will not change if the stimulus is of the wrong form or is in the wrong position. (Ch. 3)

recognition The task of memory *retrieval* in which the items to be remembered are presented and the person must decide whether or not the item was encountered in some earlier circumstance. For example, one might be asked, "Have you ever seen this person before?" or "Is this the poster you saw in the office yesterday?" Often contrasted with *recall*. (Ch. 7)

recognition by components (RBC) model A model of *object recognition*. In this model, a crucial role is played by *geons*, the (hypothesized) basic building blocks out of which all the objects we recognize are constructed. (Ch. 4)

relational (or elaborative) rehearsal A form of mental processing in which one thinks about the relations, or connections, among ideas. The connections created (or strengthened) in this way will later guide memory search. (Ch. 6)

reliability The degree of consistency with which a test measures a trait or attribute. See also *test-retest reliability.* (Ch. 14)

"remember/know" distinction A distinction between two experiences a person can have in recalling a past event. If you "remember" having encountered a stimulus before, then you usually can offer information about that encounter, including when, where, and how it occurred. If you merely "know" that you encountered a stimulus before, then you're likely to have a sense of *familiarity* with the stimulus but may have no idea when or where it was last encountered. (Ch. 7)

repetition priming A pattern of *priming* that occurs simply because a stimulus is presented a second time; processing is more efficient on the second presentation. (Ch. 4)

replication A re-running of a study in order to ask whether the results are *reliable* (i.e., emerge in the subsequent running of the study just as they did in the first). In a "direct" replication, the researchers repeat the earlier experiment with no changes. In a "conceptual" replication, the researchers use a slightly different procedure to test the hypothesis or confirm the initial result.

representativeness heuristic A strategy that is often used in making judgments about categories. This strategy is broadly equivalent to making the assumption that, in general, the instances of a category will resemble the *prototype* for that category and, likewise, that the prototype resembles each instance. (Ch. 12)

response threshold The quantity of information or activation needed to trigger a response in a *node* or *detector*, or, in a neuroscience context, a response from a *neuron.* (Ch. 4)

response time (RT) The amount of time (usually measured in milliseconds) needed for a person to respond to a particular event (such as a question or a cue to press a specific button). (Ch. 1)

retention interval The amount of time that passes between the initial learning of some material and the subsequent memory *retrieval* of that material. (Ch. 8)

retina The light-sensitive tissue that lines the back of the eyeball. (Ch. 3)

retrieval The process of locating information in memory and activating that information for use. (Ch. 6)

retrieval failure A mechanism that probably contributes to a great deal of forgetting. Retrieval failure occurs when a memory is, in fact, in long-term storage but the person is unable to locate that memory when trying to retrieve it. (Ch. 8)

retrieval paths A connection (or series of connections) that can lead to a sought-after memory in long-term storage. (Ch. 6)

retrograde amnesia An inability to remember experiences that occurred before the event that triggered the memory disruption. Often contrasted with *anterograde amnesia.* (Ch. 7)

reversible (or ambiguous) figure Drawings that can be readily perceived in more than one way. Classic examples include the vase/profiles, the duck/rabbit, and the *Necker cube.* (Ch. 3)

risk aversion A tendency toward avoiding risk. People tend to be risk averse when contemplating gains, choosing instead to hold tight to what they already have. Often contrasted with *risk seeking.* (Ch. 12)

risk seeking A tendency toward seeking out risk. People tend to be risk seeking when contemplating losses, presumably because they're willing to gamble in hopes of avoiding (or diminishing) their losses. Often contrasted with *risk aversion.* (Ch. 12)

rods *Photoreceptors* that are sensitive to very low light levels but that are unable to discriminate hues and that have relatively poor *acuity.* Often contrasted with *cones.* (Ch. 3)

sample The subset of the *population* that an investigator studies to learn about the population at large.

savant syndrome A pattern of traits in a disabled person such that the person has some remarkable talent that contrasts with their very low level of *general intelligence.* (Ch. 14)

schema Knowledge describing what is typical or frequent in a particular situation. For example, a "kitchen schema" would stipulate that a stove and refrigerator are likely to be present, whereas a coffeemaker may be or may not be present, and a piano is not likely to be present. (Ch. 8)

selection task An experimental procedure, commonly used to study reasoning, in which a person is presented with four cards with certain information on either side of the card. The person is also given a rule that may describe the cards, and the person's task is to decide which cards must be turned over to find out if the rule describes the cards or not. Also called the *four-card task*. (Ch. 12)

selective attention The skill through which a person focuses on one input or one task while ignoring other stimuli that are also on the scene. (Ch. 5)

self-report data A form of evidence in which a person is asked directly about their own thoughts or experiences. (Ch. 11)

self-schema The set of interwoven beliefs and memories that constitute one's knowledge about oneself.

self-selected group A comparison in which research participants decide for themselves which condition of the study they will be in (e.g., the *control condition* or the *experimental condition*). This situation is likely to cause concern about a *third-variable problem* because presumably participants choose one condition or another for some reason—some preference or trait or inclination that the participants have prior to the study. The concern, then, is that the preexisting preference or trait, and not the *independent variable*, might be causing the difference observed in the *dependent variable*.

semantic priming A process in which activation of an idea in memory causes activation to spread to other ideas related to the first in meaning. (Ch. 7)

sensory memory A form of memory that holds on to just-seen or just-heard input in a "raw" sensory form. (Ch. 6)

sentence A sequence of words that conforms to the rules of *syntax* (and so has the right constituents in the right sequence). (Ch. 10)

sentence verification task An experimental procedure used for studying memory in which participants are given simple *sentences* (e.g., "Cats are animals") and must respond as quickly as possible whether the sentence is true or false. (Ch. 9)

serial position A data pattern summarizing the relationship between some performance measure (often, likelihood of *recall*) and the order in which the test materials were presented (i.e., where the materials were located within the series). In memory studies, the serial-position curve tends to be U-shaped, with people being best able to recall the first-presented items (the *primacy effect*) and also the last-presented items (the *recency effect*). (Ch. 6)

serial processing A system in which only one step happens at a time (and so the steps occur in a series). Usually contrasted with *parallel processing*. (Ch. 3)

shadowing A task in which research participants repeat back a verbal input, word for word, as they hear it. (Ch. 5)

shallow processing A mode of thinking about material in which one pays attention only to appearances and other superficial aspects of the material; shallow processing typically leads to poor memory retention. Often contrasted with *deep processing*. (Ch. 6)

shape constancy The achievement of perceiving the constant shape of objects despite changes in the shape of the retinal image that result from variations in viewing angle. (Ch. 3)

short-term memory An older term for what is now called *working memory*. (Ch. 6)

single-cell recording A technique for recording the moment-by-moment *activation level* of an individual *neuron* within a healthy, normally functioning brain. (Ch. 3)

size constancy The achievement of perceiving the constant size of objects despite changes in the size of the retinal image that result from variations in viewing distance. (Ch. 3)

somatic markers States of the body used in decision making. For example, a tight stomach and an accelerated heart rate when a person is thinking about a particular option can signal to the person that the option has risk associated with it. (Ch. 12)

source confusion A memory error in which one misremembers where a bit of information was learned or where a particular stimulus was last encountered. (Ch. 7)

source memory A form of memory that enables a person to recollect the episode in which learning took place or the time and place in which a particular stimulus was encountered. (Ch. 7)

spatial attention The mechanism through which people allocate processing resources to particular positions in space, so that they more efficiently process any inputs from that region in space. (Ch. 5)

specific-language impairment (SLI) A disorder in which individuals seem to have normal intelligence but experience problems in learning the rules of language. (Ch. 10)

speech segmentation The process through which a stream of speech is "sliced" into its constituent words and, within words, into the constituent *phonemes*. (Ch. 10)

spreading activation A process through which activation travels from one *node* to another, via *associative links*. As each node becomes activated, it serves as a source for further activation, spreading onward through the network. (Ch. 7)

stereotype threat A mechanism through which a person's performance is influenced by the perception that their score will confirm stereotypes about their group. (Ch. 14)

storage The state in which a memory, once acquired, remains until it is retrieved. Many people understand storage to be a "dormant" process, so that the memory remains unchanged while it is in storage. Modern theories, however, describe a more dynamic form of storage,

in which older memories are integrated with (and sometimes replaced by) newer knowledge. (Ch. 6)

Stroop interference A classic demonstration of *automaticity* in which research participants are asked to name the color of ink used to print a word, and the word itself is the name of a different color. For example, participants might see the word "YELLOW" printed in blue ink and be required to say "blue." Considerable interference is observed in this task, with participants apparently being unable to ignore the word's content even though it is irrelevant to their task. (Ch. 5)

subcortical structures Identified pieces of the brain that are underneath the *cortex* and therefore are hidden from view in drawings of an intact brain. These structures include the *thalamus*, the *hypothalamus*, and the various components of the *limbic system*. (Ch. 2)

subliminal perception A pattern in which people perceive and are in some ways influenced by inputs they did not consciously notice. (Ch. 15)

subthreshold activation *Activation levels* below *response threshold*. Subthreshold activation, by definition, will not trigger a response; nonetheless, this activation is important because it can accumulate, leading eventually to an *activation level* that reaches (or exceeds) the *response threshold*. (Ch. 7)

subvocalization Covert speech in which one goes through the motions of speaking, or perhaps forms a detailed motor

plan for speech movements, but without making any sound. (Ch. 6)

summation The addition of two or more separate inputs so that the effect of the combined inputs is greater than the effect of any one input by itself. (Ch. 7)

synapse The area that includes the *presynaptic membrane* of one *neuron*, the *postsynaptic membrane* of another neuron, and the tiny gap between them. The presynaptic membrane releases a small amount of *neurotransmitter* that drifts across the gap and stimulates the postsynaptic membrane. (Ch. 2)

syntax Rules governing the sequences and combinations of words in the formation of phrases and *sentences*. (Ch. 10)

systematic data collection A pattern of recording and collecting data for a study in which all of the evidence is collected, or, at least, in which evidence is collected in a way that is independent of the hypothesis being considered.

tachistoscope A device that allows the presentation of stimuli for precisely controlled amounts of time, including very brief presentations. (Ch. 4)

temporal lobes The lobe of the *cortex* lying inward and down from the temples. The temporal lobe in each *cerebral hemisphere* includes the primary auditory projection area, *Wernicke's area*, and, subcortically, the *amygdala* and *hippocampus*. (Ch. 2)

testable hypothesis A supposition about the facts that may or may not turn out to be true, but that is stated in a way that allows unambiguous testing— that is, it allows a persuasive determination of whether the supposition is true.

test-retest reliability An assessment of whether a test is consistent in what it measures from one occasion to another, determined by asking whether the test's results on one occasion are correlated with results from the same test (or a close variant on it) given at a later time. (Ch. 14)

thalamus A part of the lower portion of the *forebrain* that serves as a major relay and integration center for sensory information. (Ch. 2)

theory of multiple intelligences A proposal that there are many forms of intelligence, including linguistic, spatial, musical, bodily-kinesthetic, and personal. (Ch. 14)

third-variable problem A concern that arises when two variables (say: X and Y) are *correlated*. In such cases, there is likely to be some ambiguity about whether X causes Y or Y causes X. But, in addition, it is possible that neither of these variables causes the other. Instead, X and Y might be correlated because both are the result of some other factor (the "third variable"). An example might be taking Latin in high school and doing well in college. Here, the third variable might be "being academically serious and ambitious," which both leads a student to study Latin in high school and also enables the student to do well in college.

threshold The activity level at which a cell or *detector* responds, or fires. (Ch. 2)

top-down processing A sequence of events that is heavily shaped by the knowledge and expectations that the person brings to the situation. Often contrasted with *bottom-up processing*. (Ch. 4)

TOT phenomenon An often-observed effect in which people are unable to remember a particular word, even though they are certain that the word (typically identified via its definition) is in their vocabulary. People in this state often can remember the starting letter for the word and its number of syllables, and they insist that the word is on the "tip of their tongue" (therefore, the "TOT" label). (Ch. 8)

transcendental method A type of theorizing proposed by the philosopher Immanuel Kant. To use this method, an investigator first observes the effects or consequences of a process and then asks: What must the process have been to bring about these effects? (Ch. 1)

transcranial magnetic stimulation (TMS) A technique in which a series of strong magnetic pulses at a specific location on the scalp causes temporary disruption in the brain region directly underneath this scalp area. (Ch. 2)

tree structure A style of depiction often used to indicate hierarchical relationships, such as the relationships (specified by *phrase-structure rules*) among the words in a phrase or *sentence*. (Ch. 10)

Type 1 thinking A commonly used name for judgment and reasoning strategies that are fast and effortless, but prone to error. (Ch. 12)

Type 2 thinking A commonly used name for judgment and reasoning strategies that are slower and require more effort than *Type 1 thinking*. (Ch. 12)

typicality The degree to which a particular case (an object, situation, or event) is typical for its kind. (Ch. 9)

unattended channel A stimulus (or group of stimuli) that a person is not trying to perceive. Ordinarily, little information is understood or remembered from the unattended channel. Often contrasted with *attended channel*. (Ch. 5)

unconscious inference The hypothesized steps that perceivers follow in order to take one aspect of the visual scene (e.g., viewing distance) into account in judging another aspect (e.g., size). (Ch. 3)

unilateral neglect syndrome A pattern of symptoms in which affected individuals ignore all inputs coming from one side of space. Individuals with this syndrome put only one of their arms into their jackets, eat food from only half of their plates, read only half of words (e.g., they might read "blouse" as "use"), and so on. (Ch. 2)

utility maximization The proposal that people make decisions by selecting the option that has the greatest utility. (Ch. 12)

validity The extent to which a method or procedure measures what it is supposed to measure. Validity is assessed in a variety of ways, including through *predictive validity*. (Ch. 14)

valid syllogisms A syllogism for which the conclusion follows from the *premise*, in accord with the rules of logic. (Ch. 12)

verification One of the four steps that are commonly hypothesized as part of creative *problem solving*; in this step, the problem solver confirms that a new idea really does lead to a problem solution, and then they work out the details. (The other steps are *preparation, incubation,* and *illumination.*) (Ch. 13)

viewpoint-dependent recognition A process in which the ease or success of recognition depends on the perceiver's particular viewing angle or distance with regard to the target object.

viewpoint-independent recognition A process in which the ease or success of recognition does *not* depend on the perceiver's particular viewing angle or distance with regard to the target object.

visual features The elements of a visual pattern—vertical lines, curves, diagonals, and so on—that, together, form the overall pattern. (Ch. 3)

visual search task An often-used laboratory task in which research participants are asked to search for a specific target (e.g., a shape, or a shape of a certain color) within a field of other stimuli; usually, the researcher is interested in how quickly the participants can locate the target. (Ch. 4)

visuospatial buffer One of the low-level assistants used as part of the *working-memory system.* This buffer plays an important role in storing visual or spatial representations, including visual images.

voicing One of the properties that distinguishes different categories of speech sounds. A sound is considered "voiced" if the vocal folds are vibrating while the sound is produced. If the vocal folds start vibrating sometime after the sound begins (i.e., with a long voice-onset time), the sound is considered "unvoiced." (Ch. 10)

well-formedness A measure of the degree to which a string of symbols (usually letters) conforms to the usual patterns (for letters: the rules of spelling); for example, the nonword "FIKE" is well formed in English, but "IEFK" is not. (Ch. 4)

Wernicke's area An area in the *temporal lobe* of the brain, where the temporal and *parietal lobes* meet; damage here typically causes *fluent aphasia.* (Ch. 10)

what system The system of visual circuits and pathways leading from the visual *cortex* to the *temporal lobe* and especially involved in object recognition. Often contrasted with the *where system.* (Ch. 3)

where system The system of visual circuits and pathways leading from the visual *cortex* to the *parietal lobe* and especially involved in the spatial localization of objects and in the coordination of movements. Often contrasted with the *what system.* (Ch. 3)

word-stem completion A task in which research participants are given the beginning of a word (e.g., "TOM") and must provide a word that starts with the letters provided. In some versions of the task, only one solution is possible, so performance is measured by counting the number of words completed.

In other versions of the task, several solutions are possible for each stem, and performance is assessed by determining which responses fulfill some other criterion. (Ch. 7)

word-superiority effect (WSE) The data pattern in which research participants are more accurate and more efficient in recognizing letters if the letters appear within a word (or a word-like letter string) than they are in recognizing letters appearing in isolation. (Ch. 4)

working memory The storage system in which information is held while that information is being worked on. All indications are that working memory is a system, not a single entity, and that information is held here via active processes, not via some sort of passive storage. Formerly called *short-term memory.* (Ch. 6)

working-memory capacity (WMC) A measure of *working memory* derived from *operation span* tasks. Although termed a "memory capacity," this measure can perhaps best be understood as a measure of a person's ability to store some materials while simultaneously working with other materials. (Ch. 6)

working-memory system A system of mental resources used for holding information in an easily accessible form. The central executive is at the heart of this system, and the executive then relies on a number of low-level assistants, including the *visuospatial buffer* and the *articulatory rehearsal loop.* (Ch. 6)

References

Ackermann, S., & Rasch, B. (2014). Differential effects of non-REM and REM sleep on memory consolidation? *Current Neurology and Neuroscience Reports*, *14*(2), 430.

Aggleton, J. P., & Brown, M. W. (2006). Interleaving brain systems for episodic and recognition memory. *Trends in Cognitive Sciences*, *10*(10), 455–463.

Akers, K. G., Martinez-Canabal, A., Restivo, L., Yiu, A. P., De Cristofaro, A., Hsiang, H.-L. L, Wheeler, A. L., Guskjolen, A., Niibori, Y., Shoji, H., Ohira, K., Richards, B. A., Miyakawa, T., Josselyn, S. A., & Frankland, P. W. (2014, May 9). Hippocampal neurogenesis regulates forgetting during adulthood and infancy. *Science*, *344*(6184), 598–602.

Akhtar, S., Justice, L. V., Morrison, C. M., & Conway, M. A. (2018). Fictional first memories. *Psychological Science*, *29*(10), 1612–1619.

Albers, A. M., Kok, P., Toni, I., Dijkerman, H. C., & de Lange, F. P. (2013). Shared representations for working memory and mental imagery in early visual cortex. *Current Biology*, *23*(15), 1427–1431.

Alder, H., Michel, B. A., Marx, C., Tamborrini, G., Langenegger, T., Bruehlmann, P., Steurer, J., & Wildi, L. M. (2014). Computer-based diagnostic expert systems in rheumatology: Where do we stand in 2014? *International Journal of Rheumatology*, *2014*, 1–10.

Alexander, K. W., Quas, J. A., Goodman, G. S., Ghetti, S., Edelstein, R. S., Redlich, A. D., Cordon, I. M., Jones, D. P. H. (2005). Traumatic impact predicts long-term memory for documented child sexual abuse. *Psychological Science*, *16*(1), 33–40.

Alkire, M. T., Hudetz, A. G., & Tononi, G. (2008). Consciousness and anesthesia. *Science*, *322*(5903), 876–880.

Allen, A. L., & Strand, N. K. (2015). Cognitive enhancement and beyond: Recommendations from the Bioethics Commission. *Trends in Cognitive Sciences*, *19*(10), 549–555.

Allport, D. A., Antonis, B., & Reynolds, P. (1972). On the division of attention: A disproof of the single channel hypothesis. *Quarterly Journal of Experimental Psychology*, *24*(2), 225–235.

Altmann, E. M., & Schunn, C. D. (2012). Decay versus interference: A new look at an old interaction. *Psychological Science*, *23*(11), 1435–1437.

Alvarez, M. J., Miller, M. K., & Bornstein, B. H. (2016). "It will be your duty . . .": The psychology of criminal jury instructions. In M. K. Miller & B. H. Bornstein (Eds.), *Advances in psychology and law* (Vol. 1, pp. 119–158). New York, NY: Springer.

Amer, T., Ngo, K. W. J., & Hasher, L. (2016). Cultural differences in visual attention: Implications for distraction processing. *British Journal of Psychology*, *108*(2), 244–258.

American Civil Liberties Union. (2021). *Intellectual disability and the death penalty.* https://www.aclu.org/other/intellectual-disability-and-death-penalty

Amishav, R., & Kimchi, R. (2010). Perceptual integrality of componential and configural information in faces. *Psychonomic Bulletin & Review*, *17*(5), 743–748.

Anakwah, N., Horselenberg, R., Hope, L., Amankwah-Poku, M., & van Koppen, P. (2020). Cross-cultural differences in eyewitness memory reports. *Applied Cognitive Psychology*, *34*(2), 504–515.

Anderson, J. R. (1976). *Language, memory, and thought.* Hillsdale, NJ: Erlbaum.

Anderson, J. R. (1980). *Cognitive psychology and its implications.* San Francisco, CA: Freeman.

Anderson, J. R. (1993). Problem solving and learning. *American Psychologist*, *48*(1), 35–44.

Anderson, J. R., & Bower, G. H. (1973). *Human associative memory.* Washington, DC: Winston.

Anderson, M. C., & Bell, T. (2001). Forgetting our facts: The role of inhibitory processes in the loss of propositional knowledge. *Journal of Experimental Psychology: General*, *130*(3), 544–570.

Baird, B., Smallwood, J., Mrazek, M. D., Kam, J. W. Y., Franklin, M. S., & Schooler, J. W. (2012). Inspired by distraction: Mind wandering facilitates creative incubation. *Psychological Science, 23*(10), 1117–1122.

Ball, B. H., Vogel, A., Ellis, D. M., & Brewer, G. A. (2020). Wait a second . . . Boundary conditions on delayed responding theories of prospective memory. *Journal of Experimental Psychology: Learning, Memory, & Cognition.* Advance online publication. https://doi.org/10.1037/xlm0000976

Barasch, A., Diehl, K., Silverman, J., & Zauberman, G. (2017). Photographic memory: The effects of volitional photo-taking on memory for visual and auditory aspects of an experience. *Psychological Science, 28*(8), 1056–1066.

Barclay, J. R., Bransford, J. D., Franks, J. J., McCarrell, N. S., & Nitsch, K. (1974). Comprehension and semantic flexibility. *Journal of Verbal Learning & Verbal Behavior, 13*(4), 471–481.

Bargh, J. A. (2005). Bypassing the will: Toward demystifying the nonconscious control of social behavior. In R. R. Hasslin, J. S. Uleman, & J. A. Bargh (Eds.), *The new unconscious* (pp. 37–58). New York, NY: Oxford University Press.

Barkley, R. A., Murphy, K. R., & Fischer, M. (2008). *ADHD in adults: What the science says.* New York, NY: Guilford.

Baron, J., Scott, S., Fincher, K., & Emien Metz, S. (2015). Why does the Cognitive Reflection Test (sometimes) predict utilitarian moral judgments (among other things)? *Journal of Applied Research in Memory and Cognition, 4*(3), 265–284.

Barrett, H. C. (2020). Towards a cognitive science of the human: Cross-cultural approaches and their urgency. *Trends in Cognitive Sciences, 24*(8), 620–638.

Barsalou, L. W. (1983). Ad hoc categories. *Memory, & Cognition, 11,* 211–227.

Barsalou, L. W. (1985). Ideals, central tendency, and frequency of instantiation as determinants of graded structure in categories. *Journal of Experimental Psychology: Learning, Memory, & Cognition, 11*(4), 629–654.

Barsalou, L. W. (1988). The content and organization of autobiographical memories. In U. Neisser & E. Winograd (Eds.), *Remembering reconsidered: Ecological and traditional approaches to the study of memory* (pp. 193–243). New York, NY: Cambridge University Press.

Barsalou, L. W., & Sewell, D. R. (1985). Contrasting the representation of scripts and categories. *Journal of Memory and Language, 24*(6), 646–665.

Barsalou, L. W. (2008). Grounded cognition. *Annual Review of Psychology, 59,* 617–645.

Barsalou, L. W. (2016). On staying grounded and avoiding Quixotic dead ends. *Psychonomic Bulletin & Review, 23,* 1122–1142.

Bartlett, F. C. (1932). *Remembering: A study in experimental and social psychology.* Cambridge, England: Cambridge University Press.

Bartolomeo, P., Bachoud-Lévi, A.-C., De Gelder, B., Denes, G., Barba, G. D., Brugières, P., & Degos, J.-D. (1998). Multiple-domain dissociation between impaired visual perception and preserved mental imagery in a patient with bilateral extrastriate lesions. *Neuropsychologia, 36*(3), 239–249.

Bassok, M., & Novick, L. R. (2012). Problem solving. In K. J. Holyoak & R. G. Morrison (Eds.), *The Oxford handbook of thinking and reasoning* (pp. 413–432). New York, NY: Oxford University Press.

Bate, S., Bennetts, R., Hasshim, N., Portch, E., Murray, E., Burns, E., & Dudfield, G. (2019). The limits of super recognition: An other-ethnicity effect in individuals with extraordinary face recognition skills. *Journal of Experimental Psychology: Human Perception & Performance, 45*(3), 363–377.

Bate, S., Frowd, C., Bennetts, R., Hasshim, N., Portch, E., Murray, E., & Dudfield, G. (2019). The consistency of superior face recognition skills in police officers. *Applied Cognitive Psychology, 33*(5), 828–842.

Bates, T. C., Lewis, G. J., & Weiss, A. (2013). Childhood socioeconomic status amplifies genetic effects on adult intelligence. *Psychological Science, 24*(10), 2111–2116.

Bates, T. C., & Shieles, A. (2003). Crystallized intelligence as product of speed and drive for experience: The relationship of inspection time and openness to g and *Gc. Intelligence, 31*(3), 275–287.

Batty, G. D., Deary, I. J., & Gottfredson, L. S. (2006). Premorbid (early life) IQ and later mortality risk: Systematic review. *Annals of Epidemiology, 17*(4), 278–288.

Bauer, P. J., Larkina, M., Güler, E., & Burch, M. (2019). Long-term autobiographical memory across middle childhood: Patterns, predictors, and implications for conceptualizations of childhood amnesia. *Memory, 27*(9), 1175–1193.

Bayne, T., Hohwy, J., & Owen, A. M. (2016a). Are there levels of consciousness? *Trends in Cognitive Sciences, 20*(6), 405–413.

Bayne, T., Hohwy, J., & Owen, A. M. (2016b). Response to Fazekas and Overgaard: Degrees and levels. *Trends in Cognitive Sciences, 20*(10), 716–717.

Beach, C. M. (1991). The interpretation of prosodic patterns at points of syntactic structural ambiguity: Evidence for cue trading relations. *Journal of Memory and Language, 30*(6), 644–663.

Beaty, R. E., Silvia, P. J., Nusbaum, E. C., Jauk, E., & Benedek, M. (2014). The roles of associative and executive processes in creative cognition. *Memory & Cognition, 42*(7), 1186–1197.

Bechara, A., Damasio, H., & Damasio, A. R. (2003). Role of the amygdala in decision-making. *Annals of the New York Academy of Sciences, 985,* 356–369.

Bechara, A., Tranel, D., Damasio, H., Adolphs, R., Rockland, C., & Damasio, A. R. (1995). Double dissociation of conditioning and declarative knowledge relative to the amygdala and hippocampus in humans. *Science, 269*(5227), 1115–1118.

Becker-Blease, K., & Freyd, J. J. (2017). Additional questions about the applicability of "false memory" research. *Applied Cognitive Psychology, 31,* 34–36.

Becklen, R., & Cervone, D. (1983). Selective looking and the noticing of unexpected events. *Memory & Cognition, 11,* 601–608.

Bédard, J., & Chi, M. T. H. (1992). Expertise. *Current Directions in Psychological Science, 1,* 135–139.

Begg, I. M., Anas, A., & Farinacci, S. (1992). Dissociation of processes in belief: Source recollection, statement familiarity, and the illusion of truth. *Journal of Experimental Psychology: General, 121*(4), 446–458.

Begg, I., Armour, V., & Kerr, T. (1985). On believing what we remember. *Canadian Journal of Behavioural Science, 17*(3), 199–214.

Behrmann, M. (2000). The mind's eye mapped onto the brain's matter. *Current Directions in Psychological Science, 9*(2), 50–54.

Behrmann, M., & Avidan, G. (2005). Congenital prosopagnosia: Face-blind from birth. *Trends in Cognitive Sciences, 9*(4), 180–187.

Behrmann, M., & Tipper, S. P. (1999). Attention accesses multiple reference frames: Evidence from visual neglect. *Journal of Experimental Psychology: Human Perception and Performance, 25*(1), 83–101.

Bekerian, D. A., & Baddeley, A. D. (1980). Saturation advertising and the repetition effect. *Journal of Verbal Learning & Verbal Behavior, 19*(1), 17–25.

Benjamin, L. T., Jr. (2008). *A history of psychology: Original sources and contemporary research.* New York, NY: Wiley-Blackwell.

Berger, S. A., Hall, L. K., & Bahrick, H. P. (1999). Stabilizing access to marginal and submarginal knowledge. *Journal of Experimental Psychology: Applied, 5*(4), 438–447.

Berko, J. (1958). The child's learning of English morphology. *Word, 14*(2-3), 150–177.

Bernstein, D. M., Kumar, R. Masson, M. E. J., & Levitin, D. J. (2018). Fluency misattribution and auditory hindsight bias. *Memory & Cognition, 46*(8), 1331–1343.

Berntsen, D., Hoyle, R. H., & Rubin, D. C. (2019). The autobiographical recollection test (ART): A measure of individual differences in autobiographical memory. *Journal of Applied Research in Memory and Cognition, 8*(3), 305–318.

Besken, M., & Mulligan, N. W. (2014). Perceptual fluency, auditory generation, and metamemory: Analyzing the perceptual fluency hypothesis in the auditory modality. *Journal of Experimental Psychology: Learning, Memory, & Cognition, 40*(2), 429–440.

Besner, D., Risko, E. F., Stolz, J. A., White, D., Reynolds, M., O'Malley, S., & Robidoux, S. (2016). Varieties of attention: Their roles in word recognition. *Current Directions in Psychological Science, 25*(3), 162–168.

Bever, T. (1970). The cognitive basis for linguistic structures. In J. R. Hayes (Ed.), *Cognition and the development of language* (pp. 279–362). New York, NY: Wiley.

Bialystok, E., Craik, F. I. M., Green, D. W., & Gollan, T. H. (2009). Bilingual minds. *Psychological Science in the Public Interest, 10*(3), 89–129

Bialystok, E., & Grundy, J. G. (2018). Science does not disengage. *Cognition, 170,* 330–333.

Biancarosa, G., & Griffiths, G. G. (2012). Technology tools to support reading in the digital age. *The Future of Children, 22*(2), 139–160.

Bidrose, S., & Goodman, G. S. (2000). Testimony and evidence: A scientific case study of memory for child sexual abuse. *Applied Cognitive Psychology, 14*(3), 197–213.

Biederman, I. (1987). Recognition-by-components: A theory of human image understanding. *Psychological Review, 94*(2), 115–147.

Biederman, I. (1990). Higher-level vision. In D. N. Osherson, S. M. Kosslyn, & J. M. Hollerbach (Eds.), *Visual cognition and action: An invitation to cognitive science* (Vol. 2, pp. 41–72). Cambridge, MA: MIT Press.

Biederman, I., & Shiffrar, M. M. (1987). Sexing day-old chicks: A case study and expert systems analysis of a difficult perceptual-learning task. *Journal of Experimental Psychology: Learning, Memory, & Cognition, 13*(4), 640–645.

Bilow, R. (2014, June 30). *How IBM's Chef Watson actually works.* Bon Appetit. https://www.bonappetit.com/entertaining-style/trends-news/article/how-ibm-chef-watson-works

Bindemann, M., Brown, C., Koyas, T., & Russ, A. (2012). Individual differences in face identification postdict eyewitness accuracy. *Journal of Applied Research in Memory & Cognition, 1*(2), 96–103.

Birch, S. A. J., Brosseau-Liard, P. E., Haddock, T., & Ghrear, S. E. (2017). A "curse of knowledge" in the absence of knowledge? People misattribute fluency when judging how common knowledge is among their peers. *Cognition, 166,* 447–458.

Bisby, J. A., Burgess, N., & Brewin, C. R. (2020). Reduced memory coherence for negative events and its relationship to posttraumatic stress disorder. *Current Directions in Psychological Science, 29*(3), 267–272.

Bishop, D. V. M., & Norbury, C. F. (2008). Speech and language disorders. In M. Rutter, D. Bishop, D. Pine, S. Scott, J. Stevenson, E. Taylor, & A. Thapar (Eds.), *Rutter's child and adolescent psychiatry* (pp. 782–801). Oxford, England: Blackwell.

Bisiach, E., & Luzzatti, C. (1978). Unilateral neglect of representational space. *Cortex, 14*(1), 129–133.

Bisiach, E., Luzzatti, C., & Perani, D. (1979). Unilateral neglect, representational schema, and consciousness. *Brain*, *102*(3), 609–618.

Blake, A. B., Nazarian, M., & Castel, A. D. (2015). Rapid Communication: The Apple of the mind's eye: Everyday attention, metamemory, and reconstructive memory for the Apple logo. *Quarterly Journal of Experimental Psychology*, *68*(5), 858–865.

Bleckley, M. K., Foster, J. L., & Engle, R. W. (2015). Working memory capacity accounts for the ability to switch between object-based and location-based allocation of visual attention. *Memory & Cognition*, *43*(3), 479–488.

Blinkhorn, S. (2005). A gender bender. *Nature*, *438*(7064), 31–32.

Block, N. (1997). Biology versus computation in the study of consciousness. *Behavioral and Brain Sciences*, *20*(1), 159–165.

Block, N. (2005). Two neural correlates of consciousness. *Trends in Cognitive Sciences*, *9*(2), 46–52.

Block, N., Carmel, D., Fleming, S. M., Kentridge, R. W., Koch, C., Lamme, V. A. F., Lau, H., & Rosenthal, D. (2014). Consciousness science: Real progress and lingering misconceptions. *Trends in Cognitive Sciences*, *18*(11), 556–557.

Blouin-Hudon, E.-M. C., & Pychyl, T. A. (2015). Experiencing the temporally extended self: Initial support for the role of affective states, vivid mental imagery, and future self-continuity in the prediction of academic procrastination. *Personality and Individual Differences*, *86*, 50–56.

Blount, G. (1986). Dangerousness of patients with Capgras syndrome. *Nebraska Medical Journal*, *71*(6), 207.

Bobak, A. K., Hancock, P. J. B., & Bate, S. (2015). Super-recognisers in action: Evidence from face-matching and face memory tasks. *Applied Cognitive Psychology*, *30*(1), 81–91.

Bobrow, S. A., & Bower, G. H. (1969). Comprehension and recall of sentences. *Journal of Experimental Psychology*, *80*(3), 455–461.

Boduroglu, A., Shah, P., & Nisbett, R. E. (2010). Cultural differences in allocation of attention in visual information processing. *Journal of Cross-Cultural Psychology*, *40*(3), 349–360.

Bogen, J. E. (1995). On the neurophysiology of consciousness: I. An overview. *Consciousness & Cognition*, *4*(1), 52–62.

Boole, G. (1854). *An investigation of the laws of thought, on which are founded the mathematical theories of logic and probabilities*. London, England: Maberly.

Boone, A. P., & Hegarty, M. (2017). Sex differences in mental rotation tasks: Not just in the mental rotation process! *Journal of Experimental Psychology: Learning, Memory, & Cognition*, *43*(7), 1005–1019.

Bootzin, R. (1979). *Psychology today: An introduction*, (4th ed.). New York, NY: McGraw-Hill.

Borges, J. L. (1964). *Labyrinths: Selected stories and other writings*. New York, NY: New Directions.

Borghi, A. M., Binkofski, F., Castelfranchi, C., Cimatti, F., Scorolli, C., & Tummolini, L. (2017). The challenge of abstract concepts. *Psychological Bulletin*, *143*(3), 263–292.

Bornstein, B. (1963). Prosopagnosia. In L. Halpern (Ed.), *Problems of dynamic neurology* (pp. 283–318). Jerusalem, Israel: Hadassah Medical School.

Bornstein, B., Sroka, H., & Munitz, H. (1969). Prosopagnosia with animal face agnosia. *Cortex*, *5*(2), 164–169.

Boroditsky, L. (2011, February). How language shapes thought. *Scientific American*, 63–65.

Borst, G., Thompson, W. L., & Kosslyn, S. M. (2011). Understanding the dorsal and ventral systems of the human cerebral cortex: *Beyond dichotomies*. *American Psychologist*, *66*(7), 624–632.

Botvinick, M. M., Cohen, J. D., & Carter, C. S. (2004). Conflict monitoring and anterior cingulate cortex: An update. *Trends in Cognitive Sciences*, *8*(12), 539–546.

Bouchard, T. J., Jr., Lykken, D. T., McGue, M., Segal, N. L., & Tellegen, A. (1990). Sources of human psychological differences: The Minnesota study of twins reared apart. *Science*, *250*(4978), 223–228.

Bourke, P. A., & Duncan, J. (2005). Effect of template complexity on visual search and dual-task performance. *Psychological Science*, *16*(3), 208–213.

Bower, G. H. (1970). Analysis of a mnemonic device. *American Scientist*, *58*, 496–510.

Bower, G. H. (1972). Mental imagery and associative learning. In L. W. Gregg (Ed.), *Cognition in learning and memory* (pp. 51–88). New York, NY: Wiley.

Bower, G. H., & Winzenz, D. (1970). Comparison of associative learning strategies. *Psychonomic Science*, *20*(2), 119–120.

Bower, J. M., & Parsons, L. M. (2003, August). Rethinking the "lesser brain." *Scientific American*, *289*, 50–57.

Bowles, B., Crupi, C., Mirsattari, S. M., Pigott, S. E., Parrent, A. G., Pruessner, J. C., Yonelinas, A., & Köhler, S. (2007). Impaired familiarity with preserved recollection after anterior temporal-lobe resection that spares the hippocampus. *Proceedings of the National Academy of Sciences*, *104*(41), 16382–16387.

Brackett, M. A., & Mayer, J. D. (2003). Convergent, discriminant, and incremental validity of competing measures of emotional intelligence. *Personality and Social Psychology Bulletin*, *29*(9), 1147–1158.

Brady, W. J., Gantman, A. P., & Van Bavel, J. J. (2020). Attentional capture helps explain why moral and emotional content go viral. *Journal of Experimental Psychology: General*, *149*(4), 746–756.

Brams, S., Ziv, G., Levin, O., Spitz, J., Wagemans, J., Williams, A. M., & Helsen, W. F. (2019). The relationship between gaze behavior, expertise, and performance: A systematic review. *Psychological Bulletin*, *145*(10), 980–1027.

Brandimonte, M., Einstein, G. O., & McDaniel, M. A. (Eds.) (1996). *Prospective memory: Theory and applications*. Mahwah, NJ: Erlbaum.

Brandon, S. E., Arthur, J. C., Ray, D. G., Meissner, C. A., Kleinman, S. M., Russano, M. B., & Wells, S (2019). The high-value detainee interrogation group HIG: Inception, evolution, and impact. In M. A. Staal & S. C. Harvey (Eds.), *Operational psychology: A new field to support national security and public safety* (pp. 263–286). Santa Barbara, CA: Praeger.

Bransford, J. (1979). *Human cognition: Learning, understanding and remembering*. Belmont, CA: Wadsworth.

Bransford, J., & Franks, J. J. (1971). The abstraction of linguistic ideas. *Cognitive Psychology, 2*, 331–350.

Bransford, J. D., & Johnson, M. K. (1972). Contextual prerequisites for understanding: Some investigations of comprehension and recall. *Journal of Verbal Learning and Verbal Behavior, 11*(6), 717–726.

Bransford, J. D., Brown, A. L., & Cocking, R. R. (Eds.) (1999). *How people learn: Brain, mind, experience, and school*. Washington, DC: National Academy Press.

Brase, G. L. (2008). Frequency interpretation of ambiguous statistical information facilitates Bayesian reasoning. *Psychonomic Bulletin & Review, 15*, 284–289.

Bratsberg, B., & Rogeberg, O. (2018). Flynn effect and its reversal are both environmentally caused. *Proceedings of the National Academy of Sciences, 115*(26), 6674–6678.

Braverman, M. (2020). On-demand creativity: Five ways to foster it in your law firm. *National Law Review, 10*(15).

Breen, M. (2014). Empirical investigations of the role of implicit prosody in sentence processing. *Language and Linguistics Compass, 8*(2), 37–50.

Brewer, D. D., Potterat, J. J., Muth, S. Q., Malone, P. Z., Montoya, P., Green, D. L., Rogers, H. L., & Cox, P. A. (2005). Randomized trial of supplementary interviewing techniques to enhance recall of sexual partners in contact interviews. *Sexually Transmitted Diseases, 32*(3), 189–193.

Brewer, W. F., & Treyens, J. C. (1981). Role of schemata in memory for places. *Cognitive Psychology, 13*(2), 207–230.

Brewin, C. R. (2020). Tilting at windmills: Why attacks on repression are misguided. *Perspectives on Psychological Science, 16*(2), 443–453.

Brewin, C. R., & Andrews, B. (2014). Why it is scientifically respectable to believe in repression: A response to Patithis, Ho, Tingen, Lilienfeld, and Loftus. *Psychological Science, 25*(10), 1964–1966.

Brewin, C. R., & Andrews, B. (2017). Creating memories for false autobiographical events in childhood: A systematic review. *Applied Cognitive Psychology, 31*(1), 2–23.

Brewin, C. R., Andrews, B., & Mickes, L. (2020). Regaining the consensus on the reliability of memory. *Current Directions in Psychological Science, 29*(2), 121–125.

Britton, M. K., & Anderson, B. A. (2020). Specificity and persistence of statistical learning in distractor suppression. *Journal of Experimental Psychology: Human Perception & Performance, 46*(3), 324–334.

Broadbent, D. E. (1958). *Perception and communication*. London, England: Pergamon.

Bronfman, Z. Z., Brezis, N., Jacobson, H., & Usher, M. (2014). We see more than we can report: "Cost free" color phenomenality outside focal attention. *Psychological Science, 25*(7), 1394–1403.

Bronstein, M. V., Pennycook, G., Bear, A., Rand, D. G., & Cannon, T. D (2019). Belief in fake news is associated with delusionality, dogmatism, religious fundamentalism, and reduced analytic thinking. *Journal of Applied Research in Memory and Cognition, 8*(1), 108–117.

Brown, A. S. (1991). A review of the tip-of-the-tongue experience. *Psychological Bulletin, 109*(2), 204–223.

Brown, A. S., & Halliday, H. E. (1990, November). *Multiple-choice tests: Pondering incorrect alternatives can be hazardous to your knowledge*. Paper presented at the meeting of the Psychonomic Society, 1990, New Orleans, LA.

Brown, A. S., & Marsh, E. J. (2008). Evoking false beliefs about autobiographical experience. *Psychonomic Bulletin & Review, 15*(1), 186–190.

Brown, A. S., & Murphy, D. R. (1989). Cryptomnesia: Delineating inadvertent plagiarism. *Journal of Experimental Psychology: Learning, Memory, & Cognition, 15*(3), 432–442.

Brown, D. A., & Lamb, M. E. (2018). Forks in the road, routes chosen, and journeys that beckon: A selective review of scholarship on children's testimony. *Applied Cognitive Psychology, 33*(4), 480–488.

Brown, E., Deffenbacher, K., & Sturgill, W. (1977). Memory for faces and the circumstances of encounter. *Journal of Applied Psychology, 62*(3), 311–318.

Brown, P. C., Roediger, H. L., III, & McDaniel, M. A. (2014). *Make it stick: The science of successful learning*. New York, NY: Belknap Press.

Brown, R. (1958). *Words and things: An introduction to language*. Glencoe, IL: Free Press.

Brown, R., & Kulik, J. (1977). Flashbulb memories. *Cognition, 5*(1), 73–99.

Brown, T. E. (2005). *Attention deficit disorder: The unfocused mind in children and adults*. New Haven, CT: Yale University Press.

Bruck, M., Ceci, S. J., & Francoeur, E. (1999). The accuracy of mothers' memories of conversations with their preschool children. *Journal of Experimental Psychology: Applied, 5*(1), 89–106.

Bruner, J. S. (1973). *Beyond the information given: Studies in the psychology of knowing*. New York, NY: Norton.

Carmon, Z., & Ariely, D. (2000). Focusing on the fore-gone: How value can appear so different to buyers and sellers. *Journal of Consumer Research, 27*(3), 360–370.

Carpenter, A. C., & Schacter, D. L. (2017). Flexible retrieval: When true inferences produce false memo-ries. *Journal of Experimental Psychology: Learning, Memory, & Cognition, 43*(3), 335–349.

Carpenter, P. A., & Eisenberg, P. (1978). Mental rotation and the frame of reference in blind and sighted individuals. *Perception & Psychophysics, 23*(2), 117–124.

Carpenter, P. A., Just, M. A., Keller, T. A., Eddy, W., Thulborn, K. (1999). Graded functional activation in the visuospatial system with the amount of task demand. *Journal of Cognitive Neuroscience, 11*(1), 14.

Carpenter, S. K., Pashler, H., & Cepeda, N. J. (2009). Using tests to enhance 8th grade students' retention of U.S. history facts. *Applied Cognitive Psychology, 23*(6), 760–771.

Carpenter, S. K., Witherby, A. E., & Tauber, S. K. (2020). On students' (mis)judgments of learning and teaching effectiveness. *Journal of Applied Research in Memory and Cognition, 9*, 137–151.

Carrasco, M., Ling, S., & Read, S. (2004). Attention alters appearance. *Nature Neuroscience, 7*(3), 308–313.

Carreiras, M., Armstrong, B. C., Perea, M., & Frost, R. (2014). The what, when, where, and how of visual word recognition. *Trends in Cognitive Sciences, 18*(2), 90–98.

Carroll, J. B. (1993). *Human cognitive abilities: A survey of factor-analytic studies.* New York, NY: Cambridge University Press.

Carroll, J. B. (2005). The three-stratum theory of cogni-tive abilities. In D. P. Flanagan & P. L. Harrison (Eds.), *Contemporary intellectual assessment: Theories, tests, and issues* (2nd ed., pp. 69–76). New York, NY: Guilford.

Carson, S. H., Peterson, J. B., & Higgins, D. M. (2005). Reliability, validity, and factor structure of the cre-ative achievement questionnaire. *Creativity Research Journal, 17*(1), 37–50.

Carvalho, P. F., & Goldstone, R. L. (2014). Putting category learning in order: Category structure and temporal arrangement affect the benefit of interleaved over blocked study. *Memory & Cognition, 42*(3), 481–495.

Casey, B. J., Jones, R. M., & Hare, T. A. (2008). The adolescent brain. *Annals of the New York Academy of Science, 1124*, 111–126.

Castel, A. D., Vendetti, M., & Holyoak, K. J. (2012). Fire drill: Inattentional blindness and amnesia for the location of fire extinguishers. *Attention, Perception, and Psychophysics, 74*, 1391–1396.

Castelhano, M. S., & Henderson, J. M. (2008). Stable individual differences across images in human saccadic eye movement. *Canadian Journal of Experimental Psychology, 62*(1), 1–14.

Castles, A., Rastle, K., & Nation, K. (2018). Ending the reading wars: Reading acquisition from novice to expert. *Psychological Science in the Public Interest, 19*(1), 5–51.

Castro-Alonso, J. C., & Jansen, P. (2019). Sex differences in visuospatial processing. In J. C. Castro-Alongo (Ed.), *Visuospatial processing for education in health and natural sciences.* New York, NY: Springer.

Catrambone, R., Craig, D. L., & Nersessian, N. J. (2006). The role of perceptually represented structure in analogical problem solving. *Memory & Cognition, 34*, 1126–1132.

Cattell, J. M. (1885). Über die zeit der erkennung and benennung von schriftzeichen, bildern and farben. *Philosophische Studien, 2*, 635–650.

Cave, K. R. (2013). Spatial attention. In D. Reisberg (Ed.), *The Oxford handbook of cognitive psychology* (pp. 117–130). New York, NY: Oxford University Press.

Cejudo, A. B., McDaniel, M. A., & Bajo, M. T. (2019). Event versus activity-based cues and motivation in school-related prospective memory tasks. *PLoS ONE, 14*(4), e0215845.

Chabris, C., & Simons, D. (2010). *The invisible gorilla: How our intuitions deceive us.* New York, NY: Crown Archetype.

Chalmers, D. J. (1996). *The conscious mind: In search of a fundamental theory.* New York, NY: Oxford University Press.

Chalmers, D. J. (1998). What is a neural correlate of con-sciousness? In T. Metzinger (Ed.), *Neural correlates of consciousness: Empirical and conceptual questions* (pp. 17–39). Cambridge, MA: MIT Press.

Chambers, D., & Reisberg, D. (1985). Can mental images be ambiguous? *Journal of Experimental Psychology: Human Perception and Performance, 11*(3), 317–328.

Chan, J., Paletz, S. B. F., & Schunn, C. D. (2012). Analogy as a strategy for supporting complex problem solv-ing under uncertainty. *Memory & Cognition, 40*, 1352–1365.

Chan, M. S., Jones, C. R., Hall Jamieson, K., & Albarracín, D. (2017). Debunking: A meta-analysis of the psycho-logical efficacy of messages countering misinforma-tion. *Psychological Science, 28*(11), 1531–1546.

Chang, S., & Egeth, H. E. (2019). Enhancement and suppression flexibly guide attention. *Psychological Science, 30*(12), 1724–1732.

Chao, L. L., Weisberg, J., & Martin, A. (2002). Experience-dependent modulation of category-related cortical activity. *Cerebral Cortex, 12*(5), 545–551.

Chapman, L. J., & Chapman, J. P. (1959). Atmosphere effect re-examined. *Journal of Experimental Psychol-ogy, 58*(3), 220–226.

Chapman, S. B., & Mudar, R. A. (2014). Enhancement of cognitive and neural functions through complex reasoning training: Evidence from normal and clini-cal populations. *Frontiers in Systems Neuroscience, 8*, Article 69.

Charman, S. D., Wells, G. L., & Joy, S. W. (2011). The dud effect: Adding highly dissimilar fillers increases confidence in lineup identifications. *Law & Human Behavior*, 35(6), 479–500.

Charniak, E. (1972). *Toward a model of children's story comprehension.* Unpublished doctoral dissertation, Massachusetts Institute of Technology, Cambridge, MA.

Chase, W. G., & Ericsson, K. A. (1982). Skill and working memory. In G. H. Bower (Ed.), *The psychology of learning and motivation* (Vol. 16, pp. 1–58). New York, NY: Academic Press.

Chase, W. G., & Simon, H. A. (1973). Perception in chess. *Cognitive Psychology*, 4(1), 55–81.

Cheesman, R., Hunjan, A. Coleman, J. R. I., Ahmadzadeh, Y., Plomin, R., McAdams, T. A., Eley, T. C., & Breen, G. (2020). Comparison of adopted and nonadopted individuals reveals gene-environment interplay for education in the UK Biobank. *Psychological Science*, 31(5), 582–591.

Chen, Y., & Zelinsky, G. J. (2019). Is there a shape to the attention spotlight? Computing saliency over proto-objects predicts fixations during scene viewing. *Journal of Experimental Psychology: Human Perception & Performance*, 45(1), 139–154.

Chen, Z., & Cave, K. R. (2006). Reinstating object-based attention under positional certainty: The importance of subjective parsing. *Perception and Psychophysics*, 68(6), 992–1003.

Chen, Z., & Cave, K. R. (2019). When is object-based attention not based on objects? *Journal of Experimental Psychology: Human Perception and Performance*, 45(8), 1062–1082.

Cherry, E. C. (1953). Some experiments on the recognition of speech, with one and with two ears. *Journal of the Acoustical Society of America*, 25, 975–979.

Chi, M. T. H. (1976). Short-term memory limitations in children: Capacity or processing deficit? *Memory & Cognition*, 4, 559–572.

Chi, M. T. H., Feltovich, P. J., & Glaser, R. (1981). Categorization and representation of physics problems by experts and novices. *Cognitive Science*, 5(2), 121–152.

Chincotta, D., & Underwood, G. (1997). Digit span and articulatory suppression: A cross-linguistic comparison. *European Journal of Cognitive Psychology*, 9(1), 89–96.

Choi, H.-Y., Kensinger, E. A., & Rajaram, S. (2017). Mnemonic transmission, social contagion, and emergence of collective memory: Influence of emotional valence, group structure, and information distribution. *Journal of Experimental Psychology: General*, 146(9), 1247–1265.

Chomsky, N. (1959). A review of B. F. Skinner's *Verbal behavior*. *Language*, 35(1), 26–58.

Chomsky, N., & Halle, M. (1968). *The sound pattern of English*. New York, NY: Harper & Row.

Chow, M., & Conway, A. R. A. (2015). The scope and control of attention: Sources of variance in working memory capacity. *Memory & Cognition*, 43(3), 325–339.

Christensen, B. T., & Schunn, C. D. (2005). Spontaneous access and analogical incubation effects. *Creativity Research Journal*, 17(1-2), 207–220.

Christiaansen, R., Sweeney, J. D., & Ochalek, K. (1983). Influencing eyewitness descriptions. *Law and Human Behavior*, 7, 59–65.

Christophel, T. B., Klink, P. C., Spitzer, B., Roelfsema, P. R., & Haynes, J.-D. (2017). The distributed nature of working memory. *Trends in Cognitive Sciences*, 21(2), 111–124.

Chrobak, Q. M., & Zaragoza, M. S. (2008). Inventing stories: Forcing witnesses to fabricate entire fictitious events leads to freely reported false memories. *Psychonomic Bulletin & Review*, 15(6), 1190–1195.

Chrobak, Q. M., & Zaragoza, M. S. (2013). The misinformation effect: Past research and recent advances In A. M. Ridley, F. Gabbert, & D. J. La Rooy (Eds.), *Suggestibility in legal contexts: Psychological research and forensic implications* (pp. 21–44). New York, NY: Wiley Blackwell.

Chrysikou, E. G., Cassanto, D., & Thompson-Schill, S. L. (2017). Motor experience influences object knowledge. *Journal of Experimental Psychology: General*, 146(3), 395–408.

Chuderski, A., & Jastrzębski, J. (2018). Much ado about aha!: Insight problem solving is strongly related to working memory capacity and reasoning ability. *Journal of Experimental Psychology: General*, 147(2), 257–281.

Claparède, E. (1951). Reconnaissance et moitié. In D. Rapaport (Ed.), *Organization and pathology of thought* (pp. 58–75). New York, NY: Columbia University Press. (Original work published in 1911.)

Clark, A., & Chalmers, D. (1998). The extended mind. *Analysis*, 58(1), 7–19.

Clark, H. H. (1996). *Using language*. Cambridge, England: Cambridge University Press.

Cochran, K. J., Greenspan, R. L., Bogart, D. F., & Loftus, E. F. (2016). Memory blindness: Altered memory reports lead to distortion in eyewitness memory. *Memory & Cognition*, 44(5), 717–726.

Cohen, G., & Java, R. (1995) Memory for medical history: Accuracy of recall. *Applied Cognitive Psychology*, 9(4), 273–288.

Cohen, G. L., Garcia, J., Apfel, N., & Master, A. (2006). Reducing the racial achievement gap: A social-psychological intervention. *Science*, 313(5791), 1307–1310.

Cohen, G. L., Garcia, J., Purdie-Vaughns, V., Apfel, N., & Brzustoski, P. (2009). Recursive processes in self-affirmation: Intervening to close the minority achievement gap. *Science*, 324(5925), 400–403.

Cohen, M. A., & Dennett, D. C. (2011). Consciousness cannot be separated from function. *Trends in Cognitive Sciences*, 15, 358–364.

Cohen, M. R. (2012). When attention wanders. *Science*, *338*, 58–59.

Coley, J. D., Medin, D. L., & Atran, S. (1997). Does rank have its privilege? Inductive inferences within folkbiological taxonomies. *Cognition*, *64*(1), 73–112.

Collins, A. M. C., & Quillian, M. R. (1969). Retrieval time from semantic memory. *Journal of Verbal Learning and Verbal Behavior*, *8*(2), 240–247.

Conrad, C. (1972). Cognitive economy in semantic memory. *Journal of Experimental Psychology*, *92*(2), 149–154.

Constable, M. D., Elekes, F., Sebanz, N., & Knoblich, G. (2019). Relevant for us? We-prioritization in cognitive processing. *Journal of Experimental Psychology: Human Perception & Performance*, *45*(12), 1549–1561.

Conway, A. R. A., Cowan, N., & Bunting, M. F. (2001). The cocktail party phenomenon revisited: The importance of working memory capacity. *Psychonomic Bulletin & Review*, *8*, 331–335.

Conway, M. A., Cohen, G., & Stanhope, N. (1991). On the very long-term retention of knowledge acquired through formal education: Twelve years of cognitive psychology. *Journal of Experimental Psychology: General*, *120*(4), 395–409.

Conway, M. A., Cohen, G., & Stanhope, N. (1992). Why is it that university grades do not predict very-long-term retention? *Journal of Experimental Psychology: General*, *121*(3), 382–384.

Conway, M. A., & Haque, S. (1999). Overshadowing the reminiscence bump: Memories of a struggle for independence. *Journal of Adult Development*, *6*, 35–43.

Conway, M., & Ross, M. (1984). Getting what you want by revising what you had. *Journal of Personality and Social Psychology*, *47*(4), 738–748.

Conway, M. A., Wang, Q., Hanyu, K., & Haque, S. (2005). A cross-cultural investigation of autobiographical memory: *On the universality and cultural variation of the reminiscence bump. Journal of Cross-Cultural Psychology*, *36*(6), 739–749.

Cooney, J. W., & Gazzaniga, M. S. (2003). Neurological disorders and the structure of human consciousness. *Trends in Cognitive Sciences*, *7*(4), 161–165.

Cooper, L. A., & Shepard, R. N. (1973). Chronometric studies of the rotation of mental images. In W. G. Chase (Ed.), *Visual information processing* (pp. 75–176). New York, NY: Academic Press.

Cooper, S. A., & O'Sullivan, M. (2016). Here, there and everywhere: Higher visual function and the dorsal visual stream. *Practical Neurology*, *16*(3), 176–183.

Corbetta, M., & Shulman, G. L. (2002). Control of goal-directed and stimulus-driven attention in the brain. *Nature Reviews Neuroscience*, *3*(3), 201–215.

Corbetta, M., & Shulman, G. L. (2011). Spatial neglect and attention networks. *Annual Review of Neuroscience*, *34*, 569–599.

Coricelli, G., Dolan, R. J., & Sirigu, A. (2007). Brain, emotion and decision making: The paradigmatic example of regret. *Trends in Cognitive Sciences*, *11*(6), 258–265.

Corkin, S. (2013). *Permanent present tense: The unforgettable life of the amnesic patient, H.M.* New York, NY: Basic Books.

Corneille, O., Mierop, A., & Unkelbach, C. (2020). Repetition increases both the perceived truth and fakeness of information: An ecological account. *Cognition*, *205*, Article 104470.

Cosmides, L., & Tooby, J. (1996). Are humans good intuitive statisticians after all? Rethinking some conclusions from the literature on judgment under uncertainty. *Cognition*, *58*(1), 1–73.

Cowan, R., & Carney, D. P. J. (2006). Calendrical savants: Exceptionality and practice. *Cognition*, *100*(2), B1–B9.

Coyle, T. R., Pillow, D. R., Snyder, A. C., & Kochunov, P. (2011). Processing speed mediates the development of general intelligence (*g*) in adolescence. *Psychological Science*, *22*(10), 1265–1269.

Craik, F. I. M. (2020). Remembering: An activity of mind and brain. *Annual Review of Psychology*, *71*, 1–24.

Craik, F. I. M., & Tulving, E. (1975). Depth of processing and the retention of words in episodic memory. *Journal of Experimental Psychology: General*, *104*(3), 268–294.

Creswell, J. D. (2017). Mindfulness interventions. *Annual Review of Psychology*, *68*, 491–516.

Crick, F., & Koch, C. (1990). Towards a neurobiological theory of consciousness. *Seminars in the Neurosciences*, *2*, 263–275.

Crick, F., & Koch, C. (1995). Are we aware of neural activity in primary visual cortex? *Nature*, *375*, 121–123.

Crick, F., & Koch, C. (2003). A framework for consciousness. *Nature Neuroscience*, *6*, 119–126.

Crombag, H. F. M., Wagenaar, W. A., & van Koppen, P. J. (1996). Crashing memories and the problem of "source monitoring." *Applied Cognitive Psychology*, *10*(2), 95–104.

Cruse, D., Chennu, S., Chatelle, C., Bekinschtein, T. A., Fernández-Espejo, D., Pickard, J. D., Laureys, S., & Owen, A. M. (2012). Bedside detection of awareness in the vegetative state: A cohort study. *The Lancet*, *378*(9809), 2088–2094.

Csibra, G., Davis, G., Spratling, M. W., & Johnson, M. H. (2000). Gamma oscillations and object processing in the infant brain. *Science*, *290*(5496), 1582–1585.

Cui, X., Jeter, C. B., Yang, D., Montague, P. R., & Eagleman, D. M. (2007). Vividness of mental imagery: Individual variability can be measured objectively. *Vision Research*, *47*(4), 474–478.

Cunningham, C. A., & Egeth, H. E. (2016). Taming the white bear: Initial costs and eventual benefits of distractor inhibition. *Psychological Science*, *27*(4), 476–485.

Curci, A., Lanciano, T., Maddalena, C., Mastandrea, S., & Sartori, G. (2015). Flashbulb memories of the Pope's resignation: Explicit and implicit measures across differing religious groups. *Memory, 23*(4), 529–544.

Cushen, P. J., & Wiley, J. (2018). Both attentional control and the ability to make remote associations aid spontaneous analogical transfer. *Memory & Cognition, 46*(8), 1398–1412.

Custers, R., & Aarts, H. (2010). The unconscious will: How the pursuit of goals operates outside of conscious awareness. *Science, 329*(5987), 47–50.

Daftary-Kapur, T., Penrod, S. D., O'Connor, M., & Wallace, B. (2014). Examining pretrial publicity in a shadow jury paradigm: Issues of slant, quantity, persistence and generalizability. *Law and Human Behavior, 38*(5), 462–477.

Dalenberg, C. J., Brand, B. L., Gleaves, D. H., Dorahy, M. J., Loewenstein, R. J., Cardeña, E., Frewen, P. A., Carlson, E. B., & Spiegel, D. (2012, March 12). Evaluation of the evidence for the trauma and fantasy models of dissociation. *Psychological Bulletin, 138*(3), 550–588.

Daley, T. C., Whaley, S. E., Sigman, M. D., Espinosa, M. P., & Neumann, C. (2003). IQ on the rise: The Flynn effect in rural Kenyan children. *Psychological Science, 14*(3), 215–219.

Dalton, P., & Fraenkel, N. (2012). Gorillas we have missed: Sustained inattentional deafness for dynamic events. *Cognition, 124*(3), 367–372.

Damasio, A. (1994). *Descartes' error: Emotion, reason, and the human brain.* London, England: Penguin.

Damasio, A. R. (1985). Disorders of complex visual processing. In M.-M. Mesulam (Ed.), *Principles of behavioral neurology.* Philadelphia, PA: Davis.

Damasio, A. R., Damasio, H., & Van Hoesen, G. W. (1982). Prosopagnosia: Anatomic basis and behavioral mechanisms. *Neurology, 32*(4), 331–341.

Damasio, A. R., Tranel, D., & Damasio, H. (1989). Disorders of visual recognition. In H. Goodglass & A. R. Damasio (Eds.), *Handbook of neuropsychology* (Vol. 2, pp. 317–332). New York, NY: Elsevier.

Damasio, H., Grabowski, T. J., Tranel, D., Hichwa, R. D., & Damasio, A. R. (1996). A neural basis for lexical retrieval. *Nature, 380*, 499–505.

Daniel, T. A., & Katz, J. S. (2018). Primacy and recency effects for taste. *Journal of Experimental Psychology: Learning, Memory, & Cognition, 44*(3), 399–405.

Daniloff, R. G., & Hammarberg, R. E. (1973). On defining coarticulation. *Journal of Phonetics, 1*(3), 239–248.

Danthiir, V., Roberts, R. D., Schulze, R., & Wilhelm, O. (2005). Mental speed: On frameworks, paradigms, and a platform for the future. In O. Wilhelm & R. W. Engle (Eds.), *Handbook of understanding and measuring intelligence* (pp. 27–46). Thousand Oaks, CA: Sage.

Dar-Nimrod, I., & Heine, S. J. (2006). Exposure to scientific theories affects women's math performance. *Science, 314*(5798), 435.

Davachi, L., & Dobbins, I. G. (2008). Declarative memory. *Current Directions in Psychological Science, 17*(2), 112–118.

Davachi, L., Mitchell, J. P., & Wagner, A. D. (2003). Multiple routes to memory: Distinct medial temporal lobe processes build item and source memories. *Proceedings of the National Academy of Sciences, 100*(4), 2157–2162.

Davidai, S., Gilovich, T., & Ross, L. D. (2012). The meaning of default options for potential organ donors. *Proceedings of the National Academy of Sciences, 109*(38), 15201–15205.

Davis, D., & Friedman, R. D. (2007). Memory for conversation: The orphan child of witness memory researchers. In M. P. Toglia, J. D. Read, D. F. Ross, & R. C. L. Lindsay (Eds.), *The handbook of eyewitness psychology: Vol. 1. Memory for events* (pp. 3–52). Mahwah, NJ: Erlbaum.

Davis, D., & Loftus, E. F. (2015). Remembering disputed sexual encounters: A new frontier for witness memory research. *Journal of Criminal Law and Criminology, 105*(4), 811–852.

Davis, D., Loftus, E. F., Vanous, S., & Cucciare, M. (2008). "Unconscious transference" can be an instance of "change blindness." *Applied Cognitive Psychology, 22*(5), 605–623.

Davis, J. P., Bretfelean, L. D., Belanova, E., & Thompson, T. (2020). Super-recognisers: Face recognition performance after variable delay intervals. *Applied Cognitive Psychology, 34*(6), 1350–1368.

Davis, O. S. P., Haworth, C. M. A., & Plomin, R. (2009). Dramatic increase in heritability of cognitive development from early to middle childhood: An 8-year longitudinal study of 8,700 pairs of twins. *Psychological Science, 20*(10), 1301–1308.

Dawes, R. M., Faust, D., & Meehl, P. E. (1989). Clinical versus actuarial judgment. *Science, 243*(4899), 1668–1674.

de Gelder, B. (2010, May). Uncanny sight in the blind. *Scientific American*, 60–64.

de Groot, A. (1965). *Thought and choice in chess.* The Hague, Netherlands: Mouton.

de Groot, A. (1966). Perception and memory versus thought: Some old ideas and recent findings. In B. Kleinmuntz (Ed.), *Problem solving: Research, method, and theory* (pp. 19–50). New York, NY: Wiley.

de Haan, E. H. F., & Cowey, A. (2011). On the usefulness of "what" and "where" pathways in vision. *Trends in Cognitive Sciences, 15*(10), 460–466.

De Lange, F. P., Heilbron, M., & Kok, P. (2018). How do expectations shape perception? *Trends in Cognitive Sciences, 22*(9), 764–779.

De Neys, W. (2006). Dual processing in reasoning: Two systems but one reasoner. *Psychological Science, 17*(5), 428–433.

De Neys, W., & Pennycook, G. (2019). Logic, fast and slow: Advances in dual-process theorizing. *Current Directions in Psychological Science, 28*(5), 503–509.

De Renzi, E., Faglioni, P., Grossi, D., & Nichelli, P. (1991). Apperceptive and associative forms of prosopagnosia. *Cortex, 27*(2), 213–221.

De Zeeuw, P., & Durston, S. (2017). Cognitive control in attention deficit hyperactivity disorder. In T. Egner (Ed.), *The wiley handbook of cognitive control* (pp. 602–618). Chichester, England: Wiley.

Deary, I. J. (2012). Intelligence. *Annual Review of Psychology, 63*, 453–482.

Deary, I. J. (2014). The stability of intelligence from childhood to old age. *Current Directions in Psychological Science, 23*(4), 239–245.

Deary, I. J., & Derr, G. (2005). Reaction time explains IQ's association with death. *Psychological Science, 16*(1), 64–69.

Deary, I. J., Pattie, A., & Starr, J. M. (2013). The stability of intelligence from age 11 to age 90 years: The Lothian birth cohort of 1921. *Psychological Science, 24*(12), 2361–2368.

Deary, I. J., Weiss, A., & Batty, G. D. (2010). Intelligence and personality as predictors of illness and death: How researchers in differential psychology and chronic disease epidemiology are collaborating to understand and address health inequalities. *Psychological Science in the Public Interest, 11*(2), 53–79.

Deffenbacher, K. A., Bornstein, B. H., Penrod, S. D., & McCorty, E. K. (2004). A meta-analytic review of the effects of high stress on eyewitness memory. *Law and Human Behavior, 28*(6), 687–706.

Deffenbacher, K. A., Bornstein, B., & Penrod, S. D. (2006). Mugshot exposure effects: Retroactive interference, mugshot commitment, source confusion, and unconscious transference. *Law and Human Behavior, 30*(3), 287–307.

Defife, J. A., Haggerty, G., Smith, S. W., Betancourt, L., Ahmed, Z., & Ditkowsky, K. (2015). Clinical validity of prototype personality disorder ratings in adolescents. *Journal of Personality Assessment, 97*(3), 271–277.

DeGutis, J., Wilmer, J., Mercado, R. J., & Cohan, S. (2013). Using regression to measure holistic face processing reveals a strong link with face recognition ability. *Cognition, 126*(1), 87–100.

Dehaene, S. (2014). *Consciousness and the brain: Deciphering how the brain codes our thoughts.* New York, NY: Penguin Books.

Dehaene, S. (Ed.) (2002). *The cognitive neuroscience of consciousness.* Cambridge, MA: MIT Press.

Dehaene, S., Artiges, E., Naccache, L., Martelli, C., Viard, A., Schürhoff, F., Recasens, C., Paillère Martinot, M. L., Leboyer, M., & Martinot, J.-L. (2003). Conscious and subliminal conflicts in normal subjects and patients with schizophrenia: The role of the anterior cingulate. *Proceedings of the National Academy of Sciences, 100*(23), 13722–13727.

Dehaene S., & Changeux, J.-P. (2011). Experimental and theoretical approaches to conscious processing. *Neuron, 70*(2), 200–227.

Dehaene, S., & Naccache, L. (2001). Towards a cognitive neuroscience of consciousness: Basic evidence and a workspace framework. *Cognition, 79*(1-2), 1–37.

Dehaene, S., Sergent, C., & Changeux, J.-P. (2003). A neuronal network model linking subjective reports and objective physiological data during conscious perception. *Proceedings of the National Academy of Science, 100*(14), 8520–8525.

Del Giudice, M. (2017). Pink, blue, and gender: An update. *Archives of Sexual Behavior, 46*(6), 1555–1563.

Dempster, F. N. (1981). Memory span: Sources of individual and developmental differences. *Psychological Bulletin, 89*(1), 63–100.

Dennett, D. C. (1992). *Consciousness explained.* Boston, MA: Little, Brown.

Dennison, S. M., & Thomson, D. M. (2002). Identifying stalking: The relevance of intent in commonsense reasoning. *Law & Human Behavior, 26*(5), 543–561.

DePaulo, B. M., Lindsay, J. J., Malone, B. E., Muhlenbruck, L., Charlton, K., & Cooper, H. (2003). Cues to deception. *Psychological Bulletin, 129*(1), 74–118.

Derksen, D. G., Giroux, M. E., Connolly D. A., Newman, E. J., & Bernstein, D. M. (2020). Truthiness and law: Non-probative photos bias perceived credibility in forensic contexts. *Applied Cognitive Psychology, 34*(6), 1335–1344.

Desimone, R., & Duncan, J. (1995). Neural mechanisms of selective visual attention. *Annual Review of Neuroscience, 18*, 193–222.

Deutsch, J. A., & Deutsch, D. (1963). Attention: Some theoretical considerations. *Psychological Review, 70*(1), 80–90.

Devine, D. J. (2012). *Jury decision making: The state of the science.* New York, NY: New York University Press.

Devine, D. J., Buddenbaum, J., Houp, S., Studebaker, N., & Stolle, D. P. (2009). Strength of evidence, extra-evidentiary influence, and the liberation hypothesis: Data from the field. *Law and Human Behavior, 33*(2), 136–148.

Devitt, A. L., & Schacter, D. L. (2018). An optimistic outlook creates a rosy past: The impact of episodic simulation on subsequent memory. *Psychological Science, 29*(6), 936–946.

Devue, C., Wride, A., & Grimshaw, G. M. (2018). New insights on real-world human face recognition. *Journal of Experimental Psychology: General, 148*(6), 994–1007.

Dewar, M., Cowan, N., & Della Salla, S. (2010). Forgetting due to retroactive interference in amnesia. In S. Della Sala (Ed.), *Forgetting* (pp. 185–209). New York, NY: Psychology Press.

Diamond, A., & Lee, K. (2011). Interventions shown to aid executive function development in children from 4 to 12 years old. *Science, 333*(6045), 959–964.

Diamond, N. B., Armson, M. J., & Levine, B. (2020). The truth is out there: Accuracy in recall of verifiable real-world events. *Psychological Science, 31*(12), 1544–1556.

Diamond, R., & Carey, S. (1986). Why faces are and are not special: An effect of expertise. *Journal of Experimental Psychology: General, 115*(2), 107–117.

Diana, R. A., Yonelinas, A. P., & Ranganath, C. (2007). Imaging recollection and familiarity in the medial temporal lobe: A three-component model. *Trends in Cognitive Sciences, 11*(9), 379–386.

Dickens, W. T., & Flynn, J. R. (2006). Black Americans reduce the racial IQ gap: Evidence from standardization samples. *Psychological Science, 17*(10), 913–920.

Dickinson, J. J., Schreiber Compo, N. S., Carol, R., Schwartz, B. L., & McCauley, M. R. (2019). *Evidence-based investigative interviewing: Applying cognitive principles*. New York, NY: Routledge.

Dickson, R. A., Pillemer, D. B., & Bruehl, E. C. (2011). The reminiscence bump for salient personal memories: Is a cultural life script required? *Memory & Cognition, 39*, 977–991.

Diemand-Yauman, C., Oppenheimer, D. M., & Vaughan, E. B. (2011). Fortune favors the **bold** (and the *italicized*): Effects of disfluency on educational outcomes. *Cognition, 118*(1), 111–115.

Dietrich, A. (2019). Types of creativity. *Psychonomic Bulletin & Review, 26*, 1–12.

Dijkstra, N., Bosch, S. E., & van Gerven, M. A. J. (2019). Shared neural mechanisms of visual perception and imagery. *Trends in Cognitive Sciences, 23*(5), 423–434.

Dismukes, D. K. (2012). Prospective memory in workplace and everyday situations. *Current Directions in Psychological Science, 21*(4), 215–220.

Dittrich, L. (2016, August 7). The brain that couldn't remember. *The New York Times Magazine*.

Dodds, R. A., Ward, T. B., & Smith, S. M. (2007). A review of the experimental literature on incubation in problem solving and creativity. In M. A. Runco (Ed.), *Creative research handbook* (Vol. 3). Cresskill, NJ: Hampton.

Dodier, O., Patihis, L., & Payoux, M. (2019). Reports of recovered memories of childhood abuse in therapy in France. *Memory, 27*(9), 1283–1298.

Dohle, S., & Montoya, A. K. (2017). The dark side of fluency: Fluent names increase drug dosing. *Journal of Experimental Psychology: Applied, 23*(3), 231–239.

Doré, B. P., Meksin, R., Mather, M., Hirst, W., & Ochsner, K. N. (2016). Highly accurate prediction of emotions surrounding the attacks of September 11, 2001 over 1-, 2-, and 7-year prediction intervals. *Journal of Experimental Psychology: General, 145*(6), 788–795.

Dore, K. L., Brooks, L. R., Weaver, B., & Norman, G. R. (2012). Influence of familiar features on diagnosis: Instantiated features in an applied setting. *Journal of Experimental Psychology: Applied, 18*(1), 109–125.

Douglas, A. B., & Pavletic, A. (2012). Eyewitness confidence malleability. In B. L. Cutler (Ed.), *Conviction of the innocent: Lessons from psychological research* (pp. 149–165). Washington, DC: American Psychological Association.

Drew, T., Võ, M. L. H., & Wolfe, J. M. (2013). The invisible gorilla strikes again: Sustained inattentional blindness in expert observers. *Psychological Science, 24*(9), 1848–1853.

Drews, F. A., Pasupathi, M., & Strayer, D. L. (2008). Passenger and cell phone conversations in simulated driving. *Journal of Experimental Psychology: Applied, 14*(4), 392–400.

Dror, I. E., & Charlton, D. (2006). Why experts make errors. *Journal of Forensic Identification, 56*(4), 600–616.

Duchaine, B. C., & Nakayama, K. (2006). Developmental prosopagnosia: A window to content-specific face processing. *Current Opinion in Neurobiology, 16*(2), 166–173.

Duncan, J. (1994). Attention, intelligence, and the frontal lobes. In M. S. Gazzaniga (Ed.), *The cognitive neurosciences*. Cambridge, MA: MIT Press.

Duncan, J., Parr, A., Woolgar, A., Thompson, R., Bright, P., Cox, S., Bishop, S., & Nimmo-Smith, I. (2008). Goal neglect and Spearman's g: Competing parts of a complex task. *Journal of Experimental Psychology: General, 137*(1), 131–148.

Duncan, J., Schramm, M., Thompson, R., & Dumontheil, I. (2012). Task rules, working memory, and fluid intelligence. *Psychonomic Bulletin & Review, 19*(5), 864–870.

Duncker, K. (1945). *On problem-solving* (L. S. Lees, Trans.). *Psychological Monographs, 58*(5), i–113.

Dunlap, E. E., Lynch, K. R., Jewell, J. A., Wasarhaley, N. E., & Golding, J. M. (2015). Participant gender, stalking myth acceptance, and gender role stereotyping in perceptions of intimate partner stalking: A structural equation modeling approach. *Psychology, Crime & Law, 21*(3), 234–253.

Dunn, B. D., Galton, H. C., Morgan, R., Evans, D., Oliver, C., Meyer, M., Cusack, R., Lawrence, A. D., Dalgleish, T (2010). Listening to your heart: How interoception shapes emotion experience and intuitive decision making. *Psychological Science, 21*(12), 1835–1844.

Dunning, D., & Parpal, M. (1989). Mental addition versus subtraction in counterfactual reasoning: On assessing the impact of personal actions and life events. *Journal of Personality and Social Psychology, 57*(1), 5–15.

Duyme, M., Dumaret, A. C., & Tomkiewicz, S. (1999). How can we boost IQs of "dull children"?: A late adoption study. *Proceedings of the National Academy of Sciences, 96*(15), 8790–8794.

Dygert, S. K. C., & Jarosz, A. F. (2020). Individual differences in creative cognition. *Journal of Experimental Psychology: General, 149*(7), 1249–1274.

Dysart, J. E., Lawson, V. Z., & Rainey, A. (2012). Blind lineup administration as a prophylactic against the postidentification feedback effect. *Law & Human Behavior, 36*(4), 312–319.

Easterbrook, J. A. (1959). The effect of emotion on cue utilization and the organization of behavior. *Psychological Review, 66*(3), 183–201.

Eberhardt, J. L., Dasgupta, N., & Banaszynski, T. L. (2003). Believing is seeing: The effects of racial labels and implicit beliefs on face perception. *Personality and Social Psychology Bulletin, 29*(3), 363–66.

Ecker, U. K. H., Lewandowsky, S., Chang, E. P., & Pillai, R. (2014). The effects of subtle misinformation in news headlines. *Journal of Experimental Psychology: Applied, 20*(4), 323–335.

Ecker, U. K. H., & Ang, L. C. (2019). Political attitudes and the processing of misinformation corrections. *Political Psychology, 40*(2), 241–260.

Eddy, D. M. (1982). Probabilistic reasoning in clinical medicine: Problems and opportunities. In D. Kahneman, P. Slovic, & A. Tversky (Eds.), *Judgment under uncertainty: Heuristics and biases* (pp. 249–267). Cambridge, England: Cambridge University Press.

Edelson, M., Sharot, T., Dolan, R. J., & Dudai, Y. (2011). Following the crowd: Brain substrates of long-term memory conformity. *Science, 333*(6038), 108–111.

Edelstyn, N. M. J., & Oyebode, F. (1999). A review of the phenomenology and cognitive neuropsychological origins of the Capgras Syndrome. *International Journal of Geriatric Psychiatry, 14*(1), 48–59.

Eich, J. E. (1980). The cue-dependent nature of state-dependent retrieval. *Memory & Cognition, 8*, 157–173.

Eichenbaum, H. (2017). Memory: Organization and control. *Annual Review of Psychology, 68*, 19–45.

Einstein, G. O., Morris, J., & Smith, S. (1985). Note-taking, individual differences, and memory for lecture information. *Journal of Educational Psychology, 77*(5), 522–532.

Eisen, M. L., Gabbert, F., Ying, R., & Williams, J. (2017). "I think he had a tattoo on his neck": How co-witness discussions about a perpetrator's description can affect identification decisions. *Journal of Applied Research in Memory and Cognition, 6*, 274–282.

Elliot, M. A., & Müller, H. J. (2000). Evidence for a 40-Hz oscillatory short-term visual memory revealed by human reaction-time measurements. *Journal of Experimental Psychology: Learning, Memory, & Cognition, 26*(3), 703–718.

Ellis, H. D., & de Pauw, K. W. (1994). The cognitive neuropsychiatric origins of the Capgras delusion. In A. S. David & J. C. Cutting (Eds.), *The neuropsychology of schizophrenia* (pp. 317–335). Hillsdale, NJ: Erlbaum.

Ellis, H. D., & Lewis, M. B. (2001). Capgras delusion: A window on face recognition. *Trends in Cognitive Sciences, 5*(4), 149–156.

Ellis, H. D., & Young, A. W. (1990). Accounting for delusional misidentifications. *The British Journal of Psychiatry, 157*, 239–248.

Elstein, A. S., Holzman, G. B., Ravitch, M. M., Metheny, W. A., Holmes, M. M., Hoppe, R. B., Rothert, M. L., & Rovner, D. R. (1986). Comparison of physicians' decisions regarding estrogen replacement therapy for menopausal women and decisions derived from a decision analytic model. *The American Journal of Medicine, 80*(2), 246–258.

Engle, R. W. (2018). Working memory and executive attention: A revisit. *Perspectives on Psychological Science, 13*(2), 190–193.

Engle, R. W., & Kane, M. J. (2004). Executive attention, working memory capacity, and a two-factor theory of cognitive control. In B. H. Ross (Ed.), *The psychology of learning and motivation: Advances in research and theory (Vol. 44*, pp. 145–199). New York, NY: Elsevier.

Enz, K. F., & Talarico, J. M. (2015). Forks in the road: Memories of turning points and transitions. *Applied Cognitive Psychology, 30*(2), 188–195.

Ericsson, K. A. (2003). Exceptional memorizers: Made, not born. *Trends in Cognitive Sciences, 7*(6), 233–235.

Ericsson, K. A., & Towne, T. J. (2012). Experts and their superior performance. In D. Reisberg (Ed.), *The Oxford handbook of cognitive psychology* (pp. 886–901). New York, NY: Oxford University Press.

Estes, Z. (2003). Domain differences in the structure of artifactual and natural categories. *Memory & Cognition, 31*(2), 199–214.

Evans, J. S. B. T. (2012a). Dual-process theories of deductive reasoning: Facts and fallacies. In K. J. Holyoak & R. G. Morrison (Eds.), *The Oxford handbook of thinking and reasoning* (pp. 115–133). New York, NY: Oxford University Press.

Evans, J. S. B. T. (2012b). Reasoning. In D. Reisberg (Ed.), *The Oxford handbook of cognitive psychology*. New York, NY: Oxford University Press.

Evans, J. S. B. T., Newstead, S. E., & Byrne, R. M. J. (1993). *Human reasoning: The psychology of deduction*. London, England: Erlbaum.

Evans, K. K., Birdwell, R. L., & Wolfe, J. M. (2013). If you don't find it often, you often don't find it: Why some cancers are missed in breast cancer screening. *PLoS ONE, 8*, e64366.

Eze-Nliam, C., Cain, K., Bond, K., Forlenza, I., Jankowski, R., Magyar-Russell, G., Yenokyan, G., & Ziegelstein, R. C. (2012). Discrepancies between the medical record and the reports of patients with acute coronary syndrome regarding important aspects of the medical history. *BMC Health Services Research, 12*, Article 78.

Farah, M. J. (1985). Psychophysical evidence for a shared representational medium for mental images and percepts. *Journal of Experimental Psychology: General, 114*(1), 91–103.

Farah, M. J. (1990). *Visual agnosia: Disorders of object recognition and what they tell us about normal vision.* Cambridge, MA: MIT Press.

Farah, M. J., Hammond, K. M., Levine, D. N., & Calvanio, R. (1988). Visual and spatial mental imagery: Dissociable systems of representation. *Cognitive Psychology, 20*(4), 439–462.

Farah, M. J., & Smith, A. F. (1983). Perceptual interference and facilitation with auditory imagery. *Perception & Psychophysics, 33*(5), 475–478.

Farah, M. J., Soso, M., & Dasheiff, R. M. (1992). Visual angle of the mind's eye before and after unilateral occipital lobectomy. *Journal of Experimental Psychology: Human Perception and Performance, 18*(1), 241–246.

Farmer, G. D., Warren, P. A., & Hahn, U. (2017). Who "believes" in the Gambler's Fallacy and why? *Journal of Experimental Psychology: General, 146*(1), 63–76.

Fawcett, J. M., & Hulbert, J. C. (2020). The many faces of forgetting: Toward a constructive view of forgetting in everyday life. *Journal of Applied Research in Memory and Cognition, 9*(1), 1–18.

Fawcett, J. M., Peace, K. A., & Greve, A. (2016). Looking down the barrel of a gun: What do we know about the weapon focus effect? *Journal of Applied Research in Memory and Cognition, 5*(3), 257–263.

Fazekas, P., & Overgaard, M. (2016). Multidimensional models of degrees and levels of consciousness. *Trends in Cognitive Sciences, 20*(10), 715–716.

Fedorenko, E., & Blank, I. A. (2020). Broca's area is not a natural kind. *Trends in Cognitive Sciences, 24*(4), 270–284.

Feng, J., Spence, I., & Pratt, J. (2007). Playing an action video game reduces gender differences in spatial cognition. *Psychological Science, 18*(10), 850–855.

Ferreira, F. (2021). In defense of the passive voice. *American Psychologist, 76*(1), 145–153.

Ferreira, M. B., Garcia-Marques, L., Sherman, S. J., & Sherman, J. W. (2006). Automatic and controlled components of judgment and decision making. *Journal of Personality & Social Psychology, 91*(5), 797–813.

Fiebelkorn, I. C., & Kastner, S. (2020). Functional specialization in the attention network. *Annual Review of Psychology, 71*, 221–249.

Finke, R. A. (2016). *Creative imagery: Discoveries and inventions in visualization.* New York, NY: Psychology Press.

Finke, R. A., & Pinker, S. (1982). Spontaneous imagery scanning in mental extrapolation. *Journal of Experimental Psychology: Learning, Memory, & Cognition, 8*(2), 142–147.

Finucane, M. L., Alhakami, A., Slovic, P., & Johnson, S. M. (2000). The affect heuristic in judgments of risks and benefits. *Journal of Behavioral Decision Making, 13*(1), 1–17.

First, M. B., Bhat, V., Adler, D., Dixon, L., Goldman, B., Koh, S., Levine, B., Oslin, D., & Siris, S. (2014). How do clinicians actually use the *Diagnostic and Statistical Manual of Mental Disorders* in clinical practice and why we need to know more. *Journal of Nervous and Mental Disease, 202*(12), 841–844.

Fischhoff, B., Slovic, P., & Lichtenstein, S. (1978). Fault trees: Sensitivity of estimated failure probabilities to problem representation. *Journal of Experimental Psychology: Human Perception & Performance, 4*(2), 330–344.

Fischhoff, B., & Broomell, S. B. (2020). Judgment and decision making. *Annual Review of Psychology, 71*, 331–355.

Fisher, R. P., & Geiselman, R. E. (1992) *Memory-enhancing techniques for investigative interviewing: The cognitive interview.* Springfield, IL: C. C. Thomas.

Fisher, R. P., Milne, R., & Bull, R. (2011). Interviewing cooperative witnesses. *Current Directions in Psychological Science, 20*(1), 16–19.

Fisher, R. P., & Quigley, K. L. (1992). Applying cognitive theory in public health investigations: Enhancing food recall with the cognitive interview. In J. M. Tanur (Ed.), *Questions about questions: Inquiries into the cognitive bases of surveys* (pp. 154–169). New York, NY: Russell Sage Foundation.

Fitousi, D. (2013). Mutual information, perceptual independence, and holistic face perception. *Attention, Perception, & Psychophysics, 75*(5), 983–1000.

Fivush, R. (2019). Sociocultural developmental approaches to autobiographical memory. *Applied Cognitive Psychology, 33*(4), 489–497.

Flanagan, D. P., McGrew, K. S., & Ortiz, S. O. (2000). *The Wechsler Intelligence Scales and Gf-Gc theory: A contemporary approach to interpretation.* Boston, MA: Allyn & Bacon.

Flavell, J. H. (1979). Metacognition and cognitive monitoring: A new area of cognitive-development inquiry. *American Psychologist, 34*(10), 906–911.

Fleck, J. I., Beeman, M., & Kounios, J. (2012) Insight. In D. Reisberg (Ed.), *The Oxford handbook of cognitive psychology.* New York, NY: Oxford University Press.

Fleck, J. I., & Weisberg, R. W. (2004). The use of verbal protocols as data: An analysis of insight in the candle problem. *Memory & Cognition, 32*, 990–1006.

Fletcher, J. M., Lyon, G. R., Fuchs, L. S., & Barnes, M. A. (2019). *Learning disabilities: From identification to intervention* (2nd ed.). New York, NY: Guilford Press.

Flores, A., Cobos, P. L., & Hagmayer, Y. (2018). The diagnosis of mental disorders is influenced by automatic causal reasoning. *Clinical Psychological Science, 6*(2), 177–188.

Flusberg, S. J., & McClelland, J. L. (2017). Connectionism and the emergence of mind. In S. E. F. Chipman (Ed.), *The Oxford handbook of cognitive science* (pp. 69–89). New York, NY: Oxford University Press.

Flynn, J. R. (1984). The mean IQ of Americans: Massive gains 1932 to 1978. *Psychological Bulletin, 95*(1), 29–51.

Flynn, J. R. (1987). Massive IQ gains in 14 nations: What IQ tests really measure. *Psychological Bulletin, 101*(2), 171–191.

Flynn, J. R. (1999). Searching for justice: The discovery of IQ gains over time. *American Psychologist*, *54*(1), 5–20.

Flynn, J. R. (2009). Requiem for nutrition as the cause of IQ gains: Raven's gains in Britain 1938–2008. *Economics & Human Biology*, *7*(1), 18–27.

Fong, G. T., Krantz, D. H., & Nisbett, R. E. (1986). The effects of statistical training on thinking about everyday problems. *Cognitive Psychology*, *18*(3), 253–292.

Fong, G. T., & Nisbett, R. E. (1991). Immediate and delayed transfer of training effects in statistical reasoning. *Journal of Experimental Psychology: General*, *120*(1), 34–45.

Ford, J. H., & Kensinger, E. A. (2019). The role of the amygdala in emotional experience during retrieval of personal memories. *Memory*, *27*(10), 1362–1370.

Fox, C. R. (2006). The availability heuristic in the classroom: How soliciting more criticism can boost your course ratings. *Judgment and Decision Making*, *1*(1), 86–90.

Fox, M. C., & Mitchum, A. L. (2013). A knowledge-based theory of rising scores on "cultural-free" tests. *Journal of Experimental Psychology: General*, *142*(3), 979–1000.

Fraga González, G., Žarić, G., Tijms, J., Bonte, M., Blomert, L., & van der Molen, M. W. (2015). A randomized controlled trial on the beneficial effects of training letter-speech sound integration on reading fluency in children with dyslexia. *PLoS ONE*, *10*(12), e0143914.

Frank, C. C., Iordan, A. D., Ballouz, T. L., Mikels, J. A., & Reuter-Lorenz, P. A. (2021). Affective forecasting: A selective relationship with working memory for emotion. *Journal of Experimental Psychology: General*, *150*(1), 67–82.

Frederick, S. (2005). Cognitive reflection and decision making. *Journal of Economic Perspectives*, *19*(4), 25–42.

Fredrickson, B. L. (2000). Extracting meaning from past affective experiences: The importance of peaks, ends, and specific emotions. *Cognition & Emotion*, *14*(4), 577–606.

Frenda, S. J., Nichols, R. M., & Loftus, E. F. (2011). Current issues and advances in misinformation research. *Current Directions in Psychological Science*, *20*(1), 20–23.

Friedman, A. (1979). Framing pictures: The role of knowledge in automatized encoding and memory for gist. *Journal of Experimental Psychology: General*, *108*(3), 316–355.

Friedman, A., & Brown, N. R. (2000a). Reasoning about geography. *Journal of Experimental Psychology: General*, *129*(2), 193–219.

Friedman, A., & Brown, N. R. (2000b). Updating geographical knowledge: Principles of coherence and inertia. *Journal of Experimental Psychology: Learning, Memory, & Cognition*, *26*(4), 900–914.

Fries, P., Reynolds, J. H., Rorie, A. E., & Desimone, R. (2001). Modulation of oscillatory neural synchronization by selective visual attention. *Science*, *291*(5508), 1560–1563.

Frings, C., & Wühr, P. (2014). Top-down deactivation of interference from irrelevant spatial or verbal stimulus features. *Attention, Perception, & Psychophysics*, *76*(8), 2360–2374.

Frisby, C. L., & Henry, B. (2016). Science, politics, and best practice: 35 years after Larry P. *Contemporary School Psychology*, *20*(1), 46–62.

Fukuda, K., Vogel, E., Mayr, U., & Awh, E. (2011). Quantity, not quality: The relationship between fluid intelligence and working memory capacity. *Psychonomic Bulletin & Review*, *17*(5), 673–679.

Gable, P. A., & Harmon-Jones, E. (2008). Approach-motivated positive affect reduces breadth of attention. *Psychological Science*, *19*(5), 476–482.

Gable, S. L., Hopper, E. A., & Schooler, J. W. (2019). When the Muses strike: Creative ideas of physicists and writers routinely occur during mind wandering. *Psychological Science*, *30*(3), 396–404.

Gainotti, G., & Marra, C. (2011). Differential contributions of right and left temporo-occipital and anterior temporal lesions to face recognition disorders. *Frontiers in Human Neuroscience*, *5*, 55.

Gall, S., Phan, H., Madsen, T. E., Reeves, M., Rist, P., Jimenez, M., Lichtman, J., Dong, L., Lisabeth, L. D (2018). Focused update of sex differences in patient report outcome measures after stroke. *Stroke*, *49*(3), 531–535.

Gallagher, J. (2019, April 8). Aphantasia: Ex-Pixar chief Ed Catmull says "My mind's eye is blind." BBC News.

Gallistel, C. R. (2017). The coding question. *Trends in Cognitive Sciences*, *21*(7), 498–508.

Gallo, D. A., Roberts, M. J., & Seamon, J. G. (1997). Remembering words not presented in lists: Can we avoid creating false memories? *Psychonomic Bulletin & Review*, *4*(2), 271–276.

Gallo, V., & Chittajullu, R. (2001). Unwrapping glial cells from the synapse: What lies inside? *Science*, *292*(5518), 872–873.

Galton, F. (1883). *Inquiries into human faculty and its development*. London, England: Dent.

Gamino, J. F., Motes, M. M., Riddle, R., Lyon, G. R., Spence, J. S., & Chapman, S. B. (2014). Enhancing inferential abilities in adolescence: New hope for students in poverty. *Frontiers in Human Neuroscience*, *8*, Article 924.

Garcia-Retamero, R., Petrova, D., Cokely, E. T., & Joeris, A. (2020). Scientific risk reporting in medical journals can bias expert judgment: Comparing surgeons' risk comprehension across reporting formats. *Journal of Experimental Psychology: Applied*, *26*(2), 283–299.

Gardiner, J. M. (1988). Functional aspects of recollective experience. *Memory & Cognition*, *16*, 309–313.

Gardner, H. (1974). *The shattered mind: The person after brain damage.* New York, NY: Vintage.

Gardner, H. (1983). *Frames of mind: The theory of multiple intelligences.* New York, NY: Basic Books.

Gardner, H. (2006). *Multiple intelligences: New horizons in theory and practice.* New York, NY: Basic Books.

Garrett, B. L. (2011). *Convicting the innocent: Where criminal prosecutions go wrong.* Cambridge, MA: Harvard University Press.

Garrison, T. M., & Williams, C. C. (2013). Impact of relevance and distraction on driving performance and visual attention in a simulated driving environment. *Applied Cognitive Psychology, 27*(3), 396–405.

Garry, M., Hope, L., Zajac, R., Verrall, A. J., & Robertson, J. M. (2020). Contact tracing: A memory task with consequences for public health. *Perspectives on Psychological Science, 16*(1), 175–187.

Garry, M., Manning, C. G., Loftus, E. F., & Sherman, S. J. (1996). Imagination inflation: Imagining a childhood event inflates confidence that it occurred. *Psychonomic Bulletin & Review, 3*(2), 208–214.

Gaspar, J. G., Street, W. N., Windsor, M. B., Carbonari, R., Kaczmarski, H., Kramer, A. F., & Mathewson, K. E. (2014). Providing views of the driving scene to drivers' conversation partners mitigates cell-phone-related distraction. *Psychological Science, 25*(12), 2136–2146.

Gauthier, I. (2020). What we could learn about holistic face processing only from nonface objects. *Current Directions in Psychological Science, 29*(4), 419–425.

Gauthier, I., Skudlarski, P., Gore, J. C., & Anderson, A. W. (2000). Expertise for cars and birds recruits brain areas involved in face recognition. *Nature Neuroscience, 3*(2), 191–197.

Gazzaniga, M. S., Fendrich, R., & Wessinger, C. M. (1994). Blindsight reconsidered. *Current Directions in Psychological Science, 3*(3), 93–96.

Gazzaniga, M. S., Ivry, R. B., & Mangun, G. R. (2019). *Cognitive neuroscience: The biology of the mind* (5th ed.). New York, NY: Norton.

Geary, D. C. (2019). The spark of life and the unification of intelligence, health, and aging. *Current Directions in Psychological Science, 28*(3), 223–228.

Gelman, S. A., & Wellman, H. M. (1991). Insides and essences: Early understandings of the non-obvious. *Cognition, 38*(3), 213–244.

Geng, J. J., Won, B.-Y., & Carlisle, N. B. (2019). Distractor ignoring: Strategies, learning, and passive filtering. *Current Directions in Psychological Science, 28*(6), 600–606.

Gentner, D., & Smith, L. A. (2013). Analogical learning and reasoning. In D. Reisberg (Ed.), *The Oxford handbook of cognitive psychology* (pp. 668–681). New York, NY: Oxford University Press.

Georgopoulos, A. P. (1990). Neurophysiology of reaching. In M. Jeannerod (Ed.), *Attention and performance XIII: Motor representation and control* (pp. 227–263). Hillsdale, NJ: Erlbaum.

Georgopoulos, A. P. (1995). Motor cortex and cognitive processing. In M. S. Gazzaniga (Ed.) *The cognitive neurosciences* (pp. 507–517). Cambridge, MA: MIT Press.

Geraerts, E., Lindsay, D. S., Merckelbach, H., Jelicic, M., Raymaekers, L., Arnold, M. M., Schooler, J. W. (2009). Cognitive mechanisms underlying recovered-memory experiences of childhood sexual abuse. *Psychological Science, 20*(1), 92–99.

Gerlach, C., Law, I., & Paulson, O. B. (2002). When action turns into words. Activation of motor-based knowledge during categorization of manipulable objects. *Journal of Cognitive Neuroscience, 14*(8), 1230–1239.

German, T. P., & Barrett, H. C. (2005). Functional fixedness in a technologically sparse culture. *Psychological Science, 16*(1), 1–5.

Gernsbacher, M. A., & Kaschak, M. P. (2013). Text comprehension. In D. Reisberg (Ed.), *The Oxford handbook of cognitive psychology* (pp. 462–474). New York, NY: Oxford University Press.

Geschwind, N. (1970). The organization of language and the brain. *Science, 170*(3961), 940–944.

Giacobbi, P. R., Jr., Stabler, M. E., Stewart, J., Jaeschke, A.-M., Siebert, J. L., & Kelley, G. A. (2015). Guided imagery for arthritis and other rheumatic diseases: A systematic review of randomized control trials. *Pain Management Nursing, 16*(5), 792–803.

Gibson, E. (2006). The interaction of top-down and bottom-up statistics in the resolution of syntactic category ambiguity. *Journal of Memory & Language, 54*(3), 363–388.

Gibson, E. J., Bishop, C. H., Schiff, W., & Smith, J. (1964). Comparison of meaningfulness and pronounciability as grouping principles in the perception and retention of verbal material. *Journal of Experimental Psychology, 67,* 173–182.

Gibson, J. J. (1950). *The perception of the visual world.* Boston, MA: Houghton Mifflin.

Gibson, J. J. (1966). *The senses considered as perceptual systems.* Boston, MA: Houghton Mifflin.

Gibson, J. J. (1979). *The ecological approach to visual perception.* Boston, MA: Houghton Mifflin.

Gick, M. L., & Holyoak, K. J. (1980). Analogical problem solving. *Cognitive Psychology, 12,* 306–355.

Gigerenzer, G., & Gaissmaier, W. (2011). Heuristic decision making. *Annual Review of Psychology, 62,* 451–482.

Gigerenzer, G., Gaissmaier, W., Kurz-Milcke, E., Schwartz, L. M., & Woloshin, S. (2008). Helping doctors and patients make sense of health statistics. *Psychological Science in the Public Interest, 8*(2), 53–96.

Gigerenzer, G., Hell, W., & Blank, H. (1988). Presentation and content: The use of base rates as a continuous variable. *Journal of Experimental Psychology: Human Perception and Performance, 14*(3), 513–525.

Gigerenzer, G., & Hoffrage, U. (1995). How to improve Bayesian reasoning without instruction: Frequency formats. *Psychological Review, 102*(4), 684–704.

Gilbert, D. (2006). *Stumbling on happiness.* New York, NY: Random House.

Gilbert, D. T., & Ebert, J. E. J. (2002). Decisions and revisions: The affective forecasting of changeable outcomes. *Journal of Personality and Social Psychology, 82*(4), 503–514.

Gilhooly, K. J., Georgiou, G. J., Garrison, J., Reston, J. D., & Sirota, M. (2012). Don't wait to incubate: Immediate versus delayed incubation in divergent thinking. *Memory & Cognition, 40*(6), 966–975.

Gilovich, T. (1983). Biased evaluation and persistence in gambling. *Journal of Personality & Social Psychology, 44*(6), 1110–1126.

Gilovich, T. (1991). *How we know what isn't so: The fallibility of human reason in everyday life.* New York, NY: Free Press.

Gilovich, T., & Douglas, C. (1986). Biased evaluations of randomly determined gambling outcomes. *Journal of Experimental Social Psychology, 22*(3), 228–241.

Giudice, N. A., Betty, M. R., & Loomis, J. M. (2011). Functional equivalence of spatial images from touch and vision: Evidence from spatial updating in blind and sighted individuals. *Journal of Experimental Psychology: Learning, Memory, & Cognition, 37*(3), 621–634.

Giuditta, A. (2014). Sleep memory processing: The sequential hypothesis. *Frontiers in Systems Neuroscience, 8,* 219.

Glanzer, M., & Cunitz, A. R. (1966). Two storage mechanisms in free recall. *Journal of Verbal Learning and Verbal Behavior, 5*(4), 351–360.

Glass, A., & Sinha, N. (2013). Multiple-choice questioning is an efficient instructional methodology that may be widely implemented in academic courses to improve exam performance. *Current Directions in Psychological Science, 22*(6), 471–477.

Gleitman, H. (1963, October). Place-learning. *Scientific American, 209,* 116–122.

Godden, D. R., & Baddeley, A. D. (1975). Context-dependent memory in two natural environments: On land and underwater. *British Journal of Psychology, 66*(3), 325–332.

Godfrey, R. D., & Clark, S. E. (2010). Repeated eyewitness identification procedures: Memory, decision making, and probative value. *Law and Human Behavior, 34*(3), 241–258.

Godinez v. Moran, 509 U.S. 389 (1993). https://supreme.justia.com/cases/federal/us/509/389/

Goebel, R., Khorram-Sefat, D., Muckli, L., Hacker, H., & Singer, W. (1998). The constructive nature of vision: Direct evidence from functional magnetic resonance imaging studies of apparent motion and motion imagery. *European Journal of Neuroscience, 10*(5), 1563–1573.

Gold, P. E., Cahill, L., & Wenk, G. L. (2002). Ginkgo biloba: A cognitive enhancer? *Psychological Science in the Public Interest, 3*(1), 2–11.

Goldenberg, G., Müllbacher, W., & Nowak, A. (1995). Imagery without perception: A case study of anosognosia for cortical blindness. *Neuropsychologia, 33*(11), 1373–1382.

Goldfarb, D., Goodman, G. S., Larson, R. P., & Eisen, M. L., Qin, J. (2019). Long-term memory in adults exposed to childhood violence: Remembering genital contact nearly 20 years later. *Clinical Psychological Science, 7*(2), 381–396.

Goldfarb, E. V., Tompary, A., Davachi, L., & Phelps, E. A. (2019). Acute stress throughout the memory cycle: Diverging effects on associative and item memory. *Journal of Experimental Psychology: General, 148*(1), 13–29.

Goldin-Meadow, S. (2003). *The resilience of language: What gesture creation in deaf children can tell us about how all children learn language.* New York, NY: Psychology Press.

Goldin-Meadow, S. (2017). What the hands can tell us about language emergence. *Psychonomic Bulletin & Review, 24*(1), 213–218.

Goldman-Rakic, P. S. (1987). Development of cortical circuitry and cognitive function. *Child Development, 58*(3), 601–622.

Goldman-Rakic, P. S. (1998). The prefrontal landscape: Implications of functional architecture for understanding human mentation and the central executive. In A. C. Roberts, T. W. Robbins, & L. Weiskrantz (Eds.), *The prefrontal cortex: Executive and cognitive functions* (pp. 87–102). New York, NY: Oxford University Press.

Goldsmith, S. F., & Morton, J. B. (2018). Time to disengage from the bilingual advantage hypothesis. *Cognition, 170,* 328–329.

Goldstein, N. E. S., Messenheimer, S., Riggs Romaine, C. L., & Zelle, H. (2012). Potential impact of juvenile suspects' linguistic abilities on Miranda understanding and appreciation. In L. M. Solan & P. M. Tiersma (Eds.), *The Oxford handbook of linguistics and law* (pp. 299–311). New York, NY: Oxford University Press.

Goldstone, R. L, & Son, J. Y. (2012). Similarity. In K. J. Holyoak & R. G. Morrison (Eds.), *The Oxford handbook of thinking and reasoning* (pp. 155–176). New York, NY: Oxford University Press.

Goldwater, M. B., & Jamrozik, A. (2019). Can a relational mindset boost analogical retrieval? *Cognitive Research: Principles and Implications, 4,* Article 47.

Gonthier, C., & Thomassin, N. (2015). Strategy use fully mediates the relationship between working memory capacity and performance on Raven's matrices. *Journal of Experimental Psychology: General, 144*(5), 916–924.

Goodale, M. A. (1995). The cortical organization of visual perception and visuomotor control. In S. M. Kosslyn & D. N. Osherson (Eds.), *Visual cognition: An invitation to cognitive science* (2nd ed., pp. 167–213). Cambridge, MA: MIT Press.

Goodale, M. A., & Milner, A. D. (2004). *Sight unseen: An exploration of conscious and unconscious vision.* New York, NY: Oxford University Press.

Goodale, M. A., Milner, A. D., Jacobson, L. S., & Carey, D. P. (1991). A neurological dissociation between perceiving objects and grasping them. *Nature, 349*(6305), 154–156.

Goodman, G. S., Ghetti, S., Quas, J. A., Edelstein, R. S., Alexander, K. W., Redlich, A. D., Cordon, I. M., & Jones, D. P. H. (2003). A prospective study of memory for child sexual abuse: New findings relevant to the repressed-memory controversy. *Psychological Science, 14*(2), 113–118.

Goodman, N. (1972). Seven strictures on similarity. In N. Goodman (Ed.), *Problems and projects* (pp. 437–446). New York, NY: Bobbs-Merrill.

Gordon, H. (1923). Mental and scholastic tests among retarded children. *Educational pamphlet, no. 44.* London, England: Board of Education.

Gordon, R. D. (2006). Selective attention during scene perception: Evidence from negative priming. *Memory & Cognition, 34,* 1484–1494.

Gottfredson, L. S. (1997). Why g matters: The complexity of everyday life. *Intelligence, 24*(1), 79–132.

Gottfredson, L. S. (2003). Dissecting practical intelligence theory: Its claims and evidence. *Intelligence, 31*(4), 343–397.

Gottfredson, L. S. (2004). Intelligence: Is it the epidemiologists' elusive "fundamental cause" of social class inequalities in health? *Journal of Personality and Social Psychology, 86*(1), 174–199.

Gottfredson, L. S., & Deary, I. J. (2004). Intelligence predicts health and longevity, but why? *Current Directions in Psychological Science, 13*(1), 1–4.

Grace, A., Kemp, N., Martin, F. H., & Parrila, R. (2014). Undergraduates' text messaging language and literacy skills. *Reading and Writing, 27*(5), 855–873.

Grady, R. H., Butler, B. J., & Loftus, E. F. (2016). What should happen after an officer-involved shooting? Memory concerns in police reporting procedures. *Journal of Applied Research in Memory and Cognition, 5*(3), 246–251.

Graesser, A. C., & Forsyth, C. M. (2013). Discourse comprehension. In D. Reisberg (Ed.), *The Oxford handbook of cognitive psychology* (pp. 475–491). New York, NY: Oxford University Press.

Graf, P. (2012). Prospective memory: Faulty brain, flaky person. *Canadian Psychology, 53*(1), 7–13.

Graf, P., Mandler, G., & Haden, P. E. (1982). Simulating amnesic symptoms in normal subjects. *Science, 218*(4578), 1243–1244.

Graf, P., & Schacter, D. L. (1985). Implicit and explicit memory for new associations in normal and amnesic subjects. *Journal of Experimental Psychology: Learning, Memory, & Cognition, 11*(3), 501–518.

Grainger, J., Rey, A., & Dufau, S. (2008). Letter perception: From pixels to pandemonium. *Trends in Cognitive Sciences, 12*(10), 381–387.

Grainger, J., & Whitney, C. (2004). Does the huamn mnid raed wrods as a wlohe? *Trends in Cognitive Sciences, 8*(2), 58–59.

Grant, H. M., Bredahl, L. C., Clay, J., Ferrie, J., Groves, J. E., McDorman, T. A., & Dark, V. J. (1998). Context-dependent memory for meaningful material: Information for students. *Applied Cognitive Psychology, 12,* 617–623.

Gray, K., Anderson, S., Chen, E. E., Kelly, J. M., Christian, M. S., Patrick, J., Huang, L., Kenett, Y. N., & Lewis, K. (2019). "Forward flow": A new measure to quantify free thought and predict creativity. *American Psychologist, 74*(5), 539–554.

Greenberg, D. L., & Knowlton, B. J. (2014). The role of visual imagery in autobiographical memory. *Memory & Cognition, 42*(6), 922–934.

Greenfield, P. M. (2009). Technology and informal education: What is taught, what is learned. *Science, 323*(5910), 69–71.

Gregory, A. H., Schreiber-Compo, N., Vertefeuille, L., & Zambrusky, G. (2011). A comparison of U.S. police interviewers' notes with their subsequent reports. *Journal of Investigative Psychology and Offender Profiling, 8*(2), 203–215.

Grewal, D., & Salovey, P. (2005). Feeling smart: The science of emotional intelligence. *American Scientist, 93,* 330–339.

Grice, P. (1989). *Studies in the way of words.* Cambridge, MA: Harvard University Press.

Griffin, D. W., Gonzalez, R., Koehler, D. J., & Gilovich, T. (2012). Judgmental heuristics: A historical overview. In K. J. Holyoak & R. G. Morrison (Eds.), *The Oxford handbook of thinking and reasoning* (pp. 322–345). New York, NY: Oxford University Press.

Griggs, R. A., & Cox, J. R. (1982). The elusive thematic-materials effect in Wason's selection task. *British Journal of Psychology, 73*(3), 407–420.

Grigorenko, E. L., Jarvin, I., & Sternberg, R. J. (2002). School-based tests of the triarchic theory of intelligence: Three settings, three samples, three syllabi. *Contemporary Educational Psychology, 27*(2), 167–208.

Grill-Spector, K., Knouf, N., & Kanwisher, N. (2004). The fusiform face area subserves face perception, not generic within-category identification. *Nature Neuroscience, 7*(5), 555–562.

Gross, S. R., Jacoby, K., Matheson, D. J., & Montgomery, N. (2005). Exonerations in the United States 1989 through 2003. *Journal of Criminal Law and Criminology, 95*(2), 523–560.

Grother, P., Ngan, M., & Hanaoka, K. (2019, December). *Face Recognition Vendor Test (FRVT), Part 3: Demographic Effects.* U.S. Department of Commerce, National Institute of Standards and Technology. https://nvlpubs.nist.gov/nistpubs/ir/2019/NIST.IR.8280.pdf

Gruber, H. E. (1981). *Darwin on man: A psychological study of scientific creativity* (2nd ed.). Chicago, IL: University of Chicago Press.

Grysman, A., Harris, C. B., Barnier, A. J. & Savage, G. (2020). Long-married couples recall their wedding day: The influence of collaboration and gender on autobiographical memory recall. *Memory*, 28(1), 18–33.

Guilford, J. P. (1967). *The nature of human intelligence.* New York, NY: Scribner.

Guilford, J. P. (1979). Some incubated thoughts on incubation. *The Journal of Creative Behavior*, 13(1), 1–8.

Gunnerud, H. L., ten Braak, D., Reikerås, E. K. L., Donolato, E., & Melby-Lervåg, M. (2020). Is bilingualism related to a cognitive advantage in children? A systematic review and meta-analysis. *Psychological Bulletin*, 146(12), 1059–1083.

Haas, M., Zuber, S., Kliegel, M., & Ballhausen, N. (2020). Prospective memory errors in everyday life: Does instruction matter? *Memory*, 28(2), 196–203.

Haber, R. N. (1969, April). Eidetic images. *Scientific American*, 220, 36–44.

Haber, R. N., & Haber, L. (1988). The characteristics of eidetic imagery. In L. K. Obler & D. Fein (Eds.), *The exceptional brain: Neuropsychology of talent and special abilities* (pp. 218–241). New York, NY: Guilford.

Hacker, P. M. S. (2002). Is there anything it is like to be a bat? *Philosophy*, 77(300), 435–450.

Hackman, D. A., & Farah, M. J. (2009). Socioeconomic status and the developing brain. *Trends in Cognitive Sciences*, 13(2), 65–73.

Haggerty, G., Zodan, J., Mehra, A., Zubair, A., Ghosh, K., Siefert, C. J., Sinclair, S. J., & DeFife, J. (2016). Reliability and validity of prototype diagnosis for adolescent psychopathology. *Journal of Nervous and Mental Disease*, 204(4), 287–290.

Hagoort, P., Hald, L., Bastiaansen, M., & Petersson, K. M. (2004). Integration of word meaning and world knowledge in language comprehension. *Science*, 304(5669), 438–441.

Hahn, B., Ross, T. J., & Stein, E. A. (2006). Neuroanatomical dissociation between bottom-up and top-down processes of visuospatial selective attention. *NeuroImage*, 32(2), 842–853.

Hakim, N., Simons, D. J., Zhao, H., & Wan, X. (2017). Do easterners and westerners differ in visual cognition? A preregistered examination of three visual cognition tasks. *Social Psychological and Personality Science*, 8(2), 142–152.

Halamish, V. (2018). Can very small font size enhance memory? *Memory & Cognition*, 46, 979–993.

Halamish, V., & Bjork, R. (2011). When does testing enhance retention? A distribution-based interpretation of retrieval as a memory modifier. *Journal of Experimental Psychology: Learning, Memory, & Cognition*, 37(4), 801–812.

Halberstadt, J., & Rhodes, G. (2003). It's not just average faces that are attractive: Computer-manipulated averageness makes birds, fish, and automobiles attractive. *Psychonomic Bulletin & Review*, 10, 149–156.

Hale, R. G., Brown, J. M., & McLunn, B. A. (2016). Increasing task demand by obstructing object recognition increases boundary extension. *Psychonomic Bulletin & Review*, 23(5), 1497–1503.

Halle, M. (1990). Phonology. In D. Osherson & H. Lasnik (Eds.), *Language: An invitation to cognitive science* (pp. 43–68). Cambridge, MA: MIT Press.

Halpern, D. F. (2011). *Sex differences in cognitive abilities* (4th ed.). New York, NY: Psychology Press.

Hamann, S. (2001). Cognitive and neural mechanisms of emotional memory. *Trends in Cognitive Sciences*, 5(9), 394–400.

Hampshire, A., Duncan, J., & Owen, A. M. (2007). Selective tuning of the blood oxygenation level-dependent response during simple target detection dissociates human frontoparietal subregions. *Journal of Neuroscience*, 27(23), 6219–6223.

Handel, S. (1989). *Listening: An introduction to the perception of auditory events.* Cambridge, MA: MIT Press.

Hardt, O., Einarsson, E. O., & Nader, K. (2010). A bridge over troubled water: Reconsolidation as a link between cognitive and neuroscientific memory research traditions. *Annual Review of Psychology*, 61, 141–167.

Hardt, O., Nader, K., & Nadel, L. (2013). Decay happens: The role of active forgetting in memory. *Trends in Cognitive Sciences*, 17(3), 111–120.

Harinck, F., Van Dijk, E., Van Beest, I., & Mersmann, P. (2007). When gains loom larger than losses: Reversed loss aversion for small amounts of money. *Psychological Science*, 18(12), 1099–1105.

Harley, E. M., Carlsen, K. A., & Loftus, G. R. (2004). The "saw-it-all-along" effect: Demonstrations of visual hindsight bias. *Journal of Experimental Psychology: Learning, Memory, & Cognition*, 30(5), 960–968.

Harley, T. A., & Bown, H. E. (1998). What causes a tip-of-the-tongue state? Evidence for lexical neighbourhood effects in speech production. *British Journal of Psychology*, 89(1), 151–174.

Harmon-Jones, E., Gable, P. A., & Price, T. F. (2013). Does negative affect always narrow and positive affect always broaden the mind? Considering the influence of motivational intensity on cognitive scope. *Current Directions in Psychological Science*, 22(4), 301–307.

Harris, I. M., Harris, J. A., & Corballis, M. C. (2020). Binding identity and orientation in object recognition. *Attention, Perception, & Psychophysics*, 82(1), 153–167.

Harris, J., Hirsh-Pasek, K., & Newcombe, N. S. (2013). Understanding spatial transformations: Similarities and differences between mental rotation and mental folding. *Cognitive Processing*, 14(2), 105–115.

Harrison, T. L., Shipstead, Z., & Engle, R. W. (2015). Why is working memory capacity related to matrix reasoning tasks? *Memory & Cognition*, 43(3), 389–396.

Hartanto, A., & Yang, H. (2019). Does early active bilingualism enhance inhibitory control and monitoring? A propensity-matching analysis. *Journal of Experimental Psychology: Learning, Memory, & Cognition*, 45(2), 360–378.

Hartanto, A., & Yang, H. (2020). The role of bilingual interactional contexts in predicting interindividual variability in executive functions: A latent variable analysis. *Journal of Experimental Psychology: General*, 149(4), 609–633.

Hartmann, P., Ramseier, A., Gudat, F., Mihatsch, M. J., Polasek, W., & Geisenhoff, C. (1994). Normal weight of the brain in adults in relation to age, sex, body height and weight. *Der Pathologe*, 15(3), 165–170.

Harvard Women's Health Watch. (2015, April). *6 ways to use your mind to control pain.* Harvard Health Publishing, Harvard Medical School. https://www.health.harvard.edu/mind-and-mood/6-ways-to-use-your-mind-to-control-pain

Harvey, L. O., Jr., & Leibowitz, H. W. (1967). Effects of exposure duration, cue reduction, and temporary monocularity on size matching at short distances. *Journal of the Optical Society of America*, 57(2), 249–253.

Harwood, D. G., Barker, W. W., Ownby, R. L., & Duara, R. (1999). Prevalence and correlates of Capgras syndrome in Alzheimer's disease. *International Journal of Geriatric Psychiatry*, 14(6), 415–420.

Hasel, L. E., & Kassin, S. M. (2009). On the presumption of evidentiary independence: Can confessions corrupt eyewitness identifications? *Psychological Science*, 20(1), 122–126.

Hass, R. W. (2017). Tracking the dynamics of divergent thinking via semantic distance: Analytic methods and theoretical implications. *Memory & Cognition*, 45, 233–244.

Hassin, R. R. (2013). Yes it can: On the functional abilities of the human unconscious. *Perspectives on Psychological Science*, 8(2), 195–207.

Hayward, W. G., Crookes, K., Chu, M. H., Favelle, S. K., & Rhodes, G. (2016). Holistic processing of face configurations and components. *Journal of Experimental Psychology: Human Perception & Performance*, 42(10), 1482–1489.

Healy, A. F., Jones, M., Lalchandani, L. A., & Tack, L. A. (2017). Timing of quizzes during learning: Effects on motivation and retention. *Journal of Experimental Psychology: Applied*, 23(2), 128–137.

Heckman, J. J. (2006). Skill formation and the economics of investing in disadvantaged children. *Science*, 312(5782), 1900–1902.

Hegarty, M., & Stull, A. T. (2012). Visuospatial thinking. In K. J. Holyoak & R. G. Morrison (Eds.), *The Oxford handbook of thinking and reasoning* (pp. 606–630). New York, NY: Oxford University Press.

Heine, S. J. (2015). *Cultural psychology* (3rd ed.). New York, NY: Norton.

Heit, E. (2000). Properties of inductive reasoning. *Psychonomic Bulletin & Review*, 7(4), 569–592.

Heit, E., & Bott, L. (2000). Knowledge selection in category learning. In D. L. Medin (Ed.), *The psychology of learning and motivation: Advances in research and theory* (Vol. 39, pp. 163–199). San Diego, CA: Academic Press.

Heit, E., & Feeney, A. (2005). Relations between premise similarity and inductive strength. *Psychonomic Bulletin & Review*, 12(2), 340–344.

Hélie, S., & Sun, R. (2010). Incubation, insight, and creative problem solving: A unified theory and a connectionist model. *Psychological Review*, 117(3), 994–1024.

Heller, M. A., & Gentaz, E. (2014). *Psychology of touch and blindness.* New York, NY: Psychology Press.

Helmuth, L. (2001). Boosting brain activity from the outside in. *Science*, 292(5520), 1284–1286.

Henderson, J. M. (2013). Eye movements. In D. Reisberg (Ed.), *The Oxford handbook of cognitive psychology* (pp. 69–82). New York, NY: Oxford University Press.

Henkel, L. A. (2014). Point-and-shoot memories: The influence of taking photos on memory for a museum tour. *Psychological Science*, 25(2), 396–402.

Henkel, L. A., & Milliken, A. (2020) The benefits and costs of editing and reviewing photos of one's experiences on subsequent memory. *Journal of Applied Research in Memory and Cognition*, 9(4), 480–494.

Hennessey, B. A., & Amabile, A. M. (2010). Creativity. *Annual Review of Psychology*, 61, 569–598.

Herlitz, A., & Rehnman, J. (2014). Sex differences in episodic memory. *Current Directions in Psychological Science*, 17(1), 52–56.

Hertwig, R., Herzog, S. M., Schooler, L. J., & Reimer, T. (2008). Fluency heuristic: A model of how the mind exploits a by-product of information retrieval. *Journal of Experimental Psychology: Learning, Memory, & Cognition*, 34(5), 1191–1206.

Hertwig, R., & Ortmann, A. (2003). Economists' and psychologists' experimental practices: How they differ, why they differ, and how they could converge. In I. Brocas & J. D. Carrillo (Eds.), *The psychology of economic decisions: Rationality and well-being* (Vol. 1, pp. 253–272). New York, NY: Oxford University Press.

Hicks, J. L., & Marsh, R. L. (1999). Remember-know judgments can depend on how memory is tested. *Psychonomic Bulletin & Review*, 6(1), 117–122.

Higbee, K. L. (1977). *Your memory: How it works and how to improve it.* Englewood Cliffs, NJ: Prentice-Hall.

Hill, A. L. (1978). Savants: Mentally retarded individuals with special skills. In N. R. Ellis (Ed.), *International review of research in mental retardation* (Vol. 9). New York: Academic Press.

Hill, K. (2020, January 18). The secretive company that might end privacy as we know it. *The New York Times*. https://www.nytimes.com/2020/01/18/technology/clearview-privacy-facial-recognition.html

Hillyard, S. A., & Münte, T. F. (1984). Selective attention to color and location: An analysis with event-related brain potentials. *Perception & Psychophysics*, 36(2), 185–198.

Hillyard, S. A., Vogel, E. K., & Luck, S. J. (1998). Sensory gain control (amplification) as a mechanism of selective attention: Electrophysiological and neuroimaging evidence. *Philosophical Transactions of the Royal Society of London B*, 353(1373), 1257–1270.

Hilton, D. J. (2003). Psychology and the financial markets: Applications to understanding and remedying irrational decision-making. In I. Brocas & J. D. Carrillo (Eds.), *The psychology of economic decisions: Rationality and well-being* (Vol. 1, pp. 273–297). New York, NY: Oxford University Press.

Hirst, W., Coman, A., & Stone, C. B. (2012). Memory and jury deliberation: The benefits and costs of collective remembering. In L. Nadel & W. P. Sinnott-Armstrong (Eds.), *Memory and law* (pp. 161–184). New York, NY: Oxford University Press.

Hirst, W., & Phelps, E. A. (2016). Flashbulb memories. *Current Directions in Psychological Science*, 25(1), 36–41.

Hirst, W., Phelps, E. A., Buckner, R. L., Budson, A. E., Cuc, A., Gabrieli, J. D. E., Johnson, M. K., Lustig, C., Lyle, K. B., Mather, M., Meksin, R., Mitchell, K. J., Ochsner, K. N., Schacter, D. L., Simons, J. S., & Vaidya, C. J. (2009). Long-term memory for the terrorist attack of September 11: Flashbulb memories, event memories, and the factors that influence their retention. *Journal of Experimental Psychology: General*, 138(2), 161–176.

Hirst, W., Phelps, E. A., Meksin, R., Vaidya, C. J., Johnson, M. K., Mitchell, K. J., Buckner, R. L., Budson, A. E., Gabrieli, J. D. E., Lustig, C., Mather, M. Ochsner, K. N., Schacter, D., Simons, J. S., Lyle, K. B., Cuc, A. F., Olsson, A. (2015). A ten-year follow-up of a study of memory for the attack of September 11, 2001: Flashbulb memories and memories for flashbulb events. *Journal of Experimental Psychology: General*, 144(3), 604–623.

Hirst, W., Spelke, E. S., Reaves, C. C., Caharack, G., & Neisser, U. (1980). Dividing attention without alternation or automaticity. *Journal of Experimental Psychology: General*, 109(1), 98–117.

Hirst, W., Yamashiro, J. K., & Coman, A. (2018). Collective memory from a psychological perspective. *Trends in Cognitive Sciences*, 22(5), 438–451.

Hitch, G. J., Allen, R. J., & Baddeley, A. D. (2020). Attention and binding in visual working memory: Two forms of attention and two kinds of buffer storage. *Attention, Perception, & Psychophysics*, 82(1), 280–293.

Hobson, J. A., Pace-Schott, E. F., & Stickgold, R. (2000). Dreaming and the brain: Toward a cognitive neuroscience of conscious states. *Behavioral and Brain Sciences*, 23(6), 793–842.

Hochstein, S. (2020). The gist of Anne Treisman's revolution. *Attention, Perception, & Psychophysics*, 82(1), 24–30.

Hoffman, P., McClelland, J. L., & Lambon Ralph, M. A. (2018). Concepts, control, and context: A connectionist account of normal and disordered semantic cognition. *Psychological Review*, 125(3), 293–328.

Holden, C. (2003). The practical benefits of general intelligence. *Science*, 299(5604), 192–193.

Hollingworth, A., & Luck, S. J. (2009). The role of visual working memory (VWM) in the control of gaze during visual search. *Attention, Perception, & Psychophysics*, 71(4), 936–949.

Holmberg, D., & Homes, J. G. (1994). Reconstruction of relationship memories: A mental models approach. In N. Schwarz & S. Sudman (Eds.), *Autobiographical memory and the validity of retrospective reports* (pp. 267–288). New York, NY: Springer.

Holmes, E. A., & Mathews, A. (2010). Mental imagery in emotion and emotional disorders. *Clinical Psychology Review*, 30(3), 349–362.

Holtgraves, T. M. (2002). *Language as social action: Social psychology and language use*. New York, NY: Psychology Press.

Holway, A. F., & Boring, E. G. (1947). Determinants of apparent visual size with distance variant. *American Journal of Psychology*, 54(1), 21–37.

Holyoak, K. J. (2012). Analogy and relational reasoning. In K. J. Holyoak & R. G. Morrison (Eds.), *The Oxford handbook of thinking and reasoning* (pp. 234–259). New York, NY: Oxford University Press.

Hon, N., Epstein, R. A., Owen, A. M., & Duncan, J. (2006). Frontoparietal activity with minimal decision and control. *Journal of Neuroscience*, 26(38), 9805–9809.

Hope, L., Gabbert, F., & Fraser, J. (2013). Postincident conferring by law enforcement officers: Determining the impact of team discussions on statement content, accuracy, and officer beliefs. *Law & Human Behavior*, 37(2), 117–127.

Hope, L., Lewinski, H., Dixon, J., Blocksidge, D., & Gabbert, F. (2012). Witnesses in action: The effect of physical exertion on recall and recognition. *Psychological Science*, 23(4), 386–390.

Hope, L., Memon, A., & McGeorge, P. (2004). Understanding pretrial publicity: Predecisional distortion of evidence by mock jurors. *Journal of Experimental Psychology: Applied*, 10(2), 111–119.

Hopf, J.-M., Luck, S. J., Boelmans, K., Schoenfeld, M. A., Boehler, C. N., Rieger, J., Heinze, H.-J. (2006). The neural site of attention matches the spatial scale of perception. *Journal of Neuroscience*, 26(13), 3532–3540.

Horn, J. L. (1985). Remodeling old models of intelligence. In B. B. Wolman (Ed.), *Handbook of intelligence: Theories, measurements, and applications* (pp. 267–300). New York: Wiley.

Horn, J. L., & Blankson, N. (2005). Foundations for better understanding of cognitive abilities. In D. P. Flanagan & P. L. Harrison (Eds.), *Contemporary intellectual assessment: Theories, tests, and issues* (2nd ed., pp. 41–68). New York: Guilford Press.

Horn, J. L., & Noll, J. (1994). A system for understanding cognitive capabilities: A theory and the evidence on which it is based. In D. K. Detterman (Ed.), *Current topics in human intelligence* (Vol. 4, *Theories of intelligence,* pp. 151–203). Norwood, NJ: Ablex.

Horrey, W. J., Lesch, M. F., & Garabet, A. (2008). Assessing the awareness of performance decrements in distracted drivers. *Accident Analysis & Prevention, 40*(2), 675–682.

Horry, R., Cheong, W., & Brewer, N. (2015). The other-race effect in perception and recognition: Insights from the complete composite task. *Journal of Experimental Psychology: Human Perception & Performance, 41*(2), 508–524.

Hoscheidt, S. M., Dongaonkar, B., Payne, J., & Nadel, L. (2012). Emotion, stress and memory. In D. Reisberg (Ed.), *The Oxford handbook of cognitive psychology* (pp. 557–570). New York, NY: Oxford University Press.

Hsee, C. K., & Hastie, R. (2005). Decision and experience: Why don't we choose what makes us happy? *Trends in Cognitive Sciences, 10,* 31–37.

Hubel, D. H. (1963, November). The visual cortex of the brain. *Scientific American, 209,* 54–62.

Hubel, D. H., & Wiesel, T. N. (1959). Receptive fields of single neurones in the cat's striate cortex. *Journal of Physiology, 148*(3), 574–591.

Hubel, D. H., & Wiesel, T. N. (1968). Receptive fields and functional architecture of monkey striate cortex. *Journal of Physiology, 195*(1), 215–243.

Hummel, J. E. (2013). Object recognition. In D. Reisberg (Ed.), *The Oxford handbook of cognitive psychology* (pp. 32–45). New York, NY: Oxford University Press.

Hummel, J. E., & Biederman, I. (1992). Dynamic binding in a neural network for shape recognition. *Psychological Review, 99*(3), 480–517.

Humphreys, G., & Riddoch, J. (2014). *A case study in visual agnosia: To see but not to see.* New York, NY: Psychology Press.

Hung, J., Driver, J., & Walsh, V. (2005). Visual selection and posterior parietal cortex: Effects of repetitive transcranial magnetic stimulation on partial report analyzed by Bundesen's theory of visual attention. *Journal of Neuroscience, 25*(42), 9602–9612.

Hunt, E. (1995). *Will we be smart enough? A cognitive analysis of the coming workforce.* New York, NY: Russell Sage Foundation.

Hunt, R. R., & Ellis, H. D. (1974). Recognition memory and degree of semantic contextual change. *Journal of Experimental Psychology, 103,* 1153–1159.

Huntley, J. E., & Costanzo, M. (2003). Sexual harassment stories: Testing a story-mediated model of juror decision-making in civil litigation. *Law and Human Behavior, 27*(1), 29–51.

Huntsinger, J. R. (2012). Does positive affect broaden and negative affect narrow attentional scope? A new answer to an old question. *Journal of Experimental Psychology: General, 141*(4), 595–600.

Huntsinger, J. R. (2013). Does emotion directly tune the scope of attention? *Current Directions in Psychological Science, 22*(4), 265–270.

Husain, M., & Mehta, M. A. (2011). Cognitive enhancement by drugs in health and disease. *Trends in Cognitive Sciences, 15*(1), 28–36.

Husserl, E. (1931). *Ideas: General introduction to pure phenomenology.* New York, NY: Collier.

Hyde, J. S. (2014). Gender similarities and differences. *Annual Review of Psychology, 65,* 373–398.

Hyde, T. S., & Jenkins, J. J. (1969). Differential effects of incidental tasks on the organization of recall of a list of highly associated words. *Journal of Experimental Psychology, 82*(3), 472–481.

Hyman, I. E., Jr., Boss, S. M., Wise, B. M., McKenzie, K. E., & Caggiano, J. M. (2010). Did you see the unicycling clown? Inattentional blindness while walking and talking on a cell phone. *Applied Cognitive Psychology, 24*(5), 597–607.

Hyman, I. E., Jr. (2000). Creating false autobiographical memories: Why people believe their memory errors. In E. Winograd, R. Fivush, & W. Hirst (Eds.), *Ecological approaches to cognition: Essays in honor of Ulric Neisser* pp. 229–252. Hillsdale, NJ: Erlbaum.

Hyman, I. E., Jr., Husband, T. H., & Billings, F. J. (1995). False memories of childhood experiences. *Applied Cognitive Psychology, 9*(3), 181–197.

Idan, O., Halperin, E, Hemeiri, B., & Tagar, M. R. (2018). A rose by any other name? A subtle linguistic cue impacts anger and corresponding policy support in intractable conflict. *Psychological Science, 29*(6), 972–983.

International Dyslexia Association. (2018). *Knowledge and practice standards for teachers of reading* (2nd ed.). https://app.box.com/s/21gdk2k1p3bnagdfz1xy0v98j5ytl1wk

Intons-Peterson, M. J. (1983). Imagery paradigms: How vulnerable are they to experimenters' expectations? *Journal of Experimental Psychology: Human Perception & Performance, 9*(3), 394–412.

Intons-Peterson, M. J. (1999). Comments and caveats about "scanning visual mental images." *Cahiers de Psychologie Cognitive, 18*(4), 534–540.

Intons-Peterson, M. J., & White, A. (1981). Experimenter naiveté and imaginal judgments. *Journal of Experimental Psychology: Human Perception & Performance, 7*(4), 833–843.

Intraub, H., & Bodamer, J. L. (1993). Boundary extension: Fundamental aspect of pictorial representation or encoding artifact? *Journal of Experimental Psychology: Learning, Memory, & Cognition, 19*(6), 1387–1397.

Intraub, H., & Dickinson, C. A. (2008). False memory 1/20th of a second later. What the early onset of boundary extension reveals about perception. *Psychological Science, 19*(10), 1007–1014.

Intraub, H., & Richardson, M. (1989). Wide-angle memories of close-up scenes. *Journal of Experimental Psychology: Learning, Memory, & Cognition, 15*(2), 179–187.

Ishikawa, T., & Zhou, Y. (2020). Improving cognitive mapping by training for people with a poor sense of direction. *Cognitive Research: Principles and Implications, 5*, Article 39.

Jackendoff, R. S. (1972). *Semantic interpretation in generative grammar.* Cambridge, MA: MIT Press.

Jacobson, A. F., Umberger, W. A., Palmieri, P. A., Alexander, T. S., Myerscough, R. P., Draucker, C. B., Steudte-Schmiedgen, S., Kirschbaum, C. (2016). Guided imagery for total knee replacement: A randomized, placebo-controlled pilot study. *Journal of Alternative and Complementary Medicine, 22*(7), 563–575.

Jacoby, L. L., & Hollingshead, A. (1990). Reading student essays may be hazardous to your spelling: Effects of reading incorrectly and correctly spelled words. *Canadian Journal of Psychology, 44*(3), 345–358.

Jacoby, L. L. (1978). On interpreting the effects of repetition: Solving a problem versus remembering a solution. *Journal of Verbal Learning and Verbal Behavior, 17*(6), 649–667.

Jacoby, L. L., & Dallas, M. (1981). On the relationship between autobiographical memory and perceptual learning. *Journal of Experimental Psychology: General, 110*(3), 306–340.

Jacoby, L. L., Jones, T. C., & Dolan, P. O. (1998). Two effects of repetition: Support for a dual process model of knowledge judgments and exclusion errors. *Psychonomic Bulletin & Review, 5*(4), 705–709.

Jacoby, L. L., Kelley, C., Brown, J., & Jasechko, J. (1989). Becoming famous overnight: Limits on the ability to avoid unconscious influences of the past. *Journal of Personality and Social Psychology, 56*(3), 326–338.

Jacoby, L. L., & Witherspoon, D. (1982). Remembering without awareness. *Canadian Journal of Psychology, 36*(2), 300–324.

Jaeger, C. B., Levin, D. T., & Porter, E. (2017). Justice is (change) blind: Applying research on visual metacognition in legal settings. *Psychology, Public Policy, & Law, 23*(2), 259–279.

James, L. E., & Burke, D. M. (2000). Phonological priming effects on word retrieval and tip-of-the-tongue experiences in young and older adults. *Journal of Experimental Psychology: Learning, Memory, & Cognition, 26*(6), 1378–1391.

James, W. (1890). *The principles of psychology* (Vol. 2). New York, NY: Dover.

Jang, Y., Pashler, H., & Huber, D. E. (2014). Manipulations of choice familiarity in multiple-choice testing support a retrieval practice account of the testing effect. *Journal of Educational Psychology, 106*(2), 435–447.

Jeffries, R., Polson, P. G., Razran, L., & Atwood, M. E. (1977). A process model for missionaries-cannibals and other river-crossing problems. *Cognitive Psychology, 9*(4), 412–440.

Jencks, C., & Phillips, M. (Eds.). (1998). *The Black-White test score gap.* Washington, DC: Brookings Institution.

Jenkins, R., Lavie, N., & Driver, J. (2005). Recognition memory for distractor faces depends on attentional load at exposure. *Psychological Bulletin & Review, 12*, 314–320.

Jennings, W. G., Fridell, L. A., & Lynch, M. D. (2014). Cops and cameras: Officer perceptions of the use of body-worn cameras in law enforcement. *Journal of Criminal Justice, 42*(6), 549–556.

Jensen, A. R. (1985). The nature of the Black-White difference on various psychometric tests: Spearman's hypothesis. *Behavioral and Brain Sciences, 8*(2), 193–263.

Jesse, A. (2021). Sentence context guides phonetic retuning to speaker idiosyncracies. *Journal of Experimental Psychology: Learning, Memory, & Cognition, 47*(1), 184–194.

Jewsbury, P. A., Bowden, S. C., & Strauss, M. E. (2016). Integrating the switching, inhibition, and updating model of executive function with the Cattell-Horn-Carroll model. *Journal of Experimental Psychology: General, 145*(2), 220–245.

Jiang, J., Li, X., Zhao, C., Guan, Y., & Yu, Q. (2017). Learning and inference in knowledge-based probabilistic model for medical diagnosis. *Knowledge-Based Systems, 138*, 58–68.

Joëls, M., Fernandez, G., & Roozendaal, B. (2011). Stress and emotional memory: A matter of timing. *Trends in Cognitive Sciences, 15*(6), 280–288.

Johnson, E. J., & Goldstein, D. C. (2003). Do defaults save lives? *Science, 302*(5649), 1338–1339.

Johnson, S. K., & Anderson, M. C. (2004). The role of inhibitory control in forgetting semantic knowledge. *Psychological Science, 15*(7), 448–453.

Johnson, W., Carothers, A., & Deary, I. J. (2008). Sex differences in variability in general intelligence: A new look at the old question. *Perspectives on Psychological Science, 3*(6), 518–531.

Johnson, W., te Nijenhuis, J., & Bouchard, T. J., Jr. (2007). Replication of the hierarchical visual-perceptual-image rotation model in de Wolff and Buiten's (1963) battery of 46 tests of mental ability. *Intelligence, 35*(1), 69–81.

Johnson, W., Gangestad, S. W., Segal, N. L., & Bouchard, T. J., Jr. (2008). Heritability of fluctuating asymmetry in a human twin sample: The effect of trait aggregation. *American Journal of Human Biology, 20*(6), 651–658.

Johnston, J. C., & McClelland, J. L. (1973). Visual factors in word perception. *Perception & Psychophysics, 14*, 365–370.

Jonauskaite, D., Abu-Akel, A., Dael, N., Oberfeld, D., Abdel-Khalek, A. M., Al-Rasheed, A. S., Antonietti, J.-P., Bogushevskaya, V., Chamseddine, A., Chkonia, E., Corona, V., Fonseca-Pedrero, E., Griber, Y. A., Grimshaw, G., Ahmed Hasan, A., Havelka, J., Himstein, M., Karlsson, B. S. A., Laurent, E., Lindeman, M. (2020). Universal patterns in color-emotion associations are further shaped by linguistic and geographic proximity. *Psychological Science*, *31*(10), 1245–1260.

Jones, J. L., Esber, G. R., McDannald, M. A., Gruber, A. J., Hernandez, A., Mirenzi, A., & Schoenbaum, G. (2012). Orbitofrontal cortex supports behavior and learning using inferred but not cached values. *Science*, *338*(6109), 953–956.

Jonides, J., Lacey, S. C., & Nee, D. E. (2005). Processes of working memory in mind and brain. *Current Directions in Psychological Science*, *14*(1), 2–5.

Jonides, J., Lewis, R. L., Nee, D. E., Lustig, C. A., Berman, M. G., & Moore, K. S. (2008). The mind and brain of short-term memory. *Annual Review of Psychology*, *59*, 193–224.

Jung, R. E., & Haier, R. J. (2007). The parieto-frontal integration theory (P-FIT) of intelligence: Converging neuroimaging evidence. *Behavioral and Brain Sciences*, *30*(2), 135–154.

Just, M. A., & Buchweitz, A. (2017). What brain imaging reveals about the nature of multitasking. In S. E. F. Chipman (Ed.), *The Oxford handbook of cognitive science* (pp. 265–279). New York, NY: Oxford University Press.

Kahan, D. M., Peters, E., Wittlin, M., Slovic, P., Ouellette, L. L., Braman, D., & Mandel, G. (2012). The polarizing impact of science literacy and numeracy on perceived climate change risks. *Nature Climate Change, 2*, 732–735.

Kahneman, D. (1973). *Attention and effort.* Englewood Cliffs, NJ: Prentice-Hall.

Kahneman, D. (2003). A perspective on judgment and choice: Mapping bounded rationality. *American Psychologist, 58*(9), 697–720.

Kahneman, D. (2011). *Thinking, fast and slow.* New York, NY: Farrar, Straus and Giroux.

Kahneman, D., Fredrickson, B. L., Schreiber, C. A., & Redelmeier, D. (1993). When more pain is preferred to less: Adding a better end. *Psychological Science, 4*(6), 401–405.

Kahneman, D., & Klein, G. (2009). Conditions for intuitive expertise: A failure to disagree. *American Psychologist, 64*(6), 515–526.

Kahneman, D., Knetsch, J. L., & Thaler, R. H. (1990). Experimental tests of the endowment effect and the Coase theorem. *Journal of Political Economy, 98*(6), 1325–1348.

Kahneman, D., & Tversky, A. (1973). On the psychology of prediction. *Psychological Review, 80*(4), 237–251.

Kanaya, T., Scullin, M. H., & Ceci, S. J. (2003). The Flynn effect and U.S. policies: The impact of rising IQ scores on American society via mental retardation diagnoses. *American Psychologist, 58*(10), 778–790.

Kanerva, K., & Kalakoski, V. (2016). The predictive utility of a working memory span task depends on processing demand and the cognitive task. *Applied Cognitive Psychology, 30*(5), 681–690.

Kannan, A. (2019, April 15). *The science of assisting medical diagnosis: From expert systems to machine-learned models.* Curai Health Tech blog. https://medium.com/curai-tech/the-science-of-assisting-medical-diagnosis-from-expert-systems-to-machine-learned-models-cc2ef0b03098

Kanwisher, N., McDermott, J., & Chun, M. M. (1997). The fusiform face area: A module in human extrastriate cortex specialized for face perception. *Journal of Neuroscience, 17*(11), 4302–4311.

Kanwisher, N., & Yovel, G. (2006). The fusiform face area: A cortical region specialized for the perception of faces. *Philosophical Transactions of the Royal Society of London B, 361*(1476), 2109–2128.

Kaplan, A. S., & Murphy, G. L. (2000). Category learning with minimal prior knowledge. *Journal of Experimental Psychology: Learning, Memory, & Cognition, 26*(4), 829–846.

Kaplan, R. L., Van Damme, I., & Levine, L. J. (2012). Motivation matters: Differing effects of pre-goal and post-goal emotions on attention and memory. *Frontiers in Psychology, 3*, Article 404.

Karpicke, J. D. (2012). Retrieval-based learning: Active retrieval promotes meaningful learning. *Current Directions in Psychological Science, 21*(3), 157–163.

Karr, J. E., Areshenkoff, C. N., Rast, P., Hofer, S. M., Iverson, G. L., & Garcia-Barrera, M. A. (2018). The unity and diversity of executive functions: A systematic review and re-analysis of latent variable studies. *Psychological Bulletin, 144*(11), 1147–1185.

Kaasa, S. O., Morris, E. K., & Loftus, E. F. (2011). Remembering why: Can people consistently recall reasons for their behaviour? *Applied Cognitive Psychology, 25*(1), 35–42.

Kassin, S. M, Bogart, D., & Kerner, J. (2012). Confessions that corrupt: Evidence from the DNA exoneration cases. *Psychological Science, 23*(1), (41–45).

Kassin, S. M., Drizin, S. A., Grisso, T., Gudjonsson, G. H., Leo, R. A., & Redlich, A. D. (2010). Police-induced confessions, risk factors, and recommendations: Looking ahead. *Law and Human Behavior, 34*(1), 49–52.

Kassin, S. M., Dror, I. E., & Kukucka, J. (2013). The forensic confirmation bias: Problems, perspectives, and proposed solutions. *Journal of Applied Research in Memory and Cognition, 2*(1), 42–52.

Kassin, S. M., & McNall, K. (1991). Police interrogations and confessions: Communicating promises and threats by pragmatic implication. *Law and Human Behavior, 15*(3), 233–251.

Kassin, S. M., Russano, M. B., Amrom, A. D., Hellgren, J., Kukucka, J., & Lawson, V. Z. (2019). Does video recording inhibit crime suspects? Evidence from a fully randomized field experiment. *Law & Human Behavior, 43*(1), 45–55.

Kastner, S., Schneider, K. A., & Wunderlich, K. (2006). Beyond a relay nucleus: Neuroimaging views on the human LGN. *Progress in Brain Research, 155,* 125–143.

Kaufman, J. C., & Baer, J. (2004). *Creativity across domains: Faces of the muse.* New York, NY: Psychology Press.

Kaufman, J. C., Kaufman, S. B., & Plucker, J. A. (2012). Contemporary theories of intelligence. In D. Reisberg (Ed.), *The Oxford handbook of cognitive psychology.* New York, NY: Oxford University Press.

Kay, K. N., Naselaris, T., Prenger, R. J., & Gallant, J. L. (2008). Identifying natural images from human brain activity. *Nature, 452,* 352–355.

Keefe, P. R. (2016, August 15). Total recall: The detectives who never forget a face. *The New Yorker.*

Keenan, J. M., MacWhinney, B., & Mayhew, D. (1977). Pragmatics in memory: A study of natural conversation. *Journal of Verbal Learning and Verbal Behavior, 16,* 549–560.

Keil, F. C. (1986). The acquisition of natural kind and artifact terms. In W. Demopoulos & A. Marras (Eds.), *Language learning, and concept acquisition* (pp. 133–153). Norwood, NJ: Ablex.

Kellenbach, M. L., Brett, M., & Patterson, K. (2003). Actions speak louder than functions: The importance of manipulability and action in tool representation. *Journal of Cognitive Neuroscience, 15*(1), 30–46.

Kelley, W. M., Macrae, C. N, Wyland, C. L., Cagalar, S., Inatai, S., & Heatherton, T. F. (2002). Finding the self? An event-related fMRI study. *Journal of Cognitive Neuroscience, 14*(5), 785–794.

Kemp, N., & Clayton, J. (2016). University students vary their use of textese in digital messages to suit the recipient. *Journal of Research in Reading, 40*(S1), S141–S157.

Kensinger, E. A., & Ford, J. H. (2020). Retrieval of emotional events from memory. *Annual Review of Psychology, 71,* 251–272.

Keogh, R., & Pearson, J. (2011). Mental imagery and visual working memory. *PLoS ONE, 6*(12), e29221.

Kermer, D. A., Driver-Linn, E., Wilson, T. D., & Gilbert, D. T. (2006). Loss aversion is an affective forecasting error. *Psychological Science, 17*(8), 649–653.

Kerr, N. H. (1983). The role of vision in "visual imagery" experiments: Evidence from the congenitally blind. *Journal of Experimental Psychology: General, 112*(2), 265–277.

Kerr, N. H., & Domhoff, G. W. (2004). Do the blind literally "see" in their dreams? A critique of a recent claim that they do. *Dreaming, 14*(4), 230–233.

Kershaw, T. C., & Ohlsson, S. (2004). Multiple causes of difficulty in insight: The case of the nine-dot problem. *Journal of Experimental Psychology: Learning, Memory, & Cognition, 30*(1), 3–13.

Kerssens, C., Gaither, J. R., & Sebel, P. S. (2009). Preserved memory function during bispectral index-guided anesthesia with sevoflurane for major orthopedic surgery. *Anesthesiology, 111*(3), 518–524.

Kersten, A. W., & Earles, J. L. (2017). Feelings of familiarity and false memory for specific associations resulting from mugshot exposure. *Memory & Cognition, 45*(1), 93–104.

Khemlani, S., & Johnson-Laird, P. N. (2012). Theories of the syllogism: A meta-analysis. *Psychological Bulletin, 138*(3), 427–457.

Kieras, D. E. (2017). A summary of the EPIC cognitive architect. In S. E. F. Chipman (Ed.), *The Oxford handbook of cognitive science* (pp. 27–48). New York, NY: Oxford University Press.

Kim, C.-Y., & Blake, R. (2005). Psychophysical magic: Rendering the visible "invisible." *Trends in Cognitive Sciences, 9*(8), 381–388.

Kim, N. S., & Ahn, W.-K. (2002). Clinical psychologists' theory-based representations of mental disorders predict their diagnostic reasoning and memory. *Journal of Experimental Psychology: General, 131*(4), 451–476.

Kim, N. S., & LoSavio, S. T. (2009). Causal explanations affect judgments of the need for psychological treatment. *Judgment and Decision Making, 4*(1), 82–91.

Kimberg, D. Y., D'Esposito, M., & Farah, M. J. (1997). Cognitive functions in the prefrontal cortex: Working memory and executive control. *Current Directions in Psychological Science, 6*(6), 185–192.

King, M. L., Jr. (1947/1992). The purpose of education. In C. Carson, R. Luker, & P. A. Russell (Eds.), *The papers of Martin Luther King, Jr.* (Vol. 1). Stanford, CA: University of California Press at Berkeley, The Martin Luther King, Jr., Research and Education Institute. https://kinginstitute.stanford.edu/king-papers/documents/purpose-education

King, R. N., & Koehler, D. J. (2000). Illusory correlations in graphological inference. *Journal of Experimental Psychology: Applied, 6*(4), 336–348.

Klauer, K. J., & Phye, G. D. (2008). Inductive reasoning: A training approach. *Review of Educational Research, 78*(1), 85–123.

Kleeman, A. (2016, November 28). Cooking with Chef Watson, I.B.M.'s artificial-intelligence app. *The New Yorker.* https://www.newyorker.com/magazine/2016/11/28/cooking-with-chef-watson-ibms-artificial-intelligence-app

Klein, G. (2013). *Seeing what others don't: The remarkable ways we gain insights.* New York, NY: PublicAffairs.

Knowlton, B. J., & Foerde, K. (2008). Neural representations of nondeclarative memories. *Current Directions in Psychological Science, 17*(2), 107–111.

Kocab, K., & Sporer, S. L. (2016). The weapon focus effect for person identifications and descriptions: A meta-analysis. In M. K. Miller & B. H. Bornstein (Eds.), *Advances in psychology and law* (Vol. 1, pp. 71–117). New York, NY: Springer.

Koch, C. (2008). The neuroscience of consciousness. In L. R. Squire, D. Berg, F. E. Bloom, S. du Lac, A. Ghosh, & N. C. Spitzer (Eds.), *Fundamental neuroscience* (3rd ed., pp. 1223–1236). Burlington, MA: Academic Press.

Koehler, D. J. (2016). Can journalistic "false balance" distort public perception of consensus in expert opinion? *Journal of Experimental Psychology: Applied, 22*(1), 24–38.

Koehler, D. J., Brenner, L., & Griffin, D. W. (2002). The calibration of expert judgment: Heuristics and biases beyond the laboratory. In T. Gilovich, D. Griffin, & D. Kahneman (Eds.), *Heuristics and biases: The psychology of intuitive judgment* (pp. 686–715). New York, NY: Cambridge University Press.

Koppel, J., & Rubin, D. C. (2016). Recent advances in understanding the reminiscence bump: The importance of cues in guiding recall from autobiographical memory. *Current Directions in Psychological Science, 25*(2), 135–140.

Kosslyn, S. M. (1976). Can imagery be distinguished from other forms of internal representation? Evidence from studies of information retrieval times. *Memory & Cognition, 4*(3), 291–297.

Kosslyn, S. M. (1980). *Image and mind.* Cambridge, MA: Harvard University Press.

Kosslyn, S. M. (1983). *Ghosts in the mind's machine: Creating and using images in the brain.* New York, NY: Norton.

Kosslyn, S. M. (1994). *Image and brain: The resolution of the imagery debate.* Cambridge, MA: MIT Press.

Kosslyn, S. M., Ball, T. M., & Reiser, B. J. (1978). Visual images preserve metric spatial information: Evidence from studies of image scanning. *Journal of Experimental Psychology: Human Perception and Performance, 4*(1), 1–20.

Kosslyn, S. M., Pascual-Leone, A., Felician, O., Camposano, S., Keenan, J. P., Thompson, W. L., Ganis, G., Sukel, K. E., Alpert, N. M. (1999). The role of area 17 in visual imagery: Convergent evidence from PET and rTMS. *Science, 284*(5411), 167–170.

Kosslyn, S. M., & Thompson, W. L. (2003). When is early visual cortex activated during mental imagery? *Psychological Bulletin, 129*(5), 723–746.

Kouider, S., de Gardelle, V., Sackur, J., & Dupoux, E. (2010). How rich is consciousness? The partial awareness hypothesis. *Trends in Cognitive Sciences, 14*(7), 301–307.

Kounios, J., & Beeman, M. (2014). The cognitive neuroscience of insight. *Annual Review of Psychology, 65,* 71–93.

Kounios, J., & Beeman, M. (2015). *The eureka factor: Aha moments, creative insight, and the brain.* New York, NY: Random House.

Kovacs, K., & Conway, A. R. A. (2019). What is IQ? Life beyond "general intelligence." *Current Directions in Psychological Science, 28*(2), 189–194.

Kovelman, I., Shalinsky, M. H., Berens, M. S., & Petitto, L. A. (2008). Shining new light on the brain's "bilingual signature": A functional near infrared spectroscopy investigation of semantic processing. *NeuroImage, 39*(3), 1457–1471.

Kovera, M. B., & Evelo, A. J. (2020). Improving eyewitness identification evidence through double-blind lineup administration. *Current Directions in Psychological Science, 29*(6), 563–568.

Kozhevnikov, M., Kosslyn, S., & Shephard, J. (2005). Spatial versus object visualizers: A new characterization of visual cognitive style. *Memory & Cognition, 33,* 710–726.

Kozyreva, A., Lewandowsky, S., & Hertwig, R. (2020). Citizens versus the internet: Confronting digital challenges with cognitive tools. *Psychological Science in the Public Interest, 21*(3), 103–156.

Krafnick, A. J., & Evans, T. M. (2018). Neurobiological sex differences in developmental dyslexia. *Frontiers in Psychology, 9,* Article 2669.

Kraha, A., & Boals, A. (2014). Why so negative? Positive flashbulb memories for a personal event. *Memory, 22*(4), 442–449.

Kramer, R. S. S., Young, A. W., & Burton, A. M. (2018). Understanding face familiarity. *Cognition, 172,* 46–58.

Kraus, N., & Slater, J. (2016). Beyond words: How humans communicate through sound. *Annual Review of Psychology, 67,* 83–103.

Kristjánsson, Á., & Egeth, H. (2020). How feature integration theory integrated cognitive psychology, neurophysiology, and psychophysics. *Attention, Perception, & Psychophysics, 82,* 7–23.

Kroll, J. F., & Potter, M. C. (1984). Recognizing words, pictures, and concepts: A comparison of lexical, object, and reality decisions. *Journal of Verbal Learning and Verbal Behavior, 23*(1), 39–66.

Kubricht, J. R., Lu, H., & Holyoak, K. J. (2017). Individual differences in spontaneous analogical transfer. *Memory & Cognition, 45*(4), 576–588.

Kumar, A. A., Balota, D. A., & Steyvers, M. (2020). Distant connectivity and multiple-step priming in large-scale semantic networks. *Journal of Experimental Psychology: Learning, Memory, & Cognition, 46*(12), 2261–2276.

Kunar, M. A., Carter, R., Cohen, M., & Horowitz, T. S. (2008). Telephone conversation impairs sustained visual attention via a central bottleneck. *Psychonomic Bulletin & Review, 15*(6), 1135–1140.

Kunar, M. A., Cole, L., Cox, A., & Ocampo, J. (2018). It is not good to talk: Conversation has a fixed interference cost on attention regardless of difficulty. *Cognitive Research: Principles and Implications, 3,* Article 33.

Kuncel, N. R., Hezlett, S. A., & Ones, D. S. (2004). Academic performance, career potential, creativity, and job performance: Can one construct predict them all? *Journal of Personality and Social Psychology, 86*(1), 148–161.

Küpper, C. S., Benoit, R. G., Dalgleish, T., & Anderson, M. C. (2014). Direct suppression as a mechanism for controlling unpleasant memories in daily life. *Journal of Experimental Psychology: General*, 143(4), 1443–1449.

Kurtz, K. J., & Loewenstein, J. (2007). Converging on a new role for analogy in problem solving and retrieval: When two problems are better than one. *Memory & Cognition*, 35, 334–341.

Kuster, S. M., van Weerdenburg, M., Gompel, M., & Bosman, A. M. T. (2018). Dyslexie font does not benefit reading in children with or without dyslexia. *Annals of Dyslexia*, 68(1), 25–42.

Labov, B. (2007). Transmission and diffusion. *Language*, 83, 344–387.

Labuschagne, E. M., & Besner, D. (2015). Automaticity revisited: When print doesn't activate semantics. *Frontiers in Psychology*, 6, Article 117.

Lamb, M. E., Orbach, Y., Sternberg, K. J., Hershkowitz, I., & Horowitz, D. (2000). Accuracy of investigators' verbatim notes of their forensic interviews with alleged child abuse victims. *Law and Human Behavior*, 24(6), 699–708.

Lambon Ralph, M. A., Jefferies, E., Patterson, K., & Rogers, T. T. (2017). The neural and computational bases of semantic cognition. *Nature Reviews Neuroscience*, 18(1), 42–55.

Lamme V. A. F., & Roelfsema, P. R. (2000). The distinct modes of vision offered by feedforward and recurrent processing. *Trends in Neuroscience*, 23(11), 571–579.

Lampinen, J. M., Erickson, W. B., Moore, K. N., & Hittson, A. (2014). Effects of distance on face recognition: Implications for eyewitness identification. *Psychonomic Bulletin & Review*, 21(6), 1489–1494.

Lanciano, T., Curci, A., Matera, G., & Sartori, G. (2018). Measuring the flashbulb-like nature of memories for private events: The flashbulb memory checklist. *Memory*, 26(8), 1053–1064.

Lander, K., Bruce, V., & Bindemann, M. (2018). Use-inspired basic research on individual differences in face identification: Implications for criminal investigation and security. *Cognitive Research: Principles and Implications*, 3, Article 26.

Laney, C., & Loftus, E. F. (2010). False memory. In J. M. Brown & E. A. Campbell (Eds.), *The Cambridge handbook of forensic psychology* (pp. 187–194). Cambridge, England: Cambridge University Press.

Lange, N. D., Thomas, R. P., Dana, J., & Dawes, R. M. (2011). Contextual biases in the interpretation of auditory evidence. *Law & Human Behavior*, 35(3), 178–187.

Langer, E. J. (1989). *Mindfulness*. Reading, MA: Addison-Wesley.

Lanska, M., Olds, J. M., & Westerman, D. L. (2013). Fluency effects in recognition memory: Are perceptual fluency and conceptual fluency interchangeable?

Journal of Experimental Psychology: Learning, Memory, & Cognition, 40(1), 1–11.

Lanska, M., & Westerman, D. (2018). Transfer appropriate fluency: Encoding and retrieval interactions in fluency-based memory illusions. *Journal of Experimental Psychology: Learning, Memory, & Cognition*, 44(7), 1001–1012.

Lantian, A., Bagneux, V., Delouvée, S., & Gauvrit, N. (2021). Maybe a free thinker but not a critical one: High conspiracy belief is associated with low critical thinking ability. *Applied Cognitive Psychology*. Advance online publication. https://doi.org/10.1002/acp.3790

Lapate, R. C., Rokers, B., Li, T., & Davidson, R. J. (2014). Nonconscious emotional activation colors first impressions: A regulatory role for conscious awareness. *Psychological Science*, 25(2), 349–357.

Lau, H., & Rosenthal, D. (2011). Empirical support for higher-order theories of conscious awareness. *Trends in Cognitive Sciences*, 15(8), 365–373.

Laukkonen, R. E., Kaveladze, B. T., Tangen, J. M., & Schooler, J. W. (2020). The dark side of eureka: Artificially induced aha moments make facts feel true. *Cognition*, 196, Article 104122.

Laureys, S. (2005). The neural correlate of (un)awareness: Lessons from the vegetative state. *Trends in Cognitive Sciences*, 9(12), 556–559.

Lavie, N. (2001). Capacity limits in selective attention: Behavioral evidence and implications for neural activity. In J. Braun, C. Koch, & J. L. Davis (Eds.), *Visual attention and cortical circuits* (pp. 49–68). Cambridge, MA: MIT Press.

Lavie, N. (2005). Distracted and confused? Selective attention under load. *Trends in Cognitive Sciences*, 9(2), 75–82.

Lavie, N., Lin, Z., Zokaei, N., & Thoma, V. (2009). The role of perceptual load in object recognition. *Journal of Experimental Psychology: Human Perception & Performance*, 35(5), 1346–1358.

Layard, R. (2010). Measuring subjective well-being. *Science*, 327(5965), 534–535.

Lebuda, I., Zabelina, D. L., & Karwowski, M. (2016). Mind full of ideas: A meta-analysis of the mindfulness-creativity link. *Personality and Individual Differences*, 93, 22–26.

Lee, A. J., Sidari, M. J., Murphy, S. C., Sherlock, J. M., & Zietsch, B. P. (2020). Sex differences in misperceptions of sexual interest can be explained by sociosexual orientation and men projecting their own interest onto women. *Psychological Science*, 31(2), 184–192.

Leh, S. E., Johansen-Berg, H., & Ptito, A. (2006). Unconscious vision: New insights into the neuronal correlate of blindsight using diffusion tractography. *Brain*, 129(7), 1822–1832.

Lehman, D. R., Lempert, R. O., & Nisbett, R. E. (1988). The effects of graduate training on reasoning: Formal discipline and thinking about everyday-life events. *American Psychologist*, 43(6), 431–442.

Lehman, D. R., & Nisbett, R. E. (1990). A longitudinal study of the effects of undergraduate education on reasoning. *Developmental Psychology*, 26(6), 952–960.

Lehtonen, M., Soveri, A., Laine, A., Järvenpää, J., deBruin, A., & Antfolk, J. (2018). Is bilingualism associated with enhanced executive functioning in adults? A meta-analytic review. *Psychological Bulletin*, 144(4), 394–425.

Levin, D. T., Takarae, Y., Miner, A. G., & Keil, F. (2001). Efficient visual search by category: Specifying the features that mark the difference between artifacts and animals in preattentive vision. *Perception and Psychophysics*, 63, 676–697.

Levin, D. T., & Simons, D. J. (1997). Failure to detect changes to attended objects in motion pictures. *Psychonomic Bulletin & Review*, 4(4), 501–506.

Levin, I. P., & Gaeth, G. J. (1988). How consumers are affected by the framing of attribute information before and after consuming the product. *Journal of Consumer Research*, 15(3), 374–378.

Levin, I. P., Schnittjer, S. K., & Thee, S. L. (1988). Information framing effects in social and personal decisions. *Journal of Experimental Social Psychology*, 24(6), 520–529.

Levine, L. J., & Edelstein, R. S. (2009). Emotion and memory narrowing: A review and goal relevance approach. *Cognition and Emotion*, 23(5), 833–875.

Levy, J., & Pashler, H. (2008). Task prioritisation in multitasking during driving: Opportunity to abort a concurrent task does not insulate braking responses from dual-task slowing. *Applied Cognitive Psychology*, 22(4), 507–525.

Lewandowsky, S., Ecker, U. K. H., & Cook, J. (2017). Beyond misinformation: Understanding and coping with the "post-truth" era. *Journal of Applied Research in Memory and Cognition*, 6(4), 353–369.

Lewandowsky, S., Ecker, U. K. H, Seifert, C. M., Schwarz, N., & Cook, J. (2012). Misinformation and its correction: Continued influence and successful debiasing. *Psychological Science in the Public Interest*, 13(3), 106–131.

Lewandowsky, S., Gignac, G. E., & Oberauer, K. (2013). The role of conspiracist ideation and worldviews in predicting rejection of science. *PLoS ONE*, 8(10), e75637.

Lewis, M. (2016). *The undoing project: A friendship that changed our minds*. New York, NY: Norton.

Lewis, P. A., Knoblich, G., & Poe, G. (2018). How memory replay in sleep boosts creative problem solving. *Trends in Cognitive Sciences*, 22(6), 491–503.

Li, C., Wang, J., & Otgaar, H. (2020). Creating non-believed memories for bizarre actions using an imagination inflation procedure. *Applied Cognitive Psychology*, 34(6), 1277–1286.

Liberale, L., Carbone, F., Montecucco, F., Gebhard, C., Lüscher, T. F., Wegener, S., & Camici, G. C. (2018). Ischemic stroke across sexes: What is the status quo? *Frontiers in Neuroendocrinology*, 50, 3–17.

Liberman, A. M. (1970). The grammars of speech and language. *Cognitive Psychology*, 1(4), 301–323.

Liberman, A. M., Harris, K. S., Hoffman, H. S., & Griffith, B. C. (1957). The discrimination of speech sounds within and across phoneme boundaries. *Journal of Experimental Psychology*, 54(5), 358–368.

Lichtenstein, S., Slovic, P., Fischhoff, B., Layman, M., & Combs, B. (1978). Judged frequency of lethal events. *Journal of Experimental Psychology: Human Learning and Memory*, 4(6), 551–578.

Lieberman, J. D. (2009). The psychology of the jury instruction process. In J. D. Lieberman & D. A. Krauss (Eds.), *Jury psychology: Social aspects of trial processes* (Vol. 1, pp. 129–155). Burlington, VT: Ashgate.

Lieberman, J. D., & Arndt, J. (2000). Understanding the limits of limiting instructions: Social psychological explanations for the failures of instructions to disregard pretrial publicity and other inadmissible evidence. *Psychology, Public Policy, and Law*, 6(3), 677–711.

Light, L. L., & Carter-Sobell, L. (1970). Effects of changed semantic context on recognition memory. *Journal of Verbal Learning and Verbal Behavior*, 9(1), 1–11.

Lindsay, D. S., & Hyman, I. E., Jr. (2017). Commentary on Brewin and Andrews. *Applied Cognitive Psychology*, 31(1), 37–39.

Lindsay, R. C. L., Semmler, C., Weber, N., Brewer, N., & Lindsay, M. R. (2008). How variations in distance affect eyewitness reports and identification accuracy. *Law and Human Behavior*, 32(6), 526–535.

Lisker, L., & Abramson, A. S. (1970). *The voicing dimension: Some experiments in comparative phonetics.* Paper presented at the Proceedings of the Sixth International Congress of Phonetic Sciences, Prague.

Liu, T., Stevens, S. T., & Carrasco, M. (2007). Comparing the time course and efficacy of spatial and feature-based attention. *Vision Research*, 47(1), 108–113.

Loehlin, J. C., Lindzey, G., & Spuhler, J. N. (1975). *Race difference in intelligence*. San Francisco, CA: Freeman.

Loewenstein, G. F., Weber, E. U., Hsee, C. K., & Welch, N. (2001). Risk as feelings. *Psychological Bulletin*, 127(2), 267–286.

Loftus, E. F. (2003). Make-believe memories. *American Psychologist*, 58(11), 867–873.

Loftus, E. F. (2004). Memories of things unseen. *Current Directions in Psychological Science*, 13(4), 145–147.

Loftus, E. F. (2017). Eavesdropping on memory. *Annual Review of Psychology*, 68, 1–18.

Loftus, E. F., & Palmer, J. C. (1974). Reconstruction of automobile destruction: An example of the interaction between language and memory. *Journal of Verbal Learning and Verbal Behavior*, 13(5), 585–589.

Loftus, G. R., & Harley, E. M. (2005). Why is it easier to identify someone close than far away? *Psychonomic Bulletin & Review*, *12*(1), 43–65.

Logan, G. D. (2018). Automatic control: How experts act without thinking. *Psychological Review*, *125*(4), 453–485.

Logie, R. H., & Cowan, N. (2015). Perspectives on working memory: Introduction to the special issue. *Memory & Cognition*, *43*, 315–324.

Logie, R. H., & Della Salla, S. (2005). Disorders of visuospatial working memory. In P. Shah & A. Miyake (Eds.), *The Cambridge handbook of visuospatial thinking* (pp. 81–120). New York, NY: Cambridge University Press.

Lopes, P. N., Salovey, P., Côté, S., Beers, M., & Petty, R. E. (Ed.). (2005). Emotion regulation abilities and the quality of social interaction. *Emotion*, *5*(1), 113–118.

Loup-Escande, E., Jamet, E., Ragot, M., Erhel, S., & Michinov, N. (2016). Effects of stereoscopic display on learning and user experience in an educational virtual environment. *International Journal of Human-Computer Interaction*, *33*(2), 115–122.

Loveday, C., & Conway, M. A. (2011). Using SenseCam with an amnesic patient: Accessing inaccessible everyday memories. *Memory*, *19*(7), 697–704.

Lu, X., Kelly, M. O., & Risko, E. F. (2020). Offloading information to an external store increases false recall. *Cognition*, *205*, Article 104428.

Lubinski, D. (2004). Introduction to the special section on cognitive abilities: 100 years after Spearman's (1904) "'General intelligence,' objectively determined and measured." *Journal of Personality and Social Psychology*, *86*(1), 96–111.

Luchins, A. S. (1942). Mechanization in problem solving: The effect of Einstellung. *Psychological Monographs*, *54*(6), i–95.

Luchins, A. S., & Luchins, E. H. (1950). New experimental attempts at preventing mechanization in problem solving. *Journal of General Psychology*, *42*, 279–297.

Luhby, T. (2020, June 3). *US Black-White inequality in 6 stark charts*. CNN Politics. https://www.cnn.com/2020/06/03/politics/black-white-us-financial-inequality/index.html

Luke, T. J., & Alceste, F. (2020). The mechanisms of minimization: How interrogation tactics suggest lenient sentencing through pragmatic implication. *Law & Human Behavior*, *44*(4), 266–285.

Lum, C., Stolz, M., Koper, C. S., & Scherer, J. A. (2019). Research on body-worn cameras: What we know, what we need to know. *Criminology & Public Policy*, *18*(1), 93–118.

Luminet, O., & Curci, A. (Eds.). (2009). *Flashbulb memories: New issues and new perspectives*. New York, NY: Psychology Press.

Lupyan, G., Rahman, R. A., Boroditsky, L., & Clark, A. (2020). Effects of language on visual perception. *Trends in Cognitive Sciences*, *24*(11), 930–944.

Luria, A. R. (1966). *Higher cortical functions in man*. New York, NY: Basic Books.

Luria, A. R. (1968). *The mind of a mnemonist: A little book about a vast memory*. New York, NY: Basic Books.

Lurie, R., & Westerman, D. L. (2020). Photo-taking impairs memory on perceptual and conceptual memory tests. *Journal of Applied Research in Memory and Cognition*. Advance online publication. https://doi.org/10.1016/j.jarmac.2020.11.002

Lv, H., Wang, Z., Tong, E., Williams, L. M., Zaharchuk, G., Zeineh, M., Goldstein-Piekarski, A. N., Ball, T. M., Liao, C., & Wintermark, M. (2018). Resting-state functional MRI: Everything that nonexperts have always wanted to know. *American Journal of Neuroradiology*, *39*(8), 1390–1399.

Lynn, S. J., Green, J. P., Polizzi, C. P., Ellenberg, S., Gautam, A., & Aksen, D. E. (2019). Hypnosis, hypnotic phenomena, and hypnotic responsiveness: Clinical and research foundations—a 40-year perspective. *International Journal of Clinical and Experimental Hypnosis*, *67*(4), 475–511.

Lynn, S. J., Kirsch, I., Terhune, D. B., & Green, J. P. (2020). Myths and misconceptions about hypnosis and suggestion: Separating fact and fiction. *Applied Cognitive Psychology*, *34*(6), 1253–1264.

MacCann, C., Jiang, Y., Brown, L. E. R., Double, K. S., Bucich, M., & Minbashian, A. (2020) Emotional intelligence predicts academic performance: A meta-analysis. *Psychological Bulletin*, *146*(2), 150–186.

MacDonald, M. C., Pearlmutter, N. J., & Seidenberg, M. S. (1994). The lexical nature of syntactic ambiguity resolution. *Psychological Review*, *101*(4), 676–703.

MacGregor, J. N., Ormerod, T. C., & Chronicle, E. P. (2001). Information processing and insight: A process model of performance on the 9-dot and related problems. *Journal of Experimental Psychology: Learning, Memory, & Cognition*, *27*(1), 176–201.

Mack, A. (2003). Inattentional blindness: Looking without seeing. *Current Directions in Psychological Science*, *12*(5), 180–184.

Mack, A., & Rock, I. (1998). *Inattentional blindness*. Cambridge, MA: MIT Press.

MacLean, C. L., Stinson, V., Kelloway, E. K., & Fisher, R. P. (2011). Improving workplace incident investigations by enhancing memory recall. *International Journal of Workplace Health Management*, *4*, 257–273.

Mahon, B. Z., & Caramazza, A. (2009). Concepts and categories: A cognitive neuropsychological perspective. *Annual Review of Psychology*, *60*, 27–51.

Mahon, B. Z., & Hickok, G. (2016). Arguments about the nature of concepts: Symbols, embodiment, and beyond. *Psychonomic Bulletin & Review*, *23*, 941–958.

Maia, T. V., & Cleeremans, A. (2005). Consciousness: Converging insights from connectionist modeling and neuroscience. *Trends in Cognitive Sciences*, *9*(8), 397–404.

Majid, A., Bowerman, M., Kita, S., Haun, D. B. M., & Levinson, S. C. (2004). Can language restructure cognition? The case for space. *Trends in Cognitive Sciences*, 8(3), 108–114.

Malmberg, K. J., Raaijmakers, J. G. W., & Shiffrin, R. M. (2019). 50 years of research sparked by Atkinson and Shiffrin (1968). *Memory & Cognition*, 47(4), 561–574.

Malmquist, C. P. (1986). Children who witness parental murder: Posttraumatic aspects. *Journal of the American Academy of Child Psychiatry*, 25(3), 320–325.

Malone, J. C. (2009). *Psychology: Pythagoras to present.* Cambridge, MA: MIT Press.

Malt, B. C., & Smith, E. E. (1984). Correlated properties in natural categories. *Journal of Verbal Learning and Verbal Behavior*, 23(2), 250–269.

Mandler, G. (2011). *A history of modern experimental psychology: From James and Wundt to cognitive science.* Cambridge, MA: MIT Press.

Mansour, J. K., Hamilton, C. M., & Gibson, M. T. (2018). Understanding the weapon focus effect: The role of threat, unusualness, exposure duration, and scene complexity. *Applied Cognitive Psychology*, 33(6), 991–1007.

Marcus, G. F., Pinker, S., Ullman, M., Hollander, M., Rosen, T. J., Xu, F. & Clahsen, H. (1992). *Overregularization in language acquisition* (Monographs of the Society for Research in Child Development, Vol. 57, No. 4 [serial no. 228]). Chicago, IL: University of Chicago Press.

Marcus, G. F., Vijayan, S., Rao, S. B., & Vishton, P. M. (1999). Rule learning by seven-month-old infants. *Science*, 283(5398), 77–80.

Markman, A. B., & Gentner, D. (2001). Thinking. *Annual Review of Psychology*, 52, 223–247.

Markman, A. B., & Rein, J. R. (2013). The nature of mental concepts. In D. Reisberg (Ed.), *The Oxford handbook of cognitive psychology* (pp. 321–329). New York, NY: Oxford University Press.

Markman, K. D., Lindberg, M. J., Kray, L. J., & Galinsky, A. D. (2007). Implications of counterfactual structure for creative generation and analytical problem solving. *Personality and Social Psychology Bulletin*, 33(3), 312–324.

Marmor, G. S., & Zabeck, L. A. (1976). Mental rotation by the blind: Does mental rotation depend on visual imagery? *Journal of Experimental Psychology: Human Perception and Performance*, 2(4), 515–521.

Marsh, E. J. & Rajaram, S. (2019). The digital expansion of the mind: Implications of internet usage for memory and cognition. *Journal of Applied Research in Memory and Cognition*, 8(1), 1–14.

Marsh, R. L., Ward, T. B., & Landau, J. D. (1999). The inadvertent use of prior knowledge in a generative cognitive task. *Memory & Cognition*, 27(1), 94–105.

Marslen-Wilson, W. D., & Teuber, H. L. (1975). Memory for remote events in anterograde amnesia: Recognition of public figures from news photographs. *Neuropsychologia*, 13(3), 353–364.

Masicampo, E. J., & Baumeister, R. F. (2008). Toward a physiology of dual-process reasoning and judgment: Lemonade, willpower, and expensive rule-based analysis. *Psychological Science*, 19(3), 255–260.

Massimini, M., Ferrarelli, F., Huber, R., Esser, S. K., Singh, H., & Tononi, G. (2005). Breakdown of cortical effective connectivity during sleep. *Science*, 309(5744), 2228–2232.

Maswood, R., Rasmussen, A. S., & Rajaram, S. (2019). Collaborative remembering of emotional autobiographical memories: Implications for emotion regulation and collective memory. *Journal of Experimental Psychology: General*, 148(1), 65–79.

Masuda, T., Ellsworth, P. C., Mesquita, B., Leu, J., Tanida, S., & Van de Veerdonk, E. (2008). Placing the face in context: Cultural differences in the perception of facial emotion. *Journal of Personality and Social Psychology*, 94(3), 365–381.

Masuda, T., & Nisbett, R. E. (2006). Culture and change blindness. *Cognitive Science*, 30(2), 381–399.

Mattys, S. L. (2012). Speech perception. In D. Reisberg, (Ed.), *The Oxford handbook of cognitive psychology.* New York, NY: Oxford University Press.

May, C. P., Dein, A., & Ford, J. (2020). New insights into the formation and duration of flashbulb memories: Evidence from medical diagnosis memories. *Applied Cognitive Psychology*, 34(5), 1154–1165.

Mayer, J. D., Roberts, R. D., & Barsade, S. G. (2008). Human abilities: Emotional intelligence. *Annual Review of Psychology*, 59, 507–536.

Mayer, R. E. (2013). Problem solving. In D. Reisberg (Ed.), *The Oxford handbook of cognitive psychology* (pp. 769–778). New York, NY: Oxford University Press.

Mayr, U. (2004). Conflict, consciousness, and control. *Trends in Cognitive Sciences*, 8(4), 145–148.

Mazzoni, G. A. L., Loftus, E. F., & Kirsch, I. (2001). Changing beliefs about implausible autobiographical events: A little plausibility goes a long way. *Journal of Experimental Psychology: Applied*, 7(1), 51–59.

Mazzoni, G., & Lynn, S. J. (2007). Using hypnosis in eyewitness memory: Past and current issues. In M. P. Toglia, J. D. Read, D. F. Ross, & R. C. L. Lindsay (Eds.), *Handbook of eyewitness memory* (Vol. 1, *Memory for events,* pp. 321–338). Mahwah, NJ: Erlbaum.

Mazzoni, G., & Memon, A. (2003). Imagination can create false autobiographical memories. *Psychological Science*, 14(2), 186–188.

McAdams, C. J., & Reid, R. C. (2005). Attention modulates the responses of simple cells in monkey primary visual cortex. *Journal of Neuroscience*, 25(47), 11023–11033.

McAlonan, K., Cavanaugh, J., & Wurtz, R. H. (2008). Guarding the gateway to cortex with attention in visual thalamus. *Nature*, 456(7220), 391–394.

McCabe, J. A., Redick, T. S., & Engle, R. W. (2016). Brain-training pessimism, but applied memory optimism. *Psychological Science in the Public Interest*, 17(3), 187–191.

McCaffrey, T. (2012). Innovation relies on the obscure: A key to overcoming the classic problem of functional fixedness. *Psychological Science*, *23*(3), 215–218.

McClelland, J. L., & Rumelhart, D. E. (1981). An interactive activation model of context effects in letter perception. Part 1: An account of basic findings. *Psychological Review*, *88*(5), 375–407.

McDaniel, M. A., Anderson, J. L., Derbish, M. H., & Morrisette, N. (2007). Testing the testing effect in the classroom. *European Journal of Cognitive Psychology*, *19*(4-5), 494–513.

McDaniel, M. A., Maier, S. F., & Einstein, G. O. (2002). "Brain-specific" nutrients: A memory cure? *Psychological Science in the Public Interest*, *3*(1), 12–38.

McDermott, K. B. (2021). Practicing retrieval facilitates learning. *Annual Review of Psychology*, *72*, 609–633.

McDermott, K. B., Agarwal, P. K., D'Antonio, L., Roediger, H. L., III, & McDaniel, M. A. (2014). Both multiple-choice and short-answer quizzes enhance later exam performance in middle and high school classes. *Journal of Experimental Psychology: Applied*, *20*(1), 3–21.

McDermott, K. B., & Roediger, H., III (1998). False recognition of associates can be resistant to an explicit warning to subjects and an immediate recognition probe. *Journal of Memory & Language*, *39*, 508–520.

McDunn, B. A., Siddiqui, A. P., & Brown, J. M. (2014). Seeking the boundary of boundary extension. *Psychonomic Bulletin & Review*, *21*(2), 370–375.

McGaugh, J. L. (2015). Consolidating memories. *Annual Review of Psychology*, *66*, 1–24.

McGaugh, J. L., & LePort, A. (2014, February). Remembrance of all things past. *Scientific American*, 41–45.

McGrew, K. S. (2009). CHC theory and the human cognitive abilities project: Standing on the shoulders of the giants of psychometric intelligence research. *Intelligence*, *37*(1), 1–10.

McGue, M., Bouchard, T. J., Jr., Iacono, W. G., & Lykken, D. T. (1993). Behavioral genetics of cognitive ability: A life-span perspective. In R. Plomin & G. E. McClearn (Eds.), *Nature, nurture and psychology* (pp. 59–76). Washington, DC: American Psychological Association.

McGurk, H., & MacDonald, J. (1976). Hearing lips and seeing voices. *Nature*, *264*, 746–748.

McIntosh, A. R., Rajah, M. N., & Lobaugh, N. J. (1999). Interactions of prefrontal cortex in relation to awareness in sensory learning. *Science*, *284*(5419), 1531–1533.

McKimmie, B. M., Masser, B. M., & Bongiorno, R. (2014). What counts as rape? The effect of offense prototypes, victim stereotypes, and participant gender on how the complainant and defendant are perceived. *Journal of Interpersonal Violence*, *29*(12), 2273–2303.

McKone, E., Kanwisher, N., & Duchaine, B. C. (2007). Can generic expertise explain special processing for faces? *Trends in Cognitive Sciences*, *11*(1), 8–15.

McNally, R. J. (2017). False memories in the laboratory and in life: Commentary on Brewin and Andrews (2016). *Applied Cognitive Psychology*, *31*(1), 40–41.

McNally, R. J. (2003). Recovering memories of trauma: A view from the laboratory. *Current Directions in Psychological Science*, *12*(1), 32–35.

McRae, K., & Jones, M. (2013). Semantic memory. In D. Reisberg (Ed.), *The Oxford handbook of cognitive psychology* (pp. 206–219). New York, NY: Oxford University Press.

Medeiros-Ward, N., Watson, J. M., & Strayer, D. L. (2015). On supertaskers and the neural basis of efficient multitasking. *Psychonomic Bulletin & Review*, *22*(3), 876–883.

Medin, D. L. (1989). Concepts and conceptual structure. *American Psychologist*, *44*(12), 1469–1481.

Medin, D. L., Coley, J. D., Storms, G., & Hayes, B. K. (2003). A relevance theory of induction. *Psychonomic Bulletin & Review*, *10*(3), 517–532.

Medin, D. L., Goldstone, R. L., & Gentner, D. (1993). Respects for similarity. *Psychological Review*, *100*(2), 254–278.

Medin, D. L., & Ortony, A. (1989). Psychological essentialism. In S. Vosniadou & A. Ortony (Eds.), *Similarity and analogical reasoning* (pp. 179–195). New York, NY: Cambridge University Press.

Mednick, S. (1962). The associative basis of the creative process. *Psychological Review*, *69*(3), 220–232.

Mednick, S., & Mednick, M. (1957). *Examiner's manual, Remote Associates Test*. Boston, MA: Houghton Mifflin.

Meehl, P. E. (1954). *Clinical versus statistical prediction: A theoretical analysis and a review of the evidence*. Minneapolis: University of Minnesota Press.

Meijer, E. H., Selle, N. K., Elber, L., & Ben-Shakhar, G. (2014). Memory detection with the Concealed Information Test: A meta-analysis of skin conductance, respiration, heart rate, and P300 data. *Psychophysiology*, *51*(9), 879–904.

Meissner, C. A., & Brigham, J. C. (2001). Thirty years of investigating the own-race bias in memory for faces: A meta-analytic review. *Psychology, Public Policy, and Law*, *7*(1), 3–35.

Mella, N., Fagot, D., Lecerf, T., & de Ribaupierre, A. (2015). Working memory and intraindividual variability in processing speed: A lifespan developmental and individual-differences study. *Memory & Cognition*, *43*(3), 349–356.

Meltzer, M. A., & Bartlett, J. C. (2019). Holistic processing and unitization in face recognition memory. *Journal of Experimental Psychology: General*, *148*(8), 1386–1406.

Menkel-Meadow, C. (2001). Aha? Is creativity possible in legal problem solving and teachable in legal education? *Harvard Negotiation Law Review*, *6*, 97–144.

Mervis, C. B., Catlin, J., & Rosch, E. (1976). Relationships among goodness-of-example, category norms and word frequency. *Bulletin of the Psychonomic Society*, 7(3), 268–284.

Metcalfe, J. (1986). Premonitions of insight predict impending error. *Journal of Experimental Psychology: Learning, Memory, & Cognition*, 12(4), 623–634.

Metcalfe, J., & Weibe, D. (1987). Intuition in insight and noninsight problem solving. *Memory & Cognition*, 15, 238–246.

Meyer, D. E., & Schvaneveldt, R. W. (1971). Facilitation in recognizing pairs of words: Evidence of a dependence between retrieval operations. *Journal of Experimental Psychology*, 90(2), 227–234.

Meyer, D. E., Schvaneveldt, R. W., & Ruddy, M. G. (1974). Functions of graphemic and phonemic codes in visual word-recognition. *Memory & Cognition*, 2(2), 309–321.

Milivojevic, B., Johnson, B. W., Hamm, J. P., & Corballis, M. C. (2003). Non-identical neural mechanisms for two types of mental transformation: Event-related potentials during mental rotation and mental paper folding. *Neuropsychologia*, 41(10), 1345–1356.

Mill, J. S. (1874). *A system of logic* (8th ed.). New York, NY: Harper.

Miller, D. I., & Halpern, D. F. (2014). The new science of cognitive sex differences. *Trends in Cognitive Sciences*, 18(1), 37–45.

Miller, E. K., & Cohen, J. D. (2001). An integrative theory of prefrontal cortex function. *Annual Review of Neuroscience*, 24, 167–202.

Miller, G. A. (1951). *Language and communication*. New York, NY: McGraw-Hill.

Miller, G. A. (1956). The magical number seven, plus or minus two: Some limits on our capacity for processing information. *Psychological Review*, 63(2), 81–97.

Miller, G. A. (1962). *Psychology: The science of mental life*. New York, NY: Harper & Row.

Miller, G. A., Bruner, J. S., & Postman, L. (1954). Familiarity of letter sequences and tachistoscopic identification. *Journal of General Psychology*, 50, 129–139.

Miller, G. A., Galanter, E., & Pribram, K. H. (1960). *Plans and the structure of behavior*. New York, NY: Holt, Rinehart and Winston.

Miller, L. K. (1999). The Savant Syndrome: Intellectual impairment and exceptional skill. *Psychological Bulletin*, 125(1), 31–46.

Miller, M. B., van Horn, J. D., Wolford, G. L., Handy, T. C., Valsangkar-Smyth, M., Inati, S., Grafton, S., Gazzaniga, M. S. (2002). Extensive individual differences in brain activations associated with episodic retrieval are reliable over time. *Journal of Cognitive Neuroscience*, 14(8), 1200–1214.

Miller, R. R. & Springer, A. D. (1973). Amnesia, consolidation, and retrieval. *Psychological Review*, 80(1), 69–79.

Mills, J. O., Jalil, A., & Stanga, P. E. (2017). Electronic retinal implants and artificial vision: Journey and present. *Eye*, 31, 1383–1398.

Milner, B. (1966). Amnesia following operation on the temporal lobes. In C. W. M. Whitty & O. L. Zangwill (Eds.), *Amnesia* (pp. 109–133). London, England: Butterworths.

Milner, B. (1970). Memory and the medial temporal regions of the brain. In K. H. Pribram & D. E. Broadbent (Eds.), *Biology of memory* (pp. 29–48). New York, NY: Academic Press.

Mitroff, S. R., & Biggs, A. T. (2014). The ultra-rare-item effect: Visual search for exceedingly rare items is highly susceptible to error. *Psychological Science*, 25(1), 284–289.

Miyake, A., & Friedman, N. P. (2012). The nature and organization of individual differences in executive functions: Four general conclusions. *Current Directions in Psychological Science*, 21(1), 8–14.

Moen, K. C., Beck, M. R., Saltzmann, S. M., Cowan, T. M., Burleigh, L. M., Butler, L. G., Ramanujam, J., Cohen, A. S., & Greening, S. G. (2020). Strengthening spatial reasoning: Elucidating the attentional and neural mechanisms associated with mental rotation skill development. *Cognitive Research: Principles and Implications*, 5, Article 20.

Montaldi, D., Spencer, T. J., Roberts, N., & Mayes, A. R. (2006). The neural system that mediates familiarity memory. *Hippocampus*, 16(5), 504–520.

Montoya, R. M., Horton, R. S., Vevea, J. L., Citkowicz, M., & Lauber, E. A. (2017). A re-examination of the mere exposure effect: The influence of repeated exposure on recognition, familiarity, and liking. *Psychological Bulletin*, 143(5), 459–498.

Moons, W. G., Mackie, D. M., & Garcia-Marques, T. (2009). The impact of repetition-induced familarity on agreement with weak and strong arguments. *Journal of Personality & Social Psychology*, 96(1), 32–44.

Moore, A., & Malinowski, P. (2009). Meditation, mindfulness and cognitive flexibility. *Consciousness and Cognition*, 18, 176–186.

Moore, C. M., & Egeth, H. (1997). Perception without attention: Evidence of grouping under conditions of inattention. *Journal of Experimental Psychology: Human Perception and Performance*, 23(2), 339–352.

Moore, T., & Zirnsak, M. (2017). Neural mechanisms of selective visual attention. *Annual Review of Psychology*, 68, 47–52.

Moore v. Texas, 18-443, Tex. Crim. App., Feb. 19, 2019 (OT 2018). https://www.scotusblog.com/case-files/cases/moore-v-texas-2/

Moors, A. (2016). Automaticity: Componential, causal, and mechanistic explanations. *Annual Review of Psychology*, 67, 263–287.

Moors, A., & De Houwer, J. (2006). Automaticity: A theoretical and conceptual analysis. *Psychological Bulletin*, 132(2), 297–326.

Mooser, A. E., & Evans, J. R. (2019). From the police station to the hospital bed: Using the Cognitive Interview to enhance epidemiologic interview. In J. J. Dickinson, N. Schreiber Compo, R. N. Carol, B. L. Schwartz, & M. R. McCauley (Eds.), *Evidence-based investigative interviewing: Applying cognitive principles* (pp. 93–115). New York, NY: Routledge.

Moray, N. (1959). Attention in dichotic listening: Affective cues and the influence of instructions. *Quarterly Journal of Experimental Psychology, 11*(1), 56–60.

Morewedge, C. K., & Giblin, C. E. (2015). Explanations of the endowment effect: An integrative review. *Trends in Cognitive Sciences, 19*(6), 339–348.

Morgan, C. A., III, Hazlett, G., Doran, A., Garrett, S., Hoyt, G., Thomas, P., Baranoski, M., & Southwick, S. M. (2004). Accuracy of eyewitness memory for persons encountered during exposure to highly intense stress. *International Journal of Law and Psychiatry, 27*(3), 265–279.

Morgan, C. A., III, Southwick, S., Steffian, G., Hazlett, G. A., & Loftus, E. F. (2013). Misinformation can influence memory for recently experienced, highly stressful events. *International Journal of Law and Psychiatry, 36*(1), 11–17.

Morrison, C. M., & Conway, M. A. (2010). First words and first memories. *Cognition, 116*(1), 23–32.

Morsella, E., & Bargh, J. A. (2011). Unconscious action tendencies: Sources of "unintegrated" action. In J. T. Cacioppo & J. Decety (Eds.), *The handbook of social neuroscience* (pp. 335–347). New York, NY: Oxford University Press.

Morsella, E., Godwin, C. A., Jantz, T. K., Krieger, S. C., & Gazzaley, A. (2016). Passive frame theory: A new synthesis. *Behavioral and Brain Sciences, 39*, 44–70.

Möschl, M., Fischer, R., Bugg, J. M., Scullin, M., K. Goschke, T., & Walser, M. (2020). Aftereffects and deactivation of completed prospective memory intentions: A systematic review. *Psychological Bulletin, 146*(3), 245–278.

Moscovitch, M. (1982). Multiple dissociations of function in amnesia. In L. S. Cermak (Ed.), *Human memory and amnesia* (pp. 337–370). Hillsdale, NJ: Erlbaum.

Moseley, P., Smailes, D., Ellison, A., & Fernyhough, C. (2016). The effect of auditory verbal imagery on signal detection in hallucination-prone individuals. *Cognition, 146*, 202–216.

Most, S. B., Simons, D. J., Scholl, B. J., Jimenez, R., Clifford, E., & Chabris, C. F. (2001). How not to be seen: The contribution of similarity and selective ignoring to sustained inattentional blindness. *Psychological Science, 12*(1), 9–17.

Mulligan, N. W., & Besken, M. (2013). Implicit memory. In D. Reisberg (Ed.), *The Oxford handbook of cognitive psychology* (pp. 220–231). New York, NY: Oxford University Press.

Munger, M. P., & Multhaup, K. S. (2016). No imagination effect on boundary extension. *Memory & Cognition, 44*(1), 73–88.

Munion, A. K., Stefanucci, J. K., Rovira, E., Squire, P., & Hendricks, M. (2019). Gender differences in spatial navigation: Characterizing wayfinding behaviors. *Psychonomic Bulletin & Review, 26*(6), 1933–1940.

Murdock, B. B., Jr. (1962). The serial position effect of free recall. *Journal of Experimental Psychology, 64*(5), 482–488.

Murphy, G., & Greene, C. M. (2016). Perceptual load induces inattentional blindness in drivers. *Applied Cognitive Psychology, 30*(3), 479–483.

Murphy, G., & Greene, C. M. (2017). The elephant in the road: Auditory perceptual load affects driver perception and awareness. *Applied Cognitive Psychology, 31*(2), 258–263.

Murphy, G., Groeger, J. A., & Greene, C. M. (2016). Twenty years of load theory—Where are we now, and where should we go next? *Psychonomic Bulletin & Review, 23*(5), 1316–1340.

Murphy, G., & Murphy, L. (2018). Perceptual load affects change blindness in a real-world interaction. *Applied Cognitive Psychology, 32*(5), 655–660.

Murphy, G. L. (2016). Is there an exemplar theory of concepts? *Psychonomic Bulletin & Review, 23*(4), 1035–1042.

Murphy, G. L., & Medin, D. L. (1985). The role of theories in conceptual coherence. *Psychological Review, 92*(3), 289–316.

Murphy, G. L., & Shapiro, A. M. (1994). Forgetting of verbatim information in discourse. *Memory & Cognition, 22*(21), 85–94.

Murphy, J., Gray, K. L. H., & Cook, R. (2017). The composite face illusion. *Psychonomic Bulletin & Review, 24*(2), 245–261.

Murphy, S., & Dalton, P. (2016). Out of touch? Visual load induces inattentional numbness. *Journal of Experimental Psychology: Human Perception & Performance, 42*(6), 761–765.

Murphy, S., & Dalton, P. (2018). Inattentional numbness and the influence of task difficulty. *Cognition, 178*, 1–6.

Murphy, S. T. (2001). Feeling without thinking: Affective primacy and the nonconscious processing of emotion. In J. A. Bargh & D. K. Apsley (Eds.), *Unraveling the complexities of social life: A festschrift in honor of Robert B. Zajonc* (pp. 39–53). Washington, DC: American Psychological Association.

Murray, C., Pattie, A., Starr, J. M., & Deary, I. J. (2012). Does cognitive ability predict mortality in the ninth decade? The Lothian birth cohort 1921. *Intelligence, 40*(5), 490–498.

Nadarevic, L., Reber, R., Helmecke, A. J., & Köse, D. (2020). Perceived truth of statements and simulated social media postings: An experimental investigation of source credibility, repeated exposure, and presentation format. *Cognitive Research: Principles & Implications, 5*, Article 56.

Nagel, T. (1974). What is it like to be a bat? *The Philosophical Review*, 83(4), 435–450.

Naqvi, N., Shiv, B., & Bechara, A. (2006). The role of emotion in decision making: A cognitive neuroscience perspective. *Current Directions in Psychological Science*, 15(5), 260–264.

Nash, R. A., Wade, K. A., Garry, M., Loftus, E. F., & Ost, J. (2017). Misrepresentations and flawed logic about the prevalence of false memories. *Applied Cognitive Psychology*, 31(1), 31–33.

National Academies of Sciences, Engineering, and Medicine. (2015). *Improving diagnosis in health care*. https://www.nap.edu/catalog/21794/improving -diagnosis-in-health-care

National Research Council (2014). *Identifying the culprit: Assessing eyewitness identification*. Washington, DC: National Academies Press.

National Research Council, Committee to Review the Scientific Evidence on the Polygraph, Division of Behavioral and Social Sciences and Education. (2003). *The polygraph and lie detection*. Washington, DC: National Academies Press.

Neisser, U. (1967). *Cognitive psychology*. New York, NY: Appleton-Century-Crofts.

Neisser, U., & Becklen, R. (1975). Selective looking: Attending to visually specified events. *Cognitive Psychology*, 7(4), 480–494.

Neisser, U., Boodoo, G., Bouchard, T. J., Jr., Boykin, A. W., Brody, N., Ceci, S. J., Halpern, D. F., Loehlin, J. C., Perloff, R., Sternberg, R. J., Urbina, S. (1996). Intelligence: Knowns and unknowns. *American Psychologist*, 51(2), 77–101.

Nettelbeck, T. (2003). Inspection time and g. In H. Nyborg (Ed.), *The scientific study of general intelligence: Tribute to Arthur R. Jensen* (pp. 77–92). New York, NY: Elsevier.

Newell, A., & Simon, H. A. (1972). *Human problem solving*. Englewood Cliffs, NJ: Prentice-Hall.

Newell, A., Shaw, J. C., & Simon, H. A. (1959). Report on a general problem-solving program. *Proceedings of the International Conference on Information Processing* (pp. 256–264).

Newman, E. J., Garry, M., Bernstein, D. M., Kantner, J., & Lindsay, D. S. (2012). Nonprobative photographs (or words) inflate truthiness. *Psychonomic Bulletin & Review*, 19(5), 969–974.

Newman, E. J., Garry, M., Unkelbach, C., Bernstein, D. M., Lindsay, D. S., & Nash, R. A. (2015). Truthiness and falsiness of trivia claims depend on judgmental contexts. *Journal of Experimental Psychology: Learning, Memory, & Cognition*, 41(5), 1337–1348.

Nichols, E. S., Wild, C. J., Stojanoski, B., Battista, M. E., & Owen, A. M. (2020). Bilingualism affords no general cognitive advantages: A population study of executive function in 11,000 people. *Psychological Science*, 31(5), 548–567.

Nickerson, R. S., & Adams, M. J. (1979). Long-term memory for a common object. *Cognitive Psychology*, 11(3), 287–307.

Nisbett, R. E. (2003). *The geography of thought: How Asians and Westerners think differently . . . and why*. New York, NY: Free Press.

Nisbett, R. E. (2009). *Intelligence and how to get it: Why schools and cultures count*. New York, NY: Norton.

Nisbett, R. E., Aronson, J., Blair, C., Dickens, W., Flynn, J., Halpern, D. F., & Turkheimer, E. (2012a). Group differences in IQ are best understood as environmental in origin. *American Psychologist*, 67(6), 503–504.

Nisbett, R. E., Aronson, J., Blair, C., Dickens, W., Flynn, J., Halpern, D. F., & Turkheimer, E. (2012b). Intelligence: New findings and theoretical developments. *American Psychologist*, 67(2), 130–159.

Nisbett, R. E., Krantz, D. H., Jepson, C., & Kunda, Z. (1983). The use of statistical heuristics in everyday inductive reasoning. *Psychological Review*, 90(4), 339–363.

Nisbett, R. E., Peng, K., Choi, I., & Norenzayan, A. (2001). Culture and systems of thought: Holistic versus analytic cognition. *Psychological Review*, 108(2), 291–310.

Nisbett, R. E., & Ross, L. (1980). *Human inference: Strategies and shortcomings of social judgment*. Englewood Cliffs, NJ: Prentice-Hall.

Nisbett, R. E., & Schachter, S. (1966). Cognitive manipulation of pain. *Journal of Experimental Social Psychology*, 2(3), 277–236.

Nisbett, R. E., & Wilson, T. D. (1977). Telling more than we can know: Verbal reports on mental processes. *Psychological Review*, 84(3), 231–259.

Norman, D. (1981). Categorization of action slips. *Psychological Review*, 88(1), 1–15.

Norman, D. A., & Shallice, T. (1986). Attention to action: Willed and automatic control of behavior. In R. J. Davidson, G. E. Schwartz, & D. Shapiro (Eds.), *Consciousness and self-regulation* (pp. 1–18). New York, NY: Plenum.

Norman, D. G., Wade, K. A., Williams, M. A., & Watson, D. G. (2020). Caught virtually lying—Crime scenes in virtual reality help to expose suspects' concealed recognition. *Journal of Applied Research in Memory and Cognition*, 9(1), 118–127.

Noveck, I. A., & Reboul, A. (2008). Experimental pragmatics: A Gricean turn in the study of language. *Trends in Cognitive Sciences*, 12(11), 425–431.

Noveck, I. A., & Sperber, D. (Eds.). (2005). *Experimental pragmatics*. New York, NY: Oxford University Press.

Noyes, E., Hill, M. Q., & O'Toole, A. J. (2018). Face recognition ability does not predict person identification performance: Using individual data in the interpretation of group results. *Cognitive Research: Principles and Implications*, 3, Article 23.

Nyberg, L., Habib, R., McIntosh, A. R., & Tulving, E. (2000). Reactivation of encoding-related brain activity during memory retrieval. *Proceedings of the National Academy of Sciences*, 97(20), 11120–11124.

O'Connor, K., & Cheema, A. (2018). Do evaluations rise with experience? *Psychological Science*, 29(5), 779–790.

O'Connor, M., Walbridge, M., Sandson, T., & Alexander, M. (1996). A neuropsychological analysis of Capgras syndrome. *Neuropsychiatry, Neuropsychology, and Behavioral Neurology*, 9, 265–271.

O'Craven, K. M., & Kanwisher, N. (2000). Mental imagery of faces and places activates corresponding stimulus-specific brain regions. *Journal of Cognitive Neuroscience*, 12(6), 1013–1023.

O'Kane, G., Kensinger, E. A., & Corkin, S. (2004). Evidence for semantic learning in profound amnesia: An investigation with patient H.M. *Hippocampus*, 14(4), 417–425.

O'Rear, A. E., & Radvansky, G. A. (2020). Failures to accept retractions: A contribution to the continued influence effect. *Memory & Cognition*, 48, 127–144.

Oaksford, M., & Chater, N. (2020). New paradigms in the psychology of reasoning. *Annual Review of Psychology*, 71, 305–330.

Oaksford, M., & Hall, S. (2016). On the source of human irrationality. *Trends in Cognitive Sciences*, 20(5), 336–344.

Oberauer, K., Lewandowsky, S., Awh, E., Brown, G. D. A., Conway, A., Cowan, N., Donkin, C., Farrell, S., Hitch, G. J., Hurlstone, M. J., Ma, W. J., Morey, C. C., Nee, D. E., Schweppe, J., Vergauwe, E., & Ward, G. (2018). Benchmarks for models of short-term and working memory. *Psychological Bulletin*, 144(9), 885–958.

Obrecht, N. A., Chapman, G. B., & Gelman, R. (2009). An encounter frequency account of how experience affects likelihood estimation. *Memory & Cognition*, 37, 632–643.

Ogloff, J. R. P., & Rose, V. G. (2005). The comprehension of judicial instructions. In N. Brewer & K. D. Wilson (Eds.), *Psychology and law: An empirical perspective* (pp. 407–444). New York, NY: Guilford Press.

Oldfield, R. C. (1963). Individual vocabulary and semantic currency: A preliminary study. *British Journal of Social and Clinical Psychology*, 2(2), 122–130.

Oliphant, G. W. (1983). Repetition and recency effects in word recognition. *Australian Journal of Psychology*, 35(3), 393–403.

Öllinger, M., Jones, G., Faber, A. H., & Knoblich, G. (2013). Cognitive mechanisms of insight: The role of heuristics and representational change in solving the eight-coin problem. *Journal of Experimental Psychology: Learning, Memory, & Cognition*, 39(3), 931–939.

Oppenheimer, D. M. (2006). Consequences of erudite vernacular utilized irrespective of necessity: Problems with using long words needlessly. *Applied Cognitive Psychology*, 20(2), 139–156.

Oppenheimer, D. M. (2008). The secret life of fluency. *Trends in Cognitive Sciences*, 12(6), 237–241.

Oppenheimer, D. M., & Alter A. L. (2014). The search for moderators in disfluency research. *Applied Cognitive Psychology*, 28(4), 502–504.

Ost, J. (2013). Recovered memories and suggestibility for entire events. In A. M. Ridley, F. Gabbert, & D. J. La Rooy (Eds.), *Suggestibility in legal contexts: Psychological research and forensic implications* (pp. 107–128). New York, NY: Wiley.

Ost, J., Vrij, A., Costall, A., & Bull, R. (2002). Crashing memories and reality monitoring: Distinguishing between perceptions, imaginations and "false memories." *Applied Cognitive Psychology*, 16(2), 125–134.

Otgaar, H., Bücken, C., Bogaard, G., Wade, K., Hopwood, A. R., Scoboria, A., & Howe, M. L. (2019). Non-believed memories in the False Memory Archive. *Journal of Applied Research in Memory and Cognition*, 8(4), 429–438.

Otgaar, H., Howe, M. L., & Patihis, L. (2021). What science tells us about false and repressed memories. *Memory*, 12, 1–6.

Otgaar, H., Howe, M. L., Patihis, L., Merckelbach, H., Lynn, S. J., Lilienfeld, S. O., & Loftus, E. F. (2019). The return of the repressed: The persistent and problematic claims of long-forgotten trauma. *Perspectives on Psychological Science*, 14(6), 1072–1095.

Otgaar, H., Merckelbach, H., Jelicic, M., & Smeets, T. (2017). The potential for false memories is bigger than what Brewin and Andrews suggest. *Applied Cognitive Psychology*, 31(1), 24–25.

Otsuka-Hirota, N., Yamamoto, H., Miyashita, K., & Nagatsuka, K. (2014). Invisibility of moving objects: A core symptom of motion blindness. *BMJ Case Reports*, 2014, bcr2013201233.

Overton, D. A. (1985). Contextual stimulus effects of drugs and internal states. In P. D. Balsam & A. Tomie (Eds.), *Context and learning* (pp. 357–384). Hillsdale, NJ: Erlbaum.

Owen, A. M., Coleman, M. R., Boly, M., Davis, M. H., Laureys, S., & Pickard, J. D. (2006). Detecting awareness in the vegetative state. *Science*, 313(5792), 1402.

Owens, J., Bower, G. H., & Black, J. B. (1979). The "soap opera" effect in story recall. *Memory & Cognition*, 7(3), 185–191.

Ozcan, M. S., Gronlund, S. D., Trojan, R., Khan, Q., Cure, J., & Wong, C. (2011). Does a BIS-guided maintenance of anesthetic depth prevent implicit memory? *Psychology*, 2(3), 143–149.

Özgen, E. (2004). Language, learning, and color perception. *Current Directions in Psychological Science*, 13(3), 95–98.

Pachur, T., Hertwig, R., & Steinmann, F. (2012). How do people judge risks: Availability heuristic, affect heuristic, or both? *Journal of Experimental Psychology: Applied*, 18(3), 314–330.

Paivio, A. (1969). Mental imagery in associative learning and memory. *Psychological Review*, 76(3), 241–263.

Paivio, A. (1971). *Imagery and verbal processes*. New York, NY: Holt, Rinehart & Winston.

Paivio, A., & Okovita, H. W. (1971). Word imagery modalities and associative learning in blind and sighted subjects. *Journal of Verbal Learning and Verbal Behavior, 10*, 506–510.

Paivio, A., Smythe, P. C., & Yuille, J. C. (1968). Imagery versus meaningfulness of nouns in paired-associate learning. *Canadian Journal of Psychology, 22*(6), 427–441.

Paivio, A., Yuille, J. C., & Madigan, S. A. (1968). Concreteness, imagery, and meaningfulness values for 925 nouns. [Monograph supplement]. *Journal of Experimental Psychology, 76*(1), Pt. 2. Washington, DC: American Psychological Association.

Paller, K. A., Creery, J. D., & Schechtman, E. (2021). Memory and sleep: How sleep cognition can change the waking mind for the better. *Annual Review of Psychology, 72*, 123–150.

Paller, K. A., & Suzuki, S. (2014). Response to Block et al.: First-person perspectives are both necessary and troublesome for consciousness science. *Trends in Cognitive Sciences, 18*(11), 557–558.

Palombo, D. J., Sheldon, S., & Levine, B. (2018). Individual differences in autobiographical memory. *Trends in Cognitive Sciences, 22*(7), 583–597.

Pansky, A., & Koriat, A. (2004). The basic-level convergence effect in memory distortions. *Psychological Science, 15*(1), 52–59.

Paoletti, J. B. (2012). *Pink and blue: Telling the boys from the girls in America*. Bloomington: Indiana University Press.

Parker, E. S., Cahill, L., & McGaugh, J. L. (2006, February). A case of unusual autobiographical remembering. *Neurocase, 12*(1): 35–49.

Parkhurst, D., Law, K., & Niebur, E. (2002). Modeling the role of salience in the allocation of overt visual attention. *Vision Research, 42*(1), 107–123.

Patel, N., Baker, S. G., & Scherer, L. D. (2019). Evaluating the cognitive reflection test as a measure of intuition/reflection, numeracy, and insight problem solving, and the implications for understanding real-world judgments and beliefs. *Journal of Experimental Psychology: General, 148*(12), 2129–2153.

Paterson, H. M., & Kemp, R. I. (2006). Comparing methods of encountering post-event information: The power of co-witness suggestion. *Applied Cognitive Psychology, 20*(8), 1083–1099.

Patihis, L., Cruz, C. S., & Herrera, M. E. (2019). Changing current appraisals of mothers leads to changes in childhood memories of love toward mothers. *Clinical Psychological Science, 7*(5), 1125–1143.

Patihis, L., Lilienfeld, S. O., Ho, L., & Loftus, E. F. (2014). Unconscious repressed memory is scientifically questionable. *Psychological Science, 25*(10), 197–198.

Patihis, L., & Loftus, E. F. (2015). Crashing memory 2.0: False memories in adults for an upsetting childhood event. *Applied Cognitive Psychology, 30*(1), 41–50.

Patrick, J., & Ahmed, Afia. (2014). Facilitating representation change in insight problems through training. *Journal of Experimental Psychology: Learning, Memory, & Cognition, 40*(2), 532–543.

Patrick, J., Ahmed, A., Smy, V., Seeby, H., & Sambrooks, K. (2015). A cognitive procedure for representation change in verbal insight problems. *Journal of Experimental Psychology: Learning, Memory, & Cognition, 41*(3), 746–759.

Patterson, K., & Lambon Ralph, M. A. (2016). The Hub-and-Spoke hypothesis of semantic memory. In G. Hickok & S. L. Small (Eds.), *Neurobiology of language* (pp. 765–775). New York, NY: Academic Press.

Payne, L., & Sekuler, R. (2014). The importance of ignoring: Alpha oscillations protect selectivity. *Current Directions in Psychological Science, 23*(3), 171–177.

Payton, A. (2009). The impact of genetic research on our understanding of normal cognitive ageing: 1995 to 2009. *Neuropsychology Review, 19*(4), 451–477.

Paz-Alonso, P. M., & Goodman, G. S. (2008). Trauma and memory: Effects of post-event misinformation, retrieval order, and retention interval. *Memory, 16*(1), 58–75.

Peace, K. A., & Porter, S. (2004). A longitudinal investigation of the reliability of memories for trauma and other emotional experiences. *Applied Cognitive Psychology, 18*, 1143–1159.

Pearson, D. G. (2007). Mental imagery and creative thought. *Proceedings of the British Academy, 147*, 187–212.

Pearson, J. (2014). New directions in mental-imagery research: The binocular-rivalry technique and decoding fMRI patterns. *Current Directions in Psychological Science, 23*(3), 178–183.

Pearson, J. (2019). The human imagination: The cognitive neuroscience of visual mental imagery. *Nature Reviews Neuroscience, 20*, 624–634.

Pearson, J., Naselaris, T., Holmes, E. A., & Kosslyn, S. M. (2015). Mental imagery: Functional mechanisms and clinical applications. *Trends in Cognitive Sciences, 19*(10), 590–602.

Pearson, J., Rademaker, R. L., & Tong, F. (2011). Evaluating the mind's eye: The metacognition of visual imagery. *Psychological Science, 22*(12), 1535–1542.

Pederson, E., Danziger, E., Wilkins, D., Levinson, S., Kita, S., & Senft, G. (1998). Semantic typology and spatial conceptualization. *Language, 74*(3), 557–589.

Peng, Y., & Tullis, J. G. (2020). Theories of intelligence influence self-regulated study choices and learning. *Journal of Experimental Psychology: Learning, Memory, & Cognition, 46*(3), 487–496.

Pennycook, G., Cheyne, J. A., Koehler, D. J., & Fugelsang, J. A. (2016). Is the cognitive reflection test a measure of both reflection and intuition? *Behavior Research Methods, 48*(1), 341–348.

Pennycook, G., Fugelsang, J. A., & Koehler, D. J. (2015). Everyday consequences of analytic thinking. *Current Directions in Psychological Science, 24*(6), 425–432.

Pennycook, G., McPhetres, J., Zhang, Y., Lu, J. G., & Rand, D. G. (2020). Fighting COVID-19 misinformation on social media: Experimental evidence for a scalable accuracy-nudge intervention. *Psychological Science*, 31(7), 770–780.

Pennycook, G., & Rand, D. G. (2019a). Lazy, not biased: Susceptibility to partisan fake news is better explained by lack of reasoning than by motivated reasoning. *Cognition*, 188, 39–50.

Pennycook, G., & Rand, D. G. (2019b). Who falls for fake news? The roles of bullshit receptivity, over-claiming, familiarity, and analytic thinking. *Journal of Personality*, 88(2), 185–200.

Pennycook, G., Trippas, D., Handley, S. J., & Thompson, V. A. (2014). Base rates: Both neglected and intuitive. *Journal of Experimental Psychology: Learning, Memory, & Cognition*, 40(2), 544–554.

Peru, A., & Avesani, R. (2008). To know what it is for, but not how it is: Semantic dissociations in a case of visual agnosia. *Neurocase*, 14(3), 249–263.

Petersen, S. E., van Mier, H., Fiez, J. A., & Raichle, M. E. (1998). The effects of practice on the functional anatomy of task performance. *Proceedings of the National Academy of Sciences*, 95(3), 853–860.

Peterson, M. A., Kihlstrom, J. F., Rose, P. M., & Glisky, M. L. (1992). Mental images can be ambiguous: Reconstruals and reference-frame reversals. *Memory & Cognition*, 20, 107–123.

Pezdek, K., & Blandon-Gitlin, I. (2017). It is just harder to construct memories for false autobiographical events. *Applied Cognitive Psychology*, 31(1), 42–44.

Pezdek, K., Blandon-Gitlin, I., & Gabbay, P. (2006). Imagination and memory: Does imagining implausible events lead to false autobiographical memories? *Psychonomic Bulletin & Review*, 13(5), 764–769.

Phillips, I. (2020). Blindsight is qualitatively degraded conscious vision. *Psychological Review*. Advance online publication. https://doi.org/10.1037/rev0000254

Phillips, J. A., Noppeney, U., Humphreys, G. W., & Price, C. J. (2002). Can segregation within the semantic system account for category-specific deficits? *Brain*, 125(9), 2067–2080.

Piaget, J. (1952). *The origins of intelligence in children*. New York, NY: International Universities Press.

Pietschnig, J., & Voracek., M. (2015). One century of global IQ gains: A formal meta-analysis of the Flynn Effect (1909–2013). *Perspectives on Psychological Science*, 10(3), 282–306.

Pilcher, H. (2004). Chinese dyslexics have problems of their own. *Nature*. https://doi.org/10.1038/news040830-5

Pillemer, D. B. (1984). Flashbulb memories of the assassination attempt on President Reagan. *Cognition*, 16(1), 63–80.

Pillemer, D. B., Koff, E., Rhinehart, E. D., & Rierdan, J. (1987). Flashbulb memories of menarche and adults' menstrual distress. *Journal of Adolescence*, 10(2), 187–199.

Pinker, S. (1994). *The language instinct: How the mind creates language*. New York, NY: Harper Perennial.

Pittarello, A., Conte, B., Caserotti, M., Scrimin, S., & Rubaeltelli, E. (2018). Emotional intelligence buffers the effect of physiological arousal on dishonesty. *Psychonomic Bulletin & Review*, 25, 440–446.

Pittam, J., & Scherer, K. R. (1993). Vocal expression and communication of emotion. In M. Lewis & J. M. Haviland (Eds.), *Handbook of emotions* (pp. 185–197). New York, NY: Guilford Press.

Platt, J. M., Keyes, K. M., McLaughlin, K A., & Kaufman, A. S. (2019). The Flynn effect for fluid IQ may not generalize to all ages or ability levels: A population-based study of 10,000 US adolescents. *Intelligence*, 77, Article 101385.

Plomin, R., Fulker, D. W., Corley, R., & DeFries, J. C. (1997). Nature, nurture, and cognitive development from 1 to 16 years: A parent-offspring adoption study. *Psychological Science*, 8(6), 442–447.

Plomin, R., Haworth, C. M. A., Meaburn, E. L., Price, T. S., Wellcome Trust Case Control Consortium, & Davis, O. S. P. (2013). Common DNA markers can account for more than half of the genetic influence on cognitive abilities. *Psychological Science*, 24(4), 562–568.

Plomin, R., & Spinath, F. M. (2004). Intelligence: Genetics, genes, and genomics. *Journal of Personality and Social Psychology*, 86(1), 112–129.

Pollack, I., & Pickett, J. M. (1964). Intelligibility of excerpts from fluent speech: Auditory vs. structural context. *Journal of Verbal Learning & Verbal Behavior*, 3(1), 79–84.

Popper, K. (1934). *The logic of scientific discovery*. London, England: Routledge.

Porter, S., & Peace, K. A. (2007). The scars of memory: A prospective, longitudinal investigation of the consistency of traumatic and positive emotional memories in adulthood. *Psychological Science*, 18(5), 435–441.

Posadzki, P., Lewandowski, W., Terry, R., Ernst, E., & Stearns, A. (2012). Guided imagery for non-musculoskeletal pain: A systematic review of randomized clinical trials. *Journal of Pain and Symptom Management*, 44(1), 95–104.

Posner, M. I., & Rothbart, M. K. (2007). Research on attention networks as a model for the integration of psychological science. *Annual Review of Psychology*, 58, 1–23.

Posner, M. I., & Snyder, C. R. (1975). Facilitation and inhibition in the processing of signals. In P. M. Rabbitt & S. Dornic (Eds.), *Attention and performance V* (pp. 669–682). New York, NY: Academic Press.

Posner, M. I., Snyder, C. R., & Davidson, B. J. (1980). Attention and the detection of signals. *Journal of Experimental Psychology: General*, 109(2), 160–174.

Postman, L., & Phillips, L. W. (1965). Short-term temporal changes in free recall. *Quarterly Journal of Experimental Psychology*, 17(2), 132–138.

Powers, P. A., Andriks, J. L., & Loftus, E. F. (1979). Eyewitness accounts of females and males. *Journal of Applied Psychology, 64*(3), 339–347.

Pratte, M. S. (2018) Iconic memories die a sudden death. *Psychological Science, 29*(6), 877–887.

Preston, J., & Wegner, D. M. (2007). The Eureka error: Inadvertent plagiarism by misattributions of effort. *Journal of Personality and Social Psychology, 92*(4), 575–584.

Pretz, J. E. (2008). Intuition versus analysis: Strategy and experience in complex everyday problem solving. *Memory & Cognition, 36,* 554–566.

Protzko, J., Aronson, J., & Blair, C. (2013). How to make a young child smarter: Evidence from the Database of Raising Intelligence. *Perspective on Psychological Science, 8*(1), 25–40.

Pugh, K., & McCardle, P. (Eds.). (2009). *How children learn to read: Current issues and new directions in the integration of cognition, neurobiology, and genetics of reading and dyslexia research and practice.* New York, NY: Psychology Press.

Pulvermüller, F. (2013). How neurons make meaning: Brain mechanisms for embodied and abstract-symbolic semantics. *Trends in Cognitive Sciences, 17*(9), 458–470.

Putnam, A. L., Nestojko, J. F., & Roediger, H. L., III. (2017). Improving student learning: Two strategies to make it stick. In J. C. Horvath, J. M. Lodge, & J. Hattie (Eds.), *From the laboratory to the classroom: Translating the science of learning for teachers* (pp. 94–121). Oxford, England: Routledge.

Putnam, A. L., Ross, M. Q., Soter, L. K., & Roediger, H. L., III. (2018). Collective narcissism: Americans exaggerate the role of their home state in appraising U.S. history. *Psychological Science, 29*(9), 1414–1422.

Putnam, A. L., Sungkhasettee, V. W., & Roediger, H. L., III. (2016). Optimizing learning in college: Tips from cognitive psychology. *Perspectives on Psychological Science, 11*(5), 652–660.

Pyc, M. A., & Rawson, K. A., (2012). Why is test-restudy practice beneficial for memory? An evaluation of the mediator shift hypothesis. *Journal of Experimental Psychology: Learning, Memory, & Cognition, 38*(3), 737–746.

Pylyshyn, Z. (1981). The imagery debate: Analogue media versus tacit knowledge. In N. Block (Ed.), *Imagery* (pp. 151–206). Cambridge, MA: MIT Press.

Quas, J. A., Goodman, G. S., Bidrose, S., Pipe, M.-E., Craw, S., & Ablin, D. S. (1999). Emotion and memory: Children's long-term remembering, forgetting, and suggestibility. *Journal of Experimental Child Psychology, 72*(4), 235–270.

Quiroga, R. Q., Reddy, L., Kreiman, G., Koch, C., & Fried, I. (2005). Invariant visual representation by single neurons in the human brain. *Nature, 435,* 1102–1107.

Rabagliati, H., Robertson, A., & Carmel, D. (2018). The importance of awareness for understanding language. *Journal of Experimental Psychology: General, 147*(2), 190–208.

Radel, R., Davranche, K., Fournier, M., & Dietrich, A. (2015). The role of (dis)inhibition in creativity: Decreased inhibition improves idea generation. *Cognition, 134,* 110–120.

Radoeva, P. D., Prasad, S., Brainard, D. H., & Aguirre, G. K. (2008). Neural activity within area V1 reflects unconscious visual performance in a case of blindsight. *Journal of Cognitive Neuroscience, 20*(11), 1927–1939.

Raghubir, P., & Menon, G. (2005). When and why is ease of retrieval informative? *Memory & Cognition, 33,* 821–832.

Ragni, M., Kola, I., & Johnson-Laird, P. N. (2018). On selecting evidence to test hypotheses: A theory of selection tasks. *Psychological Bulletin, 144*(8), 779–796.

Raizada, R. D. S., & Kishiyama, M. M. (2010). Effects of socioeconomic status on brain development, and how cognitive neuroscience may contribute to levelling the playing field. *Frontiers in Human Neuroscience, 5,* 1–18.

Rakover, S. S. (2013). Explaining the face-inversion effect: The face-scheme incompatibility (FSI) model. *Psychonomic Bulletin & Review, 20,* 665–692.

Ramachandran, V. S., & Blakeslee, S. (1998). *Phantoms in the brain.* New York, NY: Morrow.

Ramsden, S., Richardson, F. M., Josse, G., Thomas, M. S. C., Ellis, C., Shakeshaft, C., Seghier, M. L., & Price, C. J. (2011). Verbal and nonverbal intelligence changes in the teenage brain. *Nature, 479*(7371), 113–116.

Randhawa, G., Brocklehurst, A., Pateman, R., Kinsella, S., & Parry, V. (2010). "Opting-in or opting out?"—The views of the UK's faith leaders in relation to organ donation. *Health Policy, 96*(1), 36–44.

Ranganath, C., Yonelinas, A. P., Cohen, M. X., Dy, C. J., Tom, S. M., & D'Esposito, M. (2003). Dissociable correlates of recollection and familiarity within the medial temporal lobes. *Neuropsychologia, 42*(1), 2–13.

Rao, G. A., Larkin, E. C., & Derr, R. F. (1986). Biologic effects of chronic ethanol consumption related to a deficient intake of carbohydrates. *Alcohol and Alcoholism, 21*(4), 369–373.

Rasch, B., & Born, J. (2013). About sleep's role in memory. *Physiological Reviews, 93*(2), 681–766.

Rathbone, C. J., Moulin, C. J. A., & Conway, M. A. (2008). Self-centered memories: The reminiscence bump and the self. *Memory & Cognition, 36*(8), 1403–1414.

Rathbone, C. J., O'Connor, A. R., & Moulin, C. J. A. (2017). The tracks of my years: Personal significance contributes to the reminiscence bump. *Memory & Cognition, 45,* 137–150.

Raven, J., & Raven, J. (Eds.). (2008). *Uses and abuses of intelligence: Studies advancing Spearman and Raven's quest for non-arbitrary metrics.* Unionville, NY: Royal Fireworks Tests.

Ravenzwaaij, D. V., Brown, S., & Wagenmakers, E.-J. (2011). An integrated perspective on the relation between response speed and intelligence. *Cognition*, *119*(3), 381–393.

Ravuri, M., Kannan, A., Tso, G. J., & Amatriain, X. (2018). *Learning from the experts: From expert systems to machine-learned diagnosis models*. Cornell University. https://arxiv.org/abs/1804.08033

Rayner, K., & Pollatsek, A. (2011). Basic processes in reading. In D. Reisberg (Ed.), *Handbook of cognitive psychology*. New York, NY: Oxford University Press.

Rayner, K., Schotter, E. R., Masson, M. E. J., Potter, M. C., & Treiman, R. (2016). So much to read, so little time: How do we read, and can speed reading help? *Psychological Science in the Public Interest*, *17*(1), 4–34.

Reason, J. T. (1990). *Human error.* Cambridge, England: Cambridge University Press.

Redelmeier, D., & Shafir, E. (1995). Medical decision making in situations that offer multiple alternatives. *Journal of the American Medical Association*, *273*(4), 302–305.

Redelmeier, D. A., & Tversky, A. (1996). On the belief that arthritis pain is related to the weather. *Proceedings of the National Academic of Sciences*, *93*, 2895–2896.

Redick, T. S., Shipstead, Z., Harrison, T. L., Hicks, K. L., Fried, D. E., Hambrick, D. Z., Kane, M. J., & Engle, R. W. (2013). No evidence of intelligence improvement after working memory training: A randomized, placebo-controlled study. *Journal of Experimental Psychology: General*, *142*(2), 359–379.

Redick, T. S., Shipstead, Z., Meier, M. E., Montroy, J. J., Hicks, K. L., Unsworth, N., Kane, M. J., Hambrick, D. Z., & Engle, R. W. (2016). Cognitive predictors of a common multitasking ability: Contributions from working memory, attention control, and fluid intelligence. *Journal of Experimental Psychology: General*, *145*(11), 1473–1492.

Redlich, D., Memmert, D., & Kreitz, C. (2021). Rethinking inattentional blindness research: A systematic overview of methods, their limitations and their opportunities to investigate inattentional blindness. *Applied Cognitive Psychology*, *35*(1), 136–147.

Reed, S. K. (2017). Problem solving. In S. E. F. Chipman (Ed.), *The Oxford handbook of cognitive science* (pp. 231–247). New York, NY: Oxford University Press.

Rees, G., Kreiman, G., & Koch, C. (2002). Neural correlates of consciousness in humans. *Nature Reviews Neuroscience*, *3*(4), 261–270.

Rehder, B., & Hastie, R. (2004). Category coherence and category-based property induction. *Cognition*, *91*(2), 113–153.

Rehder, B., & Ross, B. H. (2001). Abstract coherent categories. *Journal of Experimental Psychology: Learning, Memory, & Cognition*, *27*(5), 1261–1275.

Reicher, G. M. (1969). Perceptual recognition as a function of meaningfulness of stimulus material. *Journal of Experimental Psychology*, *81*(2), 275–280.

Reisberg, D. (1996). The non-ambiguity of mental images. In C. Cornoldi, R. H. Logie, M. A. Brandimonte, G. Kaufmann, & D. Reisberg (Eds.), *Stretching the imagination: Representation and transformation in mental imagery* (pp. 119–171). New York, NY: Oxford University Press.

Reisberg, D. (2014). *The science of perception and memory: A pragmatic guide for the justice system.* New York, NY: Oxford University Press.

Reisberg, D., & Heuer, F. (2004). Memory for emotional events. In D. Reisberg & P. Hertel (Eds.), *Memory and emotion* (pp. 3–41). New York, NY: Oxford University Press.

Reisberg, D., & Heuer, F. (2020). Emotion's (varied) impact on memory for sexual misconduct. In J. Pozzulo, E. Pica, & C. Sheahan (Eds.), *Memory and sexual misconduct: Psychological research for criminal justice* (pp. 7–41). New York, NY: Routledge.

Renoult, L., Irish, M., Moscovitch, M., & Rugg, M. D. (2019). From knowing to remembering: The semantic-episodic distinction, *Trends in Cognitive Sciences*, *23*(12), 1041–1057.

Rensink, R. A. (2002). Change detection. *Annual Review of Psychology*, *53*(1), 245–277.

Rensink, R. A. (2018). To have seen or not to have seen: A look at Rensink, O'Regan, and Clark (1997). *Perspective on Psychological Science*, *13*(2), 230–235.

Rensink, R. A., O'Regan, J. K., & Clark, J. J. (1997). To see or not to see: The need for attention to perceive changes in scenes. *Psychological Science*, *8*(5), 368–373.

Repovš, G., & Baddeley, A. (2006). The multi-component model of working memory: Explorations in experimental cognitive psychology. *Neuroscience*, *139*(1), 5–21.

Repp. B. H. (1992). Perceptual restoration of a "missing" speech sound: Auditory induction or illusion? *Perception & Psychophysics*, *51*(1), 14–32.

Revelle, W., Dworak, E. M., & Condon, D. (2020). Cognitive ability in everyday life: The utility of open-source measures. *Current Directions in Psychological Science*, *29*(4), 358–363.

Rey-Mermet, A., Gade, M., Souza, A. S., von Bastian, C. C., & Oberauer, K. (2019). Is executive control related to working memory capacity and fluid intelligence? *Journal of Experimental Psychology: General*, *148*(8), 1335–1372.

Reynolds, C. R., Chastain, R. L., Kaufman, A. S., & McLean, J. E. (1987). Demographic characteristics and IQ among adults: Analysis of the WAIS-R standardization sample as a function of the stratification variables. *Journal of School Psychology*, *25*(4), 323–342.

Rhodes, G. (2013). Face recognition. In D. Reisberg (Ed.), *The Oxford handbook of cognitive psychology* (pp. 46–68). New York, NY: Oxford University Press.

Rhodes, G., Brake, S., & Atkinson, A. P. (1993). What's lost in inverted faces? *Cognition*, *47*(1), 25–57.

Rhodes, M. G., & Anastasi, J. S. (2012). The own-age bias in face recognition: A meta-analytic and theoretical review. *Psychological Bulletin*, *138*(1), 146–174.

Rich, P. R., & Zaragoza, M. S. (2016). The continued influence of implied and explicitly stated misinformation in news reports. *Journal of Experimental Psychology: Learning, Memory, & Cognition*, *42*(1), 62–74.

Richard, A. M., Lee, H., & Vecera, S. P. (2008). Attentional spreading in object-based attention. *Journal of Experimental Psychology: Human Perception & Performance*, *34*(4), 842–853.

Richie, K. L., Kramer, R. S. S., & Burton, A. M. (2018). What makes a face photo a "good likeness"? *Cognition*, *170*, 1–8.

Richler, J. J., & Gauthier, I. (2014). A meta-analysis and review of holistic face processing. *Psychological Bulletin*, *140*(5), 1281–1302.

Rinck, M. (1999). Memory for everyday objects: Where are the digits on numerical keypads? *Applied Cognitive Psychology*, *13*(4), 329–350.

Rips, L. J. (1975). Inductive judgements about natural categories. *Journal of Verbal Learning and Verbal Behavior*, *14*(6), 665–681.

Rips, L. J. (1990). Reasoning. *Annual Review of Psychology*, *41*, 321–353.

Rips, L. J., Smith, E. E., & Medin, D. L. (2012). Concepts and categories: Memory, meaning, and metaphysics. In K. J. Holyoak & R. G. Morrison (Eds.), *The Oxford handbook of thinking and reasoning* (pp. 177–209). New York, NY: Oxford University Press.

Ritchie, J. M. (1985). The aliphatic alcohols. In A. G. Gilman, L. S. Goodman, T. W. Rall, & F. Murad (Eds.), *Goodman and Gilman's the pharmacological basis of therapeutics* (pp. 372–386). New York, NY: Macmillan.

Ritchie, S. J., & Tucker-Drob, E. M. (2018). How much does education improve intelligence? A meta-analysis. *Psychological Science*, *29*(8), 1358–1369.

Rittle-Johnson, B., Star, J. R., & Durkin, K. (2020). How can cognitive-science research help improve education? The case of comparing multiple strategies to improve mathematics learning and teaching. *Current Directions in Psychological Science*, *29*(6), 599–609.

Rizzi, T. S., & Posthuma, D. (2012). Genes and intelligence. In D. Reisberg (Ed.), *The Oxford handbook of cognitive psychology*. New York, NY: Oxford University Press.

Roberson, D., Davies, I., & Davidoff, J. (2000). Color categories are not universal: Replications and new evidence from a stone-age culture. *Journal of Experimental Psychology: General*, *129*(3), 369–398.

Robertson, D. J., Black, J., Chamberlain, B., Megreya, A. M., & Davis, J. P. (2019). Super-recognisers show an advantage for other race face identification. *Applied Cognitive Psychology, 34*(1), 205–216.

Robertson, D. J., Noyes, E., Dowsett, A. J., Jenkins, R., & Burton A. M. (2016). Face recognition by metropolitan police super-recognisers. *PLoS ONE*, *11*(2), e0150036.

Robson, D. (2012, December 18). Are there really 50 Eskimo words for snow? *NewScientist*.

Roediger, H. L. (1980). The effectiveness of four mnemonics in ordering recall. *Journal of Experimental Psychology: Human Learning and Memory*, *6*(5), 558–567.

Roediger, H. L., III, & Abel, M. (2015). Collective memory: A new arena of cognitive study. *Trends in Cognitive Sciences*, *19*(7), 359–361.

Roediger, H. L., & McDermott, K. (1995). Creating false memories: Remembering words not presented in lists. *Journal of Experimental Psychology: Learning, Memory, & Cognition*, *21*(4), 803–814.

Roediger, H. L., III, & McDermott, K. (2000). Tricks of memory. *Current Directions in Psychological Science*, *9*(4), 123–127.

Röer, J. P., & Cowan, N. (2021). A preregistered replication and extension of the cocktail party phenomenon: One's name captures attention, unexpected words do not. *Journal of Experimental Psychology: Learning, Memory, & Cognition*, *47*(2), 234–242.

Rogers, R., Hazelwood, L. L., Sewell, K. W., Harrison, K. S., & Shuman, D. W. (2008). The language of Miranda warnings in American jurisdictions: A replication and vocabulary analysis. *Law & Human Behavior*, *32*(2), 124–136.

Rogers, R., Rogstad, J. E., Gillard, N. D., Drogin, E. Y., Blackwood, H. L., & Shuman, D. W. (2010). "Everyone knows their Miranda rights": Implicit assumptions and countervailing evidence. *Psychology, Public Policy, & Law*, *16*(3), 300–318.

Rogers, S. (1992). How a publicity blitz created the myth of subliminal advertising. *Public Relations Quarterly*, *37*, 12–17.

Rogers, T. T., & Patterson, K. (2007). Object categorization: Reversals and explanations of the basic-level advantage. *Journal of Experimental Psychology: General*, *136*(3), 451–469.

Rosch, E. H. (1973). On the internal structure of perceptual and semantic categories. In T. E. Moore (Ed.), *Cognitive development and the acquisition of language* (pp. 111–144). New York, NY: Academic Press.

Rosch, E. (1975). Cognitive representations of semantic categories. *Journal of Experimental Psychology: General*, *104*(3), 192–233.

Rosch, E. (1978). Principles of categorization. In E. Rosch & B. B. Lloyd (Eds.), *Cognition and categorization* (pp. 27–48). Hillsdale, NJ: Erlbaum.

Rosch, E., & Mervis, C. B. (1975). Family resemblances: Studies in the internal structure of categories. *Cognitive Psychology*, *7*(4), 573–605.

Rosch, E., Mervis, C. B., Gray, W. D., Johnson, D. M., & Boyes-Braem, P. (1976). Basic objects in natural categories. *Cognitive Psychology*, *8*(3), 382–439.

Rosenfeld, J. P., Ben-Shakhar, G., & Ganis, G. (2012). Detection of concealed stored memories with psycho-physiological and neuroimaging methods. In L. Nadel & W. P. Sinnott-Armstrong (Eds.), *Memory and law* (pp. 263–305). New York, NY: Oxford University Press.

Rosenthal, G., Levakov, G., & Avidan, G. (2018). Holistic face representation is highly orientation-specific. *Psychonomic Bulletin & Review, 25*(4), 1351–1357.

Roser, M., & Gazzaniga, M. S. (2004). Automatic brains—Interpretive minds. *Current Directions in Psychological Science, 13*(2), 56–59.

Roska, B., & Sahel, J.-A. (2018). Restoring vision. *Nature, 557*(7705), 359–367.

Ross, J., & Lawrence, K. A. (1968). Some observations on memory artifice. *Psychonomic Science, 13*(2), 107–108.

Ross, L., & Anderson, C. A. (1982). Shortcomings in the attribution process: On the origins and maintenance of erroneous social assessments. In D. Kahneman, P. Slovic, & A. Tversky (Eds.), *Judgment under uncertainty: Heuristics and biases* (pp. 129–152). New York, NY: Cambridge University Press.

Ross, L., Lepper, M. R., & Hubbard, M. (1975). Perseverance in self perception and social perception: Biased attributional processes in the debriefing paradigm. *Journal of Personality and Social Psychology, 32*(5), 880–892.

Rowland, C. A. (2014). The effect of testing versus restudy on retention: A meta-analytic review of the testing effect. *Psychological Bulletin, 140*(6), 1432–1463.

Rubin, D. C. (1997). *Memory in oral traditions: The cognitive psychology of epic, ballads, and counting-out rhymes.* New York, NY: Oxford University Press.

Rubin, D. C. (2020). The ability to recall scenes is a stable individual difference: Evidence from autobiographical remembering. *Cognition, 197*, Article 104164.

Rubin, D. C., & Kozin, M. (1984). Vivid memories. *Cognition, 16*(1), 81–95.

Rubin, D. C., & Umanath, S. (2015). Event memory: A theory of memory for laboratory, autobiographical, and fictional events. *Psychological Review, 122*(1), 1–23.

Rubin, E. (1915). *Synoplevede figuren.* Copenhagen, Denmark: Gyldendalske.

Rubin, E. (1921). *Visuell wahrgenommene figuren.* Copenhagen, Denmark: Gyldendalske.

Rubínová, E., Fitzgerald, R. J., Juncu, S., Ribbers, E., Hope, L., & Sauer, J. D. (2020). Live presentation for eyewitness identification is not superior to photo or video presentation. *Journal of Applied Research in Memory and Cognition.* Advance online publication. https://doi.org/10.1016/j.jarmac.2020.08.009

Ruch, S. & Henke, K. (2020). Learning during sleep: A dream come true? *Trends in Cognitive Sciences, 24*(3), 170–172.

Rueda, M. R., Rothbart, M. K., McCandliss, B. D., Saccomanno, L., & Posner, M. I. (2005). Training, maturation, and genetic influences on the development of executive attention. *Proceedings of the National Academy of Sciences, 102*(41), 14931–14936.

Rugg, M. D., & Curran, T. (2007). Event-related potentials and recognition memory. *Trends in Cognitive Sciences, 11*(6), 251–257.

Rumelhart, D. E., & Siple, P. (1974). Process of recognizing tachistoscopically presented words. *Psychological Review, 81*(2), 99–118.

Rundus, D. (1971). Analysis of rehearsal processes in free recall. *Journal of Experimental Psychology, 89*(1), 63–77.

Rushton, J. P. (2012). No narrowing in mean Black-White IQ differences—Predicted by heritable *g. American Psychologist, 67*(6), 500–501.

Rushton, J. P., & Jensen, A. R. (2005). Thirty years of research on race differences in cognitive ability. *Psychology, Public Policy, and Law, 11*(2), 235–294.

Russell, R., Duchaine, B., & Nakayama, K. (2009). Super-recognizers: People with extraordinary face recognition ability. *Psychonomic Bulletin and Review, 16*(2), 252–257.

Ruthruff, E., Johnston, J. C., & Remington, R. W. (2009). How strategic is the central bottleneck: Can it be overcome by trying harder? *Journal of Experimental Psychology: Human Perception & Performance, 35*(5), 1368–1384.

Ruva, C. L., & Guenther, C. C. (2015). From the shadows into the light: How pretrial publicity and deliberation affect mock jurors' decisions, impressions, and memory. *Law & Human Behavior, 39*(3), 294–310.

Saalmann, Y. B., Pigarev, I. N., & Vidyasagar, T. R. (2007). Neural mechanisms of visual attention: How top-down feedback highlights relevant locations. *Science, 316*(5831), 1612–1615.

Sackett, P. R., Borneman, M. J., & Connelly, B. S. (2008). High-stakes testing in higher education and employment: Appraising the evidence for validity and fairness. *American Psychologist, 63*(4), 215–227.

Sacks, O. (1985). *The man who mistook his wife for a hat and other clinical tales.* New York, NY: Harper & Row.

Sadeh, T., Ozubko, J. D., Winocur, G., & Moscovitch, M. (2016). Forgetting patterns differentiate between two forms of memory representation. *Psychological Science, 27*(6), 810–820.

Saffran, J. R. (2003). Statistical language learning: Mechanisms and constraints. *Current Directions in Psychological Science, 12*(4), 110–114.

Saj, A., Fuhrman, O., Vuilleumier, P., & Boroditsky, L. (2014). Patients with left spatial neglect also neglect the "left side" of time. *Psychological Science, 25*(1), 207–214.

Sala, G., & Gobet, F. (2017). Experts' memory superiority for domain-specific random material generalizes across fields of expertise: A meta-analysis. *Memory & Cognition, 45*, 183–193.

Sala, G., & Gobet, F. (2019). Cognitive training does not enhance general cognition. *Trends in Cognitive Sciences, 23*(1), 9–20.

Salthouse, T. A. (2004). What and when of cognitive aging. *Current Directions in Psychological Science, 13*(4), 140–144.

Salthouse, T. (2012). Consequences of age-related cognitive declines. *Annual Review of Psychology, 63*, 201–226.

Salvucci, D. D. (2017). ACT-R and beyond. In S. E. F. Chipman (Ed.), *The Oxford handbook of cognitive science* (pp. 15–26). New York, NY: Oxford University Press.

Samuel, A. G. (1987). Lexical uniqueness effects on phonemic restoration. *Journal of Memory and Language, 26*(1), 36–56.

Samuel, A. G. (1991). A further examination of attentional effects in the phonemic restoration illusion. *Quarterly Journal of Experimental Psychology: Human Experimental Psychology, 43A*(3), 679–699.

Samuel, S., Cole, G., & Eacott, M. J. (2019). Grammatical gender and linguistic relativity: A systematic review. *Psychonomic Bulletin & Review, 26*, 1767–1786.

Sanbonmatsu, D. M., Strayer, D. L., Biondi, F., Behrends, A. A., & Moore, S. M. (2016). Cell-phone use diminishes self-awareness of impaired driving. *Psychonomic Bulletin & Review, 23*(2), 617–623.

Sanbonmatsu, D. M., Strayer, D. L., Medeiros-Ward, N., & Watson, J. M. (2013). Who multi-tasks and why? Multi-tasking ability, perceived multi-tasking ability, impulsivity, and sensation thinking. *PloS ONE, 8*(1), e54402.

Sanders, K. E. G., Osburn, S., Paller, K. A., & Beeman, M. (2019). Targeted memory reactivation during sleep improves next-day problem solving, *Psychological Science, 30*(11), 1616–1624.

Savage-Rumbaugh, E. S., & Fields, W. M. (2000). Linguistic, cultural and cognitive capacities of bonobos (*Pan paniscus*). *Culture & Psychology, 6*(2), 131–153.

Savage-Rumbaugh, S., & Lewin, R. (1994). *Kanzi, the ape at the brink of the human mind.* New York, NY: Wiley.

Savi, A. O., Marsman, M., van der Maas, H. L. J., & Maris, G. K. J. (2019). The wiring of intelligence. *Perspectives on Psychological Science, 14*(6), 1034–1061.

Sawyer, R. K. (2006). *Explaining creativity: The science of human innovation.* New York, NY: Oxford University Press.

Schacter, D. L. (1996). *Searching for memory: The brain, the mind, and the past.* New York, NY: Basic Books.

Schacter, D. L., & Tulving, E. (1982). Amnesia and memory research. In L. S. Cermak (Ed.), *Human memory and amnesia* (pp. 1–32). Hillsdale, NJ: Erlbaum.

Schacter, D. L., Tulving, E., & Wang, P. (1981). *Source amnesia: New methods and illustrative data.* Paper presented at the meeting of the International Neuropsychological Society, 1981, Atlanta, GA.

Schellenberg, D., & Kaiser, A. (2018). The sex/gender distinction: Beyond f and m. In C. B. Travis, J. W. White, A. Rutherford, W. S. Williams, S. L. Cook, & K. F. Wyche (Eds.), *APA handbook of the psychology of women: History, theory, and battlegrounds* (pp. 165–187). American Psychological Association.

Schenk, T., Ellison, A., Rice, N., & Milner, A. D. (2005). The role of V5/MT+ in the control of catching movements: An rTMS study. *Neuropsychologia, 43*(2), 189–198.

Schlegel, A., Kohler, P. J., Fogelson, S. V., Alexander, P., Konuthula, D., & Tse, P. U. (2013). Network structure and dynamics of the mental workspace. *Proceeds of the National Academy of Sciences, 110*(40), 16277–16282.

Schmidt, F. L., & Hunter, E. (2004). General mental ability in the world of work: Occupational attainment and job performance. *Journal of Personality and Social Psychology, 86*(1), 162–173.

Schmidt, S. R. (2012). *Extraordinary memories for exceptional events.* New York, NY: Psychology Press.

Schmidt, S. R., & Qiao, L. (2019). A comparison of Chinese and American memories for public events. *Applied Cognitive Psychology, 34*(1), 217–227.

Schnuerch, R., Kreiz, C., Gibbons, H., & Memmert, D. (2016). Not quite so blind: Semantic processing despite inattentional blindness. *Journal of Experimental Psychology: Human Perception & Performance, 42*(4), 459–463.

Schubert, A.-L., & Frischkorn, G. T. (2020). Neurocognitive psychometrics of intelligence: How measurement advancements unveiled the role of mental speed in intelligence differences. *Current Directions in Psychological Science, 29*(2), 140–146.

Schubert, A.-L., Hagemann, D., & Frischkorn, G. T. (2017). Is general intelligence little more than the speed of higher-order processing? *Journal of Experimental Psychology: General, 146*(10), 1498–1512.

Schubert, A.-L., Hagemann, D., Löffler, C., Rummel, J., & Arnau, S. (2021). A chronometric model of the relationship between frontal midline theta functional connectivity and human intelligence. *Journal of Experimental Psychology: General, 150*(1), 1–22.

Schulz-Hardt, S., Frey, D., Lüthgens, C., & Moscovici, S. (2000). Biased information search in group decision making. *Journal of Personality and Social Psychology, 78*(4), 655–669.

Schwartz, B. (2003). *The paradox of choice: Why more is less.* New York, NY: Ecco.

Schwartz, B. L., & Metcalfe, J. (2011). Tip-of-the-tongue (TOT) states: Retrieval, behavior, and experience. *Memory & Cognition, 39*(35), 737–749.

Schwarz, N. (2018). Of fluency, beauty, and truth: Inferences from metacognitive experiences. In J. Proust & M. Fortier (Eds.), *Metacognitive diversity: An interdisciplinary approach* (pp. 25–46). New York, NY: Oxford University Press.

Schwarz, N., Bless, H., Strack, F., Klumpp. G., Rittenauer-Schatka, H., & Simons, A. (1991). Ease of retrieval as information: Another look at the availability heuristic. *Journal of Personality & Social Psychology, 61*(2), 195–202.

Schwitzgebel, E., & Cushman, F. (2015). Philosophers' biased judgments persist despite training, expertise and reflection. *Cognition, 141*, 127–137.

Scoboria, A., & Mazzoni, G. (2017). Invited commentary on Brewin and Andrews (2016). *Applied Cognitive Psychology, 31*(1), 28–30.

Scoboria, A., Mazzoni, G., Kirsch, I., & Jimenez, S. (2006). The effects of prevalence and script information on plausibility, belief, and memory of autobiographical events. *Applied Cognitive Psychology, 20*(8), 1049–1064.

Sedivy, J. C., Tanenhaus, M. K., Chambers, C. G., & Carlson, G. N. (1999). Achieving incremental semantic interpretation through contextual representation. *Cognition, 71*(2), 109–147.

Seegmiller, J. K., Watson, J. M., & Strayer, D. L. (2011). Individual differences in susceptibility to inattentional blindness. *Journal of Experimental Psychology: Learning, Memory, & Cognition, 37*(3), 785–791.

Segal, S. J., & Fusella, V. (1970). Influence of imaged pictures and sounds on detection of visual and auditory signals. *Journal of Experimental Psychology, 83*(3), 458–474.

Segal, S. J., & Fusella, V. (1971). Effect of images in six sense modalities on detection of visual signal from noise. *Psychonomic Science, 24*(2), 55–56.

Segal, Z. V., Williams, J. M. G., & Teasdale, J. D. (2018). *Mindfulness-based cognitive therapy for depression* (2nd ed.). New York, NY: Guilford Press.

Selfridge, O. G. (1955). *Pattern recognition and modern computers.* Proceedings of the Western Joint Computer Conference, March 1955, Los Angeles, CA.

Selfridge, O. G. (1959). Pandemonium: A paradigm for learning. In D. V. Blake & A. M. Uttley (Eds.), *The mechanisation of thought processes: Proceedings of a symposium held at the National Physics Laboratory* (pp. 511–529). London, England: H. M. Stationery Office.

Seli, P., Kane, M. J., Smallwood, J., Schacter, D. L., Maillet, D., Schooler, J. W., & Smilek, D. (2018). Mind-wandering as a natural kind: A family-resemblances view. *Trends in Cognitive Sciences, 22*, 479–490.

Seli, P., Smallwood, J., Cheyne, J. A., & Smilek, D. (2015). On the relation of mind wandering and ADHD symptomatology. *Psychonomic Bulletin & Review, 22*(6), 629–636.

Seltzer, B., & Benson, D. F. (1974). The temporal pattern of retrograde amnesia in Korsakoff's disease. *Neurology, 24*(6), 527–530.

Semmler, C., & Brewer, N. (2006). Postidentification feedback effects on face recognition confidence: Evidence for metacognitive influences. *Applied Cognitive Psychology, 20*(7), 895–916.

Senghas, A., Román, D., & Mavillapalli, S. (2006). *Simply unique.* London: Leonard Cheshire International.

Servant, M., Cassey, P., Woodman, G. F., & Logan, G. D. (2018). Neural bases of automaticity. *Journal of Experimental Psychology: Learning, Memory, & Cognition, 44*(3), 440–464.

Servos, P., & Goodale, M. A. (1995). Preserved visual imagery in visual form agnosia. *Neuropsychologia, 33*(11), 1383–1394.

Sevdalis, N., & Harvey, N. (2007). Biased forecasting of postdecisional affect. *Psychological Science, 18*(8), 678–681.

Shafir, E. (1993). Choosing versus rejecting: Why some options are both better and worse than others. *Memory & Cognition, 21*(4), 546–556.

Shafir, E., & LeBoeuf, R. A. (2002). Rationality. *Annual Review of Psychology, 53*(1), 491–517.

Shafir, E., Simonson, I., & Tversky, A. (1993). Reason-based choice. *Cognition, 49*(1–2), 11–36.

Shaklee, H., & Mims, M. (1982). Sources of error in judging event covariations: Effects of memory demands. *Journal of Experimental Psychology: Learning, Memory, & Cognition, 8*(3), 208–224.

Sharman, S. J., & Barnier, A. J. (2008). Imagining nice and nasty events in childhood or adulthood: Recent positive events show the most imagination inflation. *Acta Psychologica, 129*(2), 228–233.

Shaw, J. (2018). How can researchers tell whether someone has a false memory? Coding strategies in autobiographical false-memory research: A reply to Wade, Garry, and Pezdek (2018). *Psychological Science, 29*(3), 477–480.

Shaw, J., & Porter, S. (2015). Constructing rich false memories of committing crime. *Psychological Science, 26*(3), 291–301.

Shepard, R., & Feng, C. (1972). A chronometric study of mental paper folding. *Cognitive Psychology, 3*, 228–243.

Shepard, R. N., & Cooper, L. A. (1982). *Mental images and their transformations.* Cambridge, MA: MIT Press.

Shepard, R. N., & Metzler, J. (1971). Mental rotation of three-dimensional objects. *Science, 171*(3972), 701–703.

Sheppard, L. D., & Vernon, P. A. (2008). Intelligence and speed of information-processing: A review of 50 years of research. *Personality and Individual Differences, 44*(3), 535–551.

Shidlovski, D., Schul, Y., & Mayo, R. (2014). If I imagine it, then it happened: The implicit truth value of imaginary representations. *Cognition, 133*(3), 517–529.

Shields, G. S., Sazma, M. A., McCullough, A. M., & Yonelinas, A. P. (2017). The effects of acute stress on episodic memory: A meta-analysis and integrative review. *Psychological Bulletin, 143*(6), 636–675.

Shiffrin, R. M., & Schneider, W. (1977). Controlled and automatic human information processing: II. Perceptual learning, automatic attending, and a general theory. *Psychological Review, 84*(2), 127–190.

Shilowich, B. E., & Biederman, I. (2016). An estimate of the prevalence of developmental phonagnosia. *Brain and Language, 159*, 84–91.

Shipstead, Z., Harrison, T. L., & Engle, R. W. (2015). Working memory capacity and the scope and control of attention. *Attention, Perception & Psychophysics, 77*(6), 1863–1880.

Shipstead, Z., Redick, T. S., & Engle, R. W. (2012). Is working memory training effective? *Psychological Bulletin, 138*(4), 628–654.

Shore, D. I., & Klein, R. M. (2000). The effects of scene inversion on change blindness. *Journal of General Psychology, 127*(1), 27–43.

Siegel, J. S., Ramsey, L. E., Snyder, A. Z., Metcalf, N. V., Chacko, R. V., Weinberger, K., Baldassarre, A., Hacker, C. D., Shulman, G. L., & Borbetta, M. (2016). Disruptions of network connectivity predict impairment in multiple behavioral domains after stroke. *Proceedings of the National Academy of Sciences, 113*(30), E4367–E4376.

Signoret, C., Johnsrude, I., Classon, E., & Rudner, M. (2018). Combined effects of form- and meaning-based predictability on perceived clarity of speech. *Journal of Experimental Psychology: Human Perception & Performance, 44*(2), 277–285.

Silbersweig, D. A., Stern, E., Frith, C., Cahill, C., Holmes, A., Grootoonk, S., Seaward, J., McKenna, P., Chua, S. E., Schnorr, L., Jones, T., & Frackowiak, R. S. J. (1995). A functional neuroanatomy of hallucinations in schizophrenia. *Nature, 378*, 176–179.

Simons, D. J., & Ambinder, M. S. (2005). Change blindness: Theory and consequences. *Current Directions in Psychological Science, 14*(1), 44–48.

Simons, D. J., Boot, W. R., Charness, N., Gathercole, S. E., Chabris, C. F., Hambrick, D. Z., & Stine-Morrow, E. A. L. (2016). Do "brain-training" programs work? *Psychological Science in the Public Interest, 17*(3), 103–186.

Simons, D. J., & Chabris, C. F. (1999). Gorillas in our midst: Sustained inattentional blindness for dynamic events. *Perception, 28*(9), 1059–1074.

Simons, D. J., & Rensink, R. A. (2005). Change blindness: Past, present, and future. *Trends in Cognitive Sciences, 9*(1), 1–20.

Simonton, D. K. (2011). Creativity and discovery as blind variation: Campbell's (1960) BVSR model after the half-century mark. *Review of General Psychology, 15*(2), 158–174.

Simonton, D. K., & Damian, R. I. (2012). Creativity. In D. Reisberg (Ed.), *The Oxford handbook of cognitive psychology* (pp. 795–807). New York, NY: Oxford University Press.

Sinclair, A. H., Stanley, M. L., & Seli, P. (2020). Closed-minded cognition: Right-wing authoritarianism is negatively related to belief updating following prediction error. *Psychonomic Bulletin & Review, 27*, 1348–1361.

Singh, H., Meyer, A. N. D., & Thomas, E. J. (2014). The frequency of diagnostic errors in outpatient care: Estimations from three large observational studies involving US adult populations. *BMJ Quality & Safety, 23*(9), 727–731.

Singh, T., Laub, R., Burgard, J. P., & Frings, C. (2018). Disentangling inhibition-based and retrieval-based aftereffects of distractors: Cognitive versus motor processes. *Journal of Experimental Psychology: Human Perception and Performance, 44*(5), 797–805.

Sio, U. N., Kotovsky, K., & Cagan, J. (2017). Interrupted: The roles of distributed effort and incubation in preventing fixation and generating problem solutions. *Memory & Cognition, 45*(4), 553–565.

Skinner, B. F. (1957). *Verbal Behavior.* New York, NY: Copley Group.

Skotko, B. G., Kensinger, E. A., Locascio, J. J., Einstein, G., Rubin, D. C., Tupler, L. A., Krendl, A., & Corkin, S (2004). Puzzling thoughts for H.M.: Can new semantic information be anchored to old semantic memories? *Neuropsychology, 18*(4), 756–769.

Skotko, B. G., Rubin, D. C., & Tupler, L. A. (2008). H.M.'s personal crossword puzzles: Understanding memory and language. *Memory, 16*(2), 89–96.

Slamecka, N. J., & Graf, P. (1978). The generation effect: Delineation of a phenomenon. *Journal of Experimental Psychology: Human Learning and Memory, 4*(6), 592–604.

Slobin, D. I. (1966). Grammatical transformations and sentence comprehension in childhood and adulthood. *Journal of Verbal Learning and Verbal Behavior, 5*(3), 219–227.

Slovic, P., Finucane, M., Peters, E., & MacGregor, D. G. (2002). The affect heuristic. In T. Gilovich, D. Griffin, & D. Kahneman (Eds.), *Heuristics and biases: The psychology of intuitive judgment* (pp. 397–420). New York, NY: Cambridge University Press.

Slovic, P., & Peters, E. (2010). Risk perception and affect. *Current Directions in Psychological Science, 15*(6), 322–325.

Smalarz, L., & Wells, G. L. (2014). Confirming feedback following a mistaken identification impairs memory for the culprit. *Law & Human Behavior, 38*(3), 283–292.

Smalarz, L., & Wells, G. L. (2014). Post-identification feedback to eyewitnesses impairs evaluators' abilities to discriminate between accurate and mistaken testimony. *Law & Human Behavior, 38*(2), 194–202.

Smallwood, J., & Schooler, J. W. (2006). The restless mind. *Psychological Bulletin, 132*(6), 946–958.

Smallwood, J., & Schooler, J. W. (2015). The science of mind wandering: Empirically navigating the stream of consciousness. *Annual Review of Psychology, 66,* 487–518.

Smeets, T., Jelicic, M., Peters, M. J. V., Candel, I., Horselenberg, R., & Merckelbach, H. (2006). "Of course I remember seeing that film"—How ambiguous questions generate crashing memories. *Applied Cognitive Psychology, 20*(6), 779–789.

Smelter, T. J., & Calvillo, D. P. (2020). Pictures and repeated exposure increase perceived accuracy of news headlines. *Applied Cognitive Psychology, 34*(5), 1061–1071.

Smith, E. E., Shoben, E. J., & Rips, L. J. (1974). Structure and process in semantic memory: A featural model for semantic decisions. *Psychological Review, 81*(3), 214–241.

Smith, E. R., & Miller, F. D. (1978). Limits on perception of cognitive processes: A reply to Nisbett & Wilson. *Psychological Review, 85,* 355–362.

Smith, J. D., Zakrzewski, A. C., Johnson, J. M., & Valleau, J. C. (2016). Ecology, fitness, evolution: New perspectives on categorization. *Current Directions in Psychological Science, 25*(4), 266–274.

Smith, K. A., Huber, D. E., & Vul, E. (2013). Multiply-constrained semantic search in the Remote Associates Test. *Cognition, 128*(1), 64–75.

Smith, S. M. (1979). Remembering in and out of context. *Journal of Experimental Psychology: Human Learning and Memory, 5*(5), 460–471.

Smith, S. M., & Beda, Z. (2020a). Forgetting fixation with context change. *Journal of Applied Research in Memory and Cognition, 9*(1), 19–23.

Smith, S. M., & Beda, Z. (2020b). Old problems in new contexts: The context-dependent fixation hypothesis. *Journal of Experimental Psychology: General, 149*(1), 192–197.

Smith, S. M., & Blankenship, S. E. (1989). Incubation effects. *Bulletin of the Psychonomic Society, 27*(4), 311–314.

Smith, S. M., & Blankenship, S. E. (1991). Incubation and the persistence of fixation in problem solving. *American Journal of Psychology, 104*(1), 61–87.

Smith, S. M., Glenberg, A., & Bjork, R. A. (1978). Environmental context and human memory. *Memory & Cognition, 6*(4), 342–353.

Smith, S. M., & Vela, E. (2001). Environmental context-dependent memory: A review and meta-analysis. *Psychonomic Bulletin & Review, 8*(2), 203–220.

Smith, S. M., & Ward, T. B. (2012). Cognition and the creation of ideas. In K. J. Holyoak & R. G. Morrison (Eds.), *The Oxford handbook of thinking and reasoning* (pp. 456–474). New York, NY: Oxford University Press.

Smitizsky, G., Liu, W., & Gneezy, U. (2021). The endowment effect: Loss aversion or a buy-sell discrepancy. *Journal of Experimental Psychology: General.* Advance online publication. https://doi.org/10.1037/xge0000880

Snow, R. E. (1994). Abilities in academic tasks. In R. J. Sternberg & R. K. Wagner (Eds.), *Mind in context: Inter-actionist perspectives on human intelligence* (pp. 3–37). Cambridge, England: Cambridge University Press.

Snow, R. E. (1996). Aptitude development and education. *Psychology, Public Policy, and Law, 2*(3-4), 536–560.

Soares, J. S., & Storm, B. C. (2018). Forget in a flash: A further investigation of the photo-taking-impairment effect. *Journal of Applied Research in Memory and Cognition, 7*(1), 154–160.

Soto, D., & Silvanto, J. (2014). Reappraising the relationship between working memory and conscious awareness. *Trends in Cognitive Sciences, 18*(10), 520–525.

Sparrow, B., Liu, J., & Wegner, D. M. (2011). Google effects on memory: Cognitive consequences of having information at our fingertips. *Science, 333*(6043), 776–778.

Spearman, C. (1904). "General intelligence," objectively determined and measured. *American Journal of Psychology, 15*(2), 201–293.

Spearman, C. (1927). *The abilities of man.* New York, NY: Macmillan.

Speekenbrink, M., & Shanks, D. R. (2012). Decision making. In D. Reisberg (Ed.), *The Oxford handbook of cognitive psychology* (pp. 682–703). New York, NY: Oxford University Press.

Spelke, E., Hirst, W., & Neisser, U. (1976). Skills of divided attention. *Cognition, 4*(3), 215–230.

Spencer, S. J., Logel, C., & Davies, P. G. (2016). Stereotype threat. *Annual Review of Psychology, 67,* 415–437.

Spencer, S. J., Steele, C. M., & Quinn, D. M. (1999). Stereotype threat and women's math performance. *Journal of Experimental Social Psychology, 35*(1), 4–28.

Sperling, G. (1960). The information available in brief visual presentations. *Psychological Monographs, 74*(11), 1–29.

Squire, L. R., & McKee, R. D. (1993). Declarative and nondeclarative memory in opposition: When prior events influence amnesic patients more than normal subjects. *Memory & Cognition, 21,* 424–430.

St. Jacques, P. L., & Schacter, D. L. (2013). Modifying memory: Selectively enhancing and updating personal memories for a museum tour by reactivating them. *Psychological Science, 24*(4), 537–543.

Stanley, M. L., Bedrov, A., Cabeza, R., & De Brigard, F. (2020). The centrality of remembered moral and immoral actions in constructing personal identity. *Memory, 28*(2), 278–284.

Stanovich, K. E. (2009). *What intelligence tests miss: The psychology of rational thought.* New Haven, CT: Yale University Press.

Stanovich, K. E. (2012). On the distinction between rationality and intelligence: Implications for understanding individual differences in reasoning. In K. J. Holyoak & R. G. Morrison (Eds.), *The Oxford handbook of thinking and reasoning* (pp. 433–455). New York, NY: Oxford University Press.

Stanovich, K. E., & West, R. F. (2000). Individual differences in reasoning: Implications for the rationality debate? *Behavioral and Brain Sciences*, 23(5), 645–665.

Stanovich, K. E., West, R. F., & Toplak, M. E. (2016). *The rationality quotient: Toward a test of rational thinking*. Cambridge, MA: MIT Press.

Stark, L.-J., & Perfect, T., J. (2008). The effects of repeated idea elaboration on unconscious plagiarism. *Memory & Cognition*, 36(1), 65–73.

Stasenko, A., & Gollan, T. H. (2019). Tip of the tongue after any language: Reintroducing the notion of blocked retrieval. *Cognition*, 193, Article 104027.

Steblay, N. M. (1992). A meta-analytic review of the weapon focus effect. *Law and Human Behavior*, 16(4), 413–424.

Steblay, N. (1997). Social influence in eyewitness recall: A meta-analytic review of lineup instruction effects. *Law & Human Behavior*, 21, 283–297.

Steblay, N. M., Besirevic, J., Fulero, S. M., & Jiminez-Lorente, B. (1999). The effects of pretrial publicity on juror verdicts: A meta-analytic review. *Law and Human Behavior*, 23(2), 219–235.

Steblay, N. K., Hosch, H. M., Culhane, S. E., & McWethy, A. (2006). The impact on juror verdicts of judicial instruction to disregard inadmissible evidence: A meta-analysis. *Law and Human Behavior*, 30(4), 469–492.

Steblay, N. K., Wells, G. L., & Douglass, A. B. (2014). The eyewitness post identification feedback effect 15 year later: Theoretical and policy implications. *Psychology, Public Policy, & Law*, 20(1), 1–18.

Steele, C. (2010). *Whistling Vivaldi: And other clues to how stereotypes affect us*. New York, NY: Norton.

Steele, C. M., & Aronson, J. (1995). Stereotype threat and the intellectual test performance of African Americans. *Journal of Personality and Social Psychology*, 69(5), 797–811.

Stein, T., Reeder, R. R., & Peelen, M. V. (2016). Privileged access to awareness for faces and objects of expertise. *Journal of Experimental Psychology: Human Perception & Performance*, 42(6), 788–798.

Stephens, R. G., Dunn, J. C., & Hayes, B. K. (2019). Belief bias is response bias: Evidence from a two-step signal detection model. *Journal of Experimental Psychology: Learning, Memory, & Cognition*, 45(2), 320–332.

Sternberg, R. J., & Grigorenko, E. L. (2004). Successful intelligence in the classroom. *Theory into Practice*, 43(4), 274–280.

Sternberg, R. J., Kaufman, J. C., & Grigorenko, E. L. (2008). *Applied intelligence*. New York, NY: Cambridge University Press.

Stevens, A., & Coupe, P. (1978). Distortions in judged spatial relations. *Cognitive Psychology*, 10(4), 422–437.

Stojanoski, B., Wild, C. J., Battista, M. E., Nichols, E. S., & Owen, A. M. (2020). Brain training habits are not associated with generalized benefits to cognition: An online study of over 1000 "brain trainers." *Journal of Experimental Psychology: General*. Advance online publication. https://doi.org/10.1037/xge0000773

Stone, S. M., & Storm, B. C. (2021). Search fluency as a misleading measure of memory. *Journal of Experimental Psychology: Learning, Memory, & Cognition*, 47(1), 53–64.

Storm, B. C., & Patel, T. N. (2014). Forgetting as a consequence and enabler of creative thinking. *Journal of Experimental Psychology: Learning, Memory, & Cognition*, 40(6), 1594–1609.

Stothart, C., Mitchum, A., & Yehnert, C. (2015). The attentional cost of receiving a cell phone notification. *Journal of Experimental Psychology: Human Perception & Performance*, 41(4), 893–897.

Stough, C., & Pase, M. P. (2015). Improving cognition in the elderly with nutritional supplements. *Current Directions in Psychological Science*, 24(3), 177–183.

Strayer, D. L., Cooper, J. M., Turrill, J., Coleman, J. R., & Hopman, R. J. (2016). Talking to your car can drive you to distraction. *Cognitive Research: Principles and Implications*, 1, 1–17.

Strayer, D. L., & Drews, F. A. (2007). Cell phone–induced driver distraction. *Current Directions in Psychological Science*, 16(3), 128–131.

Strayer, D. L., & Johnston, W. A. (2001). Driven to distraction: Dual-task studies of simulated driving and conversing on a cellular telephone. *Psychological Science*, 12(6), 462–466.

Stromeyer, C. F., III. (1982). *An adult eidetiker*. In U. Neisser (Ed.), *Memory observed: Remembering in natural contexts* (pp. 399–404). New York, NY: Freeman.

Stroop, J. R. (1935). Studies of interference in serial verbal reactions. *Journal of Experimental Psychology*, 18(6), 643–662.

Strub, T., & McKimmie, B. M. (2015). Sugar and spice and all things nice: The role of gender stereotypes in jurors' perceptions of criminal defendants. *Psychiatry, Psychology and Law*, 23(4), 487–498.

Studebaker, C. A., & Penrod, S. D. (2005). Pretrial publicity and its influence on juror decision making. In N. Brewer & K. D. Williams (Eds.), *Psychology and law: An empirical perspective* (pp. 254–275). New York, NY: Guilford Press.

Su, N., Buchin, Z. L., & Mulligan, N. W. (2020). Levels of retrieval and the testing effect. *Journal of Experimental Psychology: Learning, Memory, & Cognition*. Advance online publication. http://dx.doi.org/10.1037/xlm0000962

Sulin, R. A., & Dooling, D. J. (1974). Intrusion of a thematic idea in retention of prose. *Journal of Experimental Psychology*, 103, 255–262.

Sunstein, C. R. (2016). The council of psychological advisers. *Annual Review of Psychology*, 67, 713–737.

Svartvik, J. (1966). *On voice in the English verb*. The Hague, Netherlands: Mouton.

Swanson, J., Posner, M. I., Cantwell, D., Wigal, S., Crinella, F., Filipek, P., Emerson, J., Tucker, D., & Nalcioglu, O. (1998). Attention-deficit/hyperactivity Disorder: Symptom domain, cognitive processes and neural networks. In R. Parasuraman (Ed.), *The attentive brain* (pp. 445–460). Cambridge, MA: MIT Press.

Swire, B., Ecker, U. K. H., & Lewandowsky, S. (2017). The role of familiarity in correcting inaccurate information. *Journal of Experimental Psychology: Learning, Memory, & Cognition, 43*(12), 1948–1961.

Symons, C. S., & Johnson, B. T. (1997). The self-reference effect in memory: A meta-analysis. *Psychological Bulletin, 121*(3), 371–394.

Szpunar, K. K., Khan, N. Y., & Schacter, D. L. (2013). Interpolated memory tests reduce mind wandering and improve learning of online lectures. *Proceedings of the National Academy of Sciences, 110*(63), 6313– 6317.

Tabachnick, B., & Brotsky, S. J. (1976). Free recall and complexity of pictorial stimuli. *Memory & Cognition, 4,* 466–470.

Tagg, C. (2015). *Exploring digital communication: Language in action.* New York, NY: Routledge.

Talarico, J. M., & Rubin, D. C (2007). Flashbulb memories are special after all; in phenomenology, not accuracy. *Applied Cognitive Psychology, 21*(5), 557–558.

Talmi, D. (2013). Enhanced emotional memory: Cognitive and neural mechanisms. *Current Directions in Psychological Science, 22*(6), 430–436.

Talmi, D., Grady, C. L., Goshen-Gottstein, Y., & Moscovitch, M. (2005). Neuroimaging the serial position curve: A test of single-store versus dual-store models. *Psychological Science, 16*(6), 716–723.

Tamietto, M., Cauda, F., Latini Corazzini, L., Savazzi, S., Marzi, C. A., Goebel, R., Weiskrantz, L., & de Gelder, B (2010). Collicular vision guides nonconscious behavior. *Journal of Cognitive Neuroscience, 22*(5), 888–902.

Tamir, D. I., Templeton, E. M., Ward, A. F., & Zaki, J. (2018). Media usage diminishes memory for experiences. *Journal of Experimental Social Psychology, 76,* 161–168.

Tanenhaus, M. K., & Trueswell, J. C. (2006). Eye movements and spoken language comprehension. In M. J. Traxler & M. A. Gernsbacher (Eds.), *Handbook of psycholinguistics* (2nd ed.). Amsterdam, Netherlands: Elsevier.

Tardif, J., Duchesne, X. M., Cohan, S., Royer, J., Blais, C., Fiset, D., Duchaine, B., & Gosselin, F. (2019). Use of face information varies systematically from developmental prosopagnosics to super-recognizers. *Psychological Science, 30*(2), 300–308.

Tardif, J., Fiset, D., Zhang, Y., Estéphan, A., Cai, Q., Luo, C., Sun, D., Gosselin, F., & Blais, C. (2017). Culture shapes spatial frequency tuning for face identification. *Journal of Experimental Psychology: Human Perception & Performance, 43*(2), 294–306.

Taylor, A., Jordan, K., Zajac, R., Takarangi, M. K. T., & Garry, M. (2020). Judgments of memory coherence depend on the conditions under which a memory is retrieved, regardless of reported PTSD symptoms. *Journal of Applied Research in Memory and Cognition, 9*(3), 396–409.

Taylor, J., Roehrig, A. D., Hensler, B. S., Connor, C. M., & Schatschneider, C. (2010). Teacher quality moderates the genetic effects on early reading. *Science, 328*(5977), 512–514.

Teper, R., Segal, Z. V., & Inzlicht, M. (2013). Inside the mindful mind: How mindfulness enhances emotion regulation through improvements in executive control. *Current Directions in Psychological Science, 22*(6), 449–454.

Thaler, R. H., & Sunstein, C. R. (2009). *Nudge: Improving decisions about health, wealth, and happiness.* New York, NY: Penguin.

Thaler, R. H. (2009, September 26). Opting in vs. opting out. *The New York Times.*

Tham, D. S. Y., Sowden, P. T., Grandison, A., Franklin, A., Lee, A. K. W., Ng, M., Park, J., Pang, W., & Zhao, J. (2020). A systematic investigation of conceptual color associations. *Journal of Experimental Psychology: General, 149*(7), 1311–1332.

The Sentencing Project. (2019, October 8). *Youth sentenced to life imprisonment.* https://www.sentencingproject.org/publications/youth-sentenced-life-imprisonment/

Thibaut, J.-P., Gelaes, S., & Murphy, G. L. (2018). Does practice in category learning increase rule use or exemplar use—or both? *Memory & Cognition, 46,* 530–543.

Thibodeau, P. H., & Boroditsky, L. (2011). Metaphors we think with: The role of metaphor in reasoning. *PLoS ONE, 6*(2), e16782.

Thioux, M., Stark, D. E., Klaiman, C., & Shultz, R. T. (2006). The day of the week when you were born in 700 ms: Calendar computation in an autistic savant. *Journal of Experimental Psychology: Human Perception and Performance, 32*(5), 1155–1168.

Thirion, B., Duchesnay, E., Hubbard, E., Dubois, J., Poline, J.-B., Lebihan, D., & Dehaene, S. (2006). Inverse retinotopy: Inferring the visual content of images from brain activation patterns. *NeuroImage, 33*(4), 1104–1116.

Thomas, A. K., & Loftus, E. F. (2002). Creating bizarre false memories through imagination. *Memory & Cognition, 30*(3), 423–431.

Thomas, A. K., Smith, A. M., Kamal, K., & Gordon, L. T. (2020). Should you use frequent quizzing in your college course? Giving up 20 minutes of lecture time may pay off. *Journal of Applied Research in Memory and Cognition, 9*(1), 83–95.

Thomas, J. C., Jr. (1974). An analysis of behavior in the hobbits-orcs problem. *Cognitive Psychology, 6*(2), 257–269.

Thompson, P. (1980). Margaret Thatcher: A new illusion. *Perception, 9*(4), 483–484.

Thompson, W. L., & Kosslyn, S. M. (2000). Neural systems activated during visual mental imagery: A review and meta-analyses. In A. W. Toga & J. C. Mazziotta (Eds.), *Brain mapping: The applications* (pp. 535–560). New York, NY: Academic Press.

Thompson, W. L., Kosslyn, S. M., Hoffman, M. S., & Van der Kooij, K. (2008). Inspecting visual mental images: Can people "see" implicit properties as easily in imagery and perception? *Memory & Cognition, 36*(5), 1024–1032.

Thompson, W. L., Slotnick, S. D., Burrage, M. S., & Kosslyn, S. M. (2009). Two forms of spatial imagery: Neuroimaging evidence. *Psychological Science*, 20(10), 1245–1253.

Thomsen, D. K., & Berntsen, D. (2009). The long-term impact of emotionally stressful events on memory characteristics and life story. *Applied Cognitive Psychology*, 23(4), 579–598.

Thomson, K. S., & Oppenheimer, D. M. (2016). Investigating an alternate form of the cognitive reflection test. *Judgment and Decision Making*, 11(1), 99–113.

Tinti, C., Schmidt, S., Sotgiu, I., Testa, S., & Curci, A. (2009). The role of importance/consequentiality appraisal in flashbulb memory formation: The case of the death of Pope John Paul II. *Applied Cognitive Psychology*, 23(2), 236–253.

Tinti, C., Schmidt, S., Testa, S., & Levine, L. J. (2014). Distinct processes shape flashbulb and event memories. *Memory and Cognition*, 42(4), 539–551.

Tolman, E. C. (1948). Cognitive maps in rats and men. *Psychological Review*, 55(4), 189–208.

Tong, F., Nakayama, K., Vaughan, J. T., & Kanwisher, N. (1998). Binocular rivalry and visual awareness in human extrastriate cortex. *Neuron*, 21(4), 753–759.

Tononi, G., Boly, M., Massimini, M., & Koch, C. (2016). Integrated information theory: From consciousness to its physical substrate. *Nature Reviews Neuroscience*, 17, 450–461.

Tononi, G., & Cirelli, C. (2013, August). New hypothesis explains why we sleep. *Scientific American*, 309(2).

Toplak, M. E., West, R. F. & Stanovich, K. E. (2014). Assessing miserly information processing: An expansion of the cognitive reflection test. *Thinking & Reasoning*, 20(2), 147–168.

Trahan, L. H., Stuebing, K. K., Fletcher, J. M., & Hiscock, M. (2014). The Flynn effect: A meta-analysis. *Psychological Bulletin*, 140(5), 1332–1360.

Travers, E., Rolison, J. J., & Feeney, A. (2016). The time course of conflict on the cognitive reflection test. *Cognition*, 150, 109–118.

Tree, J. J., Horry, R., Riley, H., & Wilmer, J. B. (2017). Are portrait artists superior face recognizers? Limited impact of adult experience on face recognition ability. *Journal of Experimental Psychology: Human Perception & Performance*, 43(4), 667–676.

Treffert, D. A. (2014, August). Accidental genius. *Scientific American*, 52–57.

Treisman, A. M. (1964). Verbal cues, language, and meaning in selective attention. *American Journal of Psychology*, 77(2), 206–219.

Treisman, A. M., & Gelade, G. (1980). A feature-integration theory of attention. *Cognitive Psychology*, 12(1), 97–136.

Treisman, A. M., Sykes, M., & Gelade, G. (1977). Selective attention and stimulus integration. In S. Dornic (Ed.), *Attention and performance VI* (pp. 333–361). Hillsdale, NJ: Erlbaum.

Trippas, D., Thompson, V. A., & Handley, S. J. (2017). When fast logic meets slow belief: Evidence for a parallel-processing model of belief bias. *Memory & Cognition*, 45(4), 539–552.

Trueswell, J. C., Tanenhaus, M. K., & Garnsey, S. M. (1994). Semantic influences on parsing: Use of thematic role information in syntactic ambiguity resolution. *Journal of Memory and Language*, 33(3), 285–318.

Tsai, C. I., & Thomas, M. (2011). When does feeling of fluency matter? How abstract and concrete thinking influence fluency effects. *Psychological Science*, 22(3), 348–354.

Tsuchiya, N., & Adolphs, R. (2007). Emotion and consciousness. *Trends in Cognitive Sciences*, 11(4), 158–167.

Tucker-Drob, E. M., & Bates, T. C. (2016). Large cross-national differences in gene x socioeconomic status interaction on intelligence. *Psychological Science*, 27(2), 138–149.

Tucker-Drob, E. M., Rhemtulla, M., Harden, K. P., Turkheimer, E., & Fask, D. (2011). Emergence of a gene x socioeconomic status interaction on infant mental ability between 10 months and 2 years. *Psychological Science*, 22(1), 125–133.

Tuffiash, M., Roring, R. W., & Ericsson, K. A. (2007). Expert performance in SCRABBLE: Implications for the study of the structure and acquisition of complex skills. *Journal of Experimental Psychology: Applied*, 13(3), 124–134.

Tulving, E. (1983). *Elements of episodic memory*. Oxford, England: Oxford University Press.

Turkheimer, E., Haley, A., Waldron, M., D'Onofrio, B., & Gottesman, I. I. (2003). Socioeconomic status modifies heritability of IQ in young children. *Psychological Science*, 14(6), 623–628.

Tversky, A., & Kahneman, D. (1973). Availability: A heuristic for judging frequency and probability. *Cognitive Psychology*, 5(2), 207–232.

Tversky, A., & Kahneman, D. (1974). Judgment under uncertainty: Heuristics and biases. *Science*, 185(4157), 1124–1131.

Tversky, A., & Kahneman, D. (1981). The framing of decisions and the psychology of choice. *Science*, 211(4481), 453–458.

Tversky, A., & Kahneman, D. (1982). Evidential impact of base rates. In D. Kahneman, P. Slovic, & A. Tversky (Eds.), *Judgment under uncertainty: Heuristics and biases* (pp. 153–160). New York, NY: Cambridge University Press.

Tversky, A., & Kahneman, D. (1987). Rational choice and the framing of decisions. In R. M. Hogarth & M. W. Reder (Eds.), *Rational choice: The contrast between economics and psychology* (pp. 67–94). Chicago, IL: University of Chicago Press.

Umanath, S., & Coane, J. H. (2020). Face validity of remembering and knowing: Empirical consensus and disagreement between participants and researchers. *Perspectives on Psychological Science*, 15(6), 1400–1422.

Uner, O., & Roediger, H. L. (2018). The effect of question placement on learning from textbook chapters. *Journal of Applied Research in Memory and Cognition*, 7(1), 116–122.

Ungerleider, L. G., & Haxby, J. V. (1994). "What" and "where" in the human brain. *Current Opinions in Neurobiology*, 4(2), 157–165.

Unkelbach, C., Koch, A., Silva, R. R., & Garcia-Marques, T. (2019). Truth by repetition: Explanations and implications. *Current Directions in Psychological Science*, 28(3), 247–253.

Unsworth, N. (2019). Individual differences in long-term memory. *Psychological Bulletin*, 145(1), 79–139.

U.S. Department of Agriculture. (2019, March). *Organic 101: What the USDA organic label means*. https://www.usda.gov/media/blog/2012/03/22/organic-101-what-usda-organic-label-means

Usher, M., Tsetsos, K., Glickman, M., & Chater, N. (2019). Selective integration: An attention theory of choice biases and adaptive choice. *Current Directions in Psychological Science*, 28(6), 552–559.

Uttal, D. H., Meadow, N. G., Tipton, E., Hand, L. L., Alden, A. R., Warren, C., & Newcombe, N. S. (2013). The malleability of spatial skills: A meta-analysis of training studies. *Psychological Bulletin*, 139(2), 352–402.

Valentine, T. (1988). Upside-down faces: A review of the effect of inversion upon face recognition. *British Journal of Psychology*, 79, 471–491.

Valentine, T., Davis, J. P., Memon, A., & Roberts, A. (2012). Live showups and their influence on a subsequent video line-up. *Applied Cognitive Psychology*, 26(1), 1–23.

Valentine, T., & Mesout, J. (2008). Eyewitness identification under stress in the London Dungeon. *Applied Cognitive Psychology*, 23(2), 151–161.

van der Lely, H. K. J., & Pinker, S. (2014). The biological basis for language: Insight from developmental grammatical impairments. *Trends in Cognitive Sciences*, 18(11), 586–595.

Van Essen, D. C., & DeYoe, E. A. (1995). Concurrent processing in the primate visual cortex. In M. S. Gazzaniga (Ed.), *The cognitive neurosciences* (pp. 383–400). Cambridge, MA: MIT Press.

van Gaal, S., Naccache, L., Meuwese, J. D. I., van Loon, A. M., Leighton, A. H., Cohen, L., & Dehaene, S. (2014). Can the meaning of multiple words be integrated unconsciously? *Philosophical Transactions of the Royal Society of London B,* 20130212.

van Steenburgh, J. J., Fleck, J. I., Beeman, M., & Kounios, J. (2012). Insight. In K. J. Holyoak & R. G. Morrison (Eds.), *The Oxford handbook of thinking and reasoning* (pp. 475–491). New York, NY: Oxford University Press.

van Veen, V., & Carter, C. S. (2006). Conflict and cognitive control in the brain. *Current Directions in Psychological Science*, 15(5), 237–240.

Vandierendonck, A., Liefooghe, B., & Verbruggen, F. (2010). Task switching: Interplay of reconfiguration and interference control. *Psychological Bulletin*, 136(4), 601–626.

Vansteenkiste, P., Lenoir, M., & Bourgois, J. G. (2021). Gaze behavior of experienced and novice beach lifeguards—An exploratory in situ study. *Applied Cognitive Psychology*, 35(1), 251–257.

Varshney, L. R., Pinel, F., Varshney, K. R., Bhattacharjya, D., Schörgendorfer, A., & Chee Y.-M. (2019). A big data approach to computational creativity: The curious case of Chef Watson. *IBM Journal of Research and Development*, 63(1), 7:1–7:18.

Vartanian, O., Martindale, C., & Matthews, J. (2009). Divergent thinking ability is related to faster relatedness judgments. *Psychology of Aesthetics, Creativity, and the Arts*, 3(2), 99–103.

Vergauwe, E., Barrouillet, P., & Camos, V. (2010). Do mental processes share a domain-general resource? *Psychological Science*, 21(3), 384–390.

Verheijen, L. (2013). The effects of text messaging and instant messaging on literacy. *Journal of English Studies*, 94(5), 582–602.

Verkuilen, J. (2018, June 19). *The power of the mind can help heal cancer*. Thrive Global Community. https://thriveglobal.com/stories/the-science-behind-guided-imagery-how-does-it-work/

Vernon, P. A. (Ed.). (1987). *Speed of information-processing and intelligence*. Canada: Ablex.

Verschuere, B., Ben-Shakhar, G., & Meijer, E. (Eds.). (2011). *Memory detection: Theory and application of the concealed information test*. New York, NY: Cambridge University Press.

Verstijnen, I. M., van Leeuwen, C., Goldschmidt, G., Hamel, R., & Hennessey, J. M. (1998). Creative discovery in imagery and perception: Combining is relatively easy, restructuring takes a sketch. *Acta Psychologica*, 99(2), 177–200.

Vieites, V., Pruden, S. M., & Reeb-Sutherland, B. C. (2020). Childhood wayfinding experience explains sex and individual differences in adult wayfinding strategy and anxiety. *Cognitive Research: Principles and Implications*, 5, Article 12.

Vihinen, M., & Samarghitean, C. M. (2008). Medical expert systems. *Current Bioinformatics*, 3(1), 56–65.

Vinkhuyzen, A. A. E., van der Sluis, S., & Posthuma, D. (2011). Life events moderate variation in cognitive ability (g) in adults. *Molecular Psychiatry*, 16(1), 4–6.

Visser, B. A., Ashton, M. C., & Vernon, P. A. (2006). Beyond g: Putting multiple intelligences theory to the test. *Intelligence*, 34, 487–502.

Võ, M. L.-H., & Henderson, J. M. (2009) Does gravity matter? Effects of semantic and syntactic inconsistencies on the allocation of attention during scene perception. *Journal of Vision*, 9(3), 1–15.

Vogel, T., Silva, R. R., Thomas, A., & Wänke, M. (2020). Truth is in the mind, but beauty is in the eye: Fluency effects are moderated by a match between fluency source and judgment direction. *Journal of Experimental Psychology: General*, 149(8), 1587–1596.

von Helmholtz, H. (1909). *Wissenschaftliche Abhandlungen, II* (pp. 764–843). Leipzig, Germany: Barth.

von Neumann, J., & Morgenstern, O. (1947). *Theory of games and economic behavior*. Princeton, NJ: Princeton University Press.

Vossel, S., Geng, J. J., & Fink, G. R. (2014). Dorsal and ventral attention systems: Distinct neural circuits but collaborative roles. *The Neuroscientist, 20*(2), 150–159.

Voyer, D. (2011). Time limits and gender differences on paper-and-pencil tests of mental rotation: A meta-analysis. *Psychonomic Bulletin & Review, 18*, 267–277.

Voyer, D., Saint-Aubin, J., Altman, K., & Doyle, R. A. (2020). Sex differences in tests of mental rotation: Direct manipulation of strategies with eye-tracking. *Journal of Experimental Psychology: Human Perception & Performance, 46*(9), 871–889.

Voyer, D., Voyer, S. D., & Saint-Aubin, J. (2017). Sex differences in visual-spatial working memory: A meta-analysis. *Psychonomic Bulletin & Review, 24*(2), 307–334.

Vredeveldt, A., Knol, J. W., & van Koppen, P. J. (2017). Observing offenders: Incident reports by surveillance detectives, uniformed police, and civilians. *Legal and Criminological Psychology, 22*(1), 150–163.

Vredeveldt, A., van Deuren, S., & van Koppen, P. J. (2019). Remembering with a friend or a stranger: Comparing acquainted and unacquainted pairs in collaborative eyewitness interviews. *Memory, 27*, 1390–1493.

Vredeveldt, A., & van Koppen, P. J. (2016). The thin blue line-up: Comparing eyewitness performance by police and civilians. *Journal of Applied Research in Memory & Cognition, 5*(3), 252–256.

Vrij, A., & Fisher, R. P. (2020). Unraveling the misconception about deception and nervous behavior. *Frontiers in Psychology, 11*, 1377. https//doi.org/10.3389/fpsyg.2020.01377

Vrij, A., Granhag, P. A., & Porter, S. (2010). Pitfalls and opportunities in nonverbal and verbal lie detection. *Psychological Science in the Public Interest, 11*(3), 89–121.

Vrij, A., Hartwig, M., & Granhag, P. A. (2019). Reading lies: Nonverbal communication and deception. *Annual Review of Psychology, 70*, 295–317.

Vul, E., & Pashler, H. (2007). Incubation benefits only after people have been misdirected. *Memory & Cognition, 35*, 701–710.

Wade, K. A., Garry, M., & Pezdek, K. (2017). Deconstructing rich false memories of committing crime: Commentary on Shaw & Porter (2015). *Psychological Science, 29*(3), 471–476.

Wade, K. A., Garry, M., Read, J. D., & Lindsay, D. S. (2002). A picture is worth a thousand lies: Using false photographs to create false childhood memories. *Psychonomic Bulletin & Review, 9*, 597–603.

Wagemans, J., Elder, J. H., Kubovy, M., Palmer, S. E., Peterson, M. A., Singh, M., & von der Heydt, R. (2012). A century of Gestalt psychology in visual perception: I. Perceptual grouping and figure-ground organization. *Psychological Bulletin, 138*(6), 1172–1217.

Wagemans, J., Feldman, J., Gepshtein, S., Kimchi, R., Pomerantz, J. R., van der Helm, P. A., & van Leeuwen, C. (2012). A century of Gestalt psychology in visual perception: II. Conceptual and theoretical foundations. *Psychological Bulletin, 138*(6), 1218–1252.

Wagner, A. D., Shannon, B. J., Kahn, I., & Buckner, R. L. (2005). Parietal lobe contributions to episodic memory retrieval. *Trends in Cognitive Sciences, 9*(9), 445–453.

Wagner, R. K. (2000). Practical intelligence. In R. J. Sternberg (Ed.), *Handbook of human intelligence* (pp. 380–395). New York, NY: Cambridge University Press.

Wai, J., Putallaz, M., & Makel, M. C. (2012). Studying intellectual outliers: Are there sex differences, and are the smart getting smarter? *Current Directions in Psychological Science, 21*(6), 382–390.

Wallas, G. (1926). *The art of thought*. New York, NY: Harcourt, Brace.

Wallentin, M. (2018). Sex differences in post-stroke aphasia rates are caused by age. A meta-analysis and database query. *PLoS ONE, 13*(12), e0209571.

Wallis, G. (2013). Toward a unified model of face and object recognition in the human visual system. *Frontiers in Psychology, 4*, 497.

Walter, N., & Tukachinsky, R. (2020). A meta-analytic examination of the continued influence of misinformation in the face of correction: How powerful is it, why does it happen, and how to stop it? *Communication Research, 47*(2), 155–177.

Walton, G. M., & Spencer, S. J. (2009). Latent ability: Grades and test scores systematically underestimate the intellectual ability of negatively stereotyped students. *Psychological Science, 20*(9), 1132–1139.

Wamsley, E. J. (2019). Memory consolidation during waking rest. *Trends in Cognitive Sciences, 23*(3), 171–173.

Wan, L., Crookes, K., Dawel, A., Pidcock, M., Hall, A., & McKone, E. (2017). Face-blind for other-race faces: Individual differences in other-race recognition impairments. *Journal of Experimental Psychology: General, 146*(1), 102–122.

Wan, L., Crookes, K., Reynolds, K. J., Irons, J. L., & McKone, E. (2015). A cultural setting where the other-race effect on face recognition has no social-motivational component and derives entirely from lifetime perceptual experiences. *Cognition, 144*, 91–115.

Wang, R., Li, J., Fang, H., Tian, M., & Liu, J. (2012). Individual differences in holistic processing predict face recognition ability. *Psychological Science, 23*(2), 169–177.

Wang, S.-H., & Morris, R. G. M. (2010). Hippocampal-neocortical interactions in memory formation, consolidation, and reconsolidation. *Annual Review of Psychology, 61*, 49–79.

Wang, Y., Luppi, A., Fawcett, J., & Anderson, M. C. (2019). Reconsidering unconscious persistence: Suppressing unwanted memories reduces their indirect expression in later thoughts. *Cognition, 187*, 78–94.

Wänke, M., & Hansen, J. (2015). Relative processing fluency. *Current Directions in Psychological Science*, 24(3), 195–199.

Wantz, A. L., Borst, G., Mast, F. W., & Lobmaier, J. S. (2015). Colors in mind: A novel paradigm to investigate pure color imagery. *Journal of Experimental Psychology: Learning, Memory, & Cognition*, 41(4), 1152–1161.

Ward, T. B., Finke, R. A., & Smith, S. M. (1995). *Creativity and the mind: Discovering the genius within*. New York, NY: Plenum Press.

Warne, R. T., & Burningham, C. (2019). Spearman's *g* found in 31 non-Western nations: Strong evidence that *g* is a universal phenomenon. *Psychological Bulletin*, 145(3), 237–272.

Warrington, E. K., & McCarthy, R. (1983). Category specific access dysphasia. *Brain*, *106*, 859–878.

Warrington, E. K., & McCarthy, R. A. (1987). Categories of knowledge: Further fractionations and an attempted integration. *Brain*, *110*, 1273–1296.

Wason, P. C. (1966). Reasoning. In B. M. Foss (Ed.), *New horizons in psychology* (pp. 135–151). Middlesex, England: Penguin.

Wason, P. C. (1968). Reasoning about a rule. *Quarterly Journal of Experimental Psychology*, 20(3), 273–281.

Watkins, M. W., Wilson, S. M., Kotz, K. M., Carbone, M. C., & Babula, T. (2006). Factor structure of the Wechsler Intelligence Scale for Children—Fourth edition among referred students. *Educational and Psychological Measurement*, 66(6), 975–983.

Watkins, M. J. (1977). The intricacy of memory span. *Memory & Cognition*, 5(5), 529–534.

Wattenmaker, W. D., Dewey, G. I., Murphy, T. D., & Medin, D. L. (1986). Linear separability and concept learning: Context, relational properties, and concept naturalness. *Cognitive Psychology*, 18(2), 158–194.

Waugh, N. C., & Norman, D. A. (1965). Primary memory. *Psychological Review*, 72(2), 89–104.

Wearing, D. (2011). *Forever today: A memoir of love and amnesia*. New York, NY: Doubleday.

Weatherford, D. R., Erickson, W. B., Thomas, J., Walker, M. E., & Schein, B. (2020). You shall not pass: How facial variability and feedback affect the detection of low-prevalence fake IDs. *Cognitive Research: Principles and Implications*, 5, Article 3.

Weaver, C. A. (1993). Do you need a "flash" to form a flashbulb memory? *Journal of Experimental Psychology: General*, 122(1), 39–46.

Weber, E. U., & Johnson, E. J. (2009). Mindful judgment and decision making. *Annual Review of Psychology*, 60, 53–85.

Wechsler, D. (2003). *Wechsler Intelligence Scale for Children—Fourth edition*. San Antonio, TX: Psychological Corporation.

Weidemann, C. T., Kragel, J. E., Lega, B. C., Worrell, G. A., Sperling, M. R., Sharan, A. D., Jobst, B. C., Khadjevand, F., Davis, K. A., Wanda, P. A., Kadel, A., Rizzuto, D. S., & Kahana, M. J. (2019). Neural activity reveals interactions between episodic and semantic memory systems during retrieval. *Journal of Experimental Psychology: General*, 148(1), 1–12.

Weiland, J. D., Walston, S. T., & Humayun, M. S. (2016). Electrical stimulation of the retina to produce artificial vision. *Annual Review of Vision Science*, 2, 273–294.

Weiner, K. S., & Grill-Spector, K. (2013). The improbable simplicity of the fusiform face area. *Trends in Cognitive Sciences*, 16(5), 251–254.

Weinstein, J., & Morton, L. H. (2003). Stuck in a rut: The role of creative thinking in problem solving and legal education. *Clinical Law Review*, 9, 835–877.

Weisberg, R. W., & Alba, J. W. (1981). An examination of the alleged role of "fixation" in the solution of several "insight" problems. *Journal of Experimental Psychology: General*, 110(2), 169–192.

Weisberg, R. W. (1986). *Creativity: Genius and other myths*. New York, NY: Freeman.

Weiskrantz, L. (1986). *Blindsight: A case study and implications*. New York, NY: Oxford University Press.

Weiskrantz, L. (1997). *Consciousness lost and found: A neuropsychological exploration*. New York, NY: Oxford University Press.

Wells, G. L., Kovera, M. B., Douglass, A. B., Brewer, N., Meissner, C. A., & Wixted, J. T. (2020). Policy and procedure recommendations for the collection and preservation of eyewitness identification evidence. *Law and Human Behavior*, 44(1), 3–36.

Wells, G. L., & Bradfield, A. L. (1998). "Good, you identified the suspect": Feedback to eyewitnesses distorts their reports of the witnessed experience. *Journal of Applied Psychology*, 83(3), 360–376.

Wells, G. L., Olson, E. A., & Charman, S. D. (2003). Distorted retrospective eyewitness reports as functions of feedback and delay. *Journal of Experimental Psychology: Applied*, 9(1), 42–51.

Wells, G. L., & Quinlivan, D. S. (2009). Suggestive eyewitness identification procedures and the Supreme Court's reliability test in light of eyewitness science: 30 years later. *Law and Human Behavior*, 33(1), 1–24.

Werth, R. (2019). Risk and punishment: The recent history and uncertain future of actuarial, algorithmic, and "evidence-based" penal techniques. *Sociology Compass*, 13(1), e12659.

Wessel, I., Albers, C. J., Zandstra, A. R. E., & Heininga, V. E. (2020). A multiverse analysis of attempts to replicate memory suppression with the think/no-think task. *Memory*, 28(7), 870–887.

Westen, D. (2012). Prototype diagnosis of psychiatric syndromes. *World Psychiatry*, 11(1), 16–21.

Westmacott, R., & Moscovitch, M. (2003). The contribution of autobiographical significance to semantic memory. *Memory & Cognition*, 31, 761–774.

Whalley, L. J., & Deary, I. J. (2001). Longitudinal cohort study of childhood IQ and survival up to age 76. *British Medical Journal*, 322(7290), 1–5.

Wheeler, D. D. (1970). Processes in word recognition. *Cognitive Psychology*, 1(1), 59–85.

Wheeler, M. E., Petersen, S. E, & Buckner, R. L. (2000). Memory's echo: Vivid remembering reactivates sensory-specific cortex. *Proceedings of the National Academy of Sciences*, 97(20), 11125–11129.

White, A. M., Jamieson-Drake, D. W., & Swartzwelder, H. S. (2002). Prevalence and correlates of alcohol-induced blackouts among college students: Results of an e-mail survey. *Journal of American College Health*, 51(3), 117–119, 122–131.

White, J. (2008). Illusory intelligences? *Journal of Philosophy of Education*, 42(3-4), 611–630.

White, P. A. (1988). Knowing more about what we can tell: "Introspective access" and causal report accuracy 10 years later. *British Journal of Psychology*, 79, 13–45.

Whittlesea, B. W. A. (2002). False memory and the discrepancy-attribution hypothesis: The prototype-familiarity illusion. *Journal of Experimental Psychology: General*, 131(1), 96–115.

Whittlesea, B. W. A., Jacoby, L. L., & Girard, K. (1990). Illusions of immediate memory: Evidence of an attributional basis for feelings of familiarity and perceptual quality. *Journal of Memory and Language*, 29(6), 716–732.

Whorf, B. L. (1956). *Language, thought, and reality*. Cambridge, MA: Technology Press.

Wiese, H., Tüttenberg, S. C., Ingram, B. T., Chan, C. Y. X., Gurbuz, Z., Burton, A. M., & Young, A.W. (2019). A robust neural index of high face familiarity. *Psychological Science*, 30(2), 261–272.

Willemsen, M. C., Böckenholt, U., & Johnson, E. J. (2011). Choice by value encoding and value construction: Processes of loss aversion. *Journal of Experimental Psychology: General*, 140(3), 303–324.

Williams, H. L., & Lindsay, D. S. (2019). Different definitions of the nonrecollection-based response option(s) change how people use the "remember" response in the remember/know paradigm. *Memory & Cognition*, 47(7), 1359–1374.

Williams, L. M., Liddell, B. J., Kemp, A. H., Bryant, R. A., Meares, R. A., Peduto, A. S., & Gordon, E. (2006). Amygdala-prefrontal dissociation of subliminal and supraliminal fear. *Human Brain Mapping*, 27(8), 652–661.

Wilmer, J. B. (2017). Individual differences in face recognition: A decade of discovery. *Current Directions in Psychological Science*, 26(3), 225–230.

Wilson, K., & French, C. C. (2006). The relationship between susceptibility to false memories, dissociativity, and paranormal belief and experience. *Personality and Individual Differences*, 41(8), 1493–1502.

Wilson, M. A., & Tonegawa, S. (1997). Synaptic plasticity, place cells, and spatial memory: Study with second generation knockouts. *Trends in Neuroscience*, 20(3), 102–106.

Wilson, T. D. (2002). *Strangers to ourselves: Discovering the adaptive unconscious*. Cambridge, MA: Harvard University Press.

Wilson, T. D., & Brekke, N. (1994). Mental contamination and mental correction: Unwanted influences on judgments and evaluations. *Psychological Bulletin*, 116(1), 117–142.

Wilson, T. D., & Dunn, E. W. (2004). Self-knowledge: Its limits, value, and potential for improvement. *Annual Review of Psychology*, 55, 493–518.

Wilson, T. D., Wheatley, T., Meyers, J. M., Gilbert, D. T., & Axsom, D. (2000). Focalism: A source of durability bias in affective forecasting. *Journal of Personality and Social Psychology*, 78(5), 821–836.

Wimmer, R. D., Schmitt, L. I., Davidson, T. J., Nakajima, M., Deisseroth, K., & Halassa, M. M. (2015). Thalamic control of sensory selection in divided attention. *Nature*, 526, 705–709.

Winawer, J., Witthoft, N., Frank, M. C., Wu, L., Wade, A. R., & Boroditsky, L. (2007). Russian blues reveal effects of language on color discrimination. *Proceedings of the National Academy of Sciences*, 104(19), 7780–7785.

Winograd, E., & Neisser, U. (Eds.). (1992). *Affect and accuracy in recall: Studies of "flashbulb" memories*. New York, NY: Cambridge University Press.

Wiseman, S., & Neisser, U. (1974). Perceptual organization as a determinant of visual recognition memory. *American Journal of Psychology*, 87(4), 675–681.

Witt, J. K., Kemmerer, D., Linkenauger, S. A., & Culham, J. C. (2020). Reanalysis suggests evidence for motor simulation in naming tools is limited: A commentary on Witt, Kemmerer, Linkenauger, & Culham (2010). *Psychological Science*, 31(8), 1036–1039.

Wittgenstein, L. (1953). *Philosophical investigations* (G. E. M. Anscombe, Trans.). Oxford, England: Blackwell.

Witxted, J. T., & Wells, G. L. (2017). The relationship between eyewitness confidence and identification accuracy: A new synthesis. *Psychological Science in the Public Interest*, 18(1), 10–65.

Wixted, J. T., Mickes, L., Clark, S. E., Gronlund, S. D., & Roediger, H. L., III. (2015). Initial eyewitness confidence reliably predicts eyewitness identification accuracy. *American Psychologist*, 70(6), 515–526.

Wolfe, J. M. (2020). Major issues in the study of visual search: Part 2 of "40 years of feature integration: Special issue in memory of Anne Treisman." *Attention, Perception, & Psychophysics*, 82, 383–393.

Wolfe, J. M. (1999). Inattentional amnesia. In V. Coltheart (Ed.), *Fleeting memories: Cognition of brief visual stimuli* (pp. 71–94). Cambridge, MA: MIT Press.

Wollen, K. A., Weber, A., & Lowry, D. H. (1972). Bizarreness versus interaction of mental images as determinants of learning. *Cognitive Psychology*, 3(3), 518–523.

Womelsdorf, T., Schoffelen, J.-M., Oostenveld, R., Singer, W., Desimone, R., Engel, A. K., & Fries, P. (2007). Modulation of neuronal interactions through neuronal synchronization. *Science*, 316(5831), 1609–1612.

Wong, E. M., Galinsky, A. D., & Kray, L. J. (2009). The counterfactual mind-set: A decade of research. In K. D. Markman, W. M. P. Klein, & J. A. Suhr (Eds.). *Handbook of imagination and mental simulation* (pp. 161–174). New York, NY: Psychology Press.

Wood, C., Kemp, N., & Plester, B. (2014). *Text messaging and literacy: The evidence.* New York, NY: Routledge.

Wood, N., & Cowan, N. (1995). The cocktail party phenomenon revisited: How frequent are attention shifts to one's name in an irrelevant auditory channel? *Journal of Experimental Psychology: Learning, Memory, & Cognition, 21*(1), 255–260.

World Health Organization. (2019). *International statistical classification of diseases and related health problems (ICD).* https://www.who.int/classifications /icd/en/

World Science Festival. (2019, June 2). *Can we "cure" deafness and blindness? Should we?* https://www .worldsciencefestival.com/videos/can-cure-deafness -blindness-/?gclid=EAIaIQobChMIueaw9onM5gIVkh h9Ch0sjgtzEAAYBCAAEgK2_PD_BwE

Wright, D. B., & Carlucci, M. E. (2011). The response order effect: People believe the first person who remembers an event. *Psychonomics Bulletin & Review, 18,* 805–812.

Wright, D. B., & Skagerberg, E. M. (2007). Postidentification feedback affects real eyewitnesses. *Psychological Science, 18*(2), 172–177.

Xu, F., & Garcia, V. (2008). Intuitive statistics by 8-month-old infants. *Proceedings of the National Academy of Sciences, 105*(13), 5012–5015.

Yamashiro, J. K., & Hirst, W. (2020). Convergence on collective memories: Central speakers and distributed remembering. *Journal of Experimental Psychology: General, 149*(3), 461–481.

Yan, V. X., Soderstrom, N. C., Seneviratna, G. S, Bjork, E. L, & Bjork, R. A. (2017). How should exemplars be sequenced in inductive learning? Empirical evidence versus learners' opinions. *Journal of Experimental Psychology: Applied, 23*(4), 403–416.

Yantis, S. (2008). The neural basis of selective attention: Cortical sources and targets of attentional modulation. *Current Directions in Psychological Science, 17*(2), 86–90.

Yarbus, A. L. (1967). *Eye movements and vision.* New York, NY: Plenum Press. (Translated from Russian by B. Haigh. Original Russian edition published in Moscow, 1965.)

Yechiam, E., Ashby, N. J. S., & Hochman, G. (2019). Are we attracted by losses? Boundary conditions for the approach and avoidance effects of losses. *Journal of Experimental Psychology: Learning, Memory, & Cognition, 45*(4), 591–605.

Yee, E., & Thompson-Schill, S. L. (2016). Putting concepts into context. *Psychonomic Bulletin & Review, 23,* 1015–1027.

Yeni-Komshian, G. H. (1993). Speech perception. In J. B. Gleason & N. B. Ratner (Eds.), *Psycholinguistics* (pp. 90–133). New York, NY: Harcourt Brace Jovanovich.

Yin, R. K. (1969). Looking at upside-down faces. *Journal of Experimental Psychology, 81*(1), 141–145.

Yonelinas, A. P., & Jacoby, L. L. (2012). The process-dissociation approach two decades later: Convergence, boundary conditions, and new direction. *Memory & Cognition, 40,* 663–680.

Yonelinas, A. P., & Ritchey, M. (2015). The slow forgetting of emotional episodic memories: An emotional binding account. *Trends in Cognitive Sciences, 19*(5), 259–267.

Young, A. W., & Burton, A. M. (2017). Recognizing faces. *Current Directions in Psychological Science, 26*(3), 212–217.

Young, A. W., Hellawell, D., & Hay, D. C. (1987). Configurational information in face perception. *Perception, 16*(6), 747–759.

Zaragoza, M. S., Payment, K. E., Ackil, J. K., Drivdahl, S. B., & Beck, M. (2001). Interviewing witnesses: Forced confabulation and confirmatory feedback increases false memories. *Psychological Science, 12*(6), 473–477.

Zaromb, F. M., Liu, J. H., Páez, D. Hanke, K., Putnam, A. L., & Roediger, H. L., III. (2018). We made history: Citizens of 35 countries overestimate their nation's role in world history. *Journal of Applied Research in Memory and Cognition, 7*(4), 521–528.

Zechmeister, E. B., Chronis, A. M. Cull, W. L., D'Anna, C. A., & Healy, N. A. (1995). Growth of a functionally important lexicon. *Journal of Reading Behavior, 27*(2), 201–212.

Zeki, S. (1991). Cerebral akinetopsia (visual motion blindness): A review. *Brain, 114,* 811–824.

Zeman, A., Dewar, M., & Della Sala, S. (2015). Lives without imagery—Congenital aphantasia. *Cortex, 73,* 378–380.

Zeman, A., Dewar, M., & Della Sala, S. (2016). Reflections on aphantasia. *Cortex, 74,* 336–337.

Zhao, M., Bülthoff, H. H., & Bülthoff, I. (2016). Beyond faces and expertise: Facelike holistic processing of nonface objects in the absence of expertise. *Psychological Science, 27*(2), 213–222.

Zhou, P., & Christianson, K. (2016). I "hear" what you're "saying": Auditory perceptual simulation, reading speed, and reading comprehension. *Quarterly Journal of Experimental Psychology, 69*(5), 972–999.

Zihl, J., von Cramon, D., & Mai, N. (1983). Selective disturbance of movement vision after bilateral brain damage. *Brain, 106,* 313–340

Zihl, J., von Cramon, D., Mai, N. & Schmid, C. (1991). Disturbance of movement vision after bilateral posterior brain damage. Further evidence and follow up observations. *Brain, 114,* 2235–2252.

Zillmer, E. A., Spiers, M. V., & Culbertson, W. C. (2008). *Principles of neuropsychology*. Belmont, CA: Wadsworth.

Zimler, J., & Keenan, J. M. (1983). Imagery in the congenitally blind: How visual are visual images? *Journal of Experimental Psychology: Learning, Memory, & Cognition, 9*(2), 269–282.

Zimmer, C. (2010). The brain. *Discover*, 28–29.

Zimmer, C. (2015, June 22). Picture this? Some just can't. *The New York Times*, p. D3. http://www.nytimes.com/2015/06/23/science/aphantasia-minds-eye-blind.html?emc=eta1&_r=0

Zwaan, R. A. (2016). Situation models, mental simulations, and abstract concepts in discourse comprehension. *Psychonomic Bulletin & Review, 23*(4), 1028–1034.

Credits

Photographs

CHAPTER 4

Page 102: Powerofforever/Getty Images; p. 104: James TW et al; *Ventral occipital lesions impair object recognition but not object-directed grasping: an fMRI study. Brain*, (2003), 126(11), 2463–2475. Reproduced by permission of Oxford University Press on behalf of the Guarantors of Brain; p. 105: P. Servos, M.A. Goodale and G.K. Humphrey (March 1993). *The drawing of objects by a visual form agnosia: Contribution of surface properties and memorial representations. Neuropsychologia*, 31(3), pp. 251–259. ©1993 with permission from Elsevier; p. 107: Russell Glenister/Corbis; p. 126: Quiroga et al. 2005. *Invariant visual representation by single neurons in the human brain. Nature*, 435(23), 1102–1107. ©2005 Nature Publishing Group; p. 129: Thompson, Peter. *Perception*, 9, pp. 483–484 ©1980 by SAGE Publication Ltd. Reprinted by Permission of SAGE Publication Ltd.; p. 131: Sydney Alford/Alamy Stock Photo and WFPA/Alamy Stock Photo; p. 132: Nancy Kanwisher and Galit Yovel. *The fusiform face area: a cortical region specialized for the perception of faces.* Phil. Trans R. Soc. B (2006) 361. Permission conveyed through Copyright ClearanceCenter Inc.; p. 136: M. Bar, K.S. Kassam, A.S. Ghuman, J. Boshyan, A.M. Schmid, A.M. Dale, M.S. Hamalainen, K. Markinkovic, D.L. Schacter, B.R. Rosen, and E. Halgren. *Top-down facilitation of visual recognition.* PNAS, Jan. 10, 2006, 103(2), pp. 449–454. © (2006) National Academy of Sciences U.S.A; p. 138: Fuse/Thinkstock/Getty Images.

CHAPTER 5

Page 142: Dragon Images/Shutterstock; p. 145: Courtesy of Daniel J. Simons and Christopher Chabris. Simons, D. J., & Chabris, C. F. (1999). *Gorillas in our midst: Sustained inattentional blindness for dynamic events. Perception*, 28, 1059–1074; p. 146: Javier Pierini/Getty Images; p. 148: iStockphoto/Getty Images; p. 149: Galina Barskaya/Dreamstime and Titania1980/Dreamstime; p. 150: Daniel T. Levin and Daniel J. Simons. *Failure to Detect Changes to Attended Objects in Motion Pictures.* Psychonomic Bulletin and Review, 1997, 4(4), 501–506; p. 158: Rykoff Collection/Corbis via Getty Images; p. 160: J.B. Hopfinger, M. H. Buonocore & G. R. Mangun. *The neural mechanisms of top-down attentional control.* Nature Neuroscience, volume 3, p. 28; p. 162: Unexpected, 1884–88 (oil on canvas), Repin, Ilya Efimovich (1844–1930)/Tretyakov Gallery, Moscow, Russia/Bridgeman Images and Republished with permission of Springer Science and

Bus Media B V. from '*Eye Movement and Vision*' by Alfred L. Yarbus. Trans Plenum Press New York 1967; permission conveyed through Copyright Clearance Center Inc.; p. 163: American Photo Archive/Alamy Stock Photo; p. 164: Gilles Mingasson/Getty Images; p. 171: Gaius Julius Caesar (100–44 BC.). Statue. Louvre Museum. Paris. Francia/Tarker/Bridgeman Images; p. 174: David Nelson/Alamy Stock Photo; p. 175: Kimberg, D. Y., D'Esposito, M., & Farah, M. J. (1998). *Cognitive functions in the prefrontal cortex in working memory and executive control.* Current Directions in Psychological Science, 6, 185–192. Reprinted by Permission of SAGE Publication Ltd.

CHAPTER 6

Page 186: Digital Vision/Getty Images; p. 188 (top): Ros Drinkwater/Alamy Stock Photo; p. 188 (bottom): Jiri Rezac/Polaris; p. 196: Talmi, D. et al. *Neuroimaging the serial position curve.* Psychological Science. 2005 Sep, 16(9), 716–23. Reprinted by Permission of SAGE Publication Ltd.; p. 198: Eduardo Abad/EPA/Shutterstock; p. 202: Courtesy of Dr. John Jonides; p. 205: Alberto Pomares/Getty Images; p. 211 (left): Imagic Chicago/Alamy Stock Photo; p. 211 (right): Stuart Black/Alamy Stock Photo; p. 213: Mnesmosyne, 1881 (oil on canvas), Rossetti, Dante Gabriel Charles (1828–82)/Delaware Art Museum, Wilmington, USA/Samuel and Mary R. Bancroft Memorial/Bridgeman Images; p. 219: From American Journal of Psychology. Copyright 1974 by the Board of Trustees of the University of Illinois. Used with permission of the University of Illinois Press. Wiseman, S. & Neisser, U. (1974). *Perceptual organization as a determinant of visual recognition memory.* American Journal of Psychology, 87(4), 675–681; p. 221: Blend Images/Getty Images.

CHAPTER 7

Page 226: Tim Macpherson /Cultura/Getty Images; p. 228: Photo by Project Neuron, University of Illinois at Urbana-Champaign; p. 233: Wheeler et al. (2000) *Memory's echo: Vivid remembering reactivates sensory-specific cortex.* Proceedings of the National Academy of Sciences, September 26, 2000, 97(20), 11125–11129. Copyright (2000) National Academy of Sciences, U.S.A.; p. 240 (left to right): UPI/Alamy Stock Photo, CelebrityArchaeology.com/Alamy Stock Photo, Matt Baron/Shutterstock, REUTERS/Alamy Stock Photo, and Gary Mitchell, GMP Media/Alamy Stock Photo; p. 241: Ranganath, C. et al. *Dissociable correlates of recollection and familiarity within the* medial temporal lobes. Neuropsychologia, 42(1), 2–13. © 2003 with permission from Elsevier. All rights reserved; **p. 245**: Courtesy of Daniel Reisberg; **p. 249**: Junko Kimura/Getty Images; **p. 254**: The Canadian Press/Helen Branswell; **p. 255**: Corkin et al. *H.M.'s medial temporal lobe lesion: Findings from magnetic resonance imaging.* The Journal of Neuroscience, 17, 3964–3979, Copyright © 1997 Society of Neuroscience; **p. 259**: Nick Ledger/Alamy Stock Photo.

CHAPTER 8

Page 264: Ryan McVay/Getty Images; **p. 268**: Brewer, W.F. and Treyens, J.C. *Role of schemata in memory for places.* Cognitive Psychology, 13, 207–230. ©1981 with permission from Elsevier; **p. 273**: Kevin Sullivan/The Orange County Register via AP; **p. 277**: Wade, K.A.; Garry, M.; Read, J.D.; Lindsay, D.S. (2002). *A picture is worth a thousand lies: Using false photographs to create false childhood memories.* Psychonomic Bulletin & Review, 9(3): 597–603; **p. 278**: Barney Wayne/Keystone/Getty Images; **p. 286**: Orne, M.T. (1959) *The nature of hypnosis: Artifact and essence.* Journal of Abnormal and Social Psychology, pp. 277–299; **p. 288**: W.M. Kelley, C.N. Macrae, C.L. Wyland, S. Caglar, S. Inati and T.F. Heatherton, *Finding the Self? An Event-Related fMRI Study.* Journal of Cognitive Neuroscience, (July 1 2002) 14(5), pp. 785–794. © 2002 by the Massachusetts Institute of Technology; **p. 291 (left)**: Sean Adair/Reuters/Newscom; **p. 291 (center)**: AP Photo/Joel Ryan; **p. 291 (right)**: ZUMA Press/Newscom; **p. 300**: BENSON IBEABUCHI/AFP via Getty Images.

CHAPTER 9

Page 306: Gozooma/Gallery Stock; **p. 309**: Courtesy of Daniel Reisberg; **p. 310**: Tierfotoagentur/Alamy Stock Photo; **p. 312**: GK Hart/Vikki Hart/Getty Images, Eric Isselée/Dreamstime, REX/Shutterstock, and Vanessa Grossemy/Alamy Stock Photo; **p. 315**: Adrian Lewart/Dreamstime.com; **p. 316 (top left)**: Rick & Nora Bowers/Alamy; **p. 316 (top right)**: Avalon/Photoshot License/Alamy Stock Photo; **p. 316 (bottom)**: Rob Atherton/Alamy Stock Photo; **p. 318**: Mick Tsikas/Epa/REX/ Shutterstock; **p. 319**: Michele D'Ottavio/Alamy Stock Photo; **p. 321**: Sidney Harris/CartoonStock; **p. 324**: age fotostock/Superstock; **p. 325**: Courtesy of Robert Malseed; **p. 338**: Rommel Canias/Shutterstock.

CHAPTER 10

Page 342: Photosindia/AgeFotostock; **p. 349**: © By permission of Leigh Rubin and Creators Syndicate Inc.; **p. 351**: Savushkin/Getty Images; **p. 357**: Derek Bayes/Bridgeman Images; **p. 358**: Lucasfilm/Fox/Kobal/REX/ Shutterstock; **p. 359**: mccool/Alamy Stock Photo; **p. 362**: Sidney Harris/CartoonStock; **p. 366**: Peter Dench/Getty Images; **p. 369**: Dronkers, N.F. et al, Paul *Broca's historic cases: high resolution MR imaging of the brains of Leborgne and Lelong.* Brain 2007, 130(5), 1432–1441. Reproduced by permission of Oxford University Press on behalf of the Guarantors of Brain; **p. 371**: Vikki Martin/Alamy Stock Photo; **p. 373**: Stu Porter/Alamy Stock Photo; **p. 374 (left)**: Rolls Press/Popperfoto/Getty Images; **p. 374 (right)**: Hulton Archive/Getty Images; **p. 375**: ColsTravel/Alamy Stock Photo; **p. 380**: True Images/Alamy Stock Photo.

CHAPTER 11

Page 384: © Friderike Heuer; **p. 395**: Adapted by Marcel Just from Carpenter, P.A . Just, M.A. Keller, T.A. et al. (1999). *Graded functional activation in the visuospatial system and the amount of task demand.* Journal of Cognitive Neuroscience, 11(1), p.14. © 1999 Massachusetts Institute of Technology; **p. 396**: Comstock/Getty Images; **p. 398**: Courtesy of Nancy Kanwisher; **p. 400**: Stefano Amantini/Atlantide Phototravel/Corbis via Getty Images; **p. 402**: Thompson, W. L. Slotnick, S. Burrage, M. & Kosslyn, S. (2009). *Two forms of spatial imagery: Neuroimaging evidence.* Psychological Science, 20, 1245–1253; **p. 404**: Cui, X., Jeter, C. B., Yang, D., Montague, P. R., and Eagleman, D. M. (2007). *Vividness of mental imagery: individual variability can be measured objectively.* Vision research, 47(4), 474–478; **p. 406**: Post Staff Photographer/SCMP/Newscom; **p. 410**: Tenniel, John (1820–1914)/Private Collection/The Bridgeman Art Library; **p. 412**: GL Archive/Alamy Stock Photo; **p. 419**: Intraub, H., and Richardson, M. *Boundary extension in picture memory.* Journal of Experimental Psychology, 15, 179–87. Reprinted by permission; **p. 421**: Andriy Popov/Alamy Stock Photo.

CHAPTER 12

Page 428: Sean Justice/Getty Images; **p. 431**: Paul Wicks/Public Domain; **p. 434**: Fuse/Corbis; **p. 436**: Jonathan Larsen/Diadem Images/Alamy Stock Photo; **p. 438**: AA Film Archive/Alamy Stock Photo; **p. 441**: Linus Andersson, Johan Eriksson, Sara Stillesjö, Peter Juslin, Lars Nyberg, Linnea Karlsson Wirebring. *Neurocognitive processes underlying heuristic and normative probability judgments.*

Cognition, *196*, © 2020 with permission from Elsevier; **p. 444:** Sidney Harris/CartoonStock; **p. 448:** TORSTEN BLACKWOOD/AFP via Getty Images; **p. 450:** Sidney Harris/Cartoonstock; **p. 459:** Marc Arts/Shutterstock; **p. 464:** © Mark Parisi/www.offthemark.com; **p. 465:** Cal Sport Media/Alamy Stock Photo.

CHAPTER 13

Page 473: Master1305/Shutterstock; **p. 488:** Sam Gross/CartoonStock; **p. 492:** From Kounios and Beeman (2009) *The Aha! Moment: The Cognitive Neuroscience of Insight.* Current Directions in Psychological Science 18:4 pp. 210–216; **p. 497:** Indiapicture/Alamy Stock Photo; **p. 498:** Andor Bujdoso/Alamy Stock Photo.

CHAPTER 14

Page 504: Lucidio Studio Inc./Getty Images; **p. 507:** Copyright © 1998 NCS Pearson Inc. Reproduced with permission. All rights reserved. "Wechsler Adult Intelligence Scale" "WAIS' and "Raven's Progressive Matrices" are trademarks in the US and/or other countries of Pearson Education Inc. or its affiliates(s); **p. 512:** Africa Studio/Shutterstock; **p. 514:** From Jung, R.E. and Haier, R.J., *The Parieto-Frontal Integration Theory (P-FIT) of intelligence: Converging neuroimaging evidence.* Behavioral and Brain Sciences, (2007), *30*, 135–187. Courtesy Brain and Behavioral Associates; **p. 517:** John Alex Maguire/REX/Shutterstock; **p. 518:** Tom Dymond/Thames/REX/ Shutterstock; **p. 525:** Rawpixel/Shutterstock.

CHAPTER 15

Page 534: Sarah Wilmer /Gallery Stock; **p. 542:** REUTERS/Alamy Stock Photo; **p. 544:** John Caldwell/CartoonStock; **p. 553:** Jeramey Lende/Alamy Stock Photo; **p. 559:** Naotsugu Tsuchiya and Ralph Adolphs. *Emotion and consciousness.* Trends in Cognitive Sciences, *11*(4), 158–167. © 2007 with permission from Elsevier; **p. 565:** John Springer Collection/Corbis via Getty Images; **p. 568:** Owen, A. M., Coleman, M. R., Boly, M., Davis, M. H., Laureys, S., and Pickard, J. D. (2006). *Detecting awareness in the vegetative state.* Science, *313*, 1402. ©2006 American Association for the Advancement of Science.

Figures

Figure 4.3 (p. 106): Figure 3 from Selfridge, O. G., "Pattern Recognition and Modern Computers." *AFIPS '55 (Western) Proceedings of the March 1–3,* *1955, western joint computer conference.* Copyright © 1955 by the Association for Computing Machinery, Inc. doi:10.1145/1455292.1455310. Reprinted by permission. **Figure 4.10 (p. 122):** Figure 3 from James L. McClelland and David E. Rumelhart, "An interactive model of context effects in letter perception," *Psychological Review*, 88(5), pp. 375–407, September 1981. Copyright © 1981 by the American Psychological Association. Reprinted with permission. **Figure 4.17 (p. 133):** Figure 2 from Wiese, H., Tuttenberg, S.C., Ingram, B.T., et al., "A robust neural index of high face familiarity," *Psychological Science*, 30(2), pp. 261–272, 2019. Republished with permission of SAGE; permission conveyed through Copyright Clearance Center, Inc. **Figure 5.6A (p. 153):** Figure 6.7A from *Principles of Cognitive Neuroscience*, 2nd ed. by Purves, Cabeza, Huettel, LaBar, Platt, and Woldorff. © 2012 by Sinauer Associates, Inc. Used by permission of Oxford University Press. Reproduced with permission of the Licensor through PLSclear. **Figure 5.6B (p. 153):** Figure 6.7B from *Principles of Cognitive Neuroscience*, 2nd Ed. by Purves, Cabeza, Huettel, LaBar, Platt, and Woldorff. Originally published as Figure 1, Hillyard et. al. "Electric signs of selective attention in the human brain," *Science* 182, p. 178. © 1973 AAAS. Reprinted with permission from AAAS. 10.1126/science.182.4108.177 **Figure 6.6 (p. 199):** Figure 7 from Cabeza, R., & Nyberg, L. "Imaging cognition II: An empirical review of 275 PET and fMRI studies." *Journal of Cognitive Neuroscience*, 12(1), pp. 1–47. Copyright © 2000 by the Massachusetts Institute of Technology. Reprinted by permission of MIT Press Journals. **Figure 8.9 (p. 296):** Figure 1 from Martin A. Conway, Gillian Cohen, and Nicole Stanhope, "On the very long-term retention of knowledge acquired through formal education: Twelve years of cognitive psychology," *Journal of Experimental Psychology*, 120(4): 395–409, December 1991. Copyright © 1991 by the American Psychological Association. Reprinted with permission. **Figure 8.10 (p. 297):** Figure 2 from "Life-Span Retrieval Curves from Five Countries" from Martin A. Conway, Qi Wang, Kazunori Hanyu & Shamsul Haque, "A Cross-Cultural Investigation of Autobiographical Memory." *Journal of Cross-Cultural Psychology*, 36(6), pp. 739–749, copyright © 2005 by SAGE Publications. Reprinted by permission of SAGE Publications. https://doi.org/10.1177/0022022105280512 **Figure 10.10 (p. 365):** Fig. 1 from Hagoort, et.al. "Integration of word meaning and world knowledge in language comprehension," *Science* 304, pp. 438–441. © 2004 AAAS. Reprinted with permission from AAAS. 10.1126/science.1095455 **Figure 11.4 (p. 393):** Fig. 1 from Shepard & Metzler, "Mental rotation of three-dimensional objects," *Science* 171, pp. 701–03. © 1971 AAAS. Reprinted with permission from AAAS. 10.1126/science.171.3972.701 **Figure 11.11 (p. 407):** Figure 1 reprinted from B. Milivojevic, B.W. Johnson, J.P. Hamm & M.C. Corballis, "Non-identical neural mechanisms for two types of mental transformation: event-related potentials during mental rotation and mental paper folding," *Neuropsychologia*, *31*(10), pp. 1345–1356. Copyright © 2003 Elsevier Science Ltd. Reprinted with permission from Elsevier. **Figure 12.3 (p. 443):** Figure 1 from Shane Frederick "Cognitive Reflection and Decision Making," *Journal of Economic Perspectives*, *19*(4), Fall 2005, pp. 25–42. Copyright American Economic Association; reproduced with permission of the Journal of Economic Perspectives. **Figure 12.8–12.9 (p. 455):** Problems 1 & 2 from A. Tversky & D. Kahneman. "The framing of decisions and the psychology of choice," *Science*, *211*, p. 453. © 1981 AAAS. Reprinted with permission from AAAS. 10.1126/science.7455683 **Figure 12.13 (p. 462):** Figure 14.20A from *Principles of Cognitive Neuroscience*, 2nd ed. by Purves, Cabeza, Huettel, LaBar, Platt, and Woldorff. © 2012 by Sinauer Associates, Inc. Adapted from Bechara et. al. *Cerebal Cortex* 10: 295–307. Used by permission of Oxford University Press. Reproduced with permission of the Licensor through PLSclear. **Figure 12.14 (p. 463):** Figure 13.10: Results of Kermer et. al.'s experiment republished with permission of Cengage Learning, from *Cognitive Psychology 3rd Edition*, E. Bruce Goldstein, p. 378. Copyright © 2011 Cengage Learning. **Figure 13.8 (p. 482):** Fig. 8.15 from R. Bootzin, E. Loftus, R. Zanjunc et al., *Psychology Today: An Introduction*, 4th ed. (1979), © 1979 McGraw-Hill Education. Republished with permission of McGraw-Hill Education; permission conveyed through Copyright Clearance Center, Inc. **Figure 14.1 (p. 507):** Sample item similar to those in the *Wechsler Adult Intelligence Scale*, Fourth Edition (WAIS-IV). Copyright © 2008 NCS Pearson, Inc. Reproduced with permission. All rights reserved. "Wechsler Adult Intelligence Scale," and "WAIS" are trademarks, in the US and/or other countries, of Pearson Education, Inc. or its affiliate(s). **Figure 14.2 (p. 508):** Sample item similar to those in the *Raven's Progressive Matrices (Standard Parallel, Sets A-E)*. Copyright © 1998 NCS Pearson, Inc. Reproduced with permission. All rights reserved. "Raven's Progressive Matrices" is a trademark, in the US and/or other countries, of Pearson Education, Inc. or its affiliate(s).

Author Index

(Note: Page numbers in *italics* refer to figures or tables.)

Subject Index

(Note: Page numbers in *italics* refer to figures or tables.)

flashbulb memories, 290–92, *291*, 298

fluent aphasia, 370

fluid intelligence, 513, *513*, 520

Flynn, James, 520

Flynn effect, 520–21

fMRI. *See* functional magnetic resonance imaging scans

focus
  of attention, 160–67, *162–64*, *166*, 168–69, *169*
  of spatial attention, 160–64
  when studying, 221

focus (vision), 65

fonts, 113

forebrain, *28*, 33, 45

forecasting emotions, 461, *463*

forgetting, 282–87, *283*, 493, *494*

formatting, of print words, 113

form perception, 79–86
  about: overview, 79–81
  edge enhancement and, 68–69, *70*
  Gestalt principles, 79–80, 82–84, *82–83*
  organization and features for, 84–86, *84–85*, 107

forward flow, 497

four-card (selection) task, 452–53, *452–53*

fovea, 47, 66–68, 89

fragmentary blackouts, 53

framing, 454–57, *455–56*, 459, 543–44

free recall procedure, 192, *192*

frequency estimates, 431–32

frontal lobes
  about: overview, *28*, 33
  ADHD and, *161*
  association areas of, 47, 48
  intelligence and, *514*
  lesions of, 29, *31*, 37, 47, 48, 174, 369–70, *369*
  memory processing and, *514*
  motor areas of, 45, *46*
  spatial attention and, 158

functional fixedness, 484–85, *484–85*

functional magnetic resonance imaging (fMRI) scans
  about: overview, 27, 28, 37
  combining techniques with, 41, *42*
  conceptual knowledge data, 327–28
  consciousness data, 567–68, *568*
  localization of function data, *44*

memory processing data, 196, *196*, 240
  selective attention data, *160*
  self-referencing data, *288*
  strengths and weaknesses of, 41
  vegetative states data, 567–68
  visual imagery data, 397, 404, *404*

"Funes the Memorious" (Borges), 307

fusiform face area (FFA), 41–43, *42*, 129–30, 132, *398*

g. See general intelligence

Gage, Phineas, 31, *31*, 174

Galton, Francis, 387–88, 403

gambler's fallacy, 436–37

gamma rhythm, 39

ganglion cells, 65, 68

gaps in memory. *See* memory errors

garden-path sentences, 362–66, *362*

Gardner, Howard, 516–18, *518*

gender differences
  attention and, 209
  color associations, 94
  emotional processing and, 209
  intelligence research on, 521, 525–26, 527, 529
  memory processing and, 209
  mental rotation task and, 394, *395*, 408
  selective attention and, 162

gender pronouns, 359

general and fortress problem, 480, *480*

general intelligence (*g*)
  as combined operation, 515
  executive control and, 515
  model of, 512–13
  neural basis for, 514, *514*
  specialized intelligence *vs.*, 510–11, 512–13, *512*

generativity of language, 356

generic knowledge
  conscious thought and, 542
  memory processing and, 272, 298, 418
  See also conceptual knowledge

genetics and intelligence, 518–19, *519*, 521

geons (geometric ions), 123–24, *124*

Gestalt psychology movement, 16, 79–80

Giffords, Gabby, 343

Gilbert, Charles Allan, *158*

giraffes, 259

Glasgow Coma Scale, 567

glia (glial cells), 31, 48, 50–51, *50*

global warming, 448–49, *448*

glucose, *38*

gnu, *324*

goal-derived categories, 327

goal neglect, 174–75, *175*

goals, for problem solving, 477, 482–83, *482*

good continuation, *83*

graded membership, 312–13

Graham, Martha, 497

grasp reflex, *11*

Grice, Paul, 367

grounded cognition, 328–30

group problem-solving, 498–99, *498*

gut feelings, 461, *462*

G.Y. (blind sight case study), 535–36

Hamlet (Shakespeare), *412*

happiness research, 463–64

Harrison, George, 247

Harvard Women's Health Watch website, 421

health and medicine
  application of cognitive psychology to, 20
  IQ scores and, 528–30
  medical decision making, *460*, 528–29
  medical histories, 299–301
  pain relief through visualization, 421–23
  vegetative states, 567–69

hearing
  context and, 135
  divided attention and, 171, *172*
  memory processing and, 268
  neural basis for, 46, *46*, 47
  selective listening, 144–46, *153*, 154

Helmholtz, Hermann von, 87–88, 89

hemispheres, of human brain, *28*, 35, *36*, 37, 45

"He's So Fine" (Chiffons), 247

heuristics
  consciousness and, 562
  emotional processing and, 461
  fake news processing and, 448–49
  problem solving method, 476–77, *477*, 496
  types of, 432–37, *433*, *434*

hierarchical model of intelligence, 511–13, *511–12*

as life expectancy predictor, 509, 527–30

as life outcome predictor, 509–10, 509, 526

racial bias of, 524

reliability of, 507–8

talents untested by, 505, 517–18

validity of, 508–10, 509, 512

iris, 65

"Jabberwocky" (Carroll), 357, 357

Jackman, Hugh, 131, 132

James, William, 144, 403, 536–37

Jobs, Steve, 473

judgment, 428–71

about: overview, 430–31

assessment tools, 443–44, 443

attribute substitution, 431–37, 433, 449

confirmation and disconfirmation, 444–47, 445, 449, 450

covariation and, 437–40, 438

decision making, 454–64 (See also decision making)

dual-process model, 440–42, 441

emotions and, 459–64, 462–64

errors in, 432–34, 436–37, 441, 442, 444, 449

of fake news and misinformation, 448–49

happiness and, 463–64

heuristics, 432–37, 433, 434, 448–49, 461

logic and, 450–53, 450–53

reasoning and, 437

skilled intuition, 442–44

unconscious, 548

utility maximization and, 454, 459, 460

juror bias, 465–66, 465

justification and decision making, 459

Kamala ("wolf child"), 373–74

Kant, Immanuel, 13, 13, 14

Kanzi (bonobo), 373

K. C. (amnesia patient), 254

Keane, Glen, 406

Khoisan, 348

"Kill You" (Eminem), 542

King, Martin Luther, Jr., 359

knowledge

background, 5–6

concepts and generic knowledge, 307–41 (See also conceptual knowledge)

distributed, 119–20

episodic knowledge, 191

of language, 342–82 (See also language)

memory processing and, 216–18, 218–19

schemas and, 16, 16, 271–73, 281–82, 287, 418–19

self and, 7–8

as sentence parsing guide, 363–64, 365

storage of, 191 (See also long-term memory)

study of, 3–4

visual, 384–426 (See also visual knowledge and imagery)

See also learning

knowledge networks, 330–36, 331–32

knowledge retrieval, 330–33

Korsakoff's syndrome, 227, 255, 256, 544–45, 563–64

language, 342–83

about: preview and summary, 344

acquisition of, 370–74, 371, 373–74

animal language, 351, 372–73, 373

aphasia and, 48

behaviorism on, 15

bilingualism, 378–79

biological basis for, 368–74, 369

Chomsky on, 15

clinical studies, 343–44, 369–70, 369

cultural differences and, 375–76, 375

lip reading, 354

morphemes and words, 345, 345, 355–56, 356

organization of, 344–46, 345

phonology, 346–55 (See also phonology)

pragmatic rules, 366–68

prosody, 364–66, 366

sentence parsing, 360–64, 361–62, 365 (See also sentence parsing)

sign language, 204, 371, 371

syntax, 356–60, 360 (See also syntax)

texting vocabulary, 379–80, 380

thought processes and, 374–79, 375–76

unconscious guide to, 544

"wolf children," 373–74, 374

lateral fissure (brain), 28, 33

lateral geniculate nucleus (LGN), 68, 73, 74–75, 123, 152

lateralization (brain), 35, 36

late selection hypothesis, 150–52, 151

laws. See legal system

leading questions, 274–75, 274, 279

learning

behaviorism on, 15

language acquisition, 370–74, 371, 373–74

memory processes for, 210–12, 211, 229–33, 258

neural basis for, 52

study techniques, 207–10, 208, 213–16, 218–22, 221

types of, 207–10, 208, 221, 252, 258

See also knowledge

"left-brain thinking," 35

legal system

adolescent brain development and, 56–57, 56

application of cognitive psychology to, 19, 20

cognitive interviews and, 285–86

commonsense beliefs about memory, 279

confessions, 56–57, 277

copyright infringement, 247, 542

death penalty, 57

eyewitness errors, 273–76, 273–74, 280–81, 539, 540 (See also eyewitnesses)

face recognition issues, 134

false confessions, 56–57, 277

false convictions, 273, 273

legal concepts, 337–38

life sentences, 57

photo lineups, 245–46, 245, 539

pretrial publicity, 464–66, 464

Le Guin, Ursula K., 473

lens, 65, 65, 89, 93

Leonardo da Vinci, 474, 499

lesions, defined, 37

See also specific brain lesions

letter combinations, 115–16

letter detectors, 112, 112, 115, 117, 118, 121

connections for, 210–12, *211*
cues for, 235, *236*
defined, 189
encoding for, 212–13, *213*
errors and, 268–69
forgetting, 282–87 (*See also* amnesia and memory loss; forgetting)
imagery as helpful for, 416–20, *419*
learning and, 229–33
memory network for, 235
model of, *190*
neural basis for, 196, *196*
optimal learning and, 258
recall, 238
recognition, 238–39
retrieval paths, 213, 216, 220, 221–22, 229, 238, 269
from working memory, 191
memory search, 474–76, *475*, 496
memory storage, 205–10
  about: overview, 189, 220
  consolidation process, 288–89, 292
  defined, 189
  learning and studying, 207–10, *208*, 213–16, *213–14, 216*, 220–22
  level of processing, 208–10, *208*
  memory network for, 233–38
  as modality-specific, 268
memory testing, 238–40, 242–43
mental image scanning, *390–92*, 391–92, 395–96, 399–401, 403
mental maps, *414*, 415–16
mental pictures, 213, *216*, 409–10
  See also visualization; visual knowledge and imagery
mental resources. *See* resources
mental rotation, of image, 392–96, *393–95*, 399–403, *402*, 408
metacognitive skills, 552, 556
metamemory, 552
midbrain, 33, 545
Miles, Guy, *273*
Miller, George, 197–98
Miller v. Alabama (2012), 57
mind-body problem, 566
mind's ear, 396
mind's eye
  about, 387
  assessment of, 387–96, *390–95*
  individual differences, 403, 406–7, *407*

neural basis for, 43, *44*
Shakespeare and, *412*
visual perception and, 396–97
vivid imagery, 403–4, *404*, 406–7, *406*
mind wandering, 493, 557
minimally conscious state (MCS), 567
mirror drawing, *228*
misattribution, 243–44, 538–39
misinformation effect
  dangers of, 448–49, *448*
  false memories, 273–78, *274, 277–78*
  implicit memory and, 244–45
  pretrial publicity, 464–65
misperceptions, 89–90, *90*
mnemonic strategies, 213–16, *213–14, 216*, 222, 409, 416–17
Mnemosyne, 213, *213*
modal model, 190–92, *190*, 198
Molaison, Henry "H.M.," 6–7, *7*, 18, 34, 187, 227, 255, *255*
monetary choice framing, 456–57, *456*
monocular cues, 92–95, *93*, 95–96, 98
morality, 180–81
morpheme (linguistic unit), 345, *345*, 355–56, *356*, 380
motion parallax, 95, *96*
motion perception, 63–64, *95*
motor areas, of cerebral cortex, 45, 46, *46*, 328–30, 568
Mozart, Wolfgang, 473
MPFC (medial prefrontal cortex), 288
MRI scans (magnetic resonance imaging), 27, *27*, 37, *39*, 41, *160, 255*
Müller-Lyer illusion, 151, *151, 549*
multiple intelligences, theory of, 516–18, *517–18*
multitasking, *171*
  See also divided attention
musical intelligence, 516
myelin sheath, *50*, 51–52
"My Sweet Lord" (Harrison), 247

naturalistic intelligence, 516
natural kinds (concept), 327
Necker cube, 80, *80*, 82, 410–11, *411*
negative frame, *455*, 456

neglect syndrome, 47, 143, 165–67, *165–66*, 399, *400*, 417
Neisser, Ulric, *15*
networks. *See* knowledge networks; memory network
neural correlates of consciousness, 553–55, *553*
neural synchrony, 78–79
neuroimaging data, 18, 26–29, 37, 41–43, 55, 129–30, *553*
  See also specific techniques
neuronal workspace hypothesis, 555–59, *559*, 564
neurons
  about: overview, 30–31, 48, *50*
  biased competition theory and, 152–54
  coding and, 54
  communication between, 38, 49, 52, 234–35
  communication within, 38–39, 49–52
  electrical recordings of, 38
  executive control and, 558–59
  memory network comparison, 234
  neuronal workspace hypothesis, 555–59, 564
  object recognition and, 124–27, *125–26*
  regions and structures of, 48–52, *50–51*
  rhythms of firing, 78–79
  single-cell recording of, 70–71, 124–26, *125–26*
  three-dimensional object recognition and, 123–24
  transcranial magnetic stimulation of, 43
  visual coding and, 69–79 (*See also* visual coding)
  word recognition and, 123
neuropsychology, 18, 36–37, 327–30, *329*, 368–70, *369*
neurotransmitters, 38, 49–50, *50–51*, 52
news (fake), 448–49, 464–65
N400 brain wave, *365*, 546–47
nine-dot problem, 487–89, *487*
nodes
  of knowledge network, 330–36, *335*
  of memory network, 234–38, *236*, 248, 268–69, *413*
nodes of Ranvier, *50*
nonfluent aphasia, 369–70

postsynaptic membrane, 49–50, *51*

PPA (parahippocampal place area), *42, 398, 568*

practical intelligence, 515–16

practice, 176–80

pragmatic rules, for language, 366–68

predictive validity, 508–10, *509*, 512

prefrontal cortex (PFC)
  alcohol's effect on, 53
  damage to, 28–29, 48, 174, *175*
  development of, *55–56*
  function of, 29, *558*

premises, 444, 451

preparation (creativity stage), 490

prescriptive rules, 358–59

presynaptic membrane, 49, *51*

pretrial publicity, 464–66, *464*

primacy effect, 192, *192*, 193–96, 205, *420*

primary motor projection areas, 45, 46, *46*

primary sensory projection areas, 45–47

primate communication, 373, *373*

priming
  biased competition theory on, 152–54
  expectation-based (goal-directed), 154–57, *155–56*
  implicit memory and, 241, 242–43, 247, 252, *252*
  neural basis for, 152–54, *156*
  repetition priming, 109, *109*, 114–15, 154, 156, *156*, 242
  selective attention and, 152–70
  selective attention summary, 169
  semantic priming, 235–38, *237*
  spatial attention, 157–64
  stimulus-driven, 152–54, *153, 156*
  as top-down process, 135–36
  word recognition and, 109, *109*, 114–15, 116–20, 123, 135–36

probability
  decisions made based on, *455*
  judgments based on, 432, 433, *433*, 439, 442

problem solving, 472–503
  about, 473–74
  brainstorming, 498–99, *498*
  creativity and (*See* creativity)
  defined, 474
  defining the problem, 483–89, *484–88*

experience and, 478–83, *478–80, 482*
  general methods for, 474–78, *475, 477–78*
  unconscious guide to, 543

problem-solving set, 486–89, *486–88*

problem space, 475–76, *475*

procedural memory, *252*

processing fluency, 246–50, *249*, 561–63

processing pathway (memory), 246–48

production task, 313

projection areas, 45, *46*

pronoun use, 359

propositions and propositional networks, 333–34, *334–35*, 336

prosody, 364–66, *366*, 372

prosopagnosia, 127, 129–30

prototype-based reasoning, 311–26
  about, 311–12, *312*
  basic-level categorization and, 314–15, *315*
  defined, 311–12
  exemplars comparison, 315–18, *318*
  graded membership and, 312–13
  legal concepts application of, 337–38
  neural basis for, 329–30
  new case application of, 323–25, *324–25*
  resemblance judgements, 321–23
  stereotype comparison, 326
  testing the prototype notion, 313–14, *314*
  typicality judgements, 318–21, *321*

proximity, 83, *83*

qualia, 560–61, *561, 562–63, 564, 565*

questions
  framing of, *457, 458*
  leading, 274–75, *274, 279*

race and ethnicity differences
  face recognition and, 134
  intelligence research on, 521, 524
  selective attention and, 163
  stereotypes and, 326

Ramu (wild child), *374*

random chance, 442

rare item effect, 161, *163*

rating task, 313, *314*

rationality, 516

rat maze studies, 15

Raven's Progressive Matrices Test, 507, *508*, 520

Rayner, Rosalie, *11*

RBC (recognition by components) model, 123–24

reading (speed-reading), 137–38

reading span, 199–200

"read my lips," 354

reason-based choice, 459

reasoning, unconscious, 538–41, *540, 542*
  See also judgment

recall, 238–40, 242, 265–66, 271
  See also memory retrieval

recency effect, 192–93, *192*, 194–96, *195, 420*

recognition, 238–39, 242
  See also face recognition; object recognition; word recognition

recognition by components (RBC) model, 123–24

reconstructions, 542–43, *542*

"recovered" memories, 277, 293–94

redundancy, 96

reflected light, 64–65

reflexes (mental), 550

regression hypnosis, *286*

regrets, 463–64, *464*

rehearsal loop, 201–4, *202–3*

Reisberg, Dan, 308

relational (elaborative) rehearsal, 205

relational categories (concept), 327

relational mindset, 481

reliability, of IQ tests, 507–8

remembering. *See* memory retrieval

"remember/know" distinction, 239–40, *240*

reminiscence bump, 297–98, *297*

Remote Associates Test, 496, *496*

repetition priming, 109, *109*, 114–15, 154, 156, *156*, 242

representation
  distributed, 120, 126–27, 334–36
  local, 119–20, 126, 334

representativeness heuristic, 432, 433, *433*, 435–37, 448–49